William Adolphus Wheeler

A Dictionary of the Noted Names of Fiction

Including also Familiar Pseudonyms, Surnames, Bestowed on Eminent...

William Adolphus Wheeler

A Dictionary of the Noted Names of Fiction
Including also Familiar Pseudonyms, Surnames, Bestowed on Eminent...

ISBN/EAN: 9783337205119

Printed in Europe, USA, Canada, Australia, Japan

Cover: Foto ©ninafisch / pixelio.de

More available books at **www.hansebooks.com**

A DICTIONARY OF THE NOTED NAMES OF FICTION;

INCLUDING ALSO

FAMILIAR PSEUDONYMS, SURNAMES BESTOWED ON EMINENT MEN, AND ANALOGOUS POPULAR APPELLATIONS OFTEN REFERRED TO IN LITERATURE AND CONVERSATION.

BY WILLIAM A. WHEELER, M.A.

So eine Arbeit eigentlich nie fertig wird; ... man sie für fertig erklären muß, wenn man nach Zeit und Umständen das Möglichste daran gethan hat.
                Goethe.

LONDON:
BELL & DALDY, 6, YORK STREET, COVENT GARDEN,
AND 186, FLEET STREET.
1866.

TO

RICHARD SOULE, JR.,

THE MAN, THE SCHOLAR, THE FRIEND,

This Work is Dedicated

AS A

TOKEN OF AFFECTIONATE RESPECT.

PREFACE.

The author of this volume contributed to the edition of Webster's Quarto Dictionary published in 1864 a "Vocabulary of the Names of Noted Fictitious Persons and Places;" but the present work, though based on that Vocabulary, embraces a wider range of subjects, contains nearly seventeen hundred new articles, besides important modifications of many of the others, and is furnished with an orthoëpical Introduction, and an Index to the real names of persons, places, &c., whose nicknames, pseudonyms, or popular appellations, are given in the body of the book. Notwithstanding the great pains that has been taken to secure fulness and minute accuracy, there are undoubtedly some errors and numerous omissions; but no more of either, it is hoped, than are inseparable from a work of such multiplicity. And although a casual examination or closer scrutiny may bring to light defects of both kinds, it may still be affirmed, that, with respect to a very large class of names, there can nowhere else be found in a collective form an equal amount and variety of information.

The main design of the work is to explain, as far as practicable, the allusions which occur in modern standard literature to noted fictitious persons and places, whether mythological or not. For this reason, the plan is almost entirely restricted to proper names, or such as designate individual persons, places, or things. The introduction of appellative or generic names, such as *abbot of unreason, lord of misrule, kobold,* &c., as well as the explanation of celebrated customs and phrases, such as *flap-dragon, nine-men's-morrice, philosophy of the Porch, to send to Coventry, to carry coals to Newcastle,* &c., would open too vast a field of inquiry; and, besides, there are copious special treatises on these subjects already before the public, as those of Brand, Hone, Pulleyn, Timbs, and others. The author has been urged to extend his plan so as to include the titles of famous poems, essays, novels, and other literary works, and the names of celebrated statues, paintings, palaces, country-seats, churches, ships, streets, clubs, and the like; inasmuch as such names are of very common occurrence in books and newspapers, and, for the most part, are not alphabetically entered and explained in Encyclopædias, Dictionaries, or Gazetteers. That a dictionary which should furnish succinct information upon such matters would supply a want which is daily felt by readers of every class is not to be doubted; but it should constitute an independent work. A manual of this description the author has for some time had in preparation; and he hopes to publish it, at no distant day, as a companion to the present volume.

The names from the Greek, Roman, Norse, and Hindu Mythologies that are here given, are concisely treated, mainly with a view to explain frequent allusions in the poets and other popular writers, and for the benefit of mere English readers, rather than for that of professed scholars. From the Rabbinical and Mohammedan Mythologies have been taken some names, which are occasionally made the subject of reference, and concerning which information is not readily obtainable. Prominence has been given to the departments of Angelology, Demonology, Fairy Mythology, and Popular Superstitions, which afford many of the most important names in Fiction. Parables, Allegories, Proverbs, and Mediæval Legends have also furnished a considerable number. Ecclesiastical History contributes the names of several pseudo-saints, and other imaginary personages. In the Drama, and in Poetry — including the various kinds, Epic, Romantic, Narrative, Comic, &c., — the intention has been to give the names of all such characters as are familiarly referred to by writers and speakers at the present day; and, though there may be accidental omissions, it is hoped that under this head the Dictionary will be found reasonably complete.

The principal deficiency is most likely to exist in the department of Prose Romance; for, though there is very little that is fictitious in ancient literature which is not included in ancient Mythology, yet the field of research continually widens as we come down to modern times, until it seems to be almost boundless. In fixing the limits of the work, the consideration which has determined the admission or rejection of names has not been the intrinsic merit of a book, or the reputation of its writer, but the hold which his characters have taken upon the popular mind. There are many authors of acknowledged genius, and hundreds of clever and prolific writers, who yet have not produced a single character that has so fallen in with the humour, or hit the fancy, of the time, as to have become the subject of frequent allusion. The English romancers and novelists whose creations are most familiarly known and most firmly established are Bunyan, De Foe, Swift, Richardson, Fielding, Smollett, Sterne, Goldsmith, Scott, Dickens, and Thackeray. Many of the portraitures of these writers may be safely presumed to be of more than temporary interest and importance. In regard to other and minor characters, from whatever source derived, it is to be borne in mind that a dictionary is chiefly designed for the use of the existing generation. To what extent names of secondary importance should be included was a question difficult to determine. Opinions from scholars entitled to the highest consideration were about equally divided upon this point. Some favoured a selected list of the most important names only: others, and the greater number, recommended a much wider scope. A middle course is the one that has been actually followed. It is evident that many articles which may seem to one person of very questionable importance, if not wholly unworthy of insertion, will be held by another to be of special value, as throwing light upon passages which to him would otherwise be perplexing or obscure.

This Dictionary is, of course, chiefly designed to elucidate the works of British and American writers; but names occurring in the literatures of other modern nations have been introduced whenever they have become well known to the public through the medium of translations, or when they seemed, for other reasons, to be worthy of insertion.

In accordance with the plan of the work as indicated in the title, such English, French, German, and other Pseudonyms as are frequently met with in books and newspapers have been given for the benefit of the general reader. No pretence, however, is made to completeness, or even to fulness, in this respect. The bibliographer will find here little or nothing that is new to him; and he must still have recourse to his Barbier, Quérard, Weller, and other writers of the same class. Names like *Erasmus, Melanchthon, Mercator, Œcolampadius,* &c., assumed by learned men after the revival of classical literature, being, in general, merely the Latin or Greek equivalents of their real names, and being also the only names by which they are now known in history, are excluded as not pertinent to the work. For a similar reason, no notice is taken of such names as *Masséna, Metastasio, Philidor, Psalmanazar, Voltaire,* &c.

Many eminent characters in political and literary history are often known and referred to by the surnames and sobriquets, or nicknames, which they have borne; as, the *Master of Sentences,* the *Scourge of God,* the *Stagirite,* the *Wizard of the North,* the *Little Corporal,* &c. "Nicknames," said Napoleon, "should never be despised: it is by such means mankind are governed." The Dictionary embraces the more important of these; but names like *Caligula, Guercino, Tintoretto,* &c., which have entirely superseded the real names of the persons designated by them, have not been regarded as properly coming within the purview of the present undertaking. Nor has it, as a rule, been thought advisable to admit simple epithets, such as *the Bold, the Good, the Great, the Unready, the Courtier,* &c., the omission of which can hardly be considered a defect, since their signification and the reason of their imposition are usually too obvious to excite inquiry. This rule, however, has not been uniformly observed. Here, as elsewhere in the work, that discretionary power has been freely exercised, to which every author of a dictionary or glossary is fairly entitled, and which he is often compelled to use.

A considerable space has been allotted to familiar names of Parties and Sects, of Laws, and of Battles; to poetical and popular names of Seas, Countries, States, Cities, &c.; to ancient geographical names which have become interesting from their revival in poetry or otherwise; and to certain long-established and important Personifications. In general, nicknames of Parties and Sects, such as *Chouans, Ghibellines, Gueux, Methodists, Shakers,* &c., which have been adopted by those to whom they were at first derisively applied, or which have passed into history and common use as their peculiar and appropriate names, and are to be found in any good Encyclopædia or Manual of Dates, are designedly not included. Most of the historical by-names inserted, such as *Day of Dupes, Evil May-day, Wonderful Parliament, Omnibus Bill, Western Reserve,* &c., are those which are not to be found under the proper heads in Encyclopædias and other books of reference. Popular designations connected with History and Geography have been freely given in all cases where they seemed to be well settled, and to be fitted to illustrate past or contemporary events or characters.

A slight departure from the strict limits of the plan has been thought allowable in the case of a few quasi-historical, or real but obscure, persons, places, and things, such as *Owleglass, John O' Groat, Mrs. Glasse,* the *Minerva Press,* &c., which are often referred to in literature or conversation, and of most of which no account can be obtained except through an amount of research and toil hardly possible to a majority of readers.

Illustrative citations have been copiously given from no small variety of authors; and, as many of them are gems of thought or expression, it is believed that they will be deemed greatly to enhance the value and interest of the work. Some of them, however, have purposely been taken from newspapers and magazines rather than from the classics of the language, in order to show, by such familiar examples, the popularity of the characters or other creations of fiction to which they allude.

There are also some quotations which serve no other purpose than that of justifying the insertion of names whose claim to admission might be thought doubtful, if it were not made to appear that they are referred to by authors "known and read of all men." It will probably be observed that Sir Walter Scott is more frequently cited than any other single writer; the reason, however, is not that his works have been examined with more care or to a greater extent than those of some other writers, but merely that he abounds more than most others in allusions, — often remote or recondite, but almost always apt and suggestive, — which his unusually tenacious memory enabled him to draw from the stores of a vast and most multifarious reading.

In the explanation of names, statements borrowed in great part from one author have been diligently collated with other statements derived from independent and often widely separated sources; and they have been freely enlarged, abridged, or otherwise modified, according to the necessity of the case, or as would best subserve the purpose of the work. But where the information required has been found already stated in the best way, no hesitation has been felt in making use of the exact language of the writer; and, beyond this general explanation, no acknowledgment of indebtedness seems necessary.

To determine the pronunciation of proper names is unquestionably the most difficult requirement of orthoëpy; and little or no attention has hitherto been paid to the pronunciation of such as are peculiar to the literature of fiction. In the absence, not merely of a trustworthy guide, but of any printed guide at all, the author may sometimes have gone astray; but he has been careful to avail himself of all the information he could obtain. In particular, he has made a thorough examination of such of our vernacular poets as are esteemed classics, and has occasionally adduced passages from their writings to show the accentuation adopted by these "best judges of pronunciation," as Walker styles them; or, more rarely, to show the sound they assign to particular letters or syllables. If the decisions or opinions he has given prove, in general, to be well grounded, the credit will not be wholly due to him, since he has often profited by the advice and assistance of gentlemen whose superior opportunities of becoming acquainted with the best usage both at home and abroad, and whose critical taste and familiarity with all that pertains to the subject of orthoëpy, afford the assurance that they " speak scholarly and wisely." To indicate with absolute accuracy the peculiar sounds of the principal languages of modern Europe, including the English, would necessarily require an extensive and elaborate system of arbitrary phonic signs; and such a system would be hard to understand, and still harder to remember. It has, therefore, been deemed important not to introduce into this work unnecessary and perplexing discriminations of sounds nearly identical, or to embarrass the inquirer with needless intimations of a pronunciation obvious or already familiar to him. Hence, diacritical marks are sparingly employed, except in the case of unaccented vowels, — which, in our language, are often of doubtful or variable value, — and except also in the case of foreign sounds which have no equivalent in English. Although the system of notation made use of is easy to be understood, so far as it applies to most English names, it has been thought desirable to prefix to the work observations on some points of English pronunciation not familiar to the generality of readers, or concerning which professed orthoëpists differ. In regard to the sounds occurring in the work that are peculiar to foreign languages, an explanation is given, in the Introduction, of the mode of their organic formation, or of their position and relations in a scientific classification of spoken sounds. These observations and explanations are contained in distinct paragraphs or sections, consecutively numbered, and are often referred to from the words in the Dictionary.

The Index at the end of the volume forms the counterpart of the Dictionary proper, and will, it is hoped, prove serviceable by enabling an inquirer to ascertain at once the distinguishing epithet or epithets borne by a particular person or place of which only the real name may be known to him.

PREFACE.

In the preparation of this Dictionary, the wide field of general literature has been extensively and carefully searched. Moreover, use has been made of a large number of works specially devoted to the various branches of literary history; and valuable assistance has been derived from the principal Reviews, and the published writings of the best essayists. Not a few noteworthy names and facts, incidentally mentioned in the body of the articles of Encyclopædias, Biographical Dictionaries, Gazetteers, and other works of reference, but not treated in alphabetical order, have been carefully gleaned from such works, which have been systematically searched for this purpose. These sources of information are altogether too numerous to be particularised in this place, while to specify a few and make no mention of others of equal importance would be as unjust as it would be unsatisfactory.

The author would return his sincere thanks to the many friends who have contributed in different ways to the completeness and accuracy of his work. Some of them, whose kind assistance he would gladly acknowledge, he regrets that he is not permitted to name; but it affords him unfeigned pleasure to be able to mention his great and varied obligations to Dr. Robley Dunglison and Dr. R. Shelton Mackenzie of Philadelphia, Mr. Charles Folsom of Cambridge, Mr. Samuel Porter of Hartford, and Mr. Arthur W. Wright of New Haven.

Believing that the successful accomplishment of a task like the present, in its fullest extent, is hardly to be expected of any individual, the author, in conclusion, would ask a candid criticism of his labours; and if corrections or suggestions from any quarter — especially suggestions of additional names, accompanied with explanations, references, or citations — be sent to him through his publishers, they will be gratefully received, and used in the preparation of a future edition.

MONTREAL, *November*, 1865.

CONTENTS.

	PAGE
KEY TO THE SCHEME OF PRONUNCIATION,	xiv
REMARKS ON SOME POINTS OF ENGLISH ORTHOËPY,	xvii
RULES FOR THE PRONUNCIATION OF GREEK AND LATIN WORDS,	xxi to xxiii
Vowels,	xxii
Consonants,	xxii
Accent,	xxiii
BRIEF RULES FOR THE PRONUNCIATION OF THE PRINCIPAL MODERN LANGUAGES OF CONTINENTAL EUROPE,	xxiii to xxxii
Vowels,	xxiii
Diphthongs and Vowel Combinations,	xxv
Consonants,	xxvi
Combined Consonants,	xxix
Accent,	xxxi
EXPLANATION OF ABBREVIATIONS, ETC.,	xxxiv
A DICTIONARY OF THE NOTED NAMES OF FICTION, ETC.,	1 to 398
INDEX OF THE REAL NAMES OF PERSONS, PLACES, ETC., WHOSE NICKNAMES, PSEUDONYMS, OR POPULAR APPELLATIONS, ARE GIVEN IN THE PRECEDING DICTIONARY,	399

KEY

TO THE SCHEME OF PRONUNCIATION.

VOWELS.

Ā, ā, *long*, as in .... Āle, fāte, greāt, prāy, rānge, tāste. [See § 1.]
Ă, ă, *short*, as in .... Ădd, făt, nărrow, răillery.
Ȧ, ȧ, as in .... Ȧerial, Isrȧel, chȧotic, mortmȧin.
Â, â, like ê, as in ...... Âir, fâre, peâr, prâyer, scârce. [See § 3.]
A̤, a̤, like ō, as in ...... A̤ll, broa̤d, ha̤ul, wa̤lk.
Ä, ä, like ŏ, as in ...... Wän, swällow, quädrant.
Ȧ, ȧ, as in .... Ärm, äunt, gräss, [Fr.] pâte (pät). [See § 2.]
A̍, a̍, as in .... [Ger.] mann (ma̍n), [Fr.] pas (pa̍).
Ạ, ạ, as in .... Beggạr, commạ, metạl, scholạr.

Ē, ē, *long*, as in .... Ēve, mēte, bēam, cēil, piēce, pēople.
Ĕ, ĕ, *short*, as in .... Ĕnd, mĕt, hĕad, hĕifer, lĕopard.
Ė, ė, as in .... Ėject, appėtite, sėrenity, strophė.
Ê, ê, like â, as in ...... Êre, bêar, hêir, whêre. [See § 3.]
Ē, ē, like ī, as in ...... Ērr, tērm, sērvant, defēr. [See § 4.]
Ē, ē, like ā, as in ...... Ēight, invēigh, prēy.
Ẹ, ẹ, as in .... Briẹr, geheral, robbẹr, suffẹr.

I, ī, *long*, as in .... Īvy, īce, pīne, chīld, aīsle, heīght, tīe.
Ĭ, ĭ, *short*, as in .... Ĭll, Ĭnn, pĭn, lĭly, guĭlt, sĭeve.
İ, i̇, as in .... İdea, di̇urnal, tri̇umphant.
Î, î, like ē, as in ...... Marîne, pîque, polîce, ravîne.
Ī, ī, like ē, as in ...... Īrksome, fīr, gīrl, vīrtuous. [See § 4.]
Ị, ị, as in .... Elixịr, nadịr, tapịr.

Ō, ō, *long*, as in .... Ōld, tōne, fōe, snōw, sōul, yeōman. [See § 5.]
Ŏ, ŏ, *short*, as in .... Ŏdd, ŏn, cŏt, knŏwledge, mŏral.
Ȯ, ȯ, as in .... Ȯbey, borrȯw, [Fr.] homme (ȯm). [See § 5.]
Ô, ô, like ȧ, as in ...... Ôrb, ôrder, geôrgic, bôught.
Ō, ô, like ōō, as in ...... Môve, prôve, shôe, sôup.
Ó, ó, like ŭ, as in ...... Cóme, dóes, dóne, blóod, tóuch.
Ö, ö, as in .... [Ger.] böse (bö′zä), [Fr.] jeu (zhö). [See §§ 43, 46.]
Ọ, ọ, as in .... Authọr, carọl, ransọm, connẹct.

Ū, ū, *long*, as in .... Ūse, cūbe, tūne, lūte, feūdal. [See § 6.]
Ŭ, ŭ, *short*, as in .... Ŭs, cŭb, tŭn, hŭrry.
U̇, u̇, as in .... U̇nite, agu̇e, cu̇pidity, globu̇le.
Û, û, like ōō, as in ...... Trûe, rûin, erûdite, virûlent. [See § 6.]

INTRODUCTION.

Ṳ, ṳ, like o͞o, as in ...... Fṳll, pṳll, pṳsh, coṳld.
Û, û, as in .... Ûrn, fûr, fûrry, incûr, pûrple. [See § 4.]
Ü, ü, as in .... [Ger.] grün, [Fr.] vue (vü). [See §§ 34, 51.]
Ų, ų, as in .... Sulphųr, gloriouṣ.

Ȳ, ȳ, *long*, as in .... Tȳpe, flȳ, stȳle, buȳ, rȳe.
Y̆, y̆, *short*, as in .... Ny̆mph, ly̆ric, my̆thic, sy̆mbol.
Ŷ, ŷ, as in .... Tŷphoon, hŷdraulic, lŷceum.
Ẏ, ẏ, like ē, as in ...... My̆rrh, my̆rtle, sy̆rt. [See § 4.]
Y, y, as in .... Martyr, zephyr.

Æ, æ, like e, as in ...... Cæsar (*long*), Æschylus (*short*).
Œ, œ, like e, as in ...... Crœsus (*long*), Œdipus (*short*).
EW, ew, like u, as in ... Ewe, dew, few, new (=û), crew (=o͞o).
OI, oi, as in .... Oil, foible, foist, join, loiter, poignant.
OY, oy, as in .... Oyster, boy, employ, joyous, royal.
O͞O, o͞o, as in .... Fo͞od, no͞on, mo͞od, o͞oze.
ŎŎ, ŏŏ, as in .... Fŏŏt, gŏŏd, stŏŏd, wŏŏlly.
ÔU, ôu, as in .... Ôunce, bôund, hôuse, pôut.
ÔW, ôw, as in .... Ôwl, nôw, tôwer, vôwel.

CONSONANTS.

Ç, ç, as in .... Çent, çity, çyst, açid, flaççid, suççess.
Ç, ç, as in .... Çage, çoal, çure, flaççid, suççess.
C̣H, c̣h, as in .... C̣haise, c̣hampagne, mac̣hine.
C̣H, c̣h, as in .... C̣hasm, c̣haos, c̣haracter, ec̣ho.
CH, ch, as in .... Chance, cheer, church, teacher. [See § 8.]
Ğ, ğ, as in .... Ğet, ğive, tiğer, foğğy.
Ġ, ġ, as in .... Ġem, ġender, ġiant, eleġy.
Ḥ, ḥ, as in .... [Sp.] Jorge (ḥor'ḥā), hijo (ee'ḥo). [See § 60.]
Ḵ, ḵ, as in .... [Ger.] ach (äḵ), buch (bo͞oḵ). [See § 71.]
K̇, k̇, as in .... [Ger.] ich (ik̇), durch (do͞ork̇). [See § 71.]
L̇, l̇, as in .... [Sp.] llano, (lä'no), [It.] gli (l̇ee). [See § 82.]
Ñ, ñ, as in .... [Fr.] règne (rāñ), [Sp.] ñoño. [See §§ 62, 78.]
N, n, as in .... [Fr.] vin (văⁿ), [Port.] vim (veeⁿ). [See § 62.]
Ṅ, ṅ, like ng, as in ...... Iṅk, uṅcle, aṅger, aṅxiety, laryṅx.
NG, ng, as in .... Singing, hanger, prolong, young.
PH, ph, as in .... Phantom, philosophy, seraphic.
QU, qu, as in .... Quantity, queen, quince, banquet.
Ṙ, ṙ, as in .... [Fr.] mer (mêṙ), [Sp.] rata (ṙä'tä). [See § 64.]
Ṣ, ṣ, like z, as in .... Adviṣe, preṣide, roṣe, diṣmal, spaṣm.
T̄H, t̄h, as in .... Fat̄her, t̄hen, t̄his, t̄herefore, smoot̄h.
V̇, v̇, as in .... [Ger.] schwan (shv̇än), [Sp.] cubo (koo'v̇o). [See § 68.]
WH, wh, as in .... When, which, while. [See § 11.]
X̣, x̣, like gz, as in ...... Ex̣ample, ex̣emplary, ux̣orious.
ZH, zh, as in .... Azure (ā'zhoor), usual (ū'zhoo-al), vision (vizh'un).

INTRODUCTION.

*** In addition to what appears in the Key, the following explanations will be needed for understanding the notation made use of in this Dictionary:—

Diacritical marks have been dispensed with, in the case of English names, wherever it seemed that the accentuation and the division into syllables would be sufficient to indicate the true pronunciation to any one familiar with the more general and commonly-understood principles of English orthoëpy; but, in all exceptional, doubtful, or difficult cases, the appropriate marks are used. Most of the names from modern foreign languages are respelt.

In combinations of vowels, where one letter is marked, it is to be taken as representing the sound of the combination, and the letter or letters which are not marked are to be regarded as silent; as in $gr\bar{a}in$, $d\bar{e}al$, $s\bar{e}ize$, tie, $d\bar{o}or$, $gr\acute{o}up$, $jo\acute{u}rney$, $fl\bar{o}w$, &c.

The combined letters ce, ci, sci, se, si, or ti, occurring before a vowel in a syllable immediately preceded by an accented syllable, are generally equivalent to sh; as in o′cean, sapona′ceous, coer′cion, magi′cian, an′cient, gra′cious, omni′science, nau′seous, tran′sient, pa′tience, vexa′tious, proba′tion, &c. But if, the combination si, when thus situated, is at the same time preceded by a vowel, it has the sound represented by the digraph zh; as in eli′sion, explo′sion, suffu′sion, &c. Such syllables are not usually respelt, as, in general, they will naturally be pronounced correctly by an English speaker.

In respelling for pronunciation, aw and ee are often used instead of $\bar{a}$ and $\bar{e}$ respectively.

In the notation of $\delta\hat{u}$ and $\delta\hat{w}$ (as in $ounce$, owl), the mark over the o [ˆ] is intended to suggest the first element of the diphthong, namely, a as in arm (marked $\ddot{a}$), and the circumflex [ˆ] over the u and the w, to indicate the second element, namely, u as in $true$ (marked $\dot{u}$).

The sounds represented by $\breve{a}$, $\breve{e}$, $\breve{\imath}$, $\breve{o}$, $\breve{u}$, $\breve{y}$, are essentially the same in quality as the proper long sounds of these vowels, but differ in quantity, being less protracted in utterance. In respelling foreign names for pronunciation, $\breve{a}$, $\breve{e}$ (or e), and $\breve{o}$, are generally used instead of $\bar{a}$, $\bar{e}$, and $\bar{o}$, unless a full accent falls upon the vowel.

The marked letters $ạ$, $ẹ$, $ị$, $ọ$, $ụ$, $ỵ$, represent the sound of "the neutral vowel," or u as in us, urn. They occur only in unaccented syllables. Diacritical signs placed above these letters are intended to indicate their normal or theoretical value. Thus, $salad$, $cymbal$, $altar$, $hillock$, $lion$, $sailor$, $ballot$, $confess$, would regularly be pronounced sal′ăd, cym′băl, al′tăr, hil′lŏck, li′ŏn, sail′ŏr, bal′lŏt, cŏn-fess′, but in fluent, and particularly in colloquial, utterance, the unaccented vowel is apt to suffer a corruption or change of its distinctive quality, falling into the easier sound of the neutral vowel, so that the actual or customary pronunciation of the words in question is sal′ud, cym′bul, al′tur, hil′luck, li′un, sail′ur, bal′lut, cun-fess′. They may, therefore, be printed thus:— sal′ạd, cym′bạl, al′tạr, hil′lọck, li′ọn, sail′ọr, bal′lọt, cọn-fess′.

The letter s is doubled, in the orthoëpical respelling, to indicate the "sharp" or hissing sound of this member of the alphabet, in cases where a single s would be liable to be pronounced like z; as $expense$ (eks-penss′).

In a word having more than one accent, the primary or principal accent is denoted by a heavy mark; the secondary, or subordinate, by a lighter mark; as in *Ad'amas'tor*. In the division of words into syllables, these marks, besides performing their proper office, supply the place of the hyphen.

An apostrophe ['] is used in the respelling of certain French words to show that an unaccented *e* is either entirely mute, or is pronounced with the briefest possible sound of *e* in *her*. It is also used after *y*, in some cases, to denote that this letter is to be pronounced with its consonant sound, as in *yard, yes*, &c.

A tie [⌒] placed over two or more vowels denotes that they must be pronounced without an obvious separation into distinct syllables; as, *Hauy* (ä'ü-e').

The figures which follow some of the names in the Vocabulary refer to corresponding sections in the following "Remarks" and "Rules."

REMARKS ON SOME POINTS OF ENGLISH ORTHOËPY.

Ā.

§ 1. The sound of *a* in *ale, fate* (commonly called "long *a*"), though regarded by many writers as a simple element, is in most cases diphthongal, beginning with a sound closely resembling that of the first *e* in *there*, but slightly less open, and ending with a brief sound of *e* in *me*. (See § 3.) This final *e* sound is usually omitted in unaccented syllables, and in the correct pronunciation of the common foreign equivalent of *ā*; namely, *e* as in [Fr.] *bête, née*, [Ger.] *ewig*, &c. (See § 31.)

A (as in *bath, dance*, &c.).

§ 2. There is a considerable class of words (chiefly monosyllables) ending in *aff, aft, ask, asp, ass, ast*, with a few ending in *ance, and*, and *ant* (as *staff, graft, mask, rasp, glass, last, lance, command, pant*), to which must be added *castle, advantage, half*, and some other words, in the pronunciation of which, usage, both in England and America, is far from being uniform, some speakers giving to the vowel the full, open sound of *a* in *far* (ä), and some the abrupt, flat sound of *a* in *man* (ă), while others, seeking for a compromise between these two extremes, either slightly shorten the ä, or dwell upon the ă. Of these varieties, the first and second (ä and ă) are much the most common. The drawled ä was never more than a temporary and local fashion, which — according to Smart — has been generally laid aside in England, and which seems to be going out of use in America, in those parts where it has hitherto prevailed. The brief ä, — improperly styled "intermediate," — though recommended by Worcester, Goodrich, and some other orthoëpists, differs so slightly from the fuller form of this vowel, that the distinction attempted to be set up is practically a nugatory one. Words belonging to the class under consideration are in this Dictionary marked as having the full sound of *a* in *far*; but the reader is, in every instance, referred to this section, and can decide for himself which of the sounds here described he will adopt in his own practice.

Â, Ê.

§ 3. The sound of *a* heard in *fare, lair*, &c., and of *e* in *there, heir*, &c., when these words are correctly pronounced, is a lengthened form of the *e* in *met*, or of the initial element in long *a* (*a* as in *mate*), sounds which are closely allied, and are, by some writers, regarded as identical. Instead of this, however, many speakers substitute a prolongation of the *a* in *mat*, — a mode of utterance which, notwithstanding its frequency and its equal gracefulness, is opposed by the majority of cultivated speakers, including most of the orthoëpists.

Ē, Ĭ, Ũ, Ỹ.

§ 4. The vowel *u* before *r*, in such words as *urn, fur, furry, incur, incurring*, &c. (sometimes called the "neutral vowel," from its peculiarly dull and indiscrete character), is very common in English, and has a uniform and well-known sound. According to the common practice, both in England and America, and according to most writers upon the subject, the vowels *e, i*, and *y*, and the digraph *ea*, when similarly situated, have precisely the same sound. But some speakers, particularly among the more refined and aristocratic classes of English society, give them a different and peculiar sound, which is best described as intermediate between that of *u* in *urn*, and that of *e* in *met*, being less guttural than the former, and less palatal than the latter. This "delicacy" of pronunciation, as it has been termed, is not observed in unaccented syllables, or in "very common words," even by those who are tenacious of its observance in other cases. In this work, all these vowels are marked in the same way (*ẽ, ĩ, ũ, ỹ*), but the reference-figure appended to words in the Dictionary in which they occur, will direct the reader to this section, that he may not be left in ignorance of the fact that there is a diversity of usage in their pronunciation.

Ō, Ŏ.

§ 5. The sound of *o* in *old, note*, &c. (commonly called "long *o*"), though by some writers regarded as a simple sound, is in reality diphthongal, ending in a slight sound of *oo* in *food*, or in *foot*. The initial element is the normal *o*, intermediate in quality between *aw* (as in *saw*) and *ōō*. The terminal *oo* sound is usually omitted in unaccented syllables.

In some parts of America, particularly in New England, it is very common to shorten the sound of long *o* in certain monosyllables, and in the accented syllable of some other words, by dropping the brief final element which properly belongs to the vowel, and at the same time making the initial element slightly more open in quality; but the practice is an unauthorised provincialism. This shortened form of long *o* is heard in the words *home, stone, wholly*, &c. It also occurs in some foreign languages. As it differs but little from the sound of unaccented *o* (in *car′go, ech′o*, &c.), it is, in this Dictionary, represented by the same diacritical sign (*ŏ*).

Ū.

§ 6. The sound of *u* in *unit, cube, mute*, &c. (commonly called "long *u*"), is a compound sound formed of consonant *y* as the initial element, and the *oo* in

INTRODUCTION. xix

food as the final element. The sound of consonant *y* is distinctly heard when *u* (or any of its equivalent digraphs) makes or begins an initial syllable (as in *unite, use*); when it is preceded by any one of the labial or palatal sounds *p, b, m, f, v, k, g* (as in *putrid, bugle, music, fusion, view* (= vu), *cubic, gules*); and when it is preceded by any one of the dental sounds *d, t, l, n, th*, provided the preceding vowel is short and under the accent (as in *ĕd'ucate, rĭt'ual, săl'utary, mŏn'ument, spăth'ulate*). But when it is preceded, in the same syllable, by any one of the consonants *d, t, l, n, s, th*, it is difficult to introduce the sound of *y*, and hence careless speakers omit it altogether, saying *dook, toob, loot, nood, soot, enthoosiasm*, instead of *duke, tube, lute, nude, suit, enthusiasm*. The reason is, that, after forming these dental consonants, the organs are in a position to pass directly and easily to the labial *oo;* but to insert the palatal *y* before the *oo*, is to go back from a medial to a posterior position of the organs before proceeding to an anterior position. Although the tendency to get rid of the *y*, in such cases, is a natural and legitimate one, it is only so far yielded to by the best speakers as to substitute for the *y* the closely related element short *i*, made as brief as possible, and pronounced in the same syllable as the *oo*. If, in similar situations, the *u* is preceded by the sound of *r, sh*, or *zh*, it takes the simple sound of *oo* in *food;* as, *rule* (rool), *true* (troo), *virulent* (vĭr'oo-lent), *sure* (shoor), *azure* (ā'zhoor). When preceded by *ch* or *j*, the practice of different speakers varies, some sounding the *u* as *oo*, others as *ĭ-o͞o*.

H.

§ 7. The sound of *h* in *hand, heart*, &c., is a pure aspiration produced by an emission of breath through whatever configuration of the vocal channel may be requisite for uttering a succeeding vowel or semivowel, the organs being always adjusted to the position of the next following sound before the *h* is pronounced. Yet *h* is palpably not a whisper of the following sound. If it were so, a whispered *he* would be nothing more than a prolonged whispered *e*, whereas the difference between the two elements is very marked, and is felt not only by the speaker, but by the hearer as well. Physiologically considered, *h* is formed by an expulsion of unvocalised breath through the glottis, which is opened wide through its whole extent. In simple whispering of the vowels, on the contrary, the vocal chords are brought together, — approximated, though not stretched, or but slightly so, — and the breath, in passing through, is thus not only rendered audible, but acquires a peculiar and distinctive quality of roughness, which approaches in a greater or less degree to actual sonancy.

CH, J.

§ 8. The digraph *ch* (as in *church*) is regarded by some writers as representing a simple sound; but most orthoëpists consider that it is compounded of *t* and *sh*. Neither view is quite right, nor is either wholly wrong. In forming *ch*, there is an attempt at blending *t* and *sh* in a single sound, the result of which is to modify the former of these elements by causing it to be produced, not in the ordinary way with the tip of the tongue against the gum of the upper front teeth, but with the flat surface of the tongue, near the tip, applied within the dome of the palate at the point where a slight relaxation of the contact, accompanied with an emission of breath, gives rise to the sound of *sh*. Considering the brevity of the two elements, and the peculiar closeness with which they are combined, we may regard *ch* as a consonant diphthong, or, as Müller expresses it, "only one whole consonant" consisting of "a half *t* and a half *sh*."

The sound of *j* — which is merely a vocal *ch* — is composed in like manner of a modified *d* followed by *zh*.

R.

§ 9. According to many English orthoëpists, the letter *r* has two distinct though related sounds, — the one a dental or lingual consonant, formed by a contact of the margin of the fore part of the tongue with the inner surface of the upper side teeth, the tip of the tongue touching, or nearly touching, the gum of the front teeth with a slight quivering or tremulous motion as the stream of intonated breath flows over it, heard (1.) when this letter is not preceded by a vowel, as in *rose, dream, pray, strike*; and (2.) when it is placed between two vowels of which the former is short, as in *ărĭd, pĕril, spĭrit, cŏral, lўric, sŏrry* (=sŏry), *hŭrry* (=hŭry); the other a guttural sound, nearly resembling a vowel, formed by a slight vibration of the root of the tongue and the uvula, heard when the letter *r* occurs before any consonant, or is itself the final consonant in a word, as in *part, verse, mirth, torn, surf, far, nor, slur*. In the first case, *r* is sometimes strongly trilled or rolled by a violent emission of the vocal current; but, in ordinary pronunciation, the sound is peculiarly smooth and liquid, and any decided vibration of the tongue is laborious, pedantic, and altogether un-English.

If *r* follows any one of the vowels *â, ē, ī, ō, ū, ōō, ôû*, a slight sound of the neutral vowel (*u* in *urn*) is inserted before the *r*, forming a diphthong with the preceding vowel, or, in the case of *ī, ū*, and *ôû*, a triphthong. Thus, *care, dear, wire, more, lure, boor, sour*, are pronounced câ͡'ur, de͡'ur, wi͡'ur, mo͡'ur, lu͡'ur, boo͡'ur, soû͡'ur. In English usage, the *r* is thus joined to the preceding vowel *in all cases* in which this vowel is in an accented syllable; and if, at the same time, a vowel follows, the *r* has, according to some orthoëpists, both its guttural and its lingual sound; as in *vary* (vâr′y, *or* vâr′ry), *era* (ē′ra, *or* ēr′ra), *tory* (tō′ry, *or* tōr′ry), *burin* (būr′in, *or* būr′rin), *houri* (hôûr′ĭ, *or* hôûr′rĭ), &c. In the United States, this mode of pronunciation is, for the most part, confined to words ending with *r* or *re* preceded by one of the above-mentioned vowels, and to the derivatives of such words. Thus, *dearest* (from *dear*) is pronounced dear′est, *or* dear′rest; *boorish* (from *boor*), boor′ish, *or* boor′rish; *sourer* (from *sour*), sour′er, *or* sour′rer, &c.; but *vary* is vā′ry; *era*, ē′ra; *tory*, tō′ry, &c. The Scotch, on the contrary, preserve the vowel pure even in derivatives, saying dea′rest, boo′rish, sou′rer, &c., as well as vā′ry, ē′ra, tō′ry, &c.

It must be observed that some very acute and eminent phonologists utterly deny the existence of the alleged double pronunciation of *r*, maintaining that the letter has, in English at least, one unvaried sound in all situations, produced between the tip of the tongue and the upper gum. Others allow that when *r* is preceded by a long or full vowel, a slight guttural vibration accompanies the lingual articulation; but they do not regard this modification of the sound as affording sufficient ground for its discrimination into two distinct and independent elements. It is not improbable that the disagreement of authorities in regard to the precise nature of the "guttural *r*" is owing, in some measure, to actual difference of utterance.

It is further to be observed, that, in the best style of pronunciation, *r* is never silent; but that, when it occurs after a vowel, it is commonly suppressed by careless or uneducated speakers.

W, Y.

§ 10. The sounds signified by *w* and *y*, when these letters occur at the beginning of a word or syllable, as in *woo*, *ye*, &c., are considered by some writers to be identical with the vowels *oo* and *e* respectively; they are, however, formed by a closer approximation of the articulative organs, which destroys the pure vocality of the vowel sounds, and gives them a consonantal or semi-consonantal character. They are not, however, perfect consonants; for it is impossible to prolong them, and the attempt to do so results only in the production of the vowels *oo* and *e*.

WH.

§ 11. The digraph *wh* is regarded by many modern orthoëpists as representing a simple elementary sound, which is the surd or whispered correspondent of *w*. Of those who take this view, some say that the sound of *wh* is followed by that of *w*; as in *when* (wh-w-e-n): others assert that the voice is not heard until the following vowel is commenced, *when*, for example, being pronounced wh-e-n; but such persons wrongly analyse their own pronunciation. The common opinion is, that both letters of the digraph are pronounced with their usual sounds, only in the reverse order, — *hw*, — according to the original Anglo-Saxon orthography. But *h-w* does not differ from *wh-w*, *h* being an emission of unvocalised breath through the position taken by the organs of speech in forming the next following element, as is explained in § 7.

RULES FOR THE PRONUNCIATION OF GREEK AND LATIN WORDS.

§ 12. The established English pronunciation of Latin words and of Latinised forms of Greek words is conformed to the general laws and tendencies of the English language. Hence, the proper position of the accent and the syllabication having been determined, each syllable is to be pronounced according to the usual powers or sounds of the letters in English, except in cases specially provided for in the following rules.

Vowels.

§ 13. (1.) Any vowel at the end of an accented syllable, and *e*, *o*, and *u* at the end of an unaccented syllable, have the long English sound; as, *Cā'to*, *Cē'res*, *Mī'das*, *Sō'lon*, *Nū'ma*, *Pē-lī'des*, *Hŭ-me'rus*, *Lū-ca'nus*.

§ 14. (2.) If a syllable ends with a consonant, the vowel has its short English sound; as, *Băl'bus*, *Mĕm'non*, *Mŏs'chus*, *Pŭb'lius*.

EXCEPTION. — *E*, in final *es*, has its long sound; as in *Achilles* (a-kil'lēz).

§ 15. (3.) *A*, ending an unaccented syllable, is sounded like *a* in *comma*; as, *Cre-u'sa*, *A-ri'on*.

§ 16. (4.) *E* final is always sounded; as in *He'be*, *Pe-nel'o-pe*.

§ 17. (5.) The diphthongs *œ* and *æ* are pronounced as *e* would be in the same situation; as, *Cæsar* (sē'zar), *Œnone* (e-no'ne), *Dædalus* (ded'a-lus), *Œdipus* (ed'i-pus).

§ 18. (6.) *I*, ending a final syllable, has its long English sound; as, *E-pig'o-ni*. Ending an initial unaccented syllable, it has in some cases its long sound, as in *Bī-a'nor*, *I-ū'lus*; and in some its short sound, as in *Ci-lic'i-a*, *I-ta'li-a*. In all other cases, ending an unaccented syllable, it has its short sound; as, *Fă'bĭ-us*.

§ 19. (7.) *Y* is pronounced as *i* would be in the same situation.

§ 20. (8.) When *ai*, *ei*, *oi*, and *yi*, not initial, are followed by another vowel, and take the accent on the *a*, *e*, *o*, or *y*, the *i* assumes the sound of consonant *y*, and the vowel before it has its long sound; as in *Maia* (mā'ya), *Hygeia* (hī-jē'ya), *Pompeius* (pom-pē'yus), *Latoia* (la-tō'ya), *Harpyia* (har-pī'ya).

Consonants.

§ 21. (9.) The consonants *c* and *g* have their "soft" sound, like *s* and *j*, before *e*, *i*, *y*, *œ*, and *æ*; before *a*, *o*, and *u*, or a consonant, they have their "hard" sound; as in *cot*, *go*.

EXCEPTION. — When *g*, having the sound of *j*, is preceded by another *g*, the former of the two is suppressed, or may be said to coalesce in sound with the second; as, *Aggenus* (a-je'nus).

§ 22. (10.) The combination *ch* is pronounced like *k*; as, *Charon* (kā'ron).

§ 23. (11.) Each of the three consonants *c*, *s*, and *t*, when preceded immediately by the accent, or itself ending an accented syllable, and followed by *ia*, *ie*, *ii*, *io*, or *iu*, commonly has the sound of *sh*; as in *Por'cia* (por'shi-a), *Cly'tie* (klish'i-e), *Hora'tii* (ho-rā'shi-i), *Pho'cion* (fō'shi-on), *Cas'sius* (kash'i-us). *C* has also the same sound, when following an accented vowel, and standing before *eu* and *yo*; as, *Menœ'ceus* (me-ne'she-us), *Si'cyon* (sish'i-on).

EXCEPTION. — When *si*, immediately preceded by an accented vowel, is followed by a vowel, the *s* takes the sound of *zh*; as in *He'siod* (he'zhi-od). — Though not properly an exception to the rule, it may be stated that *zi* similarly situated is pronounced in the same manner; as in *Aly'zia* (a-lizh'i-a). — *T*, when preceded by another *t*, and commonly in the termination *tion*, has its proper sound (heard in *top*, *mat*, &c.); as in *Brut'ti-i*, *Me'ti-on*: when preceded by *s* or *x*, it has, according to some authorities, the same sound; according to others, the sound of *ch* in *church*; as in *Sallus'tius* (sal-lus'ti-us, *or* sal-lus'chi-us), *Sex'tius* (seks'ti-us, *or* seks'chi-us), &c.

§ 24. (12.) *S*, when final, if preceded by *e*, has the sound of *z*; as in *Per'icles* (pĕr'i-klēz).

§ 25. (13.) *X*, ending an accented syllable, and standing before *i* followed by another vowel, has the sound of *ksh;* as, *Cinx'ia* (singk'shi-a).

§ 26. (14.) Combinations of initial consonants which are foreign to the nature and habits of our language, drop the sound of their first letter or digraph; as in *Cneius* (pronounced ne'yus), *Ctesiphon* (tes'i-fon), *Gnatho* (nā'tho), *Mnemosyne* (ne-mos'i-ne), *Pnytagoras* (nĭ-tag'o-ras), *Psyche* (sī'ke), *Ptolemy* (tol'e-me), *Phthas* (thas).

§ 27. (15.) The terminations *aus* and *ous* are always to be pronounced in two syllables; as, *Archela'us, Alcin'o-us*.

§ 28. (16.) The termination *eus*, in proper names which in Greek end in ευς, as *Orpheus, Prometheus*, &c., should be pronounced in one syllable, the *eu* being a diphthong with the sound of "long *u.*"

Accent.

§ 29. (17.) Words of two syllables invariably have the accent on the first syllable. In words of more than two syllables, if the penult is long in quantity, it takes the accent; but, if short, the accent is on the antepenult. When the penult is common, or doubtful, the accent is on the antepenult.

☞ By quantity, in Greek and Latin, is meant the relative time occupied in pronouncing a syllable, *when those languages were spoken tongues.* A syllable containing a short vowel may be lengthened by accompanying consonants; but the ancients seem to have felt the effect of these only when final, and to have made no account of initial consonants — probably because they pronounced them with extreme brevity — in estimating the duration of a syllable. The general rules in relation to quantity are as follows: — 1. Before *j, x, z,* or any two consonants except a mute followed by *l* or *r*, the vowel of the penult is *long by position.* [This is the language of the grammarians: the *vowel*, in such cases, was probably short or stopped; but the *syllable* was long, being made so by the following consonant or consonants.] The digraphs *ch, ph, rh*, and *th*, which represent simple sounds, are reckoned as single consonants. 2. A vowel before a mute and *l* or *r* is common; that is, either long or short. 3. Diphthongs are long. 4. A vowel before another vowel or *h* is short. In other cases, the quantity must be determined by etymology, metrical usage, or the orthography of the word in Greek; but every vowel which cannot be proved to be long, is arbitrarily assumed to be short. — The division of words into syllables — which depends in part upon the position of the accent, and this, in turn, upon quantity — must be understood before words can be correctly pronounced. The rules in regard to this subject may be found in any good Latin grammar.

BRIEF RULES

FOR THE PRONUNCIATION OF THE PRINCIPAL MODERN LANGUAGES OF CONTINENTAL EUROPE.

Vowels.

§ 30. (1.) In the languages of the Continent of Europe, the vowel *a*, when long, has usually the sound of the English *a* in *far, father;* when short, nearly that of *a* in *fat, man;* never that of *a* in *fate*. *Â*, in French, has a sound resembling that of *a* in *far*, but deeper and less distinct, verging toward that of *a* in *all:* its peculiar quality is due to the retraction of the tongue and the soft palate. A briefer variety of the same sound is heard in the Fr. *pas*, Ger. *mann*. In Hungarian, *a* is like *o* in *not;* *á*, like *a* in *far*. *Å*, in Swedish, has a sound intermediate between that of *a* in *all*, and that of *o* in *note*. For the sounds of *ā*, *ã*, *ą*, see §§ 37, 62.

§ 31. (2.) *E* generally has a sound similar to that of "long *a*" in *fate*, but often like that of "short *e*" in *met*, or like the latter when protracted. (See § 1.) *É*, in French, has the sound of *e* in *then*, or that of the initial element in *mate* (see § 1); *è* and *ê* have the sound of the first *e* in *there;* *e* (unaccented) is, in most cases, either entirely silent, or has a very brief sound of the neutral vowel (*u* in *up, urn*). *É*, in Swedish, when long, has a sound somewhat like that of short *i* (in *pin*), but more prolonged; when short, it is like *e* in *met*. In Hungarian and Polish, *e* (unaccented) sounds like *e* in *met;* *é* nearly like *a* in *mate*. For the sounds of *ē*, *ę*, see § 62.

§ 32. (3.) *I* has usually the sound of *i* in *marine*, which is the same as the "long *e*" in *me, she*, &c. It is often shortened in quantity, like the *e* in *bemoan*, but the quality of the sound remains the same, and should not be suffered to degenerate into that of *i* in *ill*. This latter sound, however, is heard in Dutch, and sometimes in German. In Hungarian, *í* and *i* differ only in length, the accented vowel being more protracted than the unaccented.

§ 33. (4.) *O* has, for the most part, the same, or nearly the same, sounds that it has in English in the words *note, not, north*. (See § 5.) It sometimes — as in the It. *volpe* — has a sound intermediate between that of *o* in *note* and that of *oo* in *food*. This is called, in Italian, "*o chiuso*." The "*o aperto*" of the same language is a sound intermediate between the *o* of *note* and that of *north*. In Swedish and Norwegian, at the end of a syllable, *o* has the sound of *o͞o* or of *o͝o*. *Ô*, in French, has always the full sound of "long *o*" in English. In Hungarian, *o* is nearly like long *o* in English; *ó* has a fuller and deeper sound. In Polish, *o* sounds like *o* in *note;* *ó*, like *oo* in *food*, or in *foot*. For the sound of *ō*, see § 46.

§ 34. (5.) *U*, in most of these languages, has, when long, the sound of *u* in *true* (equivalent to the *o͞o* in *food*); when short, that of *u* in *full* (equivalent to the *o͝o* in *foot*). In French, — and also in Dutch, when at the end of a syllable, — it has a sound intermediate between *o͞o* and *ē*, formed by attempting to pronounce these sounds simultaneously, the lips being placed in the position for uttering *o͞o*, and the tongue in that for *ē*. The sound is sometimes long and sometimes short, but the difference is merely one of quantity. In Dutch, *u*, when short or stopped, is sounded as in *nut*. *U*, in Swedish, is intermediate between *i* and *o͞o*, but is a pinched and very peculiar sound, differing considerably in its effect upon the ear from that of the French *u*, the lips being rounded instead of pouted. The nearest equivalent in English is *o͞o*. In Hungarian, *u* (unaccented) has the sound of *o͞o;* *ú*, a longer and fuller sound of the same general quality. For the sound of *ū*, see § 51.

§ 35. (6.) *Y*, for the most part, has the same sound that *i* has; that is, it is

INTRODUCTION. XXV

like "long *e*" in English. (See § 32.) In Dutch, it has the sound of the English "long *i*" (*i* in *pine*); but in the modern Dutch orthography it is replaced by *ij*. In Danish, Norwegian, and Swedish, it is like the French and Dutch *u*, or the German *ü*. (See § 34.)

Diphthongs and Vowel Combinations.

§ 36. (7.) *Aa*, in most languages, has the same sound as single *a*,—that is, the sound of *a* in *far*,—but is more prolonged. In Danish, it sounds nearly as *a* in *all*, but verges towards the sound of *o* in *note*.

§ 37. (8.) *Ae*, or *ä*, when long, is usually sounded like *a* in *fate*, or the first *e* in *there;* when short, like *e* in *met*. (See § 1.) In Dutch, it is like *a* in *far;* but the reformed Dutch orthography substitutes *aa* for *ae*.

§ 38. (9.) *Aeu*, or *äu*, in German, has the sound of *oi* in *toil*, but is differently pronounced in different parts of Germany.

§ 39. (10.) *Ai* and *ay* are generally sounded like the English adverb *ay* (yes); but in French they have nearly the sound of *a* in *fate*, or *e* in *there*. (See § 1.)

§ 40. (11.) *Eau*, in French, has the same sound as the French *au;* that is, of the English "long *o*."

§ 41. (12.) *Ee* has a prolonged sound of the foreign *e*, which is nearly equivalent to the English *a* in *fate*. (See § 31.)

§ 42. (13.) *Ei* and *ey* are generally like *ay* in *day*, when this word is pronounced with the full diphthongal sound of the vowel. In French, they have a more open sound, resembling that of *e* in *met*, or that of *a* in *mate* with the terminal element of the *a* omitted. (See § 1.) In German and Danish, they are like the English adverb *ay* (yes); that is, they unite the sounds of *a* in *far* and *i* in *ill*, and hence nearly resemble our "long *i*."

§ 43. (14.) *Eu*, in French and Dutch, has—with some variations of quantity, and some slight differences of quality—a sound similar to that of *u* in *urn*, but more accurately described as intermediate between the *a* in *mate* and the *o* in *note*, and formed by an attempt to pronounce these vowels simultaneously. (See § 46.) *Eu*, in German and Danish, sounds like *oi* in *toil*. In Italian, Spanish, and Portuguese, it is equivalent to $\overline{a\overline{oo}}$.

§ 44. (15.) *Ie* usually sounds like *e* in *me*, but, in German, it sometimes makes two syllables, and, in French, before *r* final, forms a diphthong which is pronounced $\hat{e\textnormal{-}\overline{a}}$.

§ 45. (16.) *Ii* is equivalent to *ī*—that is, to the English "long *e*," as in *me*—prolonged.

§ 46. (17.) *Oe*, or *ö* (in Dan. *ø*), in the Germanic languages, is *essentially* the same as *eu* in French (see § 43), though most authorities recognise a slight difference of quality between the two sounds, *ö* inclining more to the sound of *ā*, and having the lips more pursed up for its utterance, than *eu*. The *u* in *urn* is the nearest English approximation to both. In Hungarian, *ŏ* or *ő* is merely a longer variety of *ō*.

§ 47. (18.) *Œu*, in French, is like *eu* in the same language. (See § 43.)

§ 48. (19.) *Oi*, in French, sounds, in most words, nearly like *wa* in *was*. In some words, it formerly had the sound now given to *ai*, by which it is replaced in the modern French spelling. *Oi*, in Danish, is like *oi* in English; *Øi* is *o͞e*, with the *o* short, or brief.

§ 49. (20.) *Oo*, has the sound of *oo* in *door*, or *o* in *note*, somewhat prolonged, and without the final element of this sound in English.

§ 50. (21.) *Ou*, in French, when long, is like *oo* in *food;* when short, like *oo* in *foot*. In Dutch and Norwegian, it has the sound of *ou* in the English word *out*. In Portuguese, it is usually pronounced like the English "long *o*."

§ 51. (22.) *Ue*, or *ü*, in the Germanic languages, is sounded like the French *u*. (See § 34.) In Hungarian, *ü* or *ű* is merely a longer variety of *ü*.

§ 52. (23.) *Ui* and *uy*, in Dutch, resemble *oi* in English.

§ 53. (24.) *Uu* is like *oo* in *food*, but longer.

Consonants.

§ 54. (25.) *B*, in German and Danish, at the end of a word, sounds like *p*. In Spanish, between two vowels, its sound is intermediate between those of the English *b* and *w*, and may be described as a *v* made without the aid of the teeth, but with the lips alone, which are pouted and brought flatly and feebly into contact.

§ 55. (26.) *C*, in Italian, before *e* and *i*, sounds like *ch* in *church;* in Spanish, in the same position, like *th* in *thin* (though in Catalonia and in Spanish America it has the sound of *s*). In German and Danish, before *e, i, y, ä, ö* (*ø*)*, ü*, or a diphthong commencing with any one of these letters, and in Polish in all positions, it is pronounced like *ts*. *Ć*, in Polish, blends the sounds of *ts* and consonant *y*. (Compare § 74.) *Ç*, in French and Portuguese, sounds like *s*, before *a, o*, and *u*.

§ 56. (27.) *D*, in German, Dutch, and Swedish, at the end of a word, sounds like *t;* in Spanish and Danish, when occurring between two vowels, or at the end of a word, like *th* in *this*, but it is very gently pronounced, so as sometimes scarcely to be audible.

§ 57. (28.) *F*, in Swedish, at the end of a word or syllable, sounds as *v* does in English.

§ 58. (29.) *G* is always "hard" before *a, o, u*, as it is in the English words *gain, gold, gust*. In Polish, it is hard in all situations; so also in Hungarian, unless followed by *j* or *y*. (See §§ 76, 79.) In French, Spanish, and Portuguese, before *e, i*, and *y*, it is like the *j* of these languages. (See § 60.) In Italian, in the same position, it is like the English *j*, that is, like *g* in *gem*. (See § 8.) In German, the standard and best pronunciation makes *g* "hard" in every case when it is followed by a vowel in the same word; but when preceded and not followed by a vowel, it has the sound of the German *ch*. (See § 71.) In Dutch, *g*, in all positions, has a harsh guttural sound, which is the sonant or vocalised correspondent of the German guttural *ch*. (See § 71.) In Swedish, before *e, i, y, ä*, and *ö*, and when preceded by any other consonant than *n*, it sounds like the English consonant *y;* in Danish, at the end of a word, its sound is very soft, somewhat resembling that of *h*. — *Gu*, in French, Spanish, and Portuguese, before *e* and *i*, sounds like *gu* in *guest, guile*, the *u* being inserted to keep the *g* in its hard sound before these vowels.

INTRODUCTION. xxvii

§ 59. (30.) *H*, in French, Italian, Spanish, and Portuguese, is either wholly mute, or is very feebly aspirated. In the remaining languages of Continental Europe, it sounds as in English. In all of them, it is mute when it follows a vowel in the same syllable, its office being merely to show that the vowel has its long sound. In Polish, *h* is very harshly aspirated, resembling *k*, or the German guttural *ch*. (See § 71.)

§ 60. (31.) *J*, in German, Dutch, Danish, Norwegian, Swedish, Polish, and Hungarian, has the sound of the English *y* consonant. In Italian, it has rather the sound of "long *e*." In French and Portuguese, it has the sound orthoëpically represented by *zh*; that is, of *s* in *treasure*, or *z* in *azure*. In Spanish, it has a very peculiar sound, somewhat resembling that of a strongly aspirated *h*, and this is substituted for it in Spanish America. "To pronounce it," says Ellis, "the back of the mouth must be stopped by doubling up the back of the tongue, and making an effort as if to hawk up phlegm, the scrape being in the *palate*, and *not* in the pharynx." It is most nearly allied to the German palatal *ch*, but must not be confounded with it, nor with *sh*, *h*, or the guttural *ch*.

§ 61. (32.) *L*, in French, in the terminations *ble*, *nle*, *ple*, &c. (as in *table*, *branle*, *simple*), is colloquially whispered, but in serious or careful discourse, it has its usual vocal sound, and is followed by a faint sound of the neutral vowel (*u* in *up*, *urn*). *Ł*, in Polish, has a peculiar, thick sound, formed by placing the under side of the tip of the tongue firmly against the back of the upper front teeth, or the upper gum.

§ 62. (33.) *M* and *n*, in French and Portuguese, when final in a word or syllable, and also when not doubled or not followed by a vowel, have no sound of their own, but are mere diacritical letters, or signs, serving to show that the preceding vowel is nasal, that is, pronounced by opening the back nostrils and allowing the voice to enter the nose simultaneously with its passage through the mouth. The nasal vowels in French are as follows:—

1. am, an } = ŏⁿ   2. im, in, (o) in }   3. om, on } = ŏⁿ   4. um, un } = ŭⁿ
    em, en   aim, ain } = ăⁿ   aun   cum, eun
                        cim, cin
                        (i) en

In pronouncing these sounds, there must be no contact of the tongue and the soft palate, as in forming the sound of *ng* in English. By some phonetists, the first of these nasal vowels is regarded as corresponding to the pure oral vowel in *far*; by others, to that in *not*; but these two sounds are closely related, the brief open *o* of *not* (ŏ) being intermediate between the *a* of *far* (ä) and the *o* of *for* (ō, å, or *aw*), and hence differing but little from a shortened form of the open *å*. There is disagreement, also, as to the quality of the third nasal vowel, some referring it to the *o* in *note*, or to its briefer form as heard in the New England pronunciation of *whole*, *only*, &c. (as is done in this work); while others think that it corresponds to the *o* in *form*, *north*, &c. In Portuguese, the nasality of a vowel is sometimes indicated by the sign ~ (originally a superposed *m*) placed over it. The combinations representing nasal vowels are ã, ãa, am, an (pron. äⁿ); em, en (pron. ăⁿ); im (pron. ĕⁿ); õ, om, on (pron. ŏⁿ); um, un (pron. ōⁿ). Nasal diphthongs are ãe, ãi, ão, õe. The terminations *aes, oes*, were formerly written *aens, oens*. The nasal vowels o^n and a^n occur in Polish, in which language they are written *ą, ę*. — *M*, in conversational French, is whispered, and not vocalised, in such words as *schisme*; but, in formal delivery, it has its usual vocal sound, followed by an indistinct murmur of the mute *e*. — *N* before *g*, in Italian, usually preserves its pure sound; in the other Continental European languages, or in most of them, it takes the sound of the English *n* in *sink*. — *Ñ*, in Spanish, is a variety of *n*, formed by an attempt to pronounce *n* and consonant *y* simultaneously. The same is true of the Polish *ń*. The effect is very similar to that produced by the insertion of *y* after *n*; as in *minion* (min'yun). (Compare § 74.)

§ 63. (34.) *Qu*, in Spanish and Portuguese, when followed by *e* or *i*, has the sound of *k*; in other situations, that of *kŏŏ*. In French, the combination has the sound of *k* before every vowel. In German and Dutch, it is sounded as *kw* would be in those languages. (See § 68.) In most other languages, its sound is essentially the same as in English.

§ 64. (35.) *R*, at the end of a word or syllable, is sounded more distinctly, and in other positions is apt to be more strongly trilled, than in English. By us, this letter is usually pronounced with the under surface of the tip of the tongue applied within the dome of the palate, in which position the utterance is naturally very smooth and easy. By foreign nations, *r* is ordinarily produced by applying the upper surface of the tongue's tip to the upper gum at a point quite near the teeth, which occasions a peculiar harshness of sound, and most generally a decided vibration, or trill. In French, in such words as *sabre, cidre, apôtre, œuvre*, it is usually pronounced as a whisper, but is sometimes vocalised, particularly in serious discourse, forming a syllable with the obscure *e*. It never admits the interposition of the neutral vowel (*u* in *up, urn*) between it and a preceding vowel, as is often the case in English. Thus, the French *dire* is pronounced dêr or de'rṇ, whereas the English *dear* is pronounced de͡ur.

§ 65. (36.) *S*, between two vowels, has usually the sound of *z* in *zeal*. In German, it often has this sound given to it at the beginning of a syllable, but is commonly pronounced like *sz*, a hiss gliding instantaneously and almost imperceptibly into a buzz. In Hungarian, it sounds like *sh* in English. *Ś*, in Polish, blends in a single utterance the sounds of *s* and consonant *y*. (Compare § 74.)

§ 66. (37.) *T* has often a more dental sound than in English, the tip of the tongue being placed against the cutting edge of the upper front teeth, and not against the upper gum, as with us. This is particularly observable in Spanish.

§ 67. (38.) *V*, in German, sounds like *f*. In Danish, it is usually like *v* in English, but sometimes has the sound of *ŏŏ*; as in *havn* (hă'ŏŏn, *or* hŏŭn); when followed by *t*, it has the sound of *f*.

§ 68. (39.) *W*, in German and Dutch, is intermediate between the English *b* and *w*, on the one hand, and *v*, on the other, the inner surfaces of the lips being brought flat against each other, whereas in (Eng.) *w* they are rounded, in *b* the edges are compressed, and in *v* the lower lip comes in contact with the upper teeth. (See § 54.) By some writers, this peculiar utterance of *w* is said to be provincial and dialectical, in German, except in words in which *w* is preceded by a consonant, as, *schwan*. In Polish, *w*, when it precedes a whispered or mute consonant, is pronounced as *f;* in other situations, it has the sound of the German *w.*

§ 69. (40.) *X,* in French, has often the sound of *s,* and occasionally that of *z,* but more generally that of *ks* or of *gz,* as in English. In Spanish, it is equivalent to the *j* of that language. (See § 60.) In Portuguese, it is pronounced like *sh* in *shall.*

§ 70. (41.) *Z,* in German and Swedish, has the sound of *ts;* in Spanish, that of *th* in *think;* in Italian, usually that of *dz.* In Polish, *z* has the sound of this letter in the English word *zeal;* ź, the sound of *zh,* as in *azure* (ă'zhoor); ż, nearly that of *rzh.*

Combined Consonants.

§ 71. (42.) *Ch,* in Spanish (except in the Catalan dialect, where it sounds as *k*), is pronounced like the same combination in English in the word *church.* In Italian and Hungarian, it has the sound of *k;* in French and Portuguese, of *sh,* the exceptions being confined to words in which it occurs before *l* or *r,* and to a few words from the Greek, where it sounds like *k.* In German, Dutch, and Polish, when preceded in the same syllable by any one of the vowels *a, o,* or *u,* it has a harsh, guttural sound somewhat resembling a strongly aspirated *h;* as in *ach, doch, buch:* it is produced by bringing the uvula into contact with the base of the tongue, and forcing unintonated breath through the barrier thus formed, the position taken by the organs remaining in other respects unchanged. When preceded by *e, i, ä, ö, ü, ei, äu, eu, l, n,* or *r,* the sound is palatal, and approximates closely to that of the first two elements in the word *hue* (h-yoo), the tongue being considerably raised in the mouth; as in *echt, ich, mächtig, wöchentlich, bücher, reich, euch, milch, manch, durch.*

☞ *Ch,* in German and Dutch, before *s* radical, has the sound of *k;* as in *Sachsen* (săk'sn).

§ 72. (43.) *Cs,* in Hungarian, has the sound of *ch* in *church.*

§ 73. (44.) *Cz,* in Hungarian, sounds like *ts;* in Polish, like *ch* in *church.*

§ 74. (45.) *Dj* and *dy,* in Hungarian, is a peculiar sound, organically formed by placing the tip of the tongue in the position for uttering *d,* and simultaneously raising the back part into the position for sounding consonant *y,* before speaking. It closely resembles the sound of *d* and consonant *y* produced in immediate succession, as in *verdure* (vĕrd'yoor), and hence approximates the kindred sound of *j* in *just.*

§ 75. (46.) *Gh,* in Italian, is like *gh* in the English words *gherkin, ghost;* that is, like *g* in *get, begin,* &c.

§ 76. (47.) *Gj,* in Hungarian, is equivalent to *dj* or *dy* in the same language. (See § 74.)

§ 77. (48.) *Gl* before *i,* not followed by a consonant, in Italian, is a peculiar liquid sound formed from *l* in precisely the same way that the Hungarian *dy* is formed from *d.* Examples are *gli, marsigli,* &c. (See § 74.) The *i* is mute, if a vowel follows it; as in *battaglia, miglio,* &c.

§ 78. (49.) *Gn,* in French and Italian, represents a peculiar liquid sound which is identical with *ñ* in Spanish. (See § 62, and compare § 74.)

§ 79. (50.) *Gy*, in Hungarian, is like *dy* in that language. (See § 74.)

§ 80. (51.) *Kj*, in Swedish, sounds like *ch* in *church*.

§ 81. (52.) *Lh*, in Portuguese, is the same in sound with *gl* in French and Italian, and *ll* in Spanish. (See §§ 77, 82.)

§ 82. (53.) *Ll*, in Spanish, blends the sounds of *l* and consonant *y* in a single, though compound utterance, by an attempt to pronounce them simultaneously, the back part of the tongue being placed in the position for forming *y*, and the tip at the same time in that for forming *l*. The effect produced is very nearly the same as in the English words *filial* (fĭl′yal), *million* (mĭl′yun), &c., where the *y* follows the *l*, instead of being amalgamated with it. (Compare § 74.) — In French, the sound here described is, by some speakers, given to *ll*, when preceded by *i*, and followed by a vowel; but, according to the modern popular style of pronunciation, the sound of the *l* is dropped, while that of *y* is often whispered. Thus, *papillon* is pronounced pȧ′pĕl′yôⁿ′, or pȧ′pe′yôⁿ′; *fille*, fĕl, or fe͡y′; *mouillé*, mool′yȧ′, or moo′yȧ′. It is to be observed that the *i* preceding *ll* is silent, if itself preceded by a vowel.

§ 83. (54.) *Ly*, in Hungarian, is pronounced like *ll* in Spanish. (See § 82.)

§ 84. (55.) *Ng*, in German and Swedish, has the same sound as in the English words *sing, singer*.

§ 85. (56.) *Nh*, in Portuguese, corresponds to the Spanish *ñ*. *Ny*, in Hungarian, has the same sound. (See § 62.)

§ 86. (57.) *Ph*, in all the languages of Continental Europe in which it occurs, has the same sound, that of *f*.

§ 87. (58.) *Rh* is pronounced like simple *r*.

§ 88. (59.) *Rz*, in Polish, is a peculiar sound, said to be uttered by placing the tongue in the position for *zh*, and trilling the tip, which is at liberty; in other words, it is a simultaneous pronunciation of *r* and *zh*.

§ 89. (60.) *Sc*, in Italian, before *e* and *i*, is sounded like *sh* in *shall;* in other positions, like *sk*. *Śc*, in Polish, unites the sounds of *ś* and *ć*. (See §§ 65, 55.)

§ 90. (61.) *Sch*, in German, sounds like *sh* in *shall;* in Italian, before *e* and *i*, like *sch* in *school*, or *sk* in *skill;* in Dutch and Polish, before all the vowels, it resembles *sk*, but is harsher, the *ch* having the guttural or palatal sound described in § 71.

§ 91. (62.) *Ss*, in the Germanic languages, has the same sharp and hissing sound that it usually has in English.

§ 92. (63.) *Sz*, in German and Hungarian, sounds like *s* in *sun;* in Polish, like *sh* in *shall*.

§ 93. (64.) *Szcz*, in Polish, is pronounced as *shch* would be in English.

§ 94. (65.) *Th*, in all the languages of Continental Europe, except the Modern Greek (in which ϑ, the graphic equivalent of *th*, has the same sound that this digraph usually has in English), is pronounced like *th* in *thyme, Thomas*, that is, like simple *t*.

§ 95. (66.) *Tj* and *ty*, in Hungarian, blend the sounds of *t* and consonant *y* in the same manner that *dj* and *dy*, in the same language, blend the sounds of *d* and *y*. (See § 74.) The nearest English equivalent is the combination of *t* and *y* in the pronunciation sometimes given to the words *nature* (nūt'yoor), *virtue* (vĕrt'yoo), &c., though the *ch* in *church* is a very similar sound.

§ 96. (67.) *Ts*, in Hungarian, is like *ch* in *church*, being the same as the Hungarian *cs*. (See § 72.)

§ 97. (68.) *Tsch*, in German, sounds very nearly as *ch* in *church*. (See §§ 8, 90.)

§ 98. (69.) *Zs*, in Hungarian, is like *zh* in English, as heard in the pronunciation of *azure* (ā'zhoor), *confusion* (kon-fu'zhun), &c.

§ 99. (70.) *Zsch*, in German, has very nearly the sound of *ch* in *church;* thus *Zschokke* is pronounced almost like chok'kă. (See §§ 8, 70, and 90.)

§ 100. (71.) *Zz*, in Italian, usually has the sound of *ts*.

§ 101. (72.) The letters *k* and *p* have the same sound as in English.

§ 102. (73.) Double consonants, in some foreign languages, are dwelt upon in a marked manner, producing the effect of double articulation, though there is but one contact of the organs of speech. This is particularly observable in Italian words; as, *e. g.*, *hanno*, pronounced ăn'no, and not ä'no, the two *n*'s being pronounced as distinctly as in the English word *unnerve*. But if the double letters are *cc* or *gg*, and the second *c* or *g* has the power of *ch* (in *church*) or of *j*, in consequence of being followed by any one of the vowels *e, i,* and *y*, the first *c* or *g* has the sound of *t* or *d;* thus *ucciso* is pronounced oot-che'zo, not ōo-che'zo nor ooch-e'zo; *oggi* is od'jee not ŏ'jee nor oj'ee. In like manner, *zz* is equivalent to *t-ts*, sometimes to *d-dz*.

Final consonants in French — with the exception of *c, f, l, r*, in most cases — are not generally pronounced, unless immediately followed, in the same sentence, by a word beginning with a vowel. But final consonants, in classical and foreign names adopted in French, are almost always articulated.

Accent.

§ 103. (74.) The French language, — *as spoken*, — unlike the English, has no decided accent, all the syllables of a word being uttered with a nearly equal stress of voice, except those in which the mute or obscure *e* occurs, and those in which *i, u,* or *ou*, precedes a syllable commencing with a vowel. To an English ear, however, the French seem to accent the last syllable of a word, because the general tendency of our own language is to throw the accent back toward the beginning of the word. Hence, it is the usual practice in English books, in respelling French words for pronunciation, to mark the last syllable as having the accent; at the same time, secondary accents may be placed on the other syllables, to prevent them from being slurred over, or too hurriedly and indistinctly pronounced, as is often the case in the enunciation of unaccented syllables in English. It may be observed, that, in French words derived from the Latin, the final spoken syllable always represents the accented syllable of the Latin; it therefore has a right to, and, in point of fact, receives, whatever accent there is.

The Hungarian language, like the French, has no accent, the syllables of a word being distinguished from each other solely by quantity, as in Greek and Latin. (See § 29.) But in this work, as in others, an accent is placed on the long syllable, in conformity with the principle observed in the accentuation of Greek and Latin words.

In the Germanic family of languages, the principal accent falls upon the radical syllable; but, in consequence of the vast proportion of compound words, secondarily accented syllables abound, so that two, and sometimes even three or four, accents of nearly equal force may occur in the same word. It is evident, that, to those who are familiar with the meaning and composition of words in these languages, the accentuation must be easy; but no general rules can be given.

Italian words are mostly accented on the penultimate syllable; the same is true of Spanish and Portuguese words ending in a vowel, while those ending in a consonant, in these two languages, are generally accented on the last syllable. But the exceptions — especially in Italian — are so numerous that the rule is not, perhaps, of much practical utility.

Polish words are invariably accented on the penultimate syllable; while the seat of the accent in Russian words is almost always the last syllable.

xxxiii

"AS PEOPLE READ NOTHING IN THESE DAYS THAT IS MORE THAN FORTY-EIGHT HOURS OLD, I AM DAILY ADMONISHED THAT ALLUSIONS, THE MOST OBVIOUS, TO ANY THING IN THE REAR OF OUR OWN TIME NEED EXPLANATION." — DE QUINCEY.

EXPLANATION OF ABBREVIATIONS, ETC.

a.,	act.
Am., or Amer.,	American.
Ar., or Arab.,	Arabic.
A.-S.,	Anglo-Saxon.
b.,	born.
Celt.,	Celtic.
cent.,	century.
Chald.,	Chaldæan.
coll., or colloq.,	colloquially.
Comp.,	Compare.
Cyc.,	Cyclopædia.
d.,	died.
D.,	Dutch.
Dan.,	Danish.
Edin.,	Edinburgh.
Egypt.,	Egyptian.
Eng.,	English.
fem.,	feminine.
For.,	Foreign.
Fr.,	French.
Ger.,	German.
Gr.,	Greek.
Heb.,	Hebrew.
Hist.,	History.
Hung.,	Hungarian.
Icel.,	Icelandic.
Ir.,	Irish.
It., or Ital.,	Italian.
Lat.,	Latin.
Mag.,	Magazine.
Myth.,	Mythology.
Norw.,	Norwegian.
Per.,	Persian.
Pol.,	Polish.
Port.,	Portuguese.
Pr.,	Provençal.
pron.,	pronounced, pronunciation.
Prov.,	Provincial.
Qu.,	Quarterly.
q. v. (quod vide),	which see.
Rev.,	Review.
Rom.,	Roman.
Sansk.,	Sanskrit.
sc.,	scene.
Scand.,	Scandinavian.
Scot.,	Scottish.
Shak.,	Shakespeare.
Sp.,	Spanish.
Sw.,	Swedish.

☞ S p a c e d l e t t e r s are used to distinguish forms of spelling which are not so common or so well authorised as those adopted in the vocabulary.

A
DICTIONARY
OF THE
NOTED NAMES OF FICTION, ETC.

A.

Ā-bad'dŏn. [Heb., from *ábad*, to be ruined.] The Hebrew name of the evil spirit or destroying angel, called Apollyon in Greek. (*Rev.* ix. 11.) Some of the mediæval demonographers regarded him as the chief of the demons of the seventh hierarchy, and as the causer of wars, combustions, and uproars. Klopstock has made use of him in his "Messiah," under the name of Abadonna, representing him as a fallen angel, still bearing traces of his former dignity amid the disfigurements caused by sin.

Ab'ā-ris. [Gr. Ἄβαρις.] A hyperborean priest of Apollo, whose history is entirely mythical. He is said to have been endowed with the gift of prophecy; to have taken no earthly food; and to have ridden through the air on an arrow, the gift of Apollo.

    The dart of *Abaris*, which carried the philosopher wheresoever he desired it, gratifies later enthusiasts in travel as the cap of Fortunatus and the space-compelling boots of the nursery hero [Jack the Giant-killer].
    Willmott.

Ab'di-el. [Heb., servant of God.] The name of an angel mentioned by the Jewish Cabalists. He is represented, in Milton's "Paradise Lost," as one of the seraphim, who, when Satan tried to stir up a revolt among the angels subordinate to his authority, alone and boldly withstood his traitorous designs.

So spake the seraph *Abdiel*, faithful found
Among the faithless; faithful only he;
Among innumerable false, unmoved,
Unshaken, unseduced, unterrified,
His loyalty he kept, his love, his zeal.
    Par. Lost, Bk. V.

You shall invoke the Muse, — and certainly she ought to be propitious to an author, who, in an apostatising age, adheres with the faith of *Abdiel* to the ancient form of adoration.
    Sir W. Scott.

Ab-hor'son (-sn). An executioner in Shakespeare's "Measure for Measure."

Ā'bŏn Has'sǎn. The hero of one of the stories in the "Arabian Nights' Entertainments," — a young man of Bagdad, who, by a stratagem of Haroun-Al-Raschid, was twice made to believe himself caliph, and who afterward became in reality the caliph's chief favourite and companion.

    Ah! were I caliph for a day, as honest *Abon Hassan* wished to be, I would scourge me these jugglers out of the commonwealth with rods of scorpions.
    Sir W. Scott.

    Addington [Secretary of the Treasury], on the other hand, was by no means inclined to descend from his high position. He was, indeed, under a delusion much resembling that of *Abon Hassan* in the Arabian tale. His brain was turned by his short and unreal caliphate.
    Macaulay.

Abraham-Cupid. An expression occurring in Shakespeare's "Romeo and Juliet" (a. ii., sc. 1), conjectured by Upton to be a mistake for *Adam Cupid*, and to allude to Adam Bell, the celebrated archer. In Halliwell's opinion, "the conjecture is

☞ For the "Key to the Scheme of Pronunciation," with the accompanying Explanations, and for the Remarks and Rules to which the numbers after certain words refer, see pp. xiv-xxxii.

1

very plausible, as proper names are frequently abbreviated in early MSS., and it suits the sense and metre." But Dyce thinks that *Abraham* is merely a corruption of *auburn*, and supports his view by citing several passages from old books where the corruption is unquestionable. Mr. R. G. White remarks, in confirmation of Dyce's conjecture, that "Cupid is always represented by the old painters as auburn-haired."

Abraham Newland. See NEWLAND, ABRAHAM.

Ab'sa-lŏm. A name given by Dryden, in his poem entitled "Absalom and Achitophel," to the Duke of Monmouth, a natural son of Charles II. Like Absalom, the son of David, Monmouth was remarkable for his personal beauty, his popularity, and his undutifulness to his father.

Absolute, Captain. A character in Sheridan's comedy of "The Rivals;" distinguished for his gallant, determined spirit, adroit address, and dry humour.

The author will do well to profit by *Captain Absolute's* advice to his servant, and never tell him more lies than are indispensably necessary. *Sir W. Scott.*

Absolute, Sir An'tho-ny (-to-). A character in Sheridan's comedy of "The Rivals;" represented as testy, positive, impatient, and overbearing, but yet of a warm and generous disposition.

☞ "Sir Anthony is an evident copy after Smollett's kind-hearted, high-spirited Matthew Bramble." *Hazlitt.*

I will no longer avail myself of such weak ministers as you; — I will discard you; — I will unbeget you, as *Sir Anthony Absolute* says. *Sir W. Scott.*

Ab-syr'tus. [Gr. Ἄψυρτος.] (*Gr. & Rom. Myth.*) A brother of Medea, and her companion in her flight from Colchis. Finding that she was nearly overtaken by her father, she killed Absyrtus, and cut his body into pieces, which she scattered along the way, that her father might thus be detained by gathering up the remains of his murdered son. See ARGONAUTS and MEDEA.

Ā-bu'dăh. A wealthy merchant of Bagdad who figures in the "Tales of the Genii," by H. Ridley. He meets with various remarkable adventures in his quest for the talisman of Oromanes, which he is driven to seek by the threats of a little old hag who haunts him nightly, and makes his life miserable. He finds at last that the inestimable talisman is — to obey God and to love his commandments; and he finds also that all his wonderful experiences have been but the baseless fabric of a dream.

Like *Abudah*, in the Arabian story, he is always looking out for the Fury, and knows that the night will come, and the inevitable hag with it. *Thackeray.*

And there, too, was *Abudah*, the merchant, with the terrible little old woman hobbling out of the box in his bedroom. *Dickens.*

Ā-cā'di-ă. [Fr. *Acadie*, said to be derived from *Shubenacadie*, the name of one of the principal rivers of Nova Scotia; in old grants called *L'Acadie*, and *La Cadie*.] The original, and now the poetic, name of Nova Scotia, or rather of a tract extending from the fortieth to the forty-sixth degree of north latitude, which was granted, Nov. 8, 1603, to De Monts, by Henry IV. of France. The present province of Nova Scotia extends from lat. 43° 26′ to 45° 55′ N. In 1621, Acadia was granted by charter to Sir William Alexander, and its name changed to *Nova Scotia*.

☞ In the numerous disputes between the English and French colonists previous to 1763, this territory changed masters ten or a dozen times, and the boundaries were widened or narrowed according to the respective views of the opposing parties. In 1755, the French inhabitants were seized, forcibly removed, and dispersed among the English colonists on the Atlantic coast. Longfellow has made this event the subject of his poem of "Evangeline."

Ā-ces'tēs. [Gr. Ἀκέστης.] (*Gr. & Rom. Myth.*) A son of the Sicilian river-god Crinisius and of a Trojan woman of the name of Egesta or Segesta. Æneas, on his arrival in Sicily, was hospitably received by him, and, on revisiting the island, celebrated the anniversary of Anchises's death by various games and feats at arms. At a trial of skill in archery, Acestes took part, and dis-

☞ For the "Key to the Scheme of Pronunciation," with the accompanying Explanations,

charged his arrow into the air with such force that it took fire, and marked out a pathway of flame, until it was wholly consumed and disappeared from sight.

> Thy destiny remains untold;
> For, like *Acestes*' shaft of old,
> The swift thought kindles as it flies,
> And burns to ashes in the skies.
> *Longfellow.*

Ā-chā'tēṣ. [Gr. Ἀχατής.] (*Gr. & Rom. Myth.*) A companion and friend of Æneas. His fidelity was so exemplary that "fidus Achates," faithful Achates, became a proverb.

> Old enough, perhaps, but scarce wise enough, if he has chosen this fellow for his "fidus *Achates*."
> *Sir W. Scott.*

Ach'e-rŏn. [Gr. Ἀχέρων; as if ὁ ἄχεα ῥέων, the stream of woe, or from ἀ privative, and χαίρειν, to rejoice, the joyless stream.] (*Gr. & Rom. Myth.*) A son of Sol and Terra, changed into a river in hell; sometimes used in a general sense to designate hell itself.

> Abhorrèd Styx, the flood of deadly hate,
> Sad *Acheron*, of sorrow black and deep.
> *Milton.*

Ā-chĭl'lēṣ. [Gr. Ἀχιλλεύς.] (*Gr. & Rom. Myth.*) The principal hero of Homer's "Iliad," the son of Peleus, king of the Myrmidons, in Thessaly, and of Thetis, a Nereid. He was distinguished above all the rest of the Greeks in the Trojan war by his strength, beauty, and bravery. At his birth, he was dipped by his mother in the river Styx, and was thus made invulnerable except in the right heel, — or, as some say, the ankles, — by which she held him; but he was at length killed by Paris, or, according to some accounts, by Apollo. See HECTOR.

> An unfortunate country (Hanover), if the English would but think; liable to be strangled, at any time, for England's quarrels; the *Achilles-heel* to invulnerable England.
> *Carlyle.*

Ā-chĭl'lēṣ of Germany. A title given, on account of his bravery, to Albert, Margrave of Brandenburg and Culmbach (1414-1486), "a tall, fiery, tough old gentleman," says Carlyle, "in his day, . . . a very blazing, far-seen character, dim as he has now grown."

Ā-chĭt'o-phel. A nickname given to the Earl of Shaftesbury (1621-1683) by his contemporaries, and made use of by Dryden in his poem of "Absalom and Achitophel," a masterly satire, springing from the political commotions of the times, and designed as a defence of Charles II. against the Whig party. There is a striking resemblance between the character and career of Shaftesbury and those of Achitophel, or Ahitophel, the treacherous friend and counsellor of David, and the fellow-conspirator of Absalom.

> Of this denial and this apology, we shall only say that the first seems very apocryphal, and the second would justify any crime which Machiavel or *Achitophel* could invent or recommend.
> *Sir W. Scott.*

A'cis. [Gr. Ἀκίς.] (*Gr. & Rom. Myth.*) A Sicilian shepherd, beloved by the nymph Galatea, and crushed under a huge rock by Polyphemus, the Cyclops, who was jealous of him. His blood gushing forth from under the rock was changed by the nymph into a river, the Acis, or Acinius, at the foot of Mount Ætna.

> Thus equipped, he would manfully sally forth, with pipe in mouth, to besiege some fair damsel's obdurate heart, — not such a pipe, good reader, as that which *Acis* did sweetly tune in praise of his Galatea, but one of true Delft manufacture, and furnished with a charge of fragrant tobacco.
> *W. Irving.*

Ā-crā'si-ạ (ạ̄-krā'zhĭ-ạ). [From Gr. ἀκρασία, want of self-control or moderation, intemperance, from ἀ privative and κράτος, strength, power.] A witch in Spenser's "Faëry Queen," represented as a lovely and charming woman, whose dwelling is the Bower of Bliss, situated on an island floating in a lake or gulf, and adorned with every thing in nature that could delight the senses. Acrasia typifies the vice of Intemperance, and Sir Guyon, who illustrates the opposite virtue, is commissioned by the fairy queen to bring her into subjection, and to destroy her residence.

A'creṣ, Bob (ā'kẽrz). A character in Sheridan's comedy of "The Rivals;" celebrated for his cowardice, and his system of referential or allegorical swearing.

---

and for the Remarks and Rules to which the numbers after certain words refer, see pp. xiv-xxxii.

As through his palms *Bob Acres'* valor oozed,
So Juan's virtue ebbed, I know not how.
Byron.

Besides, terror, as *Bob Acres* says of its counterpart, courage, will come and go; and few people can afford timidity enough for the writer's purpose who is determined on "horrifying" them through three thick volumes.
Sir W. Scott.

Ac-tæ'ǒn. [Gr. Ἀκταίων.] (*Gr. & Rom. Myth.*) A famous hunter, who, having surprised Diana while she was bathing, was changed by her into a stag, and, in that form, was torn to pieces by his own hounds.

He [Byron], as I guess,
Had gazed on Nature's naked loveliness,
Actæon-like, and now he fled astray
With feeble steps o'er the world's wilderness;
And his own thoughts, along that rugged way,
Pursued, like raging hounds, their father and their prey.
Shelley.

Adam. 1. Formerly a jocular name for a sergeant or bailiff.

Not that Adam that kept the paradise, but that *Adam* that keeps the prison.
Shak.

2. An aged servant to Oliver, in Shakespeare's "As You Like It."

"The serving-man Adam, humbly born and coarsely nurtured, is no insignificant personage in the drama; and we find in the healthy tone of his mind, and in his generous heart, which, under reverses and wrongs, still preserves its charitable trust in his fellows, as well as in his kindly, though frosty, age, a delightful and instructive contrast to the character of Jaques, which could hardly have been accidental."
R. G. White.

Adamastor (ăd'ȧ-măs'tǒr; *Port. pron.* ä-dä-mäs-tōr', 64). The Spirit of the Stormy Cape, — *i. e.*, the Cape of Good Hope, — a hideous phantom described by Camoens, in the fifth canto of the "Lusiad," as appearing by night to the fleet of Vasco da Gama, and predicting the woes which would befall subsequent expeditions to India. Mickle supposes that by Adamastor the genius of Mohammedanism is intended. According to Barreto, he was one of the Giants who made an attack on heaven, and were killed by the gods or buried under various mountains.

Were *Adamastor* to appear to him [the "gamin" of Paris], he would shout out, "Hallo there, old Bug-a-boo!" *V. Hugo, Trans.*

Adam Kad'mǒn. In the Cabalistic doctrine, the name given to the first emanation from the Eternal Fountain. It signifies the First Man, or the first production of divine energy, or the Son of God; and to it the other and inferior emanations are subordinate.

Adam, Master. See MASTER ADAM.

Adams, Parson Abraham. A country curate in Fielding's novel of "Joseph Andrews;" distinguished for his goodness of heart, poverty, learning, and ignorance of the world, combined with courage, modesty, and a thousand oddities.

"As to Parson Adams, and his fist, and his good heart, and his Æschylus which he couldn't see to read, and his rejoicing at being delivered from a ride in the carriage with Mr. Peter Pounce, whom he had erroneously complimented on the smallness of his parochial means, let every body rejoice that there has been a man in the world called Henry Fielding to think of such a character, and thousands of good people sprinkled about that world to answer for the truth of it; for had there not been, what would have been its value? . . . He is one of the simplest, but at the same time manliest of men; is anxious to read a man of the world his sermon on 'vanity;' preaches patience under affliction, and is ready to lose his senses on the death of his little boy; in short, has 'every virtue under heaven,' except that of superiority to the common failings of humanity, or of being able to resist knocking a rascal down when he insults the innocent. He is very poor; and, agreeably to the notions of refinement in those days, is treated by the rich as if he were little better than a servant himself. Even their stewards think it a condescension to treat him on equal terms."
Leigh Hunt.

"The humanity, benevolence, and goodness of heart so conspicuous in Mr. Adams, his unswerving integrity, his zeal in the cause of the oppressed, his unaffected nature, independent of his talent and learning, win our esteem and respect, even while his virtuous simplicity provokes our smiles; and the little predicaments into which he falls, owing to his absence of mind, are such as excite our mirth without a shadow of derision or malevolence."
Thomas Roscoe.

As to his [Hugo von Trimberg's] inward man, we can still be sure that he was no mere bookworm, or simple *Parson Adams.*
Carlyle.

ADD 5 ÆG

Ad'di-son of the North (ad'dĭ-sn). An epithet sometimes given to Henry Mackenzie (1745-1831), the Scottish novelist, whose style, like Addison's, is distinguished for its refinement and delicacy.

Addle, or **Addled, Parliament.** (*Eng. Hist.*) A name given to the English Parliament which assembled at London, April 5, 1614, and was dissolved on the 7th of the following June. It was so called because it remonstrated with the King on his levying "benevolences," and passed no acts.

Ad-me'tus. [Gr. Ἄδμητος.] (*Gr. & Rom. Myth.*) A king of Thessaly, and husband of Alcestis, famous for his misfortunes and his piety. Apollo entered his service as a shepherd, having been condemned by Jupiter to become the servant of a mortal for one year as a punishment for slaying the Cyclops. Lowell has made this incident the subject of a short poem entitled, "The Shepherd of King Admetus." See ALCESTIS.

Admirable Crichton. See CRICHTON, THE ADMIRABLE.

Admirable Doctor. [Lat. *Doctor Mirabilis*.] A title bestowed upon Roger Bacon (1214-1292), an English monk, who, by the power of his genius and the extent of his learning, raised himself above his time, made many astonishing discoveries in science, and contributed much to the extension of real knowledge.

Ad'o-nā'is. A poetical name given by Shelley to the poet Keats (1796-1821), on whose untimely death he wrote a monody bearing this name for its title. The name was coined by Shelley probably to hint an analogy between Keats's fate and that of Adonis.

Ä-do'nis. [Gr. Ἄδωνις.] (*Gr. & Rom. Myth.*) A beautiful youth, beloved by Venus and Proserpine, who quarrelled about the possession of him. The dispute was settled by Jupiter, who decided that he should spend eight months in the upper world with Venus, and four in the lower with Proserpine. Adonis died of a wound received from a wild boar during the chase, and was turned into an anemone by Venus, who yearly bewailed him on the anniversary of his death. The myths connected with Adonis are of Oriental origin, and his worship was widely spread among the countries bordering on the eastern portion of the Mediterranean. The story of Venus's love for him was made the subject of a long descriptive poem by Shakespeare, and is often alluded to by other poets.

   Beds of hyacinths and roses
   Where young *Adonis* oft reposes,
   Waxing well of his deep wound
   In slumber soft.   *Milton.*

Ä-dras'tus. [Gr. Ἄδραστος.] (*Gr. & Rom. Myth.*) A king of Argos, and the institutor of the Nemean games. He was one of the heroes who engaged in the war of the "Seven against Thebes."

Ā'dri-ā'nȧ (*or* ad'ri-an'ȧ). Wife of Antipholus of Ephesus, in Shakespeare's "Comedy of Errors."

Adversity Hume. A nickname given to Joseph Hume (1777-1855), in the time of "Prosperity Robinson," and in contradistinction to him, owing to his constant presages of ruin and disaster to befall the people of Great Britain. See PROSPERITY ROBINSON.

Æ'ȧ-cus. [Gr. Αἰακος.] (*Gr. & Rom. Myth.*) A son of Jupiter and Ægina, renowned for his justice and piety. After his death he was made one of the three judges in Hades.

Æ-ġe'ŏn. 1. [Gr. Ἀιγαίων.] (*Gr. & Rom. Myth.*) A huge monster with a hundred arms and fifty heads, who, with his brothers Cottus and Gyges, conquered the Titans by hurling at them three hundred rocks at once. By some he is reckoned as a marine god living under the Ægean Sea; Virgil numbers him among the gods who stormed Olympus; and Callimachus, regarding him in the same light, places him under Mount Ætna.
2. A merchant of Syracuse, in Shakespeare's "Comedy of Errors."

Ægeria. See EGERIA.

Æ-ġe'us. [Gr. Αἰγεύς.] (*Gr. & Rom.*

and for the Remarks and Rules to which the numbers after certain words refer, see pp. xiv-xxxii.

Myth.) A king of Athens from whom the Ægean Sea received its name. His son Theseus went to Crete to deliver Athens from the tribute it had to pay to Minos, promising that, on his return, he would hoist white sails as a signal of his safety. This he forgot to do, and Ægeus, who was watching for him on a rock on the sea-coast, on perceiving a black sail, thought that his son had perished, and threw himself into the sea.

Æ-gi'nă. (*Gr. & Rom. Myth.*) A daughter of the river-god Asopus, and a favourite of Jupiter.

Æ'gis. [Gr. Αἰγίς.] (*Gr. & Rom. Myth.*) 1. The shield of Jove, fashioned by Vulcan, and described as striking terror and amazement into the beholders.

2. A sort of short cloak, worn by Minerva, which was covered with scales, set with the Gorgon's head, and fringed with snakes.

Æ-gis'thus. [Gr. Αἴγισθος.] (*Gr. & Rom. Myth.*) A son of Thyestes, and the paramour of Clytemnestra, whose husband, Agamemnon, he treacherously murdered at a repast. He was subsequently killed by Orestes, a son of Agamemnon, who thus avenged his father's death. See THYESTES.

Æg'le (eg'le). [Gr. Αἴγλη.] (*Gr. & Rom. Myth.*) 1. One of the Hesperides.

2. The most beautiful of the Naiads, and the mother of the Graces.

Æ-gyp'tus. [Gr. Αἴγυπτος.] (*Gr. & Rom. Myth.*) A son of Belus, and twin brother of Danaus. He had by several wives fifty sons, who were married to their fifty cousins, the daughters of Danaus, and all but one of whom were murdered by their wives on the bridal night.

Æ'li-ă Læ'li-ă Cris'pis. The unknown subject of a very celebrated enigmatical inscription, preserved in Bologna, which has puzzled the heads of many learned men who have attempted to explain it. It is as follows:—

Ælia Lælia Crispis,
Nec vir, nec mulier, nec androgyna;
Nec puella, nec juvenis, nec anus;
Nec meretrix, nec pudica;
Sed omnia:
Sublata neque fame, nec ferro, neque veneno;
Sed omnibus:
Nec cælo, nec aquis, nec terris;
Sed ubique jacet.
Lucius Agatho Priscus,
Nec maritus, nec amator, nec necessarius;
Neque mœrens, neque gaudens, neque flens;
Sed omnia;
Hanc neque molem, neque pyramidem, neque sepulchrum,
Scit et nescit quid posuerit.
Hoc est, sepulchrum intus cadaver non habens;
Hoc est, cadaver, sepulchrum, extrà non, habens;
Sed cadaver idem est, et sepulchrum sibi.

Ælia Lælia Crispis, neither man, nor woman, nor hermaphrodite; neither girl, nor boy, nor old woman; neither harlot nor virgin; but all of these: destroyed neither by hunger, nor sword, nor poison: but by all of them: lies neither in heaven, nor in the water, nor in the ground, but everywhere. Lucius Agatho Priscus, neither her husband, nor her lover, nor her kinsman; neither sad, glad, nor weeping, but all at once; knows and knows not what he has built,—which is neither a funeral-pile, nor a pyramid, nor a tomb; that is, a tomb without a corpse, a corpse without a tomb; for corpse and tomb are one and the same.

☞ Various explanations of the meaning of this curious epitaph have, from time to time, been put forward; but there is much reason for doubting whether it has any. Some have thought the true interpretation to be rain-water; some, the so-called "materia prima;" some, the reasoning faculty; some, the philosopher's stone; some, love; some, a dissected person; some, a shadow; some, hemp; some, an embryo. Professor Schwartz, of Coburg, explained it of the Christian Church, referring, in support of his opinion, to *Galatians* iii. 29,—"There is neither Jew nor Greek, there is neither bond nor free, there is neither male nor female; for ye are all one in Christ Jesus." Spondanus, in his "Voyage d'Italie," affirms that the inscription is only a copy, and that it is not known what has become of the original. He denies its antiquity, regarding it as the ludicrous fancy of a modern author, who, he insists, was ignorant of the principles of Latin family nomenclature. But Franckenstein says that this assertion has been confuted by Misson, in the appendix to his "Travels."

I might add what attracted considerable notice at the time,—and that is my paper in the "Gentleman's Magazine" upon the inscription *Ælia Lælia*, which I subscribed Œdipus. *Sir W. Scott.*

Bacon's system is, in its own terms, an idol of the theatre. It would scarcely guide a man to a solution of the riddle *Ælia Lælia Crispis*, or to that of the charade of Sir Hilary [by Praed]. *J. W. Draper.*

☞ For the "Key to the Scheme of Pronunciation," with the accompanying Explanations,

Æ-mil'i-ă. Wife of Ægeon, and an abbess at Ephesus, in Shakespeare's "Comedy of Errors."

Æ-ne'ăs. [Gr. 'Αινείας.] (*Gr. & Rom. Myth.*) A Trojan prince, the hero of Virgil's "Æneid." He was the son of Anchises and Venus, and was distinguished for his pious care of his father. Having survived the fall of Troy, he sailed to Italy, and settled in Latium, where he married Lavinia, the daughter of Latinus, whom he succeeded in his kingdom. See CREUSA.

Æ'o-lus. [Gr. Αἴολος.] (*Gr. & Rom. Myth.*) The ruler and god of the winds, who resided in the islands in the Tyrrhenian sea, which were called from him the Æolian Islands.

Æs'ă-cus. [Gr. Αἴσακος.] (*Gr. & Rom. Myth.*) A son of Priam, who was enamoured of the nymph Hesperia, and, on her death, threw himself into the sea, and was changed by Thetis into a cormorant.

Æs'cu-lā'pi-us. [Gr. 'Ασκληπιός.] (*Gr. & Rom. Myth.*) The son of Apollo, and the god of the medical art. He was killed with a flash of lightning by Jupiter, because he had restored several persons to life.

Æ'sŏn. [Gr. Αἴσων.] (*Gr. & Rom. Myth.*) The father of Jason. He was restored to youth by Medea.

Af'ric. A poetical contraction of *Africa*.

Where *Afric's* sunny fountains
Roll down their golden sand. *Heber.*

Ag'ă-mem'nŏn. [Gr. 'Αγαμέμνων.] (*Gr. & Rom. Myth.*) King of Mycenæ, brother of Menelaus, and commander-in-chief of the Grecian forces in the Trojan war. See ÆGISTHUS.

Ag'ă-nip'pe. [Gr. 'Αγανίππη.] (*Gr. & Rom. Myth.*) A fountain at the foot of Mount Helicon, in Bœotia, consecrated to Apollo and the Muses, and believed to have the power of inspiring those who drank of it. The Muses are sometimes called *Aganippides*.

Agapida, Fray Antonio (frī än-tō'ne-o ă-gä-pē'dä). The imaginary chronicler of the "Conquest of Granada," written by Washington Irving.

A-gā've. [Gr. 'Αγαυή.] (*Gr. & Rom. Myth.*) A daughter of Cadmus, and the mother of Pentheus, whom, in a fit of frenzy, she tore to pieces on Mount Cithæron, believing him to be a wild beast.

Ā'ġib. The third Calendar in the story of "The Three Calendars," in the "Arabian Nights' Entertainments."

Agitator, The Irish. See IRISH AGITATOR.

Ag-lā'i-ă (20). [Gr. 'Αγλαΐη.] (*Gr. & Rom. Myth.*) One of the three Graces.

Ag'něs (*Fr. pron.* ăn'yĕs'). 1. A young girl in Molière's "L'École des Femmes," who is, or affects to be, remarkably simple and ingenuous. The name has passed into popular use, and is applied to any young woman unsophisticated in affairs of the heart.

☞ Agnes is the original from which Wycherley took his Mrs. Pinchwife, in the "Country Wife," subsequently altered by Garrick into the "Country Girl."

2. A character in Dickens's novel of "David Copperfield." See WICKFIELD, AGNES.

Ag'nî. [Sansk., fire.] (*Hindu Myth.*) The god of lightning and the sun's fire.

Agramante (ä-grä-män'tä), or **Ag'rămant.** King of the Moors, in Bojardo's poem of "Orlando Innamorato," and in Ariosto's "Orlando Furioso."

Ag'rĭ-vāine, Sir. A knight of the Round Table, celebrated in the old romances of chivalry. He was surnamed "*L' Orgueilleux*," or "The Proud."

A-Green, George. See GEORGE A-GREEN.

Agricane (ä-gre-kä'nä), or **Ag'rĭ-căn.** A fabulous king of Tartary, in Bojardo's "Orlando Innamorato," who besieges Angelica in the castle of Albracca, and is killed by Orlando in single contest. In his dying moments, he requests baptism at the hand of his conqueror, who, with great tenderness, bestows it. He is represented as bringing into the field no fewer than two million two hundred thousand troops.

> Such forces met not, nor so wide a camp,
> When *Agrican*, with all his northern powers,
> Besieged Albracca, as romancers tell.
> *Milton.*

Ague-cheek, Sir Andrew. A delightful simpleton in Shakespeare's "Twelfth Night." See SLENDER.

☞ "To this straight-haired country squire, life consists only in eating and drinking; eating beef, he himself fears, has done harm to his wit; in fact, he is stupid even to silliness, totally deprived of all fashion, and thus of all self-love or self-conceit." *Gervinus, Trans.*

> I suppose I must say of Jeffrey as *Sir Andrew Ague-cheek* saith: "An I had known he was so cunning of fence, I had seen him damned ere I had fought him." *Byron.*

Ȧ-has'u-e'rus (ȧ-hazh'oo-e'rus, 10). See JEW, THE WANDERING.

Ahmed, Prince. See PRINCE AHMED.

Ah'rĭ-măn, *or* **Ah'rĭ-mā'nĕṣ.** [Per., from Sansk. *ari*, foe.] (*Myth.*) A deity of the ancient Persians, being a personification of the principle of evil. To his agency were ascribed all the evils existing in the world. Ormuzd, or Oromasdes, the principle of good, is eternal, but Ahriman is created, and will one day perish. See ORMUZD.

> recognise the evil spirit, Sir, and do honour to *Ahrimanes* in taking off my hat to this young man. *Thackeray.*

Ai'deṉ. An Anglicised and disguised spelling of the Arabic form of the word *Eden;* used as a synonym for the celestial paradise.

> Tell the soul, with sorrow laden, if, within
> the distant *Aidenn,*
> It shall clasp a sainted maiden, whom the angels name Lenore. *Poe.*

Aimwell. A gentleman of broken fortunes, master to Archer, in Farquhar's comedy, "The Beaux' Stratagem."

Ā'jăx. [Gr. Αἴας.] (*Gr. & Rom. Myth.*) 1. A son of Telamon, king of Salamis. Next to Achilles, he was the most distinguished, the bravest, and the most beautiful, of all the Greeks before Troy. Accounts differ as to the cause and manner of his death. A tradition mentioned by Pausanias states, that from his blood there sprang up a purple flower, which bore the letters *al* on its leaves, which were at once the initials of his name and a sigh.

> Gad! she shoots her glances as sharply from behind the old pile yonder, as Teucer from behind *Ajax Telamon's* shield. *Sir W. Scott.*

2. A son of Oïleus, king of the Locrians. He was one of the great heroes among the Greeks in the Trojan war, but inferior to the son of Telamon, whence he is called the *lesser Ajax.*

> His shafts, like those of the *lesser Ajax*, were discharged more readily that the archer was inaccessible to criticism, personally speaking, as the Grecian archer under his brother's sevenfold shield. *Sir W. Scott.*

Ȧ-lad'din. A character in the "Arabian Nights' Entertainments," who becomes possessed of a wonderful lamp, and an equally wonderful ring, on rubbing which two frightful genii appear, who are respectively the slave of the lamp and the slave of the ring, and who execute the bidding of any one who may have these talismans in his keeping.

☞ By means of the lamp and ring, Aladdin is enabled to marry a daughter of the sultan of China, and builds in a single night a magnificent palace containing a large hall with four-and-twenty windows in it decorated with jewels of every description and of untold value, one window only being excepted, which is left quite plain that the sultan may have the glory of finishing the apartment. But all the treasures of his empire and all the skill of his jewellers and goldsmiths are not sufficient to ornament even one side of the window; whereupon Aladdin, after having the materials which have been used removed and returned to the sultan, directs the genie to complete the window, which is immediately done. At length, a malignant magician fraudulently obtains the miraculous lamp, during the temporary absence of the owner, and instantaneously transports the palace to Africa. But the ring still remains to Aladdin, and enables him to pursue and circumvent the thief, and to recover the lamp and restore the palace to its former situation.

> The ephemeral kingdom of Westphalia, the appanage of Jerome Bonaparte, composed out of the spoils of these principalities, vanished into air, like the palace of *Aladdin,* in the Arabian tale. *Sir W. Scott.*

☞ For the "Key to the Scheme of Pronunciation," with the accompanying Explanations,

It was absolutely impossible that a family, holding a document which gave them unlimited access to the patronage of the most powerful nobleman in Scotland, should have suffered it to remain unemployed, like *Aladdin's* rusty lamp, while they struggled through three generations in poverty and disappointment. *Senior.*

Ah! who shall lift that wand of magic power,
And the lost clew regain?
The unfinished window in *Aladdin's* tower
Unfinished must remain. *Longfellow.*

Alaric Cottin (ä′lå-rĕk′ kot′tŭⁿ′). A nickname given by Voltaire to Frederick the Great, king of Prussia, who was distinguished for his military genius, and was also known as dabbler in literature, and a writer of bad French verses. The first name refers to the famous Visigothic king and warrior, while the second probably refers to the Abbé Cotin, a mediocre poet of the seventeenth century, who was severely satirised by Boileau, Molière, and other writers of his time. See TRISSOTIN.

Ă-las′năm. The hero of a story in the "Arabian Nights' Entertainments" entitled "The History of Prince Zeyn Alasnam and the Sultan of the Genii," which relates how he came into the possession of immense wealth, including eight statues of solid gold; how he was led to seek for a ninth statue more precious still, to place on an empty pedestal; and how he found it at last in the person of the most beautiful and purest woman in the world, who became his wife.

In this brilliant comedy [Congreve's "Love for Love"], there is plenty of bright and sparkling characters, rich as wit and imagination can make them; but there is wanting one pure and perfect model of simple nature, and that one, wherever it is to be found, is, like *Alasnam's* lady, ... worth them all. *Sir W. Scott.*

Ă-las′tŏr. [Gr. Ἀλάστωρ, from ἀ privative, and λαθεῖν, to forget.] In classical mythology, a surname of Zeus or Jupiter; also, in general, a punitive deity, a house-demon, the never-forgetting, revengeful spirit, who, in consequence of some crime perpetrated, persecutes a family from generation to generation. Plutarch relates that Cicero, in his hatred of Augustus, meditated killing himself by the fireside of this prince in order to become his *Alastor.* In the Zoroastrian system, Alastor is called the Executioner or Tormentor. Origen says he is the same as Azazel. Others confound him with the Exterminating Angel. By Wierus and other mediæval demonographers, Alastor is described as a devil in the infernal court, and the chief executive officer in great undertakings. Shelley, in his poem entitled "Alastor," makes him the "Spirit of Solitude."

Al-bā′ni-ą, Ál′bą-ny. A name given to Scotland, or the Scottish Highlands, in the old romances and histories. It is said to have been derived from a certain fabulous *Albanact,* who received this portion of the island of Albion, or Britain, from his father Brutus. See ALBYN.

Ál′bą-ny Regency. A name popularly given in the United States to a junto of astute Democratic politicians, having their head-quarters at Albany, who controlled the action of the Democratic party for many years, and hence had great weight in national politics. The effort to elect William H. Crawford president, instead of John Quincy Adams, was their first great struggle.

Ăl′bi-ŏn. An ancient name of Britain, said to have been given to it on account of the lofty white cliffs (Lat. *albus,* white) on the southern coast. Others trace the word to the Celtic *alb, alp,* high.

☞ In the fabulous history of England, it is related that the first inhabitants were subdued by *Albion,* a giant and a son of Neptune, who called the island after his own name, and ruled it forty-four years. Another legend derives the name from a certain *Albina,* the eldest of fifty daughters of "a strange Dioclesian king of Syria," who, having murdered their husbands on their marriage-night, one only excepted, whom his wife's loyalty saved, were by him, at the suit of his wife, their sister, not put to death, but turned out to sea in a ship unmanned, and who, as the tale goes, were driven on this island, where they had issue by the inhabitants, — none but devils, as some write, or, as others assert, a lawless crew, without head or governor. Milton characterises these stories as "too absurd and too unconscionably gross" for credence; but he remarks, "Sure

---

and for the Remarks and Rules to which the numbers after certain words refer, see pp. xiv-xxxii.

enough wo are that Britain hath been anciently termed *Albion*, both by the Greeks and Romans."

Not yet enslaved, not wholly vile,
O *Albion*, O my mother isle! *Coleridge.*

Al′bi-ŏn, New. A name formerly given to an extensive tract of land on the north-west coast of North America. It was originally applied by Sir Francis Drake, in 1578, to the whole of what was then called California; but it was afterward confined to that part of the coast which extends from 43° to 48° N. lat., and is now included within the State of Oregon and Washington Territory.

Al Borak (ăl bŏr′ăk). [Ar., the lightning.] An imaginary animal of wonderful form and qualities, on which Mohammed pretended to have performed a nocturnal journey from the temple of Mecca to Jerusalem, and thence to the seventh heaven, under the conduct of the angel Gabriel. This marvellous steed was a female, of a milk-white colour and of incredible swiftness. At every step, she took a leap as far as the longest sight could reach. She had a human face, but the cheeks of a horse; her eyes were as jacinths, and radiant as stars. She had eagle's wings, all glittering with rays of light; and her whole form was resplendent with gems and precious stones.

Albracca (ăl-brăk′kă, 102). A castle of Cathay to which Angelica, in Bojardo's "Orlando Innamorato," retires in grief at being scorned and shunned by Rinaldo, with whom she is deeply in love. Here she is besieged by Agricane, king of Tartary, who resolves to win her, notwithstanding her rejection of his suit.

Ăl′byn (ăl′bin). The ancient Celtic name of Scotland, and, until Cæsar's time, the appellation of the whole island of Great Britain. It is said to be derived from the Celtic *alp* or *alb*, meaning *high*, and *inn*, an island. The Scottish Celts denominate themselves *Gael Albinn*, or *Albinnich*, in distinction from the Irish, whom they call *Gael Eirinnich;* and the Irish themselves call the Scottish *Gael Albannaich*, while their writers, so late as the twelfth century, call the country of the Scottish Gael *Alban*. [Written also A l b i n and A l b i n n.]

The Celtic people of Erin and *Albyn* had, in short, a style of poetry properly called national, though Macpherson was rather an excellent poet than a faithful editor and translator. *Sir W. Scott.*

The pure Culdees
Were *Albyn's* earliest priests of God,
Ere yet an island of her seas
By foot of Saxon monk was trod.
Campbell.

But woe to his kindred and woe to his cause,
When *Albin* her claymore indignantly draws.
Campbell.

Alceste (ăl′sest′). The hero of Molière's comedy, "Le Misanthrope."

☞ " Alceste is an upright and manly character, but rude, and impatient even of the ordinary civilities of life, and the harmless hypocrisies of complaisance, by which the ugliness of human nature is in some degree disguised." *Sir W. Scott.*
" Molière exhibited, in his ' Misanthrope,' a pure and noble mind which had been sorely vexed by the sight of perfidy and malevolence disguised under the forms of politeness. He adopts a standard of good and evil directly opposed to that of the society which surrounded him. Courtesy seems to him a vice, and those stern virtues which are neglected by the fops and coquettes of Paris become too exclusively the objects of his veneration. He is often to blame, he is often ridiculous, but he is always a good man." *Macaulay.*

Al-ces′tis, *or* **Al-ces′te.** [Gr. Ἀλκηστις, or Ἀλκέστη.] (*Gr. & Rom. Myth.*) A daughter of Pelias, and the wife of Admetus. To save her husband's life, she died in his stead, but was brought back to the upper world by Hercules.

Methought I saw my late espousèd saint
Brought to me like *Alcestis* from the grave,
Whom Jove's great son to her glad husband gave,
Rescued from death by force, though pale and faint. *Milton.*

Al-ci′dēṣ. [Gr. Ἀλκείδης.] (*Gr. & Rom. Myth.*) A patronymic or title of Hercules, the grandson of Alcæus. See HERCULES.

Alcina (ăl-che′nă). A fairy in Bojardo's "Orlando Innamorato," where she is represented as carrying off Astolfo. She re-appears in great splendour in Ariosto's " Orlando Furioso."

The scene, though pleasing, was not quite equal to the gardens of *Alcina. Sir W. Scott.*

☞ For the "Key to the Scheme of Pronunciation," with the accompanying Explanations,

Al-cin′o-us. [Gr. 'Αλκίνοος.] (*Gr. & Rom. Myth.*) A king of Drepane, or, as some say, of Phæacia, who entertained the Argonauts on their return from Colchis, and Ulysses when he was shipwrecked.

Al′cĭ-phrọn. [Gr. 'Αλκίφρων, from ἀλκή, strength, spirit, and φρήν, heart, breast.]
1. A freethinking interlocutor in Bishop Berkeley's work of the same name,—otherwise called the "Minute Philosopher,"—a work "written with an intention to expose the weakness of infidelity."
2. The hero of Thomas Moore's romance, "The Epicurean," and also the title of a poem by the same author.

We long to see one good solid rock or tree, on which to fasten our attention; but there is none. Like *Alciphron* we swing in air and darkness, and know not whither the wind blows us. *Putnam's Mag.*

Alc-me′nặ. [Gr. 'Αλκμήνη.] (*Gr. & Rom. Myth.*) The wife of Amphitryon, and the mother of Hercules by Jupiter, who visited her in the disguise of her husband. See AMPHITRYON.

Alcofribas Nasier (ăl′ko′fre′bă′ nă′-se-ā′, 44). An anagrammatic pseudonym of François Rabelais (1483–1553), the celebrated French romancer.

Al-cy′o-ne. [Gr.'Αλκυόνη.] (*Gr. & Rom. Myth.*) A daughter of Æolus, and the wife of Ceÿx. On hearing of her husband's death by shipwreck, she threw herself into the sea, and was changed by the gods into a kingfisher. [Written also Halcyone.]

Al′da (ăl′dă̇), *or* Al-da-bel′la (ăl-dă̇-bel′lä, 102). The name given to the wife of Orlando, and sister of Oliver, in the romantic poems of Italy.

Al′dĭ-bo-ron′te-phos′co-phor′nĭ-o.
1. A character in Henry Carey's play of "Chrononhotonthologos."

I felt as if my understanding were no longer my own, but was alternately under the dominion of *Aldiborontephoscophornio*, and that of his facetious friend Rigdum Funnidos. *Sir W. Scott.*

2. A nickname given by Sir Walter Scott to his school-mate, printer, partner, and confidential friend, James Ballantyne, on account of his solemn and rather pompous manner. See RIGDUM FUNNIDOS.

Al′din-gạr, Sir. A character in an ancient legend, and the title of a celebrated ballad, preserved in Percy's "Reliques," which relates how the honour of Queen Elianor, wife of Henry Plantagenet, impeached by Sir Aldingar, her steward, was submitted to the chance of a duel, and how an angel, in the form of a little child, appeared as her champion, and established her innocence.

Ȧ-lec′to. [Gr. 'Αληκτώ.] (*Gr. & Rom. Myth.*) One of the three Furies.

Alexander of the North. An epithet conferred upon Charles XII. of Sweden (1682–1718), whose military genius and success bore some resemblance to those of the Macedonian conqueror.

Ȧ-lex′is. A youth of great beauty, of whom the shepherd Corydon, in Virgil's second Eclogue, was enamoured.

Alfadur (äl′fä′door). [That is, All-Father.] (*Scand. Myth.*) A name given to the Supreme Being, the uncreated, eternal, and omnipresent Deity, whose nature and attributes were unknown. The name was also used as a title of Odin. See ODIN.

Al′len-ặ-Dale. The hero of an old ballad which relates how his marriage to his true love — who was on the point of being forcibly wedded to an old knight — was brought about by Robin Hood. Allen-a-Dale is described as "a brave young man," gayly dressed, who

" did frisk it over the plain,
And chanted a roundelay."

Where is *Allen-a-Dale*, to chronicle me in a ballad, or if it were but a lay? *Sir W. Scott.*

Alliance, Grand. See GRAND ALLIANCE; and for HOLY ALLIANCE, QUADRUPLE ALLIANCE, TRIPLE ALLIANCE, see the respective adjectives HOLY, QUADRUPLE, &c.

All-the-Talents Administration. An administration formed by Lord Grenville on the death of Mr. Pitt (June 23, 1806). The friends of this ministry gave it the appellation of

"All-the-Talents," which, being echoed in derision by the Opposition, became fixed upon it ever after. The death of Mr. Fox, one of the members, Sept. 13, 1806, led to various changes, and this ministry was finally dissolved in March, 1807.

☞ The members composing it were as follows : —
Lord Grenville, First Lord of the Treasury.
Earl Fitzwilliam, Lord President.
Viscount Sidmouth (Henry Addington), Privy Seal.
Rt. Hon. Charles James Fox, Foreign Seal.
Earl Spencer, Home Secretary.
William Windham, Colonial Secretary.
Lord Erskine, Lord Chancellor.
Sir Charles Grey (afterwards Viscount Howick, and Earl Grey), Admiralty.
Lord Minto, Board of Control.
Lord Auckland, Board of Trade.
Lord Moira, Master - General of the Ordnance.
Mr. Sheridan, Treasurer of the Navy.
Rt. Hon. Richard Fitzpatrick.
Lord Ellenborough (Lord Chief Justice) had a seat in the Cabinet.

Allworthy, Mr. A character in Fielding's novel of "Tom Jones," distinguished for his worth and benevolence. This character was drawn for Fielding's private friend, Ralph Allen, of whom Pope said, —

"Let humble Allen, with an awkward shame,
Do good by stealth, and blush to find it fame."

The sturdy rectitude, the large charity, the good nature, the modesty, the independent spirit, the ardent philanthropy, the unaffected indifference to money and to fame, make up a character, which, while it has nothing unnatural, seems to us to approach nearer to perfection than any of the Grandisons and *Allworthys* of fiction. *Macaulay.*

Al-main'. [Low Lat. *Alemannia,* Fr. *Allemagne,* Sp. *Alemania;* from *Alemanni,* the collective name of several ancient German tribes in the vicinity of the Lower and Middle Main; from Celt. *allman,* a stranger, foreigner, from *all,* another, *man,* place.] An old English name for Germany.

I have seen *Almain's* proud champions prance;
Have seen the gallant knights of France; . . .
Have seen the sons of England true
Wield the brown bill and bend the yew.
Search France the fair, and England free,
But bonny Blue-cap still for me! *Old Song.*

Al-man'zor. A prominent character in Dryden's tragedy of "The Conquest of Granada."

After all, I say with *Almanzor,*—
"Know that I alone am king of me."
Sir W. Scott.

Almighty Dollar. A personification of the supposed object of American idolatry, intended as a satire upon the prevailing passion for gain. The expression originated with Washington Irving.

The *Almighty Dollar,* that great object of universal devotion throughout our land, seems to have no genuine devotees in these peculiar villages.
W. Irving, The Creole Village.

Alp. The hero of Byron's "Siege of Corinth."

Alph. A river mentioned by Coleridge in his poem entitled "Kubla Khan," composed during a dream, immediately after a perusal of Purchas's "Pilgrimage," and written down from memory. This name is not found in Purchas, but was invented by Coleridge, and was probably suggested by the Alpheus of classical mythology.

"In Xanadu did Kubla Khan
A stately pleasure-dome decree,
Where *Alph,* the sacred river, ran
Through caverns measureless to man,
Down to a sunless sea."

Alquife (ăl-ke'fĭ). A personage who figures in almost all the books of the lineage of Amadis as a potent wizard.

Then . . . thou hadst not, as now, . . . converted, in thy vain imagination, honest Griffiths, citizen and broker, . . . into some . . . sage *Alquife,* the mystical and magical protector of thy peerless destiny. *Sir W. Scott.*

Al Rakim (ăr rā-keem'). [Ar., from *rakam,* to write, *rakimeh,* something written or sent.] A fabulous dog connected with the legend of the Seven Sleepers. The Mohammedans have given him a place in Paradise, where he has the care of all letters and correspondence. See SEVEN SLEEPERS.

Al-sā'ti-ă (al-sā'shĭ-ă). A popular name formerly given to Whitefriars, a precinct in London, without the Temple, and west of Blackfriars. It was for a long time an asylum or sanctuary for insolvent debtors and persons who had offended against the laws. The scene of Shadwell's

☞ For the "Key to the Scheme of Pronunciation," with the accompanying Explanations,

comedy of the "Squire of Alsatia" is laid in this place; and Scott has rendered it familiar to all readers by his "Fortunes of Nigel."

☞ "It is not unlikely that the Landgraviate of Alsace [Ger. *Elsass*, Lat. *Alsatia*]—now the frontier province of France, on the left bank of the Rhine, long a cause of contention, often the seat of war, and familiarly known to many British soldiers—suggested the application of the name *Alsatia* to the precinct of Whitefriars. This privileged spot stood in the same relation to the Temple as Alsace did to France and the central powers of Europe. In the Temple, students were studying to observe the law; and in Alsatia, adjoining, debtors to avoid and violate it. The Alsatians were troublesome neighbours to the Templars, and the Templars as troublesome neighbours to the Alsatians." *Cunningham.*

The furious German comes, with his clarions and his drums,
His bravoes of *Alsatia*, and pages of Whitehall. *Macaulay.*

Al Sirat (ăs se-răt'). [Ar., the path.] A bridge extending from this world to the next, over the abyss of hell, which must be passed by every one who would enter the Mohammedan paradise. It is very narrow, the breadth being less than the thread of a famished spider, according to some writers; others compare it to the edge of a sword, or of a razor. The deceased cross with a rapidity proportioned to their virtue. Some, it is said, pass with the swiftness of lightning, others with the speed of a horse at full gallop, others like a horse at a slow pace, others still slower, on account of the weight of their sins, and many fall down from it, and are precipitated into hell.

Am'ȧ-dis de Gául. [Sp. *Amadis de Gaula*.] The hero of an ancient and celebrated romance of chivalry, originally the work of a Portuguese, Vasco de Lobeira, who died, as Ticknor conjectures, in 1403. It was translated into Spanish by Montalvo, between 1492 and 1504. The Portuguese original is no longer extant. A French version was made by Herberay, and was printed, in 1555, under the mistranslated title of "Amadis des Gaules," meaning France. In the original romance, *Gaula* is Wales; and the subject, characters, and localities are British. The other Amadises that figure in romance are represented as descendants, more or less remote, of Amadis de Gaul. He himself was a love-child of a fabulous King Perion of Wales, and of Elisena, a British princess.

A̍-mai'mŏn, *or* **A̍-māy'mŏn.** An imaginary king of the East, one of the principal devils who might be bound or restrained from doing hurt from the third hour till noon, and from the ninth hour till evening. He is alluded to in Shakespeare's "1 Henry IV." (a. ii., sc. 4), and "Merry Wives of Windsor" (a. ii., sc. 2). According to Holme, he was "the chief whose dominion is on the north part of the infernal gulf;" but Mr. Christmas says he ruled over the easternmost of the four provinces into which the world of devils was thought to be divided. Asmodeus was his lieutenant.

Am'ȧl-thæ'ȧ. [Gr. 'Αμάλθεια.] (*Gr. & Rom. Myth.*) The name of a goat with whose milk the infant Jupiter was fed, and one of whose horns he is said to have broken off, and given to the daughters of Melisseus, a Cretan king. This he endowed with such powers, that, whenever the possessor wished, it would instantaneously become filled with whatever might be desired: hence it was called the *cornucopia*, or horn of plenty. According to other accounts, Amalthæa was the name of a nymph by whom Jupiter was nursed in his infancy.

The Britannic Fountain . . . flowed like an *Amalthæa's* horn for seven years to come, refreshing Austria and all thirsty Pragmatic Nations, to defend the Key-stone of this Universe. *Carlyle.*

Am'ȧ-ryl'lis. The name of a country-girl in the Idyls of Theocritus and in the Eclogues of Virgil, adopted into modern pastoral poetry as the name of a mistress or sweetheart.

To sport with *Amaryllis* in the shade.
Milton.

Am'ȧ-zo'ni-ȧ. A name given by Francisco Orellana, in 1580, to the country on either side of the river Marañon, from the companies of

and for the Remarks and Rules to which the numbers after certain words refer, see pp. xlv-xxxii.

women in arms whom he observed on its banks. He also gave the name *Amazon* to the river, and it has since been generally known under this designation.

Ȧ-me′li-ḁ (*or* ḁ-meel′yḁ). 1. The title of one of Fielding's novels, and the name of its heroine, who is distinguished for her conjugal tenderness and affection. The character of Amelia is said to have been drawn for Fielding's wife, even down to an accident which disfigured her beauty.

☞ "To have invented that character is not only a triumph of art, but it is a good action." *Thackeray.*

2. A young woman killed in her lover's arms by a stroke of lightning, who forms the subject of a well-known episode in the poem of " Summer," in Thomson's " Seasons."

American Fā′bi-us. An appellation often given to General Washington (1732-1799), whose military policy resembled that of the Roman general Quintus Fabius Maximus Verrucosus, who conducted operations against Hannibal by declining to risk a battle in the open field, harassing him by marches, counter-marches, and ambuscades.

Ȧ-mîne′. A character in the "Arabian Nights' Entertainments" who leads her three sisters by her side as a leash of hounds.

Aminte (ȧ′mănt′, 62). The assumed name of a female character in Molière's celebrated comedy, " Les Précieuses Ridicules." Her real name is *Cathos*, which she has discarded for a more sentimental one, in accordance with the prevailing fashion. She dismisses her admirer for proposing to marry her, scolds her uncle (see GORGIBUS) for not possessing the air of a gentleman, and is taken in by a valet whom she believes to be a nobleman, and who easily imitates the foppery and sentimentalism which she so much admires.

Am′let, Richard. The name of a gamester in Vanbrugh's " Confederacy."

Richard Amlet, Esq., in the play, is a notable instance of the disadvantages to which this chimerical notion of affinity constituting a claim to acquaintance may subject the spirit of a gentleman. *Charles Lamb.*

Am′mŏn. [Gr. ᾽Αμμων.] (*Gr. & Rom. Myth.*) The name of an Ethiopian or Libyan divinity, identified by the Greeks and Romans with Jupiter. He was represented in the form of a ram, or as a human being with the head of a ram, or sometimes with only the horns. [Written also H a m m o n.]

Am′o-ret. The name of a lady married to Sir Scudamore, in Spenser's " Faëry Queen." She expresses the affectionate devotedness of a loving and tender wife.

Am-phi′ŏn. [Gr. ᾽Αμφίων.] (*Gr. & Rom. Myth.*) A son of Jupiter and Antiope, who built a wall round the city of Thebes by the music of his lyre. It is said, that, when he played, the stones moved of their own accord, and fitted themselves together so as to form the wall.

It was like a sudden pause in one of *Amphion's* country-dances, when the huts which were to form the future Thebes were jigging it to his lute. *Sir W. Scott.*

Am′phi-tri′te. [Gr. ᾽Αμφιτρίτη.] (*Gr. & Rom. Myth.*) The wife of Neptune, goddess of the sea, and mother of Triton.

Am-phit′ry-ŏn. [Gr. ᾽Αμφιτρύων.] (*Gr. & Rom. Myth.*) A son of Alcæus and Hipponome. He was king of Thebes, and husband of Alcmena, who bore at the same time Iphicles, his son, and Hercules, the son of Jupiter. See ALCMENA. [Written also A m p h i t r y o.]

Am′rī. See FATHER OF EQUITY.

Amrita (ăm-re′tȧ). (*Hindu Myth.*) A beverage of immortality, churned from the sea by the gods, who were mortal until they discovered this potent elixir.

Ā′mys and Ȧ-myl′i-ŏn. Two faithful and sorely tried friends, — the Pylades and Orestes of the feudal ages, — whose adventures are the subject of a very ancient romance bearing these names for its title. An abstract of the story is given in Ellis's " Specimens of Early English Metrical Romances."

☞ For the " Key to the Scheme of Pronunciation," with the accompanying Explanations,

An'ạ-ҫhar'sis Clōotz (klōts). A name assumed by Baron Jean Baptiste Clootz, who was born at Cleves, in 1755. He conceived the idea of reforming the human race, and travelled through England, Germany, Italy, &c., denouncing all kings, princes, and rulers, and even the Deity. He called himself *Anacharsis*, in allusion to the Scythian philosopher of this name, who flourished about six centuries before the Christian era, and who travelled to Greece and other countries for the purpose of gaining knowledge in order to improve the people of his own country.

A̱-nac're-ǫn Moore. A name sometimes given to Thomas Moore, the poet, who, in 1801, published a translation of the Odes of Anacreon.

> Julia sat within as pretty a bower
> As e'er held houri in that heathenish heaven
> Described by Mahomet and *Anacreon Moore*.
> *Byron.*

A̱-nac're-ǫn of Painters. A name given to Francesco Albani (1578–1660), a distinguished painter of Italy. He was so called on account of the softness of his style, and his avoidance of subjects which require spirited and energetic treatment.

A̱-nac're-ǫn of Persia. A title sometimes given to Hafiz (d. 1388), the Persian poet, whose odes and lyric compositions, like those of Anacreon, celebrate the pleasures of love and wine.

A̱-nac're-ǫn of the Guillotine. A name given by the French to Bertrand Barère (or Barrère) de Vieuzac (1755–1841), president of the National Convention in 1792, on account of the flowery and poetical language in which he spoke upon all the measures of the reign of terror. See WITLING OF TERROR.

An'ạs-tā'si-us (an'ạs-tā'zhĭ-us). The hero and title of a novel by Thomas Hope (1770–1831), — a work purporting to be the autobiography of a Greek, who, to escape the consequences of his own crimes and villanies of every kind, becomes a renegade, and passes through a long series of the most extraordinary and romantic vicissitudes.

Anastasius Grün. See GRÜN, ANASTASIUS.

An-cæ'us. [Gr. Ἀγκαῖος.] (*Gr. & Rom. Myth.*) A son of Neptune who, having left a cup of wine untasted to pursue a wild boar, was killed by it, which gave rise to the proverb, "There's many a slip between the cup and the lip."

An-ҫhi'sēṣ. [Gr. Ἀγχίσης.] (*Gr. & Rom. Myth.*) A son of Capys and Themis, and the father of Æneas by Venus. He survived the capture of Troy, and was carried by Æneas on his shoulders from the burning city.

Ancient Mariner. The hero of Coleridge's poem of the same name, who, for the crime of having shot an albatross, a bird of good omen to voyagers, suffers dreadful penalties, together with his companions, who have made themselves accomplices in his crime. These penalties are at last remitted in consequence of his repentance. He reaches land, where he encounters a hermit, to whom he relates his story;

> "Since then, at an uncertain hour,
> The agony returns,"

and drives him on, like the Wandering Jew, from land to land, compelled to relate the tale of his suffering and crime as a warning to others, and as a lesson of love and charity towards all God's creatures.

☞ The conception of this poem and the mystical imagery of the skeleton-ship are said by Dyce to have been borrowed by Coleridge from a friend who had experienced a strange dream. But De Quincey asserts that the germ of the story is contained in a passage of Shelvocke, one of the classical circumnavigators of the earth, who states that his second captain, being a melancholy man, was possessed by a fancy that some long season of foul weather was owing to an albatross which had steadily pursued the ship, upon which he shot the bird, but without mending their condition.

Andrews, Joseph. The title of a novel by Fielding, and the name of its hero, a footman who marries a maid-servant. To ridicule Richardson's "Pamela," Fielding made Joseph Andrews a brother of that renowned lady, and, by way of contrast to Richardson's hero, represented him as a model of virtue and excellence.

☞ "The accounts of Joseph's bravery and good qualities, his voice too musical to halloo to the dogs, his bravery in riding races for the gentlemen of the county, and his constancy in refusing bribes and temptation, have something refreshing in their *naïveté* and freshness, and prepossess one in favour of that handsome young hero." *Thackeray.*

An-drom'a-çhe. [Gr. 'Ανδρομάχη.] (*Gr. & Rom. Myth.*) A daughter of Eëtion, and the fond wife of Hector, by whom she had Astyanax. She is one of the noblest and loveliest female characters in Homer's "Iliad."

An-drom'e-dạ. [Gr. 'Ανδρομέδη.] (*Gr. & Rom. Myth.*) A daughter of Cepheus, king of Ethiopia, and of Cassiopeia. Her mother having boasted that her beauty surpassed that of the Nereids, Andromeda was exposed to a sea-monster, but was found, saved, and married by Perseus.

An-ġel'ĭ-cạ. An infidel princess of exquisite beauty and consummate coquetry, in Bojardo's "Orlando Innamorato." She is represented to have come all the way from farthest Asia to sow dissension among the Christians in Paris, who were besieged by two hosts of infidels, one from Spain, and another, which had landed in the south of France, from Africa. Among many others, Orlando falls desperately in love with her, forgetting, for her sake, his wife, his sovereign, his country, his glory, in short, every thing except his religion. She, however, cares nothing for him, having fallen madly in love with Rinaldo, in consequence of drinking at an enchanted fountain. On the other hand, Rinaldo, from drinking at a neighbouring fountain of exactly the opposite quality, cannot abide her. Various adventures arise out of these circumstances; and the fountains are again drunk, with a mutual reversal of their effects. Ariosto, in his "Orlando Furioso," took up the thread of Angelica's story where Bojardo had left it, making the jilt fall in love here with Medoro, an obscure youth squire, he represents Orlando driven mad by jealousy and ind nation. Angelica is celebrated the possession of a magic ring, whi placed on the finger, defended wearer from all spells, and, concea in the mouth, rendered the person visible. See AGRICANE.

☞ "Angelica, noted in romance the faithless lady for whose sake Orla lost his heart and his senses, was a tuitous invention of Bojardo and Ario for Spanish ballads and earlier Ita poets make him the faithful husband Alda or Belinda." *Yo*

The fairest of her sex, *Angelica*,
... sought by many prowest knights,
Both painim and the peers of Charlema
Mi

Angelic Doctor. [Lat. *Doctor geticus.*] Thomas Aquinas (12 1274), the most famous of the m æval schoolmen and divines.

☞ Aquinas was extravagantly mired by his followers. One of his c mentators endeavours to prove that wrote with a special infusion of the S of God; that he received many thing direct revelation, and that Christ given anticipatory testimony to his w ings. Peter Labbé says, that, as learned some things from the angels he taught the angels some things; he had said what St. Paul was not mitted to utter; and that he speak God as if he had seen him, and of Ch as if he had been his voice.

We extol Bacon, and sneer at Aqui But, if the situations had been chan Bacon might have been the *Angelic Do Macau*

Angélique (ŏn'zhă'lĕk', 62). 1. heroine of Molière's comedy, ' Malade Imaginaire."
2. The wife of George Dandin Molière's comedy of this name. DANDIN, GEORGE.

An'ġe-lo. 1. The deputy of Vinc tio, in Shakespeare's "Measure Measure." At first he exercises delegated power with rigour seeming conscientiousness, but to enable him the more safely to ify his base passion for Isabella, sister of a young nobleman na Claudio. His design, howeve thwarted, and his hypocrisy asked, by a counteracting intrigue of Vincentio's, which, aided and favoured by chance, rescues Isabella, and punishes Angelo by compelling him to marry Mariana, a woman whom he had a long time before seduced and abandoned.

2. A goldsmith in Shakespeare's Comedy of Errors."

rel of the Schools. A title given Thomas Aquinas, the most celebrated metaphysician of the Middle ges. See ANGELIC DOCTOR.

rurvardel (äug'gōōr-vȧ'del). [Icel., stream of anguish.] The sword of ithiof. The blade was inscribed ith runic letters, which shone dimly peace, but gleamed with a wondrous ruddy light in time of war. See FRITHIOF. [Written also Anurwadel.]

oriously known was the sword, the first of all swords in the Northland.
Bp. Tegnér, Trans.

ie, Sister. See SISTER ANNE.

tæ'us. [Gr. 'Ανταῖος.] (*Gr. & om. Myth.*) A son of Neptune and erra, a famous Libyan giant and restler, whose strength was invincible so long as he remained in contact with his mother earth. Hercules discovered the source of his might, lifted him up from the earth, and crushed in in the air.

when Earth's son *Antæus* (to compare all things with greatest) in Irassa strove with Jove's Alcides, and, oft foiled, still rose, receiving from his mother earth new strength (as from his full), and fiercer grapple joined; throttled at length in air, expired and fell: after many a foil, the tempter proud, renewing fresh assaults amidst his pride, I whence he stood to see his victor fall.
Milton.

'e-rōs. [Gr. 'Αντέρως.] (*Gr. & om. Myth.*) A deity opposed to os, or Love, and fighting against n; usually, however, regarded as a d who avenged slighted love. He sometimes represented as the symbol of reciprocal affection.

I-christ. Literally, the opponent of the anointed, or of the Messiah. e name of Antichrist was given by the Jews and Christians to the great my of true religion, who shall, according to the Holy Scriptures, appear before the coming of the Messiah in his glory. The name occurs in the Bible in the following places only: — 1 *John* ii. 18, 22; iv. 3; 2 *John* 7. The "man of sin," whose coming is foretold by St. Paul, 2 *Thess.* ii., is supposed to be the same with Antichrist. Emblematic descriptions of him occur in the 12th and 13th chapters of the *Revelation*. Theological writers have indulged in many and the most diverse and fanciful speculations respecting this great adversary of Christianity; but the prevalent opinion among Protestant divines has always connected him with the Roman Catholic church. At the Council of Gap, in 1603, the reformed ministers there assembled inserted an article in their Confession of Faith, in which the Pope is pronounced Antichrist. Grotius and most Roman Catholic divines consider Antichrist as symbolical of Pagan Rome and her persecutions; Leclerc, Lightfoot, and others, of the Jewish Sanhedrim, or of particular Jewish impostors. Many are of opinion that the kingdom of Antichrist comprehends all who are opposed to Christ, openly or secretly.

An-tig'o-ne. [Gr. 'Αντιγόνη.] (*Gr. & Rom. Myth.*) A daughter of Œdipus by his mother Jocasta. She was famous for her filial piety.

An-tin'o-us. [Gr. 'Αντίνους.] A page of the Emperor Hadrian, celebrated for his extraordinary beauty, and for Hadrian's extravagant affection for him. After his death by drowning in the Nile, — about A. D. 122, — he was enrolled among the gods, temples were erected to him in Egypt and Greece, and statues set up in almost every part of the world.

An-ti'o-pe. [Gr. 'Αντιόπη.] (*Gr. & Rom. Myth.*) A favourite of Jupiter, by whom she became the mother of Amphion and Zethus. See LYCUS.

An-tiph'o-lus of Eph'e-sus. } Twin
An-tiph'o-lus of Syr'ą-cuse. } brothers, sons of Ægeon and Æmilia, in Shakespeare's " Comedy of Errors," and
" the one so like the other
As could not be distinguished but by names."

or the Remarks and Rules to which the numbers after certain words refer, see pp. xlv-xxxii.

2

Their attendants were Dromio of Ephesus and Dromio of Syracuse, also twins, and both alike in their personal appearance.

An-to'ni-o. 1. The usurping Duke of Milan, and brother to Prospero, in Shakespeare's "Tempest." See PROSPERO.
2. The father of Proteus, in Shakespeare's "Two Gentlemen of Verona."
3. A minor character in Shakespeare's "Much Ado about Nothing."
4. The "Merchant of Venice," in Shakespeare's play of that name. See PORTIA.
5. A sea-captain, friend to Sebastian, in Shakespeare's "Twelfth Night."

Ā-nu'bis. [Gr. 'Ανουβις.] (*Egypt. Myth.*) A divinity, a son of Osiris, worshipped in the form of a dog, or of a human being with a dog's head. He accompanied the ghosts of the dead to the under-world.

Ap'e-man'tus. A churlish philosopher, in Shakespeare's play, "Timon of Athens."

Their affected melancholy showed like the cynicism of *Apemantus* contrasted with the real misanthropy of Timon. *Sir W. Scott.*

Aph'ro-di'te. [Gr. 'Αφροδίτη.] (*Gr. Myth.*) The Greek name of *Venus*, the goddess of love, beauty, and desire. See VENUS.

Ā'pis. [Gr. 'Απις.] (*Egypt. Myth.*) The chief deity of the Egyptians, worshipped under the form of a bull. He is sometimes identified with Osiris and Serapis.

Ā-pol'lo. [Gr. 'Απόλλων.] (*Gr. & Rom. Myth.*) The son of Jupiter and Latona, and the brother of Diana, portrayed with flowing hair as being ever young. He was the god of song, music, prophecy, and archery, the punisher and destroyer of the wicked and overbearing, the protector of flocks and cattle, the averter of evil, the afforder of help, and the god who delighted in the foundation of towns and the establishment of civil constitutions. By the later Greeks he was identified with the sun. His favourite residence was at Mount Parnassus, and he had oracles at Delphi and Delos.

Ā-pol'ly-ŏn, or Ā-poll'yŏn. [Gr. 'Απολλύων, from ἀπολλύναι, to destroy utterly, to ruin.] In the Jewish demonology, an evil spirit, called in Hebrew *Abaddon*, and described in *Rev.* ix. 11, as "a king, the angel of the bottomless pit." He is introduced by Bunyan in his allegorical romance of the "Pilgrim's Progress."

Apostle of Ardennes (ar'den', 64). A title given to St. Hubert (d. 727), Bishop of Maestrecht and Liege, and son of Bertrand, Duke of Aquitaine. He was so called from his zeal in destroying remnants of idolatry.

Apostle of Germany. A title given to St. Boniface (680–755), who, for more than thirty years of his life, laboured in the work of converting and civilising the rude heathen nations of Germany.

Apostle of Infidelity. A name sometimes given to Voltaire (1694–1778), a bigoted and intolerant deist, who avowed a design of destroying the Christian religion, and was unceasing in his attacks upon it and upon its defenders.

Apostle of Ireland. St. Patrick, born near the end of the fourth century, died in 483 or 493. He was moved by visions, as he relates in his confessions, to undertake the conversion of the Irish to Christianity. He established many churches and schools, and made many converts.

Apostle of Temperance. An honorary appellation given to the Rev. Theobald Mathew (1790–1856), a distinguished temperance reformer in Ireland and England.

☞ "However, as Protestants, we may question the claim of departed saints, here is a living minister, if he may be judged from one work, who deserves to be canonised, and whose name should be placed in the calendar not far below the apostles." *Dr. Channing*, 1841.

Apostle of the English. St. Augustine, or Austin, who lived during the latter part of the sixth century. He was sent with forty monks, by Pope

☞ For the "Key to the Scheme of Pronunciation," with the accompanying Explanations,

Gregory I., to carry Christianity into England. Such was his success that he is said to have baptised 10,000 persons in a single day. He has the merit of having allowed no coercive measures in the propagation of the gospel.

Apostle of the French. A name given to St. Denis, the first bishop of Paris, in the third century. He was sent from Rome, about A. D. 250, to revive the drooping churches in Gaul, and proceeded as far as Lutetia (Paris), where he made many converts. He became the patron saint of the kingdom, and his name served, for many ages, as a rallying cry in battle, — *Montjoie St. Denis!*

Apostle of the Frisians. An appellation commonly given to Saint Wilbrord, or Willibrod (657-738), a native of the Saxon kingdom of Northumbria, who spent forty-eight years of his life in Friesland in preaching Christianity, and endeavouring to convert the people from paganism to the true faith.

Apostle of the Gauls. St. Irenæus, presbyter, and afterward bishop, of Lyons, near the close of the second century.

☞ "The immortal Apostle of the Gauls, who, in his earliest youth, had sat at the feet of Polycarp, at Smyrna, started from the school of Asia Minor. It was during a great crisis that Providence brought this gem of Asia into the West. Irenæus possessed the apostolical patience, as well as the fiery zeal, of Polycarp. He learned Celtic, in order to preach the gospel to the barbarians in their own language, and rejoiced in beholding the progress of the good work in which he was engaged in the parts of Germany bordering on Gaul." *Bunsen.*

Apostle of the Gentiles. A title assumed by St. Paul, who, in conjunction with Barnabas, was divinely appointed to the work of preaching the gospel to all mankind, without distinction of race or nation. His labours lasted through many years, and reached over a vast extent of country. See *Acts* xiii., *Rom.* xi. 13, and 2 *Tim.* i. 11.

Apostle of the Highlanders. A name given to St. Columba (521-597), one of the earliest teachers of Christianity in Scotland. He established himself in the island of Iona, and is believed to have been the founder of the Culdees, who had their head-quarters there.

Apostle of the Indians. An appellation given to the Rev. John Eliot (1603-1690), a celebrated missionary among the Indians in the Colony of Massachusetts Bay, many of whom he converted to Christianity.

☞ "The Apostle, — and truly I know not who, since Peter and Paul, better deserves that name." *E. Everett.*

Apostle of the North. 1. A title bestowed upon Anschar, Anscharius, or Ansgar (801-864), because he introduced Christianity into Denmark, Sweden, and Northern Germany. At the instigation of the Emperor, Louis le Débonnaire, he went to Denmark, and, after many disappointments and persecutions, converted the king and the greater part of the nation. The Catholic church has placed him among the saints.

☞ "He [Anschar] was the Columbus and the Cortés of that unknown world whither he penetrated with no other weapon than his dauntless faith and the name of Rome." *Michelet, Trans.*

2. A title conferred upon Bernard Gilpin (1517-1583), an English reformer, and the first who undertook to preach the Protestant doctrines to the inhabitants of the Scottish Border land.

Apostle of the Peak. A title given to William Bagshaw (1628-1702), a non-conforming divine, distinguished for his zeal and usefulness in the cause of religion in the northern parts of Derbyshire, England.

Apostle of the Picts. A name given to St. Ninian, a British bishop of the latter half of the fourth and the beginning of the fifth centuries, on account of his labours for the conversion of the Teutonic inhabitants of Cumbria.

Apostle of the Scottish Reformation. A title given to John Knox (1505-1572), the most active agent in the overthrow of the Roman Catholic religion, and the establishment of the Reformed kirk, in Scotland.

Apostle of the Slaves. A title given to St. Cyril (ninth century), who converted to Christianity the Chasars, dwelling by the Caspian Sea, laboured in the same cause among the heathens of Bulgaria, Moravia, and Bohemia, and, with the assistance of some of his pupils and his brother, made a translation of the Holy Scriptures, which is still used by all Greek-Catholic Christians.

Apostle to the Indies. A title often given to St. Francis Xavier, a distinguished Roman Catholic missionary of the sixteenth century, who spent more than ten years in laborious efforts to introduce Christianity into the East.

Apostolic King. A title given by the Holy See to the kings of Hungary, on account of the extensive propagation of Christianity by Stephen I., the founder of the royal line.

Ap'po-li'no. [The same as *Apollo*, the sun.] An imaginary deity, supposed by the people of Western Europe, during the Middle Ages, to be worshipped by the Mohammedans. —See TERMAGANT.

Aq'ui-lo. (*Rom. Myth.*) A personification of the north wind; the same as *Boreas*. See BOREAS.

Arabian Tailor. See LEARNED TAILOR.

Ăr'a-by. A poetical form of *Arabia*.

Farewell, — farewell to thee, *Araby's* daughter. *T. Moore.*

Ă-rach'ne. [Gr. Ἀράχνη.] (*Gr. & Rom. Myth.*) A Lydian maiden, so proud of her skill as a weaver that she challenged Minerva to compete with her. She was successful in the contest, but, being insulted by the goddess, hung herself in despair, and was changed into a spider.

Shall we tremble before cloth-webs and cobwebs, whether woven in Arkwright looms, or by the silent *Arachnes* that weave unrestingly in our imagination? *Carlyle.*

Ar'ca-dy. A poetical form of *Arcadia*, a pastoral district of the Peloponnesus (Morea) in Greece.

Archer. Servant to Aimwell, in Farquhar's "Beaux' Stratagem."

Ar'chĭ-mā'go, or **Ar'chĭ-mâge.** [From Gr. ἀρχι, chief, in composition, and μάγος, magician.] An enchanter in Spenser's "Faëry Queen." He is a type of Hypocrisy, or Fraud, and, as opposed to Christian Holiness embodied in the Red-cross Knight, may also represent Satan, the incarnate principle of evil. He wins the confidence of the knight in the disguise of a reverend hermit, and by the help of Duessa, or Deceit, separates him from Una, or Truth.

By his mighty science he could take
As many forms and shapes in seeming wise
As ever Proteus to himself could make:
Sometime a fowl, sometime a fish in lake,
Now like a fox, now like a dragon fell;
That of himself he oft for fear would quake,
And oft would fly away. Oh, who can tell
The hidden power of herbs, and might of magic spell? *Faëry Queen.*

Him followed his companion, dark and sage,
As he, my Master, sung the dangerous *Archimage*. *Sir W. Scott.*

Whatever momentary benefit may result from satire, it is clear that its influence, in the long run, is injurious to literature. The satirist, like a malignant *Archimago*, creates a false medium, through which posterity is obliged to look at his contemporaries, — a medium which so refracts and distorts their images, that it is almost out of the question to see them correctly. *Atlantic Monthly.*

Ar'cite. A character in the "Knight's Tale," in Chaucer's "Canterbury Tales." See PALAMON.

Ar'den, Enoch. The hero of Tennyson's poem of the same name, a seaman who is wrecked on an uninhabited and rarely visited tropical island, where he spends many years, and who returns home at last only to find that his wife, believing him to be dead, has married again, and is prosperous and happy. In a spirit of heroic self-sacrifice, he determines not to undeceive her, and soon dies of a broken heart.

Ardennes, Wild Boar of. See WILD BOAR OF ARDENNES.

A'rēṣ. [Gr. Ἄρης.] (*Gr. Myth.*) The god of war; the same as *Mars*. See MARS.

Ăr'e-thu'sȧ. [Gr. Ἀρέθουσα.] (*Gr. & Rom. Myth.*) One of the Nereids, and an attendant upon Diana. She presided over a famous fountain of the same name, close by the margin of the sea in the island of Ortygia, near Syracuse. According to Ovid, the river-god Alpheus became enamoured of her while bathing in his stream in Arcadia. Diana, however, took pity on her, and changed her into a well, which flowed under the Adriatic to Ortygia. But Alpheus still pursued her, and, passing by the same under-ground channel from Greece to Sicily, re-appeared in the fountain, and mingled his waters with those of the nymph. [Written also, poetically, A r e t h u s e.]

That renownèd flood, so often sung,
Divine Alpheus, who, by secret sluice,
Stole under seas to meet his *Arethuse*.
Milton.

Aretino, The Only (ä-rä-te′no). [It. *L' Unico Aretino.*] An honorary appellation given by his admirers to Bernardo Accolti, an Italian poet of the sixteenth century, celebrated for his wonderful powers of improvisation. The designation seems to have been intended to express his superiority to his uncle, Francesco Accolti (d. 1483), surnamed *Aretinus*, who was also a poet, and to Pietro Aretino, a distinguished contemporary satirist.

Argalia (är-gä-le′ä). A brother to Angelica, in Bojardo's romantic poem, the "Orlando Innamorato." He is celebrated as the possessor of an enchanted lance which threw whomsoever it touched. Ferraù eventually killed him, and Astolfo obtained the lance.

Ar′ga-lus. An unfortunate lover in Sir Philip Sidney's "Arcadia." See PARTHENIA.

Argan (är′gŏn′, 62). The hero of Molière's comedy, "Le Malade Imaginaire," an hypochondriac patient, whose love of medicine is accompanied by a spirit of parsimony which leads him to take every mode that may diminish the expense of his supposed indisposition.

☞ "Argan . . . is discovered taxing his apothecary's bill, at once delighting his ear with the flowery language of the Pharmacopœia, and gratifying his frugal disposition by clipping off some items and reducing others, and arriving at the double conclusion, first, that, if his apothecary does not become more reasonable, he cannot afford to be a sick man any longer; and, secondly, that, as he has swallowed fewer drugs by one third this month than he had done the last, it was no wonder he was not so well. . . . [He] is at last persuaded that the surest and cheapest way of securing himself against the variety of maladies by which he is beset, will be to become a doctor in his own proper person. He modestly represents his want of preliminary study, and of the necessary knowledge even of the Latin language; but he is assured that by merely putting on the robe and cap of a physician he will find himself endowed with all the knowledge necessary for exercising the profession. . . . This leads to the interlude which concludes the piece, being the mock ceremonial of receiving a physician into the Æsculapian college, couched in macaronic Latinity."
Sir W. Scott.

Argante (är′gŏnt′, 62). A character in Molière's comedy, "Les Fourberies de Scapin."

Ar-gan′te. A terrible giantess in Spenser's "Faëry Queen;" a very monster and miracle of licentiousness.

Argantes (är-gän′tess). The bravest of the infidel heroes in Tasso's epic poem, "Jerusalem Delivered."

Bonaparte, in these disjointed yet significant threats, stood before the deputies like the *Argantes* of Italy's heroic poet, and gave them, the choice of peace and war with the air of a superior being, capable at once to dictate their fate. *Sir W. Scott.*

Ar-ġiēr′. An old form of *Algiers*, found in Shakespeare's "Tempest."

Ar′go. [Gr. Ἀργώ, from ἀργός, swift.] (*Gr. & Rom. Myth.*) A fifty-oared ship in which Jason and his companions made their voyage to Colchis in search of the golden fleece. See ARGONAUTS.

Harder beset
And more endangered, than when *Argo* passed
Through Bosporus betwixt the justling rocks.
Milton.

Ar′go-nauts. [Lat. *Argonautæ*; Gr. Ἀργοναῦται.] (*Gr. & Rom. Myth.*) The heroes and demigods who, according to the traditions of the Greeks, undertook an expedition to Colchis, a far-distant country on the coast of the Euxine, for the purpose of obtaining a golden fleece, which was guarded by a sleepless and terrible dragon.

A body of Bastille heroes, tolerably complete, did get together ;— comparable to the *Argonauts;* hoping to endure like them.
Carlyle.

Ar'gus. [Gr. Ἀργος.] (*Gr. & Rom. Myth.*) A fabulous being of enormous strength, who had a hundred eyes, of which only two were asleep at once, whence he was named *Panoptes,* or the All-seeing. Juno appointed him to watch over Io (see Io), but Mercury killed him, and Juno transferred his eyes to the tail of the peacock, her favourite bird.

Spangled with eyes more numerous than those
Of *Argus,* and more wakeful than to drowse,
Charmed with Arcadian pipe, the pastoral reed
Of Hermes, or his opiate rod. *Milton.*

A'ri-ad'ne (9). [Gr. Ἀριάδνη.] (*Gr. & Rom. Myth.*) A daughter of Minos, king of Crete, who, from the love she bore to Theseus, gave him a clew of thread, which guided him out of the Cretan labyrinth. Theseus in return promised to marry her, and she accordingly left the island with him, but was slain by Diana in Naxos. According to another tradition, she was married to Bacchus, who, after her death, gave her a place among the gods, and placed her wedding crown as a constellation in the sky.

A'ri-el (9). 1. In the demonology of the Cabala, a water-spirit; in the fables of the Middle Ages, a spirit of the air,—the guardian angel of innocence; in Shakespeare's "Tempest," an airy and tricksy spirit, represented as having been a servant to Sycorax, a foul witch, by whom, for some acts of disobedience, he was imprisoned within the rift of a cloven pine-tree, where he remained for twelve years, until released by Prospero. In gratitude for his deliverance, he became the willing messenger of Prospero, assuming any shape, or rendering himself invisible, in order to execute the commands of his master.

On the hearth the lighted logs are glowing,
And, like *Ariel* in the cloven pine-tree,
For its freedom
Groans and sighs the air imprisoned in them.
Longfellow.

2. The name of a sylph in Pope's "Rape of the Lock."

☞ "Pope's fairy region, compared with Shakespeare's, was what a drawing-room is to the universe. To give, therefore, to the sprite of the 'Rape of the Lock' the name of the spirit in the 'Tempest' was a bold christening. Prospero's Ariel could have puffed him out like a taper. Or he would have snuffed him up as an essence, by way of jest, and found him flat. But, tested by less potent senses, the sylph species is an exquisite creation. He is an abstract of the spirit of fine life; a suggester of fashions; an inspirer of airs; would be cut to pieces rather than see his will contradicted; takes his station with dignity on a picture-cord; and is so nice an adjuster of claims that he ranks hearts with necklaces. . . . The punishments inflicted on him when disobedient have a like fitness. He is to be kept hovering over the fumes of the chocolate; to be transfixed with pins, clogged with pomatums, and wedged in the eyes of bodkins." *Leigh Hunt.*

Ariodantes (*It. pron.* ä-re-o-dän'tess). The lover of Ginevra, in Ariosto's "Orlando Furioso."

A-ri'on. [Gr. Ἀρίων.] (*Gr. & Rom. Myth.*) An ancient Greek bard and musician of the isle of Lesbos. On his return to Corinth from Italy, on one occasion, the mariners formed a plot to murder him for his riches; but being forewarned of their intention, he played upon his lute, and, by the charms of his music, brought a number of dolphins around the vessel, when he threw himself into the sea, and was carried on the back of one of them to the promontory of Tænarus in the Peloponnesus.

Ar'is-tæ'us. [Gr. Ἀρισταῖος.] (*Gr. & Rom. Myth.*) An ancient Greek divinity, worshipped as the protector of vine and olive plantations, and of hunters and herdsmen. He was also thought to have instructed men in the management of bees. According to the common tradition, he was a son of Apollo and the water-nymph Cyrene.

In such a palace *Aristæus* found
Cyrene, when he bore the plaintive tale
Of his lost bees to her maternal ear.
Cowper (on the Ice-palace of Anne of Russia).

Ar'is-te'as. [Gr. Ἀριστέας.] (*Gr. & Rom. Myth.*) A fabulous being, who has been styled the "Wandering Jew" of popular tradition in ancient Greece. He appears first as a teacher of Homer, and re-appears in different ages and places in very different characters. Herodotus and Suidas assert that he was a magician, whose soul could leave and re-enter its body at pleasure.

Aristophanes, The Modern. See MODERN ARISTOPHANES.

Arlecchino (ar-lek-ke'no, 102). See HARLEQUIN.

Armada, The Invincible. (*Eng. & Sp. Hist.*) A famous naval armament, or expedition, sent by Philip II. of Spain against England, in the year 1588. It consisted of 130 vessels, 2430 great guns, 4575 quintals of powder, nearly 20,000 soldiers, above 8000 sailors, and more than 2000 volunteers. It arrived in the Channel on the 19th of July, and was defeated the next day by Admiral Howard, who was seconded by Drake, Hawkins, and Frobisher. Eight fireships having been sent into the Spanish fleet, they bore off in great disorder. Profiting by the panic, the English fell upon them, and captured or destroyed a number of their ships, and Admiral Howard maintained a running fight from the 21st of July to the 27th, with such effect, that the Spanish commander, despairing of success, resolved to return home, and, as escape through the English Channel was prevented by contrary winds, he undertook to sail around the Orkneys; but the vessels which still remained to him were dispersed by storms, or shipwrecked among the rocks and shallows, on different parts of the Scottish and Irish coast, and upwards of 5000 men were drowned, killed, or taken prisoners. Of the whole Armada, 53 ships only returned to Spain, and these in a wretched condition. The English lost but one ship.

Armado. See DON ADRIANO DE ARMADO.

Armed Soldier of Democracy. A name given to Napoleon Bonaparte.

Armida (ar-me'dä, 64). One of the most prominent female characters in Tasso's "Jerusalem Delivered." The story of Armida is founded upon a tradition related by Pierre Delancre.

☞ The poet tells us, that, when the Crusaders arrived at the Holy City, Satan held a council to devise some means of disturbing the plans of the Christian warriors, and Armida, a very beautiful sorceress, was employed to seduce Rinaldo and other Crusaders. Rinaldo was conducted by Armida to a remote island, where, in her splendid palace, surrounded by delightful gardens and pleasure-grounds, he utterly forgot his vows and the great object to which he had devoted his life. To liberate him from his voluptuous bondage, two messengers from the Christian army, Carlo and Ubaldo, came to the island, bringing a talisman so powerful that the witchery of Armida was destroyed. Rinaldo escaped, but was followed by the sorceress, who, in battle, incited several warriors to attack the hero, and at last herself rushed into the fight. She was defeated by Rinaldo, who then confessed his love to her, persuaded her to become a Christian, and vowed to be her faithful knight. The story of Armida has been made the subject of an opera by both Gluck and Rossini.

'T was but a doubt; but ne'er magician's wand
Wrought change with all *Armida's* fairy art
Like what this light touch left on Juan's heart.
    Byron.

The stage (even as it then was), after the recluseness and austerity of a college life, must have appeared like *Armida's* enchanted palace.
    Hazlitt.

The grand mansions you arrive at in this waste, howling solitude prove sometimes essentially robber-towers; and there may be *Armida* palaces and divine-looking *Armidas*, where your ultimate fate is still worse.
    Carlyle.

Arnolphe (ar'nolf'). A selfish and morose cynic in Molière's "L'École des Femmes," whose pretended hatred of the world springs from an absorbing regard to his own gratification.

Ar'oun-dight (-dīt). The sword of Lancelot of the Lake.

It is the sword of a good knight,
Though homespun was his mail;
What matter if it be not named
Joyeuse, Colada, Durindale,
Excalibar, or *Aroundight*? *Longfellow.*

Ar-sin'o-e. A prude in Molière's comedy, "Le Misanthrope."

Ar'te-gäl. 1. A mythic king of Britain mentioned in the Chronicle of Geoffrey of Monmouth, and in Milton's History of Britain. See ELIDURE.

2. [Written also Artegall, Ar-

thegal, and Artegale.] A character in Spenser's "Faëry Queen," representative of Justice, and also of the poet's friend and patron, Lord Grey. His main object is to rescue Irena from the tyranny of Grantorto; but, like a chivalrous knight-errant, he is ready to turn aside and subdue the spirit of mischief and violence wherever it may be encountered.

> Every obligation, according to the maxim of the Civil Law, is made void in the same manner in which it is rendered binding; as *Arthegal*, the emblematic champion of Justice in Spenser's allegory, decrees as law, that what the sea has brought the sea may resume. *Sir W. Scott.*

Ar'te-mis. [Gr. Ἄρτεμις.] (*Gr. Myth.*) One of the great divinities of the ancient Greeks; the same as *Diana*. See DIANA.

Artful Dodger. A sobriquet of one of the characters in Dickens's "Oliver Twist." He is a young thief, and an adept in villany.

Arthur. See KING ARTHUR.

Ar'un-del. The steed of Bevis of Southampton. See BEVIS OF SOUTHAMPTON, SIR.

Ar-vir'ā-gus. A son of Cymbeline, in Shakespeare's play of this name, passing under the assumed name of *Cadwal*, and supposed to be a son of Belarius. See BELARIUS.

As-cal'a-phus. [Gr. Ἀσκάλοφος.] (*Gr. & Rom. Myth.*) A son of Acheron, who, having declared that Proserpine — whom Pluto had given permission to return to earth, provided she had not eaten any thing while in the under-world — had tasted of a pomegranate, was turned by Ceres into an owl, for his mischief-making.

As-ca'ni-us. [Gr. Ἀσκάνιος.] (*Gr. & Rom. Myth.*) A son of Æneas and Creusa. He accompanied his father to Italy, succeeded him in the kingdom of Latinus, and built the city of Alba Longa. [Called also *Iulus*.] See ÆNEAS.

> The former belong to that class who, like the young *Ascanius*, are ever beating about in quest of a tawny lion, though they are much more successful in now and then starting a great bore. *Sir W. Scott.*

As'cā-part. The name of a giant whom Bevis of Southampton conquered, according to the old romance. His effigy may be seen on the city-gates of Southampton. He is said to have been thirty feet high, and to have carried Sir Bevis, his wife, and horse, under his arm. Allusions to him occur in Shakespeare, Drayton, and other Elizabethan writers. According to Warton, he is a character in very old French romances.

> Each man an *Ascapart*, of strength to toss For quoits both Temple-bar and Charing-cross. *Pope.*
>
> He was a man whose huge stature, thews, sinews, and bulk in proportion, would have enabled him to enact Colbrand, *Ascapart*, or any other giant of romance, without raising himself nearer to heaven even by the altitude of a chopin. *Sir W. Scott.*

As-cræ'an Sage. [Lat. *Ascræus senex*.] A name given by Virgil, in his sixth Eclogue, to Hesiod, who was born in the eighth century, B. C. at Ascra, a village of Bœotia, in Greece.

Asgard (ăs'gard). [Old Norse, yard, or abode, of the Asir, or gods.] (*Scand. Myth.*) A celestial city or territory, the dwelling of the gods, situated in the centre of the universe, and accessible only by the bridge Bifröst (the rainbow). Here each of the principal deities had a residence apart from the rest. [Written also A s a g a r d.]

Ash'fōrd, Isaac. A peasant in Crabbe's "Parish Register," described as

> "A wise good man, contented to be poor."

Ash'tā-roth. (*Myth.*) The name given in the Bible to Astarte, an ancient Syrian deity, who was adored as the goddess of the moon; hence Jeremiah calls her "the queen of heaven." Solomon built her a temple on the Mount of Olives (2 *Kings* xxiii. 13), but her chief temples were at Tyre and Sidon. Her worship, according to ancient accounts, was of a licentious character. See ASTARTE. [Written also A s t a r o t h and A s t o r e t h.]

> Moonèd *Ashtaroth*, Heaven's queen and mother both. *Milton.*

Ash'tŏn, Lucy. The heroine of Sir Walter Scott's novel, "The Bride of Lammermoor;" daughter of Sir William Ashton, and betrothed to Edgar Ravenswood.

Ash'tŏn, Sir William. The Lord Keeper of Scotland; a prominent character in Scott's "Bride of Lammermoor."

Asir (ä'sêr). (*Scand. Myth.*) The most powerful, though not the oldest, of the deities: usually reckoned as twelve gods and twelve goddesses. The gods are — Odin, Thor, Baldur, Niörd, Frey, Tyr, Bragi, Heimdall, Vidar, Vali, Ullur, and Forseti; the best-known of the goddesses — Frigga, Freyja, Iduna, and Saga. [Written also A s e r, A s a r, and Æ s i r.]

Aṣ'mo-dāi. The same as *Asmodeus*. See ASMODEUS and BELIAL.

Aṣ'mo-de'us. [Heb. *Ascmedai*, the destroyer.] In the Jewish demonology, an evil spirit, the demon of vanity, or dress, called in the Talmud "king of the devils," whence some assume him to be identical with Beëlzebub, and others with Azrael. In modern times, he has been jocularly spoken of as the destroying demon of matrimonial happiness.

☞ In the Apocryphal book of *Tobit*, he is represented as loving Sara, the daughter of Raguel, and causing the death of seven husbands, who married her in succession, on the bridal night. Tobias, instructed by Raphael, burns on "the ashes of perfume" the heart and liver of the fish which he caught in the Tigris; "the which smell when the evil spirit had smelled, he fled into the utmost parts of Egypt, and the angel bound him." Those demonographers of the Middle Ages who reckoned nine kinds of evil spirits, placed Asmodeus at the head of the fourth rank, which consisted of malicious, revenging devils. According to other authorities, he is the lieutenant of Amaimon. Wierus, in his description of the infernal court, makes him superintendent of gambling-houses. Le Sage has made him the companion of Don Cleofas, in "Le Diable Boiteux," or "The Devil on Two Sticks," in which occurs the celebrated adventure known as Asmodeus's flight. By direction of the demon, Don Cleofas takes hold of Asmodeus's cloak, and is immediately borne through the air like an arrow, and perched upon the steeple of St. Salvador. Arrived at this spot, the demon stretches out his right arm, and at once, by his diabolical power, the roofs of the houses are taken off, and, notwithstanding the darkness of the night, the interiors are made visible. The scholar beholds, as at noonday, the inside of all the houses, as one might view the inside of a pie from which the crust had been removed.

☞ "It is impossible to conceive a being more fitted to comment upon the vices, and to ridicule the follies, of humanity, than an *esprit follet* like Asmodeus [in 'Le Diable Boiteux'], who is as much a decided creation of genius, in his way, as Ariel or Caliban. Without possessing the darker powers and propensities of a fallen angel, he presides over the vices and follies, rather than the crimes, of mankind; is malicious rather than, malignant; and his delight is to gibe, and to scoff, and to tease, rather than to torture; — one of Satan's light-infantry, in short, whose business is to goad, perplex, and disturb the ordinary train of society, rather than to break in upon and overthrow it. This character is maintained in all Asmodeus says and does, with so much spirit, wit, acuteness, and playful malice, that we never forget the fiend, even in those moments when he is very near becoming amiable as well as entertaining." *Sir W. Scott.*

Could the reader take an *Asmodeus-flight*, and, waving open all roofs and privacies, look down from the roof of Notre-Dame, what a Paris were it! *Carlyle.*

Ạ-so'pus. [Gr. Ἀσωπος.] (*Gr. & Rom. Myth.*) A son of Oceanus and Tethys, changed into a river for rebelling against Jupiter.

As-pā'si-ạ (as-pā'zhĭ-ạ). A female character in Beaumont and Fletcher's play, "The Maid's Tragedy."

☞ "Her sorrows are so deep, so pure, so unmerited; she sustains the breach of plighted faith in Amyntor, and the taunts of vicious women, with so much resignation, so little of that termagant resentment these poets are apt to infuse into their heroines; the poetry of her speeches is so exquisitely imaginative, that, of those dramatic persons who are not prominent in the development of a story, scarce any, even in Shakespeare, are more interesting." *Hallam.*

Assassination Plot. (*Eng. Hist.*) The name given to a conspiracy formed in 1696, by the Earl of Aylesbury and others, to assassinate King William III., near Richmond, as he returned from the chase. It was discovered Feb. 15, the day before that fixed upon for the execution of the plot.

---

and for the Remarks and Rules to which the numbers after certain words refer, see pp. xiv-xxxii.

As'si-en'to. [Sp., seat, contract, agreement.] A treaty or convention; specifically (*Sp. Hist.*), a convention between the king of Spain and some foreign power for the supply of negroes for the Spanish American colonies. The first Assiento was concluded with the Flemings by Charles I. of Spain. In 1713, it was transferred to England by the treaty of Utrecht, and afterward made over for thirty years by the English government to the South-Sea Company, which, however, in 1750, relinquished its rights to Spain, upon the payment of £100,000, and the concession of certain commercial advantages. [Written also, though rarely in English books, A s i e n t o, which is the proper Spanish orthography.]

As-tar'te. (*Myth.*) The Punic name of the Syrian deity named Ashtaroth. See ASHTAROTH.

<blockquote>
With these in troops
Came Astoreth, whom the Phœnicians called
Astarte, queen of heaven, with crescent horns;
To whose bright image nightly by the moon
Sidonian virgins paid their vows and songs;
In Sion also not unsung, where stood
Her temple on the offensive mountain, built
By that uxorious king, whose heart, though large,
Beguiled by fair idolatresses, fell
To Idols foul.   <i>Milton.</i>
</blockquote>

As'to-lăt. The name given to Guilford, in Surrey, in the old romances of the Arthurian cycle.

As-tol'fo, or **As-tol'pho.** A celebrated character in the romantic tales and poems founded upon the supposed adventures of Charlemagne and his paladins. Astolfo is represented as the English cousin of Orlando, being equally descended with him from Charles Martel. He is a boaster, and is perpetually undertaking great feats, which he is unable to perform; but he is generous, and brave to fool-hardiness, courteous, gay, and singularly handsome. In Ariosto's "Orlando Furioso," he is made to cure Orlando's madness by bringing home his lost wits in a phial from the moon, and is noted for his magic horn, that routed armies with a blast.

<blockquote>
In the hands of Antony Van Corlear, this windy instrument [the trumpet] appeared to him as potent as the horn of the paladin <i>Astolpho</i>, or even the more classic horn of Alecto.
W. Irving.
</blockquote>

As-træ'ă. 1. [Gr. Ἀστραία.] (*Gr. & Rom. Myth.*) The goddess of justice, a daughter of Jupiter and Themis, or, according to others, of Astræus and Aurora. She was the last of all the deities who left the earth when the golden age had passed away; and, when she departed, shocked by the impiety of mankind, she took her place in heaven among the stars, as the constellation "Virgo," in the zodiac.

2. A poetical name assumed by Mrs. Aphara, or Aphra, Behn, a dramatist and miscellaneous writer of the seventeenth century, notorious for the license of her life and writings.

<blockquote>
The stage how loosely does <i>Astræa</i> tread!
Pope.
</blockquote>

As'tro-phel. [A sort of metagrammatic translation of *Phil. Sid.*, an abbreviation of *Philip Sidney*, — *Sid.* being taken as a contraction of the Latin *sidus*, a star, in Gr., ἄστρον, and *Phil.* standing for φίλος, a friend. Hence, *Astrophil*, star-friend, or friend of the star [Stella], changed to *Astrophel*, which is the name of a flowering plant called also starwort.] A name given by Sir Philip Sidney to himself in a series of poems entitled "Astrophel and Stella," in which he celebrated the praises of Penelope Devereux, to whom he was at one time betrothed. Spenser embalmed the mutual friendship of Sidney and himself in a pastoral ode entitled "Astrophel." See STELLA.

<blockquote>
The long-winded strophes of the divine <i>Astrophel.</i>   <i>Sir W. Scott.</i>
</blockquote>

As-ty'ă-nax. [Gr. Ἀστυάναξ.] (*Gr. & Rom. Myth.*) The only son of Hector and Andromache. After the capture of Troy, the Greeks hurled him down from the walls of the city to prevent the fulfilment of a decree of fate, according to which he was to restore the kingdom of Troy.

At'ă-lan'tă. [Gr. Ἀταλάντη.] (*Gr. & Rom. Myth.*) A princess of Scyros, or, according to others, of Arcadia, who was famed for her beauty.

She consented to marry that one of her numerous suitors who should outrun her; but he was to die who lost the prize. After many had perished, Hippomenes offered himself; and, by dropping at intervals three golden apples from the garden of the Hesperides, which Atalanta stopped to pick up, arrived first at the goal, and thus obtained her hand.

Ā'te. [Gr. 'Ατη.] (*Gr. & Rom. Myth.*) A daughter of Jupiter, and the goddess of discord. The tragic writers describe her as the goddess of retribution.

Ath'el-stāne. A prominent character in Sir Walter Scott's novel of "Ivanhoe." He is thane of Coningsburgh, and is surnamed "The Unready."

A-the'ne. [Gr. 'Αθήνη.] (*Myth.*) One of the great female divinities of the Greeks; the same as the *Minerva* of the Romans. See MINERVA. [Written also A t h e n a.]

Athenian Bee. A title bestowed upon Plato (B. C. 429–348), who was a native of Athens, in allusion to the sweetness and beauty of his style.

Athens of America. A name sometimes given to Boston, Massachusetts. See MODERN ATHENS, 2.

Athens of Ireland. A popular designation of the city of Cork, the birthplace or residence of very many of the most cultivated and eminent Irishmen of the present day.

Athens of the North. See NORTHERN ATHENS.

At-lan'tēs (*It. pron.* āt-lān'tess). A famous enchanter, who figures in Bojardo's "Orlando Innamorato," and Ariosto's "Orlando Furioso," as the tutor of Rogero.

Thou mayst laugh, . . . but it [the shadow of a horse with two riders] reminded me of the magician *Atlantes* on his hippogriff with a knight trussed up behind him.
Sir W. Scott.

At-lăn'tis. [Gr. 'Ατλαντίς.] A vast island supposed by the ancient Greeks and Romans to have been situated in the western ocean, beyond the Pillars of Hercules. It was first mentioned by Plato, who tells us that he obtained his information from the priests of Egypt. He gives a beautiful picture of the interior of this imaginary land, and enriches it with a fabulous history. He says, that, nine thousand years before his time, the island suddenly sank into the sea, rendering it innavigable ever since by reason of the shoals of mud caused by the submersion of so great an extent of land.

At-lăn'tis, The New. The title of an allegorical fiction by Lord Bacon, and the name of an island described in it as being situated, like the Atlantis of the ancients, in the middle of the Atlantic Ocean. Bacon represents himself as having been wrecked on this island, and as finding there an association for the cultivation of natural science and the promotion of improvements in the arts.

At'lăs. [Gr. 'Ατλας.] (*Gr. & Rom. Myth.*) One of the Titans, son of Iapetus and Clymene. Being conquered by Jupiter, he was condemned to the labour of bearing on his head and hands the heaven he had attempted to destroy. Another account makes him a man metamorphosed into a mountain by Perseus.

Atlas, Witch of. See WITCH OF ATLAS.

Ā-tos'să. [From *Atossa*, the daughter of Cyrus, queen of Cambyses, and afterward of Darius Hystaspis, by whom she had Xerxes. Herodotus speaks of her as a follower of Sappho.] A poetical name given by Pope to Sarah, Duchess of Marlborough, a great friend of Lady Mary Wortley Montagu, whom Pope calls Sappho in his "Moral Essays," Ep. II.

But what are these to great *Atossa's* mind? Scarce once herself, by turns all womankind.
Pope.

Ā'treŭs. [Gr. 'Ατρεύς.] (*Gr. & Rom. Myth.*) A son of Pelops and Hippodamia, grandson of Tantalus, and father of Agamemnon and Menelaus.

Ā-trī'dēş. [Gr. 'Ατρείδης.] (*Gr. & Rom. Myth.*) A patronymic used to designate Agamemnon, the son of Atreus.

At′ro-pŏs. [Gr. Ἄτροπος, the inflexible, from ἀ privative, and τρέπειν, to change.] (*Gr. & Rom. Myth.*) One of the three Parcæ, or Fates; the one that cut the thread of life.

Attic Bee, } Epithets conferred by
Attic Ho′mer. } the ancients upon Sophocles (495–406, B. C.), the tragic poet of Athens, on account of the unrivalled beauty and sweetness of his productions.

Attic Muse. A title bestowed by the Greeks upon Xenophon (B. C. 450), the celebrated historian, on account of the merit of his style, which was regarded as a model of simplicity and elegance. He is sometimes called *The Muse of Greece.*

At′ti-cus. 1. A poetical name given by Pope to Addison in the "Epistle to Dr. Arbuthnot" which forms the "Prologue to the Satires." *Atticus* was an epithet applied by the Romans to a person distinguished for his learning or eloquence.

2. A name given to George Faulkner (d. 1775), to whom Lord Chesterfield addressed, under this title, a series of ironical letters, which attained great celebrity.

3. A name given to Richard Heber (1773–1833), a famous English book-hunter, in Dibdin's "Bibliomania."

Attorney-General to the Lantern. [Fr. *Procureur-Général de la Lanterne.*] A title adopted by Camille Desmoulins (1762–1794), one of the earliest instigators of the French Revolution, in reference to the summary executions in the streets, when the mob took the law into their own hands, and hanged those whom they considered their opponents, by means of the long ropes to which the lamps were suspended.

Ā′tys. [Gr. Ἄτυς.] (*Gr. & Rom. Myth.*) A beautiful Phrygian shepherd, beloved by Cybele, who made him her priest on condition of perpetual chastity; but he broke his vow, became insane, unmanned himself, and was changed into a fir-tree. [Written also **Attys**, **Attis**, **Attes**, **Attin**.]

Audhumbla (ŏw̆d-hōōm′blȧ). (*Scand. Myth.*) The name of a wonderful cow formed by the fiat of Alfadur, at the creation of the universe. She fostered the giant Ymir, and, by licking the salt rocks in Ginnunga-gap (from which she obtained her own nourishment), she occasioned the birth of Buri, the progenitor of the gods. Audhumbla represents the power of nature acting upon chaos. [Written also **Audumbla** and **Audhumla**.]

Aud′ley, John. A name used by theatrical performers, in the phrase, "We will John Audley it," when they intend to abridge an act or a play. [Written also **John Orderley**.]

☞ "In the year 1749, Shuter was master of a droll at Bartholomew Fair, and it was his mode to lengthen the exhibition until a sufficient number of persons were gathered at the door to fill the house. This event was signified by a fellow popping his head in at the gallery-door, and bellowing out, '*John Audley,*' as if in act of inquiry, though the intention was to let Shuter know that a fresh audience were in high expectation below. The consequence of this notification was, that the entertainments were immediately concluded, and the gates of the booth thrown open for a new auditory."
Pulleyn.

Au′drey. A country wench, in Shakespeare's "As You Like It."

☞ "Audrey is the most perfect specimen of a wondering she-gawky. . . . She thanks the gods she is foul, and, if to be poetical is not to be honest, she thanks the gods also that she is not poetical."
Cowden Clarke.

She flourished the switch she held in her hand, dropped a courtesy as low as a lady at a birthnight introduction, recovered herself seemingly according to Touchstone's directions to *Audrey*, and opened the conversation without waiting till any questions were asked.
Sir W. Scott.

Au′ge-ăs. [Gr. Αὐγέας.] (*Gr. & Rom. Myth.*) A king of Elis, one of the Argonauts. It was the fifth of the twelve labours of Hercules to cleanse his stables in one day of the filth which had been produced in them by 3000 head of cattle during thirty years. This he accomplished by leading the waters of the Alpheus and the Peneus through them. The fable of the Augean stables is often

---

☞ For the "Key to the Scheme of Pronunciation," with the accompanying Explanations,

alluded to in declamations on political corruptions and the like. [Written also Augias.]

Auld Ane. [That is, the Old One.] A vulgar name for the Devil in Scotland and the North of England. The epithet "old," prefixed to so many of the titles of the Devil, seems to indicate the common opinion that he can only appear in the shape of an old man.

Auld Clootie. A Scottish name for the Devil, supposed to allude to his *cloven* feet.

Auld Hangie. A name popularly given in Scotland to the Devil.

Auld Hornie. Among the Scotch, a familiar name for the Devil, who is often described and represented with horns.

> O thou! whatever title suit thee,
> *Auld Hornie*, Satan, Nick, or Clootie, . . .
> Hear me, Auld Hangie, for a wee,
> And let poor damnèd bodies be. *Burns.*

Auld Reekie. A designation given to Edinburgh on account of its *smoky* appearance, as seen from a distance; or, according to others, on account of the uncleanliness of its public streets.

☞ " This designation [Auld Reekie] reminds one, that the quarter of the city to which it particularly refers, presents, even to this day, the spectacle of the most flagrant violation of the most elementary rules for the preservation of public health and the maintenance of domestic decency." *London Review.*

> Hech, sirs, but ye 've gotten a nasty, cauld, wet day for coming into *Auld Reekie*, as you kintra folks ca' Embro. *M. Lindsay.*

> When my mind was quite made up to make *Auld Reekie* my head-quarters, I began to explore, in good earnest, for the purpose of discovering a suitable habitation. *Sir W. Scott.*

Au-ro'ra (9). [Gr. Ἄυριος ὥρα, the golden hour.] (*Rom. Myth.*) The goddess of the morning, or of the dawn; sometimes described as the goddess of day. She had a passion for mortal youths, and carried off Clitus, Orion, and Tithonus.

Aus'ter. (*Rom. Myth.*) A personification of the south wind.

Austrian Hyena. An appellation given to Julius Jakob von Haynau (1786–1853), an Austrian general distinguished for his sinister appearance, and notorious for his ruthless cruelty to the prisoners — particularly the female political prisoners — captured by the forces under his command, in the wars against Charles Albert of Sardinia and the Hungarians under Kossuth and Görgey.

Authentic Doctor. [Lat. *Doctor Authenticus.*] An honorary appellation conferred upon Gregory of Rimini (d. 1357), a celebrated scholar of the Middle Ages.

Au-tol'y̆-cus. 1. [Gr. Αὐτόλυκος.] (*Gr. & Rom. Myth.*) One of the Argonauts, a son of Mercury and Chione. He is very famous in ancient story as a successful robber, who had the power of metamorphosing both the stolen goods and himself.

2. A witty rogue in Shakespeare's "Winter's Tale."

> A lively, bustling, arch fellow, whose pack and oaken ell-wand, studded duly with brass points, denoted him to be of *Autolycus's* profession, occupied a good deal of the attention, and furnished much of the amusement, of the evening. *Sir W. Scott.*

Av'a-lŏn. In Middle-Age romance, the name of an ocean island, and of a castle of loadstone upon it, "not far on this side of the terrestrial paradise;" represented as the abode of Arthur and Oberon and Morgaine la Fée. It is most fully described in the old French Romance of "Ogier le Danois."

☞ " Avalon was perhaps the Island of the Blest of the Celtic mythology, and then the abode of the Fees, through the Breton Korrigan. Writers, however, seem to be unanimous in regarding it and Glastonbury as the same place, — called an *isle*, it is stated, as being made nearly such by the 'river's embracement.' It was named *Avalon*, we are told, from the British word *aval*, an apple, as it abounded with orchards; and *Ynys gwydrin,* Saxon *Glastn-ey,* glassy isle, (Latin *Glastonia,*) from the green hue of the water surrounding it." *Keightley.*

Avenel, White Lady of. See WHITE LADY OF AVENEL.

A-ver'nus (4). [Gr. Ἄορνος.] (*Rom. Myth.*) Properly, a small, deep lake in Campania, occupying the crater of an extinct volcano, and almost completely shut in by steep and wooded heights. From its gloomy and awful aspect, it was described by the Latin poets as the entrance to the lower world; but the name was often used to designate the lower world itself. Avernus was also regarded as a divine being.

Ay'mēr, Prior. A jovial Benedictine monk, prior of Jorvaulx Abbey, in Sir Walter Scott's "Ivanhoe."

Ay'mǫn. (*Fr. pron.* à'mōn', 62.) A semi-mythical character who figures in the romances and romantic poems of the Carolian series. He is represented as Duke of Dordona (Dordogne), and father of four sons, Rinaldo, Guicciardo, Alardo, and Ricciardetto (or Renaud, Guiscard, Alard, and Richard), whose adventures are the subject of an old French romance, entitled "Les Quatre-Filz-Aymon," by Huon de Villeneuve, a French poet of the age of Philip II. (1165-1223).

Ạ-zā'zel. Among the ancient Jews, the name inscribed upon one of the lots cast by the high priest, on the day of atonement, to determine which of the two goats selected as a sin-offering should be the scape-goat, and which should be sacrificed to Jehovah. (See *Lev.* xvi.) There has been much discussion among biblical interpreters as to the meaning of the word *Azazel*. Some regard it as a designation of the goat itself; some as the name of the place to which he was sent; and others as the name of a personal being to whom he was sent. Tholuck and other critics render the word "for complete sending away." Ewald considers Azazel to have been a demon belonging to the pre-Mosaic religion. Another opinion identifies him with Satan, or the Devil. Milton makes him Satan's standard-bearer.

That proud honour claimed
Azazel as his right, a cherub tall;
Who forthwith from his glittering staff unfurled
The imperial ensign, which, full high advanced,
Shone like a meteor streaming to the wind,
With gems and golden lustre rich emblazed,
Seraphic arms and trophies. *Par. Lost, Bk.* I.

A'zǒ. The name given by Byron to the Prince of Este, in his poem of "Parisina." The poem is founded on fact, and the real name of the prince was Nicholas; but Lord Byron substituted Azo as being metrically preferable. See PARISINA.

Az'rạ-el. [Heb., help of God.] In the Jewish and the Mohammedan mythology, the name of an angel who watches over the dying, and separates the soul from the body.

☞ "The Mohammedan doctors . . . say that Azrael . . . was commissioned to inflict the penalty of death on all mankind, and that, until the time of Mahomet, he visibly struck down before the eyes of the living those whose time for death was come; and although not invariably seen by by-standers, yet he was supposed to be always visible, in the very act of inflicting the mortal blow, to those whose souls he was summoned to take away. Mahomet, struck by the terrific effect which this produced upon men, entreated that the angel of death should take away the souls of men without this visible appearance; and, in consequence of the prayers of the prophet, it was no longer permitted, that men's souls were taken without their beholding the angelic form which removed them."
. *Henry Christmas.*

Even *Azrael*, from his deadly quiver
When flies that shaft, and fly-it-must,
That parts all else, shall doom for ever
Our hearts to undivided dust. *Byron.*

Madness . . . invisible, impalpable, and yet no black *Azrael*, with wings spread over half a continent, with sword sweeping from sea to sea, could be a truer reality. *Carlyle.*

B.

Bā'al. [Heb., lord, master.] (*Myth.*) A general appellation of honour used — sometimes in the plural form, Baalim — to designate many different gods among the ancient nations of the East; but specifically applied to the principal male deity of the Phœnicians, who was also worshipped in Assyria, Egypt, Carthage, and other countries. He was the god of the sun. See 1 *Kings* xviii.

☞ "The word Baäl is frequently found coupled with some epithet, and seems, in such cases, to have denoted a different deity, or perhaps the same deity regarded as exercising a different function. Thus, we have Baäl-Bereth, "the Covenant Lord," worshipped by the people of Shechem; Baäl-Peor, the Priapus of the Moabites and Midianites; and Boëlzebub, or Baäl-zebub, — the "Fly-god," — the idol of the Philistines at Ekron.

Baba, Ali (ä'le' bä'bä). A character in the "Arabian Nights' Entertainments," which relates the story of his adventures with the Forty Thieves (*q. v.*), whom he discovers from his hiding-place in a tree, and whose cave he enters by the use of a magic pass-word, "Sesame," which he has accidentally overheard.

Baba, Cassim (käs'sim bä'bä). A character in the "Arabian Nights' Entertainments;" the brother of Ali Baba. See FORTY THIEVES.

The spell loses its power, and he who should then hope to conjure with it would find himself as much mistaken as *Cassim* . . . when he stood crying, "Open, Wheat," "Open, Barley," to the door which obeyed no sound but "Open, Sesame." *Macaulay.*

Baba, Hajji (häd'jee bä'bä). The hero of a novel of the same name, by James Morier (1780–1849); a sort of Persian picaroon, on the Gil-Blas model.

Babes in the Wood. See CHILDREN IN THE WOOD.

Babes of the Wood. (*Irish Hist.*) Insurrectionary hordes who infested the mountains of Wicklow and the woods near Enniscarthy, toward the end of the eighteenth century, and who were guilty of the greatest atrocities.

Baboon, Lewis. Louis XIV. of France; — so called in Arbuthnot's "History of John Bull."

Baboon, Philip. A nickname given, in Arbuthnot's "History of John Bull," to Philip, Duke of Anjou, grandson of Louis XIV. of France.

Bac'chus. [Gr. Βάκχος, the noisy or riotous god.] (*Gr. & Rom. Myth.*) The son of Jupiter and Semele, and the god of wine; represented as a beautiful but effeminate youth.

Bachelor of Salamanca. See DON CHERUBIM.

Backbite, Sir Benjamin. A censorious character in Sheridan's "School for Scandal."

But could this sad, thoughtful countenance be the same vacant face of folly . . . that looked out so formally flat in Foppington, so frothily pert in Tattle, so impotently busy in *Backbite?* *Charles Lamb.*

Bac'tri-an Sage. An epithet given to Zoroaster, the founder of the Magian religion, and a native of Bactria, the modern Balkh.

Badebec (båd'bek'). The wife of Gargantua, and mother of Pantagruel, whose birth was the cause of her death; which is not to be wondered at, since he came into the world accompanied by eighty-one sellers of salt, each leading a mule by a halter; nine dromedaries, laden with ham and smoked tongues; seven camels, laden with eels: besides twenty-five waggons full of leeks, garlic, onions, and shallots.

Badger State. A name popularly given to the State of Wisconsin.

Badinguet (bä'dăn'gä', 62). A nickname given in France to the emperor Napoleon III.

Bā'don, Mount (bā'dn). The scene of a battle which is said to have been fought by King Arthur against the Saxons who invaded his kingdom, and in which the latter were signally defeated. By some writers, Badon has been identified with Bath, by others with Berkshire.

Bag'stock, Joe. A wooden-featured,

and for the Remarks and Rules to which the numbers after certain words refer, see pp. xlv–xxxii.

blue-faced major in Dickens's "Dombey and Son," self-absorbed, and for ever talking of "J. B.," "old J. B.," "Joey B.," &c.

Baillie Nicol Jarvie. See JARVIE, BAILLIE NICOL.

Baiser de Lamourette, Le. See LAMOURETTE'S KISS.

Bajardo (bä-e-ar′do). See BAYARD.

Bȧl′der-stŏne, Caleb. In Sir Walter Scott's "Bride of Lammermoor," the faithful old butler of the Master of Ravenswood. He struggles most virtuously, without food, furniture, or comfort, to maintain an appearance of affluence, and is always ready with some ludicrous shift to uphold the fallen dignity of his patron.

☞ "Of all our author's fools and bores, he is the most pertinacious, the most intrusive, and, from the nature of his one monotonous note, the least pardonable in his intrusion. His silly buffoonery is always marring, with gross absurdities and degrading associations, some scene of tenderness or dignity."
Senior.

The Gallic foray was even more terrible and fatal than Roman vanity chose to avow. It was like *Caleb Balderstone's* thunder-storm, or Edward the First's destruction of charters; for it utterly ruined early Roman history.
Yonge.

Baldur (bȧl′dōōr). [Old Norse, brilliant, beautiful, powerful.] (*Scand. Myth.*) The second son of Odin and Frigga; the god of the summer sun; represented as the noblest, gentlest, and wisest of all the gods, and so fair that a brilliant white light streamed from his person. In consequence of the machinations of Loki, he was slain by his twin brother, Hödur, the blind god of war. His death typifies the disappearance of the sun from the horizon during the winter months in the North. [Written also Balder and Balldr.]

Balisardo (bä-le-sar′do). [It.] The name of a sword which, according to Ariosto, in his "Orlando Furioso," would cut even enchanted substances, and was made by a potent sorceress, named Falerina, to kill Orlando with. It became the property of Ruggiero.

Ballengeigh, Goodman of. See GOODMAN OF BALLENGEIGH.

Bȧl′mȧ-whăp′ple (-pl). A stupidly obstinate Scottish laird who figures in Scott's novel of "Waverley."

Balmung (bȧl′mōōng). A sword of great potency, belonging to Siegfried in the German epos, the "Nibelungen Lied." Von der Hagen seems to think it merely the sword Mimung under another name. See MIMUNG and WIELAND.

Young hearts, generation after generation, will think with themselves, O worthy of worship, thou king-descended, god-descended, and poor sister-woman [the Princess de Lamballe]; why was not I there [at her execution]; and some Sword *Balmung*, or Thor's Hammer in my hand? *Carlyle.*

Bȧl′ni-bar′bĭ. A land occupied by projectors, visited by Gulliver in his famous imaginary "Travels." See GULLIVER.

Bal-thaz′ar. 1. A merchant in Shakespeare's "Comedy of Errors."
2. A servant to Don Pedro, in "Much Ado about Nothing."
3. A name assumed by Portia, in Shakespeare's "Merchant of Venice." See PORTIA.
4. One of the "Kings of Cologne," — the three magi who came from the East to worship the infant Saviour.

Balwery, Great Witch of. See GREAT WITCH OF BALWERY.

Bȧl′whid-der, The Rev. Micah (bȧl′hwĭth-ur). A Scottish Presbyterian pastor in Galt's "Annals of the Parish," imbued with all old-fashioned national feelings and prejudices, but thoroughly sincere, kind-hearted, and pious. He is easy, garrulous, fond of a quiet joke, and perfectly ignorant of the world; diligent, blameless, loyal, and exemplary in his life, but without the fiery zeal and "kirk-filling eloquence" of the supporters of the Covenant.

Ban, King. The father of Lancelot du Lac, and a famous knight of the Round Table. He was a king of Brittany, and a faithful ally of King Arthur.

Banou, Peri. See PARIBANOU.

Ban′quo (bangk′wo). A Scottish thane and warrior of the eleventh century, and progenitor of the royal House of Stuart, immortalised in

Shakespeare's tragedy of "Macbeth."

<small>Like *Banquo's* murderer, there was blood on his face, as well as upon the rowels of his spurs, and the sides of his over-ridden horse.
Sir W. Scott.</small>

Ban'shee. In the popular superstitions of the Irish, a sort of tutelary female demon, called the wife of the fairies, who is thought to give warning of an approaching death by wailings and shrieks which she utters. [Written also Benshie.]

Baph'o-met. A mysterious idol, or rather symbol, which was in use among the Templars. It was a small human figure, cut out of stone, and covered with emblems of unknown signification. It had two heads, one male and the other female, with the rest of the body purely feminine. Specimens are to be found in some of the museums of Continental cities.

<small>☞ The word *Baphomet* is supposed to be a corruption — arising from the negligence of some transcriber — of the name *Mahomet*, occurring in the depositions of witnesses against the unfortunate Templars, who were accused of having a leaning to the faith of the Arabian prophet.</small>

Baptiste, Jean (zhŏⁿ bä'tēst', 62). A sobriquet given to the French Canadians, these being very common Christian names among them.

Barataria (bă-ră-tā're-ă). [Sp., from *barato*, cheap.] Sancho Panza's island-city, in Cervantes's romance of "Don Quixote." "Sancho then, with all his attendants, arrived at a town containing about a thousand inhabitants. They gave him to understand that it was called the island of Barataria, either because Barataria was really the name of the place, or because he obtained the government of it at so cheap a rate. On his arrival near the gates of the town, the municipal officers came out to receive him. Presently after, with certain ridiculous ceremonies, they presented him with the keys of the town, and constituted him perpetual governor of the island of Barataria."

<small>Sancho Panza, in his island of *Barataria*, neither administered justice more wisely, nor was interrupted more provokingly in his personal indulgences. *Shelley.*</small>

<small>I don't eat side-dishes; and as for the roast beef of Old England, why, the meat was put on the table and whisked away like Sancho's inauguration feast at *Barataria*. *Thackeray.*</small>

Bar'bă-son (-sn). The name of a fiend mentioned by Shakespeare, "Merry Wives of Windsor," a. ii., sc. 2, and "Henry V.," a. ii., sc. 1.

Barber Poet. A name sometimes given to Jacques Jasmin (1798–1864), a popular poet of Gascony, and a barber or hair-dresser by occupation.

Bar-dell', Mrs. A widow landlady in Dickens's "Pickwick Papers," celebrated for the suit which she brought against Mr. Pickwick for an alleged breach of promise to marry her.

Bard of Ā'vŏn. An epithet often applied to Shakespeare, who was born and buried in Stratford-upon-Avon.

Bard of Ayrshire. A name often given to Robert Burns, the great peasant-poet of Scotland, who was a native and resident of the county of Ayr.

Bard of Hope. A title sometimes given to Thomas Campbell (1777–1844), author of "The Pleasures of Hope," one of the most beautiful didactic poems in the language.

Bard of Memory. A name used to designate the poet Rogers (1762–1855), author of "The Pleasures of Memory."

<small>The *Bard of Memory* slumbered on his laurels, and he of Hope had scarce begun to attract his share of public attention.
Sir W. Scott.</small>

Bard of Olney. An appellation sometimes conferred upon the poet Cowper, who resided for many years at Olney, in Buckinghamshire.

Bard of Rydal Mount. An epithet sometimes applied to the poet Wordsworth (1770–1850), who resided from 1813 until his death at Rydal, a chapelry of England, in the county of Westmoreland. His dwelling commanded a beautiful view of the lake of Rydal and of a part of Windermere.

Bard of Twick'en-hăm. A name often given to the poet Pope (1688–1744), who resided at Twickenham for the last thirty years of his life.

<small>Of all the abject and despicable drivelling, ever drivelled by clerk or layman, is all that</small>

late drivelling about the eternal principles of poetry, and the genius of the *Bard of Twickenham*. *Blackwood's Mag.*

Bar'dolph. A follower of Falstaff, a bravo, and a humourist, in Shakespeare's "Merry Wives of Windsor," and in the two parts of "King Henry IV."

We are much of the mind of Falstaff's tailor. We must have better assurance for Sir John than *Bardolph's*. We like not the security. *Macaulay.*

Though, like *Bardolph*, I have nothing, and cannot even coin my nose for guineas, or my blood for drachmas, it is not the less flattering to a man's minor vanities to receive a begging letter. *Sala.*

Bâre'bŏne's Parliament. (*Eng. Hist.*) A nickname conferred upon the Parliament convened by Cromwell, July 4, 1653. It was composed of 139 persons, who resigned their authority Dec. 12, 1653; and it was so called from a fanatical leather-seller named Praise-God Barebone, who was one of the principal members, and was notorious for his long prayers and sermons. [Called also *Little Parliament*.]

Bar'guest. (*Fairy Myth.*) A frightful goblin, armed with teeth and claws, which is an object of terror in the North of England. According to Ritson ("Fairy Tales," p. 58), the Barguest, besides its many other pranks, would sometimes, in the dead of night, in passing through the different streets, set up the most horrid and continuous shrieks, in order to scare the poor girls who might happen to be out of bed. It was generally believed that the faculty of seeing this goblin was peculiar to certain individuals, but that the gift could be imparted to another, at the time of the ghost's appearance, by the mere act of touching.

Bar'kis. A carrier in Dickens's novel of "David Copperfield," in love with a servant-girl named Peggotty, whom he solicits in marriage by writing and displaying before her eyes a proposal uniquely worded, "Barkis is willin'."

Barleycorn, Sir John. In England and Scotland, a jocular name for ale or beer, which is made of barley. Sir John is the subject of a famous old ballad of the same name. In a whimsical English tract of ancient date, entitled "The Arraigning and Indicting of Sir John Barleycorn, Knt.," he is described as of "noble blood, well beloved in England, a great supporter of the crown, and a maintainer of both rich and poor." The following list of the jury is curious:—

Timothy Toss-pot.	Richard Standfast.
Benjamin Bumper.	Small Stout.
Giles Lick-spigot.	John Never-sober.
Barnaby Full-pot.	Obadiah Thirsty.
Lancelot Toper.	Nicholas Spend-thrift.
John Six-go-downs.	Edmund Empty-purse.

Sir John is tried in regular form, the jury returning a verdict of Not Guilty.

Inspiring bold *John Barleycorn*,
What dangers thou canst make us scorn!
Wi' tippenny we fear nae evil;
Wi' usquebae we'll face the devil! *Burns.*

Good *John Barleycorn*, also, who always heightens and exaggerates the prevailing passions, be they angry or kindly, was not wanting upon this occasion. *Sir W. Scott.*

John Barleycorn has given his very heart to this liquor [the "Archdeacon"]; it is a superior kind of ale, the Prince of Ales, with a richer flavour and a mightier spirit than you can find elsewhere in this weary world. *Hawthorne.*

Bar'me-cĭde, The. A prince of the illustrious family of the same name, which flourished at Bagdad contemporaneously with the Caliph Haroun-Al-Raschid and his predecessors; represented in the "Arabian Nights' Entertainments" as ordering rich viands for a famished beggar named Shacabac, and, before they could be brought, calling upon him to help himself to the different dishes,— naming them one after another. The beggar humoured the joke, pretending to eat, and praising the entertainment, and even protesting that he could eat no more. In the end, the eccentric host, pleased with the patient complaisance of his guest, ordered a real and sumptuous entertainment for him, in place of that of which he had previously partaken only in imagination.

It is, to be sure, something like the feast which *the Barmecide* served up to Ainaschar [Shacabac], and we cannot expect to get fat upon such diet. *Sir W. Scott.*

The Barmecide's dinner to Shacabac was only one degree removed from these solemn banquets. *Thackeray.*

' As for Karl Albert, he had his new pleasant dream of sovereignty at Prag: Titular of Upper Austria, and now of Böhmen as well, and enjoyed his Feast of *the Barmecide*, and glorious repose in the captured metropolis after difficulty overcome. *Carlyle.*

Bar'nă-bỹ, Widow. The title of a novel by Mrs. Trollope, and the name of its heroine, who is distinguished for her husband-hunting schemes, her pretension, vulgar assurance, and want of principle.

Barnaby Rudge. See RUDGE, BARNABY.

Bar'nă-dĭne. A dissolute and reckless character, "fearless of what's past, present, and to come," who figures in Shakespeare's "Measure for Measure."

Barn-burners. 1. Lawless individuals who secretly set fire to the barns of the great landed proprietors in the State of New York, in the first half of the nineteenth century.
2. A nickname formerly given to the more radical and progressive section of the Democratic party in the United States, who aimed at removing the abuses connected with banks and corporations, in allusion to the story of an old Dutchman who relieved himself of rats by burning his barns, which they infested.

Barn'well, George. The hero of Lillo's tragedy of the same name. Barnwell is a London apprentice hurried on to ruin and murder by an infamous woman, who at last delivers him up to justice and to an ignominious death.

Barons, War of the. See WAR OF THE BARONS.

Barrel-Mirabeau (mĭr'ȧ-bo). [Fr. *Mirabeau-Tonneau.*] A nickname given to Boniface Riquetti, Viscount de Mirabeau (1754–1792), brother to the great tribune. He was so called from his bulk, and the quantity of drink he usually held.

Băr'rett, Clerk, Walter. A pseudonym of Joseph A. Scoville (d. 1864), author of "The Old Merchants of New York."

Barriers, Battle of the. See BATTLE OF THE BARRIERS.

Bartholo (bar'to'lo'). A doctor who plays a prominent part in Beaumarchais' comedies, "Le Mariage de Figaro" and "Le Barbier de Séville."

Bar'thol'o-mew's Day, St. [Fr. *La St.-Barthélemy;* Ger. *Bartholomäusnacht*, Bartholomew's Night, or *Bluthochzeit*, Blood-wedding.] (*Fr. Hist.*) The appellation given, in English books, to a dreadful massacre of French Protestants, commenced in Paris on the eve of the festival of St. Bartholomew, August 24, 1572. The massacre was secretly ordered by the king, Charles IX., at the instigation of his mother, the queen-dowager, Catharine de' Medici, and was attended by circumstances of the most fiendish cruelty. It is estimated that in all 30,000 (some authorities say 70,000) persons were murdered. [Called also *The Bartholomew*, and *The Massacre of St. Bartholomew.*]

Basile (bä'zĕl'). A character in Beaumarchais' comedies, "Le Mariage de Figaro" and "Le Barbier de Séville;" a calumniator, a bigot, and a niggard. The name is used generically in French, to designate any similar character.

Bas'i-lis'co. A foolish and boastful knight in an old play called "Soliman and Perseda," so popular that his name became proverbial.

Bas-să'nĭ-o. The lover of Portia, in Shakespeare's "Merchant of Venice." See PORTIA.

Bastard of Orle-ăns. [Fr. *Bâtard d' Orléans.*] An appellation applied to Jean Dunois (1403–1468), a natural son of Louis, Duke of Orleans, brother of Charles VI. He was one of the most brilliant soldiers that France ever produced.

Bă-tā'vĭ-ă. The ancient Latin name of Holland, — often used in modern poetry.

Lo! where, through flat *Batavia's* willowy groves,
Or by the lazy Seine, the exile roves.
Wordsworth.

Bateman, Lord. See LORD BEICHAN.

Bath, Maid of. See MAID OF BATH.

Băth, Major (2). The name of a

character in Fielding's novel of "Amelia;" a poor and pompous, but noble-minded gentleman, who swears, "by the honour and dignity of man," and is caught cooking some gruel in a saucepan for his ailing sister.

Bath, Wife of. See WIFE OF BATH.

Bat'rặ-ḉho'my-o-mā'ḉhi-ặ. See BATTLE OF THE FROGS AND MICE.

Battle, The Tearless. [Gr. 'Αδακρυς μάχη.] (*Gr. Hist.*) An engagement between the Lacedæmonians, under Archidamus II., and the Arcadians and Argives (B. C. 367), in which the latter were defeated with great slaughter, while not one Spartan fell. Hence, says Plutarch, it was "known by the name of the Tearless Battle." [Called also *The Tearless Victory*.]

Battle of Spurs. [Fr. *Journée des Éperons*.] (*Fr. Hist.*) 1. A name given to the battle of Courtray (July 11, 1302), the first great engagement between the nobles and the burghers, which, with the subsequent battles of Bannockburn, Crecy, and Poictiers, decided the fate of feudalism. In this encounter, the knights and gentlemen of France were entirely overthrown by the citizens of a Flemish manufacturing town. The French nobility rushed forward with loose bridles, and fell headlong, one after another, into an enormous ditch, which lay between them and their enemies. The whole army was annihilated; and when the spoils were gathered, there were found 4000 golden spurs to mark the extent of the knightly slaughter, and give a name to the engagement.

I beheld the Flemish weavers, with Namur
and Julters bold,
Marching homeward from the bloody *Battle
of the Spurs* of Gold.   *Longfellow.*

2. A name given to an affair at Guinegate, near Calais (August 18, 1513), in which the English troops under Henry VIII. defeated the French forces. The allusion is said to be to the unusual energy of the beaten party in riding off the field.

Battle of the Barriers. (*Fr. Hist.*)

The name of a battle fought under the walls of Paris, on the 30th of March, 1814, between the forces under Napoleon and the armies of the allied sovereigns. The latter, after an obstinate contest, gained the victory, which led to the capitulation of Paris, and the abdication of Napoleon.

Battle of the Books. The subject of a satirical composition by Swift, entitled "The Battle . . . between the Ancient and Modern Books in St. James's Library," alluding to a celebrated controversy among the literary men of his day regarding the respective merits of ancient and modern learning.

Battle of the Frogs and Mice. [Gr. βατραχομυομαχία, Lat. *Batrachomyomachia*.] The subject of a mock-heroic poem, ascribed to Homer, but evidently of a much later origin, and apparently designed to travesty the "Iliad" and "Odyssey."

Battle of the Giants. (*Fr. Hist.*) A name given to the celebrated battle of Marignano (Melegnano), Sept. 13, 1515, in which Francis I. of France fought against the Swiss, who were led by the Duke of Milan. Francis lost, upon this occasion, 8000 of his best troops, but displayed extraordinary generalship, and acquired extensive fame.

Battle of the Herrings. (*Eng. Hist.*) A name given by historians to an engagement which took place Feb. 12, 1429, in which Sir John Fastolfe, an English general, at the head of 1500 men, gained a victory over 6000 Frenchmen near Orleans, and brought a convoy of stores in safety to the English camp before that place. The stores comprised a large quantity of herrings.

Battle of the Kegs. The subject and title of a mock-heroic poem by Francis Hopkinson (1738–1791). This ballad, very famous in the time of the American Revolution, was occasioned by a real incident.

☞ "Certain machines in the form of kegs, charged with gunpowder, were sent down the river to annoy the British

☞ For the "Key to the Scheme of Pronunciation," with the accompanying Explanations,

shipping then at Philadelphia. The danger of these machines being discovered, the British manned the wharfs and shipping, and discharged their small-arms and cannons at every thing they saw floating in the river during the ebb-tide." *Author's Note.*

Battle of the Nations. A name sometimes given to the battle of Leipsic (1813), one of the greatest and most sanguinary battles of modern times, on account of the various nationalities, French, Austrian, Russian, Prussian, &c., which were there represented.

Battle of the Poets. The subject and title of a poem (1725) by John Sheffield, Duke of Buckingham, in which he brings all the versifiers of the time into the field.

Battle of the Standard. (*Eng. Hist.*) A name given to an engagement between the English and Scotch at Northallerton, Yorkshire, Aug. 22, 1138, resulting in the defeat of the latter. It was so called on account of a high crucifix borne by the English upon a waggon as a military ensign.

Battle of the Thirty. [Fr. *Combat des Trente.*] (*Eng. & Fr. Hist.*) A name given to a celebrated engagement which took place at a spot known as Midway Oak, half-way between the castles of Josselin and Ploermel, in France, March 27, 1351. The French General Beaumanoir, commanding the former post, being enraged at the depredations committed by Bemborough, the English general, occupying the latter position, challenged him to fight. Upon this, it was agreed that thirty knights of each party should meet and decide the contest. The two chiefs presented themselves at the head of their best soldiers, and the battle began in earnest. At the first onset, the English were successful; but Bemborough having been killed, the French renewed the struggle with redoubled courage, and finally won the victory.

☞ This was one of the most heroic exploits of the age, and gained such popularity, that, more than a hundred years later, when speaking of a hard contest, it was usual to say, "There was never such hard fighting since the Battle of the Thirty."

Bau′cis. [Gr. Βαῦκις.] (*Gr. & Rom. Myth.*) An aged Phrygian woman, who, with her husband, Philemon, hospitably received Jupiter and Mercury, after every one else in the place had refused to entertain them. The gods visited the country with an inundation, but saved Baucis and Philemon, and converted their humble dwelling into a magnificent temple, of which this pious couple became the priests. Having expressed a wish to die together, when the time of their departure should come, Jupiter granted their request by changing them simultaneously into two trees before the temple.

Bavieca (bä-ve-ā′kȧ). The name of a famous steed of the Cid. He survived his master two years and a half, during which time no one was permitted to mount him. When he died, he was buried before the gate of the monastery at Valencia, in the public place, and two elms were planted upon the grave, the one at his head, the other at his feet.

Bāy′ȧrd (*Fr. pron.* bī′ar′). 1. A famous horse, of incredible swiftness, belonging to the four sons of Aymon. (See AYMON.) He was of the ordinary size when only one of them wished to ride, but, when all four were to be carried, he had the power of elongating his body till it was of the requisite dimensions. Many wonderful things are related of him. It is said that one of his foot-prints is to be seen in the forest of Soignes in Brabant, and another on a rock near Dinant.

2. The same name is given in the old romances and romantic poems to Rinaldo's famous steed, a wonderful animal of a bright bay colour, which had formerly belonged to Amadis de Gaul. He was found by Malagigi, the wizard knight and cousin to Rinaldo, in a grotto, together with a suit of arms and the sword Fusberta, under the watch of a dragon whom

he charmed. Having obtained the prize, he bestowed it upon Rinaldo. In the French romances, he is represented to be yet alive in some of the forests of France; but runs off on beholding any one; on which account all hope of securing him is vain.

Bāyes. The name of the principal character in "The Rehearsal," a witty and celebrated farce, ostensibly and chiefly written by George Villiers, Duke of Buckingham, and intended as a satire upon the heroic or rhyming plays of his time. It was first brought out in the year 1671. In its original form, the character of Bayes was meant for the Hon. Edward Howard (for whom Sir William Davenant was afterwards substituted); but, in its present form, the hero of the satire is Dryden, who had stood forth not only as a practiser, but as the champion, of this peculiar species of the drama. He is represented as greedy for applause; impatient of censure or criticism; inordinately vain, yet meanly obsequious to those who, he hopes, will gratify him by returning his flattery in kind; and, finally, as anxiously and distressingly mindful of the minute parts of what, even in the whole, is scarce worthy of attention.

In short, sir, you are of opinion with *Bayes*, — "What the devil does the plot signify, except to bring in fine things?" *Sir W. Scott.*

Bayou State. A name sometimes given to the State of Mississippi, which abounds in bayous, or creeks.

Bay State. A popular name of Massachusetts, which, before the adoption of the Federal Constitution, was called the Colony of Massachusetts Bay.

Lift again the stately emblem on the *Bay State's* rusted shield,
Give to Northern winds the pine-tree on our banner's tattered field! *Whittier.*

When first the Pilgrims landed on the *Bay State's* iron shore,
The word went forth that slavery should one day be no more. *Lowell.*

Bēan Lēan, Don'ăld. A Highland robber-chief in Sir Walter Scott's novel of "Waverley."

Béarnais, Le (lụ bā′ȧr′nā′). A surname given to Henry IV., king of France and Navarre (1553-1598), from his native province, Le Béarn. He was so called in especial by the Leaguers (see LEAGUE, THE), who refused to recognise him as king of France, or even as king of Navarre.

Bear State. A name by which the State of Arkansas is sometimes designated, on account of the number of bears that infest its forests.

Be′à-trice (*It. pron.* bā-ā-tre′chā).
1. The Christian name of a young Florentine lady of the illustrious family of Portinari, for whom the poet Dante conceived a strong but purely Platonic affection, and whom he represents, in the "Divina Commedia," as his guide through paradise.

2. The heroine of Shakespeare's "Much Ado about Nothing."

☞ "The extraordinary success of this play in Shakespeare's own day, and ever since, in England, is to be ascribed more particularly to the parts of Benedick and Beatrice, two humoursome beings, who incessantly attack each other with all the resources of raillery. Avowed rebels to love, they are both entangled in its net by a merry plot of their friends to make them believe that each is the object of the secret passion of the other." *Schlegel, Trans.* — "In Beatrice, high intellect and high animal spirits meet, and excite each other like fire and air. In her wit (which is brilliant without being imaginative) there is a touch of insolence, not infrequent in women when the wit predominates over reflection and imagination. In her temper, too, there is a slight infusion of the termagant; and her satirical humour plays with such an unrespective levity over all subjects alike, that it required a profound knowledge of women to bring such a character within the pale of our sympathy. But Beatrice, though wilful, is not wayward; she is volatile, not unfeeling. She has not only an exuberance of wit and gayety, but of heart, and soul, and energy of spirit."
Mrs. Jameson.

3. See BEAUTIFUL PARRICIDE.

Beatrix. See CASTLEWOOD, BEATRIX.

Beau′clērc (bo′-). [Fr., fine scholar.] A surname of Henry I. of England, who received a more literary education than was usually given, in his

☞ For the "Key to the Scheme of Pronunciation," with the accompanying Explanations,

time, either to the sons of kings, or to laymen of any rank.

Beau Tibbs. A prominent character in Goldsmith's "Citizen of the World;" said by Hazlitt to be "the best comic sketch since the time of Addison; unrivalled in his finery, his vanity, and his poverty."

Beautiful Corisande (ko'rc'zōⁿd', 62). [Fr. *La Belle Corisande.*] A sobriquet given to Diane d'Andouins (1554–1620), Countess of Guiche and Grammont, and widow of Philip de Grammont.

Beautiful Gardener. [Fr. *La Belle Jardinière.*] A sobriquet given to a mistress of Henry IV. of France.

Beautiful Parricide. A name given to Beatrice Cenci (d. 1599), who is alleged to have murdered her father, a wealthy Roman nobleman, on account of the revolting and incestuous brutality with which he treated her. For this crime, she was condemned and put to death. Some historians maintain that she had no part in the murder, but was the victim of an infernal plot hatched by two robbers, or by unknown persons whose agents they were. The story of Beatrice has been made the subject of a powerful tragedy by the poet Shelley.

Beautiful Ropemaker. See ROPE-MAKER, THE BEAUTIFUL.

Beauty and the Beast. [Fr. *La Belle et la Bête.*] The hero and heroine of a celebrated fairy tale — written in French by Mme. Villeneuve — which relates how a young and lovely woman saved the life of her father by putting herself in the power of a frightful, but kind-hearted monster, whose respectful affection and deep melancholy finally overcame her aversion to his hideousness, and induced her to consent to marry him, whereupon he was freed from the enchantment of which he had been a victim, and appeared to her in his proper form and character of a handsome and graceful young prince.

So she [Caroline of Anspach, afterward queen of George II. of England] lived at Berlin, brilliant though unportioned, with the rough cub Friedrich Wilhelm much following her about, and passionately loyal to her, as the *Beast* was to *Beauty;* whom she did not mind except as a cub loyal to her, being five years older than he.
Carlyle.

Beauty of But'tẽr-mẽre. A celebrated and lovely English girl, named Mary Robinson, who was married, by means of the most odious deceit, to John Hatfield, a heartless impostor, who was executed for forgery, at Carlisle, Sept. 3, 1803.

Bede, Cŭth'bẽrt. A literary cognomen adopted by the Rev. Edward Bradley, a popular English humourist of the present day.

Bede, The Venerable. A famous English monk of the eighth century, whose surname was given him in honour of his eminent talents, virtues, and learning.

☞ There is an old story that a monk in vain attempted to write an epitaph upon Bede, and fell asleep, leaving it thus: "Hâc sunt in fossâ Bedæ . . . ossa;" and that, when he awoke, he found, to his great surprise and satisfaction, the long-sought epithet supplied by an angelic hand, — the whole line standing thus:
"Hâc sunt in fossâ Bedæ *venerabilis* ossa."

Bed'i-vere, Sir. King Arthur's butler. He was a knight of the Round Table, and a prominent figure in many of the old romances of chivalry. [Written also B e d v e r.]

Bed'red-din' Has'săn. A character in the story of "Noureddin and his Son, and Shemseddin and his Daughter," in the "Arabian Nights' Entertainments."

She [Effie Deans] amused herself with visiting the dairy, in which she had so long been assistant, and was so near discovering herself to May Hetley, by betraying her acquaintance with the celebrated receipt for Dunlop cheese, that she compared herself to *Bedreddin Hassan,* whom the vizier, his father-in-law, discovered by his superlative skill in composing cream-tarts with pepper in them.
Sir W. Scott.

Beef'ing-tŏn, Mî-lŏr'. A character in "The Rovers, or The Double Arrangement," in the poetry of the "Anti-Jacobin." He is an English nobleman in exile by the tyranny of King John, previous to the signature of Magna Charta.

"Will without power," said the sagacious Cadmir to *Milor Beefington*, "is like children playing at soldiers."
Macaulay.

and for the Remarks and Rules to which the numbers after certain words refer, see pp. xlv–xxxii.

Be-el'ze-bub. [Heb. *baal*, lord, and *s'búb*, fly.] (*Myth.*) The title of a heathen deity, to whom the Jews ascribed the sovereignty of the evil spirits. Milton, in his "Paradise Lost," makes him second in rank to Satan; but Wierus, the celebrated demonographer of the sixteenth century, says, that Satan is no longer the sovereign of hell, but that Beëlzebub reigns in his place. Other mediæval writers, who reckon nine ranks or orders of demons, place Beëlzebub at the head of the first rank, which consists of the false gods of the Gentiles.

Which when *Beëlzebub* perceived, than whom,
Satan except, none higher sat, with grave
Aspect he rose, and in his rising seemed
A pillar of state: deep on his front engraven
Deliberation sat and public care;
And princely counsel in his face yet shone,
Majestic though in ruin: sage he stood,
With Atlantean shoulders fit to bear
The weight of mightiest monarchies.
Milton.

Befana, La (lä bä-fä'nä). [It., a corruption of Gr. Ἐπιφάνια, the Epiphany.] In Italy, a common personification of the Epiphany, or Festival of the Manifestation of Christ to the Gentiles, — variously represented as a saint and as a fairy. According to other accounts, she is the Italian bugbear of naughty children.

☞ The Epiphany (Jan. 6) is the day for the presentation of Christmas gifts in Italy, and there is a pleasant fiction that La Befana goes about at night like St. Nicholas, carrying presents to children. Whether from thus personifying the season, or from whatever other cause, a figure, called La Befana, is suspended outside the doors of houses at the beginning of Lent.

Beichan, Lord. See LORD BEICHAN.

Bel. (*Chald. Myth.*) The same as *Belus* and *Baäl.* See BAÄL, BELUS.

Be-lā'rī-us (9). The name of one of the characters in Shakespeare's "Cymbeline."

Belch, Sir To'by. Uncle to Olivia, in Shakespeare's "Twelfth Night." He is a type of the reckless, jolly roisterer of the Elizabethan period.

Dalmawhapple was young, stout, and active; but the Baron, infinitely more master of his weapon, would, like *Sir Toby Belch*, have tickled his opponents other gates than

he did, had he not been under the influence of "Ursa Major" [a drinking-cup so called].
Sir W. Scott.

Bel'fŏrd. A friend and correspondent of Lovelace, in Richardson's novel, "The History of Clarissa Harlow."

It is well for thee, that, Lovelace-and-*Belford*-like, we came under a convention to pardon every species of liberty which we may take with each other. *Sir W. Scott.*

Be'lī-ăl. [Heb. *b'li*, not, and *ja'al*, useful.] A Hebrew word meaning *worthlessness*, and hence *recklessness*, *lawlessness.* The translators of the Bible have frequently treated the word as a proper name, though there can be no question that in the Old Testament it is a mere appellative. In the New Testament, the apostle Paul, in order to indicate in the strongest terms the high degree of virtue after which the Christian should strive, places Christ in direct opposition to Belial. "What concord hath Christ with Belial?" (2 Cor. vi. 15.) The term as here used is generally understood as an appellative of Satan, as the personification of all that was bad; though Bengel explains it of Antichrist, as more strictly the opposite of Christ. Milton in his "Paradise Lost" expressly distinguishes Belial from Satan, and he assigns him a prominent place in Pandemonium. Those mediæval demonographers who reckoned nine ranks of evil spirits, placed Belial at the head of the third rank, which consisted of inventors of mischief and vessels of anger. According to Wierus, who, following old authorities, establishes a complete infernal court, Belial is its ambassador in Turkey.

Belial came last, than whom a spirit more lewd
Fell not from heaven, or more gross to love
Vice for itself.

A fairer person lost not heaven; he seemed
For dignity composed and high exploit;
But all was false and hollow; though his tongue
Dropped manna, and could make the worse appear
The better reason, to perplex and dash
Maturest counsels; for his thoughts were low.

Belial, the dissolutest spirit that fell,
The sensualest, and, after Asmodai,
The fleshliest Incubus. *Milton.*

But, could he make an effectual struggle, he might depend upon the aid of the servile Barrère, a sort of *Belial* in the Convention, the meanest, yet not the least able, among those fallen spirits, who, with great adroitness and ingenuity, as well as wit and eloquence, caught opportunities as they arose, and was eminently dexterous in being always strong upon the strongest, and safe upon the safest, side. *Sir W. Scott.*

Belianis. See DON BELIANIS OF GREECE.

Be-lin'dă. 1. The poetical name of the heroine of Pope's "Rape of the Lock," whose real name was Arabella Fermor. A frolic of gallantry in which Lord Petre cut off a lock of this lady's hair — a frolic so much resented that the intercourse of the two families, before very friendly, was interrupted — was the occasion of the poem, which was written with the design of bringing the parties to a better temper, and effecting a reconciliation.

2. The heroine of Miss Edgeworth's novel of the same name.

Bell, Ac'tŏn. A pseudonym of Anne Brontë (d. 1848), an English novelist, author of "Agnes Grey" and "The Tenant of Wildfeld Hall."

Bell, Adam. The hero of a famous old ballad having this name for its title; a wild, north-country outlaw, celebrated for his skill in archery.

Bell, Bessy. A character in a ballad by Allan Ramsay, founded on fact, and entitled "Bessy Bell and Mary Gray." These were daughters of two country gentlemen in the neighbourhood of Perth. When the plague of 1666 broke out, they built themselves a bower in a very retired and romantic spot called Burn Braes, where they were supplied with food and other necessaries by a young gentleman who was in love with both of them. After a time he himself caught the disease, and, having unwittingly communicated it to them, they all three sickened and died.

Mrs. Le Blanc, a young woman fair to look upon, with her young infant, has to live in greenwood, like a beautiful *Bessy Bell* of song, her bower thatched with rushes; — catching premature rheumatism. *Carlyle.*

Bell, Cŭr'rĕr. A pseudonym adopted by Mrs. Nicholls (Charlotte Brontë, — 1824-1855, — sister of Anne and Emily Brontë), wife of the Rev. Arthur Bell Nicholls, and a distinguished English novelist, author of "Jane Eyre," "Shirley," and "Villette."

Bell, Ellis. A pseudonym of Emily Brontë (d. 1849), sister of Anne and Charlotte Brontë, and author of "Wuthering Heights."

☞ "Averse to personal publicity, we veiled our names under those of Currer, Acton, and Ellis, Bell, — the ambiguous choice being dictated by a sort of conscientious scruple at assuming Christian names positively masculine, while we did not like to declare ourselves women, because — without at that time suspecting that our mode of writing and thinking was not what is called 'feminine' — we had a vague impression that authoresses are likely to be looked on with prejudice ; we had noticed how critics sometimes use for their chastisement the weapon of personality, and for their reward a flattery which is not true praise." *C. Brontë.*

Bell, Peter. The subject of Wordsworth's poem entitled "Peter Bell, a Tale in Verse." A parody on this poem appeared soon after its publication, and Shelley wrote a burlesque, entitled "Peter Bell the Third," intended to ridicule the ludicrous puerility of language and sentiment which Wordsworth often affected in the championship of the poetical system he had adopted.

Bel'lăs-tŏn, Lady. A profligate character in Fielding's novel, "The History of Tom Jones, a Foundling."

Suppose we were to describe the doings of such a person as Mr. Lovelace, or my *Lady Bellaston* . . . ? How the pure and outraged Nineteenth Century would blush, scream, run out of the room, call away the young ladies, and order Mr. Mudie never to send one of that odious author's books again! *Thackeray.*

Belle France, La (lă bel frŏⁿss, 62). [Fr., beautiful France.] A popular epithet applied to France, corresponding to the epithet "Merry England," as applied to England.

Biddy Fudge, though delighted to find herself in "*La Belle France*," was yet somewhat disappointed at the unpicturesqueness of the country betwixt Calais and Amiens. *Brit. & For. Rev.*

Bel'len-den, Lady Margaret (bel'-len-dn). An old Tory lady, mistress of the Tower of Tillietudlem, in Sir

and for the Remarks and Rules to which the numbers after certain words refer, see pp. xiv-xxxii.

Walter Scott's novel of "Old Mortality."

Bel-lĕr'o-phŏn. [Gr. Βελλεροφῶν.] (*Gr. & Lat. Myth.*) A beautiful son of the Corinthian King Glaucus, and a grandson of Sisyphus. With the help of the winged steed Pegasus, he killed the Chimæra. He afterward attempted to rise with Pegasus into heaven; but Jupiter sent a gad-fly, which stung the horse so that he threw the rider, who became lame and blind in consequence, and wandered lonely through the Aleïan field, consumed by grief, and avoiding the paths of men.

Upled by thee [Urania],
Into the heaven of heavens I have presumed,
An earthly guest. ... With like safety guided down,
Return me to my native element;
Lest from this flying steed unreined (as once
Bellerophon, though from a lower sphere),
Dismounted on the Aleïan field I fall,
Erroneous there to wander and forlorn.
Milton.

Bel-Ie'rus (9). (*Myth.*) The name of a Cornish giant.

Sleep'st by the fable of *Bellerus* old,
Where the great vision of the guarded mount
Looks toward Namancos and Bayona's hold.
Milton.

Bel-lo'nȧ. (*Rom. Myth.*) The goddess of war; the companion and sister or wife of Mars. She prepared the chariot of Mars when he was going to war; and she appeared on the battle-field with dishevelled hair, a torch in her hand, and a whip to animate the combatants.

Her features, late so exquisitely lovely in their paleness, [were] now inflamed with the fury of frenzy, resembling those of a *Bellona*. *Sir W. Scott.*

Imminent blood-thirsty Regiments camped on the Champ de Mars; dispersed National Assembly; red-hot cannon-balls (to burn Paris);—the mad War-god and *Bellona's* sounding thongs. *Carlyle.*

Bell-the-Cat. A by-name given to Archibald Douglas (d. 1514), a Scottish nobleman, from an incident that occurred at Lauder, where the great barons of the realm had assembled at the call of the king, James III., to resist a threatened invasion of the country by Edward IV. of England. They were, however, less disposed to advance against the English than to correct the abuses of King James's administration, which were chiefly to be ascribed to the influence exerted over him by mean and unworthy favourites, particularly one Cochran, an architect, but termed a mason by the haughty barons.

"Many of the nobility and barons held a secret council in the church of Lauder, where they enlarged upon the evils which Scotland sustained through the insolence and corruption of Cochran and his associates. While they were thus declaiming, Lord Gray requested their attention to a fable. 'The mice,' he said, 'being much annoyed by the persecution of the cat, resolved that a bell should be hung about puss's neck, to give notice when she was coming. But, though the measure was agreed to in full council, it could not be carried into effect, because no mouse had courage enough to tie the bell to the neck of the formidable enemy.' This was as much as to intimate his opinion, that, though the discontented nobles might make bold resolutions against the king's ministers, yet it would be difficult to find any one courageous enough to act upon them. Archibald, Earl of Angus, a man of gigantic strength and intrepid courage, and head of that second family of Douglas whom I before mentioned, started up when Gray had done speaking. 'I am he,' he said, 'who will bell the cat;' from which expression he was distinguished by the name of *Bell-the-Cat* to his dying day." *Sir W. Scott.*

He was equally worthy of blazon with him perpetuated in Scottish song and story by the surname of *Bell-the-Cat*. *W. Irving.*

Beloved Disciple. An appellation often given to John the evangelist and apostle, who enjoys the memorable distinction of having been the chosen and favoured friend of our Lord. See *John* xiii. 23; xix. 26, 27; xx. 2; xxi. 7, 20.

Beloved Merchant. A title bestowed by Edward III. of England upon Michael de la Pole, an eminent London merchant, who in the following reign became lord chancellor, and was raised to the peerage as Earl of Suffolk.

Beloved Physician. An appellation sometimes used to designate St. Luke. It was first conferred upon him by the apostle Paul (*Col.* iv. 14).

Bel'phe-gōr. (*Myth.*) A Canaanitish divinity, worshipped particularly by the Moabites. Wierus calls him the ambassador in France from the infernal court of Beëlzebub. According to Pulci, he was a Mahometan deity. According to Macchiavelli, an archfiend who had been an archangel.

Bel-phœ'be. [Fr. *belle*, beautiful, and *Phœbe*, Diana.] A huntress in Spenser's "Faëry Queen;" intended as a likeness of Queen Elizabeth, the woman, as contradistinguished from the queen, who is imaged in Gloriana.

☞ " Flattery more highly seasoned may have been offered her [Queen Elizabeth], but none more delicate and graceful than that contained in the finished portrait of Belphœbe. She represents that pure and high-spirited maidenhood which the ancients embodied in Diana; and, like her, the forest is her dwelling-place, and the chase her favourite pastime. The breezes have imparted to her their own fleetness, and the swaying foliage its graceful movement. . . . She is passionless and pure, self-sustained and self-dependent, 'in maiden meditation fancy free,' and shines with a cold lunar light, and not the warm glow of day. The author has mingled the elements of her nature so skilfully that the result is nothing harsh, unnatural, or unfeminine; and has so combined the lofty and the ideal with the graceful and attractive, that we behold in her a creature . . .

' Too fair for worship, too divine for love.' "
Geo. S. Hillard.

Belted Will. A title bestowed upon Lord William Howard (1563-1640), warden of the western marches.

His Bilboa blade, by Marchmen felt,
Hung in a broad and studded belt;
Hence, in rude phrase, the Borderers still
Called noble Howard, *Belted Will.*
Sir W. Scott.

It is within the memory of even middle-aged persons that the south-western portion of our country was in as lawless a state as ever were the borders of England and Scotland, and with no *Belted Will* to hang up ruffians to swing in the wind.
Atlantic Monthly.

Beltenebros (bel-tā-nā-brōs'). [Sp., the darkly beautiful, or fair forlorn; from *bello*, beautiful, and *tenebroso*, dark, gloomy.] A name assumed by Amadis de Gaul on retiring to a hermitage, after receiving a cruel letter from his mistress, Oriana.

Be'lus. [Gr. Βῆλος.] (*Myth.*) The ancestral hero and national divinity of several Eastern nations, especially the Chaldæans and Assyrians. He is the same as *Baäl.* See BAÄL. [Called also *Bel.*]

Bel'vi-de'rȧ (9). The heroine of Otway's tragedy of "Venice Preserved;" remarkable for her beauty, conjugal tenderness, spotless purity, and agonizing sufferings. See JAFFIER.

More tears have been shed, probably, for the sorrows of *Belvidera* and Monimia than for those of Juliet and Desdemona.
Sir W. Scott.

Bendy, Old. See OLD BENDY.

Ben'e-dick. A young lord of Padua, in Shakespeare's "Much Ado about Nothing," who combines the characters of a wit, humourist, gentleman, and soldier. He marries Beatrice (though at first he does not love her) after a courtship which is a contest of wit and raillery. The name is often used as a synonym for a newly-married man, and is sometimes written *Benedict*, though this is not Shakespeare's orthography. See BEATRICE.

All these, like *Benedick's* brushing his hat of a morning, were signs that the sweet youth was in love.
Sir W. Scott.

In the first-named place, Henry found his dear *Benedick*, the married man, who appeared to be rather out of humour with his matrimonial chain.
Thackeray.

Ben'en-ġe'lī, Cid Ham'et [Sp. *Cide Hamete Benengeli*, theed ā-mā'tā bā-nen-hā'lee]. An imaginary Moorish chronicler from whom Cervantes professes to have derived his account of the adventures of Don Quixote.

☞ " The Spanish commentators . . . have discovered that *Cid Hamet Benengeli* is, after all, no more than an Arabian version of the name of Cervantes himself. *Cid*, as all the world knows, means lord or signior. *Hamet* is a common Moorish prefix. *Benengeli* signifies *the son of a stag*, which, being expressed in Spanish, is *hijo del ciervo, cerval*, or *cervanteno.*"
Lockhart.

I vow and protest, that, of the two bad cassocks I am worth in the world, I would have given the latter of them, as freely as ever *Cid Hamet* offered his, only to have stood by and heard my Uncle Toby's accompaniment.
Sterne.

But thou, at least, mine own especial pen!—
Once laid aside, but now assumed again,—
Our task complete, like *Hamet's*, shalt be free.
Byron.

Be-nī'cī-ȧ Boy. A sobriquet given to John C. Heenan, a noted American pugilist, who resided for a time at Benicia, in California. In 1860, he had a famous fight with Tom Sayers, the "champion prize-fighter of England," which lasted for more than two hours, and was then stopped by the interference of the police.

Ben-nas'kăr. A wealthy merchant and magician of Delhi, in Ridley's "Tales of the Genii."
Like the jeweller of Delhi, in the house of the magician *Bennaskar*, I, at length, reached a vaulted room dedicated to secrecy and silence. *Sir W. Scott.*

Ben'net, Mrs. A demure, shy, intriguing, equivocal character in Fielding's novel of "Amelia."

Benshie. See BANSHEE.

Ben-vo'li-o. A friend to Romeo, and nephew to Montague, in Shakespeare's tragedy of "Romeo and Juliet."

Berchta. See BERTHA, FRAU.

Bĕrke'ley, Old Woman of. The title and subject of a ballad by Southey.

Bĕr-lin' Decree. (*Fr. Hist.*) A decree issued at Berlin, on the 21st of November, 1806, by the Emperor Napoleon I., declaring the whole of the British islands to be in a state of blockade, and all vessels trading to them to be liable to capture by French ships. It also shut out all British vessels and produce both from France, and from all the other countries which gave obedience to the French.

Bĕr-moo'thĕs. An old form of *Bermudas*, and the Spanish pronunciation of the name of the first discoverer of these islands, *Bermudez*, who sighted them in 1527.
In the deep nook, where once
Thou calledst me up at midnight to fetch dew
From the still-vexed *Bermoothes*, there she 's hid. *Shak.*

Bĕr-mu'dăs. A cant term formerly applied to certain obscure and intricate alleys in London, in which persons lodged who had occasion to live cheaply or be concealed. They are supposed to have been the narrow passages north of the Strand, near Covent Garden.

Bĕr-nar'do. The name of an officer in Shakespeare's tragedy of "Hamlet."

Bernardo del Carpio. See CARPIO, BERNARDO DEL.

Berserker (bĕr-sĕr'ker). [Old Norse *ber*, bare, naked, and *sarke*, a shirt of mail.] (*Scand. Myth.*) A redoubtable warrior who went into battle unharnessed, his strength and fury serving him instead of armour, which he despised. He had twelve sons, who inherited his name as well as his warlike ferocity.

Bertha, Frau (frŏw bĕr'tȧ). [O. Ger. *Peracta*, shining, white; from the same root as the Eng. *bright*.] In Germany, an impersonation of the Epiphany, corresponding to the Italian *Befana*, variously represented as a gentle white lady who steals softly to neglected cradles, and rocks them in the absence of careless nurses, and also as the terror of naughty children. She has, besides, the oversight of spinners. She is represented as having an immensely large foot and a long iron nose. The legend concerning her is mainly of Christian origin, but with some admixture of heathen elements. [Written also Frau Berchta and Frau Precht.]

Bĕr'thȧ with the Great Foot. [Fr. *Berthe au Grand Pied.*] The mother of Charlemagne, by King Pepin, and the great-grand-daughter of Charles Martel; — said to have been so named because she had one foot larger than the other.

Bĕr'trăm. Count of Rousillon, a character in Shakespeare's "All 's Well that Ends Well."

Bess, Good Queen. A sobriquet by which Queen Elizabeth of England is often familiarly referred to. Her reign, take it all in all, was a happy as well as a glorious one for England, and the contrast it offers to that of her predecessor is very striking.

Bes'sus. The name of a cowardly captain in Beaumont and Fletcher's play, "A King and No King."
The story which Clarendon tells of that affair [the panic of the royal troops at Naseby]

☞ For the "Key to the Scheme of Pronunciation," with the accompanying Explanations,

reminds us of the excuses by which *Bessus* and Bobadil explain their cudgellings.
Macaulay.

Bettina (bĕt'tĕ'nȧ). [A diminutive of Elizabeth.] The name under which Elizabeth Brentano (b. 1785), afterward the wife of Ludwig Achim von Arnim, corresponded with Goethe. This correspondence, under the title of "Goethe's Letters to a Child," was published in 1835, and was translated by Bettina into English.

Beulah. See LAND OF BEULAH.

Beuves d' Aygremont (böv dåg'r'-mön', 43, 62). The father of Malagigi, or Maugis, and uncle of Rinaldo. He was treacherously slain by Gano.

Be'vis of South-amp'tŏn, Sir. A famous knight of romance, whose marvellous exploits are related in the second book of Drayton's "Polyolbion." Heylin claims him as a real Earl of Southampton. He is the *Beuves de Hantone* of the French, the *Buovo d' Antona* of the Italians. [Called also *Bevis of Hampton*.]

Ycene's oaks — beneath whose shade
Their theme the merry minstrels made
Of Ascapart and *Bevis* bold. *Sir W. Scott.*

Be-zōn'iȧn (-ɣan). A name given by Pistol to Shallow in Shakespeare's "King Henry IV." (Part II., a. v., sc. 3). It comes from the Italian word, *bisogno* (need, want), and is frequently used by the old dramatists as a term of reproach, meaning *beggar*, *low fellow*, or *scoundrel*. Strictly, it is not a proper name, but it is commonly thought to be such in the instance referred to.

Bĭ-añ'cȧ. 1. A daughter to Baptista, in Shakespeare's "Taming of the Shrew."
2. Mistress to Cassio, in the tragedy of "Othello."

Bibulus, Consul. See CONSUL BIBULUS.

Bick'er-stȧff, Isaac, Esq., Astrologer (2). The assumed name under which the "Tatler" was edited.

☞ "Isaac Bickerstaff, Esquire, Astrologer, was an imaginary person, almost as well known in that age [Addison's] as Mr. Paul Pry or Mr. Pickwick in ours. Swift had assumed the name of Bickerstaff in a satirical pamphlet against Partridge, the almanac-maker. Partridge had been fool enough to publish a furious reply. Bickerstaff had rejoined in a second pamphlet, still more diverting than the first. All the wits had combined to keep up the joke, and the town was long in convulsions of laughter. Steele determined to employ the name which this controversy had made popular; and, in April, 1709, it was announced that Isaac Bickerstaff, Esquire, Astrologer, was about to publish a paper called the 'Tatler.'" *Macaulay.*

☞ "Swift is said to have taken the name of *Bickerstaff* from a smith's sign, and added that of *Isaac*, as a Christian appellation of uncommon occurrence. Yet it was said a living person was actually found who owned both names." *Sir W. Scott.*

Bicorne. See CHICHEVACHE.

Bid'den-den Maids (bid'dn-dn). A name given to two unmarried sisters, named Mary and Elizabeth Chulkhurst, born at Biddenden, in 1100, and joined together, as tradition states, by the shoulders and hips. They lived for thirty-four years, when one died, and the other, persisting in a refusal to be separated from the corpse of her sister, succumbed six hours after. They are said to have left twenty acres of land, called "Bread and Cheese Land," where, on the afternoon of Easter Sunday, six hundred rolls are distributed to strangers, and two hundred and seventy loaves, weighing three pounds and a half each, with cheese in proportion, are given to the poor of the parish, — the expense being defrayed by the rental of the land. Halstead, in his "History of Kent," rejects this story as fabulous, so far as it relates to the Chulkhurst sisters, and asserts that the "Bread and Cheese Land" was left by two maiden ladies by the name of Preston.

Bifröst (bǐf'röst, 46). [Old Norse *bifa*, to move, and *röst*, space.] (*Scand. Myth.*) The name of the bridge between heaven and earth, typified by the rainbow, and supposed to be constructed of stones of various colours. It was extremely solid, and built with great art.

Big-endians, The. The name of a religious party in the imaginary empire of Lilliput, who made it a matter

---

and for the Remarks and Rules to which the numbers after certain words refer, see pp. xiv-xxxii.

of duty and conscience to break their eggs at the large end. They were regarded as heretics by the law, which required all persons to break the smaller end of their eggs, under pain of heavy penalties in case of disobedience. Under this name the Roman Catholics of England are satirised, and under that of *Little-endians*, the English Protestants are ridiculed. See LILLIPUT.

☞ The Vatican is great; yet poor to Chimborazo or the Peak of Teneriffe; its dome is but a foolish *Big-endian* or Little-endian chip of an egg-shell compared with that starfretted Dome where Arcturus and Orion glance for ever. *Carlyle.*

Big'lŏw, Mr. Hosea. The imaginary author of a series of humourous satirical poems, in the Yankee dialect, really written by Professor James Russell Lowell, and directed mainly against slavery and the war, in 1846-7, between the United States and Mexico.

Bimini (be'me-nee). A fabulous island and said to belong to the Bahama group, but lying far out in the ocean, where, according to a tradition current among the natives of Puerto Rico, was a marvellous fountain possessing the power of restoring youth. This was an object of eager and long-continued quest to the celebrated Spanish navigator, Juan Ponce de Leon.

Bĭ'on-del'lo. A servant to Lucentio, in Shakespeare's "Taming of the Shrew."

Birch, Har'vey. A celebrated character in Cooper's novel of "The Spy."

Bireno (be-rā'no). In Ariosto's "Orlando Furioso," the lover and husband of Olimpia, whom he abandons.

Biron (be-rŏⁿ'). A "merry mad-cap lord" attending on the king of Navarre, in Shakespeare's "Love's Labour's Lost."

Bishop, Madame. The name given to a mixture of port, sugar, and nutmeg.

Bishop Bun'yăn. A sobriquet given to John Bunyan (1628-1688), because he visited his religious brethren in various parts of England, exhorting them to good works and holiness of life.

Bishop of Hip'po. A title by which St. Augustine (354-430) is often referred to, he having held the office for many years.

Black'ȧ-cre, Widow (-ȧ-kẽr). A perverse, bustling, masculine, pettifogging, and litigious character in Wycherley's comedy of "The Plain Dealer."

☞ "The Widow Blackacre, beyond comparison Wycherley's best comic character, is the Countess in Racine's 'Plaideurs,' talking the jargon of English instead of French chicane." *Macaulay.*

Black Act, The. A name given in England to an act passed in 1722 (9 Geo. I., c. 22). It was so called because it was occasioned by, and was designed to put an end to, the wanton destruction of deer, game, plantations, &c., by persons calling themselves *Blacks*, and having their faces blackened or otherwise disguised. It was repealed June 21, 1827, by 7 and 8 of Geo. IV., c. 27.

☞ The acts of the Scottish Parliament from James I. of Scotland to 1586 or 1587 were called *Black Acts*, because printed in black or Saxon characters.

Black Assize, The. A common designation of the sitting of the courts held at Oxford in 1577, during which judges, jurymen, and counsel were swept away by a violent epidemic. The term is also used to denote the epidemic.

Black Captain, The. [Fr. *Le Capitaine Noir.*] A name given by the French to Lt.-Col. Dennis Davidoff, an officer in the Russian army, in the time of the French invasion.

Black Death, The. A name given to the celebrated Oriental plague that devastated Asia, Europe, and Africa, during the fourteenth century. It took this name from the black spots, symptomatic of putrid decomposition, which, at one of its stages, appeared upon the skin.

Black Dick. A sobriquet of Richard, Earl Howe (1725-1799), the English admiral who was sent with a squadron to operate against D'Estaing,

☞ For the "Key to the Scheme of Pronunciation," with the accompanying Explanations,

who commanded the French forces on the coast of America during the war of the Revolution.

Black Hole of Calcutta. A name commonly given to a certain small and close dungeon in Fort William, Calcutta, the scene of one of the most tragic events in the history of British India. On the capture of Calcutta, by Surajah Dowlah, June 18, 1756, the British garrison, consisting of 146 men, being made prisoners, were locked up at night in this room, which was only 20 feet square, and poorly ventilated, never having been intended to hold more than two or three prisoners at a time. In the morning, of the 146 who were imprisoned, only 23 were found to have survived the excruciating agony of pressure, heat, thirst, and want of air. In the "Annual Register" for 1758, is a narrative of the sufferings of those imprisoned, written by Mr. Holwell. one of the number. The Black Hole is now used as a warehouse.

Black Knight, The. See FAINÉANT, LE NOIR.

Black Man, The. A common designation for the Devil in the time of the New England witchcraft. It is a popular belief that the Devil is black. In the "Golden Legend" there is a story representing him as appearing in the guise of a man clad in black, of great height, and mounted on a superb horse.

These wild doctors [the Indian medicine-men] were supposed to draw their pharmaceutic knowledge from no gracious source, the *Black Man* himself being the principal professor in their medical school.
Hawthorne.

Black Monday. (*Eng. Hist.*) A memorable Easter Monday in 1351, very dark and misty. A great deal of hail fell, and the cold was so extreme that many died from its effects. The name afterward came to be applied to the Monday after Easter of each year.

My nose fell a-bleeding on *Black Monday* last. *Shak.*

Black Prince, The. Edward, Prince of Wales, the son of Edward III. of England; — so called from the colour of his armour.

To portray a Roman of the age of Camillus or Curius as superior to national antipathies, as treating conquered enemies with the delicacy of the *Black Prince*, would be to violate all dramatic propriety. *Macaulay.*

Black Republicans. See REPUBLICANS, BLACK.

Black Saturday. A name given, in Scotland, to the 4th of August, 1621. On this day, the Parliament sitting at Edinburgh ratified certain articles introducing Episcopalian fashions into the church, — a proceeding highly repugnant to the religious feelings and convictions of the Scottish people. A violent storm which occurred at the same time, and was accompanied by thunder and lightning and "heavy darkness," was thought to be a manifest token of the displeasure of Heaven.

She was to remind a neighbour of some particular which she was to recall to his memory by the token, that Thome Reid and he had set out together to go to the battle which took place on the *Black Saturday*. *Sir W. Scott.*

Blā'dud. A legendary king of England, who is said to have built the city of Bath, and dedicated the medicinal springs to Minerva.

Winifred Jenkins and Tabitha Bramble must keep Englishmen on the grin for ages yet to come; and in their letters and the story of their loves there is a perpetual fount of sparkling laughter as inexhaustible as *Bladud's* well. *Thackeray.*

Blănche'fleûr. [It. *Blancafiore.*] A lady beloved by Flores. Their adventures make the principal subject of Boccaccio's "Philopoco," but they had been famous for a long time previously, as Boccaccio himself informs us. They are mentioned as illustrious lovers by Matfres Eymengau de Bezers, a Languedocian poet, in his "Breviari d' Amor," dated in the year 1288. Boccaccio repeated in the "Decameron" (Day 10, novel 5) the story of Flores and Blanchefleur, but changed the names of the lovers to Ansaldo and Dianora. Chaucer took it as the foundation of the Frankelein's tale in the "Canterbury Tales," though he professes to have derived it from "a British lay." Boccaccio's novel is unquestionably the origin of the episode of

Iroldo, Prasildo, and Tisbina, in Bojardo's "Orlando Innamorato." There is also an old English romance entitled "Flores and Blanchefleur," said to have been originally written in French. See PRASILDO.

The chronicles of Charlemagne,
Of Merlin and the Mort d'Arthure,
Mingled together in his brain
With tales of Flores and *Blanchefleur*.
Longfellow.

Blas, Gil. See GIL BLAS.

Blatant Beast, The. A bellowing monster, in Spenser's "Faëry Queen," typical of slander or calumny; or it is an impersonation of what we now call "Vox Populi," or the Voice of the People.

Ble-fus'cu. The name of an island mentioned in the imaginary "Travels" of Lemuel Gulliver, written by Swift. It is described as being "situated to the north-east side of Lilliput, from whence it is parted only by a channel of eight hundred yards wide," and as being ruled over by an emperor. The inhabitants, like the Lilliputians, were all pygmies.

☞ "Blefuscu is France, and the ingratitude of the Lilliputian court, which forces Gulliver to take shelter there rather than have his eyes put out, is an indirect reproach upon that of England, and a vindication of the flight of Ormond and Bolingbroke to Paris." *Sir W. Scott.*

Bli'fil. A noted character who figures in Fielding's novel entitled "The History of Tom Jones, a Foundling."

Blim'ber, Miss Cornelia. A character in Dickens's novel of "Dombey and Son;" a daughter of Dr. Blimber, the head of a first-class educational establishment conducted on the forcing or cramming principle. She is a very learned, grave, and precise young lady, with "no light nonsense about her," who has become "dry and sandy with working in the graves of deceased languages."

It costs her nothing to disown the slightest acquaintance with the dead languages, or science, or any thing that calls for abstract thought. In the opinion of those whose approval she most cares for, she might as well assume *Miss Blimber's* spectacles as shine in any one of them.
Essays from the Saturday Review.

Blind Harry. A name commonly given to Henry the Minstrel, a wandering Scottish poet of the fifteenth century, of whom nothing else is known except that he was blind from infancy, and composed a romantic poem entitled "The Life of that Noble Champion of Scotland, Sir William Wallace, Knight," which has been handed down to the present time.

Blind Preacher. A popular sobriquet given to William Henry Milburn (b. 1823), a blind American clergyman and lecturer, noted for his ability and eloquence.

Blind Traveller. A name given to James Holman (d. 1857), a lieutenant in the English navy, and author of various books of travels. In 1812, a disease contracted in the discharge of his duty destroyed his eyesight.

Bloody Assizes. A common designation of the horrid judicial massacre perpetrated, in 1685, by George Jeffreys, Lord Chief Justice of the King's Bench, while on a circuit through the western counties of England. About three hundred persons were executed after short trials; very many were whipped, imprisoned, and fined; and nearly one thousand were sent as slaves to the American plantations.

Bloody Bill. A name given to the statute of the "Articles" (31 Henry VIII., c. 14), by which hanging or burning was denounced against all who should deny the doctrine of transubstantiation.

Bloody-bones. The name of a hobgoblin fiend, formerly much feared by children. The "Wyll of the Devyll" is said to be "written by our faithful secretaryes hobgoblin, rawhed, and *bloodybone*, in the spiteful audience of all the court of hell."

Made children with your tones to run for 't
As bad as *Bloody-bones* or Lunsford.
Hudibras.

Bloody Butcher. A sobriquet given to the Duke of Cumberland, second son of George II., on account of his barbarities in the suppression of the rebellion excited by Charles Edward Stuart, the Younger Pretender.

Bloody Mary. A name commonly given to Mary, a Roman Catholic queen of England, whose reign is distinguished for the sanguinary persecutions of the adherents of the Church of England, no fewer than two hundred persons having been burnt at the stake within the space of four years, for their attachment to the reformed doctrines.

Blŏw̌g'ă-lĭn'dă. A country girl in Gay's pastoral poem, "The Shepherd's Week," which depicts rural life in its character of poverty and rudeness, rather than as clothed in the colours of romance.

We, fair, fine ladies, who park out our lives
From common sheep-paths, cannot help the crows
From flying over; we 're as natural still
As *Blowsalinda*. *Mrs. E. B. Browning.*

Blue-beard. [Fr. *La Barbe Bleue.*] The hero of a well-known story of the same name, originally written in French by Charles Perrault. He is represented as having a blue beard, from which he gets his designation, and as marrying a beautiful young woman, who has all the keys of a magnificent castle intrusted to her, with injunctions not to open a certain apartment. She gratifies her curiosity during the absence of her lord, and is horrified to find the remains of his former wives, the victims of his boundless lust and cruelty. Her disobedience is discovered by means of an indelible stain produced on the key which opened the door of the interdicted room, and she is told to prepare for death, but obtains the favour of a little delay, and is happily rescued by the timely arrival of friends, who instantly despatch her brutal husband.

☞ It is said that the original Bluebeard was Giles de Laval, Lord of Raiz, who was made Marshal of France in 1429. He was distinguished for his military genius and intrepidity, and was possessed of princely revenues, but rendered himself infamous by the murder of his wives, and his extraordinary impiety and debaucheries. Mézeray says that he encouraged and maintained sorcerers to discover hidden treasures, and corrupted young persons of both sexes that he might attach them to him, and afterward killed them for the sake of their blood for his charms and incantations.

At length, for some state crime against the Duke of Brittany, he was sentenced to be burned alive in a field at Nantes, in 1440. Holinshed notices another Bluebeard, in the reign of Henry VI., *anno* 1450. Speaking of the committal of the Duke of Suffolk to the Tower, he says, "This doing so much displeased the people, that, if politic provision had not been made, great mischief had immediately ensued. For the commons, in sundry places of the realm, assembled together in great companies, and chose to them a captain, whom they called Blue-beard; but ere they had attempted any enterprise their leaders were apprehended, and so the matter pacified without any hurt committed." Bluebeard is also the name by which King Henry VIII. lives in the popular superstitions of England. The German poet Tieck, in his "Phantasus," has a tragedy which is grounded upon the common nursery tale. Dunlop notices the striking resemblance between the story of Blue-beard and that of the third calendar in the "Arabian Nights' Entertainments."

A dark tragedy of Sophie's this; the *Bluebeard* chamber of her mind, into which no eye but her own must ever look. *Carlyle.*

Blue-coat School. A name popularly given to Christ's Hospital, London, — a charitable institution for the education of orphans and foundlings, — on account of the blue coats or gowns worn by the boys. Their costume has continued unchanged ever since the foundation of the school in the reign of Edward VI.

Blue Hen. A cant or popular name for the State of Delaware. This sobriquet is said to have had its origin in a certain Captain Caldwell's fondness for the amusement of cockfighting. Caldwell was for a time an officer of the First Delaware Regiment in the war of the Revolution, and was greatly distinguished for his daring and undaunted spirit. He was exceedingly popular in the regiment, and its high state of discipline was generally conceded to be due to his exertions; so that when officers were sent on recruiting service to enlist new men in order to fill vacancies caused by death or otherwise, it was a saying, that they had gone home for more of Caldwell's game-cocks;

and for the Remarks and Rules to which the numbers after certain words refer, see pp. xiv-xxxii.

but, as Caldwell insisted that no cock could be truly game unless the mother was a blue hen, the expression "Blue Hen's chickens" was substituted for "game-cocks."
Delaware State Journal, July, 1860.

Blue Laws. A nickname given to the quaint and severe regulations of the early government of New Haven Plantation, when the public authorities kept a sharp watch over the deportment of the people of the colony, and punished all breaches of good manners and good morals, often with ludicrous formality. Some account of these laws is given in a small work published in 1825 (Hartford, by Silas Andrus), entitled "The Code of 1650, being a Compilation of the earliest Laws and Orders of the General Court of Connecticut," &c. The ancient records of the New Haven colony bear witness to the stern and sombre religious spirit common to all the first settlers. The chapter of "Capitall Lawes," in the code of 1650, is almost verbally copied from the Mosaic law.

☞ "After the restoration of Charles II., the Puritans became the subject of every kind of reproach and contumely. The epithet *blue* was applied to any one who looked with disapprobation upon the licentiousness of the time. The Presbyterians, under which name all dissenters were often included, were more particularly designated by this term. Thus Butler: —

'For his religion, it was fit
To match his learning and his wit, —
'T was Presbyterian true *blue*.'
Hudibras.

That this epithet of derision should find its way to the colonies was a matter of course. It was here applied not only to persons, but to customs, institutions, and laws of the Puritans, by those who wished to render the prevailing system ridiculous. Hence, probably, a belief with some that a distinct system of laws, known as the 'blue laws,' must have somewhere a local habitation."
Kingsley.

Blue-Nose. A nickname popularly given to an inhabitant of Nova Scotia or New Brunswick. The appellation is supposed to have been originally applied from the effect upon the more prominent parts of the face of the raw easterly winds and long-continued fogs which prevail in these provinces. Others say that it was first applied to a particular kind of potatoes which were extensively produced by the inhabitants, and that it was afterward transferred to the inhabitants themselves. Others still assert that its use is accounted for by the custom among certain tribes of the aborigines of painting the nose blue as a punishment for a crime against chastity.

Blueskin. A nickname given to Joseph Blake, an English burglar, on account of his dark complexion. He was executed Nov. 11, 1723.

Blue-Skins. A nickname applied to the Presbyterians, from their alleged grave deportment.

Bluestring, Robin. See ROBIN BLUE-STRING.

Bluff, Captain Noll. A swaggering coward in Congreve's comedy of "The Old Bachelor."

Those ancients, as *Noll Bluff* might say,
Were pretty fellows in their day.
Sir W. Scott.

Bluff City. A descriptive name popularly given to the city of Hannibal, Missouri.

Bluff Hal, or **Harry.** The sobriquet by which King Henry VIII. of England is commonly known. [Called also *Burly King Harry*.]

Ere yet in scorn of Peter's pence,
And numbered bead and shrift,
Bluff Harry broke into the spence,
And turned the cowls adrift.
Tennyson.

Bo'ä-nër'ġëṣ. [Gr. Βοανεργές, from Heb. *bene-reges*, the Aramaic pronunciation of which was *boane-reges*.] A name signifying "sons of thunder," given by our Lord (*Mark* iii. 17) to the two sons of Zebedee, James and John. Probably the name had respect to the fiery zeal of the brothers, signs of which may be seen in *Luke* ix. 54, *Mark* ix. 38.

Boar of Ardennes, Wild. See WILD BOAR OF ARDENNES.

Boast of England. See TOM-A-LIN.

Bob'ä-dil, Captain. A beggarly and cowardly adventurer, in Ben Jonson's comedy, "Every Man in his Humour," who passes himself off with young and simple people for a valiant soldier. He says (a. iv., sc. 7): "I would select nineteen more to myself; . . . gentlemen they should be, of good spirit, strong and able constitution. . . . We twenty would come into the field the tenth of March, or thereabouts, and we would challenge twenty of the enemy: they could not in their honour refuse us. Well, we would kill them: challenge twenty more; kill them: twenty more; kill them: twenty more; kill them too. And thus we would kill every man his twenty a day, — that's twenty score: twenty score, that's two hundred; two hundred a day, five days, a thousand: forty thousand — forty times five — five times forty — two hundred days kills them all up by computation."

☞ "Bobadil, with his big words and his little heart, with his sword and his oath, — ' By the foot of Pharaoh!' — is a braggart of the first water. He is, upon the whole, the best invention of the author, and is worthy to march in the same regiment with Bessus and Pistol, and Parolles and the Copper Captain."
B. W. Procter.

The present author, like *Bobadil*, had taught his trick of fence to a hundred gentlemen, — and ladies, — who could fence very nearly or quite as well as himself.
Sir W. Scott.

The whole province was once thrown in amaze by the return of one of his campaigns, wherein it was stated, that, though, like *Captain Bobadil*, he had only twenty men to back him, yet in the short space of six months he had conquered and utterly annihilated sixty oxen, ninety hogs, one hundred sheep, ten thousand cabbages, one thousand bushels of potatoes, one hundred and fifty kilderkins of small beer, two thousand seven hundred and thirty-five pipes, seventy-eight pounds of sugar-plums, and forty bars of iron, besides sundry small meats, game, poultry, and garden-stuff; — an achievement unparalleled since the days of Pantagruel and his all-devouring army. *W. Irving.*

Royalism totally abandons that *Bobadilian* method of contest. *Carlyle.*

Bobbies. See PEELERS.

Bobus Smith. See SMITH, BOBUS.

Bœuf, Front de (frŏⁿ du bŏf, 43). A gigantic and ferocious personage who figures in Sir Walter Scott's novel of " Ivanhoe " as a follower of Prince John.

Bogy. See OLD BOGY.

Bo-he'mi-å. A recent cant designation of those parts of London inhabited by gay young fellows who hang loosely "about town," leading a sort of nomadic life, like the gypsies (Fr. *Bohémiens*), and living on their wits, — as journalists, politicians, artists, dancers, and the like.

☞ In France, *La Bohême* is used of Paris in a similar way.

Bohemian Tartar. Perhaps a gypsy; or a mere wild appellation designed to ridicule the appearance of Simple in Shakespeare's "Merry Wives of Windsor," a. iv., sc. 5.

Bō'hŏrt, Sir, *or* **King.** A knight of the Round Table, celebrated in the old romances of chivalry. He was the brother of King Ban, and uncle to Lancelot du Lac. [Written also Bors, Bort.]

Bois-Guilbert, Brian de (brē-ŏⁿ' du bwŏ'gĕl'bĕr'). A brave but cruel and voluptuous Preceptor of the Knights Templars, in Sir Walter Scott's " Ivanhoe."

The most resolute courage will sometimes quail in a bad cause, and even die in its armour, like *Bois-Guilbert*. *Atlantic Monthly.*

Bom'bå. A sobriquet given to Ferdinand II. (1830–1859), late king of the Two Sicilies.

☞ "Bomba is the name of children's play in Italy, a kind of prisoner's-base, or what used formerly to be called, in England, 'King by your leave;' and there was probably an allusion to this pastime in the nickname; especially as his majesty was fond of playing the king, and had a predilection for childish amusements besides, and for playing at soldiers. But the name, whatever its first cause, or its collective significance, is understood to have derived its greatest weight from a charge made against his majesty of having called upon his soldiers to ' bombard ' his people during one of their insurrections. ' Bombard 'em ! bombard 'em !' he is said to have cried out; that is to say, ' Sweep them away, — cannonade 'em !' His apologist, Mr. Macfarlane, not only denies the charge, but says his cry was the very reverse; to wit, ' Spare my misguided people! Make prisoners; do not kill; make prisoners!' . . . The book entitled ' Naples and King Ferdinand ' repeats the charge, however, in the strongest manner. It says that he kept crying out, ' Down with them ! down

and for the Remarks and Rules to which the numbers after certain words refer, see pp. xiv-xxxii.

with them!' adding, in a note, what was stated to be the particular expression, 'Bombardare;' and hence, says the author, 'arose his well-known sobriquet of *Bomba*.'" *Leigh Hunt.*

☞ "The name Bomba is often misinterpreted as having some allusion to bombardments. It is not so. In Italy, when you tell a man a thing which he knows to be false, or when he wishes to convey to you the idea of the utter worthlessness of any thing or person, he puffs out his cheek like a bagpiper's in full blow, smites it with his forefinger, and allows the pent breath to explode, with the exclamation, 'Bomb-a.' I have witnessed the gesture, and heard the sound. Hence, after 1849, when regal oaths in the name of the Most Holy Trinity were found to be as worthless as a beggar's in the name of Bacchus or the Madonna, when Ferdinand was perceived to be a worthless liar, his quick-witted people whispered his name. He was called King Bomba, King Puff-cheek, King Liar, King Knave. The name and his character were then so much in harmony that it spread widely; and they have been so much in harmony ever since, that he has retained it till now, and will retain it, I suppose, till he is bundled into his unhonoured grave." *Dublin Evening Gazette.*

After Palermo's fatal siege,
Across the western seas he fled
In good King *Bomba's* happy reign.
Longfellow.

Bom-bǎs'tēṣ Fū-ri-ō'ṣo. The hero and title of a burlesque tragic opera by Thomas Barnes Rhodes, which was intended to ridicule the bombast of modern tragedies.

Falling on one knee, [he] put both hands on his heart, and rolled up his eyes much after the manner of *Bombastes Furioso* making love to Distaffina. *Epes Sargent.*

Bo'nạ De'ȧ. [Lat., the good goddess.] (*Myth.*) A Roman divinity, otherwise called Fauna, or Fatua, and described as the sister, wife, or daughter of Faunus. Her worship was so exclusively confined to women, that men were not even allowed to know her name.

Bo-nas'sus. [Gr. βόνασυς, βόνασσος, a wild ox.] An imaginary wild beast, with which the "Ettrick Shepherd" (James Hogg), in the "Noctes Ambrosianæ" (No. XLVIII. April, 1830), is represented as having had a most remarkable adventure. A huge animal of the genus *Bison — Bison*

bonassus — had been exhibited in London and other parts of Great Britain a few years before.

I must have been the *Bonassus* himself to have mistaken myself for a genius.
Sir W. Scott.

Bon Chevalier, sans Peur et sans Reproche, Le (lu bŏn shvȧ'lē-ȧ' sŏⁿ pör ā sŏⁿ ru-prōsh'). See GOOD KNIGHT, &c.

Bo'ney. A corruption or diminutive of *Bonaparte*, often used by English writers and speakers in the first part of the present century.

No monks can be had now for love or for money,
(All owing, papa says, to that infidel *Boney*).
Moore.

Bon Gāul'tǐ-ẽr. A pseudonym adopted by Professor William Edmonstoune Aytoun and Theodore Martin, under which they published a popular book of ballads, and contributed to a number of periodicals.

Bonhomme, Jacques (zhȧk bo'-nom'). [Fr., Jack or James Goodman]. A derisive name given by the French barons of the fourteenth century to the peasants of the country. The insurrection known as the *Jacquerie* — which derived its name from this epithet — was a terrible uprising of this class against the nobles, in 1358.

Jacques Bonhomme had a longer memory than his representative on this side of the water [England]; and while the descendants of Wat Tyler's followers were comfortable church-and-king men, when the great trial came, in 1793, the men of the Jacquerie were boiling with revenge for centuries of wrong, and poured forth the concentrated wrath of generations on clergy, noble, and crown.
Rev. John White.

Bon'i-fáce. The name of a landlord in Farquhar's comedy, "The Beaux' Stratagem," — one of the best representatives of the English innkeeper in the language; hence, a landlord in general.

"Oh! I beg your pardon," replied the Yankee *Boniface;* "I meant no offence."
Putnam's Mag.

Bono Johnny. The sobriquet by which, in the East, the English are commonly designated.

Bontemps, Roger (ro'zhä' bŏn'tŏⁿ', 62). A popular personification, in France, of a state of leisure, and freedom from care. The equivalent, among the French peasantry, for the English proverb, "There's a good time coming," is "Roger Bontemps." This character is the subject of one of Béranger's most celebrated songs, written in 1814:—

To show our hypochondriacs,
In days the most forlorn,
A pattern set before their eyes,
Roger Bontemps was born.
To live obscurely at his will,
To keep aloof from strife, —
Hurrah for fat *Roger Bontemps!*
This is his rule of life.

. . . .

Ye envious poor ; ye rich who deem
Wealth still your thoughts deserving ;
Ye who in search of pleasant tracks
Yet find your cap is swerving;
Ye who the titles that ye boast
May lose by some disaster, —
Hurrah for fat *Roger Bontemps!*
Go, take him for your master.
Béranger, Trans.

Booby, Lady. A female character of frail morals, in Fielding's novel of "Joseph Andrews," who is unable to conquer the virtue of her footman. She was designed as a caricature of Richardson's "Pamela," and is represented as a vulgar upstart, whom the parson is compelled to reprove for laughing in church.

Bo-o'tēs. [Gr. Βοώτης, the ox-driver.] (*Gr. & Rom. Myth.*) A son of Ceres, and the inventor of the plough. He was translated to heaven, and made a constellation. According to another account, he was a son of Lycaon and Callisto, and was slain by his father, who set him before Jupiter for a repast, to try the omniscience of the god. Jupiter restored him to life, and placed him among the stars.

Booth. The husband of Amelia, in Fielding's novel of that name. His frailties are said to have shadowed forth some of the author's own backslidings and experiences.

Bo-rä'chĭ-o. A follower of John (bastard brother of Don Pedro, Prince of Arragon), in Shakespeare's "Much Ado about Nothing."

Borak, Al. See AL BORAK.

Border, The. In history and in popular phraseology, the common frontier of England and Scotland, which, until comparatively modern times, shifted to the north or to the south, according to the surging tide of war or diplomacy. From the eleventh century to about the beginning of the eighteenth century, ruthless wars between the two countries, and feuds and forays of clans and families, caused almost constant disturbance on the border. Strenuous efforts were made during the reigns of Elizabeth and James VI. to preserve peace; but it was not until the legislative union of 1707 took place, that the long course of misrule was finally brought to a close.

Border Minstrel. A title often given to Sir Walter Scott, who traced his descent from the great border family now represented by the dukes of Buccleuch; resided at Abbotsford on the Tweed; edited, in early life, a collection of old ballads under the title of "The Minstrelsy of the Scottish Border;" and afterward wrote "The Lay of the Last Minstrel," and other original poems upon border subjects.

When last along its banks I wandered,
Through groves that had begun to shed
Their golden leaves upon the pathways,
My steps the *Border Minstrel* led.
Wordsworth, Yarrow Revisited.

Border States. Previous to the Rebellion, a common designation of those Slave States, in the American Union, which bordered upon the line of the Free States; namely, Delaware, Maryland, Virginia, Kentucky, and Missouri. With the abolition of slavery throughout the United States, the name will soon pass out of current use.

Border-thief School. A name formerly given, to some extent, to Sir Walter Scott and his poetical imitators, who celebrated the adventures of various predatory chiefs of the Scottish border.

With your Lake Schools, and *Border-thief Schools*, and Cockney and Satanic Schools, there has been enough to do. *Carlyle.*

Bo're-as (9). [Gr. Βορέας.] (*Gr. & Rom. Myth.*) The north wind, a son of Astræus and Aurora. He is fabled to have carried off Orithyia, the daughter of Erechtheus, and by her to have had Zetes and Calais, winged

and for the Remarks and Rules to which the numbers after certain words refer, see pp. xiv-xxxii.

warriors, who accompanied the Argonautic expedition.

Bors, *or* **Bort, King.** See BOHORT, SIR.

Boston Bard. A pseudonym assumed by Robert S. Coffin (1797-1827), an American versifier who lived for some years in Boston, Massachusetts.

Boston Massacre. (*Amer. Hist.*) A name popularly given to a disturbance which occurred in the streets of Boston on the evening of March 5, 1770, when a sergeant's guard belonging to the British garrison fired upon a crowd of people who were surrounding them and pelting them with snow-balls, and killed three men, besides wounding several others. The leader of the towns-people was a black man named Crispus Attucks. The affair is of historical importance, as it prepared the minds of men for the revolutionary struggle which followed.

Boston Tea-party. A name popularly given to the famous assemblage of citizens in Boston, Dec. 16, 1773, who met to carry out the non-importation resolves of the colony, and who, disguised as Indians, went on board three English ships which had just arrived in the harbour, and destroyed several hundred chests of tea. The British parliament retaliated by closing the port of Boston.

Bottle, Oracle of the Holy. See HOLY BOTTLE, ORACLE OF THE.

Bottle Riot. A disturbance which took place at the theatre in Dublin, Dec. 14, 1822, in consequence of the unpopularity of the Marquess Wellesley (Richard Colby, the younger), Lord Lieutenant of Ireland; so called from the circumstance of a bottle being thrown into his box. [Called also *The Bottle Conspiracy*.]

Bottom, Nick. An Athenian weaver, who is the principal actor in the interlude of "Pyramus and Thisbe," in Shakespeare's "Midsummer-Night's Dream." Oberon, the fairy king, desiring to punish Titania, his queen, commissioned Puck to watch her till she fell asleep, and then to anoint her eyelids with the juice of a plant called love-in-idleness, the effect of which, when she awoke, was to make her dote upon Bottom, upon whom Puck had fixed an ass's head.

"Bottom . . . is a compound of profound ignorance and omnivorous conceit; but these are tempered by good-nature, decision, of character, and some mother-wit. That which gives him his individuality does not depend upon his want of education, his position, or his calling. All the schools of Athens could not have reasoned it out of him; and all the gold of Crœsus would have made him but a gilded Bottom after all. . . . His descendants have not unfrequently appeared among the gifted intellects of the world. When Goldsmith, jealous of the attention which a dancing monkey attracted in a coffee-house, said, 'I can do that as well,' and was about to attempt it, he was but playing Bottom." *R. G. White.*

Indeed, the caresses which this partiality leads him [Milton] to bestow on "Sad Electra's pot," sometimes remind us of the beautiful queen of fairy-land kissing the long ears of Bottom. *Macaulay.*

Pity poor Robinson [Sir Thomas Robinson], O English reader, if you can, for indignation at the business he is in. Saving the liberties of Europe! thinks Robinson confidently: Founding the English National Debt, answers Fact; and doing *Bottom the Weaver*, with long ears, in the miserablest Pickle-herring tragedy that ever was! *Carlyle.*

Bountiful, Lady. See LADY BOUNTIFUL.

Boustrapa (boo'strä'pä'). A sobriquet given to the Emperor Napoleon III., in allusion to his unsuccessful attempts at a *coup d'état* at Boulogne (in 1840) and *Str*asbourg (in 1836), and his successful attempt at *Pa*ris (in 1851), while President of the French Republic.

Bower of Bliss. 1. A garden belonging to the beautiful enchantress Armida, in Tasso's "Jerusalem Delivered." It is described as lovely beyond description, every thing in the place contributing to harmony and sweetness, and breathing forth the fulness of bliss. Here Rinaldo and Armida, in love with each other, pass their time; but at last two knights come and release Rinaldo from his enervating and dishonourable servitude. See ARMIDA.

2. The dwelling of the witch

Acrasia, in Spenser's "Faëry Queen," Bk. II., c. 12. Acrasia is represented as a beautiful and fascinating woman, and her residence, which is situated upon a floating island, is described as being embellished with every thing calculated to charm the senses and wrap the soul in oblivious indulgence.

Bōw'ling, Tom. The name of a celebrated naval character in Smollett's novel of "Roderick Random."

☞ "The character of Tom Bowling, in 'Roderick Random,' . . . will be regarded in all ages as a happy exhibition of those naval heroes to whom Britain is indebted for so much of her happiness and glory." *Dunlop.*

Box and Cox. The title of a "dramatic romance of real life," by John M. Morton, and the names of its principal characters.

Boy-bishop, The. An appellation conferred upon St. Nicholas (fourth century), on account of his early conformity to the observances of the Roman Catholic church, of which the old legends relate marvellous instances.

Boy-et'. A lord attending on the princess of France, in Shakespeare's "Love's Labour's Lost."

Bŏz (*by some pron.* bōz). A pseudonym under which Charles Dickens contributed a series of "Sketches of Life and Character" to the "London Morning Chronicle." Of this *nom de plume* he has given the following account:—

☞ "Boz, my signature in the 'Morning Chronicle,' . . . was the nickname of a pet child, a younger brother, whom I had dubbed Moses, in honour of the 'Vicar of Wakefield,' which, being facetiously pronounced through the nose, became *Boses,* and being shortened, *Boz. Boz* was a very familiar household word to me long before I was an author, and so I came to adopt it."

Though a pledge I had to shiver,
And the longest ever was,
Ere his vessel leaves our river
I would drink a health to *Boz. Hood.*

Boz'zy. A familiar diminutive of the surname of James Boswell (1740-1822), the friend and biographer of Dr. Samuel Johnson, by whom the nickname was coined.

Brȧ-ban'ti-o (brȧ-ban'shĭ-o). A senator of Venice, in Shakespeare's play of "Othello."

Brad'a-mănt, *or* **Bradamante** (brȧ-dȧ-mȧn'tȧ). A Christian Amazon, sister to Rinaldo, and mistress of Ruggiero, in Bojardo's "Orlando Innamorato" and Ariosto's "Orlando Furioso." She possessed an irresistible spear, which unhorsed every antagonist whom it touched. See RUGGIERO. [Written also B r a n-d a m a n t e.]

☞ "I do not think Bradamante or Brandamante is ever mentioned in old romances, and I greatly suspect her to be Bojardo's own invention." *Panizzi.*

Brad'wȧr-dīne, Baron. A brave and gallant, but pedantic, character in Scott's "Waverley."

Brad'wȧr-dīne, Rose. The heroine of Sir Walter Scott's novel of "Waverley;" the daughter of Baron Bradwardine, and the lover of Waverley, whom she finally marries.

Brag, Jack. The hero of a novel of the same name by Theodore Hook (1789-1841), a spirited embodiment of the arts employed by a vulgar pretender to creep into aristocratic society.

In reality, however, he was a sort of literary *Jack Brag.* As that amusing creation . . . mustered himself with sporting gentlemen through his command over the technicalities or slang of the kennel and the turf, so did Hazlewood sit at the board with scholars and aristocratic book-collectors through a free use of their technical phraseology. *J. H. Burton.*

Brag, Sir Jack. A sobriquet of General John Burgoyne (d. 1792), who figures in an old ballad entitled "Sir Jack Brag."

Bragi (brȧ'gee). [Old Norse *bragga,* to adorn, embellish. Comp. Eng. *brag.*] (*Scand. Myth.*) The son of Odin and Frigga, the husband of Iduna, and the god of poetry and eloquence; represented as an old man with a long, flowing beard, and a brow mild and unwrinkled. [Written also B r a g u r, B r a g a.]

Bragmardo, Janotus de (jȧ-no'tus

de brăg′mar-do; *Fr. pron.* zhä′no′-tüıs′ du brâg′mar′do′, 102). The name of a sophister in Rabelais' satirical romance of "Gargantua," sent by the citizens of Paris to remonstrate with Gargantua for having carried off the bells of the church of Notre-Dame, which he had taken to suspend at the neck of his mare.

Brah′mă. (*Hindu Myth.*) The supreme, self-existent god of the Hindus, usually represented with four heads and four arms. He is regarded as the creator of the universe, and forms, with Vishnu, the preserver, and Siva, the destroyer, the divine *Trimurti*, or triad, consisting of the three principal gods of the Brahminical faith. It is said that he has descended upon the earth nine times, in various forms, and is yet to appear a tenth time, in the figure of a warrior upon a white horse, to visit retribution upon all incorrigible offenders. [Written also B r a m a, and sometimes B r u h m a.]

Brainworm. A curious, tricky character in Ben Jonson's play of "Every Man in his Humour."

Bramble, Matthew. A well-known character in Smollett's novel, "The Expedition of Humphry Clinker;" described as "an odd kind of humourist," afflicted with the gout, and "always on the fret," but full of generosity and benevolence.

To have all literature swum away before us in watery extempore, and a spiritual time of Noah supervene, — that, surely, is an awful reflection, worthy of dyspeptic *Matthew Bramble* in a London fog. *Carlyle.*

Bramble, Miss Tabitha. An unmarried sister of Matthew Bramble, in Smollett's "Expedition of Humphry Clinker." She is characterised as "a maiden of forty-five, exceeding starched, vain, and ridiculous," soured by her unsuccessful endeavours to get married, proud, imperious, prying, malicious, greedy, and uncharitable. She finally succeeds in disposing of herself to Captain Lismahago, who is content to take her on account of her snug little fortune of £4000. Her personal appearance is thus described: —

☞ "She is tall, raw-boned, awkward, flat-chested, and stooping; her complexion is sallow and freckled; her eyes are not gray, but greenish, like those of a cat, and generally inflamed; her hair is of a sandy, or, rather, dusty, hue; her forehead low; her nose long, sharp, and, toward the extremity, always red in cool weather; her lips skinny; her mouth extensive; her teeth straggling and loose, of various colours and conformation; and her long neck shrivelled into a thousand wrinkles."

Bră-mine′, The. A name given by Sterne (1713–1768) to Mrs. Elizabeth Draper, a young woman of English parentage, born in India, for whom he conceived a most violent and injudicious affection. In calling her "The Bramine," he obviously intended a reference to the country of her birth. For himself he provided a corresponding name, — "The Bramin," — suggested apparently by his profession of a clergyman. In 1775, ten letters of Sterne to Mrs. Draper were published under the title of "Letters to Eliza."

Bran. The name of Fingal's dog. See FINGAL.

☞ "Our Highlanders have a proverbial saying, founded on the traditional renown of Fingal's dog. 'If it is not Bran,' they say, 'it is Bran's brother.' Now this is always taken as a compliment of the first class, whether applied to an actual cur, or, parabolically, to a biped." *Sir W. Scott.*

In process of time, the noble dog slept with *Bran*, Luarth, and the celebrated hounds of antiquity. *Sir W. Scott.*

Brandan, Island of St. See ISLAND OF ST. BRANDAN.

Bran′di-mart. [It., swords-lover.] A character in Bojardo's "Orlando Innamorato," and in Ariosto's "Orlando Furioso," king of the Distant Islands.

Brandy Nan. A nickname given to Queen Anne, in her lifetime, by the populace, in allusion to her fondness for brandy.

Brang′tŏns, The. Characters in the novel of "Evelina," by Miss Burney. Their name became a synonym for vulgarity, malice, and jealousy.

Brass, Sally. Sister to Sampson

Brass, whom she surpasses in villany. See *infra*.

Brass, Sampson. A knavish attorney in Dickens's "Old Curiosity Shop," distinguished for his servility, dishonesty, and affected sentimentality.

Bravest of the Brave. [Fr. *Le Brave des Braves*.] A title conferred upon the celebrated Marshal Ney (1769-1815) by the French troops at Friedland (1807), on account of his fearless bravery. He was in command of the right wing, which bore the brunt of the battle, and stormed the town. Napoleon, as he watched him passing unterrified through a shower of balls, exclaimed, "That man is a lion;" and henceforth the army styled him the Bravest of the Brave.

Bray, The Vicar of. See VICAR OF BRAY.

Brazen Age. [Lat. *Ænea œtas*.] (*Gr. & Rom. Myth*.) One of the four ages or eras into which the ancient poets divided the history of the human race. It was a period of wild warfare and violence, presided over by Neptune. The silver age preceded it, and the iron age followed it. See IRON AGE, SILVER AGE.

Bread and Cheese Land. See BIDDENDEN MAIDS.

Breeches Bibles. A name given to editions of the so-called Genevan Bible (first printed at Geneva, by Rowland Hall, 1560, in 4to), from the peculiar rendering of *Gen*. iii. 7.

Breeches Review. A name formerly given, among booksellers, to the "Westminster Review," from a Mr. Francis Place, a great authority with the "Westminster." This Place was at one time a leather-breeches maker and tailor at Charing-cross, London.

Bren'dă. Daughter of Magnus Troil, and sister to Minna, in Sir Walter Scott's "Pirate."

Breng'wăin. The confidante of Isolde, and a prominent character in the romances which treat of the love of Isolde and Sir Tristram. [Written

also Bringwain, Brengein, Brangwaine, Brangwayne.]

Brent'förd, The Two Kings of. Two characters in "The Rehearsal," a celebrated farce, written by George Villiers, Duke of Buckingham (1627-1688), with the assistance of Butler, Sprat, and others, in order to correct the public taste by holding up the heroic or rhyming tragedies to ridicule.

☞ The two kings are represented as walking hand in hand, as dancing together, as singing in concert, and, generally, as living on terms of the greatest intimacy and affection. There seems to have been no particular reason for making them kings of Brentford rather than of any other place. Bayes says (a. 1., sc. 1), "Look you, sirs, the chief hinge of this play . . . is, that I suppose two kings of the same place, as, for example, at Brentford; for I love to write familiarly." Colonel Henry Howard, son of Thomas, Earl of Berkshire, wrote a play called "The United Kingdoms," which began with a funeral, and had also two kings in it. It has been supposed that this was the occasion of Buckingham's setting up two kings in Brentford, though some are of opinion that he intended them for the two royal brothers, Charles II. and the Duke of York, afterward James II. Others say that they represent Boabdelin and Abdalla, contending kings of Granada. But it is altogether more probable that they were designed to burlesque the two kings contending for one and the same crown introduced by Dryden — the Bayes of the piece — into several of his serious plays. Persons who have been known to hate each other heartily for a long time, and who afterward profess to have become reconciled, and to be warm friends, are often likened to the *Two Kings of Brentford*.

This piece of generosity reminds us of the liberality of the *Kings of Brentford* to their Knightsbridge forces. *Sir W. Scott*.

Brewer of Ghent. A descriptive title bestowed upon Jacob Arteveld, a brewer of metheglin in Ghent, who became a great popular leader in the early part of the fourteenth century, drove Louis I., Count of Flanders, into France, ruled that province, and supported Edward III. of England.

Brĭ-ā'rẹ-us (9). [Gr. Βριάρεως.] (*Gr. & Rom. Myth*.) A son of Cœlus and

Terra, a giant with a hundred arms and iiity heads. According to Hesiod, he defended Jupiter against the Titans; but other poets say that he assisted the giants in their attempt to storm Olympus, and was buried alive under Mount Ætna as a punishment. [Called also *Ægeon*.]

Brick, Mr. Jef'fẽr-son (-sn). A fiery American politician, who figures in Dickens's novel of "Martin Chuzzlewit."

Jefferson Brick, the American editor, twitted me with the multifarious patented anomalies of overgrown, worthless Dukes, Bishops of Durham, &c., which poor English society at present labours under, and is made a solecism by. *Carlyle.*

Bride of the Sea. A poetical name of Venice, having its origin in the ancient ceremony of the espousal of the Adriatic, during which the doge, in the presence of his courtiers, and amid circumstances of great splendour, threw a ring into the sea, uttering the words, "*Desponsamus te, mare, in signum veri perpetuique dominii,*" We wed thee, O sea, in sign of a true and perpetual dominion.

Bridge'north, Major Ralph. A Roundhead who figures conspicuously in Scott's "Peveril of the Peak."

Bridge of Asses. See PONS ASINORUM.

Bridge of Sighs. [It. *Ponte dei Sospiri*.] The name popularly given to the covered passage-way which connects the doge's palace in Venice with the state prisons, from the circumstance that the condemned prisoners were transported over this bridge from the hall of judgment to the place of execution. Hood has used the name as the title of one of his poems.

Bridget, Mrs. The name of a character in Sterne's celebrated novel, "The Life and Opinions of Tristram Shandy, Gent."

Bridlegoose, Judge. [Fr. *Juge Bridoye*.] The name of a character in Rabelais' famous satirical romance of "Pantagruel," who decided causes by the chance of dice.

Brid'oison (brē'dwŏ'zŏn', 62). A stupid judge in Beaumarchais' "Mariage de Figaro."

Brighella (brē-ḡel'lä). [It., from *briga*, trouble, restlessness.] A masked character in the Italian popular comedy, representing a proud, bold, and crafty plebeian of Brescia.

Brigliadoro (brēl-yä-do'ro). [It., bridle of gold.] The name of Orlando's steed, one of the most famous coursers in romance, and second only to Bajardo.

Bri-se'is. [Gr. Βρισηίς.] (*Gr. & Rom. Myth.*) The daughter of Briseus, a priest at Lyrnessus. She fell into the hands of Achilles, but was afterward forced from him by Agamemnon. [Called also *Hippodamia*.]

British Ar'is-ti'dēṣ. An epithet frequently applied to Andrew Marvell (1620-1678), an influential member of the House of Commons during the reign of Charles II., and a firm opponent of the king. His integrity was such that he refused every offer of promotion and a direct bribe tendered him by the lord treasurer, and died in poverty, being buried at the expense of his constituents.

British Jeremiah. A title given by Gibbon to Gildas, a British historian, who is said to have flourished in the first half of the sixth century. Wright considers him a fabulous person.

The British Jeremiah ... is so pleased to find, or so determined to invent, topics for declamatory lamentation or praise, that it is difficult to distinguish the basis of truth from the fantastic superstructure of exaggeration and falsehood with which he has overloaded it. *Edin. Rev.*

British Pạu-sā'ni-ạs. An epithet conferred upon William Camden (1551-1623), one of the most distinguished scholars and learned antiquaries of his age.

Brit'o-mar'tis, or **Brit'o-mart.** [Gr. Βριτόμαρτις, from the Cretan words βριτύς, sweet, and μάρτις, maid.] 1. (*Gr. & Rom. Myth.*) A Cretan nymph, daughter of Jupiter and Carme; a Cretan epithet of Diana, who loved her, assumed her name, and was worshipped under it.

2. "A lady knight," representing Chastity, whose adventures are re-

BRI 59 BRO

lated in Spenser's "Faëry Queen." She is represented as being armed with a magic spear, which nothing could resist.
She charmed at once, and tamed the heart, Incomparable *Britomart!* Sir W. Scott.

rittany, Eagle of. See EAGLE OF BRITTANY.

road Bottom Ministry. (*Eng. Hist.*) A name derisively given to an administration comprising nine dukes and a grand coalition of all parties of weight and influence in the state, formed in Nov. 1744, and dissolved by the death of Mr. Pelham, March 6, 1755.

The names of the original members were,—
The Rt. Hon. Henry Pelham, First Lord of the Treasury, and Chancellor of the Exchequer.
Duke of Dorset, President of the Council.
Earl Gower, Lord Privy Seal.
Duke of Newcastle, } Secretaries of
Earl of Harrington, } State.
Duke of Montagu, Master of the Ordnance.
Duke of Bedford, First Lord of the Admiralty.
Duke of Grafton, Lord Chamberlain.
Duke of Richmond, Master of the Horse.
Duke of Argyll, Keeper of the Great Seal of Scotland.
Marquess of Tweeddale, Secretary of State for Scotland.
Lord Hardwicke, Lord Chancellor.

From this administration, the particular adherents of Pulteney (newly created Earl of Bath) and Lord Carteret were carefully excluded.

rob'ding-nag. An imaginary country described in Swift's celebrated romance entitled "Gulliver's Travels." The inhabitants are represented as giants, about "as tall as an ordinary spire-steeple." Every thing else is on the same enormous scale. [Written also Brobdignag, an orthography which, though not that of Swift, has acquired a prescriptive title to be considered well authorised.]

Greatness with Timon dwells in such a
  draught
As brings all *Brobdignag* before your thought.
  Pope.

When Sir Thomas Lawrence paints a handsome peeress, he does not contemplate her through a powerful microscope, and transfer

to the canvas the pores of the skin, the bloodvessels of the eye, and all the other beauties which Gulliver discovered in the *Brobdignagian* maids of honour. *Macaulay.*

Bron'zo-mar'te. The name of Sir Launcelot Greaves's steed, in Smollett's "Adventures" of that celebrated hero; represented to be "a fine mettlesome sorrel who had got blood in him."

Brook, Master. A name assumed by Ford, in Shakespeare's "Merry Wives of Windsor," with a design to dupe Sir John Falstaff, who is in love with Ford's wife. The amorous knight duly reports to Master Brook the progress of his suit to Mrs. Ford, and the various contrivances by which he escapes the search of her jealous husband, one of which was that of being carried out of the house concealed in a heap of foul linen.

Brother Jonathan. A sportive collective name for the people of the United States.

☞ When General Washington, after being appointed commander of the army of the Revolutionary war, went to Massachusetts to organise it, and make preparations for the defence of the country, he found a great want of ammunition and other means necessary to meet the powerful foe he had to contend with, and great difficulty in obtaining them. If attacked in such a condition, the cause might at once be lost. On one occasion, at that anxious period, a consultation of the officers and others was had, when it seemed no way could be devised to make such preparation as was necessary. Jonathan Trumbull, the elder, was then governor of Connecticut, and, as Washington placed the greatest reliance on his judgment and aid, he remarked, "We must consult Brother Jonathan on the subject." He did so, and the governor was successful in supplying many of the wants of the army. When difficulties afterward arose, and the army was spread over the country, it became a by-word, "We must consult Brother Jonathan." The origin of the expression being soon lost sight of, the name Brother Jonathan came to be regarded as the national sobriquet. The foregoing account is from the "Norwich (Connecticut) Courier;" but it has more recently been suggested that the expression originally had reference to Captain Jonathan Carver (1732-1780), an early American traveller among the Indians, from whom he received large grants

d for the Remarks and Rules to which the numbers after certain words refer, see pp. xlv-xxxii.

of lands, in the deeds conveying which he is repeatedly styled "our dear brother Jonathan." Carver published in London, in 1778, an octavo volume entitled, "Travels through the Interior Parts of North America, in the years 1766, '67, and '68." As the work was extensively read, the author became a sort of representative man of his countrymen; and it is not difficult to see how the odd designation given him by the Indians might be caught up and applied to all Americans. The following citation, however, from an old pamphlet, satirising the Puritan innovations in the arrangement and furniture of churches, would seem to imply that the name originated at a much earlier day, and that it was at first applied to the Roundheads, or parliamentary party in the time of Charles I.:—

"Queen Elizabeth's monument was put up at my charge when the regal government had fairer credit among us than now, and her epitaph was one of my *Brother Jonathan's* best poems, before he abjured the University, or had a thought of New England."
The Reformado precisely characterized by a transformed Churchwarden at a Vestry, London, 1643.

If you knock my old friend John Bull on the head, I mean to take up with *Brother Jonathan*,— who, after all, is a very decent fellow, and, in my opinion, more likely to have peace and quiet under his own fig-tree, by and by, than any other gentleman of our acquaintance. *Noctes Ambrosianæ.*

Brown the Younger, Thomas. A pseudonym under which Thomas Moore, in 1813, published the "Twopenny Post-bag," a series of witty, playful, and very popular satires, directed against the prince regent and his ministers.

Brû'in. [D. *bruin*, brown.] In the German epic poem of "Reinecke the Fox," the bear is called by this name; hence, a bear in general.

Brunehild (broo'nä-hilt'), *or* **Brunhilde** (broon-hĭl'dä). [O. H. Ger. *brunihild*, from *bruni, brunja*, coat of mail, and *Hilti*, goddess of war, from *hilt*, battle, contest.] A proud warrior-virgin in the German epic, the "Nibelungen Lied," who promised to be the bride of the man who could conquer her in three trials, in hurling the lance, in throwing the stone, and in leaping after the stone when thrown. By the arts and bravery of Siegfried, she was deluded into marrying Günther, king of Burgundy; but, discovering the trick that had been put upon her, she planned and accomplished the destruction of Siegfried, and the humiliation of Chriemhild, his wife, who was her rival. The story of Brunchild forms a large part of the cycle of ancient German romance. See CHRIEMHILD. [Written also Brunhilt, Brynhilda, and Brynhild.]

Brû-nel'lo. A thievish dwarf in Bojardo's "Orlando Innamorato," who, besides other exploits, steals Angelica's magic ring, and, by means of it, releases Rogero from a castle in which he is imprisoned.

Brute, Sir John. A character in Vanbrugh's play, "The Provoked Wife," distinguished for his absurdities and coarse, pot-house valour.

Bubble, Law's. See LAW'S BUBBLE.

Bubble, South-Sea. See SOUTH-SEA BUBBLE.

Bubble Act. (*Eng. Hist.*) The name popularly given to an act (6 Geo. I., c. 18) passed in 1719, and designed to punish unprincipled adventurers who proposed schemes — popularly called Bubbles — merely as baits to extract money from the ignorant or thoughtless. It was repealed July 5, 1825.

Bu-ceph'ȧ-lus. [Gr. βουκεφάλας, Macedonian, βουκέφαλας, bull-headed, from βους, bullock, and κεφαλή, head.] The name of a celebrated horse of Alexander the Great, who was the first to break him in, and who thus fulfilled the condition stated by an oracle as necessary for gaining the crown of Macedon.

Buckeye State. The State of Ohio; popularly so called from the buckeye-tree (*Æsculus flava*), which abounds there.

Buddha (bōōd'ȧ). [Sansk., wise, sage, from *budd*, to know.] One of the beings worshipped or venerated by the Buddhists, a sect of religionists including more than one third of the human race, and spreading over the greater part of Central and Eastern Asia, and the Indian islands. The term is used to designate either the historical founder of Buddhism, — a

☞ For the "Key to the Scheme of Pronunciation," with the accompanying Explanations,

Hindu sage named Gautama, who is thought to have lived in the sixth century, B. C., — or one of his fabulous prototypes or successors, of whom there are many, of different classes. [Written also Budha, Boodh, Bhood, Budh, and in many other ways. Hardy, in his "Manual of Buddhism," gives a list of more than fifty varieties which had fallen under his notice.]

Bull, John. A well-known collective name of the English nation, first used in Arbuthnot's satire, "The History of John Bull," usually published in Swift's works. In this satire, the French are designated as Lewis Baboon, the Dutch as Nicholas Frog, &c. The "History of John Bull" was designed to ridicule the Duke of Marlborough.

☞ "There is no species of humour in which the English more excel than that which consists in caricaturing and giving ludicrous appellations or nicknames. In this way, they have whimsically designated, not merely individuals, but nations; and, in their fondness for pushing a joke, they have not spared even themselves. One would think, that, in personifying itself, a nation would be apt to picture something grand, heroic, and imposing; but it is characteristic of the peculiar humour of the English, and of their love for what is blunt, comic, and familiar, that they have embodied their national oddities in the figure of a sturdy, corpulent old fellow, with a three-cornered hat, red waistcoat, leather breeches, and stout oaken cudgel. Thus they have taken a singular delight in exhibiting their most private foibles in a laughable point of view, and have been so successful in their delineation, that there is scarcely a being in actual existence more absolutely present to the public mind than that eccentric personage, John Bull." *W. Irving.*

Buller of Brazenose. A name given in Wilson's "Noctes Ambrosianæ" to John Hughes (of Oriel College, — not Brazenose, — Oxford), author of an "Itinerary of the Rhone," and of other works.

Bully Dawson. See DAWSON, BULLY.

Bum'ble, Mr. A character in Dickens's novel of "Oliver Twist."

Bunch, Mother. See MOTHER BUNCH.

Bun'cle, John (bungk'l). The hero of a fantastic book entitled "The Life of John Buncle, Esq.; containing various Observations and Reflections made in several parts of the World, and many Extraordinary Relations." He is said to be the representative of his author, Thomas Amory (1691-1789), an eccentric person of whose history little is known. See ENGLISH RABELAIS, 3.

☞ "John is a kind of innocent 'Henry the Eighth of private life,' without the other's fat, fury, and solemnity. He is a prodigious hand at matrimony, at divinity, at a song, at a loud 'hem,' and at a turkey and chine. He breaks with the Trinitarians as confidently and with as much scorn as Henry did with the Pope; and he marries seven wives, whom he disposes of by the lawful process of fever and small-pox. His book is made up of natural history, mathematics (literally), songs, polemics, landscapes, eating and drinking, and characters of singular men, all bound together by his introductions to, and marriages with, these seven successive ladies, every one of whom is a charmer, a Unitarian, and cut off in the flower of her youth. Buncle does not know how to endure her loss; he shuts his eyes 'for three days;' is stupefied; is in despair; till suddenly he recollects that Heaven does not like such conduct; that it is a mourner's business to bow to its decrees; to be devout; to be philosophic; — in short, to be jolly, and look out for another dear, bewitching partner, 'on Christian principles.' This is, literally, a fair account of his book." *Leigh Hunt.*

Oh for the pen of *John Buncle,* to consecrate a *petit souvenir* to their memory [Lamb's Wednesday-evening parties]! *Hazlitt.*

Bun'combe (bungk'um). A cant or popular name, in the United States, for a body of constituents, or for an oratorical display intended to win popular applause. [Written also Bunkum.]

☞ According to the Hon. William Darlington, the phrase "speaking for Buncombe" originated near the close of the debate on the famous "Missouri Question," in the sixteenth Congress. It was then used by Felix Walter, a *naïve* old mountaineer, who resided at Waynesville, in Haywood, the most western county of North Carolina, near the border of the adjacent county of Buncombe, which formed part of his district. The old man rose to speak, while the House was impatiently calling for the "question," and several members gathered round him, begging him to desist. He persevered, however, for a while, declaring that the people of his district expected it, and that he was bound to "make a speech for Buncombe."

Bundschuh (boont'shoo). [Ger., a kind of large shoe which went over the ankle and was tied up.] (*Ger. Hist.*) A name given to the insurrection of the peasants in the first half of the sixteenth century, because the insurgents carried a clouted shoe as an ensign upon a pole, and even upon their banners.

Bunsby, Jack. A commander of a ship in Dickens's "Dombey and Son," looked up to as an oracle and philosopher by his friend Captain Cuttle. He is described as wearing a "rapt and imperturbable manner," and seeming to be "always on the lookout for something in the extremest distance."

Bunyan, Bishop. See BISHOP BUNYAN.

Buovo d' Agramonte (boo-o'vo dä-grä-mon'tä). See BEUVES D'AYGREMONT.

Bur'chell, Mr. A prominent character in Goldsmith's "Vicar of Wakefield," who passes himself off as a poor man, but is really a baronet in disguise, his true name being Sir William Thornhill. He is noted for his habit of crying out "Fudge!" by way of expressing his strong dissent from, and contempt for, the opinions of others, or his disbelief of their assertions.

Burd Helen. [*Burd*, according to Jamieson, is a Scottish form of *bird*, used as a term of endearment. But see *infra*.] A heroine of Scottish ballad and tradition, renowned for her resolute constancy. She is borne away to Elfland by the fairies, and imprisoned in a castle, from which she is rescued by her brother, the Childe Rowland. See ROWLAND, CHILDE.

☞ "*Burd* is the Scottish feminine of the French *preux* or *prud'homme*. The *preux chevalier* was brave and wise, the *Burd* of Scottish song was discreet." *Yonge.*

Buri (boo'ree). [Old Norse, producer.] (*Scand. Myth.*) The progenitor of the gods. See AUDHUMBLA. [Written also **Bure**.]

Burleigh, Lord. See LORD BURLEIGH.

Burly King Harry. See BLUFF HAL.

Burnbill. A name given to Henry de Londres, Archbishop of Dublin and Lord Justice of Ireland, in the reign of Henry III. He is said to have fraudulently procured and burnt all the instruments by which the tenants of the archiepiscopal estates held their lands.

Bū-si'ris (9). [Gr. Βούσιρις.] (*Myth.*) An Egyptian king, son of Neptune. He was a monstrous giant, who fed his horses on human flesh. He was finally slain by Hercules.

Buttermere, Beauty of. See BEAUTY OF BUTTERMERE.

Buz'fuz, Sergeant. A character in Dickens's "Pickwick Papers."

Byb'lis. [Gr. Βυβλίς.] (*Gr. & Rom. Myth.*) A daughter of Miletus, who wept herself into a fountain from a hopeless passion for her brother Caunus.

Bycorne. See CHICHEVACHE.

By'ron, Miss Harriet (9). A beautiful and accomplished woman of high rank, devotedly attached, and finally married, to Sir Charles Grandison, in Richardson's novel of this name.

☞ For the "Key to the Scheme of Pronunciation," with the accompanying Explanations,

C.

Cabal, The. (*Eng. Hist.*) A name given to a famous cabinet council formed in 1670, and composed of five unpopular ministers of Charles II.; namely, Lords Clifford, Ashley, Buckingham, Arlington, and Lauderdale. The word "cabal"—at that time in common use to denote a *junto*, or *set of men united for political purposes*—having been popularly applied to this ministry as a term of reproach, it was soon discovered to be a sort of anagram made up of the initials of the names of the several members.

Caballero, Fernan (fēr-nȧn′ kȧ-bȧl-yȧ′ro, 82). A *nom de plume* of Doña Cecilia Arrom, one of the most popular living writers of Spain. She is the author of various tales, which present truthful and lively pictures of Andalusian manners.

Cȧ-bi′rï (9). [Gr. Κάβειροι.] (*Myth.*) Mystic divinities anciently worshipped in Egypt, Phœnicia, Asia Minor, and Greece. They were regarded as inferior in dignity to the great gods, and were probably representatives of the powers of nature. [Written also C a b e i r e i.]

Cā′cus. (*Rom. Myth.*) An Italian shepherd, usually called a son of Vulcan, and described by Ovid as a fearful giant. He was a most notorious robber, and was slain by Hercules for stealing his oxen.

> There you will find the Lord Rinaldo of Montalban, with his friends and companions, all of them greater thieves than *Cacus*.
> *Cervantes, Trans.*

> Our hero, feeling his curiosity considerably excited by the idea of visiting the den of a Highland *Cacus*, took, however, the precaution to inquire if his guide might be trusted.
> *Sir W. Scott.*

Caddee. See LEAGUE OF GOD'S HOUSE.

Cȧ-de′nus. A name under which Swift describes himself in his poem of "Cadenus and Vanessa." *Cadenus* is the Latin word *decanus* (dean), by transposition of letters. See VANESSA.

Cadenus, indeed, believe him who will, has assured us, that, in such a perilous intercourse, he himself preserved the limits which were unhappily transgressed by the unfortunate Vanessa, his more impassioned pupil.
Sir W. Scott.

Cad′mus. [Gr. Κάδμος.] (*Gr. & Rom. Myth.*) A son of Agenor, king of Phœnicia, and a brother of Europa. He is the reputed founder of the city of Thebes, in Bœotia; and he is said to have invented, or at least to have brought from Phœnicia, the old Greek alphabet of sixteen letters, namely, α β γ δ ε ι κ λ μ ν ο π ρ σ τ υ. These are called *Cadmean letters*. They were afterward increased by the addition of eight more, named *Ionic letters*, namely, ς η θ ξ φ χ ψ ω.

Cȧ-du′ce-us. [Lat., from Gr. κηρύκειον, a herald's wand, Æolic καρύκειον (r being changed into its cognate, d), from κήρυξ, a herald.] (*Gr. & Rom. Myth.*) A winged staff or rod, with two serpents entwined about it; an attribute of Mercury.

Cad′wạl. A feigned name assumed by Arviragus in Shakespeare's "Cymbeline." See ARVIRAGUS.

Cæc′u-lus. (*Rom. Myth.*) A son of Vulcan, a robber, and the reputed founder of Præneste.

Cagliostro, Count de (kȧl-yos′tro). The assumed name of Joseph Balsamo (1743–1795), one of the most impudent and successful impostors of modern times.

Cā′ius, Dr. A French physician, in Shakespeare's "Merry Wives of Windsor."

Bad in themselves [certain portions of Boswell's "Life of Johnson"], they are good dramatically, like . . . the clipped English of Dr. *Caius*.
Macaulay.

Calandrino (kȧ-lȧn-dre′no). The subject of a story in Boccaccio's "Decameron" (Day 8, Tale 9). His mishaps, as Macaulay states, "have made all Europe merry for more than four centuries."

Cal′chas. [Gr. Κάλχας.] (*Gr. & Rom. Myth.*) A famous soothsayer

and for the Remarks and Rules to which the numbers after certain words refer, see pp. xiv-xxxii.

who accompanied the Greeks to Troy.

Cal'e-dŏn. A poetical contraction of *Caledonia*. See CALEDONIA.

Not thus, in ancient days of *Caledon*,
Was thy voice mute amid the festal crowd.
Sir W. Scott.

Cal'e-do'ni-ā. The ancient Latin name of Scotland, often used as a synonym of Scotland in modern poetry.

O *Caledonia*, stern and wild,
Meet nurse for a poetic child!
Sir W. Scott.

Calendars, The Three. See THREE CALENDARS, THE.

Cal'ī-bȧn. [A metathesis of *cannibal*.] A savage and deformed slave of Prospero, in Shakespeare's "Tempest." He is represented as being the "freckled whelp" of Sycorax, a foul hag, who was banished from Argier (or Algiers) to the desert island afterward inhabited by Prospero.

☞ "Caliban ... is all earth, all condensed and gross in feelings and images: he has the dawnings of understanding, without reason or the moral sense; and in him, as in some brute animals, this advance to the intellectual faculties, without the moral sense, is marked by the appearance of vice."
Coleridge.

The quantity of furious abuse poured out against the Bourbons might have authorised the authors to use the words of *Caliban*,—
"You taught me language, and my profit
  on 't
Is—I know how to curse." *Sir W. Scott.*

Cal'ī-burn. See EXCALIBUR.

Cal'ī-dore. [Gr., beautifully gifted.] A knight in Spenser's "Faëry Queen," typical of courtesy, and supposed to be intended as a portrait of Sir Philip Sidney.

In reality, he [Sir Gawain] was the *Calidore* of the Round Table. *Southey.*

Cȧ-lip'o-lis. A character in "The Battle of Alcazar" (1594), an inflated play attributed by Dyce to George Peele, a dramatist of the Elizabethan age;—referred to by Pistol, in Shakespeare's "2 Henry IV.," a. ii., sc. 4.

Hark ye, most fair *Calipolis*, ... if thou takest all that trouble of skewering thyself together, like a trussed fowl, that there may be more pleasure in the carving, even save thyself the labour. *Sir W. Scott.*

Cȧ-lis'tȧ. The name of the heroine of Rowe's "Fair Penitent," characterised as

"haughty, insolent,
And fierce with high disdain."

No high *Calista* that ever issued from story-teller's brain will impress us more deeply than this meanest of the mean, and for a good reason,—that she issued from the maker of men. *Carlyle.*

Cal-lī'o-pe. [Gr. Καλλιόπη, the beautiful-voiced.] (*Gr. & Rom. Myth.*) One of the nine Muses. She presided over eloquence and epic poetry, or poetry in general, and was the mother of Orpheus and Linus. She was usually represented with a style and waxen tablets.

Cal-lis'to. [Gr. Καλλιστώ.] (*Gr. & Rom. Myth.*) An Arcadian nymph, and a favourite of Jupiter, who metamorphosed her into a she-bear, that their intimacy might not become known to Juno. Her son Arcas having met her in the chase, one day, was on the point of killing her, but Jupiter prevented him by placing both of them in the heavens as the Great Bear and the Little Bear.

Cal'ȳ-dŏn. A forest supposed to have occupied the northern portion of Great Britain; very celebrated in the romances relating to King Arthur and Merlin.

Cȧ-lyp'so. [Gr. Καλυψώ.] (*Gr. & Rom. Myth.*) A daughter of Atlas. She was one of the Oceanides, and reigned in the island of Ogygia, whose situation and even existence are doubted. Here she received Ulysses, on his way home from Troy, entertaining him with great hospitality, and promising him immortality if he would remain with her as a husband. Ulysses refused, and, after seven years' delay, he was permitted to depart by order of Mercury, the messenger of Jupiter.

A solitary rover, in such a voyage, with such nautical tactics, will meet with adventures. Nay; as we forthwith discover, a certain *Calypso*-island detains him at the very outset, and, as it were, falsifies and oversets his whole reckoning. *Carlyle.*

Camacho (kä-mä'cho.) A character in an episode in Cervantes's "Don Quixote," who gets cheated out of his bride after having made great preparations for their wedding.

☞ For the "Key to the Scheme of Pronunciation," with the accompanying Explanations,

Camaralzaman, Prince. See PRINCE CAMARALZAMAN.

Cam′bā-lū. In the "Voyages" of Marco Polo, the chief city of the province of Cathay. It is now identified with Pekin.

Cam′brī-ạ. The ancient Latin name of Wales, often used by modern poets. It is derived from *Camber*, the son of Brutus, a legendary king of Britain. Brutus at his death left the isle to his three sons, one of whom, Camber, received the western part.

When stars through cypress-boughs are gleaming,
And fire-flies wander bright and free,
Still of thy harps, thy mountains dreaming,
My thoughts, wild *Cambria*, dwell with thee.
Mrs. Hemans.

Cam′bus-can, or **Cam-bus′căn.** A king of Tartary, in Chaucer's "Squier's Tale," to whom, upon the anniversary of his birthday, the king of Araby and Ind sends as presents a brazen horse capable of transporting his rider into the most distant region of the world in the space of twenty-four hours; a mirror of glass endued with the power of discovering the most hidden machinations of treason, and of showing any disasters which might threaten to befall the possessor; a naked sword which could pierce armour deemed impenetrable; and a ring — intended for Canace, Cambuscan's daughter — which would enable the owner to understand the language of every species of birds, and the virtues of every plant. The poem ends abruptly, the conclusion of the story having either been lost, or never written.

☞ "I think that it is not unlikely that Chaucer had seen 'The Travels of Marco Polo,' and that *Cambuscan*, or Cambu's Can, is a contraction of *Cambalu Can*. We may observe that the name of one of his sons is *Camballo*. Of Algarsif, the other son, I can give no account. The name of his daughter, Canace, is Greek. *Keightley.*

☞ "It is strange that Milton should have pronounced the word *Cambus′can*; nor is it pleasant, when his robust line must be resounding in the ear of every one to whom the story is called to mind, to be forced to obey even the greater dictation of the original, and throw the accent, as undoubtedly it ought to be thrown, on the first and last syllable. On no theory, as respects Chaucer's versification, does it appear intelligible how Milton could have thrown the accent on the second syllable, when the other reading stares us in the face throughout Chaucer's poem."   *Leigh Hunt.*

This noble king, this Tartre *Cambuscan*,
Hadde two sones by Elfleta, his wif,
Of which the eldest sone highte Algarsif,
That other was ycleped Camballo.
Chaucer.

Or call up him that left half told
The story of *Cambuscan* bold,
Of Camball and of Algarsife,
And who had Canace to wife,
That owned the virtuous ring and glass;
And of the wondrous horse of brass
On which the Tartar king did ride. *Milton.*

I have still by me the beginnings of several stories, . . . which, after in vain endeavouring to mould them into shape, I threw aside, like the tale of *Cambuscan*, "left half told."
T. Moore.

Cambyses, King. See KING CAMBYSES.

Cam′de-o. (*Hindu Myth.*) The god of love.

The tenth Avatar comes! at Heaven's command,
Shall Seriswattee wave her hallowed wand,
And *Camdeo* bright and Ganesa sublime
Shall bless with joy their own propitious clime!   *Campbell.*

Cam′e-lŏt. A parish in Somersetshire, England (now called Queen's Camel), where King Arthur is said to have held his court, and where the vast intrenchments of an ancient town or station — called by the inhabitants "King Arthur's Palace" — are still to be seen. It is sometimes erroneously identified with Winchester. Shakespeare alludes to Camelot as being famous for a breed of geese.

Goose, if once I had thee upon Sarum plain,
I'd drive thee cackling home to *Camelot.*
Lear.

Ca-me′næ. (*Rom. Myth.*) Prophetic nymphs, of whom Egeria was the most celebrated. The Roman poets often apply the name to the Muses. [Written also, but improperly, C a- m œ n æ.]

Că-mil′lạ. A virgin queen of the Volscians, famous for her fleetness of foot and her grace. She assisted Turnus in his war against Æneas, and signalised herself by undaunted bravery.

☞ "The first female warrior is the Camilla of Virgil." *Dr. Johnson.*

When Ajax strives some rock's vast weight
  to throw,
The line, too, labours, and the words move
  slow.
Not so when swift *Camilla* scours the plain,
Flies o'er the unbending corn, or skims along
  the main. *Pope.*

Candido (kŏn'dĕd', 62). The hero of Voltaire's celebrated novel of the same name, in which he collects together the most dreadful misfortunes, and heaps them upon the head of a single individual, with the intention, probably, of inculcating a philosophical indifference to the disasters and disappointments and sorrows which inevitably beset human life.

The boy-author [Beckford] appears already to have rubbed all the bloom off his heart; and, in the midst of his dazzling genius, one trembles to think that a stripling of years so tender should have attained the cool cynicism of a *Candide*. *Lond. Qu. Rev.*

Candour, Mrs. A noted slanderer in Sheridan's comedy of "The Rivals."

☞ "The name of 'Mrs. Candour' has become one of those formidable by-words which have more power in putting folly and ill-nature out of countenance than whole volumes of the wisest remonstrance and reasoning." *T. Moore.*

His [Sterne's] friends, ... wrote to him of the rumour [that he had accepted a bribe], and of how the Yorkshire *Mrs. Candours* were circulating that he had furnished all the details of that complacent sketch. *Percy Fitzgerald.*

Că-nid'i-ă. A sorceress often mentioned by Horace. She used wax figures in working her spells and enchantments, and, by her conjurations, she made the moon descend from the heavens.

The savour is sweet, but it hath been cooked by a *Canidia* or an Erichtho. *Sir W. Scott.*

Can-nucks'. A nickname applied to Canadians by people in the United States. [Written also Cunnucks.]

Că-no'pus. [Gr. Κάνωπος.] (*Gr. & Rom. Myth.*) The pilot of Menelaus, killed in Egypt by the bite of a poisonous serpent, when returning from Troy. He was buried by Menelaus on the site of the town of Canopus, which derived its name from him. According to some accounts, Canopus was worshipped in Egypt as a divine being, and was represented in the shape of a jar with small feet, a thin neck, a swollen body, and a round back. [Written also Canobus.]

Capability Brown. Launcelot Brown, a famous English gardener of the last century; — so called from his constant use of the word "capability," as well as on account of his genius for making sterile or naked grounds fruitful and beautiful.

There is a very large artificial lake [at Blenheim], which was created by *Capability Brown*, and fills the basin that he scooped for it, just as if Nature had poured these broad waters into one of her own valleys. *Hawthorne.*

Cap'ă-neûs. [Gr. Καπανεύς.] (*Gr. Myth.*) One of the seven heroes who marched from Argos against Thebes. He was killed with a thunder-bolt by Jupiter for impiously saying that not even the fire of Jupiter should prevent him from scaling the walls of the city. See EVADNE.

Cape of Storms. See STORMY CAPE.

Capitan (kă'pe'tŏn', 62). A boastful, swaggering, cowardly fellow, who figured in almost all the French farces and comedies previous to the time of Molière.

Caps and Hats. See HATS AND CAPS.

Captain, The Black. See BLACK CAPTAIN, THE.

Captain Loys. [Fr. *Le Capitaine Loys.*] A sobriquet given, by her contemporaries, to Louise Labé (1526–1566), who, in early life, embraced the profession of arms, and gave repeated proofs of the greatest valour.

Captain Right. A fictitious commander — like the Captain Rock of more recent times — whom the peasants in the south of Ireland, in the last century, were sworn to obey.

Captain Rock. The fictitious name of a leader of Irish insurgents about the year 1822, who appeared continually in large masses, among the hills and valleys, and might, at almost any time of night, be met with in the highways. They were said to be under the command of a Captain, or General, Rock, and all the lawless notices they issued were signed in his name. The term is supposed to have been a common imaginary title

☞ For the "Key to the Scheme of Pronunciation," with the accompanying Explanations,

CAP 67 CAR

adopted by the chief confederates,— whose identity was never established.

Cap'u-let. The head of a noble house of Verona, in Shakespeare's tragedy of "Romeo and Juliet,"—hostile to the house of Montague. He is represented as a jovial, testy old man, self-willed, violent, and tyrannical.

Cap'u-let, Lady. Wife of Capulet, in Shakespeare's tragedy of "Romeo and Juliet."

☞ "Then Lady Capulet comes sweeping by with her train of velvet, her black hood, her fan, and her rosary,— the very *beau-ideal* of a proud Italian matron of the fifteenth century, whose offer to poison Romeo in revenge for the death of Tybalt stamps her with one very characteristic trait of the age and country. Yet she loves her daughter; and there is a touch of remorseful tenderness in her lamentation over her which adds to our impression of the timid softness of Juliet and the harsh subjection in which she has been kept." *Mrs. Jameson.*

☞ The Capulets and Montagues (*Capelletti* and *Montecchi*, or *Monticoli*) were two rival houses of Verona in the latter part of the thirteenth and the early part of the fourteenth centuries. The familiar expression, "the tomb of the Capulets," does not occur in Shakespeare. It has not been found in any author previous to Burke, and probably originated with him. In a letter to Matthew Smith, he says, "I would rather sleep in the corner of a little country church-yard than in *the tomb of all the Capulets.*"

Căr'ȧ-băs, Marquis of. [Fr. *Marquis de Carabas*, mar'ke' dü kȧ'rȧ'bȧ']. A fanciful title employed to designate a man who possesses, or makes a boast of possessing, large estates; a feudal lord; or, in general, any pompous and purse-proud individual. The name occurs in the nursery tale, "Puss in Boots," and Béranger has adopted it as the title of one of his most popular lyrics. See PUSS IN BOOTS.

"See this old marquis treating us
As if a conquered race:
His raw-boned steed has brought him back
From distant hiding-place.
With sabre brandished o'er his head
That never dealt a blow,
The noble mortal marches on,
And seeks his old chateau.
Hats off, hats off! near and far,
Bow to the *Marquis of Carabas.*"
Béranger, Trans.

The States General assembled May 1, 1789. The delegates of the poor were to meet under the same roof with the titled aristocrats who had trampled on their social rights and domestic affections so long, with the mitred lords who had extracted their last sheaves of corn. The opponents sat face to face—the pale, thoughtful, and emaciated face of the suffering and revengeful *tiers-état*, the bloated, handsome, and contemptuous face of the high-born bishop and polished duke. They must have looked at each other with strangely ominous eyes when they met for the first time, and Jacques Bonhomme examined the *Marquis de Carabas* across the gulf of so many hundred years. *Rev. J. White.*

In Vivian Grey, his [Disraeli's] views seemed bounded by a desire to find a *Marquis de Carabas*. *Smiles.*

Căr'ȧ-doc. A knight of the Round Table, distinguished for his valour, but yet more as the husband of a chaste and constant lady, the only dame in Queen Guinever's train who could wear a certain mantle designed to prove matrimonial fidelity. He was surnamed *Brief-Bras*, or "Shrunken-Arm," a Norman corruption of *Friech-Fras*, or "Strong-Arm." To explain the reason of the former epithet, the later romancers feigned that a wicked enchanter caused a serpent to fasten on Caradoc's arm, and suck his flesh and blood, and that no human power was able to assuage his pain, or remove the reptile. Caradoc is the hero of an old ballad entitled "The Boy and the Mantle."

Căr'ȧ-this. The mother of the Caliph Vathek, in Beckford's tale of this name; represented as an adept in judicial astrology and magic.

Cardenio (*Sp. pron.* kar-dā'ne-o). A distracted lover— the dupe of a perfidious friend — whose adventures form an episode in the history of "Don Quixote."

Car'du-el (6). A name given, in the old romances about Arthur and his knights, to the city of Carlisle.

Car'kẽr, Mr. A plausible villain in Dickens's "Dombey and Son."

Car'lo Khan. A nickname given to Charles James Fox (1749–1806), on account of a bill which he brought into Parliament, in 1783, for a new regulation of the East Indies, from the supposition that he aimed to establish a dictatorship in his own person.

---

and for the Remarks and Rules to which the numbers after certain words refer, see pp. xiv-xxxii.

Carlyle, Jupiter. See JUPITER CARLYLE.

Carmilhan. See KLABOTERMANN.

Car'pi-o, Ber-nar'do del. A very ancient mythical, or semi-mythical, hero of Christian Spain, who signalised himself, chiefly in the Moorish army, by his chivalrous deeds. He is said to have been an illegitimate son of Don Sancho, Count of Saldaña, and of Doña Ximena, a sister of King Alfonso, surnamed The Chaste. He is a favourite hero in the old Spanish romances and ballads, in which the honour is claimed for him of slaying the famous Orlando, or Roland, on the fatal field of Roncesvalles.

Car-răs'co, Samson. [Sp. *Sanson Carrasco*, sän-sōn' kaŕ-räs'ko.] A waggish bachelor of Salamanca who figures in Cervantes's romance, "Don Quixote."

He may perhaps boast of arresting the general attention, in the same manner as the bachelor *Samson Carrasco*, of fixing the weather-cock La Giralda of Seville for weeks, months, or years, that is, for as long as the wind shall uniformly blow from one quarter.
Sir W. Scott.

Car-taph'i-lus. See JEW, THE WANDERING.

Casella (kä-zel'lä). The name of a musician and old friend of Dante, immortalised by him in his poem entitled "La Divina Commedia." Dante, on his arrival in Purgatory, sees a vessel approaching freighted with souls, under the conduct of an angel, to be cleansed from their sins, and made fit for Paradise. When they are disembarked, the poet recognises in the crowd his old friend Casella. In the course of an affectionate interview, the poet requests a soothing air, and Casella sings, with enchanting sweetness, Dante's second canzone.

Dante shall give fame leave to set thee higher
Than his *Casella*, whom he wooed to sing,
Met in the milder shades of Purgatory.
Milton.

Cas'ĭ-mere. A Polish emigrant in "The Rovers, or The Double Arrangement," in the poetry of the "Anti-Jacobin." See BEEFINGTON, MILOR.

Cas-san'drᾰ. [Gr. Κασσάνδρα.] (*Gr. & Rom. Myth.*) A beautiful daughter of Priam and Hecuba. According to the poets, she possessed the gift of prophecy, but none believed her predictions.

Cassim Baba. See BABA, CASSIM.

Cas'si-o (kash'i-o). Lieutenant of Othello, and a tool of Iago, in Shakespeare's tragedy of "Othello."

Indeed, I have so poor a brain myself, when I impose upon it the least burden beyond my usual three glasses, that I have only, like honest *Cassio*, a very vague recollection of the confusion of last night. *Sir W. Scott.*

Cas-si'o-pe, *or* **Cas'si-o-pe'i-ᾰ** (20). [Gr. Κασσιόπη, Κασσιόπεια.] (*Gr. & Rom. Myth.*) The wife of Cepheus, and the mother of Andromache. She was an Ethiopian by birth, and was so proud of her beauty that she even exalted it above that of the sea-nymphs, and thus incurred their enmity. After death she was placed among the stars, forming the constellation popularly known as "The Lady in her Chair." [Written also Cassiepeia.]

That starred Ethiop queen that strove
To set her beauty's praise above
The sea-nymphs, and their powers offended.
Milton.

Cas'tᾰ-lȳ. A poetical form of *Castalia*, the name of a spring at the foot of Mt. Parnassus, sacred to Apollo and the Muses. The poets feigned that its waters filled the mind of those who drank of it with poetic inspiration.

Cas-tā'rᾰ. [Probably from Lat. *casta*, fem. of *castus*, chaste; perhaps *casta ara*, sacred altar.] A poetical name under which William Habington (1605-1654) celebrated the praises of Lucia, daughter of the first Lord Powis, the lady whom he married.

Castle, Doubting. See DOUBTING CASTLE.

Castle of Indolence. The title of a poem by Thomson, and the name of a castle described in it as situated in a pleasing land of drowsiness, where every sense was steeped in the most luxurious and enervating delights. The owner of this castle was a powerful enchanter, who sought by the exercise of magical arts to entice unwary passers-by within the gate, that he might deprive them of their manly strength, take away all their high hopes and aims, and engage them in a constant round of sensual amusements.

<small>The effect of the climate, the air, the serenity and sweetness of the place, is almost as seductive as that of the *Castle of Indolence*.
W. Irving.</small>

Castles in Spain. See CHÂTEAUX EN ESPAGNE.

Castlewood, Beatrix. The heroine of Thackeray's novel of "Esmond;" "perhaps the finest picture of splendid, lustrous physical beauty ever given to the world."

Cas'tŏr. [Gr. Κάστωρ.] (*Gr. & Rom. Myth.*) A son of Leda, and a brother of Pollux, or Polydeuces. According to some writers, they were twins, and Jupiter was their father; others assert that they were the sons of Tyndareus, king of Lacedæmon; others, again, say that Pollux was the son of Jupiter, and Castor of Tyndareus. Hence Pollux was immortal, while Castor was subject to old age and death, like other men. But such was the mutual affection of the two brothers, that Jupiter granted the prayer of Pollux, and consented that they should share each other's lot, by living, alternately, one day in the under-world, and the next in heaven. According to a different form of the story, he rewarded their attachment by placing them among the stars as *Gemini*, or "The Twins," which never appear together, but when one rises the other sets. [Castor and Pollux are sometimes called the *Dioscuri*, or "Sons of Jove," and *Tyndaridæ*, or "Sons of Tyndareus."]

Ca̧-thāy'. An old name for China, said to have been introduced into Europe by Marco Polo, the celebrated Venetian traveller. It is corrupted from the Tartar appellation *Khitai* (ke-tī'), that is, the country of the Khitans, who occupied the northern portions of the empire at the period of the Mongol invasion. The heroine of Bojardo's "Orlando Innamo-

rato," the beautiful Angelica, was a princess of Cathay.

<small>Through the shadow of the globe we sweep Into the younger day ;
Better fifty years of Europe than a cycle of Cathay.
Tennyson.</small>

Catholic Majesty. A title first given in 739 by Gregory III. to Alfonso I. of Spain, who was thereupon surnamed The Catholic. The title was also given to Ferdinand V., in 1474. It was bestowed upon Ferdinand and his queen by Innocent VIII., on account of their zeal for the Roman Catholic religion, and their establishment of the Inquisition in Spain.

Cā'to-Street Conspiracy. (*Eng. Hist.*) A plot of a gang of low and desperate politicians to murder the ministers of the crown at a cabinet-dinner at Lord Harrowby's, with the view of raising an insurrection in London, and overthrowing the government. The conspirators were arrested in Cato Street, Feb. 23, 1820, and Thistlewood — one of the ringleaders — and four of his chief associates, having been convicted of treason, were executed May 1.

Caudle, Mrs. Margaret. The feigned author of a series of "Curtain Lectures" delivered in the course of thirty years, between eleven at night and seven in the morning, to her husband, Mr. Job Caudle, "one of the few men whom Nature, in her casual bounty to women, sends into the world as patient listeners." The real author of these humourous and famous lectures was Douglas Jerrold.

<small>Violante was indeed a bewitching child, — a child to whom I defy *Mrs. Caudle* herself (immortal *Mrs. Caudle !*) to have been a harsh step-mother.
Sir E. Bulwer Lytton.</small>

Câu'line, Sir. The hero of an ancient English ballad of the same name, preserved in Percy's "Reliques."

Câu'nus. [Gr. Καῦνος.] See BYBLIS.

Caustic, Christopher. A pseudonym adopted by Thomas Green Fessenden (1771-1837) in his Hudibrastic poem called "Terrible Tractoration."

Caustic, Colonel. A prominent char-

<small>and for the Remarks and Rules to which the numbers after certain words refer, see pp. xiv-xxxii.</small>

acter in "The Lounger," sketched by Henry Mackenzie. He is "a fine gentleman of the last age, somewhat severe in his remarks upon the present."

Cautionary Towns. (*Eng. Hist.*) A name given to the towns of Briel, Flushing, Rammekins, and Walcheren, which were placed, in 1585, in Queen Elizabeth's possession as security for the payment of troops furnished by her to the Netherlands. Only one third of the sum was refunded; but the Cautionary Towns were, notwithstanding, delivered up, July 14, 1616, a treaty for this purpose having been signed May 22.

Cave of Mam'mǒn. The abode of the god of riches, described in the seventh canto of the second book of Spenser's "Faëry Queen."

☞ "By what subtle art of tracing the mental processes it is effected, we are not philosophers enough to explain ; but in that wonderful episode of the Cave of Mammon, in which the Money God appears first in the lowest form of a miser, is then a worker of metals, and becomes the god of all the treasures of the world, and has a daughter, Ambition, before whom all the world kneels for favours, — with the Hesperian fruit, the waters of Tantalus, with Pilate washing his hands vainly, but not impertinently, in the same stream, — that we should be at one moment in the cave of an old hoarder of treasures, at the next at the forge of the Cyclops, in a palace and yet in hell, all at once, with the shifting mutations of the most rambling dream, and our judgment yet all the time awake, and neither able nor willing to detect the fallacy, is a proof of that hidden sanity which still guides the steps in the wildest seeming aberrations." *Charles Lamb.*

Cave of Montesinos. See MONTESINOS.

Ce'crops. [Gr. Κέκρωψ.] (*Gr. Myth.*) The first king of Attica, described as an autochthon, the upper part of whose body was human, while the lower part was that of a dragon. He is said to have instituted marriage, altars, and sacrifices, and to have introduced agriculture, navigation, and commerce.

Cĕd'ric. A Saxon thane, of Rotherwood, in Sir Walter Scott's novel of "Ivanhoe."

Cel'a-dǒn. 1. The hero of an episode in the poem of "Summer," in Thomson's "Seasons;" in love with Amelia, who is described as having been killed in his arms by a stroke of lightning.

2. A poetical name for any swain, or rustic lover.

Had we been the *Celadon* and Chloe of a country village, he could not have regarded us as more equal, so far as the world went.
Sir E. Bulwer Lytton.

Ce-læ'no. [Gr. Κελαινώ.] (*Gr. & Rom. Myth.*) One of the Harpies. See HARPIES.

Celestial City. In Bunyan's "Pilgrim's Progress," the city toward which Christian makes his pilgrimage; — the heavenly Jerusalem, whose splendours are portrayed in the Apocalypse.

Celestial Empire. A name often used, in Europe and America, as a popular designation of China. It is derived, according to Williams, from the Chinese words *Tien Chan*, that is, Heavenly Dynasty, meaning the kingdom ruled over by the dynasty appointed by Heaven.

Celia. 1. Daughter of Frederick, the usurping duke, in Shakespeare's "As You Like It."

2. The name given by Thomas Carew, an English poet of the seventeenth century, to his lady-love, whose real name is unknown.

Célimène (sā'le'mān', 31, 103). 1. A misanthrope in Molière's "Les Précieuses Ridicules."

2. A coquette in Molière's "Misanthrope," — an admirable portrait.

Cen'taurs. [Lat. *Centauri*, Gr. Κένταυροι, bull-killers.] (*Gr. & Rom. Myth.*) According to the earliest accounts, a rude and savage people of Thessaly, afterward described as monsters half man and half horse, and particularly celebrated for their contest with the Lapithæ. See LAPITHÆ.

Century White. A sobriquet given to John White (1590–1645), a barrister and political writer of the time of the English Commonwealth, from his principal publication, "The First Century of Scandalous Malignant Priests, Made and Admitted into Benefices by the Prelates," &c.

Ceph'ạ-lus. [Gr. Κέφαλος.] (*Gr. & Rom. Myth.*) The husband of Procris. See PROCRIS.

Ce'pheūs (28). [Gr. Κηφεύς.] (*Gr. & Rom. Myth.*) 1. One of the Argonauts.
2. King of Ethiopia, husband of Cassiopeia, and father of Andromeda.

Cẽr'be-rus (4). [Gr. Κέρβερος.] (*Gr. & Rom. Myth.*) A dog with three heads, a serpent's tail, and a snaky mane, who guarded the portal of Hades, into which he admitted the shades, but from which he never let them out again. Hercules overcame him, and brought him away.

Ce'res (9). (*Gr. & Rom. Myth.*) The daughter of Saturn and Ops, sister of Jupiter, Pluto, Neptune, Juno, and Vesta, mother of Proserpine, and goddess of corn, harvest, and flowers. She is usually represented as riding in a chariot drawn by dragons; with a torch or a basket in her hand, and crowned with poppies or ears of corn.

Cẽr'ĭ-mŏn. A lord of Ephesus, in Shakespeare's "Pericles."

Ce'yx. [Gr. Κήϋξ.] (*Gr. & Rom. Myth.*) See ALCYONE.

Chad'band, The Rev. Mr. A character in Dickens's "Bleak House;" a type of hypocritical piety.

Chạ-mont'. One of the *dramatis personæ* in Otway's tragedy of "The Orphan."

Why, Heaven love you! I would as soon invite a fire-brand into my stack-yard.—he's an Almanzor, a *Chamont*. *Sir W. Scott.*

Champion of the Virgin. A title given to St. Cyril of Alexandria. See DOCTOR OF THE INCARNATION.

Chăr'ĭ-tḗṣ. [Gr. Χάριτες.] (*Gr. & Rom. Myth.*) The Graces. See GRACES.

Charlies. A sobriquet given to the members of the London police force previous to its reorganisation by Sir Robert Peel in 1829. They were so called from King Charles I., who, in 1640, extended and improved the police system of the metropolis.

Char'mĭ-ạn. A kind-hearted but simple-minded female attendant on Cleopatra, in Shakespeare's play of "Antony and Cleopatra."

Chā'rŏn. [Χάρων.] (*Gr. & Rom. Myth.*) A god of Hades, son of Erebus and Nox. He was an aged and dirty ferry-man, who conducted the souls of the buried dead across the river Styx. See STYX.

Chạ-ryb'dis. [Gr. Χάρυβδις.] (*Gr. & Rom. Myth.*) A ravenous woman, turned by Jupiter into a dangerous gulf or whirlpool on the coast of Sicily, opposite to Scylla, on the coast of Italy. See SCYLLA.

Scylla wept,
And chid her barking waves into attention,
And fell *Charybdis* murmured soft applause.
Milton.

Châteaux en Espagne (shä'tōz' ŏn nes'păn', 62, 78). [Fr., castles in Spain.] Groundless or visionary projects; a French phrase sometimes used in English. In the fifteenth century, they said, in the same sense, "*faire des châteaux en Asie*," to build castles in Asia.

Chauvin (shō'văn', 62). The principal character in Scribe's "Soldat Laboureur;" represented as a veteran soldier of the time of the first Empire, having an unbounded admiration of Napoleon, and a blind idolatry of all that pertains to him.

Cherubim, Don. See DON CHERUBIM.

Chevalier de St. George. See ST. GEORGE, CHEVALIER DE.

Chev'y Chase. The subject and the title of a famous old English ballad. The event which is commemorated is probably the battle of Otterburn, which happened in August, 1388, and is declared by Froissart to have been the bravest and most chivalrous which was fought in his day; but it is impossible to reconcile the incidents of the poem with history.

☞ "According to the ballad, Percy vowed that he would enter Scotland, and

---

and for the Remarks and Rules to which the numbers after certain words refer, see pp. xiv-xxxii.

take his pleasure for three days in the woods of his rival, and slay the deer therein at will. Douglas, when he heard the vaunt, exclaimed: 'Tell him he will find one day more than enough.' Accordingly, at the time of the hay-harvest, Percy, with stag-hounds and archers, passed into the domains of his foe, and slew a 'hundred fallow-deer and harts of grice.' When the English had hastily cooked their game, and were about to retire, Earl Douglas, clad in armour and heading his Scottish peers, came on the scene. Haughty challenge and defiance passed between the potentates, and the battle joined. In the centre of the fray the two leaders met. 'Yield thee, Percy!' cried Douglas. 'I will yield to no Scot that was ever born of woman!' cried Percy. During this colloquy, an English arrow struck Douglas to the heart. 'Fight on, my merry men!' cried he, as he died. Percy, with all the chivalrous feeling of his race, took the dead man by the hand, and vowed that he would have given all his lands to save him, for a braver knight never fell by such a chance. Sir Hugh Montgomery, having seen the fall of Douglas, clapped spurs to his horse, dashed on Percy, and struck his spear through his body a long cloth-yard and more. Although the leaders on both sides had fallen, the battle, which had begun at break of day, continued till the ringing of the curfew-bell. When the battle ended, representatives of every noble family on either side of the border lay on the bloody greensward."
Chambers.

☞ "I never heard the old song of Percy and Douglas, that I found not my heart moved more than with a trumpet."
Sir Philip Sidney.

Chicaneau (she′kȧ′nō′). A litigious tradesman in Racine's comedy, "Les Plaideurs."

Chicard (she′kar′, 64). [From the originator, a M. Chicard.] The Harlequin of the modern French carnival. His costume is composed of the most various and incongruous articles, but generally includes a helmet, a postilion's wig, a flannel shirt, and cavalry trousers. His arms are half bare, and are thrust into buff gloves with large cuffs.

Chichevache (shĕsh′văsh′). [Fr., said to signify literally, "melancholy, or sour visage."] [Written also Chichefache and Chinch-

vache.] A fabulous monster. Chaucer alludes to it near the close of "The Clerkes Tale." The following is Tyrwhitt's note on the place: —

☞ "This excellent reading is restored upon the authority of the best MSS. Instead of the common one, *Chechivache*. The allusion is to the subject of an old ballad, which is still preserved in MS. Harl. 2251, fol. 270, b. It is a kind of pageant, in which two beasts are introduced, called Bycorne and Chichevache. The first is supposed to feed upon obedient husbands, and the other upon patient wives; and the humour of the piece consists in representing Bycorne as pampered with a superfluity of food, and Chichevache as half starved."

Childe Harold. See HAROLD, CHILDE.

Childe Rowland. See ROWLAND, CHILDE.

Child of Hale. A name often given to John Middleton, a famous English giant, who was born at Hale, in Lancashire, in 1578. His height was nine feet and three inches, " wanting but six inches," says Dr. Plott, " of the size of Goliath."

Children in the Wood. Two characters in an ancient and well-known ballad entitled " The Children in the Wood, or The Norfolk Gent.'s Last Will and Testament," which is thought by some to be a disguised recital of the alleged murder of his nephews by Richard III. It is certain that the ballad corresponds essentially with the narrative of the chroniclers. Addison says of the ballad referred to, that it is " one of the darling songs of the common people, and the delight of most Englishmen at some part of their age." See the " Spectator," Nos. 85 and 179.

Chi-mæ′rȧ (9). [Gr. Χίμαιρα.] (*Gr. & Rom. Myth.*) A strange, fire-breathing monster of Lycia, killed by Bellerophon. See BELLEROPHON.

Chinaman, John. A cant or popular name for the Chinese. The earliest known instance of its use is in " A Letter to the Committee of Management of Drury-Lane Theatre, London, 1819," p. 64.

Çhi'rǒn (9). [Gr. Χείρων.] (*Gr. & Rom. Myth.*) The wisest and most famous of all the Centaurs; noted for his skill in music, medicine, and hunting. He was the instructor of Achilles, and many other heroes of Grecian story. Jupiter placed him among the stars, as the constellation *Sagittarius*, or "The Archer."

Çhlo'e. Formerly a very common name, in pastoral poetry, for a mistress or sweetheart, but of late generally appropriated to negresses and spaniels.

Çhlo'ris (9). [Gr. Χλωρίς.] (*Gr. Myth.*) The wife of Zephyrus, and the goddess of flowers; the same with the Roman *Flora*. See FLORA.

Chriemhild (kreem'hilt), *or* Chriemhilde (kreem-hil'då). The heroine of the German epic poem, the "Nibelungen Lied," represented as a woman of the rarest grace and beauty, and rich beyond conception. By the treacherous murder of her husband, she becomes changed from a gentle and loving woman into a perfect fury of revenge. See BRUNEHILD, HAGEN, SIEGFRIED. [Written also Kriemhilt.]

Çhris'tå-bel. 1. The heroine of the old romance of "Sir Eglamour of Artois."
2. A lady in the ancient ballad of "Sir Cauline," the daughter of a "bonnye kinge" in Ireland.
3. A lady in Coleridge's poem of the same name.

Christian. The hero of Bunyan's spiritual romance, "The Pilgrim's Progress." This celebrated allegory describes the awakening of Christian's spiritual fears; his resolution to depart from the City of Destruction, where he had resided; his ineffectual attempts to induce his wife and family and neighbours to accompany him; his departure; and all the incidents, whether of a discouraging or a comforting nature, which befall him on his journey, until he arrives at the Celestial City; the whole being designed to represent the various experiences, internal and external, in the life of a real Christian.

We seem to have fallen among the acquaintances of our old friend *Christian*: sometimes we meet Mistrust and Timorous, sometimes Mr. Hategood and Mr. Lovelust, and then again Prudence, Piety, and Charity.
Macaulay.

Chris'ti-an'å (krist'yǐ-an'å). The wife of Christian, in Bunyan's "Pilgrim's Progress," who sets out with her children to rejoin her husband in the Celestial City, under the guidance of Mr. Great-heart.

One, like the white robes seen by *Christiana* on the Delectable Mountains, is protected from impurity by an inherent virtue; the other, like a virgin fortress, is secured against assault by its forbidding frown and its terrible powers of resistance.
R. G. White.

Christian Çiç'e-ro. A name conferred upon Lucius Cœlius Lactantius, an eminent Christian author of the early part of the fourth century, on account of the remarkable purity and eloquence of his style.

Christian Sen'e-cå. A title sometimes given to Joseph Hall (1574–1656), Bishop of Norwich, an eminent divine, highly esteemed as a moralist.

Christian Vir'ġil. A title given to Marco Girolamo Vida (1490-1566), one of the most learned scholars and most elegant Latin writers of his time. He was the author of a Latin poem in six books, on the life of Christ, the "Christias," which is as close an imitation of the "Æneid" as the great difference in the nature of the subject would permit.

Çhris'tie of the Clint Hill. A character in Scott's novel of "The Monastery;" one of Julian Avenel's retainers.

Christopher, St. See ST. CHRISTOPHER.

Chroniclers, The Rhyming. A series of writers who arose in England about the end of the thirteenth century, and related in verse the fabulous and the authentic history of that country. The most celebrated of them were Layamon, Robert of Gloucester, and Robert de Brunne.

Çhro-non'ho-ton-thol'o-gos. 1. A pompous character in a burlesque tragedy of the same name by Henry Carey.

---
and for the Remarks and Rules to which the numbers after certain words refer, see pp. xiv-xxxii.

2. A nickname given to General John Burgoyne (d. 1792), on account of an inflated address which he delivered to the American Indians during the war of the Revolution.

Chrysalde (kre′sâld′). A character in Molière's "L'École des Femmes;" a friend of Arnolphe.

Chrysale (kre′sâl′). An honest, simple-minded, hen-pecked tradesman, in Molière's comedy, "Les Femmes Savantes."

Chrys′ā-or. [Gr. Χρυσάωρ.] (*Gr. & Rom. Myth.*) A son of Neptune and Medusa, and the father of Geryon by Callirrhoë.

*Chrysaor, rising out of the sea,
Showed thus glorious and thus emulous,
Leaving the arms of Callirrhoë,
For ever tender, soft, and tremulous.*
                  Longfellow.

Chrȳ-se′is. [Gr. Χρυσηίς.] (*Gr. & Rom. Myth.*) Daughter of Chryses, a priest of Apollo. She was famed for her beauty, and for her skill in embroidery. In the course of the Trojan war, she was taken prisoner, and given to Agamemnon, who, however, was obliged to restore her to her father, in order to stop a plague which Apollo sent into the Grecian camp in answer to the prayer of Chryses.

Chuz′zle-wit, Jonas. A character in Dickens's novel of "Martin Chuzzlewit;" distinguished for his mean brutality and small tyranny.

Chuz′zle-wit, Martin. The hero of Dickens's novel of the same name.

Ciç′e-ro of Germany. [Lat. *Cicero Germaniæ*.] A title given to John III., margrave and elector of Brandenburg (1455–1499).

☞ "Nothing struck a discerning public like the talent he had for speaking: spoke 'four hours at a stretch in Kaiser Max's Diets, in elegantly flowing Latin,' with a fair share of meaning too, and had bursts of parliamentary eloquence in him that were astonishing to hear. . . . His bursts of parliamentary eloquence, once glorious as the day, procured him the name of 'Johannes Cicero,' and that is what remains of them, for they are sunk now, irretrievable he and they, into the belly of eternal Night, the final resting-place, I do perceive, of much Ciceronian ware in this world." *Carlyle.*

Ciç′e-ro of the Senate. A title popularly given to George Canning (1770–1827), a distinguished British statesman, and a very eloquent orator.

Ciç′e-ro's Mouth. [Fr. *La Bouche de Cicéron*.] A surname given, for his eloquence, to Philippe Pot (1428–1494), prime minister of Louis XI.

Cid, The. [Sp., lord, from Arab. *seid*.] A title given to Don Rodrigo Laynez, a Spanish nobleman of the eleventh century, by five Moorish generals whom he had vanquished. The title was confirmed by his king. He was also known by the abbreviated name of Ruy Diaz (*i. e.,* Rodrigo, the son of Diego), and was Count of Bivar. In 1065, he was placed by King Sancho at the head of all his armies, whence he acquired the appellation of *Campeador, i. e.,* warrior, champion. He is said to have died at Valencia, in 1100, in the seventy-fourth year of his age. The details of his history are lost in a cloud of romantic fiction. He is regarded as the model of the heroic virtues of his age, and the flower of Spanish chivalry.

Cid Hamet Benengeli. See BEN-ENGELI, CID HAMET.

Cim-me′ri-ąns (9). [Lat. *Cimmerii*, Gr. Κιμμέριοι.] (*Gr. & Rom. Myth.*) In the poems of Homer, a people dwelling " beyond the ocean-stream," in a land where the sun never shines, and where perpetual darkness reigns. Later writers placed them in Italy, near Lake Avernus, and described them as living in dark caverns, exploring metals, and never coming into the light of day.

Cin′dēr-el′lā. [That is, little *cinder-girl*; Fr. *Cendrillon*, Ger. *Aschenbrödel, Aschenputtel*.] The heroine of a well-known fairy tale, represented as the daughter of a king or a rich man, and condemned by a cruel step-mother to act the part of a household drudge, sitting in the ashes, while her more favoured sisters are dressed in finery and live in splendour.

☞ For the "Key to the Scheme of Pronunciation," with the accompanying Explanations,

The story recounts how, by a fairy's help, Cinderella presents herself before a young prince, and gains his love, to the chagrin of her sisters, who had sought to win his favour, and how, when he would pursue her, he loses sight of her, and, at last, by means of a glass slipper, or, as some say, a golden shoe, (the gift of the fairy,) which she had dropped in her flight, and which would fit no other foot but hers, he discovers her, and then marries her.

☞ The story is very wide-spread, and is told with variations in different languages. It is of great antiquity, and probably derived from the East. Among the Germans, the story is mentioned as early as the sixteenth century, in Rollenhagen's "Froschmäuseler." In France, Perrault and Madame D'Aunoy have included it in their "Fairy Tales." A similar story, of Grecian or Egyptian origin, is told of Rhodopis and Psammitichus in Egypt.

Ci-păn'go. A marvellous island, described in the "Voyages" of Marco Polo, the Venetian traveller. It is represented as lying in the eastern seas, some 1500 miles from land, and of its beauty and wealth many stories are related. The island of Cipango was an object of diligent search with Columbus and the early navigators. It is supposed by some to be the same as Japan. [Written also Zipangi and Zipangri.]

Nor will I bestow any more attention or credit to the idea that America is the fairy region of *Zipangri*, described by that dreaming traveller, Marco Polo, the Venetian.
W. Irving.

Cir'ce (4). [Gr. Κίρκη.] (*Gr. & Rom. Myth.*) A daughter of Sol and the oceanid Perse, and a noted sorceress. She lived in the island of Æœa, surrounded with numbers of human beings, whom she had changed by her drugs and incantations into the shape of wolves and lions. When Ulysses, in his wanderings, came to this island, she turned two-and-twenty of his companions into swine; but Ulysses himself, having obtained from Mercury a sprig of the herb *moly*, — of wonderful power to resist sorceries, — went boldly to the palace of the enchantress, remained uninjured by her drugs, and induced her to disenchant his comrades.

Who knows not *Circe*,
The daughter of the Sun, whose charmèd cup
Whoever tasted lost his upright shape,
And downward fell into a grovelling swine?
Milton.

Circumlocution Office. A designation made use of by Dickens in "Little Dorrit," in ridicule of official delays and indirectness. The Circumlocution Office is described as the chief of "public departments in the art of perceiving *how not to do it*." The name has come into popular use as a synonym for governmental routine, or "red tape," or a roundabout way of transacting public business.

☞ "The Administrative Reform Association might have worked for ten years without producing half of the effect which Mr. Dickens has produced in the same direction, by flinging out the phrase, 'The Circumlocution Office.'"
Masson.

Cirongillio of Thrace (the-rŏn-hēl'-ye-o). The hero of an old romance of chivalry by Bernardo de Vargas.

Cities of the Plain. The name often given to Sodom and Gomorrah, the chief of the five cities which were destroyed by fire from heaven (*Gen.* xix.), and their sites covered by the Dead Sea.

Citizen King. A surname popularly given to Louis Philippe, who, in 1830, was placed on the throne of France as the elective king of a constitutional monarchy.

City of Brotherly Love. [Gr. Φιλαδέλφεια, brotherly love.] Philadelphia, the metropolis of Pennsylvania, is sometimes so called, with reference to the signification of the name in Greek.

City of Churches. A name popularly given to the city of Brooklyn, New York, from the unusually large number of churches which it contains.

City of David. A name given to Jerusalem by, King David, who wrested it from the Canaanites, B. C. 1049.

City of Destruction. In Bunyan's "Pilgrim's Progress," the imaginary

and for the Remarks and Rules to which the numbers after certain words refer, see pp. xiv-xxxii.

city, typifying the world, from which Christian started on his pilgrimage to the Celestial City.

City of Elms. A familiar denomination of New Haven, Connecticut, many of the streets of which are thickly shaded with lofty elms.

<small>When happier days shall return, and the South, awakening from her suicidal delusion, shall remember who it was that sowed her sunny fields with the seeds of those golden crops with which she thinks to rule the world, she will cast a veil of oblivion over the memory of the ambitious men who have goaded her to her present madness, and will rear a monument of her gratitude in the beautiful *City of Elms*, over the ashes of her greatest benefactor, — Eli Whitney.
Edward Everett (1861).</small>

City of Enchantments. A magical city described in the story of Beder, Prince of Persia, in the "Arabian Nights' Entertainments."

City of God. The subject and title of St. Augustine's celebrated work ("De Civitate Dei"), written after the sack of Rome by Alaric, to answer the assertion of the pagans that the disasters to their country were a consequence of the desertion of the national deities by the Christians. The City of God comprehends the body of Christian believers, in distinction from the City of the World, which comprises those who do not belong to the Church. The work treats of both cities, but it takes its name from the former only.

<small>The City of the World, whose origin and vicissitudes Augustine had traced, appeared to him under very dismal aspects, and it was toward the *City of God*, of which he was also the Catholic Homer, that all his hopes were turned. *Poujoulat, Trans.*</small>

City of Lanterns. An imaginary cloud-city spoken of in the "Veræ Historiæ" of Lucian, a romance written with a satirical purpose. The voyagers, whose adventures are the subject of the work, sail through the Pillars of Hercules, and are wrecked upon an enchanted island. They next travel through the Zodiac, and arrive at the City of Lanterns. After further adventures, the voyage terminates at the Islands of the Blest. Rabelais probably borrowed his conception of the Island of Lanterns (see ISLAND OF LANTERNS) from this source, which also undoubtedly furnished hints to Le Sage and to Swift.

City of Magnificent Distances. A popular designation given to the city of Washington, the capital of the United States, which is laid out on a very large scale, being intended to cover a space of four miles and a half long, and two miles and a half broad, or eleven square miles. The entire site is traversed by two sets of streets from 70 to 100 feet wide, at right angles to one another, the whole again intersected obliquely by fifteen avenues from 130 to 160 feet wide.

City of Masts. A name often bestowed upon London, in allusion to the magnitude of its commerce.

City of Notions. In the United States, a popular name for the city of Boston, Massachusetts, the metropolis of Yankeedom.

City of Palaces. 1. An appellation frequently given to Calcutta, the capital of British India. The southern portion of the city comprises the principal European residences, many of which are very elegant and even palatial edifices.

<small>The City of Palaces really deserves that appellation. Nothing can be more imposing than the splendid houses of Chowringhee, viewed from the Course, which is a broad carriage-road on the esplanade of Fort William, adjoining the race-course, from which, I presume, it derives its name. *Blackwood's Mag.*</small>

2. A title sometimes given to Edinburgh, but with no great propriety.

City of Peace. A name sometimes given to Jerusalem, which was anciently called *Salem*, a word meaning "peace."

City of Rocks. A descriptive name popularly given, in the United States, to the city of Nashville, Tennessee.

City of Spindles. A name popularly given to the city of Lowell, Massachusetts, the largest cotton-manufacturing town in the United States.

City of the Great King. A name sometimes given to Jerusalem, which is so called in *Psalm* xlviii. 2, and in *Matt.* v. 35.

City of the Prophet. [Arab. *Medinat al Nabi.*] A name given to Medina, in Arabia, because here Mahomet was protected when he fled from Mecca, July 16, 622,—a flight known in history as the *Hegira*, and forming an important epoch in chronology.

City of the Straits. A name popularly given to Detroit, which is situated on the west bank of the river or strait connecting Lake St. Clair with Lake Erie. *Détroit* is a French word, meaning "strait."

City of the Sun. 1. A translation of *Baalbec*, or *Balbec*, a ruined town of Syria, once of great size, magnificence, and importance. Its Greek name, *Heliopolis*, has the same signification.

2. [Lat. *Civitas Solis*, Fr. *Cité du Soleil.*] A city placed by Thomas Campanella (1568-1639) in the ideal republic which he constructed after the manner of Plato, and in which he depicts a perfect society organised somewhat like a convent, and established upon the principles of a theocratic communism.

City of the Tribes. A name given to Galway, in Ireland, as having been the residence of thirteen "tribes," or chief families, who settled here about the year 1235, and whose names were Burke, Blake, Budkin, Martin, Athy, Browne, D'Arcy, Joyce, Kirwan, Lynch, Morris, Ffont, Skerrett.

City of the Violated Treaty. A name given to the city of Limerick, in Ireland, on account of the repeated violations of a treaty signed Oct. 1691, the first article of which was, that the Roman Catholics should enjoy such privileges in the exercise of their religion as they enjoyed in the reign of Charles II.

☞ " Years of unjust and vindictive penal laws, which are now, happily, swept away, show that this name was well founded." *Knight.*

City of the Violet Crown. An epithet of Athens. The origin of the name is obscure, and its meaning doubtful. It may possibly have reference to the situation of Athens in the central plain of Attica, surrounded by hills or lofty mountains on every side but the south,—where it is open to the sea,—and to the gorgeous rosy and purple tints in which they are bathed by the rising and setting sun. But it is to be observed that the epithet ἰοστέφανος, violet-crowned, is applied to the people of Athens as well as to the city itself.

He [Pitt] loved England as an Athenian loved the *City of the Violet Crown.*
Macaulay.

City of the West. A name generally given in Scotland to Glasgow, the largest city, and the manufacturing and commercial metropolis, of the kingdom. It is situated on the Clyde, the principal river on the west coast, and far surpassing, in navigable importance, all the other Scottish rivers.

City of Victory. Cairo, the capital city of Egypt;—sometimes so called with reference to the signification of its Arabic name, *El Kahira*, or " The Victorious."

Clärchen (klěr'ken). A female character in Goethe's "Egmont;" celebrated for her constancy and devotion.

Clăr'Ice (*It. pron.* klā-re'chee). Wife of Rinaldo, and sister of Huon of Bordeaux, frequently mentioned in the romances and romantic poems of France and Italy.

Clarissa. See HARLOW, CLARISSA.

Clău'di-o. 1. A young gentleman in love with Juliet, in Shakespeare's "Measure for Measure."

2. A young lord of Florence, in Shakespeare's "Much Ado about Nothing."

Clău'di-us. A usurping king of Denmark, in Shakespeare's " Hamlet."

But Tom Tusher, to take the place of the noble Castlewood—faugh! 't was as monstrous as King Hamlet's widow taking off her weeds for *Claudius.* *Thackeray.*

Claus, Peter. See KLAUS, PETER.

Claus, Santa. See ST. NICHOLAS.

Clav'er-house (klav'ĕr-us). The name under which the unrelenting Jacobite partisan and persecutor, John Graham, Viscount Dundee (d. 1689), eldest son of Sir William Graham, of Claverhouse, was generally

and for the Remarks and Rules to which the numbers after certain words refer, see pp. xiv-xxxii.

known in the time of James II., and is still known in history.

Clavileño, Aligero (klä-ve-lān'yo ä-le-hā'ro, 58, 62). [Sp., wooden-pin wing-bearer.] A celebrated steed which enabled Don Quixote and his faithful squire to achieve the deliverance of the Dolorida Dueña and her companions in misfortune from their beards.

Cléante (klā'ǒnt', 62). 1. A character in Molière's celebrated comedy, "Le Tartuffe," distinguished for his sound and genuine piety.
2. A character in the "Malade Imaginaire" of the same author.

Clean the Causeway Riot. (*Scot. Hist.*) The name popularly given to a skirmish or encounter in Edinburgh, in the year 1515, between the rival factions of the Earl of Angus — chief of the Douglases — and the Earl of Arran — the head of the great family of the Hamiltons. In this contest, the partisans of Angus were worsted, and fled from the city in great confusion, being, as it were, swept from the streets.

Cleishbotham, Jedediah (kleesh'-bŏth-ăm). An imaginary editor of the "Tales of My Landlord," written by Sir Walter Scott, but represented as the composition of a certain Mr. Peter Pattieson, assistant teacher at Gandercleuch. See PATTIESON.

<small>Richter tried all Leipsic with his MS. in vain; to a man, with that total contempt of grammar which *Jedediah Cleishbotham* also complains of, they "declined the article."
Carlyle.</small>

Clélie (klā'le'). A principal character in a romance — "Clélie, Histoire Romaine" — written by Mme. Scudery, though the first volumes were originally published under the name of her brother, George de Scudery. The action of the story is placed in the early ages of Roman history, and the heroine is that Clœlia who escaped from the power of Porsena by swimming across the Tiber.

<small>High-flown compliments, profound bows, sighs, and ogles, in the manner of the *Clélie* romances. *Thackeray.*</small>

Clem'en-ti'nå, The Lady. An amiable, beautiful, and accomplished woman, deeply in love with Sir Charles Grandison, in Richardson's novel of this name. Sir Charles finally marries Harriet Byron, though he is represented as having little or no partiality for her.

<small>I shall be no *Lady Clementina*, to be the wonder and pity of the spring of St. Ronan's, — no Ophelia, neither, — though I will say with her, "Good-night, ladies; good-night, sweet ladies!"
Sir W. Scott.</small>

Cleofas. See DON CLEOFAS.

Cle-om'bro-tus. [Gr. Κλεόμβροτος.] An Academic philosopher of Ambracia, who is said to have been so enraptured by the perusal of Plato's "Phædon" that he threw himself down from a high wall, or, according to some accounts, jumped into the sea, in order to exchange this life for a better.

<small>Others came single; ... he who, to enjoy Plato's Elysium, leaped into the sea, *Cleombrotus;* and many more too long.
Milton.</small>

Clif'fọrd, Paul. The title of a novel by Sir Edward Lytton Bulwer (now Sir Edward Bulwer Lytton), and the name of its hero, a romantic highwayman, familiar with the haunts of low vice and dissipation, but afterward reformed and elevated by the power of love.

Clim of the Clough. [That is, Clement of the Glen.] A north-country archer, celebrated in the legendary literature of England.

Clinker, Humphry. The hero of Smollett's novel entitled, "The Expedition of Humphry Clinker." He is introduced as a destitute and shabby fellow, who had been brought up in the work-house, put out by the parish as apprentice to a blacksmith, and afterward employed as an hostler's assistant and extra postilion. Having been dismissed from the stable, and reduced to great want, he at length attracts the notice of Mr. Bramble, who takes him into his family as a servant. He becomes the accepted lover of Winifred Jenkins, and at length turns out to be a natural son of Mr. Bramble.

<small>☞ "Humphry Clinker" is, I do believe, the most laughable story that has ever been written since the goodly art of novel-writing began. *Thackeray.*</small>

☞ For the "Key to the Scheme of Pronunciation," with the accompanying Explanations,

Cli'o. [Gr. Κλεώ, the proclaimer.] (*Gr. & Rom. Myth.*) 1. One of the nine Muses. She presided over history, and was represented as bearing a half-opened roll of a book.
2. A name formed from the four letters used by Addison as his signature in the "Spectator." His most admired papers were marked by one or other of these letters, signed consecutively. But it is not probable that he meant to adopt the name of one of the Muses. With greater likelihood, the letters are supposed to refer to the places where the essays were composed; namely, Chelsea, London, Islington, and the Office. The contrary opinion, however, has generally prevailed; and Addison was often called "Clio" by his contemporaries, as well as by later writers.

When panting virtue her last efforts made,
You brought your *Clio* to the virgin's aid.
Somerville.

Cloacina. See CLUACINA.

Clo-an'thus. One of the companions of Æneas in his voyage to Italy, and the reputed ancestor of the Cluentii family at Rome.

The strong Gyas and the strong *Cloanthus* are less distinguished by the poet than the strong Percival, the strong John, Richard, and Wilfred Osbaldistones [characters in "Rob Roy"] were by outward appearance.
Sir W. Scott.

Cloe'li-ā. See CLÉLIE.

Clootie, or **Cloots.** See AULD CLOOTIE.

Clorinda (klo-rĕn'dȧ). The heroine of the infidel army in Tasso's epic poem, "Jerusalem Delivered." She is an Amazon, and is represented as inspiring the most tender affection in others, especially in the Christian chief Tancred; yet she is herself susceptible of no passion but the love of military fame. See SOFRONIA.

Clō'ten. A rejected lover of Imogen, in Shakespeare's play of "Cymbeline;" "a compound of the booby and the villain; an 'irregulous devil.'"

☞ Miss Seward, in one of her letters, assures us, that, singular as the character of Cloten may appear, it is the exact prototype of a person whom she once knew. "The unmeaning frown of the countenance; the shuffling gait; the burst of voice; the bustling insignificance; the fever-and-ague fits of valour; the froward tetchiness; the unprincipled malice; and — what is most curious — those occasional gleams of good sense, amidst the floating clouds of folly which generally darkened and confused the man's brain, and which, in the character of Cloten, we are apt to impute to a violation of unity in character; but, in the sometime Captain C——n, I saw the portrait of Cloten was not out of nature."

Justice may even sometimes class him [Pope] with those moral assassins who wear, like *Cloten,* their dagger in their months.
E. P. Whipple.

Clothier of England. See JACK OF NEWBURY.

Clo'tho. [Gr. Κλωθώ, spinster.] (*Gr. & Rom. Myth.*) One of the three Parcæ, or Fates; the one who presides over birth, and spins the thread of life.

Mean criminals go to the gallows for a purse cut; and this chief criminal, guilty of a France cut, of a France slashed asunder with *Clotho*-scissors and civil war, ... he, such chief criminal, shall not even come to the bar?
Carlyle.

Cloudeslie, William of. See WILLIAM OF CLOUDESLIE.

Clout, Col'in. The subject of a scurrilous satire by John Skelton (d. 1529), but better known as a name applied by Spenser to himself in the "Faëry Queen" and the "Shepherd's Calendar." Colin Clout figures also in Gay's "Pastorals."

Clu'ā-ci'nȧ. [From Lat. *cluere*, to purify.] (*Rom. Myth.*) A surname of Venus, who was so called because, when the Romans and Sabines were reconciled, they purified themselves with sacred myrtle-branches, in the vicinity of a statue of the goddess, and afterward erected a temple there in honour of her. [Often written Cloacina, from a mistaken notion that she presided over the *cloacæ,* or sewers.]

Club, The. 1. (*Eng. Hist.*) A knot of disappointed Whigs, of whom Sir James Montgomery, the Earl of Annandale, and Lord Ross were the most conspicuous, formed themselves, in Edinburgh, into a society, called "The Club," in William the Third's time. They were, according to Macaulay, dishonest malcontents, whose object was merely to annoy the government and get places. They formed a coalition with the Jacobites; gave great trouble to William and Mary; and broke up in disgrace, the chiefs betraying each other.

2. Under the name of "The Club," — at Garrick's funeral, in 1779, entitled the "Literary Club," — flourished a celebrated association, proposed first by Sir Joshua Reynolds, and acceded to by Dr. Johnson; of which the original members were Sir Joshua, Dr. Johnson, Mr. Edmund Burke, Dr. Nugent, Mr. Beauclerk, Mr. Langton, Dr. Goldsmith, Mr. Chamier, and Sir John Hawkins. It has reckoned amongst its members some of the most distinguished literary and scientific characters.

Clumsy, Sir Tun'bel-ly. A character in Vanbrugh's "Relapse."

Clu'rī-cáune. (*Fairy Myth.*) A famous Irish elf, of evil disposition, who usually appears as a wrinkled old man, and has a knowledge of hidden treasure.

Clut'tĕr-buck, Captain Cuth'bĕrt. A sort of pseudonym of Sir Walter Scott, it being the name of an imaginary editor of his "Fortunes of Nigel," and of an equally imaginary patron to whom he dedicated his "Abbot."

Clyt'em-nes'trā. [Gr. Κλυταιμνήστρα.] (*Gr. & Rom. Myth.*) The faithless wife of Agamemnon, killed by her son Orestes for her crimes. See ÆGISTHUS, ORESTES.

Clyt'i-e (klish'ĭ-e). [Gr. Κλυτία.] (*Gr. & Rom. Myth.*) A water-nymph who fell in love with Apollo, or the Sun-god. Meeting with no reciprocation of her passion, she became changed into a sunflower, and still keeps her face constantly turned towards him throughout his daily course.

I will not have the mad *Clytie*,
Whose head is turned by the sun;
The tulip is a courtly quean,
Whom therefore I will shun. *Hood.*

Coalition Ministry. (*Eng. Hist.*) 1. A designation given to the administration of Lord North and Mr. Charles James Fox, as being an extraordinary political union of statesmen who had previously always displayed a strong personal dislike toward each other. It was formed April 5, 1783, and dissolved Dec. 19, in the same year.

☞ "Not three quarters of a year had elapsed since Fox and Burke had threatened North with impeachment, and had described him, night after night, as the most arbitrary, the most corrupt, the most incapable of ministers. They now allied themselves with him for the purpose of driving from office a statesman [Shelburne] with whom they cannot be said to have differed as to any important question." *Macaulay.*

2. The same appellation was given to the "Broad Bottom Administration" (*q. v.*), and to the Aberdeen Administration (formed Dec. 28, 1852, resigned Jan. 30, 1855).

Cockade City. A title popularly given to the city of Petersburg, in Virginia.

Cockagne (kok-ān'). [Fr. (also *pays de cocagne*); Old Fr. *cocaigne*, Sp. *cucaña*, It. *cucagna, cuccagna, cuggagna*, from It. *cucca*, sweetmeats, dainties, Prov. Fr. *couque*, Catalan *coca*, cake, from Latin *coquere*, to cook, because it was fancied that the houses in Cockagne were covered with cakes.] An imaginary country of idleness and luxury; hence, in burlesque, London and its suburbs. It is the subject of a celebrated satirical poem of the same name, which Warton holds to have been "evidently written soon after the Conquest," but which is probably not older than the year 1300. Boileau applies the name to the French capital. The *mât de Cocagne* (or greased pole) is one of the amusements of the Champs Élysées, in Paris. The Neapolitans have a festival which they call *Cocagna*. In Germany, Hans Sachs has made the "Land of Cockagne" the subject of a humourous poem under the name of *Schlaraffenland.* See LUBBERLAND. [Written also C o c a i g n, C o c k a i g n e, and anciently C o k a y g n e.]

☞ For the "Key to the Scheme of Pronunciation," with the accompanying Explanations,

COC 81 CŒ

☞ "'Cokaygne' seems to have been a sort of mediæval Utopia. Perhaps the earliest specimen of English poetry which we possess . . . is the humourous description of it, beginning, —
'Fur in see, by-west Spaygne,
Is a lond ihote Cockaygne.'
Whatever may be the origin of the word, it is evidently connected with the much-debated *cockney*, which probably implied an undue regard for luxury and refinement in the persons to whom it was applied — generally to Londoners as contrasted with 'persons rusticall.'"
Lower.

Even the Grand Elector himself was liable to this fate of "absorption," as it was called, although he held his crown of *Cockagne* in the common case for life.   *Sir W. Scott.*

It was for the reader not the El Dorado only, but a beatific land of *Cockaigne* (and paradise of Do-nothings).   *Carlyle.*

Cock-Lane Ghost. The name given to the imagined cause of certain strange phenomena which took place in the year 1762 about the bed of a young girl by the name of Parsons, at house No. 33 Cock Lane, West Smithfield, London, and were the cause of much excitement. The rector of the parish, with "a number of gentlemen of rank and character," of whom Dr. Johnson was one, undertook to solve the mystery. Their examination satisfied them that the whole was an imposture originating in a malignant conspiracy, and the parents of the girl were condemned to the pillory and to imprisonment. The supposed presence of the ghost was indicated by certain mysterious scratchings and knockings produced on a piece of board which the girl concealed about her person. Dr. Johnson wrote a statement of the affair, which was published in the "Gentleman's Magazine." See vol. xxxii., pp. 43 and 81.

Cockney School. A name formerly given by some of the English critics to a literary coterie whose productions were said "to consist of the most incongruous ideas in the most uncouth language." In this sect were included Leigh Hunt, Hazlitt, Shelley, Keats, and others; and the "Quarterly Review" (April, 1818) charged the first with aspiring to be the "hierophant" of it.

☞ "While the whole critical world is occupied with balancing the merits, whether in theory or execution, of what is commonly called the Lake School, it is strange that no one seems to think it at all necessary to say a single word about another new school of poetry which has of late sprung up among us. This school has not, I believe, as yet received any name; but, if I may be permitted to have the honour of christening it, it may henceforth be referred to by the designation of the Cockney School. Its chief Doctor and Professor is Mr. Leigh Hunt, a man certainly of some talents, of extraordinary pretensions both in poetry and politics, and withal of exquisitely bad taste and extremely vulgar modes of thinking and manners in all respects. . . . He is the ideal of a Cockney poet. He raves perpetually about 'green fields,' 'jaunty streams,' and 'o'erarching leafiness,' exactly as a Cheapside shopkeeper does about the beauties of his box on the Camberwell road."
Z. (i. e. *J. G. Lockhart*), in *Blackwood's Mag.*, Oct. 1817.

Cock of the North. A sobriquet given to the late and last Duke of Gordon (d. 1836). He is so called on a monument erected in his honour at Fochabers, in Aberdeenshire, Scotland.

Coc'lēs, Ho-ra'ti-us. [Lat., Horatius the one-eyed.] A hero of the old Roman lays, who defended a bridge against the whole Etruscan army under Porsena, until his countrymen had broken down the end of it which was behind him, when he plunged into the stream, and swam, amid the arrows of the enemy, to a place of safety.

Co-cy'tus. [Gr. Κωκυτός, lamentation.] (*Gr. & Rom. Myth.*) One of the rivers that washed the shores of hell, and prevented imprisoned souls from returning to earth. It was a branch of the Styx.

Cocytus, named of lamentations loud
Heard on the rueful stream.   *Milton.*

Cœ'lebs. [Lat., a bachelor.] The hero of a novel by Hannah More (1744-1833), entitled "Cœlebs in Search of a Wife."

Ready command of money, he feels, will be extremely desirable in a wife, — desirable and almost indispensable in present straitened

---

and for the Remarks and Rules to which the numbers after certain words refer, see pp. xiv-xxxii.

6

circumstances. These are the notions of this ill-situated *Cœlebs*. *Carlyle*.

Cœ′lus. (*Rom. Myth.*) Son of Æther (air) and Dies (day), and one of the most ancient of the gods; the same as *Uranus*. See URANUS.

Cœur de Lion (kūr de lĭ′ŏn; *Fr. pron.* kör dụ le′ôn′, 47, 62). [*Fr.*, lionhearted.] A surname given to Richard I. of England, on account of his dauntless courage, about A. D. 1192. This surname was also conferred on Louis VIII. of France, who signalised himself in the Crusades about his wars against England, about 1223, and on Boleslas I., king of Poland.

Coffin, Tom. See LONG TOM COFFIN.

Co′I-lŭ̇s. A Latin or Latinised name of Kyle, a district of Scotland, county of Ayr, celebrated in the lyric poetry of Burns. According to tradition, it is derived from *Coilus*, a Pictish monarch. Burns also uses the name as a poetical synonym for *Scotland*.

Farewell, old *Coila's* hills and dales,
Her heathy moors, and winding vales.
Burns.

Colada (*Sp. pron.* ko-lä′thä, 56). The name of one of the Cid's two swords, which were of dazzling brightness, and had hilts of solid gold.

Cŏld′brand. A Danish giant vanquished and slain in an encounter with Guy of Warwick. See GUY, SIR, EARL OF WARWICK. [Written also Colbran, Colbrand.]

"It is false!" said Gregory; "*Colbrand* the Dane was a dwarf to him." *Sir W. Scott.*

Coldstream, Sir Charles. The name of a character in Charles Mathews's play entitled "Used Up;" distinguished for his utter *ennui*, his mental inanity, and his apparent physical imbecility.

Colin Tampon (ko′lăn′ tŏn′pŏn′, 62). A reproachful epithet said to have been anciently given to the Swiss, and to represent the sound of their drums.

Col-lēan′, May. The heroine of a Scottish ballad, which relates how a "fause Sir John" carried her to a rock by the sea for the purpose of drowning her, and how she outwitted him, and subjected him to the same fate he had intended for her.

Colloquy of Poissy (pwŏ′se′). [Fr. *Colloque de Poissy.*] (*Fr. Hist.*) The name commonly given to a national synod of Catholics and Calvinists held at Poissy, in 1561, to settle the religious controversies by which France was then agitated. The conference, however, was mutually unsatisfactory, and was brought to a premature conclusion. Both parties became more embittered against each other than ever, and the desolating wars of religion soon followed.

Cologne, The Three Kings of. A name given to the three magi who visited the infant Saviour, and whose bodies are said to have been brought by the Empress Helena from the East to Constantinople, whence they were transferred to Milan. Afterward, in 1164, on Milan being taken by the Emperor Frederick, they were presented by him to the Archbishop of Cologne, who placed them in the principal church of the city, where, says Cressy, "they are to this day celebrated with great veneration." Their names are commonly said to be Jaspar, Melchior, and Balthazar; but one tradition gives them as Apellius, Amerus, Damascus; another as Magalath, Galgalath, Sarasin; and still another as Ator, Sator, Peratoras. See MAGI, THE THREE.

Colonel Caustic. See CAUSTIC, COLONEL.

Cŏ-lum′bi-ȧ. A name often given to the New World, from a feeling of poetic justice to its discoverer. The application of the term is usually restricted to the United States. It has not been found in any writer before Dr. Timothy Dwight (1752–1818); and it probably originated with him. He wrote a song, formerly very popular, which began, —

"Columbia, Columbia, to glory arise,
The queen of the world and the child of the skies."

☞ The ballad "Hail, Columbia, happy land," was written by Joseph Hop-

☞ For the "Key to the Scheme of Pronunciation," with the accompanying Explanations,

kinson (1770-1842), for the benefit of an actor named Fox, and to an air entitled "The President's March," composed in 1789, by a German named Teyles, on the occasion of General Washington's first visit to a theatre in New York.

Col'um-bĭne. [It. *Columbina*, pretty little dove, — used as a diminutive term of endearment.] The name of a female mask in pantomimes, with whom Harlequin is represented as in love. Their marriage usually forms the *dénoûment* of the play. In the old Italian comedy, she appeared as a maid-servant, and a perfect coquette.

Commander of the Faithful. [Ar. *Emir-al-Mumenin*.] A title assumed by Omar I. (d. 644), and retained by his successors in the caliphate.

Company, John. A popular nickname, among the native East-Indians, for the East India Company, the abstract idea involved in the name being above their comprehension. [Called also *Mother Company*.]

I have gone to the leeward of *John Company's* favour.
C. Reade.

Co'mus. [From Gr. κῶμος, a revel, from κώμη, a country town, whence also *comedy*.] (*Myth.*) In the later age of Rome, a god of festive joy and mirth. In Milton's poem entitled "Comus: a Masque," he is represented as a base enchanter, who endeavours, but in vain, to beguile and entrap the innocent by means of his "brewed enchantments."

Con-cor'di-ạ. (*Rom. Myth.*) The goddess of concord, or harmony.

Conqueror, The. A title given to William, Duke of Normandy, who, by the battle of Hastings, in 1066, became the sovereign of England.

Talk of "coming over with *the Conqueror!*" The first Browns came over with Hengist and Horsa.
Lower.

Con'răde. A follower of John (bastard brother of Don Pedro, Prince of Arragon), in Shakespeare's "Much Ado about Nothing."

Constable de Bourbon. [Fr. *Connétable de Bourbon.*] (*Fr. Hist.*) A name given to Charles, Duc du Bourbonnais (1489-1527), a brilliant military leader, famous for his austere morality and his misfortunes.

Con'stans. A legendary king of Britain, celebrated in the old romances of chivalry. He was the grandfather of Arthur.

Consuelo (kŏnˈsū-āˈlo', 34, 62). The heroine of George Sand's (Mme. Dudevant's) novel of the same name, an impersonation of noble purity sustained amidst great temptaions.

Consul Bib'u-lus. (*Rom. Hist.*) A colleague of Julius Cæsar in the consulship in the year 59 B. C. He was a man of small ability and little influence. After an ineffectual attempt to oppose an agrarian law brought forward by Cæsar, he shut himself up in his own house, and neither appeared in public nor took part in the affairs of state during the remainder of his consulship; whence it was said in joke that it was the consulship of Julius and Cæsar. The name of Bibulus is used proverbially to designate any person who fills a high office, and yet is a mere cipher in the conduct of affairs.

Continental System. (*Fr. Hist.*) The name given to a plan by which Napoleon I. endeavoured to shut England out from all connection with the continent of Europe. See BERLIN DECREE, DECREE OF FONTAINEBLEAU, MILAN DECREE.

Conversation Sharpe. A sobriquet bestowed upon Richard Sharpe, (1759-1835), well known by this name in London society.

Conway Cabal. (*Amer. Hist.*) A name given to a faction organised in 1777, for the purpose of placing General Gates at the head of the Continental army.

Cŏ-phet'u-ạ. An imaginary African king, of whom a legendary ballad told that he fell in love with the daughter of a beggar, and married her. The piece is extant in Percy's "Reliques," and is several times alluded to by Shakespeare and others. A modernised version of the story is given by Tennyson in his poem entitled "The Beggar Maid."

Young Adam Cupid, he that shot so trim When King *Cophetua* loved the beggar-maid.
Shak.

May not a monarch love a maid of low degree? Is not King *Cophetua* and the beggar-maid a case in point? *Sir W. Scott.*

How it would sound in song, that a great monarch had declined his affections upon the daughter of a beggar! Yet, do we feel the imagination at all violated when we read the "true ballad" where King *Cophetua* wooes the beggar-maid? *Charles Lamb.*

Co'pi-ă. (*Rom. Myth.*) The goddess of plenty.

Copper Captain. Michael Perez, a celebrated character in Beaumont and Fletcher's comedy, "Rule a Wife and Have a Wife."

To this *Copper Captain* [General Van Poffenburgh], therefore, was confided the command of the troops destined to protect the southern frontier. *W. Irving.*

Cop'per-field, David. The hero of Dickens's novel of the same name.

Copperheads. A popular nickname originating in the time of the great civil war in the United States, and applied to a faction in the North, which was very generally considered to be in secret sympathy with the Rebellion, and to give it aid and comfort by attempting to thwart the measures of the government. The name is derived from a poisonous serpent called the copperhead (*Trigonocephalus contortrix*), whose bite is considered as deadly as that of the rattlesnake, and whose geographical range extends from 45° N. to Florida. The copperhead, unlike the rattlesnake, gives no warning of its attack, and is, therefore, the type of a concealed foe.

Cordelia. The youngest and favourite daughter of Lear, in Shakespeare's tragedy of this name. See LEAR.

Cordière, La Belle. See ROPE-MAKER, THE BEAUTIFUL.

Cor-flam'bo. [That is, heart of flame.] A character in Spenser's "Faëry Queen," representing sensual passion. See TIMIAS.

Corinne (ko'rĕn'). The heroine of Mme. de Staël's novel of the same name, a young maiden whose lover proves false, and who, in consequence, lives miserably a few years, and then closes her eyes for ever on a world grown dark and solitary.

Cormoran, Giant. See GIANT CORMORAN.

Corn-cracker, The. A popular nickname or designation for the State of Kentucky. The inhabitants of the State are often called *Corn-crackers.*

Corn-law Rhymer, The. Ebenezer Elliott, an English writer (1781–1849), who, in a volume of poems entitled " Corn-law Rhymes," set forth the mischief which he believed the corn laws were actually producing, and the greater dangers which they were threatening. These rhyming philippics materially assisted in producing that revolt of the manufacturing population of the British islands against the corn laws which led to their final abolition in 1846.

Is not the *Corn-Law Rhymer* already a king, though a belligerent one, — king of his own mind and faculty? and what man in the long run is king of more? *Carlyle.*

Corn'wall, Bar'ry. An imperfectly anagrammatic *nom de plume* adopted by Bryan Waller Procter, a distinguished English poet of the present century.

Co-ro'nis. [Gr. Κορωνίς.] (*Gr. & Rom. Myth.*) A daughter of Phoroneus, king of Phocis. She was metamorphosed by Minerva into a crow, having implored her protection on one occasion when pursued by Neptune.

Corporal, The Little. See LITTLE CORPORAL.

Corporal Nym. See NYM, CORPORAL.

Corporal Trim. See TRIM, CORPORAL.

Corporal Violet. See VIOLET, CORPORAL.

Corrector, Alexander. A name assumed by Alexander Cruden (1701–1770), the author of the well-known "Concordance to the Bible," who found employment for some years as corrector of the press, in London. He believed himself divinely commissioned to reform the manners of the world, and petitioned Parliament to constitute him by act the "Corrector of the People," hoping by this

☞ For the "Key to the Scheme of Pronunciation," with the accompanying Explanations,

means to influence the people more effectually.

It appears to him that the seeming modesty connected with the former mode of writing [in the third person] is overbalanced by the inconvenience and affectation which attends it during a narrative of some length, and which may be observed in every work in which the third person is used, from the "Commentaries" of Cæsar to the "Autobiography of Alexander the Corrector."
Sir W. Scott.

Corrouge (kor-rooj'). The sword of Sir Otuel;—so called in the romances of chivalry.

Corsica Paoli (på'o-lee). A name popularly given to Pasquale de Paoli (1726–1807), a native of Corsica, and leader in the war which his countrymen made against Genoa, and subsequently against France, in the effort to gain their independence. After the conquest of the island by the French, he took refuge in England, where he was received with much respect, and passed many years in honourable friendship with Burke, Johnson, and other distinguished men of the time.

Cortana. See CURTANA.

Cŏr'y-ban'tēs. [Gr. Κορύβαντες.] Priests of Cybele whose religious services consisted in noisy music and wild armed dances.

Cŏr'y-dŏn. A shepherd in one of the Idyls of Theocritus, and one of the Eclogues of Virgil;—hence used to designate any rustic, more especially a rustic swain.

To obtain speech of him, I must have run the risk of alarming the suspicions of Dorcas, if not of her yet more stupid Corydon.
Sir W. Scott.

Hardly a shiftless Corydon falls in walks of art that demand the loftiest endowments of the mind,—and what crowds of such there are every year!—that he or his friends do not parade him as another example of melancholy shipwreck, as if he deserved, or could fairly have anticipated, any other end.
Putnam's Mag.

Coryphæus of Grammarians. [Gr. ὁ κορυφαῖος τῶν γραμματικῶν.] An appellation given to Aristarchus, a native of Samothrace, the most celebrated grammarian and critic in all antiquity. His life was devoted to the correction of the text of the ancient poets of Greece,—Homer, Æschylus, Sophocles, &c.

Cos'tard. A clown, in Shakespeare's "Love's Labour's Lost," who apes the display of wit, point, and sententious observation affected by the courtiers of Queen Elizabeth's time, and who misapplies, in the most ridiculous manner, the phrases and modes of combination in argument that were then in vogue.

Co-tyt'to. [Gr. Κοτυττώ.] (*Gr. & Rom. Myth.*) The goddess of licentiousness, originally worshipped in Thrace, later in Athens also. Her rites were celebrated with great indecency in private and at midnight.

Dark-veiled Cotytto! to whom the secret flame Of midnight torches burns.
Milton.

Country Parson. A pseudonym, or rather a sobriquet, of the Rev. A. K. H. Boyd, a popular English essayist of the present time.

Courtney Melmoth. See MELMOTH, COURTNEY.

Cousin Michael. [Ger. *Vetter Michel.*] A sportive and disparaging designation of the German people, intended to indicate the weaknesses and follies of the national character, and especially the proverbial national slowness, heaviness, and credulity. In Germany, the name *Michel* is often used as a contemptuous designation of any simple, coarse rustic, and has probably acquired this signification through a mingling of the Hebrew with the Old German *michel,* gross.

Coventry, Peeping Tom of. See PEEPING TOM OF COVENTRY.

Cŏv'er-leў, Sir Roger de. The name of one of the members of the imaginary club under whose direction the "Spectator" was professedly edited; a genuine English gentleman of the time of Queen Anne.

☞ *"The characters of the club, not only in the 'Tatler,' but in the 'Spectator,' were drawn by Steele. That of Sir Roger de Coverley is among the number. Addison has, however, gained himself immortal honour by his manner of filling up this last character. Who is there that can forget, or be insensible to, the inimitable, nameless graces, and various traits of nature and of old English character in it,—to his unpretending virtues and*

and for the Remarks and Rules to which the numbers after certain words refer, see pp. xlv–xxxii.

amiable weaknesses, — to his modesty, generosity, hospitality, and eccentric whims, — to the respect of his neighbours and the affection of his domestics, — to his wayward, hopeless, secret passion for his fair enemy, the widow, in which there is more of real romance and true delicacy than in a thousand tales of knight-errantry, (we perceive the hectic flush of his cheek, the faltering of his tongue in speaking of her bewitching airs and the 'whiteness of her hand,') — to the havock he makes among the game in his neighbourhood, — to his speech from the bench, to show the 'Spectator' what is thought of him in the country, — to his unwillingness to be put up as a sign-post, and his having his own likeness turned into the Saracen's head, — to his gentle reproof of the baggage of a gypsy that tells him 'he has a widow in his line of life,' — to his doubts as to the existence of witchcraft, and protection of reputed witches, — to his account of the family pictures, and his choice of a chaplain, — to his falling asleep at church, and his reproof of John Williams, as soon as he recovered from his nap, for talking in sermontime?" *Hazlitt.*

☞ "What would Sir Roger de Coverley be without his follies and his charming little brain-cracks? If the good knight did not call out to the people sleeping in church, and say 'Amen' with such a delightful pomposity; if he did not make a speech in the assize court *apropos des bottes,* and merely to show his dignity to Mr. Spectator; if he did not mistake Madam Doll Tearsheet for a lady of quality in Temple Garden; if he were wiser than he is; if he had not his humour to salt his life, and were but a mere English gentleman and game-preserver, — of what worth were he to us? We love him for his vanities as much as his virtues. What is ridiculous is delightful in him; we are so fond of him because we laugh at him so." *Thackeray.*

The greatest risk which he seems to have incurred, in his military capacity, was one somewhat resembling the escape of *Sir Roger de Coverley's* ancestor at Worcester, who was saved from the slaughter of that action by having been absent from the field.
Sir W. Scott.

Coviello (ko-ve-el'lo, 102). A Calabrian clown who figures in the "*commedia dell' arte,*" or Italian popular comedy.

Crabshaw, Timothy. The name of Sir Launcelot Greaves's squire, in Smollett's "Adventures" of that redoubted and quixotic knight.

Crabtree. A character in Smollett's novel, "The Adventures of Peregrine Pickle."

Cradle of Liberty. A popular name given to Faneuil (fun'il) Hall, a large public edifice in Boston, Massachusetts, celebrated as being the place where the orators of the Revolution roused the people to resistance to British oppression.

Crane, Ichabod. The name of a credulous Yankee schoolmaster, whose adventures are related in the "Legend of Sleepy Hollow," in Irving's "Sketch-book."

☞ "The cognomen of *Crane* was not inapplicable to his person. He was tall, but exceedingly lank, with narrow shoulders, long arms and legs, hands that dangled a mile out of his sleeves, feet that might have served for shovels, and his whole frame most loosely hung together. His head was small, and flat at top, with huge ears, large, green, glassy eyes, and a long, snipe nose, so that it looked like a weather-cock perched upon his spindle neck, to tell which way the wind blew. To see him striding along the profile of a hill on a windy day, with his clothes bagging and fluttering about him, one might have mistaken him for the genius of famine descending upon the earth, or some scarecrow eloped from a corn-field."
W. Irving.

Crapaud, Jean, *or* **Johnny** (zhön krä'pō', 62). [Sometimes incorrectly written Crapeau.] A sportive designation of a Frenchman, or of the French nation collectively considered. The following account has been given of the origin of this name: —

☞ "When the French took the city of Aras from the Spaniards, under Louis XIV., after a long and most desperate siege, it was remembered that Nostradamus had said, —

'Les anciens crapauds prendront Sara.' (The ancient toads shall Sara take).

This line was then applied to this event in a very roundabout manner. *Sara* is *Aras* backward. By *the ancient toads* were meant the French; as that nation formerly had for its armorial bearings three of those odious reptiles instead of the three flowers-de-luce which it now bears." *Seward's Anecdotes.*

☞ In Elliott's "Horæ Apocalypticæ" (vol. iv. p. 64, ed. 1847), may be

---

☞ For the "Key to the Scheme of Pronunciation," with the accompanying Explanations,

found a very full presentation of the reasons for believing that three toads, or three frogs, were the old arms of France.

Crayon, Geoffrey, Esq. A pseudonym under which Washington Irving published "The Sketch-book."

Crazy Poet. See MAD POET.

Creakle, Mr. A tyrannous schoolmaster in Dickens's novel of "David Copperfield;" represented as bullying the little David's incipient manliness out of him.

Creole State. A name sometimes given to the State of Louisiana, in which the descendants of the original French and Spanish settlers constitute a large proportion of the population.

Crescent City. A popular name for the city of New Orleans, the older portion of which is built around the convex side of a bend of the Mississippi River. In the progress of its growth up-stream, however, the city has now so extended itself as to fill the hollow of a curve in the opposite direction, so that the river-front presents an outline resembling the character ʃ.

Cres'si-dā. The heroine of Shakespeare's play, "Troilus and Cressida," founded upon Chaucer's "Troilus and Cresseide;" represented as beautiful, witty, and accomplished, but impure.

☞ "It is well known that there is no trace of the particular story of 'Troilus and Cressida' among the ancients. I find not so much as the name Cressida once mentioned." *Knight.*

Cre-u'sā. [Gr. Κρέουσα.] (*Gr. & Rom. Myth.*) A daughter of Priam and Hecuba, and the wife of Æneas, who became by her the father of Ascanius. When Æneas made his escape from the flames of Troy, with his father Anchises and his son Ascanius, she followed him, but was unable to keep him in sight, and became lost in the streets of the city.

So when Æneas through the flames of Troy
Bore his pale sire, and led his lovely boy;
With loitering step the fair *Creusa* stayed,
And death involved her in eternal shade.
Darwin.

Crēy'ton, Paul (-tn). A pseudonym of J. T. Trowbridge, a popular American novelist of the present day.

Crichton, The Admirable (kri'tn). James Crichton, a Scottish gentleman of the sixteenth century, who, at the early age of fourteen, took his degree of Master of Arts, and was considered a prodigy, not only in abilities, but in actual attainments. [Written also **Creighton**.]

The editor of the translation before us has collected some anecdotes, one of which is truly singular, and has to mind the marvellous stories which are told of *the Admirable Creighton*. *Edin. Rev.*

He [Keyserling] carried off all manner of college prizes, and was *the Admirable Crichton* of Königsberg University and the graduates there. *Carlyle.*

Crisp. One of the names of Puck, or Robin Goodfellow.

Cris'pin. 1. The patron of shoe-makers, represented as such in the ceremonial processions of the craft. He is also worshipped as a saint and martyr by the Catholic church. About the middle of the third century, under the reign of Diocletian, Crispin, with his brother Crispian, accompanied St. Quentin when he preached the gospel in France. The two brothers settled at Soissons, and, while pursuing their mission, supported themselves by making shoes, until their martyrdom, A. D. 287.

2. The name of a valet in French comedy; — popularly used to designate a wag or jester.

Cris'pin-Cat'i-līne. A nickname fastened by Mirabeau upon D'Eprémenil, in ridicule of his conspiracies. He seems to have thought the name of Catiline alone too respectable, and therefore prefixed that of Crispin, which probably alludes to a comedy in one act, published in 1707 by Le Sage, and called "Crispin the Rival of his Master." The story turns on the tricks of Crispin to gain the affections of his master's mistress.

Note further our old Parlementary friend *Crispin-Catiline* d'Esprémenil. *Carlyle.*

Criss Kringle. See KRISS KRINGLE.

Croaker. A character in Goldsmith's comedy, "The Good-natured Man;"

intended as a caricature on men who are always filled with groundless and ludicrous apprehensions.

<small>The young traveller expected a burst of indignation; but whether, as *Croaker* says, . . . our hero had exhausted himself in fretting away his misfortunes beforehand, so that he did not feel them when they actually arrived, or whether he found the company in which he was placed too congenial to lead him to repine at any thing which delayed his journey, it is certain that he submitted to his lot with much resignation. *Sir W. Scott.*</small>

Cro′cus. [Gr. Κρόκος.] (*Gr. & Rom. Myth.*) A young man who was enamoured of the nymph Smilax, and was changed by the gods into a saffron-plant, because he loved without being loved again.

Croe′sus. [Gr. Κροῖσος.] The last king of Lydia, and the richest man of his time.

Crof′tań-gry, Chrys′tặl. A pseudonym of Sir Walter Scott; the name of the imaginary editor of his "Chronicles of the Canongate."

Cro′nos. [Gr. Κρόνος.] (*Gr. Myth.*) The youngest of the Titans; identified by the Romans with *Saturn.* See SATURN.

Crŏw̆-de′ro (9). [From *crowd*, an ancient kind of violin.] A fiddler who figures in Butler's "Hudibras."

<small>To confirm him in this favourable opinion, I began to execute such a complicated flourish as I thought must have turned *Crowdero* into a pillar of stone with envy and wonder.
Sir W. Scott.</small>

Crŏwe, Captain. A celebrated nautical personage in Smollett's "Adventures of Sir Launcelot Greaves."

<small>☞ "Captain Crowe had commanded a merchant ship in the Mediterranean trade for many years, and saved some money by dint of frugality and traffic. He was an excellent seaman, — brave, active, friendly in his way, and scrupulously honest; but as little acquainted with the world as a sucking child; whimsical, impatient, and so impetuous that he could not help breaking in upon the conversation, whatever it might be, with repeated interruptions, that seemed to burst from him by involuntary impulse. When he himself attempted to speak, he never finished his period, but made such a number of abrupt transitions that his discourse seemed to be an unconnected series of unfinished sentences, the meaning of which it was not easy to decipher."
Smollett.</small>

Crowfield, Christopher. A pseudonym of Mrs. Harriet Beecher Stowe.

Crowquill, A. A pseudonym adopted by Alfred Henry Forrester (b. 1805), a popular English humourist of the present day.

Crummles, Mr. (krŭm′lz). The eccentric manager of a theatrical company in Dickens's novel of "Nicholas Nickleby."

Crū′sŏe, Rob′in-son (-sn). The hero of De Foe's great novel; a shipwrecked sailor who for many years leads a solitary existence on an uninhabited island of the tropics, and who alleviates his long reclusion by an inexhaustible prodigality of contrivance.

<small>☞ De Foe founded this story upon the adventures of Alexander Selkirk (b. 1676), a Scottish sailor who was left on the uninhabited island of Juan Fernandez in 1704, by his captain, one Straddling, to whom he had given some cause of offence. Here he resided for four years and four months, when he was rescued by Captain Woods Rogers, and taken to England. De Foe has often been charged with having surreptitiously taken the story of Crusoe from the papers of Selkirk, but he can have borrowed little beyond the mere idea of a man being left alone on a desert isle, there being scarcely any thing common to the adventures of the real and the fictitious solitary.

There are *Robinson Crusoes* in the moral as well as physical world . . . ; men cast on desert islands of thought and speculation; without companionship; without worldly resources; forced to arm and clothe themselves out of the remains of shipwrecked hopes, and to make a home for their solitary hearts in the nooks and corners of imagination and reading. *Leigh Hunt.*

What man does not remember with regret the first time that he read *Robinson Crusoe?* *Macaulay.*

It soon became evident to me, that, like *Robinson Crusoe* with his boat, I had begun on too large a scale, and that, to launch my history successfully, I must reduce its proportions. *W. Irving.*</small>

Crystal Hills. An old name for the White Mountains, in New Hampshire, sometimes used by modern writers.

<small>We had passed
The high source of the Saco; and, bewildered
In the dwarf spruce-belts of the *Crystal Hills*.
Had heard above us, like a voice in the cloud,
The horn of Fabyan sounding. *Whittier.*</small>

Cu′bit-op′o-lis. See MESOPOTAMIA.

☞ For the "Key to the Scheme of Pronunciation," with the accompanying Explanations,

Cuddie, Headrigg. See HEADRIGG, CUDDIE.

Cuf'fee, *or* **Cuf'fey.** A familiar or contemptuous name applied to negroes. The word is said to be of African origin, and it has been borne as a surname. See SAMBO.

Africa alone, of all nations, — though Turkey has a leaning that way, — sets up fatness as a standard of beauty. But *Cuffey* is not acknowledged by the rest of the world as the *arbiter elegantiarum.* *Putnam's Mag.*

Cunc-tā'tŏr. [Lat., the delayer.] A surname given to the illustrious Roman general, Quintus Fabius Maximus Verrucosus (d. B. c. 203), on account of his cautious but salutary measures in opposing the progress of Hannibal. He avoided all direct engagements, tantalised the enemy with marches and counter-marches, watched his movements with unremitting vigilance, cut off his stragglers and foragers, and compelled him to weary his allies by necessary exactions, and to dishearten his soldiers by fruitless manœuvres, while Rome gained by the delay, and assembled her forces in greater strength.

If Wellington found it judicious to play the *Cunctator* in Portugal and Spain, he would hardly have followed the Fabian tactics, if he had met the French in England. *Szabad.*

Cunégonde, Mmle. (kü'nȧ'gōⁿd', 34, 62). The mistress of Candide in Voltaire's novel of this name.

Bright goddess [the moon], if thou art not too busy with Candid and *Miss Cunegund's* affairs, take Tristram Shandy's under thy protection also. *Sterne.*

Cu'pid. [Lat. *Cupido.*] (*Gr. & Rom. Myth.*) The son of Mars and Venus; the god of love. He was the constant companion of his mother, and, armed with bow and arrows, he shot the darts of desire into the bosoms of both gods and men. He was represented as a winged child or youth, and often with a bandage covering his eyes.

Cu'răn. A courtier, in Shakespeare's tragedy of "Lear."

Curate of Meudon (mö'dŏⁿ', 43, 62). [Fr. *Le Curé de Meudon.*] A name by which Rabelais (1483-1553), the French satirist, is often referred to. He was, during the latter part of his life, the parish priest of Meudon.

Cu'ri-ā'ti-ī (9, 23). Three Albanian brothers, who, according to an old Roman legend, fought, in the time of Tullus Hostilius, with three Roman brothers, the Horatii, and were conquered by the cunning and bravery of one of them.

Cu'ri-o. A gentleman attending on the Duke of Illyria in Shakespeare's "Twelfth Night."

Curious Impertinent, The. [Sp. *El Curioso Impertinente.*] The title of a "novel" or tale introduced by Cervantes into his "Don Quixote" by way of episode, and a designation of one of the characters in it, an Italian gentleman who is foolish enough to make trial of his wife's virtue — of which he is firmly convinced — by persuading a trusted friend to seem to lay siege to it. He suffers the deserved penalty of his impertinent curiosity in the treachery of his friend and the infidelity of his wife.

Cur-tā'nȧ. [It., the shortener; — so called from its being used to cut off heads.] 1. The sword of Ogier the Dane.

2. The sword of Edward the Confessor, which is borne before the kings of England at their coronation. It has a blunted edge as being emblematical of mercy, and is carried between the swords of justice temporal and justice spiritual.

Cur'ti-o (kur'shĭ-o). A servant to Petruchio, in Shakespeare's "Taming of the Shrew."

Cutpurse, Moll, *or* **Mȧll.** A pseudonym of Mary Frith, a notorious character frequently mentioned or alluded to by the older English writers. She is the heroine of Middleton's comedy entitled "The Roaring Girl," and is introduced by Nat. Field, a contemporary dramatist, in his piece called "Amends for Ladies."

Cuttle, Captain. A character in Dickens's "Dombey and Son," combining great humour, eccentricity, and pathos. He is distinguished for his simplicity, credulity, and generous trustfulness. One of his famous expressions is, "When found, make a note of."

Are there any of you, my readers, who have not read the "Life of Robert Hall"? If so, in the words of the great *Captain Cuttle*, "When found, make a note of it." Never mind what your theological opinion is, ... send for Robert Hall. *Sir E. Bulwer Lytton.*

Cyb'e-le. (*Rom. Myth.*) The daughter of Cœlus and Terra, and the wife of Saturn; the same as the *Rhea* and *Ops* of the Greeks. She is represented as wearing a mural crown, and riding in a chariot drawn by lions, or seated on a throne with lions at her side. [Called also *Bona Dea* and *Mother of the Gods.*]

Might she the wise Latona be,
Or the towered *Cybele*,
Mother of a hundred gods?
Juno dares not give her odds. *Milton.*

She looks a sea-*Cybele*, fresh from ocean,
Rising with her tiara of proud towers,
At airy distance, with majestic motion,
A ruler of the waters and their powers.
Byron (on Venice).

Cy'clops. [Lat. *Cyclopes*, Gr. Κύκλωπες, the round-eyed.] (*Gr. & Rom. Myth.*) A gigantic one-eyed race of men inhabiting the sea-coasts of Sicily, sons of Cœlus and Terra. According to Hesiod, they were three in number, and their names were Arges, Steropes, and Brontes. Homer describes them as wild, insolent, lawless shepherds, who devoured human beings. A later tradition represents them as Vulcan's assistants in fabricating the thunderbolts of Jupiter. See POLYPHEMUS.

Cyl-le'ni-us. [Gr. Κυλλήνιος.] (*Gr. & Rom. Myth.*) A surname of Mercury, derived from Mount Cyllene, in Arcadia, where he was born.

Cym'be-line, *or* **Cym'be-line.** A legendary or mythical king of Britain, and the hero of Shakespeare's play of the same name.

Cyn'o-sure. [Lat. *Cynosura*, Gr. Κυνοσουρά.] (*Gr. & Rom. Myth.*) An Idæan nymph, and one of the nurses of Jupiter, who placed her in the constellation *Ursa Minor*, as the pole-star.

Towers and battlements it sees
Bosomed high in tufted trees,
Where perhaps some beauty lies,
The *Cynosure* of neighbouring eyes.
Milton.

Cyn'thi-å. [Gr. Κυνθία.] ⎱ (*Gr. &*
Cyn'thi-us. [Gr. Κύνθιος.] ⎰ *Rom. Myth.*) Surnames respectively of Diana and Apollo, derived from Mount Cynthus, in the island of Delos, their birthplace. See APOLLO, DIANA.

Even *Cynthia* looks haggard of an afternoon, as we may see her sometimes in the present winter season, with Phœbus staring her out of countenance from the opposite side of the heavens. *Thackeray.*

Cyp'å-ris'sus. [Gr. Κυπάρισσος.] (*Gr. & Rom. Myth.*) A beautiful youth, beloved by Apollo, whose favourite stag he inadvertently killed, in consequence of which immoderate grief seized upon him, and he was metamorphosed into a cypress.

Cȳ-re'ne. [Gr. Κυρήνη.] (*Gr. & Rom. Myth.*) A water-nymph, the mother of Aristæus. Her residence under the Peneus, and the visit of her son to her, are described in a beautiful episode in the fourth book of Virgil's "Georgics."

Cȳ-the'rå. [Gr. Κυθήρα.] ⎱ (*Gr. &*
Cyth'e-re'å. [Gr. Κυθέρεια.] ⎰ *Rom. Myth.*) Different forms of a surname of Venus, derived from the town of Cythera, in Crete, or the isle of Cythera, where the goddess was said to have first landed, and where she had a celebrated temple.

Violets dim,
But sweeter than the lids of Juno's eyes,
Or *Cytherea's* breath. *Shak.*

☞ For the "Key to the Scheme of Pronunciation," with the accompanying Explanations,

D.

Dæd'ȧ-lus (17). [Gr. Δαίδαλος.] (*Gr. & Rom. Myth.*) A most ingenious artist of Athens, who formed the famous Cretan labyrinth, and who, by the help of wings which he constructed, fled from Crete across the Ægean Sea, to escape the resentment of Minos. He was thought to be the inventor of carpentry and of most of its tools, such as the saw, the axe, the gimlet, and the like. See ICARUS.

Dā'gŏn. [A diminutive of the Heb. *dag*, a fish.] (*Myth.*) A Phœnician or Syrian divinity, who, according to the Bible, had richly adorned temples in several of the Philistine cities. In profane history, the name by which he is known is *Derceto*. He is represented as having the face and hands of a man and the tail of a fish; and he seems to have been generally regarded as a symbol of fertility and reproduction. See *Judges* xvi. 23; 1 *Sam.* v. 4.

> Next came one
> Who mourned in earnest, when the captive ark
> Maimed his brute image, head and hands lopped off
> In his own temple, on the grunsel edge,
> Where he fell flat, and shamed his worshippers:
> *Dagon* his name; sea-monster, upward man
> And downward fish: yet had his temple high
> Reared in Azotus, dreaded through the coast
> Of Palestine, in Gath and Ascalon,
> And Accaron and Gaza's frontier bounds.
> *Milton.*

Dag'o-net, Sir. The attendant fool of King Arthur. [Written also D a g u e n e t.]

> I was then *Sir Dagonet* in Arthur's show.
> *Shak.*

Dal-gar'no, Lord. A prominent character in Sir Walter Scott's "Fortunes of Nigel;" a profligate young Scottish lord, thoroughly heartless and shameless, who carried "the craft of gray hairs under his curled love-locks."

Dal-ġet'ty, Rittmaster Dü'gȧld. A mercenary soldier of fortune in Sir Walter Scott's "Legend of Montrose," distinguished for his pedantry, conceit, cool intrepidity, vulgar assurance, knowledge of the world, greediness, and a hundred other qualities, making him one of the most amusing, admirable, and natural characters ever drawn by the hand of genius.

> ☞ "The general idea of the character is familiar to our comic dramatists after the Restoration, and may be said in some measure to be compounded of Captain Fluellen and Bobadil; but the ludicrous combination of the *soldado* with the divinity student of Marcschal College is entirely original." *Jeffrey.*

> Our second remark is of the circumstance that no Historian or Narrator, neither Schiller, Strada, Thuanus, Monroc, nor *Dugald Dalgetty*, makes any mention of Ahasuer's having been present at the battle of Lützen. *Carlyle.*

> He [a hack author] lets out his pen to the highest bidder, as *Captain Dalgetty* let out his sword. *E. P. Whipple.*

Damis (dȧ'me'). A character in Molière's comedy of "Tartuffe," distinguished by his self-willed impetuosity.

Dam'o-clēs̱. [Gr. Δαμοκλῆς.] A courtier of the elder Dionysius, the tyrant of Syracuse. Having extolled the happiness caused by the possession of wealth and power, Dionysius gave him a striking illustration of the real nature of such seeming happiness, by placing him at a table loaded with delicacies, and surrounded by all the insignia of royalty, but, in the midst of his magnificent banquet, Damocles, chancing to look upward, saw a sharp and naked sword suspended over his head by a single horse-hair. A sight so alarming instantly changed his views of the felicity of kings.

> Like *Damocles* at his celebrated banquet, Rebecca perpetually beheld, amid the gorgeous display, the sword which was suspended over the heads of her people by a single hair.
> *Sir W. Scott.*

> On what *Damocles*-hairs must the judgment-sword hang over this distracted earth.
> *Carlyle.*

Dą̊-mœ'tąs. A herdsman in Theocritus and Virgil; hence, any herdsman or rustic.

> Rough satyrs danced, and fauns with cloven heel

---

and for the Remarks and Rules to which the numbers after certain words refer, see pp. xiv-xxxii.

Dā'mŏn. [Gr. Δάμων.] 1. A noble Pythagorean of Syracuse, memorable for his friendship for Pythias, or Phintias, a member of the same sect. The latter, having been condemned to death by Dionysius I., the tyrant of Syracuse, begged leave to go home for the purpose of arranging his affairs, Damon pledging his own life for the return of his friend. Dionysius consented, and Pythias came back just in season to save Damon from death. Struck by so rare and noble an example of mutual friendship, the tyrant pardoned Pythias, and entreated to be admitted as a third into their sacred fellowship.

2. A goat-herd in the third Eclogue of Virgil; hence, any rustic or swain.

Damsel of Brittany. A name given to Eleanora, daughter of Geoffrey, second son of Henry II. of England, and Duke of Brittany by marriage with Constance, the daughter and heiress of Duke Conan IV.

☞ Richard, the successor of Henry, dying without issue, the English crown rightfully devolved upon Arthur, the son of Geoffrey; but John, the brother of Richard, and the youngest of the sons of Henry, determined to secure it to himself. He, therefore, managed to capture the young prince, his nephew, and consigned him to close custody, first in the castle of Falaise, and afterward at Rouen, where he is supposed to have murdered him by his own hand. Arthur being dead, the next in the order of succession was Eleanor, his sister. John, however, obtained possession of her person, carried her to England, and confined her in the castle of Bristol, in which prison she remained till her death, in 1241.

Dan'ā-e. [Gr. Δανάη.] (*Gr. & Rom. Myth.*) The daughter of Acrisius, and the mother of Perseus by Jupiter, who visited her in the form of a shower of gold when she was shut up in a tower by her father.

Dă-nā'ĭ-dēṣ. [Lat.; Gr. Δαναΐδες.] (*Gr. & Rom. Myth.*) The fifty daughters of Danaus, king of Argos, betrothed to the fifty sons of Ægyptus, all of whom they killed on the first night after marriage, in fulfilment of a promise exacted by Danaus, Lynceus alone excepted, who was spared by his wife Hypermnestra. Her guilty sisters were punished for their crime, in Hades, by being compelled everlastingly to draw water out of a deep well, and pour it into a vessel full of holes.

Dandie Dinmont. See DINMONT, DANDIE.

Dandin, George (zhŏrzh dŏn'dăn', 58, 62, 64). The title of a comedy by Molière, and the name of its hero, a wealthy French citizen, who has had the impudence to marry a sprig of quality, daughter of an old noble called Monsieur de Sotenville, and his no less noble spouse, Madame de la Prudoterie, and who, in consequence, is exposed at once to the coquetry of a light-headed wife, and to the rigorous sway of her parents, who, called upon to interpose with their authority, place their daughter in the right, and the unhappy *roturier*, their son-in-law, in the wrong, on every appeal which is made to them. Falling, in consequence of this *mésalliance*, into many disagreeable situations, he constantly exclaims, "*Tu l'as voulu, George Dandin,*" You would have it so, George Dandin. The expression has hence become proverbial to denote self-inflicted pain, and the name is commonly applied to any silly, simple-minded fellow.

If you have really been fool enough to fall in love there, and have a mind to play *George Dandin*, I'll find you some money for the part. *C. Reade.*

Dandin, Perrin (pĕr'răn' dŏn'dăn', 62.) 1. The name of an ignorant rustic judge in Rabelais, who heard causes sitting on the first trunk of a tree which he met, instead of seating himself, like other judges, on the fleurs-de-lis.

2. The name of a ridiculous judge, in Racine's comedy, "Les Plaideurs," and in La Fontaine's " Fables."

Dangle. A prominent character in Sheridan's farce, "The Critic ; " one of those theatrical amateurs who besiege a manager with impertinent flattery and gratuitous advice. He is said to have been intended for a Mr. Thomas Vaughan, author of "The Hotel," an indifferently successful play.

Daniel, The Well-languaged. A name given by William Browne (1590-1645), in his "Britannia's Pastorals," to the English poet Samuel Daniel (1562-1619), whose writings are remarkable for their modern style and pervading purity of taste and grace of language.

Daph'ne. [Gr. Δάφνη.] (*Gr. & Rom. Myth.*) A beautiful maiden beloved by Apollo, and metamorphosed into a laurel-tree while attempting to escape from him.

Nay, lady, sit; if I but wave this wand,
Your nerves are all chained up in alabaster,
And you a statue, or, as *Daphne* was,
Root-bound, that fled Apollo. *Milton.*

Daph'nis. [Gr. Δάφνις.] (*Gr. & Rom. Myth.*) A beautiful young Sicilian shepherd, a son of Mercury. He was the inventor of bucolic poetry, and a favourite of Pan and Apollo.

Dapper. A clerk in "The Alchemist," a play by Ben Jonson.

This reminds us of the extreme doting attachment which the queen of the fairies is represented to have taken for *Dapper*.
Sir W. Scott.

Dapple. The name of Sancho's ass, in Cervantes's romance of "Don Quixote."

Dar'by and Jōan. A married couple said to have lived, more than a century ago, in the village of Healaugh, in the West Riding of Yorkshire, and celebrated for their long life and conjugal felicity. They are the hero and heroine of a ballad called "The Happy Old Couple," which has been attributed to Prior, but is of uncertain authorship. Timperley says that Darby was a printer in Bartholomew Close, who died in 1730, and that the ballad was written by one of his apprentices by the name of Henry Woodfall.

You might have sat, like *Darby and Joan*, and flattered each other; and billed and cooed like a pair of pigeons on a perch. *Thackeray.*

Indeed now, if you would but condescend to forgive and forget, perhaps some day or other we may be *Darby and Joan*,— only, you see, just at this moment I am really not worthy of such a *Joan*. *Sir E. Bulwer Lytton.*

Dar'dạ-nus. [Gr. Δάρδανος.] (*Gr. & Rom. Myth.*) The son of Jupiter and Electra of Arcadia, and ancestor of the royal race of Troy.

Dā'rḗs (9). One of the competitors at the funeral games of Anchises in Sicily, described in the fifth book of Virgil's "Æneid." He was overcome at the combat of the cestus by Entellus.

A Trojan combat would be something new:
Let *Dares* beat Entellus black and blue.
Cowper.

Dark and Bloody Ground, The. An expression often used in allusion to Kentucky, of which name it is said to be the translation. The phrase is an epitome of the early history of the State, of the dark and bloody conflicts of the first white settlers with their savage foes; but the name originated in the fact that this was the grand battle-ground between the northern and southern Indians.

Dark Day, The. May 19, 1780;— so called on account of a darkness on that day extending over all New England. In some places, persons could not see to read common print in the open air for several hours together. Birds sang their evening song, disappeared, and became silent; fowls went to roost; cattle sought the barn-yard; and candles were lighted in the houses. The obscuration began about ten o'clock in the morning, and continued till the middle of the next night, but with differences of degree and duration in different places. For several days previous, the wind had been variable, but chiefly from the southwest and the northeast. The true cause of this remarkable phenomenon is not known.

David. See JONATHAN.

Dā'vus. The name commonly given to slaves in Latin comedies. The proverb, "*Davus sum, non Œdipus*," I am Davus, not Œdipus, (that is, a simple servant, not a resolver of riddles,) occurs in Terence.

Dā'vy. Servant to Shallow, in the Second Part of Shakespeare's "King Henry IV."

---

and for the Remarks and Rules to which the numbers after certain words refer, see pp. xlv-xxxii.

Davy Jones. See JONES, DAVY.

Daw'son, Bully (-sn). A noted London sharper, swaggerer, and debauchee, especially in Blackfriars and its infamous purlieus. He lived in the seventeenth century, and was a contemporary of Rochester and Etherege. An allusion to him occurs in the "Spectator," No. 2.

> Tom Brown had a shrewder insight into this kind of character than either of his predecessors. He divides the palm more equably, and allows his hero a sort of dimidiate pre-eminence: — "*Bully Dawson* kicked by half the town, and half the town kicked by *Bully Dawson.*" This was true retributive justice.
> *Charles Lamb.*

> When, in our cooler moments, we reflect on his [Homer's] Jove-protected warriors, his invulnerable Achilles, they dwindle into insignificance, and we are ready to exclaim, in the quaint language of another, "*Bully Dawson* would have fought the Devil with such advantages."
> *Jones Very.*

Day of Barricades. [Fr. *Journée des Barricades.*] (*Fr. Hist.*) 1. May 12, 1588, on which day the Duke of Guise entered Paris, when Henry III., at his instigation, consented to take severe measures against the Huguenots, on the promise that the duke would assist him in purging Paris of strangers and obnoxious persons. No sooner, however, was an attempt made to carry out this plan, than the populace arose, erected barricades, and attacked the king's troops with irresistible fury. Henry III., having requested the Duke of Guise to put a stop to the conflict, fled from Paris, and the moment the duke showed himself to the people, they pulled down the barricades.

2. August 26, 1648; — so called on account of a riot, instigated by the leaders of the Fronde, which took place in Paris on that day.

Day of Corn-sacks. [Fr. *Journée des Farines.*] (*Fr. Hist.*) A name given to the 3d of January, 1591, from an attempt made by Henry IV. to surprise Paris on that day. Some of his officers, disguised as corn-dealers, with sacks on their shoulders, endeavoured to get possession of the gate St. Honoré; but they were recognised, and obliged to make a hasty retreat.

Day of Dupes. [Fr. *Journée des Dupes.*] (*Fr. Hist.*) 1. A name given to the 11th of November, 1630, in allusion to a celebrated imbroglio by which the opponents of the prime minister Richelieu — at the head of whom were Maria de' Medici and Anne of Austria — were completely worsted in an attempt to effect his removal from office, and the power of the cardinal was established upon a firmer basis than ever.

> Richelieu himself could not have taken a gloomier view of things, when his levees were deserted, and his power seemed annihilated before the *Day of Dupes.*
> *Sir E. Bulwer Lytton.*

2. August 4th, 1789; — so called on account of the renunciation by the nobles and clergy in the French National Convention of their peculiar immunities and feudal rights.

Day of Gold Spurs. [Fr. *Journée des Éperons d' Or.*] See BATTLE OF SPURS.

Day of the Sections. [Fr. *Journée des Sections.*] (*Fr. Hist.*) The name commonly given to an affray which occurred on the 4th of October, 1793, between the troops under the control of the Convention and the National Guard acting in the interest of the sections of Paris. The contest resulted in the success of the Convention.

Dean of St. Patrick's. A title of Jonathan Swift (1667-1745), the celebrated English satirist, by which he is often referred to. The deanery of St. Patrick's is in Dublin. Swift was appointed to the place in 1713, and retained it until his death.

Deans, Douce Dā'vie. A poor cow-feeder at Edinburgh, and the father of Effie and Jeanie Deans, in Sir Walter Scott's novel, "The Heart of Mid-Lothian." He is remarkable for his religious peculiarities, for his magnanimity in affliction, and his amusing absurdities in prosperity.

Deans, Effie. A character in Scott's "Heart of Mid-Lothian," whose lover abandons her after effecting her ruin.

Deans, Jēan'ïe. The heroine of Scott's "Heart of Mid-Lothian." The circumstances of her history are based upon facts communicated to the author by a correspondent.

☞ "She is a perfect model of sober heroism; of the union of good sense with strong affections, firm principles, and perfect disinterestedness; and of the calm superiority to misfortune, danger, and difficulty, which such a union must create." *Senior.*

We follow the travellers [in the "Pilgrim's Progress"] through their allegorical progress with interest not inferior to that with which we follow Elizabeth from Siberia to Moscow, or *Jeanie Deans* from Edinburgh to London. *Macaulay.*

Debatable Land, The. A tract of land on the western border of England and Scotland, between the Esk and Sark, which was at one time claimed by both kingdoms, and was afterward divided between them. It was long the residence of thieves and banditti, to whom its dubious state afforded a refuge.

Decree of Fontainebleau (fon'tān-blo'). (*Fr. Hist.*) An edict of the Emperor Napoleon I., dated at Fontainebleau, October 18, 1810, ordering the burning of all English goods.

Ded'lock, Sir Lĕices'tẽr (les'tẽr). A character in Dickens's novel of "Bleak House." "He is an honourable, obstinate, truthful, high-spirited, intensely prejudiced, perfectly unreasonable man."

Deerslayer. The hero of Cooper's novel of the same name.

☞ "This character ... is the author's ideal of a chivalresque manhood, of the grace which is the natural flower of purity and virtue; not the Stoic, but the Christian of the woods, the man of honourable act and sentiment, of courage and truth." *Duyckinck.*

Defender of the Faith. [Lat. *Fidei Defensor.*] A title conferred, in 1521, by Pope Leo X. upon King Henry VIII. of England, in consequence of a Latin treatise "On the Seven Sacraments" which the latter had published in confutation of Luther, and had dedicated to that pontiff. The title was not made heritable by his heirs, and Pope Paul III., in 1535, upon the king's apostasy in turning suppressor of religious houses, formally revoked and withdrew it. Henry, however, continued to use it as a part of the royal style, and, in 1543, parliament annexed it for ever to the crown by stat. 35 Hen. VIII. c. 3.

☞ It has been shown that the same title was popularly applied to, or was assumed by, some of the kings of England who preceded Henry VIII., as Richard II. and Henry VII.

Deg'o-re', Sir. [A corruption of *Dégaré*, or *L'égaré*, meaning a person "almost lost."] The hero of a romance of high antiquity, and formerly very popular, an abstract of which may be seen in Ellis's "Specimens of the Early English Poets."

De-id'ă-mi'ă. [Gr. Δηϊδάμεια.] (*Gr. & Rom. Myth.*) The daughter of Lycomedes, king of Scyros, and the mother of Pyrrhus by Achilles.

De-iph'o-bus. [Gr. Δηΐφοβος.] (*Gr. & Rom. Myth.*) A son of Priam and Hecuba. After the death of Paris, he married Helen, but was betrayed by her to the Greeks. Next to Hector, he was the bravest among the Trojans.

Dej'ă-ni'r̆ă (9). [Gr. Δηϊάνειρα.] (*Gr. & Rom. Myth.*) A daughter of Œneus, and the wife of Hercules, whose death she involuntarily caused by sending him a shirt which had been steeped in the poisoned blood of Nessus, who falsely told her that his blood would enable her to preserve her husband's love. On hearing that Hercules had burnt himself to death to escape the torment it occasioned, she killed herself in remorse and despair.

Delauney, Le Vicomte (lŭ ve'kŏⁿt' d'lō'nā', 62). A *nom de plume* of Mme. Delphine de Girardin (1804–1855), under which she published her best-known work, the "Parisian Letters" ("*Lettres Parisiennes*"), which originally appeared in "La Presse," a newspaper edited by her husband, Émile de Girardin.

Delectable Mountains. In Bunyan's allegory of "The Pilgrim's Progress," a range of hills from whose summit might be seen the Celestial City.

"When the morning was up, they had him to the top of the house, and bid him look south. So he did, and behold, at a great distance he saw a most pleasant mountainous country, beautified with woods, vineyards, fruits of all sorts, flowers also, with springs and fountains, very delectable to behold. *Isa.* xxxiii. 16, 17. . . . They then went till they came to the Delectable Mountains. . . . Now there were on the tops of these mountains shepherds feeding their flocks. The pilgrims, therefore, went to them, and, leaning on their staffs (as is common with weary pilgrims when they stand to talk with any by the way), they asked, 'Whose delectable mountains are these, and whose be the sheep that feed upon them?'" The shepherds answered, "These mountains are Emmanuel's land, and they are within sight of his city, and the sheep are his, and he laid down his life for them."

On the Muses' hill he is happy and good as one of the shepherds on the *Delectable Mountains.* *Charles Lamb.*

Delia. A poetical name given by the Roman poet Tibullus (d. about B. C. 18) to his lady-love, whose real name is not certainly known, but is thought to have been *Plania* (from *planus*), of which the Greek *Delia* (from δῆλος, clear, manifest, plain) is a translation.

De′li-ă. [Gr. Δηλία.] } (*Gr. & Rom.*
De′li-us. [Gr. Δήλιος.] } *Myth.*) Surnames respectively of Diana and Apollo, as born in Delos. See DELOS.

Delight of Mankind. A name given by his subjects to Titus, emperor of Rome (40–81), whose liberality, affability, mildness, and virtuous conduct were the subject of general admiration.

Del′lă Crŭs′căns, *or* **Della Crusca School** (del′lă kroōs′kă). A collective appellation applied to a class of sentimental poetasters of both sexes, who arose in England toward the close of the last century, and who were conspicuous for their affectation and bad taste, and for their high-flown panegyrics on one another.

Their productions consisted of odes, elegies, epigrams, songs, sonnets, epistles, plays, &c.

☞ Some of these persons had, by chance, been jumbled together for a while at Florence, where they put forth a volume of rhymes, under the title of "The Florence Miscellany," the insipidity and fantastic silliness of which transcend all belief. Afterward, they and a number of other persons, their admirers and imitators, began to publish their effusions in England, chiefly in two daily newspapers called "The World" and "The Oracle;" from which they were soon collected, and, with vast laudation, recommended to the public attention in a volume entitled "The Album," by Bell, the printer. An end was at length put to these inanities by the appearance, in 1794, of Gifford's "Baviad," which, in 1796, was followed by its continuation, the "Mæviad," — both powerful and extremely popular satires, which lashed the Della Crusca authors with merciless but deserved severity. One of the founders of this school of poetry, Mr. Robert Merry, wrote under the signature of *Della Crusca,* and this name was given to the whole brood of rhymsters to which he belonged, probably because he became the most noted of them. Merry had travelled for some years on the Continent, and had made a long residence in Florence, where he was elected a member of the celebrated Academy *Della Crusca,* — that is, Academy of the Sieve, — which was founded for the purpose of purifying and refining the Italian language and style. In adopting the name of this Academy as a *nom de plume,* Merry may not only have alluded to the fact of his membership, but very possibly intended to intimate that what he should write would be quite exquisite, and free from chaff. It would appear that Merry was not the first of the writers whose lucubrations came out in "The Oracle" and "The World;" for, says Gifford, "While the epidemic malady was spreading from fool to fool, Della Crusca came over [from Italy], and immediately announced himself by a sonnet to Love. Anna Matilda wrote an incomparable piece of nonsense in praise of it; and the two 'great luminaries of the age,' as Mr. Bell calls them, fell desperately in love with each other. From that period, not a day passed without an amatory epistle, fraught with lightning and thunder, *et quicquid habent telorum armamentaria cæli.* The fever turned to frenzy: Laura, Maria, Carlos, Orlando, Adelaide, and a thousand other nameless names, caught

of the Middle Ages. In the old mysteries and miracle-plays, he was often represented on the stage as a sort of satyr or faun, with flaming saucer eyes, sooty complexion, horns, tail, hooked nails, the cloven hoof of a goat or horse, and a strong sulphurous odour. At the present day, the doctrine of the existence of a personal Devil, the chief of evil spirits, and directly or indirectly the author of at least all moral evil, is maintained by most Christians, but rejected by many. See ABADDON, BEËLZEBUB, SATAN, &c.

Devils' Parliament. [Lat. *Parliamentum Diabolicum.*] (*Eng. Hist.*) A name given to the Parliament assembled by Henry VI. at Coventry, 1459, because it passed attainders against the Duke of York and his chief supporters.

Devil's Wall. A name given by the inhabitants of the neighbourhood to the old Roman wall separating England from Scotland, because they supposed, that, from the strength of the cement and the durability of the stone, the Devil must have built it. The superstitious peasantry are said to be in the habit of gathering up the fragments of this wall to put in the foundation of their own tenements to insure an equal solidity.

Devonshire Poet. A sobriquet or pseudonym of O. Jones, an uneducated journeyman wool-comber, author of "Poetic Attempts," London, 1786.

Diable, Le (lụ de-ȧ'bl, 61). [Fr., the Devil.] A surname given to Robert I., Duke of Normandy. See ROBERT THE DEVIL.

Diabolical Parliament. See DEVILS' PARLIAMENT.

Diafoirus, Thomas (to'mȧ' de'ȧ'fwŏ'-rüss', 34, 102). A young and pedantic medical student, about to be dubbed doctor, who figures in Molière's "Malade Imaginaire" as the lover of Angélique.

The undoubting faith of a political *Diafoirus.*
    Macaulay.

Diamond State. A name sometimes given to the State of Delaware, from its small size and its great worth, or supposed importance.

Di-ā'nă, or **Di-an'ȧ.** (*Gr. & Rom. Myth.*) Originally, an Italian divinity, afterward regarded as identical with the Greek *Artemis*, the daughter of Jupiter and Latona, and the twin sister of Apollo. She was the goddess of hunting, chastity, marriage, and nocturnal incantations. She was also regarded as the goddess of the moon. See LUNA. Her temple at Ephesus was one of the Seven Wonders of the World. [Written also, poetically, D i a n.]

Hence [from chastity] had the huntress *Dian*
  her dread bow,
Fair silver-shafted queen, for ever chaste,
Wherewith she tamed the brinded lioness
And spotted mountain pard, but set at nought
The frivolous bow of Cupid ; gods and men
Feared her stern frown, and she was queen of
  the woods.   *Milton.*

Diavolo, Fra. See FRA DIAVOLO.

Dicky Sam. A cant name applied to the inhabitants of Liverpool.

Diddler, Jeremy. A character in Kenny's farce of "Raising the Wind," where he is represented as a needy and seedy individual, always contriving, by his songs, *bon-mots,* or other expedients, to borrow money or obtain credit.

Di'do. [Gr. Διδώ.] The daughter of Belus, king of Tyre, and the wife of Sichæus, whom her brother Pygmalion murdered for his riches. Escaping to Africa, she purchased as much land as could be encompassed with a bullock's hide, which — after the bargain was completed — she craftily cut into small shreds, and thus secured a large piece of territory. Here, not far from the Phœnician colony of Utica, she built the city of Carthage. According to Virgil, when Æneas was shipwrecked upon her coast, in his voyage to Italy, she hospitably entertained him, fell in love with him, and, because he did not requite her passion, stabbed herself in despair. [Called also *Elisa,* or *Elissa.*]

Dig'go-ry. A talkative, awkward servant in Goldsmith's comedy, "She Stoops to Conquer,"—"taken from the barn to make a show at the sidetable."

You might as well make Hamlet (or *Digory*) "act mad" in a strait-waistcoat, as trammel my buffoonery, if I am to be a buffoon. — *Byron.*

Dimanche, M. (mos′e-ŏ′ de′mŏⁿsh′, 43, 62). [Fr., Mr. Sunday.) A sobriquet popularly given, in France, to a creditor or dun, in allusion to an honest merchant of this name, introduced by Molière into his "Don Juan," (a. iv., sc. 3). He is so called, doubtless, because merchants and working-men, having no other day in the week to themselves, take Sunday for presenting their bills and collecting the money which is due to them.

Dinah, Aunt. Mr. Walter Shandy's aunt, in Sterne's novel of "Tristram Shandy." She bequeathed to him a thousand pounds, which he had as many schemes for expending.

Din′mont, Dan′die (or **Andrew**). A humourous and eccentric storefarmer in Sir Walter Scott's novel of "Guy Mannering;" one of the best of rustic portraits.

Di′o-med, or **Di′o-mēde.** [Lat. *Diomedes*, Gr. Διομήδης.] (*Gr. & Rom. Myth.*) A son of Tydeus, king of Ætolia. He was one of the most renowned of the Grecian chiefs at the siege of Troy, where he performed many heroic deeds. He vanquished in fight Hector and Æneas, the most valiant of the Trojans, and, along with Ulysses, carried off the Palladium, on which the safety of Troy depended. [Called also *Tydides.*]

Di-o′ne. [Gr. Διώνη.] (*Gr. & Rom. Myth.*) A nymph who was, according to some accounts, the mother of Venus.

Di-on′y̆-sus. [Gr. Διόνυσος, or Διώνυσος.] (*Gr. Myth.*) The youthful, beautiful, and effeminate god of wine; the same as *Bacchus.* See BACCHUS.

Di-os′cu-ri. [Gr. Διόσκουροι, sons of Zeus, or Jupiter.] (*Gr. & Rom. Myth.*) The well-known heroes Castor and Pollux, or Polydeuces. See CASTOR.

Di′ræ (9). (*Rom. Myth.*) A name or title of the Furies, given to them from their dreadful appearance.

Dir′ce (4). [Gr. Δίρκη.] Wife of the Theban prince Lycus. For cruel treatment of Antiope, she was tied to a mad bull, and dragged about till dead. See ANTIOPE and LYCUS.

Dis. [Lat., kindred with *divus*, god.] (*Rom. Myth.*) A name sometimes given to Pluto, and hence also to the infernal world.

Quick is the movement here! And then so confused, unsubstantial, you might call it almost spectral, pallid, dim, inane, like the kingdoms of *Dis!* — *Carlyle.*

Dis-cor′di-ă. (*Rom. Myth.*) A malevolent deity corresponding with the Greek *Eris*, the goddess of contention. See PARIS.

Dī′vēs. A Latin word meaning *rich*, or *a rich man.* It is a common or appellative noun, or, more strictly, an adjective used substantively; but it is often erroneously regarded as a proper name, when allusion is made to our Lord's parable of the rich man and Lazarus. (See *Luke* xvi.) It has been suggested that the mistake originally arose from the fact, that, in old pictures upon this subject, the inscription, or title, was in Latin, "*Dives et Lazarus,*" and that uneducated persons probably supposed that the first word was the name of the rich man, as the last unquestionably was that of the beggar.

Lazar and *Dives* liveden diversely,
And divers guerdon hadden they thereby. — *Chaucer.*

Nor have you, O poor parasite, and humble hanger-on, much reason to complain! Your friendship for *Dives* is about as sincere as the return which it usually gets. — *Thackeray.*

Divine Doctor. An appellation given to Jean Ruysbroek (1294–1381), a celebrated mystic.

Dix′ie. An imaginary place somewhere in the Southern States of America, celebrated in a popular negro melody as a perfect paradise of luxurious ease and enjoyment. The term is often used as a collective designation of the Southern States. A correspondent of the "New Orleans Delta" has given the following account of the original and early application of the name:—

☞ For the "Key to the Scheme of Pronunciation," with the accompanying Explanations,

"I do not wish to spoil a pretty illusion, but the real truth is, that Dixie is an indigenous Northern negro refrain, as common to the writer as the lamp-posts in New York city seventy or seventy-five years ago. It was one of the every-day allusions of boys at that time in all their out-door sports. And no one ever heard of Dixie's land being other than Manhattan Island until recently, when it has been erroneously supposed to refer to the South from its connection with pathetic negro allegory. When slavery existed in New York, one 'Dixy' owned a large tract of land on Manhattan Island, and a large number of slaves. The increase of the slaves, and the increase of the abolition sentiment, caused an emigration of the slaves to more thorough and secure slave sections; and the negroes who were thus sent off (many being born there) naturally looked back to their old homes, where they had lived in clover, with feelings of regret, as they could not imagine any place like Dixy's. Hence, it became synonymous with an ideal locality, combining ease, comfort, and material happiness of every description. In those days, negro singing and minstrelsy were in their infancy, and any subject that could be wrought into a ballad was eagerly picked up. This was the case with 'Dixie.' It originated in New York, and assumed the proportions of a song there. In its travels, it has been enlarged, and has 'gathered moss.' It has picked up a 'note' here and there. A 'chorus' has been added to it; and, from an indistinct 'chant' of two or three notes, it has become an elaborate melody. But the fact that it is not a Southern song 'cannot be rubbed out.' The fallacy is so popular to the contrary, that I have thus been at pains to state the real origin of it."

Diz'zy. A nickname given to Benjamin Disraeli (b. 1805), an eminent living English statesman.

Djinnestan (jin'nes-tăn'). The name of the ideal region in which *djinns*, or genii, of Oriental superstition reside. [Written also Jinnostan.]

Doctor, The. A nickname often given to the first Lord Viscount Sidmouth (1757-1844), on account of his being the son of Doctor Anthony Addington of Reading.

Doctor, The Admirable. See ADMIRABLE DOCTOR; and for ANGELIC DOCTOR, AUTHENTIC DOCTOR, DIVINE DOCTOR, DULCIFLUOUS DOCTOR, ECSTATIC DOCTOR, ELOQUENT DOCTOR, EVANGELICAL or GOSPEL DOCTOR, ILLUMINATED DOCTOR, INVINCIBLE DOCTOR, IRREFRAGABLE DOCTOR, MELLIFLUOUS DOCTOR, MOST CHRISTIAN DOCTOR, MOST METHODICAL DOCTOR, MOST RESOLUTE DOCTOR, PLAIN AND PERSPICUOUS DOCTOR, PROFOUND DOCTOR, SCHOLASTIC DOCTOR, SERAPHIC DOCTOR, SINGULAR DOCTOR, SOLEMN DOCTOR, SOLID DOCTOR, SUBTLE DOCTOR, THOROUGH DOCTOR, UNIVERSAL DOCTOR, VENERABLE DOCTOR, WELL-FOUNDED DOCTOR, and WONDERFUL DOCTOR, see the respective adjectives.

Doctor Dóve. The hero of Southey's "Doctor."

Doctor Dulcamara (dŏŏl-kȧ-mä'rȧ). An itinerant physician in Donizetti's opera, "L'Elisir d'Amore" ("The Elixir of Love"); noted for his charlatanry, boastfulness, and pomposity.

Doctor My-book. A sobriquet very generally bestowed upon John Abernethy (1765-1830), the eminent English surgeon. "I am christened *Doctor My-book*, and satirised under that name all over England." The celebrated "My-book," to which he was so fond of referring his patients, was his "Surgical Observations."

Doctor of the Incarnation. A title given to St. Cyril of Alexandria (d. 444), on account of his long and tumultuous dispute with Nestorius, bishop of Constantinople, who denied the mystery of the hypostatic union, and contended that the Deity could not have been born of a woman; that the divine nature was not incarnate in, but only attendant on, Jesus as a man; and therefore that Mary was not entitled to the appellation then commonly used of Mother of God.

Doctor Slop. 1. The name of a choleric and uncharitable physician in Sterne's novel, "The Life and Opinions of Tristram Shandy, Gent." He breaks down Tristram's nose, and crushes Uncle Toby's fingers to a jelly, in attempting to demonstrate the use and virtues of a newly invented pair of obstetrical forceps. Under this name Sterne ridiculed one Doctor Burton, a man-midwife at York, against whom he had some pique.

☞ "The annals of satire can furnish nothing more cutting and ludicrous than this consummate portrait, so farcical, and yet so apparently free from satire."
Elwin.

2. The name was applied to Doctor (afterward Sir John) Stoddart (1773–1856), in caricature pamphlets, on account of his violent prejudices, and the rancorous denunciations with which he assailed the first Napoleon and his policy in the London "Times" newspaper, — of which he was editor from 1812 to 1816, — and also on account of the part he took at the time of the Queen-Caroline *émeute* in 1820–21.

Doctor Squintum. A name under which the celebrated George Whitefield (1714–1770) was ridiculed in Foote's farce of "The Minor." It was originally given to him by Theodore Hook, who afterwards applied it to the Rev. Edward Irving (1792–1834), who had a strong cast in his eyes.

Doctor Syntax. The hero of a work by William Combe (1741–1823), entitled "The Tour of Dr. Syntax in Search of the Picturesque," formerly very popular.

Do-do'nă. [Gr. Δωδώνη.] A very famous oracle of Jupiter in Epirus, situated in an oak grove; said to have been founded in obedience to the command of a black dove with a human voice, which came from the city of Thebes in Egypt.

And I will work in prose and rhyme,
And praise thee more in both
Than bard has honoured beech or lime,
Or that Thessalian growth
In which the swarthy ringdove sat
And mystic sentence spoke. *Tennyson.*

Dods, Meg. 1. An old landlady in Scott's novel of "St. Ronan's Well;" one of his best low comic characters.

· ☞ "Meg Dods, one of those happy creations, approaching extravagance but not reaching it, formed of the most dissimilar materials without inconsistency, . . . excites in the reader not the mere pleasure of admiring a skilful copy, but the interest and curiosity of an original, and recurs to his recollection among the real beings whose acquaintance has enlarged his knowledge of human nature."
Senior.

2. An *alias*, or pseudonym, under which Mrs. Johnstone, a Scottish authoress, published a well-known work on cookery.

Dod'son and Fogg (-sn). Pettifogging lawyers in partnership, who figure in the famous case of "Bardell *vs.* Pickwick," in Dickens's "Pickwick Papers."

Doe, John. A merely nominal plaintiff in actions of ejectment at common law; usually associated with the name of *Richard Roe.*

☞ The action of ejectment is a species of mixed action, which lies for the recovery of possession of real estate, and damages and costs for the detention of it. It was invented either in the reign of Edward II., or in the beginning of the reign of Edward III., in order to enable suitors to escape from "the thousand niceties with which," in the language of Lord Mansfield, "real actions [that is, actions for the recovery of real estate] were embarrassed and entangled." In order to foster this form of action, the court early determined (*circiter* A. D. 1445–1499) that the plaintiff was entitled to recover not merely the damages claimed by the action, but also, by way of collateral and additional relief, the land itself. This form of action is based entirely upon a legal fiction, introduced in order to make the trial of the lessor's title, which would otherwise be only incidentally brought up for examination, the direct and main object of the action. A sham plaintiff — John Doe — pretends to be the lessee of the real claimant, and alleges that he has been ousted by a sham defendant, — Richard Roe, — who is called the "casual ejector." Notice of this action is then given to the actual tenant of the lands, together with a letter from the imaginary Richard Roe stating that he shall make no appearance to the action, and warning the tenant to defend his own interest, or, if he be only the tenant of the real defendant, to give the latter due notice of the proceeding. If no appearance is made, judgment is given in favour of the plaintiff, who thereupon becomes entitled to turn out the party in possession. But if the latter makes appearance, the first step in the action is a formal acknowledgment by him of his possession of the lands, of the

☞ For the "Key to the Scheme of Pronunciation," with the accompanying Explanations,

lease in favour of Doe, of Doe's entry, and of the ouster by the tenant himself. This elaborate tissue of fictions having been introduced to comply with the technical rules of legal title, when the real question at issue presents itself, John Doe and Richard Roe disappear, the names of the real parties are substituted, and the action proceeds in the ordinary way at once to trial. The action of ejectment is still retained, with all its curious fictions, in several of the United States; in New York, Pennsylvania, and other States, the fictitious part of the action has been abolished. It has also been abolished, in England, by the Common Law Procedure Act of 1852 (15 and 16 Victoria, c.,76). *Warren. Chambers.*

☞ "Those mythical parties to so many legal proceedings, John Doe and Richard Roe, are evidently of forest extraction, and point to the days when forest laws prevailed, and venison was a sacred thing." *Lower.*

It was then I first became acquainted with the quarter which my little work will, I hope, render immortal, and grew familiar with these magnificent wilds through which the kings of Scotland once chased the dark-brown deer, but which were chiefly recommended to me, in those days, by their being inaccessible to those metaphysical persons whom the law of the neighbouring country terms *John Doe* and *Richard Roe.* *Sir W. Scott.*

While the patriotic author is weeping and howling, in prose, in blank verse, and in rhyme, and collecting the drops of public sorrow into his volume, as into a lachrymal vase, it is more than probable his fellow-citizens are eating and drinking, fiddling and dancing, as utterly ignorant of the bitter lamentations made in their name as are those men of straw, *John Doe* and *Richard Roe,* of the plaintiffs for whom they are generously pleased to become sureties. *W. Irving.*

Dō'eg. [From *Doeg*, chief of Saul's herdsmen, "having charge of the mules." 1 *Sam.* xxi. 7.] A nickname under which Dryden, in the second part of his "Absalom and Achitophel," satirised Elkanah Settle (1648-1743), a contemptible poetaster, who was for a time Dryden's successful rival.

Doeg, though without knowing how or why,
Made still a blundering kind of melody,
Spurred boldly on, and dashed through thick and thin,
Through sense and nonsense, never out nor in;
Free from all meaning, whether good or bad,
And, in one word, heroically mad. *Dryden.*

Dōe'sticks, Q. K. Phi-lan'dẽr. A pseudonym adopted by Mortimer Thompson, an American comic writer of the present day.

Dog'bẽr-ry. An ingeniously absurd, self-satisfied, and loquacious night-constable, in Shakespeare's "Much Ado about Nothing."

It is an important examination, and therefore, like *Dogberry*, we must spare no wisdom. *Sir W. Scott.*

Dŏm'bey, Florence. The heroine of Dickens's novel of "Dombey and Son;" a motherless child, of angelic purity and loveliness of character.

Dŏm'bey, Mr. A prominent character in Dickens's novel of "Dombey and Son;" a proud, self-sufficient, and wealthy merchant, who is disciplined and made better by a succession of disasters.

Dom-dan'ĭ-el. A cave in the region adjoining Babylon, the abode of evil spirits, by some traditions said to have been originally the spot where the prophet Daniel imparted instruction to his disciples. In another form, the Domdaniel was a purely imaginary region, subterranean, or submarine, the dwelling-place of genii and enchanters.

In the *Domdaniel* caverns,
Under the roots of the ocean,
Met the Masters of the Spell. *Southey.*

We find it written, "Woe to them that are at ease in Zion;" but surely it is a double woe to them that are at ease in Babel, in *Domdaniel.* *Carlyle.*

Dominic, Friar. See FRIAR DOMINIC.

Dominie Samp'son (-sn). A schoolmaster in Sir W. Scott's novel of "Guy Mannering;" "a poor, modest, humble scholar," says the author, "who had won his way through the classics, but fallen to the leeward in the voyage of life, — no uncommon personage in a country where a certain portion of learning is easily attained by those who are willing to suffer hunger and thirst in exchange for acquiring Greek and Latin." His usual ejaculation when astonished was, "Pro-di-gi-ous!" [Called also *Abel Sampson.*]

Poor Jnng [Stilling], a sort of German *Dominic Sampson*, awkward, honest, irascible, in old-fashioned clothes and bag-wig. *Carlyle.*

Don Ä'dri-ä'no de Ar-mä'do. A

and for the Remarks and Rules to which the numbers after certain words refer, see pp. xlv-xxxii.

pompous, fantastical Spaniard, in Shakespeare's "Love's Labour's Lost;" represented as a lover and a retainer of the court, and said to have been designed as a portrait of John Florio, surnamed "The Resolute." See RESOLUTE, THE.

☞ "Armado, the military braggart in the state of peace, as Parolles is in war, appears in the ridiculous exaggeration and affectation of a child of hot Spanish fancy, assuming a contempt toward every thing common, boastful but poor, a coiner of words, but most ignorant, solemnly grave and laughably awkward, a hector and a coward, of gait majestical and of the lowest propensities."
Gervinus, Trans.

Don Belianis of Greece (bā'le-à'-nĕss). The hero of an old romance of chivalry founded upon the model of the "Amadis," but with much inferior art, and on a coarser plan. An English abridgment of this romance was published in 1673. It is often referred to in "Don Quixote."

He called you "le grand sérieux," *Don Belianis of Greece,* and I don't know what names, mimicking your manner. *Thackeray.*

Don Chĕr'ŭ-bim. The "Bachelor of Salamanca," in Le Sage's novel of this name; a man placed in different situations of life, and made to associate with all classes of society, in order to give the author the greatest possible scope for satire.

Don Cle'o-făs. The hero of Le Sage's novel, "Le Diable Boiteux" (commonly called in English "The Devil on Two Sticks"); a fiery young Spaniard, proud, high-spirited, and revengeful, but interesting from his gallantry and generous sentiments. See ASMODEUS. [Written also Cleophas.]

Farewell, old Granta's spires;
No more, like *Cleofas,* I fly. *Byron.*

Come away though, now, *Don Cleophas:* we must go further afield. *Sala.*

Don Jū'ăn (*Sp. pron.* dŏn hoo-än'). A mythical personage who figures largely in drama, melodrama, and romance, as the type of refined libertinism.

☞ There are two legends connected with the name, both of Spanish origin, but in course of time these have become so blended together that they cannot easily be separated. Don Juan Tenorio of Seville, whose life has been placed in the fourteenth century, is the supposed original of the story. The traditions concerning him were long current in Seville, in an oral form, and were afterward dramatised by Gabriel Tellez (Tirso de Molina). He is said to have attempted the seduction of the daughter of the governor of Seville, or of a nobleman of the family of the Ulloas. Her father detects the design, and is killed in a duel which ensues. A statue of the murdered man having been erected in the family tomb, Don Juan forces his way into the vault, and invites the statue to a feast which he has caused to be prepared. The stony guest makes his appearance at table, as invited, to the great amazement of Don Juan, whom he compels to follow him, and delivers over to hell. The legend, in its earliest known form, involved the same supernatural features, the ghostly apparition, the final reprobation and consignment to hell, which have, in general, characterised the modern treatment of the subject. From the Spanish the story was translated by the Italian playwrights; thence it passed into France, where it was adopted and brought upon the stage by Molière and Corneille. In Italy, Goldoni made it the basis of a play. The first instance of a musical treatment of the subject was by Gluck, in his ballet of "Don Juan," about the year 1765. Afterward Mozart immortalised the tradition in his great opera, "Don Giovanni," which first appeared at Vienna in 1787. The name has been rendered most familiar to English readers by the use which Byron has made of it in his poem entitled "Don Juan." But the distinguishing features of the old legend, those which separate Don Juan from the multitude of vulgar libertines, Byron has omitted, and he can hardly be said to have done more than borrow the name of the hero.

☞ "As Goethe has expressed the eternal significance of the German legend of Faust, so has Mozart best interpreted the deep mystery of the Spanish legend; the one by language, the other by music. Language is the interpreter of thought, music of feeling. The *Faust-sage* belongs to the former domain; the legends of Don Juan to the latter."
Scheible, Trans.

We could, like *Don Juan,* ask them [Dante's ghosts and demons) to supper, and eat heartily in their company. *Macaulay.*

Don't break her heart, Jos, you rascal, said another. Don't trifle with her affections, you *Don Juan!* *Thackeray.*

Don Pedro. A Prince of Arragon who figures in Shakespeare's "Much Ado about Nothing."

The author of "Hajji Baba" returned an answer of a kind most likely to have weight with a Persian, and which we can all observe is, like *Don Pedro's* answer to Dogberry, "rightly reasoned; and in his own division."
Sir W. Scott.

Don Quix'ŏte. [Sp. *Don Quijote,* or *Don Quixote,* dŏn ke-ho'tä]. The hero of a celebrated Spanish romance of the same name, by Cervantes. Don Quixote is represented as "a gaunt country gentleman of La Mancha, full of genuine Castilian honour and enthusiasm, gentle and dignified in his character, trusted by his friends, and loved by his dependents," but "so completely crazed by long reading the most famous books of chivalry, that he believes them to be true, and feels himself called on to become the impossible knight-errant they describe, and actually goes forth into the world to defend the oppressed and avenge the injured, like the heroes of his romances."

☞ "To complete his chivalrous equipment, — which he had begun by fitting up for himself a suit of armour strange to his century, — he took an esquire out of his neighbourhood ; a middle-aged peasant, ignorant and credulous to excess, but of great good-nature ; a glutton and a liar ; selfish and gross, yet attached to his master ; shrewd enough occasionally to see the folly of their position, but always amusing, and sometimes mischievous, in his interpretations of it. These two sally forth from their native village in search of adventures, of which the excited imagination of the knight, turning windmills into giants, solitary inns into castles, and galley-slaves into oppressed gentlemen, finds abundance wherever he goes ; while the esquire translates them all into the plain prose of truth with an admirable simplicity, quite unconscious of its own humour, and rendered the more striking by its contrast with the lofty and courteous dignity and magnificent illusions of the superior personage. There could, of course, be but one consistent termination of adventures like these. The knight and his esquire suffer a series of ridiculous discomfitures, and are at last brought home, like madmen, to their native village, where Cervantes leaves them, with an intimation that the story of their adventures is by no means ended. In a continuation, or Second Part, published in 1615, the Don is exhibited in another series of adventures, equally amusing with those in the First Part, and is finally restored, ' through a severe illness, to his right mind, made to renounce all the follies of knight-errantry, and die, like a peaceful Christian, in his own bed.'"
Ticknor.

☞ "Some say his surname was Quixada, or Quisada (for authors differ in this particular). However, we may reasonably conjecture he was called Quixada, that is, Lantern-jaws. . . . Having seriously pondered the matter eight whole days, he at length determined to call himself Don Quixote. Whence the author of this most authentic history draws the inference that his right name was Quixada, and not Quisada, as others obstinately pretend." *Quixote* means literally a cuish, or piece of armour for the thigh. Cervantes calls his hero by the name of this piece of armour, because the termination *ote,* with which it ends, generally gives a ridiculous meaning to words in the Spanish language.

Be this law and this reasoning right or wrong, our interfering to arrange it would not be a whit more wise or rational than *Don Quixote's* campaign against the windmills.
Noctes Ambrosianæ.

Don'zel del Phe'bo. [It., *donzello,* a squire, a young man.] A celebrated hero of romance, in the "Mirror of Knighthood," &c. He is usually associated with Rosiclear.

Defend thee powerfully, marry thee sumptuously, and keep thee in spite of Rosiclear or *Donzel del Phebo.* *Malcontent,* Old Play.

Doo'lin of Māy-ence' (*Fr. pron.* dō'lăⁿ). The hero of an old French romance of chivalry which relates his exploits and wonderful adventures. He is chiefly remarkable as the ancestor of a long race of paladins, particularly Ogier le Danois.

Dora. The "child-wife" of David Copperfield, in Dickens's novel of that name.

Doralice (*It. pron.* do-rä-le'chä). A female character in Ariosto's "Orlando Furioso." She is loved by Rodomont, but marries Mandricardo.

Dorante (do'rŏⁿt', 62.) 1. A count in Molière's comedy, "Le Bourgeois Gentilhomme."

2. A courtier devoted to the chase, who figures in Molière's comedy, "Les Fâcheux."

3. A character in Molière's "L'École des Femmes."

I am going to make it known bluntly to that . . . old beau, to that *Dorante* become a Géronte. *Victor Hugo, Trans.*

Do-ras′tus. The hero of an old popular "history" or romance, upon which Shakespeare founded his "Winter's Tale." It was written by Robert Greene, and was first published in 1588, under the title of "Pandosto, the Triumph of Time," an example, according to Hallam, of "quaint, affected, and empty euphuism."

Do′rax (9). A character in Dryden's play of "Don Sebastian;" represented as a noble Portuguese turned renegade.

☞ "Dorax is the *chef-d'œuvre* of Dryden's tragic characters, and perhaps the only one in which he has applied his great knowledge of human kind to actual delineation." *Edin. Review*, 1808.

But some friend or other always advised me to put my verses in the fire, and, like *Dorax* in the play, I submitted, "though with a swelling heart." *Sir W. Scott.*

Dorchester, Patriarch of. See PATRIARCH OF DORCHESTER.

Doria D'Istria (do′re-ä dĕs′tre-ä). A pseudonym of Princess Koltzoff-Massalsky (*née* Helena Ghika, b. 1829), a distinguished Wallachian authoress.

Dŏr′I-cōurt. A character in Congreve's "Way of the World."

Dŏr′I-mănt. A character in Etherege's play entitled "The Man of Mode;" a genteel witty rake, designed as a portrait of the Earl of Rochester.

I shall believe it when *Dorimant* hands a fish-wife across the kennel. *Charles Lamb.*

Dorine (do′rĕn′). A hasty and petulant female in Molière's "Tartuffe;" represented as ridiculing the family that she yet serves with sincere affection.

Do′ris (9). [Gr. Δωρίς.] (*Gr. & Rom. Myth.*) The daughter of Oceanus and Tethys, and the wife of her brother Nereus, by whom she became the mother of the Nereids.

Dŏr′o-the′ä (*Ger. pron.* do-ro-tā′ä). 1. The heroine of Goethe's celebrated poem of "Hermann und Dorothea."

2. [Sp. *Dorotea*, do-ro-tā′ä.] A beautiful and unfortunate young woman whose adventures form an episode in the romance of "Don Quixote."

Do′ry, John (9). 1. The title and hero of an old ballad, formerly a great favourite, and continually alluded to in works of the sixteenth and seventeenth centuries.

2. A character in "Wild Oats, or The Strolling Gentleman," a comedy by John O'Keefe.

Do what I might, he interfered with the resolute vigour of *John Dory*. *Hood.*

Dô′the-boyş Hall. [That is, the hall where boys are taken in and "done for."] A model educational establishment described in Dickens's "Nicholas Nickleby," kept by a villain named Squeers, whose system of tuition consisted of alternate beating and starving.

Oliver Twist in the parish work-house, Smike at *Dotheboys Hall*, were petted children when compared with this wretched heir-apparent of a crown [Frederick the Great]. *Macaulay.*

Dotted Bible. A name given among bibliographers to an edition of the Bible published in London, in folio, 1578, by assignment of Chr. Barker. It is printed page for page with that of 1574.

Doubting Castle. In Bunyan's spiritual romance of "The Pilgrim's Progress," a castle belonging to Giant Despair, in which Christian and Hopeful were confined, and from which at last they made their escape by means of the key called Promise, which was able to open any lock in the castle.

Conceive the giant Mirabeau locked fast, then, in *Doubting Castle* of Vincennes; his hot soul surging up, wildly breaking itself against cold obstruction, the voice of his despair reverberated on him by dead stone-walls. *Carlyle.*

Douloureuse Garde, La (lä doo′loo′-rōz′ gård, 43). [Fr.] The name of a castle at Berwick-upon-Tweed, won by Lancelot of the Lake in one of the most terrific adventures related in romance, and thenceforth called

La Joyeuse Garde. See JOYEUSE GARDE, LA.

Dôus'tĕr-swiv'el (-swiv'l). 1. (Herman.) A German schemer, in Sir Walter Scott's novel of "The Antiquary." 2. A nickname given by the Scotch reviewers to Dr. John Gaspar Spurzheim (1766–1832), a native of Germany, a distinguished craniologist, and an active promulgator of the doctrines of phrenology in Great Britain.

Dove, Doctor. See DOCTOR DOVE.

Dŏw, Jr. A pseudonym adopted by Eldridge F. Paige (d. 1859), an English humourist, author of "Patent Sermons," &c.

Down'ing, Jack. A pseudonym under which Seba Smith, an American writer, wrote a series of humourous and popular letters (first published collectively in 1833), in the Yankee dialect, on the political affairs of the United States.

Dra'co. [Gr. Δράκων.] An Athenian lawgiver, whose code punished almost all crimes with death; whence it was said to be not that of a man but of a dragon (δράκων), and to have been written not in ink but in blood.

Dragon of Wănt'ley. The subject of an old comic ballad, — a frightful and devouring monster, killed by More of More-Hall, who procured a suit of armour studded all over with long sharp spikes, and, concealing himself in a well resorted to by the dragon, kicked him in the mouth, where alone he was mortal. This legend has been made the foundation of a burlesque opera by Henry Carey. *Wantley* is a vulgar pronunciation of Warncliff, the name of a lodge and a wood in the parish of Penniston, in Yorkshire.

Drā'pi-ĕr, M. B.,. A pseudonym under which Swift addressed a series of celebrated and remarkable letters to the people of Ireland, relative to a patent right granted by George I., in 1723, to one William Wood, allowing him, in consideration of the great want of copper money existing in Ireland at that time, to coin halfpence and farthings to the amount of £108,000, to pass current in that kingdom. As the patent had been obtained in what may be termed a surreptitious manner, through the influence of the Duchess of Kendal, the mistress of George I., to whom Wood had promised a share of the profits; as it was passed without consulting either the lord lieutenant or the privy council of Ireland; and as it devolved upon an obscure individual the right of exercising one of the highest privileges of the crown, thereby disgracefully compromising the dignity of the kingdom, — Swift, under the assumed character of a draper (which for some reason he chose to write *drapier*), warned the people not to receive the coin that was sent over to them. Such was the unequalled adroitness of his letters, such their strength of argument and brilliancy of humour, that, in the end, they were completely successful: Wood was compelled to withdraw his obnoxious patent, and his copper coinage was totally suppressed, while the Drapier — for whose discovery a reward of £300 had been offered in vain — was regarded as the liberator of Ireland; his health became a perpetual toast, his head was adopted as a sign, a club was formed in honour of him, and his portrait was displayed in every street.

Draw'can-sir. The name of a blustering, bullying fellow in the celebrated mock-heroic play of "The Rehearsal," written by George Villiers, Duke of Buckingham, assisted by Sprat and others. He is represented as taking part in a battle, where, after killing all the combatants on both sides, he makes an extravagantly boastful speech. From the popularity of the character, the name became a synonym for a braggart.

☞ "*Johnson.* Pray, Mr. Bayes, who is that Drawcansir?
Bayes. Why, sir, a great hero, that frights his mistress, snubs up kings, baffles armies, and does what he will, without regard to numbers, good sense, or justice." *The Rehearsal.*

and for the Remarks and Rules to which the numbers after certain words refer, see pp. xiv–xxxii.

The leader was of an ugly look and gigantic stature; he acted like a *Drawcansir*, sparing neither friend nor foe. *Addison.*

In defiance of the young *Drawcansir's* threats, with a stout heart and dauntless accent, he again uplifted the stave, —
" The Pope, that pagan full of pride,
Hath blinded ——." *Sir W. Scott.*

How they [the actors in the French Revolution] bellowed, stalked, and flourished about, counterfeiting Jove's thunder to an amazing degree! terrific *Drawcansir*-figures, of enormous whiskerage, unlimited command of gunpowder; not without ferocity, and even a certain heroism, stage heroism, in them.
Carlyle.

Drish-een' City. A name popularly given to the city of Cork, from a dish peculiar to the place, and formerly a very fashionable one among the inhabitants. Drisheens are made of the serum of the blood of sheep mixed with milk and seasoned with pepper, salt, and tansy. They are usually served hot for breakfast, and are eaten with drawn butter and pepper.

Dro'gi-o. The name given, by Antonio Zeno, a Venetian voyager of the fourteenth century, to a country of vast extent, equivalent to a new world. It is represented as lying to the south and west of Estotiland, and, by those who confided in the narrative, was identified with Nova Scotia and New England. The whole story is thought to be fabulous.

Dro'mi-o of Eph'e-sus. } Twin
Dro'mi-o of Syr'a-cūse. } brothers, attendants on the two Antipholuses in Shakespeare's "Comedy of Errors."

Drugger, Abel. A character in Ben Jonson's farce of " The Tobacconist."

Drum, John. A name used in the phrase, " John Drum's entertainment," which seems to have been formerly a proverbial expression for ill treatment, probably alluding originally to some particular anecdote. Most of the allusions seem to point to the dismissing of some unwelcome guest, with more or less of ignominy and insult. [Written also, though rarely, Tom Drum.]

Oh, fo, the love of laughter, let him fetch his drum; he says he has a stratagem for it; when your lordship sees the bottom of his success in 't, and to what metal this counterfeit lump of ore will be melted, if you give him not *John Drum's* entertainment, your inclining cannot be removed. *Shak.*

Tom Drum his entertainment, which is to hale a man in by the head, and thrust him out by both the shoulders. *Stanihurst.*

Drunken Parliament. (*Scot. Hist.*) A name given to the Parliament which assembled at Edinburgh, Jan. 1, 1661, soon after the restoration of the Stuarts. Burnet says, " It was a mad, warring time, full of extravagance; and no wonder it was so when the men of affairs were almost perpetually drunk."

Dry'ǎds. [Lat. *Dryades*, Gr. Δρυάδες.] (*Gr. & Rom. Myth.*) Nymphs who presided over the woods, and were thought to perish with the trees which were their abode.

Dry'as-dust, The Rev. Dr. An imaginary personage who serves as a sort of introducer of some of Scott's novels to the public, through the medium of prefatory letters, purporting to be written either to him or by him, in relation to their origin and history. The name is sometimes used to stigmatise a dull, plodding author, particularly an historian or a writer upon antiquities.

Nobody, he must have felt, was ever likely to study this great work of his, not even *Dr. Dryasdust.* *De Quincey.*

There was a Shandean library at Skelton that would have captivated the most ascetic of *Dryasdusts.* *Percy Fitzgerald.*

Truth is, the Prussian *Dryasdust*, otherwise an honest fellow, excels all other *Dryasdusts* yet known. I have often sorrowfully felt as if there were not in Nature, for darkness, dreariness, immethodic platitude, any thing comparable to him. *Carlyle.*

Dry'o-pe. [Gr. Δρυόπη.] (*Gr. & Rom. Myth.*) A daughter of King Dryops, and the wife of Andræmon, — turned into a poplar or a lotus by the Hamadryads. She had a son Amphissos by Apollo.

'T was a lay
More subtle-cadenced, more forest-wild
Than *Dryope's* lone lulling of her child.
Keats.

Du-es'sȧ. [That is, double-minded.] A foul witch, in Spenser's " Faëry Queen," who, under the assumed name of Fidessa, and the assumed character of a distressed and lovely woman, entices the Red-cross Knight into the House of Pride, where, enervated by self-indulgence, he is attacked, defeated, and imprisoned by

☞ For the " Key to the Scheme of Pronunciation," with the accompanying Explanations,

the giant Orgoglio. Duessa becomes the paramour of Orgoglio, who decks her out in gorgeous ornaments, gives her a gold and purple robe to wear, puts a triple crown on her head, and sets her upon a monstrous beast with seven heads,—from which circumstances the poet is supposed to typify the Roman Catholic church. Una, having heard of the Red-cross Knight's misfortune, sends Prince Authur to his rescue, who slays the giant, wounds the beast, releases the knight, and strips Duessa of her splendid trappings, upon which she flees into the wilderness to hide her shame from the world.

At present, though her eyes [those of "popish bigotry"] are blindfolded, her hands are tied behind her, like the false *Duessa's*.
Hazlitt.

The people had now to see tyranny naked. That foul *Duessa* was stripped of her gorgeous ornaments. *Macaulay.*

Compassion and romantic honour, the prejudices of childhood, and the venerable names of history, threw over them a spell as potent as that of *Duessa*; and, like the Red-cross Knight, they thought they were doing battle for an injured beauty, while they defended a false and loathsome sorceress. *Macaulay.*

Duke Humphrey. 1. A name used in an old expression, "To dine with Duke Humphrey," that is, to have no dinner at all. This phrase is said to have arisen from the circumstance that a part of the public walks in old Saint Paul's, London, was called Duke Humphrey's Walk, and that those who were without the means of defraying their expenses at a tavern were formerly accustomed to walk here in hope of procuring an invitation.

☞ "In the form *Humfrey*, it [Hunifred] was much used by the great house of Bohun, and through his mother, their heiress, descended to the ill-fated son of Henry IV., who have left it an open question whether 'dining with Duke Humphrey' alludes to the report that he was starved to death, or to the Elizabethan habit for poor gentility to beguile the dinner-hour by a promenade near his tomb in old St. Paul's." *Yonge.*

It distinctly appears . . . that one Diggory Chuzzlewit was in the habit of perpetually dining with *Duke Humphrey*. So constantly was he a guest at that nobleman's table, indeed, and so unceasingly were his Grace's hospitality and companionship forced, as it were, upon him, that we find him uneasy, and full of constraint and reluctance; writing his friends to the effect, that, if they fail to do so and so by bearer, he will have no choice but to dine again with *Duke Humphrey*. *Dickens.*

2. **Duke Humphrey, the Good.** See GOOD DUKE HUMPHREY.

Dulcamara, Doctor. See DOCTOR DULCAMARA.

Dulcifluous Doctor. [Lat. *Doctor Dulcifluus*.] A name given to Antony Andreas (d. 1320), a Spanish Minorite, and a theologian of the school of Duns Scotus.

Dulcinea del Toboso (dul-sin′e-ä del to-bo′zo; *Sp. pron.* dool-thē-nä′ä del to-bo′zo). In Cervantes's romance, the mistress of Don Quixote. "Her name was Aldonza Lorenzo, and her he pitched upon to be the lady of his thoughts; then casting about for a name which should have some affinity with her own, and yet incline toward that of a great lady and princess, he resolved to call her Dulcinea del Toboso (for she was born at that place), a name, to his thinking, harmonious, uncommon, and significant." The name *Dulcinea* is often used as synonymous with mistress or sweetheart.

I must ever have some *Dulcinea* in my head,—it harmonises the soul. *Sterne.*

If thou expectest a fine description of this young woman, in order to entitle thee to taunt me with having found a *Dulcinea* in the inhabitant of a fisherman's cottage on the Solway Frith, thou shalt be disappointed.
Sir W. Scott.

His moodiness must have made him perfectly odious to his friends under the tents, who like a jolly fellow, and laugh at a melancholy warrior always sighing after *Dulcinea* at home. *Thackeray.*

Du-māine′. A lord attending on the king of Navarre, in Shakespeare's "Love's Labour's Lost."

Dum′ble-dikes. A young and bashful Scotch laird, in love with Jeanie Deans, in Sir Walter Scott's novel, "The Heart of Mid-Lothian."

Dumb Ox. [Lat. *Bos Mutus*.] St. Thomas Aquinas;—said to have been so named by his fellow-pupils at Cologne, on account of his silence and apparent stupidity. His teacher, however, detected the genius that was wrapped up under his taciturnity, and remarked, that, if that ox should once begin to bellow, the world would be filled with the noise. He was afterwards known as the "Angel of the Schools" and the "Angelic Doctor."

☞ "He was the Aristotle of Christianity, whose legislation he drew up, endeavouring to reconcile logic with faith for the suppression of all heresy. . . . His overpowering task utterly absorbed this extraordinary man, and occupied his whole life, to the exclusion of all else, — a life that was entirely one of abstraction, and whose events are ideas. From five years of age he took the Scriptures in his hand, and henceforward never ceased from meditation. In the schools, he was called by his companions *the great dumb ox of Sicily*. He only broke this silence to dictate; and when sleep closed the eyes of his body, those of his soul remained open, and he went on still dictating. One day, at sea, he was not conscious of a fearful tempest; another, so deep was his abstraction, he did not let fall a lighted candle which was burning his fingers." *Michelet, Trans.* Michelet, in a note, says of this surname, that it is "full of meaning to all who have noticed the dreamy and monumental appearance of the ox of Southern Italy." St. Thomas is described as a large-bodied man, fat and upright, of a brown complexion, and with a large head, somewhat bald.

Of a truth it almost makes me laugh,
To see men leaving the golden grain,
To gather in piles the pitiful chaff
That old Peter Lombard thrashed with his brain,
To have it caught up and tossed again
On the horns of the *Dumb Ox* of Cologne!
Longfellow.

Dun'cán (dŭngk'ăn). A king of Scotland immortalised in Shakespeare's tragedy of "Macbeth." Shakespeare represents him as murdered by Macbeth, who succeeds to the Scottish throne; but, according to veritable history, he fell in battle.

Dunces' Parliament. See PARLIAMENT OF DUNCES.

Dundas, Starvation. See STARVATION DUNDAS.

Dun-drĕar'y, Lord. A grotesque character in Taylor's comedy, "Our American Cousin;" noted for his aristocratic haughtiness of manner, his weakness and excessive indolence of mind, his habit of discontinuit in expression, his great admiratio of "Brother Sam," and his suspi cion of insanity in his friends, in from any motive which he does no understand, they constantly cross hi convenience. The name is used al lusively to characterise any empty swell.

Dun Ed'in. A Celtic assimilation of the name Edinburgh (*i. e.*, Edwin's burgh), serving at the same time as a descriptive designation of its site, the words meaning "the face of a rock." In Scottish poetry, the name is often used as a synonym for *Edinburgh*. [Written also D u n e d i n, as a single word.]

When the streets of high *Dunedin*
Saw lances gleam, and falchions redden,
And heard the slogan's deadly yell,—
Then the Chief of Branksome fell.
Sir W. Scott.

No, not yet, thou high *Dun Edin*,
Shalt thou totter to thy fall;
Though thy bravest and thy strongest
Are not there to man the wall. *Aytoun.*

Dun-shun'nĕr, Augustus. A *nom de plume* of Professor William Edmonstoune Aytoun (1813–1865), in "Blackwood's Magazine."

Durandal (doo'rŏn'dál'). [Of uncertain etymology. The root is probably the Fr. *dur*, hard, *durer*, to resist.] The name of a marvellous sword of Orlando, the renowned hero of romance. It is said to have been the workmanship of the fairies, who endued it with such wonderful properties that its owner was able to cleave the Pyrenees with it at a blow. See ORLANDO. [Written also D u r a n d a r t, Durindane, Durindale, Durindana, Durenda, Durendal, and D u r l i n d a n a.]

Durandarte (doo-răn-dar'tă). A fabulous hero of Spain, celebrated in the ancient ballads of that country, and in the romances of chivalry. Cervantes has introduced him, in "Don Quixote," in the celebrated adventure of the knight in the Cave of Montesinos. He is represented as a cousin of Montesinos, and, like him, a peer of France. At the battle of Roncesvalles, he expires in the arms of Montesinos. Both of these characters are regarded by Ticknor as imaginary personages.

<small>In the mean time, as *Durandarte* says in the Cave of Montesinos, "Patience, and shuffle the cards."   *Byron.*</small>

Dur'den, Dame (dur'dn). 1. The heroine of a popular English song. She is described as a notable housewife, and the mistress of numerous serving-girls and labouring men.
2. A sobriquet applied to Esther Summerson, the heroine of Dickens's "Bleak House."

Durga (dōōr'gȧ). (*Hindu Myth.*) The consort of Siva, represented as having ten arms.

Dur'wȧrd, Quen'tin. The hero of Scott's novel of the same name; a young archer of the Scottish guard in the service of Louis XI. of France.

and for the Remarks and Rules to which the numbers after certain words refer, see pp. xlv-xxxii.

E.

Eagle of Brittany. [Fr. *L'Aigle de Bretagne.*] A title bestowed upon Bertrand du Guesclin (d. 1380), a native of Brittany, and constable of France, renowned for his gallantry and military skill.

Eagle of Divines. A title bestowed upon Thomas Aquinas, the famous theologian of the thirteenth century. See DUMB OX.

Eagle of French Doctors. [Fr. *L'Aigle des Docteurs de France.*] A surname given to Pierre d'Ailly (1350–1425), a celebrated French cardinal and theological disputant.

Eagle of Meaux (mō). [Fr. *L'Aigle de Meaux.*] A name popularly given to Jacques Bénigne Bossuet (1627–1704), a French divine celebrated for his extraordinary powers of pulpit eloquence, and for many years bishop of Meaux.

Eastern States. A name popularly given, in America, to the six New England States,—Maine, New Hampshire, Vermont, Massachusetts, Rhode Island, and Connecticut.

Eb′lis (*Arab. pron.* ib-lees′). The name given by the Arabians to the prince of the apostate angels, whom they represent as exiled to the infernal regions for refusing to worship Adam at the command of the Supreme. Eblis alleged, in justification of his refusal, that he himself had been formed of ethereal fire, while Adam was only a creature of clay. To gratify his revenge, Eblis tempted Adam and Eve, and succeeded in leading them to their fall from innocence, in consequence of which they were separated. The Mohammedans say, that, at the moment of the birth of their prophet, the throne of Eblis was precipitated to the bottom of hell, and the idols of the Gentiles were overturned. According to some, he is the same as the *Azazel* of the Hebrews. [Written also Iblis.]

Ebony. [That is, Black wood.] A humorous appellation given to Mr.

William Blackwood (1777–1834), original publisher of "Blackwood Magazine." He was so called James Hogg, the "Ettrick Shepherd," in a famous *jeu d'esprit*, titled "The Chaldee Manuscript, which appeared in the number October, 1817, but was immediately suppressed on account of its personalities and alleged immorality. T name is sometimes used as a synonym for the magazine itself.

Ech′o (*Lat. pron.* e′ko). [Gr. 'Ηχώ (*Gr. & Rom. Myth.*) An oread, w fell desperately in love with Narcissus. As her love was not returned she pined away in grief, until at l. there remained of her nothing l her voice.

Eckhardt, The Faithful (ek′ha 64). [Ger. *Der treue Eckhardt.*] legendary hero of Germany, represented as an old man with a white staff, who, in Eisleben, appears the evening of Maundy-Thursday and drives all the people into th houses, to save them from bei harmed by a terrible procession dead men, headless bodies, and tw legged horses, which immediate after passes by. Other traditic represent him as the companion the knight Tannhäuser, and as wa ing travellers from the Venusberg, mountain of fatal delights in the mythology of Germany. Tieck I founded a story upon this legen which has been translated into E1 lish by Carlyle, in which Eckha is described as the good servant w perishes to save his master's child from the seducing fiends of the mon tain. The German proverb, "Th art the faithful Eckhardt; thou wa est every one," is founded upon t tradition. See TANNHÄUSER.

Ecstatic Doctor. [Lat. *Doctor Ecstaticus.*] An honorary appellation co ferred upon Jean Ruysbroek (129 1381), one of the old schoolmen. was prior of the Canons Regular

the infection; and from one end of the kingdom to the other, all was nonsense and Della Crusca." Other writers of this school, besides Merry, whose names have been preserved, are Mr. Bertie Greathead, a man of property and good family; Mr. William Parsons, another gentleman of fortune; Mr. Edward Jerningham (" The Bard "), author of numerous plays and poems; Miles Peter Andrews, a writer of prologues and epilogues; Mr. Edward Topham, the proprietor of "The World;" the Rev. Charles Este (" Morosoph Este," as Gifford calls him), principal editor of that paper; Mr. Joseph Weston, a small magazine-critic of the day; James Cobbe, a now-forgotten farce-writer; Frederick Pilon, said to have been a player by profession; a Mr. Timothy, or Thomas, Adney (who wrote under the anagram of "Mit Yenda," or "Mot Yenda"); Mr. Thomas Vaughan (" Edwin "); Mr. John Williams (" Tony — or Anthony — Pasquin "); the celebrated James Boswell, who had not yet established his reputation as the prince of biographers; and the dramatists O'Keefe, Morton, Reynolds, Holcroft, Sheridan, and the Younger Colman, who survived and recovered from their discreditable connection with the Della Cruscan folly. Of the female [illegible text] principal names [illegible text] the widow of [illegible text] ut at that time [illegible text] le-master; [illegible text] Mr. [illegible] "), the [illegible] — s Stra[illegible] not rious Mrs. [illegible] her levity, in[illegible], was of ajo[illegible] and poeti[illegible] to the "Mr[illegible] he had been [illegible] —tterfl[illegible] [illegible] n,' he adds, [illegible] for was ing [illegible] ing imbecility, [illegible] hea[illegible] these poems with th[illegible] their praises with delight." On the other hand, the great patron, Bell, the printer, accused him of "bespattering nearly all the poetical eminence of the day." "But, on the whole," says Gifford, " the clamour against me was not loud, and was lost by insensible degrees in the applause of such as I was truly ambitious to please. Thus supported, the good effects of the satire (*gloriose loquor*) were not long in manifesting themselves. Della Crusca appeared no more in 'The Oracle,' and, if any of his followers ventured to treat the town with a soft sonnet, it was not, as before, introduced by a pompous preface.

Pope and Milton resumed their superiority, and Este and his coadjutors silently acquiesced in the growing opinion of their incompetency, and showed some sense of shame."

De'lŏs. [Gr. Δῆλος.] A small island in the Ægean Sea, one of the Cyclades. Here Apollo and Diana were born, and here the former had a famous oracle. Delos was at first a floating island, but Neptune fixed it to the bottom of the sea, that it might be a secure resting-place for Latona. See LATONA.

Del'phī. [Gr. Δελφοί.] [illegible] oracle of Apollo in Phoc[illegible] of Mount Parnassus. L[illegible] written Delphos by early Engl[illegible] writers.]

Apollo from his shrine
Can no more divine,
  With hollow shriek the steep of *Delphos* leaving.
No nightly trance, or breathèd spell,
Inspires the pale-eyed priest from the prophetic cell.   *Milton.*

Delphine (del'fēn'). The title of a novel by Mme. de Staël (1766–1817), and the name of its heroine, whose character is full of charm, and [illegible] to have been an [illegible] t [illegible] author [illegible] D[illegible]ne has a fa[illegible]le ve[illegible] nd di[illegible] [illegible] rted.

Del'tă. The signatur[illegible] under w[illegible]h Dr[illegible] M[illegible]beth Muir[illegible] a [illegible] tish writer (1778–1851), c[illegible]tributed a series of poems t[illegible] Blackwood's Magazine."

Del'ville, Mr O[illegible] [illegible] of C[illegible]ilia in Miss B[illegible]rt[illegible]ey s n[illegible]l of this name: a gentleman of wealth [illegible]gnifi[illegible]nt a d ostentatious in h[illegible] style of living, and distinguished for an air of haughty affability in his intercourse with his inferiors.

Even old *Delville* received Cecilia, though the daughter of a man of low birth.
    Sir W. Scott.

De-me'tĕr. [Gr. Δημήτηρ.] (*Myth.*) One of the great divinities of the Greeks, corresponding to the *Ceres* of the Romans. See CERES.

De-moc'rĭ-tus, Junior. A pseudonym under which Robert Burton (1576–1640) published his "Anatomy of Melancholy," a work which pre-

and for the Remarks and Rules to which the numbers after certain words refer, see pp. xiv-xxxii.

sents, in quaint language, and with many shrewd and amusing remarks, a view of all the modifications of that disease, and the manner of curing it. The name of Democritus, Junior, is introduced in the inscription on his monument in Christ-Church Cathedral. It alludes to Democritus of Abdera, the celebrated "Laughing Philosopher" of antiquity. See LAUGHING PHILOSOPHER.

De-mod'o-cus. [Gr. Δημόδοκος.] A famous bard mentioned in Homer's "Odyssey" as delighting the guests of King Alcinous, during their repast, by singing the loves of Mars and Venus, and the stratagem of the Wooden Horse, by means of which the Greeks gained entrance into Troy.

Then sing of secret things that came to pass
When beldam Nature in her cradle was;
And last of kings, and queens, and heroes old,
Such as the wise *Demodocus* once told
In solemn songs at King Alcinous' feast.
Milton.

De'mo-gor'gon. [Gr., from δαίμων, a god, and γοργός, fearful.] (*Myth.*) A formidable and mysterious deity, superior to all others, mentioned by Lutatius, or Lactantius, Placidus, the scholiast on Statius, and made known to modern readers by the account of Boccaccio, in his "Genealogia Deorum." According to Ariosto, the fairies were all subject to Demogorgon, who inhabited a splendid palatial temple on the Himalaya Mountains, where every fifth year he summoned them to appear before him, and give account of their deeds. The very mention of this deity's name was said to be tremendous; wherefore Lucan and Statius only allude to it.

Thou wast begot in *Demogorgon's* hall,
And saw'st the secrets of the world unmade.
Spenser.

The dreaded name
Of *Demogorgon*. *Milton.*

Derrydown Triangle. A sobriquet given to Lord Castlereagh (1769-1822), afterwards Marquess of Londonderry, in a parody on the Athanasian Creed by William Hone; the triangle referring, according to him, to "a thing having three sides; the meanest and most tinkling of all musical *instruments*; machinery used in military torture. DICTIONARY." See

the "Third Trial of William Hone before Lord Ellenborough," 3d edition, p. 9, London, 1818.

Des'de-mo'na. The heroine of Shakspeare's tragedy of "Othello," daughter of Brabantio, a Venetian senator, and wife of Othello, a Moorish general, who kills her in a groundless belief of her infidelity. See OTHELLO.

She was never tired of inquiring if sorrow had his young days faded; and was ready listen and weep, like *Desdemona*, at the story of his dangers and campaigns. *Thackeray.*

Deu-ca'li-on. [Gr. Δευκαλίων.] (*Gr. & Rom. Myth.*) A son of Prometheus, king of Phthia, in Thessaly. With his wife Pyrrha, he was preserved from a deluge sent upon the earth by Jupiter; and he became the progenitor of a new race of men, by throwing stones behind him, as directed by an oracle. From stones thrown by Pyrrha there sprang up women, and thus the world was repeopled.

Nor important less
Seemed their petition than when the ancient pair
In fables old, — less ancient yet than these,—
Deucalion and chaste Pyrrha, to restore
The race of mankind drowned, before the shrine
Of Themis stood devout. *Milton.*

Devil, The. In the Bible, and in Jewish and Christian theology, the sovereign spirit of evil, who is ever in active opposition to God. A majority of the early Christians, literally interpreting certain passages of Scripture, regarded him as an apostate angel, the instigator of a rebellion among the heavenly host, and their ruler in a kingdom of darkness opposed to Christ's kingdom of light. To his agency was ascribed all evil, physical as well as moral, and it was believed, that, save crimes, he was doomed to suffer less torment in a material hell, though his power was supreme if not guarded by Christian fall rites, over those who were thus armed, it was so weak that they easily rise superior to his influence. As prince of the demons, and as the ideal of evil, vice, heresy, subtlety and knavery, he has figured prominently in literature, especially the

ial in Brabant,

ir, in Shake-
ear."
: PERPETUAL

, or nŏnt, 62).
rated decree,
98, by which
ranted tolera-
bjects. It was
., on the 18th
result of this
, rather than
shed religion,
- among the
gent, and re-
uitted France,
ireat Britain,
tzerland, and

(*Ger. Hist.*)
), by the Em-
Germany, re-
lent of many

poetical name
have been in-
, the Scottish

at!
towers,
onarch's feet,
n powers.
    Burns.

See WITCH

)n of Gloster,
ly of "Lear."
f Goldsmith's
ermit."
et's ballad of

's "Minstrel."
Fr., equality.]
792, by Louis
: of Orleans
1793), in place
in order to
populace.
4.) A nymph
na Pompilius
eived his in-
forms of pub-
established in

Rome. Their interviews took place in a grove near Aricia, or, according to some versions of the story, near Rome.

E-ġe'us. Father to Hermia, in Shakespeare's "Midsummer-Night's Dream."

Eg'lȧ-môur. 1. A character in Shakespeare's "Two Gentlemen of Verona," who is an agent of Silvia in her escape.

2. (Sir.) A valiant knight of the Round Table, celebrated in the romances of chivalry, and in an old ballad. [Written also E g l a m o r e.]

Eg'lan-tĭne, Madame. The name of the prioress, in Chaucer's "Canterbury Tales." She is distinguished for the mixture, in her manners and costume, of gentle worldly vanities and ignorance of the world; for her gayety, and the ever-visible difficulty she feels in putting on an air of courtly hauteur; for the lady-like delicacy of her manners at table; and for her partiality to lap-dogs.

Egypt. A cant popular designation of the southern portion of the State of Illinois, — being a figurative allusion to the "thick darkness" in which ancient Egypt was involved for three days, in the time of Moses; or, as some say, to the extraordinary fertility of that country. The inhabitants of Southern Illinois have had the reputation of being, in general, extremely ignorant. In its agricultural capabilities, and in actual fruitfulness, this region is unsurpassed, if not unequalled, by any other in the United States.

Egypt, Little. See LORDS OF LITTLE EGYPT.

Egyptian Thief. A personage alluded to by the Duke in Shakespeare's "Twelfth Night" (a. v., sc. 1). The reference is to the story of Thyamis, a robber-chief and native of Memphis, who, knowing he must die, would have stabbed his captive Chariclea, a woman whom he loved.

E-lāine'. A mythic lady connected with the romances of King Arthur's court. Her story is treated by Tennyson in his "Idylls of the King."

Elbow. A constable, in Shakespeare's "Measure for Measure," — ignorant and feeble-minded, but modest and well-meaning.

El Do-rā'do, *or* **El Do-rä'do.** [Sp., *the golden land.*] A name given by the Spaniards to an imaginary country, supposed, in the sixteenth century, to be situated in the interior of South America, between the rivers Orinoco and Amazon, and to abound in gold and all manner of precious stones. Expeditions were fitted out for the purpose of discovering this fabulous region; and, though all such attempts proved abortive, the rumours of its existence continued to be believed down to the beginning of the eighteenth century.

☞ It is said that the name was at first applied not to a country, but to a man, "*el rey dorado.*" Sir Walter Raleigh, in his "Discovery of the Large, Rich, and Beautiful Empire of Guiana," gives a description of the rising of this gilded king, whose chamberlains, every morning, after having rubbed his naked body with aromatic oils, blew powdered gold over it through long canes. After the name came to be used as the designation of a country, it seems to have been variously applied, and the expeditions in search of the golden land had different destinations. The whole of Guiana was sometimes included in the term. Humboldt, while exploring the countries upon the Upper Orinoco, was informed that the portion of Eastern Guiana lying between the rivers Essequibo and Branco was "the classical soil of the Dorado of Parima." Francis Orellana, a companion of Pizarro, first spread in Europe the account of this fabulous region.

In short, the whole comedy is a sort of *El Dorado* of wit, where the precious metal is thrown about by all classes as carelessly as if they had not the least idea of its value.
T. Moore.

There stoodest thou, in deep mountain amphitheatre, on umbrageous lawns, in the serene solitude; stately, massive, all of granite, glittering in the western sunbeams, like a palace of *El Dorado*, overlaid with precious metal.
Carlyle.

E-lec'trā. [Gr. Ἠλέκτρα.] (*Gr. & Rom. Myth.*) A daughter of Agamemnon and Clytemnestra, and the sister of Iphigenia. She became the accomplice of Orestes in the murder of their mother. See CLYTEMNESTRA and ORESTES.

Eleven Thousand Virgins, The. Celebrated characters in Roman Catholic history. The legend concerning them — which underwent some enlargements in the course of time — can be traced back as far as the ninth century, and is substantially as follows: Ursula, a saint of the Catholic church, being demanded in marriage by a pagan prince, and fearing to refuse him, apparently consented, but obtained a respite of three years, and a grant of ten triremes and ten noble companions, each, as well as herself, attended by one thousand virgins. She passed the three years with her virgins in nautical exercises; and when the marriage-day arrived, a sudden wind arose, and wafted them to the mouth of the Rhine, and thence to Basel. Here they left their vessels, and made a pilgrimage on foot to Rome. On their return, they encountered at Cologne an army of Huns, by whom they were massacred, Ursula having refused an offer of marriage from the prince. Their corpses were buried by the people of Cologne, and a church was erected to their honour, in which bones, said to be those of Ursula and her companions, are exhibited to this day.

☞ "This extravagant number of martyred virgins, which is not specified in the earlier legends, is said [Maury, 'Légendes Picuses,' p. 214] to have arisen from the name of one of the companions of Ursula being *Undecimella*, — an explanation very plausible, though I must confess that I have not been able to find any authority for the name *Undecimella.*"
Max Müller.

E'li-ā. A pseudonym under which Charles Lamb wrote a series of celebrated essays, which were begun in the "London Magazine," and were afterward collected and published by themselves.

☞ "The establishment of the 'London Magazine,' under the auspices of Mr. John Scott, occasioned Lamb's introduction to the public by the name and colour of which he acquired his most brilliant reputation, — 'Elia.' The adoption of this signature was purely accidental. His first contribution to the magazine was a description of the old South-Sea House, where Lamb had passed a few

months' novitiate as a clerk, thirty years before, and of its inmates who had long passed away; and, remembering the name of a gay, light-hearted foreigner, who fluttered there at that time, he subscribed his name to the essay." *Talfourd.*
Lamb's second paper was unsigned, and the printer repeated the signature which had been affixed to the first paper. This led to its being attached to subsequent contributions; and Lamb used it until, in his "Last Letters of Elia," he bade it a reluctant farewell.

He is also the true *Elia,* whose essays are extant in a little volume published a year or two since, and rather better known from that name without a meaning than from any thing he has done, or can hope to do, in his own. *Charles Lamb, Autobiographical Sketch,* 1827.

Comfort thee, O thou mourner, yet a while;
Again shall *Elia's* smile
Refresh thy heart, where heart can ache no more.
What is it we deplore? *Landor.*

l'i-dûre. A legendary king of Britain, fabled to have been advanced to the throne in place of his brother Artegal, or Arthgallo, who was deposed by powerful nobles to whom he had given great offence. Returning to the country after a long exile, Artegal accidentally encountered his brother, who received him with open arms, took him home to the palace, and reinstated him in his old position, abdicating the throne himself, after feigning a dangerous illness, by which he succeeded in inducing his peers once more to swear allegiance to his brother. Artegal reigned for ten years, wisely and well, and, after his death, was succeeded by Elidure. Wordsworth has taken the story of these two brothers for the subject of a poem. See ARTEGAL.

l'i-ŏt, George. The literary cognomen of Mrs. Mary A. (Evans) Lewes, a popular and very able novelist of the present day, author of "Adam Bede," "The Mill on the Floss," and other works.

-li'sḁ̊, or E-lis'sḁ̊. Another name of *Dido.* See DIDO.

livâgar (ä-le-vä'gar̃). [Old Norse *elf,* stream, and *vaga,* to wander.] (*Scand. Myth.*) The name of a great chaotic river flowing from a fountain in Niflheim. [Written also Elivaga and Elivagor.]

Elm City. The same as *City of Elms.* See CITY OF ELMS.

Elocution Walker. A name popularly given, in his lifetime, to John Walker, the English orthoëpist and lexicographer (1732–1807), who was for a long time a distinguished teacher of elocution among the higher classes in London.

Eloquent Doctor. [Lat. *Doctor Facundus.*] An honorary appellation given to Peter Aureolus, Archbishop of Aix in the fourteenth century.

El'shen-dĕr the Recluse. The " Black Dwarf," in Scott's novel of this name. [Called also *Canny Elshie.*]

El'speth. 1. A character in Sir Walter Scott's "Antiquary."
2. An old servant to Dandie Dinmont, in Scott's " Guy Mannering."

E-ly'sĭ-um (e-lizh'ĭ-um). [Gr. Ἠλύσιον.] (*Gr. & Rom. Myth.*) The blissful abode of the virtuous dead, placed by Homer in the west, on the border of the Ocean stream; by Hesiod and Pindar in the Fortunate Islands, or Isles of the Blest, in the Western Ocean; by Virgil in the under-world, with an entrance from a cave on the shore of Lake Avernus, in Campania. [Called also *Elysian Fields.*]

Em'bro. A common Scottish corruption of *Edinburgh.*

Emerald Isle. A name sometimes given to Ireland, on account of the peculiar bright green look of the surface of the country. It was first used by Dr. William Drennan (1754–1820), author of " Glendalloch, and other Poems." It occurs in his poem entitled " Erin."

" When Erin first rose from the dark-swelling flood,
God blessed the green island; he saw it was good.
The *Emerald* of Europe, it sparkled, it shone,
In the ring of this world the most precious stone.
. . . .
" Arm of Erin, prove strong; but be gentle as brave,
And, uplifted to strike, still be ready to save;
Nor one feeling of vengeance presume to defile
The cause or the men of the *Emerald Isle.*"

---

d for the Remarks and Rules to which the numbers after certain words refer, see pp. xiv–xxxii.

Émile (ā'mēl'). The subject of Jean Jacques Rousseau's novel of the same name, and his ideal of a perfectly educated young man.

E-mil'i-ā. 1. The lady-love of Palamon and Arcite in Chaucer's "Knight's Tale." See PALAMON.
2. A lady attending Hermione, in Shakespeare's "Winter's Tale."
3. Wife to Iago, and waiting-woman to Desdemona, in Shakespeare's tragedy of "Othello;" a woman of thorough vulgarity, loose principles, and low cunning, united to a high degree of spirit, energetic feeling, and strong sense.
4. The sweetheart of Peregrine Pickle, in Smollett's novel entitled "The Adventures of Peregrine Pickle."

Em-ped'o-clēṣ. [Gr. 'Εμπεδοκλῆς.] A famous Sicilian philosopher who flourished about the year 450 B. C., and was the reputed possessor of miraculous powers. There was a tradition that he secretly threw himself into the crater of Mount Ætna, in order that his mysterious disappearance might be taken as a proof of his divine origin. Lucian says that the volcano threw out his sandals, and thus destroyed the popular belief in his divinity.

Others came single; he who, to be deemed
A god, leaped fondly into Etna flames,
Empedocles; . . . and many more too long.
Milton.

Emperor of Believers. A title of Omar I. (634), father-in-law of Mohammed, and second caliph of the Mussulmans. He was one of the most zealous apostles of Islamism.

Emperor of the West. A sobriquet given to John Murray (1778-1843), an eminent London publisher, because he changed his place of business from Fleet Street, in "the City," to Albemarle Street, at the West End.

Empire City. The city of New York, the chief city of the western world, and the metropolis of the Empire State.

Empire State. A popular name of the State of New York, the most populous and the wealthiest State in the Union.

Lo! the *Empire State* is shaking
The shackles from her hand;
With the rugged North is waking
The level sunset land! *Whittier.*

En-cel'ā-dus. [Gr. 'Εγκέλαδος.] (*Gr. & Rom. Myth.*) A son of Titan and Terra, and the most powerful of all the giants who conspired against Jupiter, and attempted to scale heaven. He was struck by Jupiter's thunderbolts, and overwhelmed under Mount Ætna. According to the poets, the flames of Ætna proceeded from the breath of Enceladus, and, as often as he turned his weary side, the whole island of Sicily felt the motion, and shook from its very foundations.

She holds her adversary as if annihilated; such adversary being, all the while, like some buried *Enceladus*, who, to gain the smallest freedom, must stir a whole Trinacria [Sicily] with its Etnas. *Carlyle.*

Endor, Witch of. See WITCH OF ENDOR.

En-dym'i-ǒn. [Gr. 'Ενδυμίων.] (*Gr. & Rom. Myth.*) A beautiful shepherd-youth of Caria, who spent his life in perpetual sleep, for which the old legends assign various causes. Diana is fabled to have come down to him nightly, as he lay in a cave of Mount Latmus, that she might kiss him unobserved.

He stood,
Fine as those shapely spirits, heaven-descended,
Hermes, or young Apollo, or whom she,
The moon-lit Dian, on the Latmian hill,
When all the woods and all the winds were still,
Kissed with the kiss of immortality.
B. W. Procter.

England, Boast of. See TOM-A-LIN.

England, Clothier of. See JACK OF NEWBURY.

England's Pride and Westminster's Glory. An honorary title or sobriquet given for a long time to Sir Francis Burdett (1770-1844), the most popular English politician of his time, and in particular the idol of Westminster, which he represented in Parliament for nearly thirty years.

English Ar'is-toph'ā-nēṣ. A title assumed by Samuel Foote (1722-1777), the comic dramatist. [Called also *The Modern Aristophanes.*]

English Bas-tīle'. A nickname given, about the first of the present

☞ For the "Key to the Scheme of Pronunciation," with the accompanying Explanations,

century, to the jail of Cold-Bath Fields, in London, from the number of state-prisoners in it.

English Hob'be-må. A designation popularly given to Patrick (or Peter) Nasmyth (d. 1831), a Scottish landscape-painter whose style was thought to resemble that of the great Flemish master Minderhout Hobbema (1611-1699), though it really had little in common with it except minuteness of detail.

English Jus-tin'i-ąn. A name often given to Edward I., whose reign is remarkable for the progress which was made in it toward the settlement of the laws and constitution of England. Sir Matthew Hale remarks, that more was done in the first thirteen years of this reign to settle and establish the distributive justice of the kingdom than in all the next four centuries. And similarly Blackstone says, " Upon the whole, we may observe that the very scheme and model of the administration of common justice between party and party was entirely settled by this king."

English Ju've-nål. An appellation given to John Oldham (1653-1683), a distinguished poet, on account of the severity of his satires, and his spirited delineation of contemporary life and manners.

English Mersenne (mĕr'sen'). John Collins, an English mathematician and physicist (1624-1683); — so called from Marin Mersenne, a contemporary French philosopher and mathematician, who was celebrated for the wonderful extent of his erudition.

☞ " In short, Mr. Collins was like the register of all the new acquisitions made in the mathematical sciences; the magazine to which the curious had frequent recourse; which acquired him the appellation of the English Mersenne."
Hutton.

English Opium-eater. A name often given to Thomas De Quincey, one of the most remarkable English writers of the present century, celebrated for his eccentricities, induced — at least in part — by the habit of eating opium, and proclaimed by himself to the world in a well-known volume of " Confessions."

English Pale. See PALE, THE.

English Palladio (păl-lä'de-o, 102). An epithet given to Inigo Jones (1573-1653), who introduced into England the Italian or "classic" style of architecture as exemplified in the works of Andrea Palladio (1518-1580) and his school. [Called also *The English Vitruvius.*]

English Pe'trarçh. A name given by Sir Walter Raleigh to Sir Philip Sidney (1554-1586), who, like Petrarch (1304-1374), was one of the earliest cultivators and refiners of his native language. His writings, as well as those of his Italian predecessor, are characterised by a rare delicacy of poetical feeling, and great brilliancy of imagination.

English Rabelais (răb'lā'). 1. A name often given to Jonathan Swift (1667-1745), whose writings resemble in some points those of the great French satirist.

2. A name sometimes given to Lawrence Sterne (1713-1768), the author of "Tristram Shandy" and " The Sentimental Journey," and the most airy and graceful of English humourists. " The cast of the whole Shandean history," says Fitzgerald, " its tone and manner and thought, is such as would come from one saturated, as it were, with Rabelais, and the school that imitated Rabelais."

3. The same name has been given to Thomas Amory (1691-1789), author of " The Life and Opinions of John Buncle, Esq." See BUNCLE, JOHN.

☞ " The soul of Francis Rabelais passed into John Amory. . . . Both were physicians, and enemies of too much gravity. Their great business was to enjoy life." *Hazlitt.* " In point of animal spirits, love of good cheer, and something of a mixture of scholarship, theology, and profane reading, he may be held to deserve the title; but he has no claim to the Frenchman's greatness of genius, freedom from bigotry, and profoundness of wit and humour. He might have done very well for a clerk to Rabe-

---

and for the Remarks and Rules to which the numbers after certain words refer, see pp. xlv-xxxii.

lais; and his master would have laughed quite as much at, as with, him."
Leigh Hunt.

English Ros'ci-us (rosh'I-us). An honorary epithet bestowed upon David Garrick (1716-1779), the most eminent actor of his day upon the English stage.

English Sap'pho (saf'fo). A title given to Mrs. Mary Darby Robinson (1758-1800), mistress of George IV. She acquired a brilliant reputation for beauty and wit, and was the author of some well-esteemed lyric poems. See DELLA CRUSCANS.

English Sen'e-cạ. A name given to Joseph Hall (1574-1656), an English bishop remarkable for his scholarship, piety, and misfortunes. [Called also *The Christian Seneca*.]

☞ "He was commonly called our English Seneca, for the pureness, plainness, and fulness of his style." *Thomas Fuller.* "It is much to our present purpose to observe that the style of his prose is strongly tinctured with the manner of Seneca. The writer of the Satires is perceptible in some of his gravest polemical or scriptural treatises, which are perpetually interspersed with excursive illustrations, familiar allusions, and observations in life." *Thomas Warton.*

English Solomon. See SOLOMON OF ENGLAND.

English Tĕr'ence. A title sometimes given to Richard Cumberland (1732-1811), an English dramatist and miscellaneous writer.

The *Terence* of England, the mender of hearts.
Goldsmith.

English Tin'to-ret. A name given by Charles I. to William Dobson (1610-1646), a distinguished English portrait and historical painter. [Called also *The English Vandyck*.]

E'nid. A mythical lady mentioned in a Welsh triad as one of the three celebrated ladies of Arthur's court; a beautiful picture of conjugal patience and affection. Her story — which is not included in the general cycle of romances — has lately been rescued from obscurity by Tennyson, in his "Idylls of the King."

Enlightened Doctor. See ILLUMINATED DOCTOR.

Entéléchie (ŏn'tā'lā'she', 62). The name given by Rabelais to an imaginary kingdom, which he represents as governed by Queen Quintessence, and as visited by Pantagruel and his companions in their search to find the oracle of the Holy Bottle. This country symbolises the taste for speculative science, and is, without doubt, the foundation of the island of Laputa, in Swift's fictitious "Travels" of Lemuel Gulliver. In the Peripatetic philosophy, *entelechy* signified an actuality, or an object completely actualised, in contradistinction to mere potential existence.

En-tel'lus. See DARES.

E'ŏs. [Gr. Ἠώς.] (*Gr. Myth.*) The goddess of the dawn; the same as *Aurora.* See AURORA.

Eph'ĭ-al'tēs. [Gr. Ἐφιάλτης.] (*Gr. & Rom. Myth.*) One of the giants who made war upon the gods. He was deprived of his left eye by Apollo, and of the right by Hercules.

E-pig'o-ni. [Gr. Ἐπίγονοι, the afterborn.] A name given to the sons of the seven Grecian heroes who laid siege to Thebes. See SEVEN AGAINST THEBES.

Ep'ĭ-men'ĭ-dēṣ. [Gr. Ἐπιμενίδης.] A philosopher and poet of Crete, who lived in the sixth or seventh century B. C. His history has reached us only in a mythical form. He is said to have fallen asleep in a cave, when a boy, and to have remained in that state for fifty-seven years. On waking and going out into the broad daylight, he was greatly perplexed and astonished to find every thing around him altered. But what was more wonderful still, during his long period of slumber, his soul, released from its fleshly prison, had been busily engaged in the study of medicine and natural philosophy; and when it again became incarnated, Epimenides found himself a man of great knowledge and wisdom. Goethe has written a poem on the subject, "Des Epimenides Erwachen." See KLAUS, PETER, and WINKLE, RIP VAN.

Like *Epimenides*, I have been sleeping in a cave; and, waking, I see those whom I left

☞ For the "Key to the Scheme of Pronunciation," with the accompanying Explanations,

children are bearded men; and towns have sprung up in the landscapes which I left as solitary wastes. *Sir E. Bulwer Lytton.*

Ep̆ĭ-me'theŭs. [Gr. 'Επιμηθεύς.] (*Gr. & Rom. Myth.*) A brother of Prometheus, and the husband of Pandora. See PANDORA.

Éraste (ā'rȧst'). The heroine in Molière's comedy entitled "Les Fâcheux."

Ĕr'ȧ-to. [Gr. 'Ερατώ.] (*Gr. & Rom. Myth.*) One of the nine Muses. She presided over lyric, tender and amatory poetry.

Ĕr'ȧ-tos'trȧ-tus. See HEROSTRATUS.

Ĕr'e-bus. [Gr. 'Ερεβος, darkness.] (*Gr. & Rom. Myth.*) A son of Chaos, and a god of hell. The name is used by the poets to denote the dark and gloomy cavern under the earth, passed through by the shades in going to Hades.

E-re'tri-ạn Bull. An appellation of Menedemus of Eretria, in Eubœa, a Greek philosopher of the fourth century B. C., and founder of the Eretrian school, which was a branch of the Socratic. He was so called on account of the gravity of his countenance.

E-rĭch'tho. [Gr. 'Εριχθώ.] A famous Thessalian witch consulted by Pompey.

Such a subject even the powerful *Erichtho* was compelled to select, as alone capable of being re-animated even by her potent magic. *Sir W. Scott.*

E'rin (9). An early name of Ireland, now used as a poetic appellative. See EMERALD ISLE.

E-rĭn'nys (*pl.* **E-rĭn'ny-ĕṣ**). [Gr. 'Εριννύς; *pl.* 'Εριννύες, 'Εριννῦς.) [*Gr. Myth.*) An avenging deity, one of the Eumenides, or Furies. See FURIES.

E'ris (9). [Gr. 'Ερις.) (*Gr. Myth.*) The goddess of discord; a sister of Mars, and a daughter of Night; the same as the Roman *Discordia*.

Erl-king. [Ger. *Erl-könig, Erlenkönig*, derived by some from the root *erle*, alder; by others supposed to be identical with *Elfen König*, King of the Elves.] A name applied to a personified natural power or elementary spirit, which, according to German poetical authorities, prepares mischief and ruin for men, and especially for children, through delusive seductions. It is fabled to appear as a goblin, haunting the Black Forest in Thuringia. The existence of such elementary spirits, and their connection with mankind, have, in the earliest times, occupied the imagination of the most widely different races. The Erl-king was introduced into German poetry from the sagas of the North, through Herder's translation of the Danish ballad of "Sir Olaf and the Erl-king's Daughter;" and it has become universally known through Goethe's ballad of the "Erlkönig."

Erminia (ĕr-me'ne-ȧ). The heroine of Tasso's epic poem, "Jerusalem Delivered," in love with Tancred.

She read of fair *Erminia's* flight,
Which Venice once might hear
Sung on her glittering seas at night
By many a gondolier. *Mrs. Hemans.*

E'ros (9). [Gr. 'Ερως.] (*Gr. Myth.*) The Greek name of the deity called *Cupido*, or Cupid, by the Romans. See CUPID.

Ĕr'rȧ Pā'tĕr. The name of some old astrologer; but who was meant by it has not been determined. Some of the old almanacs say an eminent Jewish astrologer. William Lilly was so called by Butler.

In mathematics he was greater
Than Tycho Brahe or *Erra Pater.*
Hudibras.

Ĕr'ў-ci'nȧ. [Gr. 'Ερυκίνη.] (*Gr. & Rom. Myth.*) A surname of Venus, derived from Mount Eryx, in Sicily, where she had a famous temple.

Ĕr'ў-man'thi-ạn Boar. See HERCULES.

Ĕr'ў-sĭch'thŏn. [Gr. 'Ερυσίχθων.] (*Gr. & Rom. Myth.*) A profane person who cut down trees in a grove sacred to Ceres, for which he was punished by the goddess with raging and unappeasable hunger.

E'ryx (9). [Gr. 'Ερυξ.] (*Gr. & Rom. Myth.*) A king of Sicily who challenged Hercules to fight with the gauntlet, and lost both his life and his crown, which he staked on the issue of the contest.

Es'că-lus. 1. An ancient and kind-hearted lord, in Shakespeare's "Measure for Measure," whom Vincentio, the Duke of Vienna, joins with Angelo, but in an inferior rank, as his deputy during a pretended absence on a distant journey.

We do not blame him [Leigh Hunt] for not bringing to the judgment-seat the merciless rigour of Lord Angelo, but we really think that such flagitious and impudent offenders as those now at the bar, deserved, at the least, the gentle rebuke of *Escalus*. *Macaulay.*

2. Prince of Verona, in Shakespeare's "Romeo and Juliet."

Es'că-nĕṣ. A lord of Tyre, in Shakespeare's "Pericles."

Eṣ'mǫnd, Henry. The title of a novel by Thackeray, and the name of its hero, a chivalrous cavalier and Jacobite of the time of Queen Anne.

Esplandian (es-plăn-de-ân'). In the old romances of chivalry, the son of Amadis and Oriana. Montalvo has made him the subject of an original work, which is a continuation of his translation of the "Amadis," and which, in the preface, he announces to be the fifth book of the same.

Espriella (es-pre-el'yȧ). The name of an imaginary Spaniard, whose "Letters" from England, about the year 1810, were written by Southey.

Es-tel'lȧ. The heroine of Dickens's novel of "Great Expectations."

Estermere, King. See KING ESTERMERE.

Est-il-possible (ȧ'tĕl' pos'se'bl, 61). [Fr., Is it possible?] A name given by King James II. of England to Prince George of Denmark, the husband of James's daughter, the Princess Anne, afterwards Queen Anne. These words had been a common phrase with the prince at the time of the Revolution of 1688, as reports of one desertion of the king after another came to his ears. When he also went over to William and Mary, James is reported to have said, "What! *Est-il-possible* gone too?"

Es-tot'i-lănd, or **Es-tot'i-land'i-ȧ.** According to the "Geographical Dictionary" of Edmund Bohun (1695), "a great tract of land in the north of America, toward the arctic circle and Hudson's Bay, having New France on the south, and James's Bay on the west, the first of American shores discovered, being found by some Friesland fishers, that were driven hither by a tempest, almost two hundred years before Columbus." Alcedo says of it, "An imaginary country which some authors suppose to have been discovered in 1477 by a native of Poland named John Scalve, and that the same was part of the land of Labrador. The fact is, that this country never had any existence but in the imaginations of the two brothers of the name of Zeno, Venetian noblemen, who had no particular information whatever respecting the expedition of this Polish adventurer; and that, in 1497, John Cabot, or Gabot, left England with three of his sons, under the commission of Henry VII., when he discovered Newfoundland and part of the immediate continent where this country is supposed to exist."

Else ... the low sun ...
Had rounded still the horizon, and not known
Or east or west: which had forbid the snow
From cold *Estotiland*, and south as far
Beneath Magellan. *Milton.*

The learned Grotius marches his Norwegians by a pleasant route across frozen rivers and arms of the sea, through Iceland, Greenland, *Estotiland*, and Norumbega.
W. Irving.

E-te'o-clĕṣ. [Gr. Ἐτεοκλῆς.] (*Gr. & Rom. Myth.*) A son of Œdipus, king of Thebes. He and his brother Polynices agreed to reign alternately, each holding the power a year at a time. Eteocles did not adhere to his engagement, and hence arose the Theban war. The brothers at last agreed to finish the war by a duel: in this they both fell.

Like fated *Eteocles*-Polynices Brothers, embracing, though in vain ; weeping that they must not love, that they must hate only, and die by each other's hands! *Carlyle.*

Eternal City. A popular and very ancient designation of Rome, which was fabled to have been built under the favour and immediate direction of the gods. The expression, or its equivalent, frequently occurs in classic authors, as Livy, Tibullus, Quintilian, &c. In the "Æneid," Virgil, following the received tradition, represents Jupiter as holding the following language to Venus, in reference to the Romans, who were supposed to be the descendants of her son Æneas:—

"Ilis ego nec metas rerum, nec tempora pono:
Imperium sine fine dedi." *Bk. I., v. 78, 79.*
"To them no bounds of empire I assign,
Nor term of years to their immortal line."
Dryden's Trans.

Ettrick Shepherd. A name commonly given to James Hogg (1772–1835), the Scottish poet, who was born in the forest of Ettrick, in Selkirkshire, and in early life followed the occupation of a shepherd.

When first, descending from the moorlands,
I saw the stream of Yarrow glide
Along a bare and open valley,
The *Ettrick Shepherd* was my guide.
Wordsworth.

Eu'cli-o. A character in Plautus's comedy of "Aulularia," celebrated for his penuriousness.

Now you must explain all this to me, unless you would have me use you as ill as *Euclio* does Staphyla, in the "Aulularia."
Sir W. Scott.

Eu-ġe'ni-us. An amiable monitor and counsellor of Yorick, in Sterne's "Life and Opinions of Tristram Shandy." He is said to have been intended as a portrait of the author's friend, John Hall Stevenson.

Eulenspiegel (oi-len-spe'ġel, 43, 58). See OWLE-GLASS.

Eu-mæ'us. [Gr. Εὔμαιος.] (*Gr. & Rom. Myth.*) A swine-herd and slave of Ulysses, famed for his fidelity to his master.

This second *Eumæus* strode hastily down the forest-glade, driving before him, with the assistance of Fangs, the whole herd of his inharmonious charge. *Sir W. Scott.*

Eu-men'i-dēṣ. [Gr. Εὐμενίδες, *i. e.*, the gracious or benign goddesses.] (*Gr. Myth.*) A euphemistic name given by the Greeks to the Furies, whose true name of *Erinnyes* they were afraid to utter. See FURIES.

They lie always, those subterranean *Eumenides,*—fabulous, and yet so true,—in the dullest existence of man; and can dance, brandishing their dusky torches, shaking their serpent hair. *Carlyle.*

Eu-mol'pus. [Gr. Εὔμολπος.] (*Gr.*

& Rom. Myth.) A son of Neptune and Chione, celebrated as a singer or bard, and as the founder of the Eleusinian mysteries.

Eu-phor'bus. [Gr. Εὔφορβος.] (*Gr. & Rom. Myth.*) A Trojan, son of Panthous, slain by Menelaus in the Trojan war.

Eu-phros'y-ne. [Gr. Εὐφροσύνη, cheerfulness, mirth.] (*Gr. & Rom. Myth.*) One of the three Graces.

Come, thou goddess fair and free,
In heaven y-clept *Euphrosyne,*
And by men, heart-easing Mirth.
Milton.

Eu'phu-ēṣ. [Gr. Εὐφυής, of good figure, comely, clever.] The principal character in Lyly's two famous works entitled "Euphues, or The Anatomy of Wit," and "Euphues and his England." These works are remarkable for their pedantic and fantastical style, and for the monstrous and overstrained conceits with which they abound. Euphues is represented as an Athenian gentleman, distinguished for the elegance of his person and the beauty of his wit, and for his amorous temperament and roving disposition.

Eu-ro'pḁ. [Gr. Εὐρώπη.] (*Gr. & Rom. Myth.*) A beautiful daughter of Phœnix, or of Agenor, carried off by Jupiter, under the form of a white bull, from Phœnicia to Crete. By him she became the mother of Minos and Sarpedon.

Europe, The Nightmare of. See NIGHTMARE OF EUROPE.

Eu-ry'ạ-le. [Gr. Εὐρυάλη.] (*Gr. & Rom. Myth.*) 1. One of the three Gorgons. See GORGONS.
2. A queen of the Amazons.
3. A daughter of Minos, and the mother of Orion.

Eu-ry'ạ-lus. [Gr. Εὐρύαλος.] A Trojan youth, immortalised by Virgil as the faithful friend of Nisus. See NISUS.

We have been Nisus and *Euryalus,* Theseus and Pirithous, Orestes and Pylades, and—to sum up the whole with a puritanic touch—David and Jonathan, all in one breath.
Sir W. Scott.

Eu-ryd'i-ce. [Gr. Εὐρυδίκη.] (*Gr. & Rom. Myth.*) The wife of Orpheus,

and for the Remarks and Rules to which the numbers after certain words refer, see pp. xiv–xxxii.

killed by a serpent on her bridal day. See ORPHEUS.

> Orpheus' self may heave his head
> From golden slumber on a bed
> Of heaped Elysian flowers, and hear
> Such strains as would have won the ear
> Of Pluto, to have quite set free
> His half-regained Eurydice. *Milton.*

Eu-ryl'o-chus. [Gr. Εὐρύλοχος.] (*Gr. & Rom. Myth.*) One of the companions of Ulysses in his wanderings, and the only one of them who was not changed by Circe into a hog.

Eu-ryn'o-me. [Gr. Εὐρυνόμη.] (*Gr. & Rom. Myth.*) A daughter of Oceanus and Tethys, and mother of the Graces.

Eu-rys'theûs. [Gr. Εὐρυσθεύς.] (*Gr. & Rom. Myth.*) A son of Sthenelus, and grandson of Perseus, king of Mycenæ. At Juno's instigation, he imposed upon his cousin Hercules twelve difficult labours, which he had a right to do on account of his priority of birth. See HERCULES.

Eu-ter'pe. [Gr. Εὐτέρπη.] (*Gr. & Rom. Myth.*) The Muse of music; represented in ancient works of art with a flute in her hand. See MUSES.

E-vad'ne. [Gr. Εὐάδνη.] 1. (*Gr. & Rom. Myth.*) Wife of Capaneus, and mother of Sthenelus. Her husband having been killed at the siege of Thebes, she threw herself upon the funeral pile, and was consumed with him.

2. A female character in Beaumont and Fletcher's play, "The Maid's Tragedy."

E-van'dẹr. [Gr. Εὔανδρος.] (*Gr. & Rom. Myth.*) A son of Mercury by an Arcadian nymph. He is fabled to have led a Pelasgian colony from Arcadia into Italy, about sixty years before the Trojan war. Æneas, when he arrived in Italy, found him still alive, and formed an alliance with him against the Latins.

Evangelical Doctor. [Lat. *Doctor Evangelicus.*] See GOSPEL DOCTOR.

E-van'ge-line. The heroine of Longfellow's poem of the same name, founded upon the historical incident of the expulsion of the inhabitants of Acadia from their homes in the year 1755. See ACADIA.

Ev'ạnṣ, Sir Hugh. A pedantic Welsh parson and schoolmaster, in Shakespeare's "Merry Wives of Windsor," of childish simplicity and ignorance.

> The reader may well cry out, with honest Sir Hugh Evans, "I like not when a 'ooman has a great peard; I spy a great peard under her muffler." *Macaulay.*

Ev'e-lī'nạ. The title of a novel by Miss Burney (Madame D'Arblay), and the name of its heroine, afterward Lady Orville.

Ever-memorable John Hales, The. See HALES, THE EVER-MEMORABLE JOHN.

Evil May-day. (*Eng. Hist.*) A name given to the 1st of May, 1517, on account of the dreadful excesses committed on that day by the apprentices and populace against foreigners, particularly the French.

Evil One, The. A name often applied to the Devil. See DEVIL, THE.

Ex-cal'i-bar. The name of Arthur's famous sword, which he pulled out of a miraculous stone, in which it was inserted as in a sheath, though previously two hundred and one of the most puissant barons in the realm had singly been unable to withdraw it. An inscription on the stone around the sword stated that whoever should be able to draw it out was rightful heir to the throne of Britain; and Arthur, in consequence of his remarkable success, was immediately chosen and proclaimed king by general acclamation. When about to die, he sent an attendant to throw the weapon into a lake hard by. Twice eluding the request, the knight at last complied. A hand and arm arose from the water, and caught the sword by the hilt, flourished it thrice, and then sank into the lake, and was seen no more. Tennyson has admirably versified this incident in his poem entitled "Morte d'Arthur." [Written also Excalibor, Excalibur, Escalibar, Escalibor, and Caliburn.]

☞ For the "Key to the Scheme of Pronunciation," with the accompanying Explanations,

☞ "According to the English metrical romance of 'Merlin,' this celebrated sword bore the following inscription:—
'Ich am y-hote Escalibore;
Unto a king a fair tresore.'
And it is added, in explanation,—
'On Inglis is this writing,
"Kerve steel and yren and al thing."'
When Arthur first used this sword in battle, 'it cast forth a great light full splendant, with such force that all those who beheld it thought that they were burning torches which issued from the sword; but they were the golden letters on the sword which shone so mightily.'"

"No, surely," replied the king; "no sword on earth, were it the *Excalibar* of King Arthur, can cut that which opposes no steady resistance to the blow. *Sir W. Scott.*

Excelsior State. The State of New York, sometimes so called, from the motto "Excelsior" upon its coat of arms.

Expounder of the Constitution. A title popularly given to Daniel Webster (1782-1852), on account of his elaborate expositions of the Constitution of the United States.

Expunging Resolution. (*Amer. Hist.*) A resolution introduced in the senate of the United States, on the 26th of December, 1836, by the Hon. Thomas H. Benton, of Missouri, by which a resolution adopted by the senate on the 28th of March, 1834, charging "that the president [Jackson], in the late executive proceedings in relation to the public revenue, [had] assumed authority and power not conferred by the Constitution and laws, but in derogation of both," was ordered to be expunged from the journal of the senate by drawing black lines round the resolve, and writing across the face of it, in strong letters, the following words: "Expunged, by order of the senate, this —— day of ——, A. D. 1837." Mr. Benton's resolution was adopted on the 16th of March, 1837.

Exterminator, The. [Fr. *L'Exterminateur*, Sp. *El Exterminador*.] A name given by the Spaniards to Montbars (b. 1645), a notorious French adventurer, who signalised himself by his intense hatred of that people, and by the atrocities he committed in the Antilles and other Spanish colonies.

Eyes of Greece, The Two. See TWO EYES OF GREECE, THE.

Eyre, Jane (êr, 3). The heroine of Miss Charlotte Brontë's novel of the same name, a governess, coping bravely with adverse circumstances, and finally proving her genuine force of character by winning the respect and love of a man in whom, though he had exhausted the world, and been exhausted by it, the instincts and promptings of a noble nature were not dead, but only suppressed.

and for the Remarks and Rules to which the numbers after certain words refer, see pp. xiv-xxxii.

F.

Fac-to'tum, Jo-han'nĕṣ. One who is good at any thing, who can turn his hand to any kind of work;— the Latin equivalent of *Jack-at-all-trades*.

> There is an upstart crow [Shakespeare], beautiful with our feathers, that, with his tiger's heart wrapped in a player's hide, supposes he is as well able to bombast out a blank verse as the best of you, and, being an absolute *Johannes Factotum*, is, in his own conceit, the only Shake-scene in a country.
> *Greene's Groatsworth of Wit,* 1592.

Fad'lă-deen'. The grand chamberlain of the harem in Moore's "Lalla Rookh,"—magnificent, infallible, sententious, and shrewd.

Fag. A subordinate character, in Sheridan's comedy of "The Rivals." He is a lying servant to Captain Absolute, and "wears his master's wit as he does his lace, at second-hand."

> I am quite conscious of my own immunities as a tale-teller. But even the mendacious *Mr. Fag* . . . assures us, that, though he never scruples to tell a lie at his master's command, yet it hurts his conscience to be found out. *Sir W. Scott.*

Fā'ğin. An old Jew in Dickens's "Oliver Twist," who employs young persons of both sexes to carry on a systematic trade of robbery.

Fainall, Mr. and Mrs. Noted characters in Congreve's comedy, "The Way of the World."

Fainéant, Le Noir (lu nwŏr fā'nā'-ŏn', 62). [Fr., the Black Sluggard.] In Sir Walter Scott's "Ivanhoe," a name applied to the disguised Richard Cœur de Lion by the spectators of a tournament, on account of his indifference during a great part of the action, in which, however, he was finally victorious.

Fainéants, Les Rois (lā rwŏ fā'nā'-ŏn', 62). [Fr., the Do-nothing Kings.] A sarcastic designation applied to monarchs who delegate their authority to their ministers, or from whom, by reason of incapacity and weakness, the power has been wrested, while they are still permitted nominally to reign. The usual application of the term is to the later Merovingian sovereigns of France, under whose name the "Mayors of the Palace" really governed the country. The epithet *Fainéant* was also given in contempt to Louis V., the last of the Carlovingian dynasty.

Fair City. A name popularly given in Scotland to the town of Perth, which is remarkable for the beauty of its situation, and for its elegant appearance.

Fair Gĕr'ăl-dīne. A supposed mistress of the Earl of Surrey (Henry Howard, 1516–1547), whose praises he celebrates in a famous sonnet, and in other poems, and who has been the occasion of much controversy among his biographers and critics. There is no doubt, however, that the lady called Geraldine in the sonnet was an Irish lady named Elizabeth Fitzgerald, the daughter of Gerald Fitzgerald, ninth Earl of Kildare, and afterward the wife of the Earl of Lincoln.

Fair Im'o-gīne'. The heroine of a popular ballad by Matthew Gregory Lewis, entitled "Alonzo the Brave and the Fair Imogine."

Fair Mag'ue-lone'. The heroine of an old chivalric romance, entitled "The History of the Fair Magalona, daughter of the king of Naples, and Peter, son of the Count of Provence." This romance was originally written in French, but was translated into Spanish before the middle of the sixteenth century. Cervantes alludes to Magalona, or Maguelone, in "Don Quixote." In Germany, her history has been reproduced by Tieck.

Fair Maid of An'joû. A name given to the Lady Edith Plantagenet, a kinswoman of Richard Cœur de Lion, and an attendant of his queen, Berengaria. She married David, Earl of Huntingdon, prince royal of Scotland.

☞ For the "Key to the Scheme of Pronunciation," with the accompanying Explanations,

Fair Maid of Gǎl'lo-wây. A name popularly given to Margaret, the only daughter of Archibald V., Earl of Douglas. She became the wife of her cousin, William, to whom the earldom had passed in the year 1443; and, after his death, in reluctant obedience to the royal command, married his brother and successor, James, the last Earl of Douglas.

Fair Maid of Kent. A name given to Joan, only daughter of Edmond Plantagenet, Earl of Kent, on account of her great beauty. She was married three times: first, to William de Montacute, Earl of Salisbury, from whom she was divorced; secondly, to Sir Thomas Holland; thirdly, after his death, to her second cousin, Edward, the Black Prince, under a dispensation from the pope, rendered necessary by reason of their consanguinity. By the prince she was mother of Richard II., in whose reign she died.

Fair Maid of Norway. See MAIDEN OF NORWAY.

Fair Maid of Pêrth (4). The title of a novel by Sir Walter Scott, and a sobriquet given to the heroine, Catherine, or Katie, Glover, "who was universally acknowledged to be the most beautiful young woman of the city or its vicinity."

Fair Roṣ'ȧ-mǒnd. The name popularly given to a daughter of Lord Clifford, famous in the legendary history of England as the mistress of Henry II. shortly before his accession to the throne, and the subject of an old ballad. The facts of her history are not well ascertained; but she is said to have been kept by her royal lover in a secret bower at Woodstock, the approaches to which formed a labyrinth so intricate that it could only be discovered by the clew of a silken thread, which the king used for that purpose. Here Queen Eleanor discovered and poisoned her, about 1173.

Fairservice, Andrew. A shrewd and humourous Scotch gardener at Osbaldistone Hall, in Sir Walter Scott's novel of "Rob Roy."

Fair-Star, Princess. See PRINCESS FAIR-STAR.

Faith, Defender of the. See DEFENDER OF THE FAITH.

Faithful. One of the allegorical personages in Bunyan's "Pilgrim's Progress," who dies a martyr before completing his journey.

Faithful, Jacob. The hero of a popular novel, by Marryatt, having this name for its title.

Fȧlk'lȧnd (fawk'lȧnd). 1. A character in Sheridan's comedy of "The Rivals," noted for his wayward, captious jealousy.
2. The true hero of William Godwin's novel of "Caleb Williams," and an impersonation of honour, intellect, benevolence, and a passionate love of fame; but a man driven in a moment of ungovernable passion, and under the provocation of the most cruel, persevering, and tyrannical insult, to commit a murder. His fanatical love of reputation urges him to conceal the crime; and, in order to do this more effectually, he allows an innocent man to be executed, and his family ruined. Williams, an intelligent peasant-lad taken into the service of Falkland, obtains, by an accident, a clew to the guilt of his master; when the latter, extorting from him an oath that he will keep his secret, communicates to his dependent the whole story of his double crime, his remorse, and misery. The youth, finding his life insupportable from the perpetual suspicion to which he is exposed, and the restless surveillance of his master, escapes, and is pursued through the greater part of the tale by the unrelenting persecution of Falkland, who is led, by his frantic and unnatural devotion to fame, to annihilate, in Williams, the evidence of his accumulated guilt. At last Williams is formally accused by Falkland of robbery, and naturally discloses before the tribunal the dreadful secret which had caused his long persecution, and Falkland dies of shame and a broken heart.

Fall City. Louisville, Kentucky;—

and for the Remarks and Rules to which the numbers after certain words refer, see pp. xiv-xxxii.

popularly so called from the falls which, at this place, impede the navigation of the Ohio River.

Fal'staff, Sir John (2). A famous character in Shakespeare's comedy of the "Merry Wives of Windsor," and in the First and Second Parts of his historical drama of "Henry IV.;" the most perfect comic portrait that was ever drawn by the pen of genius. In the former play, he is represented as in love with Mrs. Ford and Mrs. Page, who make a butt and a dupe of him: in the latter, he figures as a soldier and a wit: in both he is exhibited as a monster of fat, sensual, mendacious, boastful, and cowardly. See BROOK, MASTER.

☞ In this character, Shakespeare is thought to have ridiculed Sir John Fastolfe, an English general of the time of Henry VI., who had part of the command before Orleans, in France, and, at the village of Patay, set the example of an inglorious flight before Joan of Arc, causing great destruction of his men, for which cowardice he was degraded from his rank as a Knight of the Garter. The opinion that Shakespeare intended to caricature this personage has been very generally received. Fuller, the church historian, says, "Nor is our comedian excusable by some alteration of his name, writing him Sir John *Falstafe*, and making him the property and pleasure of King Henry V. to abuse, seeing the vicinity of sounds [doth] intrench on the memory of that worthy knight." Shakespeare introduces the historical Fastolfe in "The First Part of Henry VI.," and represents his conduct at Patay, and his subsequent degradation, with historical accuracy. But recent commentators deny that he was the original of the "valiant Jack Falstaff" of Shakespeare's other plays, and treat the supposition as a gross absurdity. In the first draught of "King Henry IV.," Sir John Falstaff was called *Sir John Oldcastle*, a name borne by a distinguished Wycliffite who was born under Edward III., and put to death in the fourth year of Henry V. The change in the surname is attributed to remonstrances on the part of Oldcastle's descendants. That Shakespeare was desirous to do away with any impression that Falstaff and Oldcastle were one and the same personage under different names, appears from the Epilogue to "The Second Part of King Henry IV.," in which, after promising that the play shall be continued "with Sir John in it," he says, "For any thing I know, Falstaff shall die of a sweat, unless already he be killed with your hard opinions; for Oldcastle died a martyr, *and this is not the man*."

All novelists have had occasion, at some time or other, to wish, with *Falstaff*, that they knew where a commodity of good names was to be had. *Sir W. Scott.*

Fang. A sheriff's officer, in the Second Part of Shakespeare's "King Henry IV."

Farinata (degli Uberti) (fä-re-nä'tä del'yee oo-bĕr'tee). A Ghibelline noble of Florence (d. 1624), placed by Dante in hell, as a punishment for his infidelity and epicurism. He is represented as occupying a red-hot tomb, the lid of which is suspended over him till the day of judgment, yet looking as lofty as if he scorned hell itself.

They [the Italians of the fourteenth century] said little of those awful and lovely creations on which later critics delight to dwell, — *Farinata*, lifting his haughty and tranquil brow from his couch of everlasting fire, the lion-like repose of Sordello, or the light which shone from the celestial smile of Beatrice.
Macaulay.

Farmer George. A name popularly given to George III. of England, on account of his parsimonious disposition, plain dress, familiar manners, and hearty and homely good-nature. He is said to have kept a farm at Windsor, not for amusement, but because he derived a small profit from it.

Fata Morgana (fä'tä moṙ-gä'nä). The name of a potent fairy, celebrated in the tales of chivalry, and in the romantic poems of Italy. She was a pupil of the enchanter Merlin, and the sister of Arthur, to whom she discovered the intrigue of his queen, Geneura, or Guinever, with Lancelot of the Lake. In the "Orlando Innamorato" of Bojardo, she appears at first as a personification of Fortune, inhabiting a splendid residence at the bottom of a lake, and dispensing all the treasures of the earth; but she is afterward found in her proper station, subject, with the other fairies and the witches, to the all-potent Demogorgon. [Called also *Morgaine la Fée* and *Morgue the Fay*.]

☞ For the "Key to the Scheme of Pronunciation," with the accompanying Explanations,

☞ At the present day, the appellation of Fata Morgana is given to a strange meteoric phenomenon, nearly allied to the mirage, witnessed, in certain states of the tide and weather, in the Straits of Messina, between Calabria and Sicily, and occasionally, though rarely, on other coasts. It consists in the appearance, in the air over the surface of the sea, of multiplied inverted images of objects on the surrounding coasts, — groves, hills, towers, houses, and people, — all represented as in a moving picture. The spectacle is popularly supposed to be produced by the fairy whose name is given to it.

Not a stream did he mention but flowed over sands of gold, and not a palace that was inferior to those of the celebrated *Fata Morgana*.
Sir W. Scott.

Fat Boy, The. A laughable character in Dickens's "Pickwick Papers;" a youth of astonishing obesity, whose employment consists in alternate eating and sleeping.

Fates. [Lat. *Fata*.] See PARCÆ.

Father of Angling. A title sometimes given to Izaak Walton (1593–1683), the celebrated author of "The Complete Angler."

Father of British Inland Navigation. A name often given to Francis Egerton, Duke of Bridgewater (1736–1803), the originator of the first navigable canal constructed in Great Britain in modern times, and a zealous promoter of other schemes of artificial water communication.

☞ "By that title he will ever be known." *H. Martineau*.

Father of Comedy. A name given to Aristophanes (444–380, B. C.), one of the most celebrated of the Greek dramatists, and the only writer of the old Greek comedy of whom any entire works have been preserved. He is remarkable for the richness of his fancy, the exuberance of his wit and humour, and the Attic purity and great simplicity of his style.

Father of Dutch Poetry. A title bestowed upon Jakob Maerlant (1235–1300), an early Belgic poet. [Called also *Father of Flemish Poets*.]

Father of Ecclesiastical History. A name commonly given to Eusebius of Cæsarea (264–340), a very learned patristic divine, author of "Historia Ecclesiastica," an important and valuable record of the Christian Church, in ten books, reaching from the birth of our Saviour to the defeat of Licinius by Constantine in 324.

Father of English Geology. An honorary appellation given to William Smith (1769–1840), author of the first geological map of England, and the original discoverer and teacher, in that country, of the identification of strata, and of the determination of their succession by means of their imbedded fossils.

Father of English Poetry. A title given by Dryden to Chaucer (fourteenth century), as the first great English poet.

Father of English Prose. An epithet bestowed upon Roger Ascham (1515–1568), one of our earliest miscellaneous writers. His style is regarded as a fine example of genuine English.

Father of Epic Poetry. An epithet applied to Homer, the reputed author of the "Iliad" and the "Odyssey," the earliest national heroic poems extant.

The former compares him [Samuel Richardson] to Homer, and predicts for his memory the same honours which are rendered to the *Father of Epic Poetry*. *Sir W. Scott*.

Father of Equity. An epithet conferred upon Heneage Finch, Lord Nottingham (1621–1682), an English lawyer and statesman of the time of the Restoration, who had a very high reputation for eloquence, sound judgment, and integrity. His character is drawn by Dryden, in his "Absalom and Achitophel," under the name of Amri : —

"To whom the double blessing does belong,
With Moses' inspiration, Aaron's tongue."

Father of French History. [Fr. *Le Père de l'Histoire de France*.] A title given to André Duchesne (1584–1640), an early and celebrated French historian.

Father of German Literature. A name frequently given to Gotthold Ephraim Lessing (1729–1781), an illustrious author, and the admitted reviver of the national character of

and for the Remarks and Rules to which the numbers after certain words refer, see pp. xiv-xxxii.

German literature, which before his time was corrupted and enslaved by French influences.

☞ "Lessing was the Frederick [the Great] of thought. By nature wholly Teutonic, he too sounded a trumpet-call; and, with a restless energy in no wise inferior to Frederick's, an activity and plenitude of resources that overlooked no opportunity, he dashed, now into this region of dormant literature, now into that unpenetrated department of philosophy, until he had laid the foundation of almost every conquest that has illustrated the recent ever-memorable career of his kindred." *J. P. Nichol.*

Father of Greek Music. An epithet applied to Terpander, of Lesbos, who lived about the year 676 B. C. He first reduced to rules the different modes of singing which prevailed in different countries, and formed out of these rude strains a connected system, from which the Greek music never departed throughout all the improvements and refinements of later ages.

Father of his Country. [Lat. *Pater Patriæ,* or *Parens Patriæ.*] A title given by the Roman senate and forum to Cicero, on account of the zeal, courage, and prudence he displayed in unmasking the famous Catilinarian conspiracy, and bringing the leaders to punishment. This title was offered to Marius, but was refused by him. It was subsequently bestowed upon several of the Cæsars, and was borne by Andronicus Palæologus (Andronicus II.), by Cosmo de' Medici, and by some other European princes. The same appellation has been popularly conferred in America upon Washington, of whom Jefferson said, "His was the singular destiny and merit of leading the armies of his country successfully through an arduous war for the establishment of its independence," and "of conducting its councils through the birth of a government new in its forms and principles, until it had settled down into a quiet and orderly train."

Father of his People. [Fr. *Le Père de la Peuple.*] 1. A title given by courtly historians to Louis XII. of France (1462-1515), who has the reputation of having been a kind-hearted and generous king.

2. A title conferred upon Christian III. of Denmark (1502-1559).

Father of History. [Lat. *Pater Historiæ.*] A name given by Cicero (*Leg.* i. i. v.) to Herodotus (484-408, B. C.), because he was, if not the first historian, the first who brought history to any great degree of perfection.

Father of Jests. A sobriquet bestowed upon Joseph Miller (1684-1738), an English comic actor, whose name has become widely known from its connection with a celebrated jest-book, the authorship of which was ascribed to him, though it was not published, or even compiled, until after his death.

☞ Miller was himself proverbial for dulness ; and it is said, that, when any risible saying was recounted, his neighbours would derisively apply it to him on account of his taciturnity and imperturbable gravity. When he died, his family were left entirely unprovided for ; and a Mr. Motley, a well-known dramatist of that day, was employed to collect all the stray jests current about town, and to publish them for their benefit. Joe Miller's name was prefixed, and, from that time to this, the man who never uttered a jest has been the reputed author of every jest, past, present, and to come.

Father of Letters. [Fr. *Le Père des Lettres.*] 1. An appellation sometimes given to Francis I. (1494-1547), king of France, a distinguished patron of literature and literary men.

2. A title conferred upon Lorenzo de' Medici (d. 1492), the ruler of Florence, and a munificent patron of learning and art.

Father of Lies. 1. A popular name for Satan, or the Devil, the supposed instigator of all falsehood. See DEVIL, THE.

2. A name sometimes given to Herodotus (484-408 B. C.), the Greek historian, on account of the wonderful stories he relates. But the title is not merited, and has been given by "the half-learned, who measure his experience by their own ignorance." Incidental confirmations of his veracity have been accumulating of late years on all sides.

☞ For the "Key to the Scheme of Pronunciation," with the accompanying Explanations,

Father of Medicine. A title often applied to Hippocrates (b. B. c. 460), the most famous among the Greek physicians, and author of the first attempt at a scientific treatment of medicine.

Father of Monks. A title conferred upon Ethelwold of Winchester (d. 984) by his contemporaries. He is celebrated as a reformer of the monastic orders in England.

Father of Moral Philosophy. An appellation bestowed upon Thomas Aquinas (1227-1274), the famous scholastic theologian, on account of his original, clear, and comprehensive treatment of Christian ethics.

Father of Music. A title bestowed upon Giambattista Pietro Aloisio da Palestrina (1529-1594), a celebrated Italian composer of church music. "By his fine taste and admirable skill in harmony," says Burney, he "brought choral music to a degree of perfection that has never been exceeded."

Father of Ornithologists. A name sometimes given to George Edwards (1693-1773), an eminent English naturalist, whose works, according to Swainson, "are assuredly the most valuable on general ornithology that have ever appeared in England."

Father of Orthodoxy. A name often given to Athanasius (296-373), archbishop of Alexandria, one of the brightest ornaments of the early Church, and the great defender of "orthodoxy" against all heretics, especially the Arians.

Father of Peace. A title conferred by the Genoese senate upon Andrea Doria (1468-1560), the celebrated ruler and admiral. He entered the service of Charles V. against Francis I., and became the deliverer of his country by expelling the French from Genoa. After the conclusion of peace, Doria was invested with supreme power, and the senate awarded him the title above named.

Father of Poetry. 1. A title sometimes given to Orpheus, of Thrace, an ancient Greek poet who is said to have flourished before Homer, and before the siege of Troy, but whose existence has been called in question, besides others by Aristotle.
2. The same title is sometimes given to Homer. See FATHER OF EPIC POETRY.

He whom all civilised nations now acknowledge as the *Father of Poetry*, must have himself looked back to an ancestry of poetical predecessors, and is only held original because we know not from whom he copied.
Sir W. Scott.

Father of Ridicule. A name sometimes given to François Rabelais (1483-1553), the first noteworthy comic romancer of modern times, and the most original and remarkable of all humourists.

Father of Song. A title sometimes bestowed upon Homer, the supposed author of the earliest Greek heroic poems extant, and of some hymns in praise of different gods.

Father of the Faithful. A name often given to Abraham, the progenitor of the Jewish nation, and the first depositary of the divine promises in favour of the chosen people. See *Rom.* iv.; *Gal.* iii. 6-9.

Father of the Poor. An appellation given to Bernard Gilpin (1517-1583), a celebrated English reformer, on account of his pious and unwearied exertions among the poorer classes.

Father of the Rondo. [Fr. *Le Père aux Rondeaux.*] A title sometimes given to J. B. Davaux (d. 1822), a celebrated French musical composer.

Father of the Vaudeville. [Fr. *Le Père Joyeux du Vaudeville.*] A name given to Oliver Basselin, a Norman poet and artisan, who flourished in the fifteenth century, and gave to his convivial songs the name of his native valley, the *Val-de-Vire*, or, in Old French, *Vau-de-Vire*. This name was afterward corrupted into the modern *vaudeville*.

Father of Tragedy. A title bestowed by the Athenians upon the poet Æschylus (B. C. 525-426). The alterations made by him in the composition and representation of tragedy were so great, that he was justly considered the originator of it.

Father of Waters. A popular name

given to the river Mississippi on account of its great length (3160 miles), and the very large number of its tributaries, of which the Red, the Arkansas, the Ohio, the Missouri, the Illinois, the Des Moines, the Wisconsin, and the St. Peter's or Minnesota, are the most important. The literal signification of the name, which is of Indian origin, is said to be "*great river*."

☞ The name of the great river of Farther India, the Irrawaddy, is said to mean "Father of Waters." The course of this river is estimated at 1200 miles in length.

Father Paul. The name usually given to Peter Sarpi (1552–1628), a native of Venice, and a celebrated ecclesiastic, historian, anatomist, and astronomer. He is best known by his work entitled "A History of the Council of Trent." He was a father of the order of Servites in Venice, and, on assuming the religious habit, changed his baptismal name of Peter for that of Paul.

Father Prout. A pseudonym adopted by Francis Mahony, a popular English journalist and author of the present day.

Father Thoughtful. [Fr. *Père de la Pensée.*] A title given to Nicholas Catinat (1637–1712), marshal of France, by his soldiers, on account of his caution and judgment.

Father Violet. [Fr. *Le Père la Violette.*] A nickname given by the Parisian populace to the Emperor Napoleon I. See VIOLET, CORPORAL.

Fathom, Ferdinand, Count. The title of a novel by Smollett, and the name of its principal character, a complete villain, who proceeds step by step to rob his benefactors and pillage mankind, and who finally dies in misery and despair.

The sturdy genius of modern philosophy has got her in much the same situation that *Count Fathom* has the woman that he lashes before him from the robbers' cave in the forest.
Charles Lamb.

Fat'I-mȧ. 1. A female miracle-worker, in the story of "Aladdin," in the "Arabian Nights' Entertainments."

2. The last of the wives of Bluebeard, and the only one who escaped being murdered by him. See BLUEBEARD.

"Well, guardian," said I, "without thinking myself a *Fatima*, or you a Blue-beard, I am a little curious about it." *Dickens.*

Fáun, or **Fáu'nus.** (*Rom. Myth.*) A king of Italy, said to have flourished about 1300 years B. C., and regarded as the promoter of agriculture among his subjects, and as one of the great founders of the religion of the country. After his death, he was worshipped as the protecting god of woods, fields, and shepherds, and as an oracular and prophetic divinity. As a rural deity, he corresponded in many of his attributes to the Greek Pan; and hence arose the idea of a plurality of Fauns, or Fauni, assimilated to the Greek Panes or satyrs, and represented as monster deities, with tails, short horns, pointed ears, and goats' legs and feet, with the rest of the body human, to whom all terrifying sounds and appearances were ascribed.

In shadier bower,
More sacred and sequestered, though but feigned,
Pan or Sylvanus never slept; nor nymph
Nor *Faunus* haunted. *Milton.*

Fáu'nṡ. (*Rom. Myth.*) The prophesying wife or sister of Faunus.

Faust (Ger. pron. fȯwst; Anglicised fawst.) The hero and title of a celebrated drama of Goethe, the materials of which are drawn in part from the popular legends of Dr. Faustus. Faust is a student who is toiling after knowledge beyond his reach, and who afterward deserts his studies, and makes a pact with the Devil (Mephistopheles), in pursuance of which he gives himself up to the full enjoyment of the senses, until the hour of his doom arrives, when Mephistopheles re-appears upon the scene, and carries off his victim as a condemned soul. On one occasion, Mephistopheles provided him with a mantle by which he was wafted through the air whithersoever he desired. See MARGARET, MEPHISTOPHELES, and WAGNER.

☞ The mythical Faust dates from the

☞ For the "Key to the Scheme of Pronunciation," with the accompanying Explanations,

period of the Reformation. The numerous legends connected with the name all refer to a certain Dr. Faustus, reputed to be a celebrated magician and necromancer, who flourished during the latter half of the fifteenth and the beginning of the sixteenth centuries, and who is often confounded with Johann Faust, or Fust, the associate of Gutenberg in the invention of the art of printing. It has been by many strenuously maintained that no such person ever existed, and that the name has been fancifully imputed to some magician *ob faustum in rebus peractu difficillimis successum.* As long ago as the seventeenth century, two books were written with the purpose of proving the historical nonentity of Dr. Faustus. Modern criticism, however, leaves little room for doubting that there was a real person of this name. Faustus occupies the same place in reference to the popular superstitions of Germany that the enchanter Merlin does to those of England, that Don Juan holds in Spain, Robert of Normandy in France, and Virgil in Italy. The Goethean Faust is the highest form which the tradition has attained. See *infra.*

☞ "As in Germany all popular wit clusters about Eulenspiegel, so all that is weird, mysterious, and magical, — all that foretokens the terrible abyss of hell, — groups itself about the story of Faust."
Scheible, Trans.

He says, in so many words, . . . "Society sails through the infinitude on cloth, as on a *Faust's* mantle . . . ; and, without such . . . mantle, would sink to endless depths, or mount to inane limbos, and in either case be no more." *Carlyle.*

Fāus'tus. The hero of Marlowe's tragedy of the same name ; represented as a vulgar sorcerer tempted to sell his soul to the Devil (Mephostophilis) on condition of having a familiar spirit at his command, the possession of earthly power and glory, and unlimited gratification of his sensual appetites, for twenty-four years, at the end of which time, when the forfeit comes to be exacted, he shrinks and shudders in agony and remorse, imploring yet despairing of the mercy of Heaven.

☞ The tradition of the magician Faustus was early transplanted to England from Germany. In the same year (1587-8) in which the first history of Faust appeared in Germany, one appeared in England written by Bishop Aylmer. The transition from history to the drama was soon made, Marlowe's "Faustus" having been composed not later, probably, than 1589 or 1590, and having been entered in the Stationers' books in 1600-1. See FAUST.

Fȧ-vo'ni-us. [Lat., from *favere,* to favour.] (*Rom. Myth.*) A personification of the west wind, regarded as the harbinger and attendant of spring, and a promoter of vegetation; the same as *Zephyrus.* See ZEPHYRUS.

Ye delicate! . . . for whom
The winter rose must blow, . . . and silky soft
Favonius breathe still softer or be chid.
Young.

Faw'ni-ḁ. The mistress or lady-love of Dorastus, in the old romance of this name. See DORASTUS.

Feeble. A recruit, in the Second Part of Shakespeare's " King Henry IV." Falstaff calls him "most forcible Feeble;" and this expression is sometimes used to stigmatise writers whose productions are characterised by great apparent vigour, though really tame or jejune.

He [Aytoun] would purge his book of much offensive matter, if he struck out epithets which are in the bad taste of the *forcible-feeble* school.
North Brit. Rev.

Felicians, The (fe-lish'ănz). An imaginary people described by Mercier de la Rivière (1720-1794), the French economist, in his work entitled " L' Heureuse Nation;" represented as free and sovereign, and living under the absolute empire of laws.

Fe'lix-mar'te of Hȳr-cā'ni-ḁ. The hero of an old romance of chivalry, written by Melchior de Orteza Caballero de Ubeda, and printed at Valladolid in the year 1566. His father's name being *Florisan,* and his mother's *Martedina,* it was suggested that he should be called *Florismarte,* after both of his parents. His mother, however, preferred *Felixmarte.*

☞ The curate, in "Don Quixote," condemned this work to the flames, and Lockhart speaks of it as a "dull and affected folio ;" but Dr. Johnson was of a different opinion, according to Boswell, who relates the following anecdote of him, on the authority of Bishop Percy : " The bishop said the doctor, when a boy, was immoderately fond of romances of chivalry, and he had retained his fondness for them through life ; so that, spending part of a summer at my parsonage-house in the country, he chose for his regular reading the old Spanish romance of 'Felixmarte of Hyrcania,' in folio, which he read quite through."

Female Hŏw'ărd. A title often given to Mrs. Elizabeth Fry (1780–1844), an Englishwoman celebrated for her benevolent exertions to improve the condition of lunatics and prisoners.

Fe-nel'lā. A fairy-like creature — a deaf and dumb attendant on the Countess of Derby — in Sir Walter Scott's "Peveril of the Peak," taken from the sketch of Mignon in Goethe's "Wilhelm Meister." See MIGNON.

Fenrir (fen'rĕr). (*Scand. Myth.*) A frightful demon wolf, the offspring of Loki, chained by the gods, and cast down into Niflheim, where he is to remain until Ragnarök. [Written also, but erroneously, Fenris.]

Fen'ton (-tn). A character in Shakespeare's "Merry Wives of Windsor," who wooes the rich Anne Page for her money, but soon discovers inward treasures in her which quite transform him.

Ferdinand. 1. A character in Shakespeare's "Tempest." He is son of the king of Naples, and falls in love with Miranda, the daughter of Prospero, a banished Duke of Milan. See PROSPERO and MIRANDA.

Yet oft to fancy's chapel she would go
To pay her vows, and count the rosary o'er
Of her love's promised graces: — haply so
Miranda's hope had pictured *Ferdinand*
Long ere the gaunt wave tossed him on the shore. *Lowell.*

2. King of Navarre, a character in "Love's Labour 's Lost."

Fĕr'gus (4). The same as *Ferracute.* See FERRACUTE.

Fern, Fanny. A pseudonym adopted by Mrs. Sarah Payson (Willis) Parton (b. 1811), a popular American authoress.

Fernan Caballero. See CABALLERO, FERNAN.

Fe-ro'ni-ă. (*Rom. Myth.*) An ancient Italian deity, the patroness of plants and of freedmen.

Fĕr'rā-cūte, or **Fĕr'rā-cu'tus.** [It., sharp-iron.] The name of a giant in Turpin's "Chronicle of Charlemagne," the prototype of Pulci's Morgante, and a very famous character in all the old chivalric romances. He was of the race of Goliath, had the strength of forty men, and was twenty cubits high. His skin was so thick that no lance or sword could pierce it. During the suspension of a mortal combat with Orlando, the two antagonists discussed the mysteries of the Christian faith, which its champion explained by a variety of similes and the most beautiful beggings of the question; after which the giant staked the credit of their respective beliefs on the event of their encounter, which was, that he was disarmed and put to death by Orlando, who was divinely endowed with irresistible strength for this express purpose.

Fĕr'rā-gus. A giant who flourished in romantic fable; the same as *Ferracute.* See FERRACUTE.

My sire's tall form might grace the part
Of *Ferragus* or Ascapart. *Sir W. Scott.*

Ferraù (fĕr-rä-ōō'). The same as *Ferracute.* See FERRACUTE.

Fĕr'rex. A son of a fabulous king of Britain, Gorbogudo or Gorbodego, and brother of Porrex, by whom he was driven out of the country, and, on attempting to return, with a large army, was defeated and slain. But Porrex himself was shortly after put to death by his mother, with the assistance of some of her women. The two brothers figure in an old tragedy, commonly called after them "Ferrex and Porrex," but sometimes named "Gorboduc," after their father. Halliwell says that it was "the first regular historical play in the English language." The first three acts were written by Thomas Norton; the last two by Thomas Sackville, afterwards Lord Buckhurst.

Fĕr'um-brăs, Sir. The hero of an old English metrical romance of the same name, professedly translated from a French original, probably "Fierabras." (See FIERABRAS.) An analysis of the story may be found in Ellis's "Specimens of Early English Metrical Romances," vol. ii.

Fiammetta (fe-ăm-met'tä, 102). [It., little flame, from *fiamma*, Lat. *flamma*, flame.] A name given by Boccaccio to a lady whom he loved, and who is generally believed to have been Maria, a natural daughter of Robert, king of Naples. It is used by him in many of his works.

Fi-de'le. A feigned name assumed by Imogen, in Shakespeare's "Cymbeline." See IMOGEN.

Field of Blood. 1. A translation of the Hebrew word *Aceldama*, the name given to the piece of land purchased by the chief priests with the thirty pieces of silver for which Judas betrayed his Master, and which he afterward, in remorse, carried back and cast down in the temple before those who had bribed him. (*Matt.* xxvii. 5.)
2. [It. *Pezzo di Sangue*.] A name — not of classical origin — given to the battle-field of Cannæ, on which Hannibal, in the year 216 B. C., defeated the Romans with great slaughter.

Field of Mourning. A name given to the place of a battle, near the city of Aragon, between the Christians and the Moors, July 17, 1134.

Field of Peterloo. See PETERLOO, FIELD OF.

Field of the Cloth of Gold. A name given to an open plain, between Ardres and Guisnes, where Henry VIII. of England had an interview, in 1520, with Francis I. of France, in a pavilion of golden cloth. The nobility of both kingdoms embraced the opportunity to display their magnificence with the utmost emulation and profuseness of expense.

I supposed you must have served as a yeoman of the guard since Bluff King Henry's time, and expected to hear something from you about the *Field of the Cloth of Gold*.
Sir W. Scott.

They [Petrarch's best compositions] differ from them [his bad ones] as a May-day procession of chimney-sweepers differs from the *Field of the Cloth of Gold*. *Macaulay.*

Fierabras (fe'ä'rä-brä'). The hero of various old romantic poems that relate the conquest of Spain by Charlemagne and his Twelve Peers. Fierabras, who was a Saracen, made himself master of Rome, and carried away from it various sacred relics, especially the crown of thorns, and the balsam which was used in embalming the body of the Saviour, and which possessed medicinal properties of sovereign virtue, a single drop, taken internally, being sufficient to restore the continuity of the most cruelly mangled skin.

Conveyances more rapid than the hippogriff of Ruggiero, arms more formidable than the lance of Astolfo, remedies more efficacious than the balsam of *Fierabras*. *Macaulay.*

Fifth Doctor of the Church. A title bestowed upon Thomas Aquinas, the most celebrated schoolman of the Middle Ages. See ANGELIC DOCTOR.

Fifth Monarchy. A universal monarchy, which, in the belief of a strange religious sect of England, in the time of the Civil War and the Protectorate, was to succeed the fall of the Roman Empire, the fourth of the four great monarchies of Antichrist marked out by the prophet Daniel. This monarchy, it was believed, was to be given into the hands of the saints of the Most High; and, under it, all the forms of violence and suffering hitherto attendant on the governments of this world were to cease. In other words, it was to be the kingdom of Christ on earth. But it was to be set up with the sword, and the usual worldly expedients were to be employed for the purpose of securing partisans. In politics, the Fifth Monarchy men were republicans of the extremest views, and conspired to murder the Protector and revolutionise the government. It is said that they actually proceeded to elect JESUS CHRIST king at London! Cromwell dispersed them in 1653.

Figaro (fe'gä'ro'). The hero of Beaumarchais' celebrated comedies, "Le Barbier de Séville" and "Le Mariage de Figaro." In the first of these plays, Figaro is a barber; in the second, a valet-de-chambre. In both characters, he coolly outwits every one with whom he has any dealings. The name has passed into common speech, and is used to designate an intriguer, a go-between; in general, any adroit and unscrupulous person. Mozart, Paesiello, and Rossini have made Figaro the hero of operas.

☞ "In Figaro, Beaumarchais has personified the *tiers-état*, superior in wit, industry, and activity to birth, rank, or fortune, in whose hand lies the political power; so that the idea of the piece is not only a satirical allegory upon the government and nobility of that epoch, but a living manifesto upon the inequality, just or unjust, of society." *Rose.*

Fighting Prelate. A sobriquet given to Henry Spenser, bishop of Norwich, in the reign of Richard II. During the rebellion of Wat Tyler, he distinguished himself by his decisive style of dealing with the insurgents; first meeting them in the field, and then, when he had routed them, exchanging his sword and armour for a crucifix and sacerdotal robes, and, thus arrayed, confessing and absolving his prisoners as he hurried them to the gibbet. In 1383, he went over to the Continent to assist the burghers of Ghent in their contest with the Count of Flanders and the French king, and in support of the cause of Urban VI., in the general European war excited by the struggle between that pope and his rival, Clement VII.

The Bishop of Norwich, the famous *Fighting Prelate*, had led an army into Flanders. Being obliged to return, with discomfiture, he had been charged with breach of the conditions on which a sum of money was granted to him, and the temporalities of his see were sequestered. *Lord Campbell.*

Filomena, St. See ST. FILOMENA.

Finality John. A sobriquet given to Lord John Russell (b. 1792), a distinguished English statesman, and an earnest advocate of the Reform Bill of 1831, which he regarded as a "finality."

Fin'gàl, *or* **Fin-gàl'.** A mythical hero, whose name occurs in Gaelic ballads and traditions, and in Macpherson's "Poems of Ossian."

First Gentleman of Europe (9). A title given by many, during his lifetime, to King George IV. of England (1762-1830), on account of his position and personal attractions.

First Scotch Reformer. A title conferred upon Patrick Hamilton (1503-1527), who was burnt at the stake for his dissemination of Lutheran doctrines.

Fitz-Boo'dle, George. A pseudonym under which Thackeray (1811-1863) contributed to "Fraser's Magazine" a variety of tales, criticisms, descriptive sketches, and verses, all of which were characterised by a delicate irony, a profound knowledge of the world, and a playful but vigorous and trenchant style.

Flam'bor-oughs, The Miss (flăm'-bŭr-ǒz). Snobbish female characters in Goldsmith's novel, "The Vicar of Wakefield."

Flăn'dẽrs, Moll. The subject of De Foe's novel of the same name, a tale of low vice.

Fle'ănçe. A son of Banquo, in Shakespeare's tragedy of "Macbeth."

Fle'tâ. A Latinised name of the Fleet prison in London, and the title of a disquisition by John Selden (1584-1654), who was for a time confined in this prison.

Flib'bẽr-ti-ġib'bet. 1. The name of a fiend mentioned by Edgar, in Shakespeare's tragedy of "King Lear."

☞ About the time of the attempted Spanish invasion of England, some Jesuits, for the sake of making converts, pretended to cast out a large number of evil spirits from the family of Mr. Edmund Peckham, a Roman Catholic. By order of the privy council, Bishop Harsnet wrote and published a full account of the imposture. Most of the fiends mentioned by Edgar are to be found in that work.

Fraterretto, *Flibcrdigibet*, Hoberdidance, Tocobatto, were four devils of the round, or morice; these four had forty assistants under them, as themselves do confesse.

Harsnet, Declaration of Egregious Popish Impostures.

This is the foul fiend *Flibbertigibbet;* he begins at curfew, and walks till the first cock; he gives the web and the pin, squints the eye, and makes the harelip, mildews the white wheat, and hurts the poor creature of earth.

Shak.

— *Flibbertigibbet,* [the fiend] of mopping and mowing, who since possesses chamber-maids and waiting-women. *Shak.*

2. A name given to Dickon Sludge,

a boy who figures in Sir Walter Scott's novel of "Kenilworth," and acts the part of an imp at the entertainments given to Queen Elizabeth by the Earl of Leicester.

Flo'ra (9). (*Rom. Myth.*) The goddess of flowers and spring-time.

Then, with voice
Mild, as when Zephyrus on *Flora* breathes,
Her hand soft touching, whispered thus.
Milton.

Flor'de-lice. The mistress of Brandimart, in Ariosto's "Orlando Furioso." See BRANDIMART.

Flordespina (flor-des-pe'nä), *or* **Flor'des-pine.** A female character in Ariosto's "Orlando Furioso," daughter of Marsiglio.

Flo-ren'ti-us. A knight whose story is related in the first book of Gower's "Confessio Amantis." He bound himself to marry a deformed hag, provided she taught him the solution of a riddle on which his life depended.

Be she foul as was *Florentius'* love. *Shak.*

Flo'res. The lover of Blanchefleur in Boccaccio's "Philopoco," and in other old tales and poems. See BLANCHEFLEUR.

Flŏr'i-mel. A female character in Spenser's "Faëry Queen." A malignant witch is represented as having fabricated, out of snow, tempered "with fine mercury and virgin wax," a counterfeit Florimel so like the true one that it was next to impossible to perceive any difference between them; but, on being placed side by side,—

"The enchanted damsel vanished into naught;
Her snowy substance melted as with heat;
No of that goodly hue remained aught
But the empty girdle which about her waist
was wrought."

☞ "Her name is compounded of two Latin words [*flos*, genitive *floris*, and *mel*] meaning *honey* and *flowers*, thus betokening the sweet and delicate elements of which her nature is moulded. She seems to express the gentle delicacy and timid sensitiveness of woman; and her adventures, the perils and rude encounters to which those qualities are exposed in a world of passion and violence. She flees alike from friend and foe, and finds treachery in those upon whom she had thrown herself for protection; and yet she is introduced to us under circumstances not altogether consistent with feminine delicacy, as having left the court of the fairy queen in pursuit of a knight who did not even return her passion."
Geo. S. Hillard.

To prove the whole system of this school absurd, it is only necessary to apply the test which dissolved the enchanted *Florimel.*
Macaulay.

Flŏr'is-mart. The name of one of Charlemagne's Twelve Peers, and the faithful friend of Orlando, or Roland.

Flŏr'i-zel. A prince of Bohemia, in Shakespeare's "Winter's Tale," in love with Perdita. See PERDITA.

Flour City. A popular designation, in the United States, for the city of Rochester, New York, a place remarkable for its extensive manufactories of flour.

Flower City. A name familiarly given to Springfield, Illinois, the capital of the State. It is distinguished for the beauty of its environs.

Flower of Chivalry. A name given by his contemporaries to William of Douglas, lord of Liddesdale, in the fourteenth century.

Flower of Kings. [Lat. *Flos Regum.*] An epithet applied to Arthur, the renowned and half-fabulous king of ancient Britain;—first given to him by Joseph of Exeter, a Latin poet of the twelfth century.

Flower of Poets. A title conferred upon Chaucer by his contemporaries.

Flowery Kingdom. A translation of the words *Hwa Kwoh*, a name often given to China by the inhabitants, who consider themselves to be the most polished and civilised of all nations, as the epithet *hwa* intimates.

Flŭ-el'len. A Welsh captain who is an amusing pedant, in Shakespeare's historical play of "Henry V."

Lord Mahon will find, we think, that his parallel is, in all essential circumstances, as incorrect as that which *Fluellen* drew between Macedon and Monmouth. *Macaulay.*

The architect worked hard for weeks
In venting all his private peaks
Upon the roof, whose crop of leaks
Had satisfied *Fluellen.* *Lowell.*

Flying Dutchman. The name given by sailors to a spectral ship, which is supposed to cruise in storms off the Cape of Good Hope, and the sight of which is considered the worst of all possible omens. She is distinguished from earthly vessels by bearing a press of sail when all others are unable, from stress of weather, to show an inch of canvas. The cause of her wandering is variously explained: according to one account, a Dutch captain, bound home from the Indies, met with long-continued head-winds and heavy weather off the Cape of Good Hope, and refused to put back as he was advised to do, swearing a very profane oath that he would beat round the Cape, if he had to beat there until the Day of Judgment. He was taken at his word, and doomed to beat against head-winds all his days. His sails are believed to have become thin and sere, his ship's sides white with age, and himself and crew reduced almost to shadows. He cannot heave to, or lower a boat, but sometimes hails vessels through his trumpet, and requests them to take letters home for him. Dr. John Leyden, who introduces the story of the Flying Dutchman into his "Scenes of Infancy," imputes, with poetical ingenuity, the doom of the ship to its having been the first to engage in the slave-trade. But the common tradition is, as stated by Sir Walter Scott, "that she was originally a vessel loaded with great wealth, on board of which some horrid act of murder and piracy had been committed; that the plague broke out among the wicked crew, who had perpetrated the crime, and that they sailed in vain from port to port, offering, as the price of shelter, the whole of their ill-gotten wealth; that they were excluded from every harbour, for fear of the contagion which was devouring them; and that, as a punishment of their crimes, the apparition of the ship still continues to haunt those seas in which the catastrophe took place." The superstition has its origin, probably, in the looming, or apparent suspension in the air, of some ship out of sight,—a phenomenon sometimes witnessed at sea, and caused by unequal refraction in the lower strata of the atmosphere. Marryatt's novel entitled "The Phantom Ship" is founded upon this legend.

That Phantom Ship, whose form
Shoots like a meteor through the storm;
When the dark scud comes driving hard,
And lowered is every top-sail yard,
And canvas, wove in earthly looms,
No more to brave the storm presumes;
Then, 'mid the war of sea and sky,
Top and top-gallant hoisted high,
Full-spread and crowded every sail,
The Demon Frigate braves the gale;
And well the doomed spectators know
The harbinger of wreck and woe.
Sir W. Scott.

Let this simple word [No, in answer to a claim for "recognition" on the part of the "Confederate States"] be uttered, and the audacious Slave-Power will be no better than the *Flying Dutchman*, that famous craft, which, darkened by piracy and murder, was doomed to a perpetual cruise, unable to enter a port.
Charles Sumner.

Flying Highwayman. A sobriquet given to William Harrow, a noted highway robber, executed at Hertford (Eng.), March 28, 1763. He was so called from his practice of leaping his horse over the turnpikes, which enabled him for a time to escape detection.

Foible. An intriguing lady's-maid in Congreve's "Way of the World," who plays her mistress false.

Foi'gard. A mendacious and hypocritical priest, in Farquhar's "Beaux' Stratagem," who acts the part of a pimp.

We remember no Friar Dominic, no *Father Foigard*, among the characters drawn by those great poets [the dramatists of the Elizabethan age]. *Macaulay.*

Fondlewife. An uxorious banker in Congreve's "Old Bachelor."

Fontainebleau, Decree of. See DECREE OF FONTAINEBLEAU.

Fool, Tom. A popular nickname for a fool, or foolish person.

☞ "Englishmen bestowed upon Kent the reproach that the tails cut from Becket's mules by his enemies had been transferred to themselves, and foreigners extended the imputation to the whole nation, insomuch that, as Joinville tells us, the stout Earl of Salisbury and his men were goaded on to perish in their last fatal charge on the banks of the Nile by the French scoff that they would not take the front lest their tails should be detected. It is just possible that *Tom*

Fool may be connected with this story, though more probably with some jester of forgotten fame." *Yonge.*

The ancient and noble family of *Tom Fool,* which has obtained such pre-eminence and dignity in Church and State throughout all Christendom. *Qu. Rev.*

Fools' Paradise. See LIMBO.

Foot-breadth. The sword of Thoralf Skolinson the Strong, a companion of Hako I. of Norway, distinguished for his strength and bravery. See QUERN-BITER.

Fop'ping-ton, Lord. An empty coxcomb, intent only on dress and fashion, in Vanbrugh's comedy, "The Relapse."

The shoe-maker in "The Relapse" tells *Lord Foppington* that his lordship is mistaken in supposing that his shoe pinches. *Macaulay.*

Förd, Master. A jealous gentleman dwelling at Windsor, in Shakespeare's comedy of "The Merry Wives of Windsor."

Förd, Mrs. One of the "Merry Wives of Windsor," in Shakespeare's play of that name. Sir John Falstaff is in love with her, and she encourages his attentions for a time, in order to betray and disgrace him. See BROOK, MASTER.

Forest City. 1. A name popularly given to Cleveland, Ohio, from the many ornamental trees with which the streets are bordered.

2. A name given to Portland, Maine, a city distinguished for its many elms and other beautiful shade-trees.

3. A name given to Savannah, Georgia, the streets of which are closely shaded with pride-of-India (*Margosa Azedarak*) trees.

Forester, Fanny. A *nom de plume* of Miss Emily Chubbuck (1817-1854), a popular American authoress, afterward the wife of Adoniram Judson, the missionary.

Forester, Frank. A pseudonym under which Henry William Herbert (1807-1858), a versatile English author, long resident in America, published a number of works on fowling, fishing, and field-sports in general.

For'nax. (*Rom. Myth.*) A goddess of corn, and the patroness of bakers.

Forseti (for'sä-tee). [Old Norse, president, from *fyr*, before, and *sitja*, to sit.] (*Scand. Myth.*) The god of justice, a son of Baldur. [Written also F o r s e t c.]

For'tin-brăs. Prince of Norway, in Shakespeare's tragedy of "Hamlet."

For-tu'nă. (*Rom. Myth.*) The goddess of chance or luck, particularly of good luck, success, and prosperity; said to be blind.

Fortunate Islands. See ISLANDS OF THE BLEST.

For'tu-nā'tus. The hero of a German popular romance of the fifteenth century, based upon legends of an earlier date.

☞ The story recounts how, when he had been exposed to great dangers from wild beasts, and was in a state of starvation, he suddenly beheld a beautiful lady standing by his side, with a bandage over her eyes, leaning upon a wheel, and looking as if she were going to speak. The lady did not wait long before she addressed him in these words: "Know, young man, that my name is Fortune. I have power to bestow wisdom, strength, riches, health, beauty, and long life. One of these I am willing to bestow on you. Choose for yourself which it shall be." Fortunatus immediately answered, "Good lady, I wish to have riches in such plenty that I may never again know what it is to be so hungry as I now find myself." The lady then gave him a purse, and told him, that, in all the countries where he might happen to be, he need only put his hand into the purse, as often as he pleased, and he would be sure to find in it pieces of gold; that the purse should never fail of yielding the same sum as long as it should be kept by himself and children. It is further related, that a certain sultan led Fortunatus to a room almost filled with jewels, opened a large closet, and took out a *cap*, which he said was of greater value than all the rest. Fortunatus thought the sultan was joking, and told him he had seen many a better cap than that. "Ah," said the sultan, "that is because you do not know its value. Whoever puts this cap on his head, and wishes to be in any part of the world, will find himself there in a moment." The story has a moral ending, inasmuch as the possession of this inexhaustible purse and wishing-cap are the cause of ruin to Fortunatus, and to his sons after him. The subject was dramatised by Hans Sachs in 1553, and by Thomas Dekker in his "Pleasant Comedie of Old Fortunatus" (1600); and in modern times it has been poetically treated by Ludwig Tieck in his "Phantasus" (1816).

With a miraculous *Fortunatus's* purse in his treasury, it might have lasted longer.
Carlyle.

For-tu'ni-o (6). The hero of a popular tale, closely allied to that of Fortunatus, — with whom he is perhaps identical, — but which has generally been treated as an independent story. He is famous for his adventure with a dragon, in the pursuit of which he made use of those marvellous servitors, Fine-ear, who, "putting his ear to the ground, informed his master that the dragon was seven leagues off;" Tippler, who "drank up all the rivers which were between;" Strong-back, who "carried wine enough to fill them all;" Light-foot, Boisterer, and Gormand.

Forty Thieves. Characters of a celebrated tale in the "Arabian Nights' Entertainments," represented as inhabiting a secret cave in a forest, the door of which would open and shut only at the sound of the magic word "Sesame," — the name of a kind of grain. See BABA, ALI.

All Baba, when he entered the cave of the *Forty Thieves*, could not have been more amazed by the wealth of its contents than some people will be when they first read the title of this book. *Putnam's Mag.*

Forwards, Marshal. See MARSHAL FORWARDS.

Foul-weather Jack. A name given to Commodore Byron (1723–1786), by the men who sailed under him, in allusion to his ill fortune at sea.

Fountain of Life. A title given to Alexander Hales, an English friar of the thirteenth century, and a distinguished schoolman. He was more commonly styled *The Irrefragable Doctor.*

Fountain of Youth. A miraculous fountain, whose waters were fabled to have the property of renewing youth. See BIMINI.

Four Masters, The. [Lat. *Quatuor Magistri.*] A name given to the authors of an ancient Irish history called "The Annals of Donegal." Their names were Michael O'Clerigh, or Clerk, Maurice and Fearfeasa Conry, and Cucoirighe, or Peregrine, O'Clerighe.

Fra Diavolo. (frä de-ä'vo-lo). [It., Brother Devil.] A sobriquet of Michele Pezza (1760–1806), a native of Calabria. According to some accounts, he was in early life a goatherd, afterward a monk, under the name of *Fra Angelo.* Others say that he was apprenticed to a stockinger. Escaping from the workshop or the monastery, he joined himself to a band of robbers, of which he soon became the leader. On the arrival of the French, he declared for the king of Naples, and in 1799 received pardon and office from Cardinal Buffo, organised his band, and made an incursion into the Roman territory. Subsequently he repaired to Palermo, where he took part in an insurrection under the leadership of Commodore Sidney Smith. Being taken prisoner by treachery at San Severino, he was hanged at Naples, Nov. 1806, notwithstanding the intercession of the English on his behalf, prompted by respect for his military prowess. He has been made the subject of various traditions and songs, and of an opera by Auber, entitled "Fra Diavolo," in which, however, nothing of the character but the name has been retained.

Fran-ces'cȧ of Rim'i-ni (*It. pron.* frän-ches'kä). A daughter of Guido da Polenta, lord of Ravenna in the latter part of the thirteenth century. She was married to Lanciotto, son of Malatesta da Rimini, a brave but deformed and hateful person, who, having discovered a criminal intimacy between her and his own brother, revenged himself by putting them both to death. The story of Francesca forms one of the most admired episodes in Dante's "Inferno," and has also been made the subject of a poem by Leigh Hunt.

Frank'en-stein. A monster, in Mrs. Shelley's romance of the same name, constructed by a young student of physiology out of the horrid remnants of the church-yard and dissecting-room, and endued, apparently through the agency of galvanism, with a sort of spectral and convulsive life. This existence, rendered insupportable to the monster by his vain craving after human sympathy, and by his consciousness of his own deformity, is employed in inflicting the most dreadful retribution upon the guilty philosopher.

It [the Southern "Confederacy"] will be the soulless monster of *Frankenstein*,— the wretched creation of mortal science without God; endowed with life and nothing else; for ever raging madly, the scandal to humanity; powerful only for evil; whose destruction will be essential to the peace of the world.
Charles Sumner.

Frat'ẽr-et'to. The name of a fiend mentioned by Edgar, in Shakespeare's tragedy of "King Lear." See FLIBBERTIGIBBET.

Free-born John. John Lilburne (1613–1657), a famous English republican; — popularly so called on account of his intrepid defence, before the tribunal of the Star Chamber, of his rights as a free-born Englishman.

Freeman, Mrs. An assumed name under which the Duchess of Marlborough corresponded with Queen Anne. See MORLEY, MRS.

Freeport, Sir Andrew. The name of one of the members of the imaginary club under whose direction the "Spectator" was professedly published. He is represented as a London merchant of great eminence and experience, industrious, sensible, and generous.

Freestone State. The State of Connecticut; — sometimes so called from the quarries of freestone which it contains.

Freischütz (frī'shüts, 51). [Ger., the free-shooter ; Fr. *Robin des Bois.*] The name of a legendary hunter, or marksman, who, by entering into a compact with the Devil, procures balls, six of which infallibly hit, however great the distance, while the seventh, or, according to some of the versions, one of the seven, belongs to the Devil, who directs it at his pleasure. Legends of this nature were rife among the troopers of Germany of the fourteenth and fifteenth centuries, and during the Thirty Years' war. The story first appeared in a poetic form in 1810, in Apel's "Gespensterbuch" ("Ghostbook"), and F. Kind adapted the story to the opera composed by Weber in 1821, which has made it known in all civilised countries. *Pierer.*

French Devil. An opprobrious title given by the English, Dutch, and Spanish to Jean Barth, or Bart (1651–1702), a French naval hero celebrated for his boldness and success in battle.

French Fā'bi-us. A surname bestowed upon Anne (1493–1567), first Duke of Montmorency, grand constable of France, on account of his success in nearly destroying the imperial army which had invaded Provence, by the policy of laying waste the country and skilfully prolonging the campaign. See AMERICAN FABIUS.

French Fury. (*Hist.*) A name given to the attempt made by the Duke of Anjou to carry Antwerp by storm, Jan. 17, 1583. The whole of his force was either killed or taken captive in less than an hour.

French Phid'i-ąs. 1. A title bestowed upon Jean Gougon (d. 1572), a celebrated Parisian sculptor and architect, in the reigns of Francis I. and Henry II.

2. A title conferred upon Jean Baptiste Pigalle (1714–1785), an eminent French sculptor; but not happily, as his taste cannot be said to be classical.

French Pin'dar. A title bestowed upon Jean Dorat, a French poet of the sixteenth century. Charles IX. created expressly for him the office of *Poëte Royal.* He died at Paris in 1582, aged 80 years.

French Răph'ā-el. A title conferred upon Eustace Le Sieur (1617–1655), a distinguished French painter.

French Ros'ci-us (rosh'ĭ-us). Michael Baron (1653–1727), a celebrated French actor.

and for the Remarks and Rules to which the numbers after certain words refer, see pp. xiv-xxxii.

French Solomon. See SOLOMON OF FRANCE.

French Ti-bŭl'lus. [Fr. *Le Tibulle Français.*] A surname given to Évariste Désiré Desforges, Chevalier de l'Arny (1753–1814), a French elegiac and erotic poet.

Fres'tǫn. An enchanter or necromancer who figures in many terrible scenes of the old romance of "Don Beliauis of Greece."

Not Munlaton, but *Freston*, you should have said, cried Don Quixote. Truly, quoth the niece, I can't tell whether it was *Freston*, or Friston, but sure I am that his name ended with a "ton." *Cervantes, Trans.*

Frey (frī, 42). (*Scand. Myth.*) The god of the sun and of rain, and hence of fertility and peace. He was one of the most popular of the Northern divinities. [Written also F r e y r.]

Freyja (frī'yȧ). (*Scand. Myth.*) The goddess of love, beauty, pleasure, and fecundity. She was the sister of Frey, and the wife of Odur, who abandoned her on her loss of youth and beauty, and was changed into a statue by Odin, as a punishment. [Written also F r e y i a and F r e y a.]

Friar Dom'i-nic. The chief personage in Dryden's play, "The Spanish Friar," designed to ridicule the vices of the priesthood. It is the best of his comic characters.

Friar Gĕr'und. The hero of a celebrated Spanish satirical romance by Padre Isla (1703–1781), designed to ridicule the style of pulpit oratory in vogue in his day, — oratory degraded by bad taste, by conceits, puns, and tricks of composition, and even by low buffoonery, indulged in merely to win the applause and increase the contributions of vulgar audiences. "The famous preacher, Friar Gerund," is one of these popular orators; and Isla describes his life from his birth in an obscure village, through his education in a fashionable convent, and his adventures as a missionary about the country, the fiction ending abruptly with his preparation to deliver a course of sermons in a city that seems intended to represent Madrid.

Friar John. The name of one of the most celebrated characters in Rabelais' romance of "Pantagruel."

☞ "Throughout the book, he dashes on, regardless of every thing in this world or the next. If there is a shipwreck or a skirmish, Friar John is foremost in the bustle; fear is unknown to him; if a joke more than usually profane is to be uttered, Friar John is the spokesman. The swearing, bullying phrases are all put in the mouth of Friar John. Rabelais loved this lusty friar, this mass of lewdness, debauchery, profanity, and valour. He is the 'fine fellow' of the book; and the author always seems in a good humour when he makes him talk." *For. Qu. Rev.*

And as to a dinner, they can no more do without him than they could without *Friar John* at the roistering revels of the renowned Pantagruel. *W. Irving.*

Then came the Rebellion, and, presto! a flaw in our titles was discovered, ... and we were ... no relations of theirs after all, but a dreggy hybrid of the basest bloods of Europe. Panurge was not quicker to call *Friar John* his "former" friend. *Lowell.*

Friar Lȧu'rence. A Franciscan who undertakes to marry Romeo and Juliet, in Shakespeare's tragedy of that name.

Friar Rush. [Lat. *Frater Rauschius*, Ger. *Bruder Rausch*, Dan. *Broder Ruus.* His name signifies either *noise*, as Grimm thinks, or, as Wolf deems, *drunkenness.* Comp. Old Eng. *rouse.*] A house-spirit, celebrated in the marvellous legends of old times. His history was printed in 1620, and had probably been often printed before. The whole tale is designed as a severe satire upon the monks, the pretended friar being sent from hell in consequence of news, brought to the prince of devils, " of the great misrule and vile living of these religious men; to keep them still in that state, and worse if it might be."

Quis non legit quid *Frater Rauschius* egit? *Bruno Seidelius.*

Friar Tuck. One of the constant associates of Robin Hood, to whom Ben Jonson (in his "Sad Shepherd") makes him chaplain and steward. According to some, he was a real monk. Sir Walter Scott has introduced him in "Ivanhoe," with great success, as the Holy Clerk of Copmanhurst.

Frib'ble (-bl). A feeble-minded coxcomb in Garrick's farce entitled "Miss in her Teens;" much given to coddling himself, and "sadly troubled with weak nerves."

Could this sad, thoughtful countenance be the same . . . that had looked out . . . so blankly divested of all meaning, or resolutely expressive of none, in Acres, in *Fribble*, and a thousand agreeable impertinences?
Charles Lamb.

The fashionable *Fribbles* of the day, the chat, scandal, and amusements of those attending the wells, and the canting hypocrisy of some sectarians, are depicted, sometimes with indelicacy, but always with force and liveliness. *R. Chambers.*

Friday, Man. The name of a young Indian whom Robinson Crusoe saved from death on a Friday, and kept for a companion and servant.

Even before they were acquainted, he had admired Osborne in secret. Now he was his valet, his dog, his *Man Friday*. *Thackeray.*

Friend of Man. [Fr. *L'Ami des Hommes.*] A name popularly given to Victor Riquetti, Marquis de Mirabeau (1715–1789), from the title of one of his works. He was a distinguished political economist, and was father of the great tribune, Mirabeau.

Frig'gā. (*Scand. Myth.*) The wife of Odin, the queen of the gods, and the mother of Baldur, Thor, &c. She sometimes typifies the earth, as Odin does the heavens. The Anglo-Saxons worshipped her as *Frea*. The name survives in *Friday.*

Fris'co-bāl'do. A character in Dekker's "Honest Whore." Hazlitt pronounces it perfect, in its way, as a picture of a broken-hearted father with a sneer on his lips and a teardrop in his eye.

Frithiof (frith'ī-ŏf, *or* frith'yŏf). [Icel. *Fridhthjofr*, peace-destroyer.] The hero of an ancient Icelandic "saga," which records his love for the beautiful Ingeborg, the daughter of a petty Norwegian king. After being rejected by the brothers of Ingeborg, and having committed various acts of revenge on his enemies, he comes to the court of the old King Hring, to whom Ingeborg has been married, and is received with kindness. At the death of her husband, Ingeborg is married to her lover, who acquires with her hand the dominions of Hring, over which he rules prosperously to the end of his days. The distinguished Swedish poet, Bishop Tegnér, has made use of this myth as the groundwork of a poem of his own ("Frithjof's Saga"), which has obtained a wide reputation, and has been translated into various modern languages. [Written also Frithjof.]

Fritz, Der Alte (dĕr äl'tŭ frits). [Ger., Old Fritz, Old Fred.] A sobriquet given by the Germans to Frederick I. (1712–1786) king of Prussia, commonly called Frederick the Great.

Frog, Nic. A sportive collective name applied to the Dutch, in Arbuthnot's "History of John Bull."

I back your *Nic Frog* against Mother Partington. *Noctes Ambrosianæ.*

Frol'lo, Archdeacon Claude (*Fr. pron.* klōd frol'lo'). A noted character in Victor Hugo's "Notre-Dame de Paris," absorbed in a bewildering search after the philosophers' stone. He has a great reputation for sanctity, but falls in love with a gypsy girl, and pursues her with unrelenting persecution, because she will not yield to his desires.

Front de Bœuf. See BŒUF, FRONT DE.

Frontino (fron-te'no). The name given, in the old romances of chivalry, to the horse of Ruggiero, or Rogero.

Go, Rozinante, . . . go rear thy awful front wherever thou pleasest, secure that neither the hippogriffon of Astolpho, nor the renowned *Frontino*, which Bradamante purchased at so high a price, could ever be thought thy equal. *Cervantes, Don Quixote.*

Frost, Jack. A popular personification of frost.

☞ Frost is the name of a dwarf in the Scandinavian mythology, and Ferguson suggests that our nursery hero, Jack Frost, may be derived from that source.

Froth. 1. (Master.) A foolish gentleman, in Shakespeare's "Measure for Measure." His name explains his character, which is without solidity enough for deep crime, and far too light for virtue.

We have dealt with the tale very much according to the clown's argument in favour of *Master Froth:* "Look upon his face. I'll be

and for the Remarks and Rules to which the numbers after certain words refer, see pp. xiv–xxxii.

sworn upon a book that his face is the worst part about him; and if his face be the worst part about him, how could *Master Froth* do the constable's wife any harm?" *Sir W. Scott.*

2. (Lord.) A solemn coxcomb, in Congreve's comedy of "The Double Dealer."

Fudge, Mr. A contemptuous designation bestowed upon any absurd or lying writer or talker. See BURCHELL, MR.

☞ " There was, sir, in our time, one Captain Fudge, commander of a merchantman, who, upon his return from a voyage, how ill fraught soever his ship was, always brought home to his owners a good cargo of *lies*, insomuch that now aboard ship the sailors, when they hear a great lie told, cry out, 'You *fudge* it.'" *Remarks upon the Navy* (London, 1700). " In the year 1664, we were sentenced for banishment to Jamaica by Judges Hyde and Twisden, and our number was 55. We were put on board the ship Black Eagle; the master's name was Fudge, by some called Lying Fudge." *A Collection of some Papers of William Crouch* (8vo, 1712).

☞ " With a due respect to their antiquity, and the unchanged reputation always attached to the name, we have long held in high consideration the ancient family of Fudges. Some of them, as we know, have long resided in England, and have been ever ready to assist in her domestic squabbles and political changes. But their favourite place of residence we understand to be in Ireland. Their usual modes of expression, indeed, are akin to the figurative talk of the Emerald islanders." *Brit. & For. Rev.*

Fudge Family. A name under which the poet Moore, in a series of metrical epistles, purporting to be written by the members of a family of English tourists visiting Paris, satirised the absurdities of his travelling countrymen, who, having been long confined at home by the wars waged by Napoleon, flocked to the continent in swarms, after his defeat at Waterloo. The family is composed of a hack writer and spy, devoted to legitimacy, the Bourbons, and Lord Castlereagh; his son, a young dandy of the first water; and his daughter, a sentimental damsel, rapturously fond of "romance, and high bonnets, and Madame Le Roy," in love with a Parisian linen-draper, whom she has mistaken for one of the Bourbons in disguise. There is also a tutor and "poor relation" of this egregious family, who is an ardent Bonapartist and Irish patriot.

No sooner are we seated at the gay saloon In Dessin's, than we call, like Biddy *Fudge*, for " French pons and French ink." *Mrs. Jameson.*

Funk, Peter. A person employed at petty auctions to bid on articles put up for sale, in order to raise their price;— probably so called from such a name having frequently been given when articles were bought in. To *funk,* or *funk out,* is a vulgar expression, meaning to slink away, to take one's self off. In some localities, it conveys the added notion of great fear.

☞ " By thus running up goods, Peter is of great service to the auctioneers, though he never pays them a cent of money. Indeed, it is not his intention to purchase, nor is it that of the auctioneer that he should. Goods, nevertheless, are frequently struck off to him; and then the salesman cries out the name of Mr. Smith, Mr. Johnson, or some other among the hundred aliases of Peter Funk, as the purchaser. But the goods, on such occasions, are always taken back by the auctioneer, agreeably to a secret understanding between him and Peter."
Asa Greene.

Furies. [Lat. *Furiæ.*] (*Gr. & Rom. Myth.*) The three goddesses of vengeance, daughters of Acheron and Nox. They were armed with lighted torches, their heads were wreathed with snakes, and their whole appearance was terrific and appalling. Their names were Alecto, Megæra, and Tisiphone. [Called also *Erinnyes* and *Eumenides.*]

Furioso, Bombastes. See BOMBASTES FURIOSO.

Furioso, Orlando. See ORLANDO.

Fusberta (fŏŏs-bĕr'tă.) The name of the sword of Rinaldo. See BAYARD, 2, and RINALDO. [Written also Frusberta, Fushberta, and Floberge.]

This " awful sword," as the common people term it, was as dear to him as Durindana or *Fushberta* to their respective masters, and was nearly as formidable to his enemies as those renowned falchions proved to the foes of Christendom. *Sir W. Scott.*

☞ For the "Key to the Scheme of Pronunciation," with the accompanying Explanations,

G.

Gā'bri-el. [Heb., mighty one of God.] The name of an angel described in the Scriptures as charged with the ministration of comfort and sympathy to man. He was sent to Daniel to interpret in plain words the vision of the ram and the he-goat, and to comfort him, after his prayer, with the prophecy of the "seventy weeks." (See *Dan.* viii. and ix.) In the New Testament (*Luke* i.), he is the herald of good tidings, declaring as he does the coming of the predicted Messiah, and of his forerunner, John the Baptist. In the ordinary traditions, Jewish and Christian, Gabriel is spoken of as one of the seven archangels. According to the Rabbins, he is the angel of death for the people of Israel, whose souls are intrusted to his care. The Talmud describes him as the prince of fire, and as the spirit who presides over thunder, and the ripening of fruits. Gabriel has the reputation, among the Rabbins, of being a distinguished linguist, having taught Joseph the seventy languages spoken at Babel, and being, in addition, the only angel who could speak Chaldee and Syriac. The Mohammedans hold him in even greater reverence than the Jews. He is called the spirit of truth, and is believed to have dictated the Koran to Mohammed. Milton posts him at "the eastern gate of Paradise," as "chief of the angelic guards," keeping watch there.

Gads'hill. A companion of Sir John Falstaff, in the First Part of Shakespeare's "King Henry IV."

Gā'hĕr-is, Sir. A brother of Sir Gawain, and a knight of the Round Table, celebrated in old romances of chivalry.

Găl'ȧ-hăd, Sir. The son of Lancelot of the Lake, and a knight of the Round Table, remarkable for the purity of his life. His successful adventures in search of the sangreal were celebrated by the old romancers, and have been made the subject, in modern times, of one of the most exquisite of Tennyson's minor poems. [Written also G a l a a d.]

Galalon. See GAN.

Găl'ȧ-ŏr. A brother of Amadis de Gaul. His exploits are recounted in the romance of that name.

Gă-laph'ro-ne, *or* **Gal'ȧ-frŏn.** A king of Cathay, and father of Angelica, in Bojardo's "Orlando Innamorato," Ariosto's "Orlando Furioso," and other romantic poems and tales of the Carlovingian cycle.

Găl'ȧ-te'ȧ. [Gr. Γαλάτεια.] (*Gr. & Rom. Myth.*) A sea-nymph, the daughter of Nereus and Doris. She was passionately loved by Polyphemus, but her own affections were bestowed upon Acis. See ACIS.

Ga-lā'tian. A character in the Christmas gambols of the olden time.

Găl'lĭ-ȧ. The ancient Latin name of France, often used in modern poetry.

> For gold let *Gallia's* legions fight,
> Or plunder's bloody gain:
> Uubribed, unbought, our swords we draw,
> To guard our king, to fence our law,
> Nor shall their edge be vain.
> *Sir W. Scott.*

Galloping Dick. A name popularly given to Richard Ferguson, a celebrated highway robber, — executed at Aylesbury (England), April 4, 1800, — on account of his bold riding when pursued.

Galloway, Fair Maid of. See FAIR MAID OF GALLOWAY.

Gammer Gurton. See GURTON, GAMMER.

Gamp, Mrs. Sarah. A monthly nurse who is a prominent character in Dickens's novel of "Martin Chuzzlewit." She is celebrated for her constant reference to a certain Mrs. Harris, a purely imaginary person, for whose feigned opinions and utterances she professes the greatest respect, in order to give the more

---
and for the Remarks and Rules to which the numbers after certain words refer, see pp. xiv-xxxii.

weight to her own. See HARRIS, MRS.

Gan (gän), **Ganelone** (gä-nä-lo′nä), **Ganelon** (găn′lŏn′, 62), *or* **Gano** (gä′no). A count of Mayence, and one of the paladins of Charlemagne, by whom he is perpetually trusted, and whom he perpetually betrays; always represented as engaged in machinations for the destruction of Christianity. Spite, patience, obstinacy, dissimulation, affected humility, and inexhaustible powers of intrigue are the chief elements of his character. He figures in the romantic poems of Italy, and is placed by Dante in his Inferno. See MARSIGLIO. [Written also Galalon.]

Have you not, all of you, held me at such a distance from your counsels, as if I were the most faithless spy since the days of *Ganelon*?
Sir W. Scott.

Helmer the fierce, who was the *Ganelon* of the society, sat upon the left. *H. Weber.*

Gan′dẽr-cleugh (-klōok). [That is, gander-cliff, or gander-ravine.] An imaginary town situated on the imaginary river Gander, in "the central part, the navel of Scotland." It was the residence of Jedediah Cleishbotham (see CLEISHBOTHAM, JEDEDIAH), who speaks of it as "a place frequented by most at one time or other in their lives."

Gä′nem. The name of a young merchant who is the hero of one of the tales in the "Arabian Nights' Entertainments." He incurs the vengeance of Caliph Haroun-Al-Raschid, and has his house levelled to the ground in consequence, but escapes being made a prisoner by disguising himself like a slave belonging to an eating-house, and putting on his head the dishes from which he had just eaten dinner, — a trick which effectually deceives the guards, who permit him to pass without examination.

Gan′e-sä. (*Hindu Myth.*) The god of policy and prudence, or wisdom. He is represented with the head of an elephant, and with four arms; sometimes with three arms.

The tenth Avatar comes! at Heaven's command,
Shall Seriswattee wave her hallowed wand,

And Camdeo bright and *Ganesa* sublime
Shall bless with joy their own propitious clime!
Come, Heavenly Powers! primeval peace restore!
Love, — Mercy, — Wisdom, — rule for evermore! *Campbell.*

Gan′y̆-mede. [Gr. Γανυμήδης, Lat. *Ganymedes.*] (*Gr. & Rom. Myth.*) A son of Tros, king of Troy, by Callirrhoë. He was the most beautiful of mortals; and Jupiter, charmed with his appearance, assumed the form of an eagle, snatched him away from his playmates on Mount Ida, and carried him up to heaven, where he became the cup-bearer of the gods in the place of Juno's daughter Hebe. See HEBE. [Written also, poetically, Ganymed.]

Tall stripling youths rich clad, of fairer hue
Than *Ganymed* or Hylas. *Milton.*

Pour forth heaven's wine, Idæan *Ganymede*,
And let it fill the Dædal cups like fire.
Shelley.

There, too, flushed *Ganymede*, his rosy thigh
Half buried in the eagle's down,
Sole as a flying star shot through the sky
Above the pillared town. *Tennyson.*

Garcias, Pedro (pä′dro gaŕ-the′ăss). A mythical personage, of whom mention is made in the preface to "Gil Blas," in which it is related how two scholars of Salamanca discovered a tombstone with the inscription, "Here lies interred the *soul* of the licentiate Pedro Garcias," and how, on digging beneath the stone, they found a leathern purse containing a hundred ducats.

Then it was like the soul of the licentiate *Pedro Garcias*, which lay among the ducats in his leathern purse. *Sir W. Scott.*

On the other hand, does not his soul lie enclosed in this remarkable volume much more truly than *Pedro Garcias*' did in the buried bag of doubloons? *Carlyle.*

Garden City. A popular name for Chicago, a city in Illinois which is remarkable for the number and beauty of its private gardens.

Garden of England. A name generally applied to the county of Worcester, on account of its beauty and fertility.

If the county of Worcester, which has hitherto been accounted the *Garden of England*, is now (as the Report of the Home Missionary assures us) become, for want of preachers, "a waste and howling wilderness," what must the mountains of Macgillicuddy be? *T. Moore.*

larden of Europe. An appellation sometimes given to Italy, a country remarkable for the extreme fertility of its soil, the variety of its vegetable productions, the general salubrity of its climate, and the unsurpassed loveliness and magnificence of its scenery.

larden of France. [Fr. *Jardin de la France.*] A name given to the department of Indre-et-Loire, including Tourraine, part of Anjou, Poitou, and the Orléanais, a region celebrated for its beauty and fertility.

Garden of Italy. A name sometimes given to the island of Sicily, which is distinguished for the romantic beauty of its scenery, and the luxuriance of its crops.

Garden of the West. A name usually given to Kansas, but sometimes applied to Illinois and others of the Western States, which are all noted for their productiveness.

Garden of the World. A name frequently given to the vast country, comprising more than 1,200,000 square miles, which is drained by the Mississippi and its tributaries,— a region of almost unexampled fertility.

Gargamelle (gȧr'gȧ'mel'). [Fr., throat.] The mother of Gargantua, in Rabelais' celebrated romance of this name.

Gargantua (gar-gant'yoo-ȧ; *Fr. pron.* gȧr'gŏⁿ-tü-ȧ', 34, 62). [Fr., from Sp. *garganta*, throat, gullet.] The hero of Rabelais' celebrated romance of the same name, a gigantic personage, about whom many wonderful stories are related. He lived for several centuries, and at last begot a son, Pantagruel, as wonderful as himself.

☞ Rabelais borrowed this character from an old Celtic giant story. The water-giants were all great guzzlers. Gargantua, in the legend, when a child, sucks the milk from ten nurses. He stands with each foot upon a high mountain, and bending down, drinks up the river which flows between.

You must borrow me *Gargantua's* mouth first; 'tis a word too great for any mouth of this age's size. *Shak.*

Gar'ğĕr-y, Joe. An illiterate blacksmith, in Dickens's "Great Expectations," remarkable for his simplicity, generosity, and kindness of heart.

Gar'ğĕr-y, Mrs. Joe. A virago, who figures in Dickens's novel of "Great Expectations."

Gate City. 1. Keokuk, Iowa;— popularly so called. It is situated at the foot of the lower rapids of the Mississippi (which extend twelve miles, with a fall of twenty-four feet), and is the natural head of navigation. A portion of the city is built on a bluff one hundred and fifty feet high.

2. Atlanta, a city in Georgia, and the terminus of four of the principal railroads of the State;— so called by Jefferson Davis, as being, in a military point of view, the most important inland position in the lower part of the South.

Gate of Tears. A literal translation of the word *Babelmandeb*, the straits of which name were so called on account of the number of shipwrecks which occur in them.

Like some ill-destined bark that steers
In silence through the *Gate of Tears.*
T. Moore.

Gaudentio di Lucca (gow-dent'se-o dee lōōk'kȧ). The name of a celebrated romance,—written by Simon Berington,— and also of its hero, who is represented as making a journey to Mezzorania, an imaginary country in the interior of Africa.

Gautier et Garguille (gō'te-ȧ' ă gȧr'-ğēl', 82). Two proper names having a signification equivalent to *tout le monde*, or every body, found in the French proverbial expression, " *Se moquer de Gautier et Garguille*," to make game of Gautier and Garguille, that is, to make game of every body.

For the rest, spare neither *Gautier* nor *Garguille*. *Regnier, Trans.*

Gaw'aĭn, Sir. [Written also G a u - v a i n.] A nephew of King Arthur, and one of the most celebrated knights of the Round Table, noted for his sagacity, his habitual courtesy, and his wonderful strength, which is said to have been greater at certain hours of the day than at others. Chaucer, in his "Squire's Tale," describing the entrance of a strange knight, says that he

"Salueth king and lordès alle,
lly order as they sat in the hall,
With so high reverence and observance,
As well in speech as in his countenance,
That *Gawain* with his olde curtesie,
Though he were come again out of faërie,
Ne coude him not amenden with a word."

Gawkey, Lord. See LORD GAWKEY.

Gaw'rey. A name given, in the romance of "Peter Wilkins," to the flying women among whom the hero of the work was thrown. See WILKINS, PETER.

She spread out her beautiful arms, as if indeed she could fly off like the pretty *Gawrey* whom the man in the story was enamoured of. *Thackeray.*

Gefion (gä'fe-on), } (*Scand. Myth.*)
Gefjon (gäf'yon). } The goddess of virginity, to whom all maidens repair after death.

Gel'ert. The name of a favourite greyhound of Llewellyn, son-in-law to King John of England. On one occasion, during the absence of his master in the chase, he destroyed a ferocious wolf, who attacked Llewellyn's infant son. Returning from the field, and not finding the child,—who was sound asleep under a confused heap of bedclothes,—Llewellyn rashly concluded that the dog, whose lips were bloody from his struggle with the wolf, had killed him; and, without waiting to examine or inquire, plunged his sword to the hilt in Gelert's side. With the dying yell of the dog, the infant awoke, and Llewellyn, smitten with remorse for his rash and frantic deed, erected an elegant monument over the remains of the faithful animal; whence the place was called *Bethgelert*, or "the grave of the greyhound," a name which it bears to the present day. It is in a parish of the same name in North Wales. This legend has been versified by William Robert Spencer.

Llewellyn's greyhound has a second grave very distant from that of *Bethgelert*. It sleeps and points a moral in Persia. *Willmott.*

Gel'l&t-ley, Dä'vIe. The name of an idiot servant of the Baron of Bradwardine, in Scott's novel of "Waverley."

Gem of Normandy. A name given to Emma, daughter of Richard I., duke of Normandy, married to Ethelred II., king of England. She died in 1052.

General Undertaker, The. [Fr. *Le Général Entrepreneur.*] A nickname given by the populace of Paris to the Emperor Napoleon Bonaparte, on account of the immense public works which he entered upon, but did not always complete.

Ge-neu'rĭ. The same as *Guinever*, King Arthur's queen, notorious for her infidelity to him. See GUINEVER.

Gen'e-vieve'. 1. The heroine of a ballad by Coleridge.
2. Under the form *Genoveva*, or *Genovefa*, the name occurs in a German myth as that of the wife of the Count Palatine Siegfried of Mayenfeld, in the time of Charles Martel. According to the tradition, she was left behind by her husband while on a march against the Saracens. Upon false accusations made to him, he gave orders to put her to death; but the servant intrusted with the commission suffered her to escape into the forest of Ardennes, where she lay concealed a long time, until by accident her husband discovered her retreat, and recognised her innocence. This legend furnished the material of one of the earliest "Volksbücher," or popular tales. In modern times, Tieck and Müller have redacted the tradition, and Raupach has made it the subject of a drama.

☞ "St. Genevieve is the patron saint of Paris, and the name has always been held in high esteem in France. There is a German form of the name borne by the apocryphal saint Genovefa, of Brabant, to whom has attached the story, of suspicious universality, of the wife who was driven by malicious accusations to the woods, there to give birth to an infant, and to be nourished by a white doe until the final discovery of her innocence."
Yonge.

Ge'nĭ-ĭ. (*Gr. & Rom. Myth.*) Protecting spirits or tutelar deities analagous to the guardian angels of the Christian faith.

☞ For the "Key to the Scheme of Pronunciation," with the accompanying Explanations,

Gentle Shepherd. A nickname, derived from a line of a well-known song, fastened upon George Grenville (1712-1770), by William Pitt, Earl of Chatham, in a celebrated debate in Parliament.

George a-Green. The subject of an English prose romance entitled "The History of George a-Green, Pindar of the town of Wakefield." In its MS. form, it is supposed to be as old as the days of Queen Elizabeth. "Pindar" is a corruption of *pinner*, or *penner*, that is, keeper of the public pen or pound for the confinement of estrays.

Look before you leap,
For as you sow, you're like to reap;
And were y' as good as *George a-Green*,
I shall make bold to turn again;
Nor am I doubtful of the issue
In a just quarrel, and mine is so. *Hudibras.*

I will presently order you a rundlet of Rhenish, with a corresponding quantity of neats' tongues and pickled herrings, to make you all as glorious as *George a-Green*.
Sir W. Scott.

Ge-raint', Sir. A legendary hero, connected with the romances of the Round Table. His story is treated in Tennyson's "Idylls of the King."

Gĕr'ăl-dĭne. A name of frequent occurrence in romantic poetry. Lady Elizabeth Fitzgerald was the lady who was made by Surrey the heroine of his poetry, under the title of the "Fair Geraldine," thus leading to the adoption of this latter as one of the class of romantic names. See FAIR GERALDINE.

Gĕr'dă (4). (*Scand. Myth.*) The wife of Frey. She was accounted the most beautiful of all the goddesses, and was renowned for her piety and virtue.

German Achilles. See ACHILLES OF GERMANY.

German Cicero. See CICERO OF GERMANY.

German Hector. See HECTOR OF GERMANY.

German Mil'ton (-tn). A title bestowed upon Friedrich Gottlieb Klopstock (1724-1803), author of "The Messiah," an epic poem. Coleridge said of him, that he was "a *very* German Milton, indeed!"

While Klopstock was called our Milton, Wieland our Voltaire, and others in the same way, Goethe and Schiller were never other than themselves. *Gervinus, Trans.*

German Plā'to. Friedrich Heinrich Jacobi (1743-1819), a distinguished German philosopher, so called on account of the high religious tone of his metaphysical writings.

German Vol-tâire' (3). 1. A title often given to Christoph Martin Wieland (1733-1813), one of the great poets who are the pride of Germany.

He [Wieland] had imbibed so much of the taste of the French along with their philosophy, that he bore the name of the *German Voltaire*, in Germany and out of Germany.
Bouterwek, Trans.

2. An epithet sometimes applied to Goethe.

☞ "Goethe has been called the German Voltaire; but it is a name which does him wrong, and describes him ill. Excepting in the corresponding variety of their pursuits and knowledge, in which, perhaps, it does Voltaire wrong, the two cannot be compared. Goethe is all, or the best of all, that Voltaire was, and he was much that Voltaire did not dream of." *Carlyle.*

Géronte (zhā'rônt', 62). [Fr., from the Gr. γέρων, γέροντος, an old man.] A character in Molière's comedies, "Le Médecin malgré Lui" and "Les Fourberies de Scapin." The name is commonly used in French comedies to designate any old man, particularly one who for any reason makes himself ridiculous.

Gerund, Friar. See FRIAR GERUND.

Ge'ry-ŏn (9). [Gr. Γηρυόνης.] (*Gr. & Rom. Myth.*) A king of Hesperia, son of Chrysaor and Callirrhoë, described as a being with three bodies and three heads. He possessed magnificent oxen, but, as he fed them with human flesh, he was killed by Hercules.

Ghent, Pacification of. See PACIFICATION OF GHENT.

Giant Cor'mo-răn. A Cornish giant, slain by Jack the Giant-killer. See JACK THE GIANT-KILLER.

Giant Despair. In Bunyan's "Pilgrim's Progress," a giant who is the owner of Doubting Castle, and who, finding Christian and Hopeful asleep

and for the Remarks and Rules to which the numbers after certain words refer, see pp. xiv-xxxii.

upon his grounds, takes them prisoners, and thrusts them into a dungeon.

> Since the time of John Milton, no braver heart had beat in any English bosom than Samuel Johnson now bore. ... No *Giant Despair* ... appals this pilgrim; he works resolutely for deliverance, in still defiance steps resolutely along. *Carlyle.*

> The monotonous desolation of the scene increased to that degree, that, for any redeeming feature it presented to their eyes, they might have entered in the body on the grim domains of *Giant Despair*. *Dickens.*

Giant Grim. In the "Pilgrim's Progress" of John Bunyan, a giant who seeks to stop the march of the pilgrims to the Celestial City, but is slain in a duel by Mr. Great-heart, their guide.

Giant-killer, The. See JACK THE GIANT-KILLER.

Giants. [Gr. Γίγαντες, Lat. *Gigantes*.] 1. (*Gr. & Rom. Myth.*) Sons of Tartarus and Terra, beings of monstrous size, with dragons' tails and fearful countenances. They attempted to storm heaven, being armed with huge rocks and the trunks of trees, but were killed by the gods with the assistance of Hercules, and were buried under Mount Ætna and other volcanoes.

2. (*Scand. Myth.*) Evil genii of various forms and races, enemies of the gods. They dwelt in a territory of their own, called *Jötunheim*, or Giant-land. They had the power of assuming divers shapes, and of increasing or diminishing their stature at will. See JÖTUNHEIM.

Giant Slay-good. In Bunyan's "Pilgrim's Progress," a giant slain in a duel by Mr. Great-heart.

Gib'bet. A foot-pad in the "Beaux' Stratagem," a comedy by George Farquhar.

> Like *Gibbet* ... [they] piqued themselves on being the best-behaved men on the road, and on conducting themselves with all appropriate civility in the exercise of their vocation. *Sir W. Scott.*

Gib'bie, Goose. A half-witted lad in Lady Bellenden's service, in Scott's novel of "Old Mortality."

> A great companion of my younger days was Johnny Stykes, who, like *Goose Gibbie* of famous memory, first kept the turkeys,

and then, as his years advanced, was promoted to the more important office of minding the cows. *Keightley.*

Gibraltar of America. A name often given to the city of Quebec, which, from its position, and natural and artificial means of defence, is, perhaps, the most strongly fortified city in America.

Gil Blas (zhĕl blâss). The title of a famous romance by Le Sage (1668–1747), and the name of its hero, by whom, and with whose commentaries, the story is professedly told.

> "Gil Blas ... is naturally disposed toward honesty, though with a mind unfortunately too ductile to resist the temptations of opportunity or example. He is constitutionally timid, and yet occasionally capable of doing brave actions; shrewd and intelligent, but apt to be deceived by his own vanity; with wit enough to make us laugh with him at others, and follies enough to turn the jest frequently against himself. Generous, good-natured, and humane, he has virtues sufficient to make us love him, and, as to respect, it is the last thing which he asks at his reader's hand." *Sir W. Scott.*

Gill, Harry. A character in Wordsworth's ballad entitled "Goody Blake and Harry Gill," smitten with perpetual cold for his hard-heartedness toward an old dame. See GOODY BLAKE.

Gills, Sol. A warm-hearted, simple-minded ships'-instruments maker in Dickens's "Dombey and Son."

Gil Morrice. See MORRICE, GIL.

Gil'pin, John. A citizen of London, and "a train-band captain," whose adventures are related in Cowper's humourous poem entitled "The Diverting History of John Gilpin, showing how he went further than he intended, and came safe home again." The story was related to Cowper by a Mrs. Austen, who remembered to have heard it in her childhood. The poem first appeared anonymously in the "Public Advertiser," in 1782, and was first published as Cowper's avowed production in the second volume of his poems.

> "John Gilpin is said to have been

Mr. Bayer, an eminent linen-draper, superlatively polite, who figured, in the visible order of things, at the top of Paternoster Row, or rather at the corner of Cheapside. Quoth Mr. John Gilpin,—

'I am a linen-draper bold,
As all the world doth know.'"
Notes and Queries.

Gines de Passamonte (hē-nes' dā pās-sā-mon'tā, 58). The name of a galley-slave and puppet-show man in "Don Quixote."

In that case, replied I, painting excels the ape of the renowned *Gines de Passamonte*, which only meddled with the past and the present. *Sir W. Scott.*

He manages his delightful puppet-show without thrusting his head beyond the curtain, like *Gines de Passamonte*, to explain what he is doing. *Sir W. Scott.*

Gī-nev'rā. 1. A lady whose story has been interwoven with the adventures of Rinaldo, in Ariosto's chivalrous romance, the "Orlando Furioso." Ginevra, falsely accused, is doomed to die, unless a true knight comes within a month to do battle for her honour. Her lover, Ariodantes, has fled, and is reported to have perished. The wicked duke who has brought the accusation appears secure in his treachery; but the woman who has been his instrument, meeting with Rinaldo, discloses the truth; then comes a combat, in which the guilty duke is slain by the champion of innocence, and the lover re-appears and recovers his lady. This incident was derived by Ariosto from the popular traditions of the South of Europe. Spenser has a similar story in the "Faëry Queen," and Shakespeare availed himself of the main incident in his comedy of "Much Ado about Nothing."

2. The title and subject of a metrical tale by Samuel Rogers, which relates how a young Italian lady, upon her wedding-day, secreted herself, from motives of frolic, in a self-locking oaken chest, the lid of which shut down and buried her alive.

Phœbus, sitting one day in a laurel-tree's shade,
Was reminded of Daphne, of whom it was made,
For the god being one day too warm in his wooing,
She took to the tree, to escape his pursuing;

Be the cause what it might, from his offers she shrunk,
And, *Ginevra*-like, shut herself up in a trunk.
Lowell.

3. See GUINEVER.

Gingerbread, Giles. The hero of an old and celebrated English nursery tale.

☞ "The world is probably not aware of the ingenuity, humour, good sense, and sly satire contained in many of the old English nursery tales. They have evidently been the sportive productions of able writers, who would not trust their names to productions that might be considered beneath their dignity. The ponderous works on which they relied for immortality have perhaps sunk into oblivion, and carried their names down with them; while their unacknowledged offspring, 'Jack the Giant-killer,' 'Giles Gingerbread,' and 'Tom Thumb,' flourish in wide-spreading and never-ceasing popularity." *W. Irving.*

Ginnunga-gap (gin-noon'gā-gāp). [Old Norse *ginn*, wide, expanded (used only in composition), and *gapi*, to gape, yawn, open.] (*Scand. Myth.*) The vast chaotic abyss which existed before the present world, and separated Nifiheim, or the region of fog, from Muspelheim, or the region of heat.

Gjallar (gyäl'lär). [Old Norse *gala*, to sing, call out. Comp. Eng. *call.*] (*Scand. Myth.*) The horn of Heimdall, which he blows to give notice to the gods of those who arrive at the bridge Bifröst, and attempt to cross it. [Written also G i a l l a r.]

Glāsse, Mrs. (2). The real or fictitious author of a cookery-book, formerly very famous. It is said by some to have been written by one Hannah Glasse, a habit maker and seller in the early part of the last century. Others attribute it to the scribatious Dr. Hill (Sir John Hill, 1716–1775), considering the name a pseudonym. The first edition was published in 1747, and, very appropriately, in what is termed "pot" folio. Mrs. Glasse is popularly thought to begin a receipt for cooking a hare with the pithy advice, "First catch your hare;" but this expression is not found in any known edition of her book.

They [the Crim-Tartars] have so far relin-

and for the Remarks and Rules to which the numbers after certain words refer, see pp. xiv-xxxii.

quished their ancient food of horse-flesh that they will only feed upon colts; and to this diet is added ... a great variety of learned dainties, which *Mrs. Glasse* herself would not disdain to add to her high-flavoured catalogue. *Edin. Rev.*

Semmes took a pinch of snuff, and replied, "You remember *Mrs. Glasse's* well-worn receipt for cooking a hare,— First catch your hare." *Epes Sargent.*

Glāu'cus. [Gr. Γλαῦκος.] (*Gr. & Rom. Myth.*) 1. A son of Sisyphus, torn to pieces by his own horses.

2. A fisherman of Anthedon, in Eubœa, who was changed into a sea-deity.

3. A son of Minos, king of Crete, by Pasiphaë. He met his death by falling into a cask of honey, but was miraculously restored to life.

Glen-cōe'. A name commonly given to Macdonald of Glencoe, who was the chief of a Scottish clan, and known among the mountains by the hereditary name of Mac Ian. He was one of the most impracticable rebel chiefs in the time of William and Mary, and met with a disastrous death.

Glen'do-veer. (*Hindu Myth.*) The most beautiful of the good spirits.

Glen-găr'ry. The name under which Macdonald of Glengarry — one of the great Scottish chieftains who ultimately gave in his adhesion to the government of William III. — is generally mentioned in history.

Glen-var'loch, Lord. See OLIFAUNT, NIGEL.

Glō'rĭ-ā'nă (9). In Spenser's "Faëry Queen," the "greatest glorious queen of Faëry-lond."

☞ "In that Faëry Queen, I mean *Glory* in my general intention, but in my particular, I conceive the most excellent and glorious person of our sovereign, *the Queen* [Elizabeth], and her kingdom in *Faërye-land.*"

Introductory "Letter of the Author."

Glorious Preacher. A title popularly given to St. John Chrysostom, or the "Golden-mouth" (354—407), the most renowned of the Greek fathers, and a very eloquent Church orator.

☞ He preached several times a week to crowded audiences, and his sermons were received by the people with such shouts and acclamations of applause, that his church became a sort of theatre, which attracted great numbers who had hitherto attended only the circus and other places of amusement.

Glos'sin, Gilbert. A villanous lawyer in Scott's "Guy Mannering."

Glover, Catherine. See FAIR MAID OF PERTH.

Glub-dub'drib. An imaginary island fabled to have been visited by Gulliver in his famous "Travels." It is represented to have been peopled by sorcerers or magicians, who evoked, for Gulliver's amusement, the spirits of many great men of antiquity.

Glum-dal'clitch. A little girl only nine years old, and barely forty feet high, who had charge of Gulliver while he was in Brobdingnag. See BROBDINGNAG, and GULLIVER, LEMUEL.

Soon as *Glumdalclitch* missed her pleasing care,
She wept, she blubbered, and she tore her hair. *Pope.*

He took it [a letter] up wonderingly and suspiciously, as *Glumdalclitch* took up Gulliver. *Sir E. Bulwer Lytton.*

Glyn'dŏn, Hŏw'ard. A pseudonym of Laura C. Redden, an American authoress of the present day.

Gnā'tho (nā'tho, 26). [Gr. Γνάθων, puff-cheek, from γνάθος, jaw, mouth.] A celebrated parasite in Terence's comedy entitled "Eunuchus." The name is used proverbially in the Roman and the later Greek comedy to designate a parasite.

Gob'bo, Lăun'çe-lot. A clown, in Shakespeare's "Merchant of Venice."

Gob'bo, Old. A subordinate character in Shakespeare's "Merchant of Venice;" father to Launcelot Gobbo.

Goddess of Reason. See REASON, GODDESS OF.

Go-dī'vă, Lady. See PEEPING TOM OF COVENTRY.

Godon (gŏ'dôn', 62), *or* **Godam** (gŏ'-dăⁿ'). A nickname (with some variations of spelling and pronunciation) applied by the French to the English, who are thus characterised by their

☞ For the "Key to the Scheme of Pronunciation," with the accompanying Explanations,

national oath. The name has been long in use.

☞ "At the trial of Joan of Arc, a French witness named Colette, having used the name Godon, was asked who Godon was, and replied that it was not the designation of any particular person, but a sobriquet applied generally to the English, on account of their continual use of the exclamation, *God damn it.*"
Sharon Turner.

Goetz of the Iron Hand (güts, 46). See IRON HAND.

Gog and Mā'gog. Popular names for two colossal wooden statues in the Guildhall, London. It is thought that these renowned figures are connected with the Corinæus and Gotmagot of the Armorican chronicle quoted by Geoffrey of Monmouth. The former name has gradually sunk into oblivion, and the latter has been split by popular corruption to do duty for both.

☞ "Our Guildhall giants boast of almost as high an antiquity as the Gog and Magog of the Scriptures, as they, or their living prototypes, are said to have been found in Britain by Brute, a younger son of Anthenor of Troy, who invaded Albion, and founded the city of London (at first called Troy-novant), 3000 years ago. However the fact may have been, the two giants have been the pride of London from time immemorial. The old giants were burned in the great fire, and the new ones were constructed in 1708. They are fourteen feet high, and occupy suitable pedestals in Guildhall. There can be little doubt that these civic giants are exaggerated representatives of real persons and events." *Chambers.*

Goldemar, King (gŏlt'ȧ-mar). A famous German kobold, or domestic fairy servant, fabled to be the intimate friend of Neveling von Hardenberg.

Golden Age. [Lat. *Aurea ætas.*] (*Gr. & Rom. Myth.*) One of the four ages into which the life of the human race was divided; the simple and patriarchal reign of Saturn, a period of perpetual spring, when the land flowed with milk and honey, and all things needed to make life happy were produced spontaneously; when beasts of prey lived peaceably with other animals, and man had not yet, by indulging his vices and passions, lapsed from a state of innocence. It was succeeded by the ages of silver, brass, and iron; but a belief prevailed, that, when the stars and planets had performed a complete revolution around the heavens, the Golden Age would return.

Golden Bull. [Lat. *Bulla Aurea*, Ger. *Goldene Bulle.*] 1. (*Ger. Hist.*) An edict issued by the Emperor Charles IV. in the year 1336, mainly for the purpose of settling the law of imperial elections.

2. (*Hung. Hist.*) A constitutional edict issued by Andrew II. in the early part of the thirteenth century. It changed the government of Hungary from absolutism to an aristocratic monarchy, and, until recent times, was the charter of the liberties of the Hungarians. It remained in force until the dissolution of the German empire in 1806.

Golden Fleece. (*Gr. & Rom. Myth.*) The fleece of the ram Chrysomallus, the acquisition of which was the object of the Argonautic expedition. See ARGONAUTS.

Golden State. A popular name for the State of California, which is one of the most important gold-producing regions in the world.

Golden, *or* **Yellow, Water.** See PARIZADE.

Gŏl'dy. An affectionate nickname sometimes given to Oliver Goldsmith by his friends. It originated with Dr. Johnson.

Go-li'ăth. A famous Philistine giant, a native of Gath, and a formidable opponent of the armies of Israel. He was slain by the stripling David with pebbles hurled from a sling. [Written also, but less properly, G o l i a h.]

Gon'ēr-il. A daughter of Lear, in Shakespeare's tragedy of this name. See LEAR.

The edicts of each succeeding set of magistrates have, like those of *Goneril* and *Regan*, diminished this venerable band with the similar question, "What need we five and twenty? — ten? — or five?" *Sir W. Scott.*

Gonnella (gon-nel'lä, 102.) An Ital-

---

and for the Remarks and Rules to which the numbers after certain words refer, see pp. xiv-xxxii.

ian buffoon of great celebrity, who was domestic jester to the Margrave Nicolaus of Este, and to his son Borso, the Duke of Ferrara. He was accustomed to ride upon a miserable horse, to which the Duke upon one occasion applied a line from Plautus, "*Ossa atque pellis totus est.*" ("Aulularia," a. iii., sc. 6.) "The Jests of Gonnella" was published in 1506, at Bologna. See ROZINANTE.

Gon-zā′lo. An honest old counsellor, in Shakespeare's "Tempest."

Good Duke Humphrey. A name popularly given, by his contemporaries, to Humphrey Plantagenet, Duke of Gloucester, and youngest son of Henry IV.

> He wrought his miracles like a second *Duke Humphrey*; and by the influence of the beadle's rod, caused the lame to walk, the blind to see, and the palsied to labour.
> *Sir W. Scott.*

Good Earl. A name commonly given to Archibald, the eighth Earl of Angus (d. 1588), who was distinguished for his virtues.

Goodfellow, Robin. A kind of merry domestic spirit, whose character and achievements are recorded in the well-known ballad beginning "From Oberon in Fairy-land." Wright, in his "Essays on the Literature, Superstitions, and History of England in the Middle Ages," suspects Robin Goodfellow to have been the Robin Hood of the old popular morris-dance. See HOBGOBLIN.

> ☞ "The constant attendant upon the English fairy court was the celebrated Puck, or Robin Goodfellow, who, to the elves, acted in some measure as the jester or clown of the company, — a character then to be found in the establishment of every person of quality, — or, to use a more exact comparison, resembled the Pierrot of the pantomime. His jests were of the most simple, and, at the same time, the broadest comic character; to mislead a clown on his path homeward, to disguise himself like a stool, in order to induce an old gossip to commit the egregious mistake of sitting down on the floor when she expected to repose on a chair, were his special employments."
> *Sir W. Scott.*
> That shrewd and knavish sprite Called *Robin Goodfellow.* *Shak.*

She was pinched and pulled, she said;
And he, by friar's lantern led,
Tells how the drudging goblin sweat,
To earn his cream-bowl, duly set,
When in one night, ere glimpse of morn,
His shadowy flail had threshed the corn
That ten day-labourers could not end:
Then lies him down the lubber fiend,
And, stretched out all the chimney's length,
Basks at the fire his hairy strength;
And crop full out of doors he flings,
Ere the first cock his matin rings. *Milton.*

Good King René (ru-nā′, *or* rā′nā). — [Fr. *Le Bon Roi René.*] The designation by which René d'Anjou (1408-1480) is commonly known in history.

Good Knight, without Fear and without Reproach, The. [Fr. *Le Bon Chevalier, sans Peur et sans Reproche.*] An appellation conferred upon Pierre de Terrail Bayard (1476-1524), a French knight celebrated for his valour and loyalty.

Goodman of Ballengeigh (bal′lengik). [That is, tenant of Ballengeigh, which is a steep pass leading down behind the castle of Stirling.] A *nom de guerre* employed by the Scottish king, James V., who was accustomed to make disguised expeditions through the midnight streets of Edinburgh, as Haroun-Al-Raschid did through those of Bagdad.

Goodman Palsgrave. } Contempt-
Goody Palsgrave. } uous nicknames given respectively to Frederick V., elector palatine (Ger. *pfalzgraf,* Eng. *palsgrave*), and to his wife Elizabeth, daughter of James I. of England. See WINTER KING and WINTER QUEEN.

Good Physician. A title applied to Christ, doubtless in allusion to the passage in *Mark* ii. 17, — "They that are whole have no need of the physician, but they that are sick: I came not to call the righteous, but sinners, to repentance."

Good Queen Bess. See BESS, GOOD QUEEN.

Good Regent. A name given to James Stewart, Earl of Murray, or Moray (1531-1570), appointed regent of Scotland in 1567, after the imprisonment of his sister, Mary Queen of Scots, in Lochleven castle. He was distinguished for his zeal and prudence, and for the prompt and vigor-

☞ For the "Key to the Scheme of Pronunciation," with the accompanying Explanations,

ous measures he adopted to secure the peace of the kingdom.

Good Samaritan. The principal character in a well-known parable of our Lord. See *Luke* x. 30–37.

Good Shepherd. A title often applied to Christ.

I am the *good shepherd*, and know my sheep, and am known of mine. ... and I lay down my life for the sheep. And other sheep I have, which are not of this fold: them also I must bring, and they shall hear my voice; and there shall be one fold, and one shepherd. — *John* x. 14–16.

Goody Blake. A character in Wordsworth's poem entitled "Goody Blake and Harry Gill," which purports to be "A True Story." She is represented as a poor old dame, who, driven by necessity to pilfer a few sticks of wood from her neighbour's ground, in the winter-cold, is detected by him in the act, and forced to relinquish what she had taken. In requital, she invokes upon him the curse that he may "never more be warm;" and ever after, "his teeth they chatter, chatter still."

Goody Two-shoes. The name of a well-known character in the literature of the nursery. Her "History" was first published by Newbery, a bookseller in St. Paul's Church-yard, renowned throughout the latter half of the last century for his picturebooks for children; and it is thought to have been written by Goldsmith.

☞ "The famous nursery story of 'Goody Two-shoes' ... appeared in 1765, at a moment when Goldsmith was scribbling for Newbery, and much pressed for funds. Several quaint little tales introduced in his Essays show that he had a turn for this species of mock history; and the advertisement and title-page bear the stamp of his sly and playful humour.

"'We are desired to give notice that there is in the press, and speedily will be published, either by subscription or otherwise, as the public shall please to determine, the History of Little Goody Two Shoes, otherwise Mrs. Margery Two Shoes; with the means by which she acquired learning and wisdom, and, in consequence thereof, her estate; set forth at large for the benefit of those

"Who from a state of rags and care,
And having shoes but half a pair,
Their fortune and their fame should fix,
And gallop in a coach and six."'"

Pray don't go on in that *Goody Two-shoes* sort of way. *A. Trollope.*

Goosey Go'de-rich. A popular nickname given by Cobbett to Frederick Robinson (created Viscount Goderich in 1827, and Earl of Ripon in 1833), on account of his incapacity as a statesman. He was premier for a short time in 1827–28. See PROSPERITY ROBINSON.

Gor'di-us. [Gr. Γόρδιος.] A peasant who became king of Phrygia, and father of Midas. He tied an inextricable knot on the yoke of his chariot, and an oracle declared that whoever should untie it would reign over all Asia. Alexander the Great cut the knot with his sword, and applied the prophecy to himself.

Gorgibus (gor'zhe-büss', 34). The name of an honest, simple-minded burgess, in Molière's comedy, "Les Précieuses Ridicules." His distress, perplexity, and resentment are represented as being extreme, and as all occasioned by the perverse affectation of elegance of his daughter and niece.

Gor'gons. [Gr. Γοργόνες, Lat. *Gorgones*.] (*Gr. & Rom. Myth.*) Three daughters of Phorcus and Ceto, named Stheno, Euryale, and Medusa. Their hair was entwined with hissing serpents, and their bodies were covered with impenetrable scales; they had wings, and brazen claws, and enormous teeth, and whoever looked upon them was turned to stone. The name *Gorgon* was given more especially to Medusa, the only one of the sisters who was mortal. She was killed by Perseus, and her head was fixed on the shield of Minerva. From her blood sprang the winged horse Pegasus.

Gosling, Giles. Landlord of the "Black Bear" inn at Cumnor, in Scott's novel of "Kenilworth."

Gospel Doctor. [Lat. *Doctor Evangelicus.*] A title given to Wycliffe (d. 1384), the celebrated reformer, on account of his ardent attachment to the Holy Scriptures.

Go'tham. A popular name for the

city of New York;— first given to it in "Salmagundi" (a humourous work by Washington Irving, William Irving, and James K. Paulding), because the inhabitants were such wiseacres.

☞ The allusion to the "three wise men of Gotham" who "went to sea in a bowl" is very obvious. The Gotham here referred to is a parish in Nottinghamshire, England, which has long been celebrated — like the Phrygia of the Asiatics, the Abdera of the Thracians, the Bœotia of the Greeks, and the Swabia of the modern Germans — for the remarkable stupidity of its inhabitants. They are said to have heard the cuckoo upon a certain occasion, but, never having seen her, hedged the bush from which the note proceeded. A bush is still shown there called the "cuckoo-bush." Fuller says, "The proverb of 'as wise as a man of Gotham' passeth publicly for the periphrasis of a fool; and a hundred fopperies are forged and fathered on the townsfolk of Gotham." Wharton, speaking of "the idle pranks of the men of Gotham," observes, that "such pranks bore a reference to some customary law tenures belonging to that place or its neighbourhood, now grown obsolete." Hearne, in allusion to this subject, also remarks, "Nor is there more reason to esteem 'The Merry Tales of the Mad Men of Gotham' (which were much valued and cried up in the time of Henry VIII., though now sold at ballad-singers' stalls) as altogether romance; a certain skilful person having told me, more than once, that they formerly held lands there by such customs as are touched upon in this book." The book is that noticed by Walpole, — "'The Merry Tales of the Mad Men of Gotham,' a book extremely admired, and often reprinted in that age, written by Lucas de Heere, a Flemish painter, who resided in England at the time of Elizabeth." Wood, however, tells us that the tales were written by one Andrew Borde (or Andreas Perforatus, as he calls himself), a sort of travelling quack, from whom the name and occupation of the "Merry-andrew" are said to be derived. There is an ancient blackletter edition of the work in the Bodleian Library at Oxford, called "Certeine Merry Tales of the Mad Men of Gotham, compiled in the reign of Henry VIII., by Dr. Andrew Borde, an eminent physician of that period." Another derivation of the phrase "wise men of Gotham," given in Thoroton's "Nottinghamshire," is, that when King John, in one of his "progresses," was about to pass through Gotham toward Nottingham, he was prevented by the inhabitants, who thought that the ground over which a king passed became for ever after a public road. The king was naturally incensed at this incivility, and sent some persons to punish the inhabitants, who bethought themselves of an expedient for avoiding the king's wrath. The messengers, on their arrival, found all the people engaged in some foolish occupation or other, so that they returned to the court, and reported that Gotham was a village of fools.

☞ The Germans have an old tale called the "Schildbürger," which corresponds to our "Wise Men of Gotham," and which first appeared in 1598.

Gott'helf, Jeremias. A poor villager who is the hero of a touching story entitled "The Mirror of Peasants," written by Albert Bitzius (1797-1854), a very popular Swiss author, who afterwards used the name as a pseudonym.

Governor of Tilbury. See TILBURY, GOVERNOR OF.

Gŏw'ẽr, The Moral. A name given by Chaucer, in the dedication of his "Troilus and Cresseide," and subsequently by Lydgate and others, to John Gower, a celebrated English poet of the fourteenth century, who wrote a poem called "*Confessio Amantis*," which discusses, in a solemn and sententious style, the morals and metaphysics of love.

O *Moral Gower!* this book I direct
To thee and to the philosophical Strood,
To vouchsauf there need is to correct
Of your benignities and zealès good.
Chaucer.

Gowk-thrap'ple, Maister. A covenanting preacher referred to as a "chosen vessel," in Sir Walter Scott's novel of "Waverley."

[Naigeon, author of a life of Diderot] a man of coarse, mechanical, perhaps rather intrinsically feeble intellect, and then with the vehemence of some pulpit-drumming *Gowkthrapple*, or precious Mr. Jabesh Rentowel, — only that *his* kirk is of the other complexion.
Carlyle.

Graal. See ST. GRAAL.

Graces. [Lat. *Gratiæ.*] (*Gr. & Rom. Myth.*) Three sister-goddesses, daughters of Jupiter and Eurynome, represented as beautiful and modest virgins attendant upon Venus. They were the source of all favour, loveliness, and grace. Their names were Aglaia, Euphrosyne, and Thalia.

Grā'ci-o'sạ̈ (grü'shĭ-o'sụ̈). A lovely princess in an old and popular fairy tale, — the object of the implacable ill-will of a step-mother named Grognon, whose malicious designs are perpetually thwarted by Percinet, a fairy prince, who is in love with Graciosa.

Gracioso (grä-the-o'zo). A pantomimic character in the popular comedy of Spain, noted for his drollery, and corresponding with the Italian Harlequin and English clown.

☞ Amid all these, and more acceptable than almost the whole put together, was the all-licensed fool, the Gracioso of the Spanish drama, who, with his cap fashioned into the resemblance of a coxcomb, and his bauble, a truncheon terminated by a carved figure wearing a fool's-cap, in his hand, went, came, and returned, mingling in every scene of the piece, and interrupting the business, without having any share himself in the action, and ever and anon transferring his gibes from the actors on the stage to the audience who sat around, prompt to applaud the whole. *Sir W. Scott.*

Gradasso (grä-däs'so, 102). The name of a king of Sericana, who figures in Bojardo's "Orlando Innamorato" and Ariosto's "Orlando Furioso" as a wonder of martial prowess. Instigated by a desire of winning the sword and courser of Rinaldo, he invades France, followed by his vassals, "crowned kings," who never dare to address him but on their knees. The name is popularly used by the Italians to designate a bully.

Grad'grind, Thomas. A practical, utilitarian character in Dickens's novel of "Hard Times." "A man of realities. A man of facts and calculations. A man who proceeds upon the principle that two and two are four, and nothing over, and who is not to be talked into allowing for any thing over. . . . With a rule and a pair of scales and the multiplication-table always in his pocket, sir, ready to weigh and measure any parcel of human nature, and tell you exactly what it comes to."

The *Gradgrinds* undervalue and disparage it, and the Jesuits and their sympathisers are enraged at it. *Church Review.*

Grail, The Holy. See ST. GRAAL.

Graim (grăm). A sword of trenchant sharpness owned by Siegfried. See SIEGFRIED.

Granary of Europe. A name anciently given to the island of Sicily, on account of its fertility.

Grand Alliance. (*Hist.*) A treaty between England, Leopold I., emperor of Germany, and the States General, signed at Vienna, May 12, 1689. To this treaty the king of Spain (Charles II.) and the Duke of Savoy (Victor Amadeus II.) acceded in 1690. Its objects were "to procure satisfaction to his imperial majesty in regard to the Spanish succession, obtain security to the English and Dutch for their dominions and commerce, prevent a union of the monarchies of France and Spain, and hinder the French from possessing the Spanish dominions in America."

Grand Corrupter. A name given to Sir Robert Walpole (1676-1745) in the libels of his time, and by his political opponents.

Grand Elector. See GREAT ELECTOR.

Grand Gousier, *or* Grangousier (grŏn'goo'sē-ä'). [Fr., great gullet.] The father of Gargantua, in Rabelais' romance of this name; thought by some to have been designed to represent Louis XII. of France, by others, John d'Albret, king of Navarre.

Gran'dĭ-son, Sir Charles (-sn). The hero of Richardson's novel entitled "The History of Sir Charles Grandison." In this character, Richardson designed to represent his ideal of a perfect hero, — a union of the good Christian and the perfect English gentleman.

☞ "All this does well enough in a funeral sermon or monumental inscription, where, by privilege of suppressing the worst qualities and exaggerating the better, such images of perfection are sometimes presented. But, in the living world, a state of trial and a valley of tears,

and for the Remarks and Rules to which the numbers after certain words refer, see pp. xiv-xxxii.

such unspotted worth, such unvarying perfection, is not to be met with; it could not, if we suppose it to have existence, be attended with all those favours of fortune which are accumulated upon Richardson's hero; and hence the fatal objection of Sir Charles Grandison being the 'faultless monster that the world ne'er saw.'"
Sir W. Scott.

If we are by accident alone, I become as silent as a Turk, as formal as *Sir Charles Grandison.* *Sir E. Bulwer Lytton.*

Gran'di-son Cróm'well (-sn). A nickname given by Mirabeau to Lafayette, whom he looked upon as an ambitious man without power, and one who would coquet with the supreme authority without daring to seize it, or, indeed, possessing the means of doing so.

☞ "There are nicknames of Mirabeau's worth whole treatises. 'Grandison Cromwell' Lafayette, — write a volume on the man, as many volumes have been written, and try to say more. It is the best likeness yet drawn of him." *Carlyle.*

Grand Monarque, Le (lŭ grŏⁿ mo'-nar̄k', 62). [Fr., the great monarch.] A title often applied to Louis XIV. (1638-1715), one of the most remarkable rulers that ever sat on the throne of France. In his long reign of seventy-two years, he reared the fabric of the absolute monarchy which continued for nearly as many years more after his death, when it was shaken to pieces in the storms of the Revolution; yet the ruling principles of his administration — uniformity and centralisation — survived the wreck, and France is still governed by them.

When it came to courtship, and your field of preferment was the Versailles Œil-de-Bœuf, and a *Grand Monarque* walking encircled with scarlet women and adulators there, the course of the Mirabeaus grew still more complicated. *Carlyle.*

Grandmother's Review, My. A nickname given to the "British Review," a quarterly periodical owned and edited by a Mr. Roberts, whom Byron jocosely accused of having received a bribe from him. Mr. Roberts was foolish enough to take the matter quite seriously, declared that the charge was an absolute falsehood, and challenged Byron to name how and when the bribe was given. Byron responded in an amusing letter, and turned the laugh against his opponent.

"I bribed *My Grandmamma's Review,* the British." *Don Juan.*

Am I flat, — I tip *My Grandmother* a bit of prose. Am I dunned into sourness, — I cut up some deistical fellow for the Quarterly.
Noctes Ambrosianæ.

Grane (grä'nĕ). A horse of marvellous swiftness owned by Siegfried. See SIEGFRIED.

Granite State. A popular name for the State of New Hampshire, the mountainous portions of which are largely composed of granite.

Gratiano. 1. (grä'she-ä'no.) A friend to Antonio and Bassanio, in Shakespeare's "Merchant of Venice."
2. Brother to Brabantio, in Shakespeare's tragedy of "Othello."
3. (grä-tse-ä'no.) A character in the Italian popular dramatic entertainment called "*commedia dell' arte.*" He is represented as a Bolognese doctor, and has a mask with a black nose and forehead and red cheeks; his character is that of a pedantic and tedious proser.

Gray. 1. (Auld Robin.) The title of an ancient and celebrated ballad by Lady Anne Lindsay (afterward Lady Barnard), and the name of its hero, a good old man married to a poor young girl whose lover was thought to have been lost at sea, but who returns to claim her hand a month after her marriage.
2. (**Barry.**) A pseudonym of Robert Barry Coffin, an American writer whose sketches first appeared in the "Home Journal."
3. (**Duncan.**) The hero of a ballad of the same name by Burns.
4. (**Mary.**) See BELL, BESSY.

Greal. See ST. GRAAL.

Great Bastard. [Fr. *Le Grand Bâtard.*] A sobriquet or epithet given to Antoine de Bourgogne (1421-1504), a natural son of Philip the Good, Duke of Bourgogne. He was celebrated for his bravery.

Great Captain. [Sp. *El Gran Capitan.*] 1. Gonsalvo de Cordova (1453-1515), a distinguished general of

☞ For the "Key to the Scheme of Pronunciation," with the accompanying Explanations,

Spain. He was sent by Ferdinand and Isabella to assist their kinsman, Ferdinand II. of Naples, in recovering his kingdom from the French. It was in the campaign of 1496, in which he drove the French (who a year before had possessed the whole kingdom) entirely out of Sicily, that he was hailed by his soldiers as the Great Captain, a name by which he was ever afterward familiarly known throughout Europe.

They [the people of India] could show bankers richer than the richest firms of Barcelona and Cadiz, viceroys whose splendour far surpassed that of Ferdinand the Catholic, myriads of cavalry, and long trains of artillery which would have astonished the *Great Captain*. *Macaulay*.

The great Castilian heroes, such as the Cid, Bernardo del Carpio, and Pelayo, are even now an essential portion of the faith and poetry of the common people of Spain, and are still in some degree honoured, as they were honoured in the age of the *Great Captain*. *Ticknor*.

2. A surname of Manuel I. (1120–1180), emperor of Trebizond.

Great Cham of Literature. A name given to Dr. Johnson by Smollett, in a letter to John Wilkes. See Boswell's "Life of Johnson," vol. ii. chap. iii.

This [a prologue for the comedy of " The Good-natured Man "] immediately became an object of great solicitude with Goldsmith, knowing the weight an introduction from the *Great Cham of Literature* would have with the public. *W. Irving.*

Great Commoner. William Pitt (Earl of Chatham), a famous parliamentary orator, and for more than thirty years (1735–1766) a leader in the House of Commons.

We leave the *Great Commoner* in the zenith of his glory. *Macaulay.*

Great Dauphin. [Fr. *Le Grand Dauphin*.] A name given by French historians to the son of Louis XIV. He was born in 1661, and died in 1711. See LITTLE DAUPHIN.

Great Duke. A title by which the Duke of Wellington (1769–1852) is often distinguished.

Bury the *Great Duke*
With an empire's lamentation,
Let us bury the *Great Duke*
To the noise of the mourning of a mighty
 nation. *Tennyson.*

Great Earl. A surname sometimes given to Archibald Douglas (d. 1514),

Earl of Angus. He is better known as *Archibald Bell-the-Cat*. See BELL-THE-CAT.

Great Earl of Cork. A title bestowed upon Richard Boyle (1566–1643), Earl of Cork, a nobleman who, possessing the largest estate of any English subject at that period, devoted it, in the most generous manner, to promoting public improvements.

Great Elector. [Ger. *Grosse Kurfürst*.] A surname given to Frederick William, elector of Brandenburg (1620–1688), a sovereign distinguished for his military genius and his private virtues, for the prudence and wisdom with which he administered the civil government, and for the zeal and success with which he laboured to augment the prosperity of his dominions, and to promote the welfare of his people. He is regarded as the founder of the Prussian greatness, and his reign gave to the country the military character which it still bears.

Great-heart, Mr. A character in the "Pilgrim's Progress" of Bunyan, represented as the guide of Christian's wife and children upon their journey to the Celestial City.

Great Magician. An appellation of Sir Walter Scott, given to him on account of the singular fascination he exercises over his readers by his remarkable power of description and his charming style. The designation was originated by Professor John Wilson in a poem called " The Magic Mirror," addressed to Scott, and published in the Edinburgh "Annual Register " for 1812.

And when once more the gracious vision
 spoke,
I felt the voice familiar to mine ear;
While many a banded dream of earth awoke,
Connected strangely with that unknown
 seer,
Who now stretched forth his arm, and on the
 sand
A circle round me traced, as with magician's
 wand. *Prof. J. Wilson.*

See WIZARD OF THE NORTH.

Then spake the man clothed in plain apparel to the *Great Magician* who dwelleth in the old fastness, hard by the river Jordan (Tweed), which is by the Border.
 Chaldee MS., Blackwood's Mag. (1817).

Great Marquis. 1. A title given to

and for the **Remarks** and **Rules** to which the numbers after certain words refer, see pp. xiv-xxxii.

James Graham, Marquis of Montrose (1612-1650), on account of his heroic deeds in the cause of Charles I.

> I've told thee how we swept Dundee,
> And tamed the Lindsay's pride,
> But never have I told thee yet
> How the *Great Marquis* died. *Aytoun.*

2. A name given by the Portuguese peasantry to Dom Sebastião Jose de Carvalho, Marquis de Pombal (1699-1782), the greatest of all Portuguese statesmen, and one of the ablest men of his time.

Great Mogul. The title by which the chief of the Moguls, or of the empire founded in Hindostan by Baber in the fifteenth century, was known in Europe. The last person to whom this title of right belonged was Shah Allum, at whose death, in 1806, the Mogul empire came to an end.

Great Moralist. A title often applied to Dr. Samuel Johnson (1709-1784), in allusion to the ethical character of his writings, particularly his essays, from which Goldsmith said a complete system of morals might be drawn.

> Dr. Johnson thought life had few things better than the excitation produced by being whirled rapidly along in a post-chaise; but he who has in youth experienced the confident and independent feeling of a stout pedestrian in an interesting country, and during fine weather, will hold the taste of the *Great Moralist* cheap in comparison. *Sir W. Scott.*

Great Unknown. A name given to the author of the "Waverley Novels," which, on their first appearance, were published anonymously, and which immediately acquired an extraordinary degree of popularity. The epithet was originated by James Ballantyne.

☞ " The circumstance of Scott's having published a poem in the same year in which ' Waverley ' appeared, and his engagement in other literary undertakings, being known, combined with the common prejudice that a poet cannot excel as a prose-writer, to avert from him for a time the suspicion of the authorship of the ' Waverley' novels. The taciturnity of the few intrusted with the secret defeated all attempts to obtain direct evidence as to who was the author. From the first, however, suspicion pointed strongly toward Scott; and so, many circumstances tended to strengthen it, that the disclosures from Constable's and Ballantyne's books, and his own confession, scarcely increased the moral conviction which had long prevailed, that he was the ' *Great Unknown.*' " *Eng. Cyc.*

Great Witch of Bal-wĕr'y. A name popularly given to one Margaret Aiken, a Scotchwoman of the latter part of the sixteenth century, who, on being accused of witchcraft, and subjected to torture, made a pretended confession of guilt, and, in order to save her life, informed upon others, asserting that they had a secret mark in their eyes by which she knew them for witches. She was carried about the country for the sake of detecting such emissaries of the Devil.

Greāveş, Sir Lâun'ce-lŏt. The title of a novel by Smollett (a sort of travesty of "Don Quixote"), and the name of its hero, a well-born young English squire of the time of George II., handsome, virtuous, and enlightened, but crack-brained, who sets out, attended by an old sea-captain for his Sancho Panza, to act "as coadjutor to the law, and even to remedy evils which the law cannot reach; to detect fraud and treason, abase insolence, mortify pride, discourage slander, disgrace immodesty, and stigmatise ingratitude."

Greece, The Two Eyes of. See TWO EYES OF GREECE, THE.

Greek Commentator. A title given to Fernan Nunez de Guzman (1488-1552), on account of his philological lectures, delivered in the University of Salamanca.

Green, George a-. See GEORGE A-GREEN.

Green-Bag Inquiry. (*Eng. Hist.*) A name given to an investigation into the nature of a green bag containing Reports on the state of the country (alleged to be papers of seditious import), which was laid before parliament by the prince regent, Feb. 3, 1817. These Reports were referred to secret committees, and in accordance with their recommendations the Habeas Corpus Act was suspended (March 3), and other coercive measures adopted.

Green-eyed Monster. A common personification of jealousy. The expression originated with Shakespeare.

Oh, beware, my lord, of jealousy;
It is the *Green-eyed Monster* which doth mock
The meat it feeds on. *Shak.*

Green Isle. Same as the *Emerald Isle.* See EMERALD ISLE.

If the Irish elves are anywise distinguished from those of Britain, it seems to be by their disposition to divide into factions, and fight among themselves, — a pugnacity characteristic of the *Green Isle. Sir W. Scott.*

Green-Mountain State. A popular name of Vermont, the Green Mountains being the principal mountain-range in the State.

Greenwood, Grace. A *nom de plume* adopted by Mrs. Sara Jane (Clarke) Lippincott, a popular American authoress of the present day.

Gre′mi-o. A suitor to Bianca, in Shakespeare's "Taming of the Shrew."

Gretchen (gret′ken). See MARGARET.

Grethel, Gammer (grĕth′el; *Ger. pron.* grā′tel). The imaginary narrator of a series of German nursery tales, said to have been taken down by the brothers Grimm, from the lips of Frau Viehmänin, wife of a peasant in the neighbourhood of Hesse Cassel. They have been translated into English.

Gride, Arthur. An old usurer in Dickens's "Nicholas Nickleby."

Grimes, Old. See OLD GRIMES.

Griñ′go, Harry. A *nom de plume* of Henry Augustus Wise (b. 1819), an American writer, author of "Los Gringos," "Captain Brand," and other works. *Gringo* is a Spanish word meaning *unintelligible.*

Gri-sel′dả, The Patient. A lady in Chaucer's "Clerk of Oxenford's Tale," immortalised by her virtue and her patience. The model of womanly and wifely obedience, she comes victoriously out of the most cruel and repeated ordeals to which her conjugal and maternal affections are subjected. [Written also Griseld, Grissell, Grizzell, Griseldis.]

☞ The story of Griselda was first told in the "Decameron." Boccaccio derived the incidents from Petrarch, who seems to have communicated them also to Chaucer. About the middle of the sixteenth century (1565), a song of "Patient Grissel" appeared, and a prose history the same year. The theme has subsequently been treated in a great variety of ways.

For patience she will prove a second *Grissel,*
And Roman Lucrece for her chastity.
Shak.

He might cut
My body into coins to give away
Among his other paupers; change my sons,
While I stood dumb as *Griseld,* for black babes
Or piteous foundlings.
Mrs. E. B. Browning.

Grognon (grôn′yôn′, 62). See GRACIOSA.

Grub Street. The former name of a street near Moorfields, in London, much inhabited by literary hacks (among whom Dr. Johnson includes "the writers of Dictionaries"), whence it was proverbially used to characterise any worthless author, or any mean production. Foxe, the martyrologist, and Speed, the historian, resided in this street. In 1830, the name was changed to Milton Street.

Let Budgell charge low *Grub Street* with his quill,
And write whate'er he please — except my will.
Pope.

I'd sooner ballads write, and *Grub-Street* lays. *Gay.*

Grum′ble-to′ni-ặns. A nickname sometimes given to those who were not of the Court party in the time of William and Mary. They were at times honoured with the name of "Country party."

Grû′mi-o. A servant to Petruchio, in Shakespeare's "Taming of the Shrew."

Grün, Anastasius (ä-nä-stä′se-ŏŏs grün, 34.) A *nom de plume* of Anton Alexander von Auersperg (b. 1806), a German poet.

Grun′dy, Mrs. A person frequently referred to in Morton's comedy, "Speed the Plough," but not introduced as one of the *dramatis personæ.* The solicitude of Dame Ashfield, in this play, as to *what will Mrs. Grundy* *say*, has given the latter great celebrity, the interrogatory having acquired a proverbial currency.

> You will be pleased to hear that I have hit upon a mode of satisfying the curiosity of our friend, *Mrs. Grundy*, — that is "the world,"— without injury to any one.
> *Sir E. Bulwer Lytton.*

Gudrun (goo-droon'). **1.** A famous mythical female character in the Edda of Sämund, married, by the magic arts of her mother, to Sigurd, who was betrothed to Brynhild. After the death of Sigurd, she married King Atli [Attila], at the instance of her mother. She did not love him, however; and soon coming to hate him for his cruelty, she took his life, having first caused him to drink out of the skulls, and eat the wasted hearts, of their two children, whom she had murdered. She then sought to put an end to her own wretched existence by throwing herself into the sea; but the waves bore her to the castle of King Jonakur, whom she married.

2. The heroine of a celebrated North-Saxon poem supposed to have been composed in the thirteenth century, and still extant at Vienna in a MS. of the fifteenth century. It was translated into the modern High German in 1838. Gudrun is the daughter of King Hettel [Attila], and is betrothed to Herwig, king of Heligoland; but her rejected suitor, Hartmuth, king of Norway, invades the dominions of Hettel, kills him, and carries off Gudrun. As she still treats Hartmuth with contempt, and refuses to marry him, she is put to menial service, and is treated with great indignity by his mother, Gerlinda, or Gerlint. As she is one day washing linen by the sea, she learns that a fleet is bringing her brother and her lover to her rescue. She flings the linen into the sea, and, in order to escape punishment for doing so, feigns that she is willing to marry Hartmuth. But Herwig now appears on the scene, gains a decisive victory, puts Gerlinda to death, marries Gudrun. and, at her intercession, pardons Hartmuth. Gudrun is distinguished as a perfect model of angelic mercy, heroic fortitude, and pious resignation.

Guen'do-len (gwen'-). A divorced wife of Locrine. See SABRINA.

Gui-de'ri-us (gwî-, 9). A son of Cymbeline, in Shakespeare's play of this name, passing under the assumed name of Polydore, and supposed to be a son of Belarius. Guiderius, as well as Cymbeline, was a legendary or fabulous king of Britain.

Guil'den-stĕrn (g̃il'-). The name of a courtier, in Shakespeare's tragedy of "Hamlet."

> "Rosencrantz and Guildenstern are favourable samples of the thoroughpaced, time-serving court-knave; servants of all work, ticketed, and to be hired for any hard or dirty job."
> *Cowden Clarke.*

Guinart, Roque. See ROQUE GUINART.

Guin'e-vẽr (gwin'-). Queen to King Arthur, celebrated for her amours with Lancelot du Lac, and others. Hence the name was frequently applied to any wanton woman. Geoffrey of Monmouth says that she was of a noble Roman family, and the most beautiful woman in all Britain. [Written also G u e n e v e r, G u i n e v e r e (gwin'e-veer'), G u a n h u m a r a (gwan'hu-mä'rạ̈), G e n e u r a (g̃e-nu'rạ̈), G a n o r a (gạ̈-no'rạ̈, 9), G e n i e v r e (g̃e'ni-e'vẽr), and G i n e v r a (g̃i-nev'rạ̈).]

Gul'li-ver, Lemuel. The imaginary hero of Swift's celebrated satirical romance entitled "Travels into several Remote Nations of the World, by Lemuel Gulliver." He is represented as being first a surgeon in London, and then a captain of several ships. After having followed the sea for some years, he makes in succession four extraordinary voyages, in the first of which he gets wrecked on the coast of Lilliput, a country inhabited by pygmies; in the second, he is thrown among the people of Brobdingnag, who are giants of a tremendous size; in the third, he is driven to Laputa, an empire of quack pretenders to science, knavish projectors, and sorcerers; and in the fourth, he visits the Houyhnhnms, a race of horses endowed with reason.

☞ For the "Key to the Scheme of Pronunciation," with the accompanying Explanations,

Gul-nâre'. 1. A female character in Byron's poem of "The Corsair." She is rescued from a burning harem by Conrad, and, becoming passionately enamoured of him, repays the service he has done her by taking the life of the pasha, Seyd, into whose hands Conrad falls.
2. A character in one of the tales of the "Arabian Nights' Entertainments."

Gum'mĕr's Ore. A marvellous island, fabled to float in the northern seas, — a fiction probably based upon the existence of some partly submerged reef or shoal. The geographer Buræus placed this island on his map in view of Stockholm.

☞ "There is a tradition in the northern seas, and upon the coast of Norway, that floating islands may often be seen rising out of the bosom of the waves, with trees fully formed, having branches from which hang shells instead of fruits, but which disappear after some hours. Torfæus, in his history of Norway, alludes to these. The sailors and inhabitants of the coast regard these places as the submarine habitations of evil spirits, who cause these islands to rise to taunt navigators, confuse their reckonings, and embarrass their voyages." *Pichot.*

Gungnir (gŏŏng'nĕr). (*Scand. Myth.*) The name of Odin's spear or lance.

Gunpowder Plot. (*Eng. Hist.*) A memorable conspiracy for overthrowing the government by blowing up the king, lords, and commons, at the opening of parliament on the 5th of November, 1605. This diabolical scheme was projected by Robert Catesby, a Roman Catholic, who leagued with himself Guy Fawkes and several other persons, of the same faith, who were exasperated by the intolerant and persecuting spirit of James I. and his ministers. It was discovered, however, on the evening before it was to have been carried into execution, and the principal conspirators were put to death.

Günther, King (gün'tĕr, 34). A hero whose adventures are related in the ancient German epic, the "Nibelungen Lied;" brother to Chriemhild.

Gurth. A Saxon swine-herd, the thrall of Cedric of Rotherwood, in Sir Walter Scott's "Ivanhoe."

Gur'ton, Gammer (-tn). The heroine of an old English comedy, long supposed to be the earliest in the language, but now ranked as the second in point of time. It was written about 1561, by John Still, afterward Bishop of Bath and Wells. The plot turns upon the loss of a needle by Gammer Gurton, — a serious event at that period, especially in a remote village, — and the subsequent discovery of it sticking in the breeches of her man Hodge.

Guzman de Alfarache (gooth-män' dā äl-fä-rä'chä). The hero of a celebrated Spanish novel written by Mateo Aleman, and first printed at Madrid, in 1599. He begins his career as a dupe, but afterward becomes a consummate knave, and exhibits a rich variety of gifts in the various characters he is compelled by circumstances to assume, such as stable-boy, beggar, thief, coxcomb, mercenary, valet, pander, merchant, and the like.

Guy, Sir, Earl of Warwick. The hero of a famous English legend, which celebrates his surpassing prowess and the wonderful achievements by which he obtained the hand of his lady-love, the Fair Felice, as well as the adventures he subsequently met with in a pilgrimage to the Holy Land, and on his return home. He is reputed to have lived in the reign of the Saxon King Athelstan. The romance of Sir Guy, mentioned by Chaucer in the "Canterbury Tales," cannot be traced further back than the earlier part of the fourteenth century. His existence at any period is very doubtful.

☞ Among the romances of the Anglo-Danish cycle, by no means the least celebrated is that of Guy of Warwick. It is one of the few which have been preserved in the Anglo-Norman form ; and it has gone through an extraordinary number of versions. Chaucer enumerated it among the *romances of pris*, or those which in the fourteenth century were held in the highest estimation.
Wright.

The Lord-keeper was scared by a dun cow,

and for the Remarks and Rules to which the numbers after certain words refer, see pp. xiv-xxxii.

and he takes the young fellow who killed her for *Guy of Warwick*. *Sir W. Scott.*

The conduct of the expedition was intrusted to a valiant Dutchman, who for size and weight might have matched with Colbrand, the Danish champion slain by *Guy of Warwick*. *W. Irving.*

Guy'on, Sir (gī'on). A knight whose adventures are related in the second book of Spenser's "Faëry Queen." To him was assigned the task of bringing into subjection a witch, Acrasia, and of destroying her residence, the Bower of Bliss. Sir Guyon represents the quality of Temperance in its largest sense; meaning that virtuous self-government which holds in check not only the inferior sensual appetites, but also the impulses of passion and the movements of revenge.

Gy'as. A mythical personage in Virgil's "Æneid;" a companion of Æneas, noted for his bravery. At the naval games exhibited by Æneas in honour of his father Anchises, Gyas commanded the ship "Chimæra," of which Menœtes was the pilot. See MENŒTES.

Gy'ges. [Gr. Γύγης.] (*Gr. & Rom. Myth.*) A son of Cœlus and Terra, a monstrous hundred-handed giant, who, with his brothers, made war upon the gods, and was slain by Hercules, and subjected to everlasting punishment in Tartarus.

☞ For the "Key to the Scheme of Pronunciation," with the accompanying Explanations,

H.

Hā′dēṣ. [Gr. Ἅιδης, Ἀΐδης.] (*Gr. & Rom. Myth.*) The god of the nether world, the son of Saturn and Rhea, and the brother of Jupiter and Neptune. He is the same as *Pluto*. The name is also applied to his kingdom, the abode of the departed spirits, or shades. See PLUTO.

Hœ′mǒn. [Gr. Αἵμων.] (*Gr. & Rom. Myth.*) A son of Creon of Thebes, and a lover of Antigone. He is said to have destroyed himself on hearing that Antigone was condemned by her father to be entombed alive.

Hagen (hä′gen). The murderer of Siegfried in the German epic, the "Nibelungen Lied;" represented as a pale-faced and one-eyed dwarf, of demon origin, who knows every thing, and whose sole desire is mischief. He is at last killed by Chriemhild, Siegfried's wife, who strikes off his head with Siegfried's own sword.

Haidee (hī-dē′). A beautiful young Greek girl, in Byron's poem of "Don Juan."

Hajji Baba. See BABA, HAJJI.

Halcyone. See ALCYONE.

Hales, The Ever-memorable John. A name often given to John Hales (1584–1656), an able scholar and divine of the church of England. The epithet of "ever-memorable" was first applied to him after his decease, in the title prefixed to a collection of his writings, called his "Golden Remains," published in 1659.

Ham′ȧ-dry′ȧdṣ. [Gr. Ἁμαδρυάδες, Lat. *Hamadryades*.] (*Gr. & Rom. Myth.*) Nymphs of the woods who were born and died with particular trees.

Ham′il-tŏn, Gail. A pseudonym adopted by Miss Mary Abigail Dodge, of *Hamilton*, Masssachusetts, a popular American writer of the present day.

Ham′let. In Shakespeare's tragedy of the same name, son to the former, and nephew to the reigning king of Denmark.

☞ "This is that Hamlet the Dane whom we read of in our youth, and whom we seem almost to remember in our afteryears; he who made that famous soliloquy on life, who gave the advice to the players, who thought 'this goodly frame, the earth, a sterile promontory, and this brave, o'erhanging firmament, the air, this majestical roof, fretted with golden fire, a foul and pestilent congregation of vapours;' whom 'man delighted not, nor woman neither;' he who talked with the grave-diggers, and moralised on Yorick's skull; the schoolfellow of Rosencrantz and Guildenstern at Wittenberg; the friend of Horatio; the lover of Ophelia; he that was mad and sent to England; the slow avenger of his father's death; who lived at the court of Horwendillus five hundred years before we were born, but all whose thoughts we seem to know as well as we do our own, because we have read them in Shakespeare." *Hazlitt.*

☞ The critics have been greatly divided in regard to Shakespeare's intent in this tragedy and character. Coleridge thinks that Shakespeare's purpose was "to exhibit a character flying from the sense of reality, and seeking a reprieve from the pressure of its duties in that ideal activity, the overbalance of which, with the consequent indisposition to action, is Hamlet's disease." Hazlitt says, "It is not a character marked by strength of passion or will, but by refinement of thought and feeling. . . . His ruling passion is to think, not to act; and any vague pretence that flatters this propensity instantly diverts him from his previous purposes." In Mr. R. G. White's view, "Hamlet is a man of contemplation, who is ever diverted from his purposed deeds by speculation upon their probable consequences or their past causes, unless he acts too quickly, and under too much excitement, for any reflection to present itself." Goethe thought that Shakespeare designed to exhibit "a lovely, pure, noble, and most moral nature, without the strength of nerve which forms a hero, sinking beneath a burden which it cannot bear, and must not cast away." According to Schlegel, "the whole [play] is intended to show that a calculating consideration, which exhausts all the relations and possible consequences of a deed, must cripple the power of action."

Hammer of Heretics. [Fr. *Le Marteau des Hérétiques.*] 1. A sobriquet given to Pierre d'Ailly (1350–1425), a noted French cardinal and polemic. He was president of the council of Constance, by which John Huss was condemned.
2. A surname applied to John Faber (d. 1541), from the title of one of his works. He was a native of Swabia, and an eminent Roman Catholic divine.

Hammon. See AMMON.

Handsome Englishman. [Fr. *Le Bel Anglais.*] A name given by the French troops under Turenne to John Churchill (1650–1722), afterward the celebrated Duke of Marlborough, who was no less distinguished for the singular graces of his person, than for his brilliant courage and his consummate ability both as a soldier and a statesman.

Handsome Swordsman. [Fr. *Le Beau Sabreur.*] A title popularly given to Joachim Murat (1767–1815), who was highly distinguished for his handsome person, accomplished horsemanship, and daring bravery as a cavalry officer.

Hanging Judge. An epithet fastened upon the Earl of Norbury (d. 1831), who was Chief Justice of the Common Pleas in Ireland, from 1820 to 1827. He is said to have been in the habit of jesting with criminals, on whom he was pronouncing sentence of death.

Hans von Rippach (hănss fon rĭp'-păk, 67, 71). A fictitious personage, to ask for whom was an old joke among the German students. *Hans* is the German *Jack*, and *Rippach* is a village near Leipsic.

Hanswurst (hănss'ṫoorst, 68). [Ger., Jack Pudding.] A pantomimic character formerly introduced into German comedies, and originally intended as a caricature of the Italian *Harlequin*, but corresponding more particularly with the Italian *Macaroni*, the French *Jean Potage*, the English *Jack Pudding*, and the Dutch *Pickelherringe*, — all favourite characters with the lower classes of the population, and called after favourite national dishes. Hanswurst was noted for his clumsiness, his gormandising appetite, and his Falstaffian dimensions. He was driven from the German stage by Gottsched, about the middle of the eighteenth century.

Happy Valley. In Johnson's "Rasselas," a delightful valley, situated in Abyssinia.

To his recollection, this retired spot was unparalleled in beauty by the richest scenes he had visited in his wanderings. Even the *Happy Valley* of Rasselas would have sunk into nothing upon the comparison.
Sir W. Scott.

Hard'cas-tle, Mr. (härd'kŭs-sl). A character in Goldsmith's comedy of "She Stoops to Conquer;" represented as prosy and hospitable.

Har'le-quin (här'le-kin *or* här'lekwin). [Fr. *Harlequin, Arlequin,* Sp. *Arlequin,* It. *Arlecchino;* probably from Old Fr. *hierlekin, hellequin,* goblin, elf, Low Lat. *harlequinus, hellequinus,* from D. and Old Ger. *helle,* hell. — *Mann.*] 1. The name of a well-known character in the popular extemporised Italian comedy, in which he originally figured as a servant of Pantaleone, the comic representative of Venetian foibles, and as the lover of Columbina, or the *Arlechinetta.* He appeared before the public with a shaven head, a masked face, unshod feet, and a coat of many colours. He also carried a light sword of lath, and his hat was in a deplorable condition. He was noted for his agility, and for being a great gourmand, though his gluttony had no effect upon the size of his person. In this character were satirised the roguery and drollery of the Bergamasks, who were proverbial for their intriguing knavery. Harlequin is accordingly represented as a simple, ignorant person, who tries very hard to be witty, even at the expense of being malicious. He is a parasite, cowardly, yet faithful and active, but easily induced, by fear or interest, to commit all sorts of tricks and knaveries. From the Italian stage he was transferred to that of other countries. In England, he was first introduced on the stage by Rich, in the eighteenth century. The harlequin, in its original conception, has almost ceased to possess a legitimate existence in comedy, being confined, at the present day, to the sphere of Christmas pantomimes and puppet-shows, and to the improvised plays of the Italians.

2. A punning nickname conferred upon Robert *Harley* (1661-1724), Earl of Oxford and Mortimer, an English statesman of the time of Queen Anne, noted for his restless, intriguing disposition.

Har′ley. "The Man of Feeling," in Mackenzie's novel of that name. He is remarkable for his fine sensibility and benevolence, and his bashfulness resulting from excessive delicacy. See MAN OF FEELING.

☞ "The principal object of Mackenzie, in all his novels, has been to reach and sustain a tone of moral pathos, by representing the effect of incidents, whether important or trifling, upon the human mind, and especially those which were not only just, honourable, and intelligent, but so framed as to be responsive to those finer feelings to which ordinary hearts are callous. This is the direct and professed object of Mackenzie's first work, which is in fact no narrative, but a series of successive incidents, each rendered interesting by the mode in which they operate on the feelings of Harley."
Sir W. Scott.

Harlot, The Infamous Northern. See NORTHERN HARLOT, THE INFAMOUS.

Har′lŏwe, Clarissa. The heroine of Richardson's novel entitled "The History of Clarissa Harlowe;" a young lady, who, to avoid a matrimonial union to which her heart cannot consent, and to which she is urged by her parents, casts herself on the protection of a lover, who scandalously abuses the confidence she reposes in him, and finally succeeds in gratifying his passion, though he fails in insnaring her virtue. She rejects the reparation of marriage, which is at length tendered, and retires to a solitary abode, where she expires, overwhelmed with grief and shame.

☞ "It was reserved to Richardson to show there is a chastity of the soul, which can beam out spotless and unsullied even after that of the person has been violated; and the dignity of Clarissa, under her disgrace and her misfortunes, reminds us of the saying of the ancient poet, that a good man, struggling with the tide of adversity, and surmounting it, was a sight upon which the immortal gods might look down with pleasure."
Sir W. Scott.

Har-mo′ni-å. [Gr. 'Αρμονία.] (*Gr. & Rom. Myth.*) A daughter of Mars and Venus, and the wife of Cadmus. She is renowned in ancient story on account of a necklace which she received from her husband on her wedding-day, and which wrought mischief to all who came into possession of it.

Hăr′ŏld, Childe (child, *or* chīld). The hero of Lord Byron's poem, "Childe Harold's Pilgrimage;" represented as a man of gentle birth, lofty bearing, and peerless intellect, who, having exhausted all the pleasures of youth and early manhood, and feeling the fulness of satiety, loathes his fellow-bacchanals, and the "laughing dames in whom he did delight." To banish his disgust and melancholy, he determines to travel; but, though he traverses some of the fairest portions of the earth, the feelings of bitterness and desolation still prey upon him, without for one moment lightening the weight upon his heart, or enabling him to lose his own wretched identity.

☞ "Childe Harold may not be, nor do we believe he is, Lord Byron's very self; but he is Lord Byron's picture, sketched by Lord Byron himself, arranged in a fancy dress, and disguised perhaps by some extrinsic attributes, but still bearing a sufficient resemblance to the original to warrant the conclusion that we have drawn."
Sir W. Scott.

The feelings arising from so rich a landscape as is displayed by the valley of the Rhine, must have been the same in every bosom, from the period when our Englishman took his solitary journey through it, in doubt and danger, till that in which it heard the indignant *Childe Harold* bid a proud farewell to his native country, in the vain search of a land in which his heart might throb less fiercely. *Sir W. Scott.*

Harpagon (ar'pá'gōn', 62). The hero of Molière's comedy of "L'Avare;" represented as a wretched miser, whose avarice has reached that point where it is without pride, and whose dread of losing his wealth has overpowered the desire of being thought to possess it.

Some [part of the treasure] went to stop for a time the mouths of such claimants, who, being weary of fair promises, had become of opinion with *Harpagon*, that it was necessary to touch something substantial. *Sir W. Scott.*

Harpagon is not more unlike to Jourdain ... than every one of Miss Austen's young divines to all his reverend brethren. *Macaulay.*

Har'pi-ĕr, or **Har'pĕr.** Some mysterious personage referred to by the witches, in Shakespeare's tragedy of "Macbeth," a. iv., sc. 1. Collier suggests that the word may be a corruption of *harpy*. The orthography of the first folio, and of the best modern editions, is *Harpier*.

Harpies. [Gr. Ἅρπυαι, swift robbers; Lat. *Harpyiæ*.] (*Gr. & Rom. Myth.*) Three daughters of Neptune and Terra, considered as ministers of the vengeance of the gods. They were disgusting winged monsters, of fierce and loathsome aspect, with the bodies of vultures, the heads of maidens, hands armed with long claws, and faces pale with hunger. They lived in an atmosphere of filth and stench, and polluted every thing they approached. Their names are commonly given as Aëllo, Celæno, and Ocypete.

Har-poc'rạ-tḕs. [Gr. Ἁρποκράτης.] (*Myth.*) The Greek name of the Egyptian *Horus*, the god of the sun and of silence, represented with his finger on his mouth.

Harris, Mrs. An imaginary personage to whom Mrs. Gamp — a monthly nurse who figures in Dickens's novel of "Martin Chuzzlewit" — constantly refers as an authority for her own fabrications and fancies. See GAMP, MRS. SARAH.

☞ " Mrs. Harris was a glorious creation, or, rather, conception. Only, the numerous and respectable persons who bear that name must feel themselves aggrieved; for their very existence is now made a matter of doubt. By one breath of the magician, the solid flesh-and-blood of all the Harrises has been volatilised into a hypothetical phantom." *Fraser's Mag.*

Now, hitherto, though the bandit was the nominal hero of the piece; though you were always hearing of him, — his wrongs, virtues, hair-breadth escapes, — he had never been seen. Not *Mrs. Harris*, in the immortal narrative, was more quoted and more mythical. *Sir E. Bulwer Lytton.*

Hatch'way, Lieutenant Jack. The name of a retired naval officer, on half-pay, in Smollett's novel, " The Adventures of Peregrine Pickle." He is represented as living with Commodore Trunnion as a companion.

He who can read the calamities of Trunnion and *Hatchway*, when run away with by their mettled steeds, ... without a good hearty burst of honest laughter, must be well qualified to look sad and gentleman-like with Lord Chesterfield or Master Stephen. *Sir W. Scott.*

Hats and Caps. (*Swed. Hist.*) Popular names given to two political factions by which Sweden was distracted in the middle of the eighteenth century. The former party was favourable to France, the latter was in the interest of Russia. They were both broken up, and their names prohibited, in 1771, by Gustavus III., who desired to exclude foreign influence.

☞ "'Faction of Hats,' 'Faction of Caps' (that is, *night*-caps, as being somnolent and disinclined to France and War): seldom did a once valiant, far-shining nation sink to such depths!" *Carlyle.*

Hat'tĕr-ḋick, Dirk. A Dutch smuggler captain, and a thorough and desperate villain, in Scott's novel of "Guy Mannering." His character is redeemed from utter sordidness and depravity only by his one virtue of integrity to his employers. "I was always faithful to my ship-owners, always accounted for cargo to the last stiver."

Hav'e-lŏk the Dane. [Fr. *Havelok le Danois*.] The hero of an early French romance, the original of an ancient English romance of the same name, founded upon a story of the

Saxon era relating to the town of Grimsby, in Lincolnshire.

Hawk'ạ-bites. The same as *Tityre Tus.* See TITYRE TUS.

Hawk'eye State. The State of Iowa;—said to be so named after an Indian chief, who was once a terror to *voyageurs* to its borders.

Head of Africa. A name formerly given to the Cape of Good Hope.

Hĕad'rigg, Cud'dIe (*or* **Cuthbert**). A ploughman in Lady Bellenden's service, in Scott's novel of "Old Mortality."

Heart of Mid-Lo'thi-ạn. A poetical and popular name of the old jail in Edinburgh, the capital of the county of Mid-Lothian. It was taken down in 1817. One of Scott's novels bears this name as its title.

He'be. [Gr. 'Ηβη.] (*Gr. & Rom. Myth.*) The goddess of youth, a daughter of Jupiter and Juno, and the cup-bearer of the gods. She was banished from heaven on account of an unlucky fall.

Wreathèd smiles,
Such as hang on *Hebe's* cheek,
And love to live in dimple sleek. *Milton.*

Hec'ạ-te (*sometimes Anglicised* hek'-ăt). [Gr. 'Εκάτη.] (*Gr. & Rom. Myth.*) The daughter of Jupiter and Latona; a mysterious divinity called *Luna* in heaven, *Diana* on earth, and *Hecate*, or *Proserpina*, in hell. In the latter character, she is described as a powerful and cruel goddess, of hideous appearance, having all the magical powers of the universe at her command, and sending upon the earth all kinds of demons and terrible phantoms.

Hec'tọr. [Gr. 'Εκτωρ.] (*Gr. & Rom. Myth.*) The son of Priam, king of Troy, by Hecuba, and the bravest and ablest of all the Trojan chiefs who fought against the Greeks. For a long time he gloriously defended Troy, but was at last slain in single combat by Achilles, who dragged his body in insulting triumph three times around the tomb of Patroclus and the walls of the beleaguered city. His exploits are sung by Homer in the "Iliad." One of the most beautiful and affecting as well as celebrated episodes in this poem is that in which Hector takes leave of his wife and child at the Scaean gate before going into battle.

Hec'tọr de Mā'rys, Sir. A knight of the Round Table, brother of Lancelot du Lac.

Hec'tọr of Germany. A title given by the old chroniclers to Joachim II., elector of Brandenburg (d. 1571).

Hec'tọrṣ. See TITYRE TUS.

Hec'u-bḁ. [Gr. 'Εκάβη.] (*Gr. & Rom. Myth.*) The second wife of Priam, king of Troy, and the mother of Paris and Hector. After the fall of Troy, she fell into the hands of the Greeks as a slave, and, according to one account, threw herself in despair into the sea.

Heep, Uriah. A detestable character in Dickens's novel of "David Copperfield," who, under the garb of the most abject humility, conceals a diabolic hatred and malignity. "I am well aware," quoth he, "that I am the umblest person going; let the other be who he may. My mother is likewise a very umble person. We live in a numble abode, Master Copperfield, but have much to be thankful for. My father's former calling was umble; he was a sexton."

Heimdall (hīm'dȧl). (*Scand. Myth.*) A god who stands as sentinel at the bridge of Bifröst, to prevent the giants from forcing their way into heaven. It is said of him, that he requires less sleep than a bird, that he can see to a distance of one hundred leagues, as well by night as by day, and that he can hear the grass grow and also the wool on sheep's backs. See GJALLAR. [Written also H e i m d a l.]

Heir of the Republic. A name given to Napoleon Bonaparte, "the plebeian child of the Revolution," who, in 1799, by a bold *coup d'état*, overthrew the Directory, and made himself First Consul of France with sovereign powers; and who, in 1804,

and for the Remarks and Rules to which the numbers after certain words refer, see pp. xiv-xxxii.

assumed the title of emperor, and destroyed the last vestiges of democracy and freedom.

Hel, or He'lả. (*Scand. Myth.*) The queen of the dead, daughter of the evil-hearted Loki and a giantess named Angurboda. She was frightful to behold, her aspect being ferocious, and the upper part of her body black or livid from congealed blood. Her abode (Helheim) was a vast castle in Niflheim, in the midst of eternal damp, snow, ice, and darkness. Here she received all who died of old age or disease. She was an inexorable divinity, and would release no one who had once entered her domain.

> Uprose the king of men with speed,
> And saddled straight his coal-black steed;
> Down the yawning steep he rode,
> That leads to Hela's drear abode,
> Till full before his fearless eyes,
> The portals nine of hell arise. *Gray.*

Helen. [Gr. Ἑλένη, Lat. *Helena.*] (*Gr. & Rom. Myth.*) A daughter of Jupiter and Leda, and the wife of Menelaus, king of Sparta. She was the most beautiful woman of her age. In the absence of her husband, Paris, son of King Priam, carried her off to Troy, which was the cause of the ten years' war against that city, and of its final destruction.

Helen, Burd. See BURD HELEN.

Hel'e-nả. 1. See HELEN.
2. A lady in Shakespeare's "Midsummer-Night's Dream," in love with Demetrius.
3. The heroine of Shakespeare's "All 's Well that Ends Well," distinguished for her romantic passion for Bertram, and her patient endurance of the most adverse fortune.

> ☞ "There was never, perhaps, a more beautiful picture of a woman's love, cherished in secret; not self-consuming in silent languishment; not pining in thought; not passive and 'desponding over its idol;' but patient and hopeful; strong in its own intensity, and sustained by its own fond faith. . . . The situation of Helena is the most painful and degrading in which a woman can be placed. She is poor and lowly; she loves a man [Bertram] who is far her superior in rank, who repays her love with indifference, and rejects her hand with scorn. She marries him against his will; he leaves her, with contumely, on the day of their marriage, and makes his return to her arms depend on conditions apparently impossible. All the circumstances and details with which Helena is surrounded are shocking to our feelings, and wounding to our delicacy; and yet the beauty of the character is made to triumph over all." *Mrs. Jameson.*

Hel'e-nả, The Patient. A character in an old popular tale, reproduced in Germany by Tieck.

Hel'e-nus. [Gr. Ἕλενος.] (*Gr. & Rom. Myth.*) A son of Priam and Hecuba, and a celebrated soothsayer.

He-li'ạ-dẹ̄ṣ. [Gr. Ἡλιάδες.] (*Gr. & Rom. Myth.*) Daughters of Helios or Sol (the sun), changed into poplars on account of their grief at the death of their brother Phaëthon. Their names were Lampethusa, Lampetia, and Phæthusa.

Hel'ĭ-cǫn. [Gr. Ἑλικών.] A mountain of Bœotia, in Greece, sacred to Apollo and the Muses.

> From *Helicon's* harmonious springs
> A thousand rills their mazy progress take.
> *Gray.*

He'li-os. [Gr. Ἥλιος.] (*Gr. Myth.*) The sun-god; identified in later times with Apollo or Phœbus. He corresponds to the Roman *Sol.*

Hel'le. [Gr. Ἕλλη.] (*Gr. & Rom. Myth.*) A daughter of Athamas and Nephele. With her brother Phrixus, she fled, on a golden-fleeced ram, from her step-mother Ino to Calchas, but fell into the strait called after her the Hellespont.

Hel-ve'ti-ạ (23). The Latin name of Switzerland; sometimes used in modern poetry.

> See from the ashes of *Helvetia's* pile
> The whitened skull of old Servetus smile!
> *Holmes.*

Henriette (*Fr. pron.* ŏn're-et', 62). A daughter of Chrysale in Molière's comedy, "Les Femmes Savantes." Her name has become proverbial in the French language as a type of a perfect woman.

He-phæs'tus. [Gr. Ἥφαιστος.] (*Myth.*) The Greek name of the god called *Vulcan* by the Romans. See VULCAN.

☞ For the "Key to the Scheme of Pronunciation," with the accompanying Explanations,

He'rĕ (9). [Gr. Ἥρα, Ἥρη.] (*Myth.*) The Greek name of the wife of Jupiter, called *Juno* by the Romans. See JUNO.

Hĕr'ȧ-cleï'dæ. [Gr. Ἡρακλεῖδαι.] (*Gr. & Rom. Myth.*) The descendants of Hercules. See HERCULES.

Heracles. See HERCULES.

Hĕr'cu-lĕs̱. [Gr. Ἡρακλῆς.] (*Gr. & Rom. Myth.*) A son of Jupiter and Alcmena, the most famous hero of fabulous history, remarkable for his great strength, and for his many wonderful achievements, particularly his performance of twelve labours imposed upon him by his kinsman Eurystheus. These were, 1. To destroy a lion which haunted the mountain valley of Nemea. 2. To kill a formidable hydra which infested the forest and marsh of Lerna. (See HYDRA.) 3. To capture a swift stag, with golden antlers and brazen feet, which belonged to Diana. 4. To take alive a wild boar which ravaged the neighbourhood of Erymanthus. 5. To cleanse the Augean stables. (See AUGEAS.) 6. To slay certain frightful carnivorous birds that desolated the country near Lake Stymphalis, in Arcadia. 7. To bring alive to Eurystheus a remarkable mad bull belonging to Minos, king of Crete. 8. To obtain the mares of Diomedes, king of the Bistones in Thrace, which fed on human flesh. 9. To procure the girdle of Hippolyta, queen of the Amazons. 10. To kill the monster Geryon, and bring his herds to Argos. (See GERYON.) 11. To obtain certain golden apples which were concealed in the gardens of the Hesperides. (See HESPERIDES.) 12. To bring from the infernal regions the three-headed dog Cerberus. (See CERBERUS.) To these "twelve labours" must be added many other exploits, such as his strangling two serpents sent by Juno to destroy him while yet an infant; his battles with the Centaurs and with the Giants; his participation in the Argonautic expedition; his liberation of Prometheus and Theseus; and the like. It is related by the sophist Prodicus, that Hercules in his youth met the goddesses of Pleasure and Virtue at the cross-ways, and that each endeavoured to persuade him to become her votary; but he rejected the charms of Pleasure, and chose Virtue to be the constant companion of his life. (See DEJANIRA and HYLAS.) [Called also *Alcides*, after his grandfather Alcæus.]

☞ The old world knew nothing of Conversion; instead of an "Ecce Homo" [Behold the Man! See *John* xix. 5], they had only some Choice of *Hercules*. *Carlyle*.

Heretics, Hammer of. See HAMMER OF HERETICS.

Hermann (hĕr'mȧn). The hero of Goethe's poem entitled "Hermann und Dorothea."

☞ The aim of the "Hermann and Dorothea" is "in an epic crucible to free from its dross the pure human existence of a small German town, and at the same time mirror in a small glass the great movements and changes of the world's stage." *Goethe, Trans.*

Hĕr'mĕs̱. [Gr. Ἑρμῆς.] (*Myth.*) The Greek name of *Mercury*. See MERCURY.

Hĕr'mi-ȧ. A lady in Shakespeare's "Midsummer-Night's Dream," in love with Lysander.

Hĕr-mï'o-ne. [Gr. Ἑρμιόνη.] (*Gr. & Rom. Myth.*) 1. The only daughter of Menelaus and Helen, celebrated for her beauty. She became the wife of Pyrrhus (Neoptolemus), the son of Achilles; but, having been previously promised to Orestes, whom she loved, the latter procured the assassination of Pyrrhus, and carried her off and married her.

2. The heroine of the first three acts of Shakespeare's "Winter's Tale."

☞ "She is the wife of Leontes, king of Sicilia, and, though in the prime of beauty and womanhood, is not represented in the first bloom of youth. Her husband, on slight grounds, suspects her of infidelity with his friend Polixenes, king of Bohemia. The suspicion once admitted, and working on a jealous, passionate, and vindictive mind, becomes a settled and confirmed opinion. Hermione is thrown into a dungeon; her new-born infant is taken from her, and, by the order of her husband, frantic with jealousy,

and for the Remarks and Rules to which the numbers after certain words refer, see pp. xlv–xxxii.

exposed to death on a desert shore; she is herself brought to a public trial for treason and incontinency, defends herself nobly, and is pronounced innocent by the oracle. But, at the very moment that she is acquitted, she learns the death of the prince, her son, who,
' Conceiving the dishonour of his mother,
Had straight declined, drooped, took it deeply,
Fastened and fixed the shame on 't in himself,
Threw off his spirit, appetite, and sleep,
And downright languished.'
She swoons away with grief, and her supposed death concludes the third act. The two last acts are occupied with the adventures of her daughter Perdita; and with the restoration of Perdita to the arms of her mother, and the reconciliation of Hermione and Leontes, the piece concludes. Such, in few words, is the dramatic situation. The character of Hermione exhibits what is never found in the other sex, but rarely in our own,—yet sometimes, —dignity without pride, love without passion, and tenderness without weakness." *Mrs. Jameson.*

Hermod (hĕr'mŏd, *or* hĕr'mŏd). (*Scand. Myth.*) A son of Odin, and the messenger of the gods.

He'ro (9). [Gr. Ἡρώ.] 1. (*Gr. & Rom. Myth*). A beautiful priestess of Venus at Sestos, in Thrace, beloved by Leander of Abydos, who repeatedly swam across the Hellespont to visit her; but, he being at length unfortunately drowned, she threw herself, in despair, into the sea.
2. Daughter of Leonato, and a friend of Beatrice, in Shakespeare's "Much Ado about Nothing."

☞ " The character of Hero is well contrasted with that of Beatrice, and their mutual attachment is very beautiful and natural. When they are both on the scene together, Hero has but little to say for herself; Beatrice asserts the rule of a master-spirit, eclipses her by her mental superiority, abashes her by her raillery, dictates to her, answers for her, and would fain inspire her gentle-hearted cousin with some of her own assurance. ... But Shakespeare knew well how to make one character subordinate to another, without sacrificing the slightest portion of its effect; and Hero, added to her grace and softness, and all the interest which attaches to her as the sentimental heroine of the play, possesses an intellectual beauty of her own. When she has Beatrice at an advantage, she repays her, with interest, in the severe, but most animated and elegant picture she draws of her cousin's imperious character and unbridled levity of tongue."
Mrs. Jameson.

Hĕr'ŏn, Robert. A pseudonym under which John Pinkerton (1758-1826) published a work, entitled " Letters on Literature," distinguished for its strange system of spelling, as well as for the singular opinions advanced in it on the value of the Greek and Roman writers.

Hero of the Nile. An epithet often given to Horatio Nelson (1758-1805), the illustrious naval commander of England, who, on the first of August, 1798, with a greatly inferior force, attacked, and nearly destroyed, a French fleet under the command of Brueys, in Aboukir Bay.

He-ros'tra̤-tus. [Gr. Ἡρόστρατος.] An Ephesian, who, to acquire imperishable fame, set fire to the magnificent temple of Diana, at Ephesus, B. C. 356. He was tortured to death for the deed, and a decree was passed that no one should mention his name under pain of capital punishment; but the effect produced was exactly the opposite of that which was intended. [Called also *Eratostratus*.]

Hĕr'tha̤. (*Teutonic Myth.*) A personification of the earth. Hertha was worshipped by the ancient Germans and the Anglo-Saxons, as well as by the Norsemen. The name is sometimes used as a synonym of *Frigga*. See FRIGGA.

Her Trippa (ĕr trĕp'pa̤'). The name of one of the characters in Rabelais' "Pantagruel."

☞ " Her Trippa is undoubtedly Henricus Cornelius Agrippa burlesqued. *Her* is *Henrieus*, or *Herricus*, or perhaps alludes to *Herr*, because he was a German, and *Agrippa* is turned into *Trippa*, to play upon the word *tripe*." *Motteux.*

He-si'o-ne. [Gr. Ἡσιόνη.] (*Gr. & Rom. Myth.*) A daughter of Laomedon, king of Troy, rescued from a sea-monster by Hercules, and given in marriage to Telamon, to whom she bore Teucer.

Hes-pĕr'ĭ-dēṣ. [Gr. Ἑσπερίδες.] (*Gr. & Rom. Myth.*) Three nymphs, daughters of Hesperus, — or, as some say, of Erebus and Nox, — and guardians of the golden apples which Juno, on her marriage with Jupiter, received from Terra, and which were kept in a garden on an island beyond Mount Atlas, in Africa. The tree which bore them was watched by a huge dragon.

Hes'pe-rus. [Gr. "Εσπερος.] (*Gr. & Rom. Myth.*) A personification of the evening star, worshipped with divine honours. According to one form of the legend, he was the son of Cephalus and Aurora; according to another form, the son of Iapetus and Asia. Diodorus calls him a son of Atlas, and says that he was fond of astronomy, and that once, after having ascended Mount Atlas to observe the stars, he disappeared, and was seen on earth no more.

Hes'ti-å. [Gr. 'Εστία.] (*Gr. Myth.*) The Greek name of the goddess worshipped by the Romans as *Vesta.* See VESTA.

Hi'å-wå'thå. A mythical personage of miraculous birth, believed by the North American Indians to have been sent among them to clear their rivers, forests, and fishing-grounds, and to teach them the arts of peace. The story of Hiawatha has been made the subject of a poem by Longfellow.

Hī-bēr'ni-å. The Latin name of Ireland, often used in modern poetry.

Hick'å-thrift, Thomas, *or* **Jack.** The name of a famous character in an old legendary tale of the same name, doubtless a popular corruption of an ancient Northern romance. He is described as a poor labourer of the time of William the Conqueror, and the possessor of superhuman strength, which enabled him to accomplish achievements so wonderful, and of such public importance and benefit, that he was knighted by his grateful king, and made governor of East Anglia, or Thanet. See "Qu. Rev.," No. XLI. art. V.

When a man sits down to write a history, though it be but the history of *Jack Hickathrift* or Tom Thumb, he knows no more than his heels what lets and confounded hindrances he is to meet with in his way.
Sterne.

Hieronymo. See JERONIMO.

High-heels. A faction or party in Lilliput opposed to the Low-heels. These parties were so called from the high and low heels of their shoes, by which they respectively distinguished themselves. The High-heels, it was alleged, were most agreeable to the ancient constitution of the empire, but the emperor made use only of Low-heels in the administration of the government. Under these designations, Swift satirised the High-church and Low-church parties of his time, or the Whigs and Tories. See GULLIVER and LILLIPUT.

Highland Mary. Mary Campbell, Burns's first love, the subject of some of his most beautiful songs, and of the elegy, "To Mary in Heaven."

Hin'doos. A cant name given to the "Know-nothing" or Native-American party in the United States, Daniel Ullman, their candidate for the Presidency, having been charged with being a native of Calcutta.

Hip'po-cre'ne (*the English poets sometimes pronounce it in three syllables,* hip′po-kreen). [Gr. 'Ιπποκρήνη.] A fountain near Mount Helicon, sacred to the Muses, and fabled to have been produced by a stroke of Pegasus's hoof. Longfellow has made use of this myth in his "Pegasus in Pound." See PEGASUS.

Oh for a beaker full of the warm South,
Full of the true, the blushful *Hippocrene*,
With beaded bubbles winking at the brim!
Keats.

Hip'po-då-mi'å. [Gr. 'Ιπποδάμεια.] (*Gr. & Rom. Myth.*) The real name of Briseis, the beloved slave of Achilles. See BRISEIS.

Hip-pol'ў-tå. [Gr. 'Ιππολύτη.] 1. (*Gr. & Rom. Myth.*) A queen of the Amazons, and daughter of Mars, slain by Hercules, according to one account, but, according to another, conquered by Theseus, who married her, and had by her his son Hippolytus. [Written also H i p p o l y t e.]

The worthy Doctor . . . magnanimously suppressed his own inclination to become the Theseus to this *Hippolyta*, in deference to the

and for the Remarks and Rules to which the numbers after certain words refer, see pp. xiv-xxxii.

rights of hospitality, which enjoined him to forbear interference with the pleasurable pursuits of his young friend. *Sir W. Scott.*

2. Queen of the Amazons, in Shakespeare's "Midsummer-Night's Dream."

Hip-pol'y̆-tus. [Gr. Ἱππόλυτος.] (*Gr. & Rom. Myth.*) A son of Theseus, king of Athens, by Antiope or Hippolyta. His step-mother, Phædra,— the second wife of Theseus,—fell in love with him, but, finding that her passion was not responded to, she accused him to her husband of attempts upon her chastity; the king in his rage cursed him, and prayed for his destruction, whereupon he was thrown from his chariot and dragged to death by his horses. Æsculapius, however, restored him to life, and Diana placed him, under the name of Virbius, and under the protection of the nymph Egeria, in the grove of Aricia, where he afterward received divine honours.

Hip-pom'e-don. [Gr. Ἱππομέδων.] (*Gr. & Rom. Myth.*) One of the seven Grecian chiefs who engaged in the siege of Thebes.

Hip-pom'e-nĕṣ. [Gr. Ἱππομένης.] (*Gr. & Rom. Myth.*) A Grecian prince who conquered Atalanta in a race, and thus obtained her as his wife. See ATALANTA.

Even here, in this region of wonders, I find
That light-footed Fancy leaves Truth far behind;
Or, at least, like *Hippomenes*, turns her astray
By the golden illusions he flings in her way.
T. Moore.

Hip-pot'ă-dēṣ. [Gr. Ἱπποτάδης.] (*Gr. & Rom. Myth.*) A name given to Æolus, as the grandson of Hippotes. See ÆOLUS.

He ... questioned every gust of rugged wings
That blows from off each beakèd promontory; ...
And made *Hippotades* their answer brings,
That not a blast was from his dungeon strayed.
Milton.

Hī'ren (9). [A corruption of *Irene*.] The heroine of an old play by George Peele, entitled "The Turkish Mahomet, and Hiren, the fair Greek;" referred to by Pistol, in Shakespeare's "King Henry IV.," Part II., a. ii., sc. 4. The name is proverbially used by the writers of that day to designate a strumpet.

"Come, come," exclaimed Oldbuck; "what is the meaning of all this? Have we got *Hiren* here? We'll have no swaggering here, youngsters." *Sir W. Scott.*

His-pā'ni-ă̇. The ancient Latin name of Spain; sometimes used in modern poetry.

Hob'bĭ-did'ănçe. The name of one of the fiends mentioned by Shakespeare in "Lear" (a. iv., sc. 1), and taken from Harsnet's "Declaration of Egregious Popish Impostures." See FLIBBERTIGIBBET. [Written H o p d a u c e in a. iii., sc. 6.]

Hobbididance, prince of dumbness. *Shak.*

Hob'gob'lin. A name formerly given to the merry spirit usually called *Puck*, or *Robin Goodfellow.*

☞ " Goblin is the French *gobelin*, German *kobold;* Hob is Rob, Robin, Bob ; just as *Hodge* is Roger." *Keightley.*

Those that *Hobgoblin* call you, and sweet Puck,
You do their work, and they shall have good luck. *Shak.*

Hob'ĭ-nol. A name given by Spenser, in his "Shepherd's Calendar," to Gabriel Harvey (1545–1630), a personal friend, a respectable poet and prose-writer, and one of the most learned persons of his age. [Written also H o b b i n o l.]

Hob'o-mok'ko. The name of an evil spirit among the North American Indians.

Hob'son, Tobias (-sn). A carrier who lived at Cambridge (Eng.) in the seventeenth century. He kept a stable, and let out horses, but obliged each customer to take the one which stood next to the door. Hence the proverbial expression, "Hobson's choice," used to denote a choice without an alternative.

Hocus, Humphrey. A nickname used to designate the Duke of Marlborough, in Arbuthnot's "History of John Bull."

Hödeken (hö'dä-ken, 46). [Ger., little hat.] A famous German kobold, or domestic fairy servant;—so called because he always wore a little felt hat pulled down over his face.

Hodge. The goodman of Gammer Gurton, in the old play of "Gammer

☞ For the "Key to the Scheme of Pronunciation," with the accompanying Explanations,

Gurton's Needle." See GURTON, GAMMER.

Hödur (hö'döor, 46). (*Scand. Myth.*) A blind god who destroyed his brother Baldur, at the instigation of Loki, without meaning to do so. He is the type of night and darkness, as Baldur is of light and day. [Written also Höd, Höder.]

Hol'o-fĕr'nĕṣ. 1. See JUDITH.
2. [Fr. (*Thubal*) *Holoferne.*] The name of a pedant living in Paris, under whose care Gargantua, in Rabelais' romance of this name, is placed for instruction.
3. [An imperfect anagram of *Joh. nes Floreo*, or Johannes Florio.] A pedantic schoolmaster, in Shakespeare's "Love's Labour's Lost," fantastically vain of his empty knowledge. See EUPHUES.

☞ "Under the name of *Holofernes*, Shakespeare ridicules John Florio (d. 1625), the philologist and lexicographer, called by himself 'The Resolute.' ... The character of Holofernes, however, while it caricatures the peculiar folly and ostentation of Florio, holds up to ridicule, at the same time, the general pedantry and literary affectations of the age; and amongst these, very particularly, the absurd innovations which Lyly had introduced. *Drake.*

Holy Alliance. [Fr. *La Sainte Alliance.*] (*Hist.*) A league of the sovereigns of Europe, proposed by the Emperor Alexander of Russia, Sept. 26, 1815, after the defeat of Napoleon at Waterloo, and founded upon the idea that religion should be made the basis of international politics. The act establishing this alliance was signed by Alexander, Francis of Austria, and Frederick William of Prussia, and consisted of a declaration that the principles of Christianity should be the basis of internal administration and of public policy. Principles so indefinite led in time to violations of justice, and the league soon became a conspiracy of the governments against the peoples. The kings of England and France acceded to the alliance, and, in 1818, a congress was held at Aix-la-Chapelle, in which a Declaration of the five monarchs was issued, stating that the object of the alliance was peace and *legitimate stability.* England and France afterward withdrew from this union, as its views became more pronounced, and France at the present time occupies a position hostile to it. A special article of the treaty of alliance excluded for ever the members of the Bonaparte family from any European throne!

Holy Bottle, Oracle of the. An imaginary oracle in search of which Pantagruel, in Rabelais' romance of this name, visits various islands, accompanied by his friend Panurge. See PANURGE.

☞ The last place at which they arrive is Lantern-land (see ISLAND OF LANTERNS), where the oracular bottle is kept in an alabaster fount in a magnificent temple. Being conducted hither, the attendant priestess throws something into the fount, on which the water begins to bubble, and the word *Trinc!* (Drink) is heard to proceed from the bottle, which the priestess declares to be the most auspicious response pronounced while she has officiated in the temple. They accordingly all partake of Falernian wine; and with their ravings and prophesyings under the inspiration of Bacchanalian enthusiasm the romance ends.

They were left in all the distresses of desire unsatisfied, — saw their doctors, the Parchmentarians, the Brassarians, the Turpentarians, on one side, the Popish doctors on the other, like Pantagruel and his companions in quest of the *Oracle of the Bottle*, all embarked out of sight. *Sterne.*

Holy City. A designation bestowed by various nations upon the city which is regarded as the centre of their religious worship and traditions. By the Jews and Christians, Jerusalem is so called. By the Mohammedan nations, the name is applied to Mecca and Medina. By the Hindus, Benares is regarded as the Holy City. By the Indian Mohammedans, Allahabad is so called. In the time of the Incas, the name was given to Cuzco, where there was a great temple of the sun, to which pilgrims resorted from the furthest borders of the empire.

Holy Graal. See ST. GRAAL.

Holy Island. 1. A name formerly given to Ireland, on account of its innumerable multitude of saints.

2. Guernsey was so called, in the tenth century, on account of its many monks.

3. Rügen was so called by the Slavonic Varini.

4. A synonym of Lindisfarne, a peninsula on the north-east coast of England, remarkable as having been the seat of a Saxon abbey over which the famous St. Cuthbert presided as bishop.

Holy Land. 1. A name commonly applied to Palestine; — first given to it in Zech. ii. 12.

2. A name given to Elis, in ancient Greece.

Holy League. [Fr. *La Sainte Ligue.*] (*Hist.*) 1. A celebrated combination against the republic of Venice, formed in 1508 by Pope Julius II., — whence the epithet of "Holy," — and including the emperor of Germany (Maximilian), the king of France (Louis XII.), the king of Spain (Ferdinand III.), and various Italian princes. By this league, Venice was forced to cede to Spain her possessions in the kingdom of Naples.

2. A treaty concluded, in 1533, between Pope Clement VII., the Venetians, the Duke of Milan (Francesco Maria Sforza), and Francis I. of France, to compel the Emperor Charles V. to release the French king's sons on the payment of a reasonable ransom, and to re-establish Sforza in the possession of Milan. It was so called because the Pope was at the head of it.

3. A politico-religious association formed by the Roman Catholic party in France, in the reign of Henry III., the object of which was to overthrow the Protestants, prevent the accession of Henry IV., and place the Duke of Guise on the throne. [Called also *The League*, by way of eminence.]

Holy Maid of Kent. Elizabeth Barton, a woman once popularly believed to possess miraculous endowments, and to be an instrument of divine revelation. She was beheaded at Tyburn, on the 21st of April, 1534, for high treason in having predicted that direful calamities would befall the English nation, and that Henry VIII. would die a speedy and violent death if he should divorce Queen Catharine and marry Anne Boleyn. Her imposture was for a time so successful that even Sir Thomas More was disposed to be a believer.

Honeycomb, Will. One of the members of the imaginary club by whom the "Spectator" was professedly edited. He is distinguished for his graceful affectation, courtly pretension, and knowledge of the gay world.

Honeyed Teacher. An appellation bestowed upon St. Bernard (1091-1153), one of the most eloquent and distinguished ecclesiastics of the Middle Ages. See MELLIFLUOUS DOCTOR.

Hŏn'ey-măn, Charles. A free-and-easy clergyman in Thackeray's novel of "The Newcomes."

In the *Honeyman* of the parish, even where that person is of ordinary qualifications, a more familiar tone both of speech and writing is tolerated. *Percy Fitzgerald.*

Hŏn'ey-wŏŏd. A character in Goldsmith's comedy of "The Good-natured Man;" distinguished for his exaggerated generosity and self-abnegation.

Honour, Mrs. The waiting-maid of Sophia Western, in Fielding's novel, "The History of a Foundling."

Stop, stop; fold up the bedclothes again, if you please. Upon my word, this is worse than Sophy Western and *Mrs. Honour* about Tom Jones's broken arm. *Prof. J. Wilson.*

Hood, Robin. See ROBIN HOOD.

Hŏŏk'ẽr, The Judicious. Richard Hooker, an eminent English divine (1553-1600), to whom the surname of "The Judicious" has been given on account of his wisdom and judgment. Of his "Ecclesiastical Polity" Pope Clement VIII. said, "There are in it such seeds of eternity as will continue till the last fire shall devour all learning."

Hookey Walker. The popular name of an out-door clerk at Longman, Clementi, & Co.'s, in Cheapside, London, where a great number of persons were employed. His real name was *John* Walker, and the epithet

"*Hookey*" was given him on account of his hooked or crooked nose. He occupied the post of a spy upon the other workmen, whose misdemeanours were numerous. Of course it was for their interest to throw discredit upon all Jack's reports to the head of the firm; and numbers could attest that those reports were fabrications, however true. Jack, somehow or other, was constantly outvoted, his evidence superseded, and of course disbelieved; and thus his occupation ceased, but not the fame of "*Hookey Walker*," who often forms a subject of allusion when the testimony of a person of tried and well-known veracity is impeached. The name is also often used as an ejaculation, to express incredulity.

☞ According to the London "Saturday Review," the expression is derived from an aquiline-nosed Jew, named Walker, an out-door astronomical lecturer of some local notoriety in his day. Another authority refers it to "a magistrate of dreaded acuteness and incredulity," whose hooked nose gave the title of "beak" to all judges, constables, and policemen.

Hoosier State (hoo'zhur). The State of Indiana, the inhabitants of which are often called *Hoosiers*. This word is said to be a corruption of *husher*, formerly a common term for a bully, throughout the West.

Hopeful. A pilgrim in Bunyan's "Pilgrim's Progress," who, after the death of Faithful, accompanies Christian to the end of his journey.

Hop-o'-my-Thumb. A character in the tales of the nursery, often confounded with Tom Thumb. See THUMB, TOM.

Ho'ræ (9). [Gr. 'Ωραι.] (*Gr. & Rom. Myth.*) The Hours, daughters of Jupiter and Themis, goddesses that presided over the changes of the seasons and the works of man, and kept watch at the gates of heaven; represented in art as blooming maidens carrying flowers, fruits, &c. Their names are usually given as Eunomia, Dice, and Irene.

Lo! where the rosy-bosomed *Hours*,
Fair Venus' train, appear.   *Gray.*

Ho-rā'ti-i (-shǐ-ī). See CURIATII.

Ho-rā'ti-o (ho-rā'shǐ-o). A friend to Hamlet, in Shakespeare's tragedy of this name.

Hŏr'i-cŏn. A fanciful name sometimes given to Lake George, and commonly supposed to be the original Indian name, but really an invention of the American novelist, James Fenimore Cooper. The ancient Iroquois name of this lake was *Andialarocte*, which is said to mean, "there the lake shuts itself." The French missionary, Father Jogues, called it *Saint Sacrement*, because he discovered it on the eve of that festival.

Horn, King. See KING HORN.

Hor'nĕr, Jack. The name of a celebrated personage in the literature of the nursery. The full history of his "witty tricks and pleasant pranks" is given in Halliwell's "Nursery Rhymes of England."

☞ According to a writer in "Notes and Queries" (xvi. 156), "There is a tradition in Somersetshire that the Abbot of Glastonbury, hearing that Henry VIII. had spoken with indignation of his building such a kitchen as the king could not burn down, — it being domed over with stone, — sent up his steward, Jack Horner, to present the king with an acceptable dish; namely, a dish, which, when the crust was lifted up, was found to contain deeds transferring twelve manors to his sovereign; and that, as Jack Horner travelled up to town in the Abbot's waggon, he lifted up the crust, and stole out the gift of the manor of Wells, still possessed by his descendants, and, when he returned, told the Abbot that the king had given it to him, but was found, or suspected, to have imposed upon his patron. Hence the satire vested under the nursery lines, —

'Little *Jack Horner*
Sat in a corner [namely, that of the waggon],
Eyeing his Christmas pie;
He put in his thumb,
And pulled out a plum [the deed of the manor of Wells],
And said, "What a brave boy am I!"'"

Another correspondent of the same work (xvii. 83) gives a different version of this story. "When the monasteries and their property were seized, orders were given that the title-deeds of the abbey estates at Mells [Wells?], which were very extensive and valuable, and partly consisted of a sumptuous grange built by Abbot John Sellwood, should be given up to the commissioners. After some delay, it was determined by the Abbot of Glastonbury to give them up; and, for want of a safe mode of conveying them, it was decided that the most likely to avoid their being seized by any but those for whom they were intended, was to send them in a pasty, which should be forwarded as a present to one of the commissioners in London. The safest messenger, and least likely to excite suspicion, was considered to be a lad named Jack Horner, who was a son of poor parents living in the neighbourhood of the grange. The lad set out on his journey on foot, laden with the pasty. It was a weary road, and England not being so thickly inhabited as now, he sat down to rest in as snug a corner as he could find by the way-side. Hunger, too, overcame him, and he was at a loss what to do, when he bethought himself that there would be no harm in tasting ever so little of the pasty which he was carrying. He therefore inserted his thumb under the crust, when, lo! there was nothing but parchments. Whether that allayed his hunger then or not, I cannot say; but, although he could not read or understand these parchments, yet he thought they might be valuable. He therefore took one of the parchments and pocketed it, and pursued his journey with the rest of his pasty. Upon his delivering his parcel, it was perceived that one of the chief deeds (the deed of the Mells [Wells?] Abbey estates) was missing; and, as it was thought that the Abbot had withheld it, an order was straightway sent for his execution. But the sequel was, that, after the monasteries were despoiled, there was found in the possession of the family of Jack Horner a piece of parchment which was, in fact, the title-deed of Mells [Wells?] Abbey and lands; and that was 'the plum' which little Jack Horner had unwittingly become possessed of. The Abbot Whiting was executed for withholding the deeds. This is the tale as told to me."

"No, I a'n't, sir," replied the fat boy, starting up from a remote corner, where, like the patron saint of fat boys,—the immortal Horner,—he had been devouring a Christmas pie, though not with the coolness and deliberation which characterised that young gentleman's proceeding. *Dickens.*

Horn Gate. One of "two gates of sleep" in the under-world, spoken of by Virgil in the "Æneid," Book VI., one of which is made of horn, the other of shining white ivory. Through that of horn, true visions or dreams are sent up to men.

So too the Necklace, though we saw it vanish through the *Horn Gate* of Dreams, and in my opinion man shall never more behold it yet its activity ceases not, nor will. *Carlyle.*

Hornie, Auld. See AULD HORNIE.

Horse Latitudes. A name given by seamen to a bank or region of calm in the Atlantic Ocean, between the parallels of 30° and 35° N. The name is said to be derived from the circumstance that vessels formerly bound from New England to the West Indies, with a deck-load of horses, were often delayed in this calm belt, and, for want of water, were obliged to throw the animals overboard.

Hor-ten'si-o. A suitor to Bianca, in Shakespeare's "Taming of the Shrew."

Ho'rus (9). [Gr. *Ὧρος*.] (*Myth.*) The Egyptian god of the sun, corresponding to the Grecian *Apollo.* He was a son of Osiris and Isis, and along with his mother avenged his father's death by vanquishing Typhon in a great battle (see OSIRIS), and taking his place as king of the gods. He is often represented as a child seated on a lotus-flower, with his finger on his lips, and hence has been regarded as the god of silence. His worship extended to Greece, and even to Rome.

Hot'spur. An appellation for a person of a warm or vehement disposition, and therefore given to the famous Harry Percy. The allusion is to one who rides in hot haste, or spurs hotly.

It is probable that he . . . forgot, amid the hundreds of thousands which Paris contains, what small relation the number of his own faithful and devoted followers bore, not only to those who were perilously engaged in factions hostile to him, but to the great mass, who, in *Hotspur's* phrase, loved their own shops or barns better than his house.
Sir W. Scott.

Hot'spur of Debate. A sobriquet given by Macaulay to the Earl of Derby (b. 1799), on account of his fiery invective and vehemence of declamation.

Hours. See HORÆ.

House of Fame. The title of a celebrated poem of Chaucer's, and the name of a magnificent palace described in it as built upon a mountain of ice, and supported by rows of pillars, on which are inscribed the names of the most illustrious poets. Here the goddess Fame, seated on her throne, dispenses her capricious and unjust judgments to the crowds who come to solicit her favours.

Houssain, Prince. See PRINCE HOUSSAIN.

Houyhnhnms. A name given by Swift, in his imaginary "Travels into several Remote Nations of the World, by Lemuel Gulliver," to a race of horses endowed with reason. The word seems intended to be suggestive of the *whinnying* of a horse. It is a dissyllable, and may be pronounced hoo-inmz', or hoo'inmz, but the voice should properly be quavered in sounding the *n*.

Nay, would kind Jove my organs so dispose
To hymn harmonious *Houyhnhnms* through the nose.
I'd call thee *Houyhnhnm*, that high-sounding name;
Thy children's noses all should twang the same.
Pope.

"True, true, — ay, too true," replied the Dominie, his *Houyhnhnm* laugh sinking into an hysterical giggle. *Sir W. Scott.*

If the *Houyhnhnms* should ever catch me, and, finding me particularly vicious and unmanageable, send a man-tamer to Rarey-fy me, I'll tell you what drugs he would have to take, and how he would have to use them. *Holmes.*

Höwe, Miss. A personage who figures in Richardson's novel of "Clarissa Harlowe."

☞ "Miss Howe is an admirably sketched character drawn in strong contrast to that of Clarissa, yet worthy of being her friend, with more of worldly perspicacity, though less of abstracted principle, and who, when they argue upon points of doubt and delicacy, is often able, by going directly to the question at issue, to start the game, while her more gifted correspondent does but beat the bush. Her high spirit and disinterested devotion for her friend, acknowledging, as she does on all occasions, her own inferiority, show her in a noble point of view." *Sir W. Scott.*

Hubbard, *and* Hubberd, Mother. See MOTHER HUBBARD, and MOTHER HUBBERD.

Hub of the Universe. A jocular designation of the state-house in Boston, Massachusetts, originating with the American humorist, Oliver Wendell Holmes; sometimes extended, in its application, to the city itself.

Hu'di-bras. The title and hero of a celebrated satirical poem by Samuel Butler (1600–1680). Hudibras is a Presbyterian justice, of the time of the Commonwealth, who, fired with the same species of madness as the Don Quixote of Cervantes, sets out (in company with his squire, Ralph, an Independent clerk, with whom he is almost always engaged in controversy) to correct abuses, and to enforce the observance of the strict laws enacted by parliament for the suppression of the sports and amusements of the people.

☞ Butler is said to have taken the name of his hero from the old romances of chivalry, Sir Hugh de Bras being the appellation of one of the knights of Arthur's fabulous Round Table. A "Sir Huddibras" figures in Spenser's "Faëry Queen," and is described as "an hardy man," but "more huge in strength than wise in works." "Huddibras" was also the name of a fabulous king of England, who is said to have founded Canterbury, Winchester, and Shaftesbury.

He became wretched enough. As was natural, with haggard scarcity threatening him in the distance, and so vehement a soul languishing in restless inaction, and forced thereby, like *Sir Hudibras's* sword by rust,

"To eat into itself, for lack
Of something else to hew and hack!"
Carlyle.

Hug'gins and Mug'gins. A jocular embodiment of vulgar pretension.

☞ It has been suggested that these names are a corruption of *Hooge en Mogende* (high and mighty), words occurring in the style of the States General of Holland, much ridiculed by English writers of the latter part of the seventeenth century, as, for example, in the following couplet:—

But I have sent him for a token
To your Low-Country *Hogen Mogen*.
Hudibras.

☞ "Although we have never felt the least inclination to indulge in conjectural etymology, . . . we cannot refrain, for once, from noticing the curious coincidence between the names of Odin's ravens, Hugin and Munin,—Mind and Memory,—and those of two personages who figure so often in our comic literature as Messrs. Huggins and Muggins. . . . Should this *conjecture*, for it is nothing else, be well founded, one of the most

and for the Remarks and Rules to which the numbers after certain words refer, see pp. xiv-xxxii.

poetical ideas in the whole range of mythology would, in this plodding, practical, spinning-jenny age of ours, have thus undergone a most singular metamorphosis." *Blackwell.*

Whitford and Mitford joined the train,
Huggins and Muggins from Chick Lane,
And Clutterbuck, who got a sprain
Before the plug was found.
Rejected Addresses.

Hugh of Lincoln. A legendary personage who forms the subject of Chaucer's "Prioress's Tale," and also of an ancient English ballad. The story has its origin in the chronicle of Matthew Paris, who, in his account of the reign of Henry III., relates, that, in the year 1255, the Jews of Lincoln stole a boy named Hugh, of the age of eight years, whom, after torturing for ten days, they crucified before a large number of their people, in contempt of the death of the Founder of Christianity. Eighteen of the richest and most distinguished Jews of Lincoln were hanged for participation in this murder, while the body of the child was buried with the honours of a martyr, in Lincoln Cathedral. The story has been generally discredited by modern historians. Wordsworth has given a modernised version of Chaucer's tale.

Hugh Roe. [That is, Red Hugh.] The eldest son of Sir Hugh O'Donnell, of Ireland, who flourished at the time of the intestine wars of that country, in the reign of Elizabeth. He was a man of great abilities and ambition.

Hugin (hoo'gin). [Old Norse, thought, intellect.] (*Scand. Myth.*) One of Odin's two ravens, who carried him news from earth, and who, when not thus employed, perched upon his shoulders. See HUGGINS AND MUGGINS.

Hugon (ü'gôn', 34, 62). A kind of evil spirit, in the popular superstition of France, a sort of ogre made use of to frighten children. It has been said that from him the French Protestants were called "Huguenots," on account of the desolation resulting from the religious wars which were imputed to them; but the assertion is an incorrect one.

Huguenot Pope. [Fr. *Le Pape des Huguenots.*] A title bestowed upon Philippe de Mornay (1549-1623), a distinguished French nobleman, and an able supporter of the Protestant cause. He was so called on account of the ability of his arguments and the weight of his personal influence in behalf of the reformed religion.

Humphrey, Duke. See DUKE HUMPHREY.

Humphrey, Master. See MASTER HUMPHREY.

Humphrey, Old. See OLD HUMPHREY.

Hundred Days. [Fr. *Les Cent Jours.*] A name given to the period which intervened between the entrance of Napoleon Bonaparte into Paris (March 20, 1815), after his escape from the island of Elba, and his abdication in favour of his son (June 22).

Hunkers. See OLD HUNKERS.

Hunter, Mr. and Mrs. Leo. Characters in Dickens's "Pickwick Papers," distinguished, as the name indicates, for their desire to make the acquaintance of all the "lions" of the day.

Mr. Dickens was the grand object of interest to the whole tribe of *Leo Hunters*, male and female, of the metropolis. *Qu. Rev.*

Huon of Bordeaux, Sir (bor'do'). The hero of one of the romances of chivalry bearing his name. He is represented as having been a great favourite of Oberon, the fairy king. An abstract of this romance may be found in Dunlop's "History of Fiction," or in Keightley's "Fairy Mythology." The adventures of Sir Huon form the subject of Wieland's beautiful poem of "Oberon," known to the English reader by Sotheby's translation.

I will carry him off from the very foot of the gallows into the land of faëry, like King Arthur, or *Sir Huon of Bordeaux*, or Ogero the Dane. *Sir W. Scott.*

Hurlo-thrum'bo. The chief character in a play, entitled "Hurlo thrumbo, or The Supernatural," by Samuel Johnson (d. 1773), an English actor and dramatic writer. The whimsicalness and originality of this play, which is an absurd compound of extravagant incidents and unconnected dialogues, gave it great success.

Consider, then, before, like *Thurlothrumbo*,
You aim your club at any creed on earth,
That, by the simple accident of birth,
You might have been high-priest to Mumbo Jumbo. *Hood.*

Hy'ạ-cin'thus. [Gr. Ὑάκινθος.] (*Gr. & Rom. Myth.*) A Spartan boy of extraordinary beauty, beloved by Apollo, who unintentionally killed him in a game of quoits. Another form of the myth is that he was beloved also by Zephyrus or Boreas, who, from jealousy of Apollo, drove the quoit of the god against the head of the boy, and thus killed him. Apollo changed the blood that was spilt into a flower called the hyacinth, on the leaves of which there appeared the exclamation of woe, AI, AI (alas, alas), or the letter Y, the initial of Ὑάκινθος.

Hy'ạ-dēṣ. [Gr. Ὑάδες, the rainy.] (*Gr. & Rom. Myth.*) A class of nymphs commonly said to be seven in number, and their names to be Ambrosia, Eudora, Pedile, Coronis, Polyxo, Phyto, and Thyene or Dione. They were placed among the stars (forming the constellation *Taurus*), and were thought to threaten rain when they rose with the sun.

Hy'dră. [Gr. Ὕδρα.] (*Gr. & Rom. Myth.*) A many-headed water-serpent which inhabited the marshes of Lerna, in Argolis, near the sea-coast. As fast as one of its heads was cut off, two sprang up in its place. Hercules, however, killed it with the assistance of his friend Iolaus.

Hȳ-ġe'ī-ặ (20). [Gr. Ὑγίεια, Ὑγεία.] (*Gr. & Rom. Myth.*) The goddess of health, a daughter of Æsculapius. In works of art, she is usually represented as a blooming virgin, with a snake, the symbol of health, drinking from a cup held in her hand. [Written also **Hygea** and **Hygia**.]

Hy'lặs. [Gr. Ὕλας.] (*Gr. & Rom. Myth.*) A beautiful youth passionately loved by Hercules, whom he accompanied on the Argonautic expedition. He was carried off by the nymphs on the coast of Mysia, as he was drawing water from a fountain. Hercules long sought for him in vain.

The self-same lay
Which melted in music, the night before,
From lips as the lips of *Hylas* sweet,
And moved like twin roses which zephyrs meet. *Whittier.*

Hy'mon, *or* **Hym'e-næ'us.** [Gr. Ὑμήν, Ὑμέναιος.] (*Gr. & Rom. Myth.*) The god of marriage, a son of Bacchus and Venus, or, according to some, of Apollo and one of the Muses. He is represented as a winged boy crowned with a garland, and having a bridal torch and a veil in his hand.

There let *Hymen* oft appear
In saffron robe, with taper clear. *Milton.*

Hyperboreans. [Gr. Ὑπερβόρεοι, *i. e.* dwellers beyond Boreas, or the north wind; Lat. *Hyperborei*.] (*Gr. & Rom. Myth.*) A fabulous people living at the farthest north, supposed by the Greeks to be the favourites of Apollo, and therefore in the enjoyment of a terrestrial paradise and everlasting youth and health.

Hȳ-pe'rī-ŏn (9) (*classical pron.* hip'e-rī'ŏn). [Gr. Ὑπερίων]. (*Gr. & Rom. Myth.*) One of the Titans, a son of Cœlus and Terra, and the father of Sol, Luna, and Aurora.

and for the Remarks and Rules to which the numbers after certain words refer, see pp. xiv-xxxii.

I.

Ï-ac'çhus. [Gr. 'Ιακχος]. (*Gr. & Rom. Myth.*) A poetic surname of Bacchus.

Iăçh'ï-mo (yăk'ĭ-mo). The name of an Italian villain, in Shakespeare's "Cymbeline," celebrated for the art, address, audacity, and ill success, with which he attempts the chastity of Imogen, the wife of Posthumus, and for the daring imposture by which he conceals the defeat of his project.

I know where she kept that packet she had, — and can steal in and out of her chamber like Iachimo. *Thackeray.*

Iago (e-ä'go). The "ancient," or ensign, of Othello, in Shakespeare's tragedy of this name; "a being of motiveless malignity, passionless, self-possessed, sceptical of all truth and purity, — the abstract of the reasoning power in the highest state of activity, but without love, without veneration, a being next to devil, and only not quite devil, and yet a character which Shakespeare has attempted and executed without scandal."

Richard Plantagenet was one of those, who, in Iago's words, would not serve God because it was the Devil who bade him. *Sir W. Scott.*

Ï-ap'e-tus. [Gr. 'Ιαπετός.] (*Gr. & Rom. Myth.*) A Titan or a giant, the father of Atlas, Prometheus, and Epimetheus, regarded by the Greeks as the ancestor of the human race.

Ï-be'ri-ȧ (9). [Gr. 'Ιβηρία.] The Greek name of Spain; sometimes used by ancient Latin authors, and also in modern poetry.

Art thou too fallen, Iberia? Do we see The robber and the murderer weak as we? *Cowper.*

Ic'ȧ-rus. [Gr. 'Ικαρος.] (*Gr. & Rom. Myth.*) A son of Dædalus, who, flying with his father out of Crete, soared so high that the sun melted his wings, and he fell into the sea, — which was called after him the Icarian Sea.

Belleisle is an imaginary sun-god; but the poor Icarus, tempted aloft in that manner into the earnest elements, and melting at once into quills and rags, is a tragic reality! *Carlyle.*

Ï-dom'e-neûs. [Gr. 'Ιδομενεύς.] (*Gr. & Rom. Myth.*) A king of Crete, celebrated for his beauty, and for his bravery at the siege of Troy, whither he led the Cretans. He was banished from his dominions by his own subjects for bringing a plague upon them in consequence of sacrificing his son on account of a vow which he had made to Neptune in a tempest.

Iduna (e-doo'nȧ.) (*Scand. Myth.*) The goddess of youth, and the wife of Bragi. She was the guardian of the apples of immortality, the juice of which gave the gods perpetual youth, health, and beauty. [Written also Idun, Idunna.]

Ï-ğĕr'nȧ (4). The beautiful wife of Gorlois, Duke of Tintadiel, or Tintagel, in Cornwall, and mother of the illustrious Arthur, by Uther, a legendary king of Britain, whom Merlin, the renowned magician, changed into the semblance of Gorlois, thus enabling him to impose upon the duke's wife, for whom he had conceived a violent passion. [Written also I g e r n e and Y g u e r n e.]

Ï-li'o-neûs. [Gr. 'Ιλιονεύς.] (*Gr. & Rom. Myth.*) 1. A son of Niobe, unintentionally killed, while praying, by Apollo.

2. A Trojan, distinguished for his eloquence.

Il'i-thy'ï-ȧ (20). [Gr. Ειλείθυια.] (*Gr. Myth.*) The goddess of birth, who came to women in travail, and shortened or protracted the labour, according as she happened to be kindly disposed or the reverse. She corresponds with the Roman *Lucina*. Homer mentions more than one, and calls them daughters of Hera, or Juno.

Il'i-um, *or* Il'i-ŏn. [Gr. 'Ιλιον.] A poetical name for Troy, which was founded by Ilus.

Ill-grounded Peace. (*Fr. Hist.*) The name commonly given to a treaty between the Huguenots and the Roman Catholics, concluded March 23, 1568. It was a mere stratagem on the part of the latter to weaken their opponents, and was soon broken. [Called also *Lame and Unstable Peace* and *Patched-up Peace*.]

Illuminated Doctor. [Lat. *Doctor Illuminatus*.] 1. A title bestowed upon Raymond Lulle, or Lully (1235-1315), a distinguished scholastic, and author of the system called "Ars Lulliana," which was taught throughout Europe for several centuries, and the purpose of which was to prove that the mysteries of faith are not contrary to reason.

2. A title conferred upon John Tauler (1294-1361), a celebrated German mystic, on account of the visions he professed to have seen, and the spiritual voices he professed to have heard.

3. An honorary appellation given to François de Mairone (d. 1327), a French religious writer.

Illuminator, The. A surname commonly given to St. Gregory of Armenia, a celebrated bishop of the primitive church, whose memory is held in great reverence by the Greek, Coptic, Abyssinian, Armenian, and Roman Catholic churches.

Im'lac. A character in Dr. Johnson's "Rasselas."

Im'o-gen. The wife of Posthumus, and the daughter of Cymbeline by a deceased wife, in Shakespeare's play of this name. She is distinguished for her unalterable and magnanimous fidelity to her mistaken husband, by whom she is unjustly persecuted. "Of all Shakespeare's women," says Hazlitt, "she is, perhaps, the most tender and the most artless."

Imogine, The Fair. See FAIR IMOGINE.

Imperial City. One of the names by which Rome — for many ages the seat of empire — is familiarly known.

Impertinent, The Curious. See CURIOUS IMPERTINENT, THE.

Ind. A poetical contraction of *India*.

High on a throne of royal state, which far
Outshone the wealth of Ormus and of *Ind*,...
Satan exalted sat. *Milton.*

In'drȧ. [Sansk., the discoverer, *scil.*, of the doings of the world.] (*Hindu Myth.*) The ever youthful god of the firmament, and the omnipotent ruler of the elements. He is a most important personage in Indian fable. In the Vedic period of the Hindu religion, he occupied a foremost rank, and, though degraded to an inferior position in the Epic and Purânic periods, he long enjoyed a great legendary popularity. In works of art, he is represented as riding on a gigantic elephant.

" Then," as *Indra* says of Kehama, " then
was the time to strike." *Macaulay.*

In'gŏlds-bỹ, Thomas. A pseudonym adopted by the Rev. Richard Barham (1788-1845), author of a series of humourous tales in verse entitled " The Ingoldsby Legends," — wild and wondrous stories of chivalry, witchcraft, and *diablerie*, related in singularly rich and flexible metre, and in language in which the intermixture of the modern cant phrases of society with antiquarian pedantry produces a truly comic effect.

Iniquity, The. A personage who figured in the old English moralities, mysteries, and other dramas; the same as *The Vice*. See VICE, THE.

Iṅ'kle, Mr. Thomas (ingk'l). The hero of a story by Sir Richard Steele in the "Spectator" (No. 11); a young Englishman who got lost in the Spanish main, where he fell in love with a young Indian maiden named Yarico, with whom he lived for many months; but, having discovered a vessel on the coast, he went with her to Barbadoes, and there sold her into slavery. The story of Inkle and Yarico has been made the subject of an opera by George Colman.

Innamorato, Orlando. See ORLANDO.

In'nis-fāil. An ancient name of Ireland, signifying *the isle of destiny*.

Oh! once the harp of *Innisfail*
Was strung full high to notes of gladness;
But yet it often told a tale
Of more prevailing sadness. *Campbell.*

Innocents, The. A name given, from early times, to the infants whom

Herod massacred at Bethlehem. They were termed in Latin *innocentes*, from *in*, not, and *nocere*, to hurt. These harmless ones were revered by the Church from the first, and honoured, on the third day after Christmas, as martyrs; and with them were connected many strange observances, such as the festival of the boy-bishop, and, in opposition to this, the whipping children out of their beds on that morning. In the modern Church, the feast of the Holy Innocents is celebrated as a special holiday by the young, and many curious and sportive customs connected with it prevail in Catholic countries. The relics of the Holy Innocents were great favourites in the Middle Ages. The Massacre of the Innocents is the subject of a poem by John Baptist Marino (1569-1625), the Italian poet.

I′no. [Gr. Ἰνώ.] (*Gr. & Rom. Myth.*) A daughter of Cadmus and Hermione, sister of Semele, and wife of Athamas, king of Thebes. Being pursued by her husband,—who had become raving mad,—she threw herself into the sea with her son Melicertes, whereupon they were both changed into sea-deities.

Inspired Idiot. An epithet applied by Horace Walpole to Oliver Goldsmith (1728-1774), on account of his exquisite genius, his ungainly person, his awkward manners, and his frequent blunders and absurdities.

Interpreter, The. A personage in Bunyan's allegorical romance, "The Pilgrim's Progress," designed to symbolise the Holy Spirit. Christian, on his way to the Celestial City, called at the Interpreter's house, where he was shown many wonderful sights, the remembrance of which was "as a goad in his sides to prick him forward" in his journey.

Invincible Armada. See ARMADA, THE INVINCIBLE.

Invincible Doctor. [Lat. *Doctor Invincibilis*.] An appellation conferred upon William of Occam, a celebrated English scholastic of the fourteenth century, on account of his rigorously logical and rational treatment of Nominalism, of which he was a zealous advocate.

I′o. [Gr. Ἰώ.] (*Gr. & Rom. Myth.*) A daughter of Inachus, king of Argos. She was beloved by Jupiter, who turned her into a cow, fearing the jealousy of Juno. Juno, however, set the hundred-eyed Argus to watch her, and Jupiter in return had him killed by Mercury. Thereupon Io was smitten with madness by Juno, and, wandering about, came at last to Egypt, where she was restored to her own form, married King Osiris, and, after death, was worshipped by the Egyptians under the name of Isis.

I′o-lā′us. [Gr. Ἰόλαος.] (*Gr. & Rom. Myth.*) A son of Iphicles, and a faithful friend and servant of Hercules. He assisted his master in destroying the Lernæan hydra. See HERCULES and HYDRA.

Iph′ī-ġe-nī′ȧ. [Gr. Ἰφιγένεια.] (*Gr. & Rom. Myth.*) A daughter of Agamemnon and Clytemnestra. Her father having killed in Aulis a favourite deer belonging to Diana, the soothsayer Calchas declared that Iphigenia must be sacrificed to appease the wrath of the goddess. But when she was on the point of being slain, Diana carried her in a cloud to Tauris, and made her a priestess in her temple.

I′phis. [Gr. Ἶφις.] (*Gr. & Rom. Myth.*) A Cyprian youth who hanged himself because his love for the highborn Anaxarete was not reciprocated, and whose fate the gods avenged by changing Anaxarete to stone.

I′rȧs (9). An attendant on Cleopatra, in Shakespeare's tragedy of "Antony and Cleopatra."

I-re′ne. [Gr. Εἰρήνη.] (*Myth.*) The goddess of peace among the Greeks.

I′ris (9). [Gr. Ἶρις.] (*Gr. & Rom. Myth.*) The daughter of Thaumas and Electra, and sister of the Harpies. She was one of the Oceanides, and messenger of the gods, more particularly of Juno. She is generally regarded as a personification of the rainbow; but the prevalent notion among the ancients seems to have been that the rainbow was only the path on which Iris travelled between heaven and earth, and that it therefore appeared whenever the goddess wanted it, and vanished when it was no longer needed.

Irish Agitator. An epithet applied to Daniel O'Connell (1775–1847), the leader of the political movements in Ireland for the emancipation of Roman Catholics from civil disabilities, and for the repeal of the Act of Union between Great Britain and Ireland, which was passed on the 2d of July, 1800.

Irish Night. (*Eng. Hist.*) A night of agitation and terror in London, after the flight of James II., occasioned by an unfounded report that the Irish Catholics of Feversham's army had been let loose to murder the Protestant population, men, women, and children.

Iroldo (e-rŏl′do). A character in Bojardo's "Orlando Innamorato," distinguished for his friendship for Prasildo. See PRASILDO.

Iron Age. [Lat. *Ferrea ætas.*] (*Gr. & Rom. Myth.*) The last of the four ages into which the ancients divided the history of the human race; the age of Pluto, characterised by the prevalence of crime, fraud, cunning, and avarice, and the absence of honour, truth, justice, and piety.

Iron Arm. [Fr. *Bras de Fer.*] A surname or sobriquet given to François de Lanoue (1531–1591), a famous Calvinistic captain, who died at the siege of Lamballe, in the service of Henry IV.

Iron City. A name popularly given, in the United States, to Pittsburg, Pennsylvania, a city distinguished for its numerous and immense iron manufactures.

Iron Duke. A familiar title given to the Duke of Wellington. According to his biographer, the Rev. George Robert Gleig, this sobriquet arose out of the building of an iron steamboat, which plied between Liverpool and Dublin, and which its owners called the " Duke of Wellington." The term " Iron Duke " was first applied to the vessel; and by and by, rather in jest than in earnest, it was transferred to the Duke himself. It had no reference whatever, at the outset, to any peculiarities, or assumed peculiarities, in his disposition; though, from the popular belief that he never entertained a single generous feeling toward the masses, it is sometimes understood as a figurative allusion to his supposed hostility to the interests of the lower orders.

Iron Hand. A surname of Gottfried, or Goetz, von Berlichingen, a famous predatory burgrave of the sixteenth century, who, at the siege of Landshut, lost his right hand, which was replaced by one of iron, yet shown at Jaxthausen. Goethe has made him the subject of an historic drama.

Iron Mask. See MASK, IRON.

Ironside. 1. An epithet conferred upon Edmund II. (989–1016), king of the Anglo-Saxons, on account either of his great strength, or else of the armour which he wore. [Written also I r o n s i d e s.]
2. (Nes′tŏr.) A name under which Sir Richard Steele, assuming the character of an astrologer, set up the " Guardian."
3. (Sir.) A knight of the Round Table.

Ironsides. 1. A name given to the English soldiers who served under Cromwell at Marston Moor, on account of the great victory they there gained over the royalist forces, a victory which gave them a world-wide renown for invincible courage and determination.
2. An appellation popularly conferred upon the United States frigate "Constitution." See OLD IRONSIDES.

Irrefragable Doctor. [Lat. *Doctor Irrefragabilis.*] An honorary title bestowed upon Alexander Hales, an English friar of the thirteenth century, distinguished as a scholastic divine and philosopher.

Isabella. 1. Sister to Claudio, in Shakespeare's "Measure for Measure," and the heroine of the drama. See ANGELO.

2. The lady-love of Zerbino, in Ariosto's poem of "Orlando Furioso."

Isaie le Triste. See YSAIE LE TRISTE.

Isengrin (e'zen-grên'). The name of the wolf in the ancient and famous animal-epos of Germany, "Reinhard, or Reinecke, Fuchs." See RENARD.

I'sis. [Gr. *Ἶσις.] (*Myth.*) An Egyptian divinity, regarded as the goddess of the moon, and the queen of heaven. She was the mother of Horus, and the wife of Osiris. She was sometimes represented with the head veiled, a symbol of mystery. Her worship spread from Egypt to Greece, Rome, and other parts of ancient Europe. The Greeks identified her with *Io*. See IO, OSIRIS.

The drift of the maker is dark, an *Isis* hid by the veil. *Tennyson.*

Island, The Ringing. See RINGING ISLAND.

Island City. A popular synonym for Montreal, the largest city of British America, built on an island of the same name.

Island of Lanterns. [Fr. *L' Île des Lanternes.*] In the celebrated satire of Rabelais, an imaginary country inhabited by false pretenders to knowledge, called *Lanternois*. The name was probably suggested by the "City of Lanterns," in the Greek romance of Lucian. See CITY OF LANTERNS.

Island of St. Bran'dăn. A marvellous flying island, the subject of an old and widely spread legend of the Middle Ages, which exercised an influence on geographical science down to a late period. It is represented as about ninety leagues in length, lying west of the Canaries. This island appears on most of the maps of the time of Columbus, and is laid down in a French geographical chart of as late a date as 1755, in which it is placed 5° W. of the island of Ferro, in lat. 29° N. The name *St. Brandan*, or *Borandan*, given to this imaginary island, is said to be derived from an Irish abbot who flourished in the sixth century, and concerning whose voyage in search of the Islands of Paradise many legends are related. Many expeditions were sent forth in quest of this mysterious island, the last being from Spain in 1721; but it always eluded the search, though it was sometimes seen by accident. A king of Portugal is said to have made a conditional cession of it to another person, "when it should be found." The Spaniards believe this lost island to have been the retreat of their King Rodrigo; the Portuguese assign it to their Don Sebastian. "Its reality," says Irving, "was for a long time a matter of firm belief. The public, after trying all kinds of sophistry, took refuge in the supernatural to defend their favourite chimera. They maintained that it was rendered inaccessible to mortals by divine Providence, or by diabolical magic. Poetry, it is said, owes to this popular belief one of its beautiful fictions; and the garden of Armida, where Rinaldo was detained enchanted, and which Tasso places in one of the Canary Isles, has been identified with the imaginary San Borandan." The origin of this illusion has been ascribed to certain atmospherical deceptions, like that of the Fata Morgana.

Island of the Seven Cities. An imaginary island, the subject of one of the popular traditions concerning the ocean, which were current in the time of Columbus. It is represented as abounding in gold, with magnificent houses and temples, and high towers that shone at a distance. The legend relates, that, at the time of the conquest of Spain and Portugal by the Moors, when the inhabitants fled in every direction to escape from slavery, seven bishops, followed by a great number of people, took shipping, and abandoned themselves to their fate upon the high seas. After tossing about for a time, they landed upon an unknown island in the midst of the ocean. Here the bishops burned the ships to prevent the desertion of their followers, and founded seven cities. This mysterious island is said to have been visited at different times by navigators, who, however, were never permitted to return.

Islands of the Blest. [Gr. Τῶν Μακάρων Νῆσοι, Lat. *Fortunatæ Insulæ*.] (*Gr. & Rom. Myth.*) Imaginary islands in the west, abounding with the choicest products of nature. They were supposed to be situated on the confines of the earth, in an ocean warmed by the rays of the near setting sun. Hither the favourites of the gods were conveyed without dying, and dwelt in never ending joy. The name first occurs in Hesiod's "Works and Days." Herodotus applies the name to an oasis in the desert of Africa. It is also of common occurrence in modern literature.

Their place of birth alone is mute
To sounds that echo further west
Than your sires' *Islands of the Blest.*
Byron.

Isle of Saints, or **Island of Saints.** [Lat. *Insula Sanctorum.*] A name by which Ireland was designated in the Middle Ages, on account of the rapid progress which Christianity made in that country, and the number of learned ecclesiastics which it furnished. See HOLY ISLAND, 1.

"My lord," uttered with a vernacular richness of intonation, gave him an assurance that we were from "the *Island of Saints,* and on the right road to heaven." *Sheil.*

Ismeno (ĕz-mä'no). The name of a sorcerer in Tasso's "Jerusalem Delivered."

Isólde. The wife of King Mark of Cornwall, and the mistress of her nephew, Sir Tristram, of whom she became passionately enamoured from having drunk a philter by mistake. Their illicit love is celebrated in many an ancient romance, and became proverbial during the Middle Ages. References to it are innumerable. She is often called *Isolde the Fair,* to distinguish her from *Isolde of the White Hands,* a Breton princess whom Tristram married after he undertook the conquest of the Holy Grail. See TRISTRAM, SIR. [Written also I s o u l t, I s o u d e, Y s e u l t, Y s o l d e, Y s o l t, Y s o u d e, and, very erroneously, Y s o n d e.]

No art the poison might withstand;
No medicine could be found
Till lovely *Isolde's* lily hand
Had probed the rankling wound.
Sir W. Scott.

Is'râ-feel. (*Mohammedan Myth.*) The name of the angel whose office it will be to sound the trumpet at the resurrection. He is said to have the most melodious voice of any of God's creatures. [Written also I s r a f i l.]

Is'um-brás, Sir. The hero of an old romance of chivalry, which celebrates the painful labours and misfortunes visited upon him as a punishment for his pride and presumption, and the happiness and blessings with which his penitence was finally rewarded.

Italian Molière (mo'lē-ĕr'). A title given to Carlo Goldoni (1707-1793), a distinguished Italian dramatist.

Italian Pin'dar. A name given to Gabriello Chiabrera (1552-1637), a celebrated Italian lyric poet, and one of the best modern imitators of Pindar.

Ĭ-thu'ri-el (6). [Heb., the discovery of God.] In Milton's "Paradise Lost," an angel commissioned by Gabriel to search through Paradise, in company with Zephon, to find Satan, who had eluded the vigilance of the angelic guard, and effected an entrance into the garden.

Him . . . they found,
Squat like a toad, close at the ear of Eve,
Assaying by his devilish art to reach
The organs of her fancy, and with them forge
Illusions as he list, phantasms and dreams;
Or if, inspiring venom, he might taint
The animal spirits ; . . . thence raise,
At least, distempered, discontented thoughts,
Vain hopes, vain aims, inordinate desires,
Blown up with high conceits engendering pride.
Him thus intent, *Ithuriel* with his spear
Touched lightly; for no falsehood can endure
Touch of celestial temper, but returns,
Of force, to its own likeness; up he starts,
Discovered and surprised.
Par. Lost, Bk. IV.

Such spirits have nothing to do with the detecting spear of *Ithuriel.* *Macaulay.*

He who argues against it [Christianity], or for it, in this manner, may be regarded as mistaking its nature; the *Ithuriel,* though to our eyes he wears a body and the fashion of armour, cannot be wounded by material aid.
Carlyle.

I'van-hŏe. The hero of Sir Walter Scott's novel of the same name. He figures as Cedric of Rotherwood's disinherited son, the favourite of King Richard I., and the lover of the Lady Rowena, whom, in the end, he marries.

Ivanovitch, Ivan (e-vân' e-vân'o-vitch). An imaginary personage, who is the embodiment of the peculiarities of the Russian people, in the same way as John Bull represents the English, and Jean Crapaud the French character. He is described as a lazy, good-natured person.

Ivory Gate. According to Virgil, a gate of sleep in the under-world, wrought of shining white ivory, through which the infernal gods send up false dreams to earth. See HORN GATE.

Ix-i'ŏn. [Gr. 'Ιξίων.] (*Gr. & Rom. Myth.*) A king of the Lapithæ in Thessaly, and father of the Centaurs. For his presumptuous impiety he was sent to hell, and there bound to a perpetually revolving fiery wheel.

☞ For the "Key to the Scheme of Pronunciation," with the accompanying Explanations,

J.

Jack. [An Anglicised form of the Fr. *Jacques* (from Lat. *Jacobus*, James), the commonest Christian name in France, and hence a contemptuous expression for a peasant or common man; introduced in the same sense into England, where it got into use as a diminutive or nickname of *John*, the commonest of all English Christian names.] A general term of ridicule or contempt for a saucy or a paltry fellow, or for one who puts himself forward in some office or employment; hence, any mechanical contrivance that supplies the place of an attendant; as, a boot-*jack*. Taylor, the "Water-Poet," in his "Jack-a-lent," thus enumerates some of the persons and things to which the name has been applied:—

"Of *Jack-an-apes* I list not to indite,
Nor of *Jack Daw* my goose's quill shall write:
Of *Jack of Newbury* I will not repeat,
Nor of *Jack-of-both-sides*, nor of *Skip-Jack* create.
To praise the turnspit *Jack* my Muse is mum,
Nor of the entertainment of *Jack Drum*
I'll not rehearse; nor of *Jack Dog*, *Jack Date*,
Jack Fool, or *Jack-a-dandy*, I relate;
Nor of *Black-jack* at garth buttery bars,
Whose liquor oftentimes breeds household wars;
Nor *Jack of Dover*, that Grand-Jury *Jack*,
Nor *Jack Sauce*, the worst knave amongst the pack."

[*Jack-a-lent*, a stuffed puppet, dressed in rags, formerly thrown at in Lent. *Jack-an-apes*, or *Jack-a-napes*, a monkey, a buffoon, a fop. *Jack Daw*, the daw, a common English bird. *Jack of Newbury*. See below. *Jack-of-both-sides*, one who is or tries to be neutral. *Skip-Jack*, an upstart. *Jack Drum*. See DAUM, JOHN. *Jack Fool*, a foolish person. See FOOL, TOM. *Juck-a-dandy*, a fop, a coxcomb. *Black-jack*, a leathern jug for household service. *Jack of Dover*, a fish, the sole. *Jack Sauce*, a saucy fellow.]

Jack, Colonel. The hero of De Foe's novel entitled "The History of the Most Remarkable Life and Extraordinary Adventures of the truly Hon. Colonel Jacque, vulgarly called Colonel Jack;" a thief, whose portrait is drawn with great power. He goes to Virginia, and passes through all the gradations of colonial life, from the state of a servant to that of an owner of slaves and plantations.

Jack, Sixteen-string. See SIXTEEN-STRING JACK.

Jack and Gill. Characters in an ancient and popular nursery song. [Written also J a c k a n d J i l l.]

☞ "*Julienne* was in vogue among the Norman families, and it long prevailed in England as *Julyan*; and, indeed, it became so common as *Gillian*, that *Jill* [or *Gill*] was the regular companion of Jack, as still appears in nursery rhyme, though now this good old form has entirely disappeared, except in the occasional un-English form of *Juliana*." *Yonge.*

How gallantly he extended, not his arm, in our modern *Jack-and-Jill* sort of fashion, but his right hand, to my mother.
Sir E. Bulwer Lytton.

Jack and the Bean-stalk. A legend of the nursery, which, like Jack the Giant-killer, is of ancient, and probably of Teutonic, origin. A boy was sent by his mother to sell a cow, and met with a butcher, to whom he parted with her for a few coloured beans. His mother was very angry, and threw them away. One of them fell into the garden, and grew so rapidly in one night, that by morning the top reached the heavens. Jack ascended the vine, and came to an extensive country. After divers adventures, a fairy met him, and directed him to the house of a giant, from whom he acquired great wealth. He descended the vine, and as the giant attempted to follow him, he seized his hatchet and cut away the vine, when the giant fell and was killed. Jack and his mother lived afterward in comfort.

Jack-in-the-Green. A character — a puppet — in the May-day games of England. Dr. Owen Pugh says that Jack-in-the-Green, on May-day, was once a pageant representing Melva, or Melvas, king of the country now called Somersetshire, disguised in green boughs, as he lay in ambush to steal King Arthur's wife, as she went out hunting.

<small>Yesterday, being May-day, the more secluded parts of the metropolis were visited by *Jack-in-the-Green*, and the usual group of grotesque attendants. *London Times*, 1844.</small>

Jack of Newbury. A title given to John Winchcomb, the greatest clothier in England, in the time of Henry VIII. He kept one hundred looms in his own house at Newbury, and armed and clothed at his own expense one hundred of his men, to march in the expedition against the Scots at Flodden Field.

Jack Pudding. See HANSWURST.

Jackson, Stonewall. See STONEWALL JACKSON.

Jack the Giant-killer. The name of a famous hero in the literature of the nursery, the subject of one of the Teutonic or Indo-European legends, which have become nationalised in England. Jack was "a valiant Cornishman." His first exploit was the killing of a huge giant named Cormoran, which he accomplished, when a mere child, by artfully contriving to make him fall into a deep pit, and then knocking him on the head with a pick-axe. He afterward destroyed a great many Welsh monsters of the same sort, being greatly aided in his task by a coat of invisibility, a cap of knowledge, an irresistible sword, and shoes of incredible swiftness,— treasures which he tricked a foolish giant into giving him. For his invaluable services in ridding the country of such undesirable inhabitants, he was made a knight of Arthur's Round Table, married to a duke's daughter, and presented with a large estate.

<small>☞ "Before we dismiss the giganticide, we must remark that most of his giants rest upon good romance authority; or, to speak more correctly, Jack's history is a popular and degraded version of the traditions upon which our earliest romances are founded." *Qu. Rev.*
"Not only single words come to attest our common ancestry; but many a nursery legend or terse fable crops out in one country after another, either in lofty mythology or homely household tale. For instance, the Persian trick of Ameen and the Ghoul recurs in the Scandinavian visit of Thor to Loki, which has come down to Germany in 'The Brave Little Tailor,' and to us in 'Jack the Giant-killer.'" *Yonge.*
"Our 'Jack the Giant-killer' . . . is clearly the last modern transmutation of the old British legend, told in Geoffrey of Monmouth, of Corineus the Trojan, the companion of the Trojan Brutus when he first settles in Britain; which Corineus, being a very strong man, and particularly good-humoured, is satisfied with being king of Cornwall, and killing out the aboriginal giants there, leaving to Brutus all the rest of the island, and only stipulating, that, whenever there is a peculiarly difficult giant in any part of Brutus's dominions, he shall be sent for to finish the fellow." *Masson.*

While he [Junius] walks, like *Jack the Giant-killer*, in a coat of darkness, he may do much mischief with little strength. *Johnson.*

They say she [Meg Merrilies] . . . can gang any gate she likes, like *Jack the Giant-killer* in the ballant, with his coat o' darkness and his shoon o' swiftness. *Sir W. Scott.*

He made up for this turnspit construction by striding to such an extent, that you would have sworn he had on the seven-leagued boots of *Jack the Giant-killer*; and so high did he tread on parade, that his soldiers were sometimes alarmed lest he should trample himself under foot. *W. Irving.*</small>

Jack-with-the-Lantern. In the superstition of former times, an evil spirit who delighted in leading benighted and unwary travellers astray from their path, by assuming the appearance of a light like that of a candle. This superstition, as is well known, had its origin in the *ignis-fatuus*, a luminous meteor seen in summer nights over morasses, graveyards, and other spots where there is a great accumulation of animal or vegetable substances, and caused, as is supposed, by the spontaneous ignition of a gaseous compound of phosphorus and hydrogen, resulting from their decomposition. [Written also **Jack o' Lantern.**]

Jacob's Ladder. A ladder seen in a vision by Jacob, the Jewish patriarch. "And he dreamed, and behold, a ladder set upon the earth, and the top of it reached to heaven: and behold, the angels of God ascending and descending on it." (*Gen.* xxviii. 12.)

<small>All of air they were, all soul and form, so lovely, like mysterious priestesses, in whose hand was the invisible *Jacob's Ladder*, whereby man might mount into very heaven. *Carlyle.*</small>

Jaf'fiêr. A prominent character in Otway's "Venice Preserved." He joins with Pierre and others in a conspiracy against the Venetian senate, but communicates the secret to his wife, Belvidera, and she, anxious to save the life of her father, a senator, prevails on Jaffier to disclose the plot. This he does upon the solemn assurance of pardon for himself and friends; but, on discovering the perfidy of the senate, who condemn the conspirators to death, he stabs his friend Pierre, to prevent his being broken on the wheel, and then stabs himself.

"I have it!" said Bunce, "I have it!" and on he went in the vein of *Jaffier*.
Sir W. Scott.

Janot, *or* **Jeannot** (zhă'no'). A French proper name, the diminutive of *Jean* (John), used proverbially to designate a simpleton, a quiddler, one who exercises a silly ingenuity.

Without being a *Janot*, who has not sometimes, in conversation, committed a Janotism?
Ourry, Trans.

January Searle. See SEARLE, JANUARY.

Jā'nus. (*Rom. Myth.*) A very ancient Italian deity who presided over the beginning of the year, and of each month and day, and over the commencement of all enterprises. He was originally worshipped as the sun-god. He was represented with two faces, one on the front, the other on the back of his head, one youthful, and the other aged. A gateway — often erroneously called a temple — which stood close by the Forum in Rome, and had two doors opposite to each other, which, in time of war, were always open, and in time of peace were closed, was dedicated to Janus by Numa. The myth makes him to have been the most ancient king of Latium or Etruria, where he hospitably received Saturn when expelled from Crete by Jupiter.

Jaques (jă'kwes *or* jāks; *Fr. pron.* zhăk). A lord attending upon the exiled duke, in Shakespeare's "As You Like It."

☞ "Jaques is the only purely contemplative character in Shakespeare. He thinks, and does — nothing. His whole occupation is to amuse his mind; and he is totally regardless of his body and his fortunes. He is the prince of philosophical idlers; his only passion is thought; he sets no value on any thing but as it serves as food for reflection. He can 'suck melancholy out of a song, as a weasel sucks eggs;' the motley fool, 'who morals on the time,' is the greatest prize he meets with in the forest. He resents Orlando's passion for Rosalind as some disparagement of his own passion for abstract truth; and leaves the duke, as soon as he is restored to his sovereignty, to seek his brother, who has quitted it and turned hermit." *Hazlitt.* "Jaques is a morose, cynical, querulous old fellow, who has been a bad young one. He does not have sad moments, but 'sullen fits,' as the duke says. His melancholy is morbid, and is but the fruit of that utter loss of mental tone which results from years of riot and debauchery. He has not a tender spot in his heart. There is not a gentle act attributed to him, or a generous sentiment, or a kind word put into his mouth by Shakespeare."
R. G. White.

Indeed, my lord,
The melancholy *Jaques* grieves at that.
Shak.

That motley clown in Arden wood,
Whom humourous *Jaques* with envy viewed,
Not even that clown could amplify
On this trite text so long as I. *Sir W. Scott.*

The forest-walks of Arden's fair domain,
Where *Jaques* fed his solitary vein,
No pencil's aid as yet had dared supply,
Seen only by the intellectual eye.
Charles Lamb.

Jarn'dўçe. A prominent figure in Dickens's "Bleak House," distinguished for his philanthropy, easy good-nature, and good sense, and for always saying, "The wind is in the east," when any thing went wrong with him. The famous suit of "Jarndyce *vs.* Jarndyce," in this novel, is a satire upon the Court of Chancery.

Jar'vĭe, Baillie Nic'ŏl. A prominent and admirable character in Sir Walter Scott's novel of "Rob Roy." He is a magistrate of Glasgow, and a kinsman of Rob Roy.

☞ "Nothing can promise less originality and interest than the portrait of a conceited, petulant, purse-proud tradesman, full of his own and his father's local dignity and importance, and of mercantile and Presbyterian formalities, totally without tact or discretion, who does nothing in the story but give bail,

and for the Remarks and Rules to which the numbers after certain words refer, see pp. xiv-xxxii.

take a journey, and marry his maid. But the courage, the generosity, and the frank naïveté and warm-heartedness, which are united to these unpromising ingredients, and above all, perhaps, the 'Hieland blude of him that warms at thae daft tales o' venturesome deeds and escapes, tho' they are all sinfu' vanities,' and makes him affirm before the council that Rob Roy, 'set apart what he had done again the law o' the country, and the hership o' the Lennox [i. e. the laying waste and plundering a whole county], and the misfortune o' some folk losing life by him, was an honester man than stude on any o' their hauks,' make him both original and interesting." *Senior.*

Jā'son (-sn). [Gr. 'Ιάσων.] (*Gr. & Rom. Myth.*) A famous Grecian hero, king of Thessaly, leader of the Argonautic expedition, and a sharer in the Calydonian boar-hunt. He married Medea, and afterward Creusa.

Javert (zhȧ'věȓ', 64). A character in Victor Hugo's "Les Misérables;" an impersonation of the inexorableness of law.

Jēameṣ. An old English form of *James*, so pronounced, and often so spelt, in the best society, till the end of the last century, when it became confined to the lower classes. Recently, owing to the popularity of Thackeray's "Jeames's Diary," it has acquired a proverbial currency as a designation of a footman, or of a flunky. It has also been applied to the London "Morning Post," the organ of the "haristocracy."

A poor clergyman, or a poor military man, may have no more than three hundred a year; but I heartily venerate his endeavours to preserve his girls from the society of the servants' hall, and the delicate attention of *Jeames*.
A. K. H. Boyd.

Jean d'Épée (zhŏⁿ dā'pā' 31, 62). [Fr., John with the sword.] A symbolical name given to Bonaparte by his partisans in France who conspired to effect his restoration to power after the allied sovereigns had banished him to Elba, in 1814.

Jean Jacques (zhŏⁿ zhȧk, 30, 62). Christian names of Rousseau (1712-1778), the distinguished French philosopher, by which alone he is often designated by English writers, particularly those of the last century.

Years ago, at Venice, poor *Jean Jacques* was Legation Secretary to him [Couut de Herni*], as some readers may remember. *Carlyle.*
That is almost the only maxim of *Jean Jacques* to which I can cheerfully subscribe!
Sir E. Bulwer Lytton.

Jeanjean (zhŏⁿ'zhŏⁿ', 62). A popular name in France for a conscript.

Jēan Pȧul (*or* zhŏng pȯwl). The name under which the eminent German author, Jean Paul Friedrich Richter (1763-1825), wrote, and by which he is most familiarly known.

Jef'frey's Campaign. A name given by King James II. to the judicial expedition through the west of England, headed by Lord Chief Justice Jeffreys, in 1685. See BLOODY ASSIZES.

Jel'lȳ-bȳ, Mrs. A character in Dickens's novel of "Bleak House;" a type of sham philanthropy.

Jenk'ins. A cant name for any snobbish penny-a-liner. It was first given, in "Punch," to a writer for the London "Morning Post," — said to have been originally a footman, — whose descriptions of persons and events in fashionable and aristocratic society betrayed the ingrained servility, priggishness, and vulgarity of his character.

Jenk'ins, Win'i-fred. The name of Miss Tabitha Bramble's maid, in Smollett's "Expedition of Humphry Clinker."

Jenk'in-son, Ephraim (-sn). A swindling rascal in Goldsmith's "Vicar of Wakefield," who wins the confidence of Dr. Primrose by his venerable appearance, his great apparent devoutness, his learned talk about "cosmogony," and his loudly professed admiration of the good Doctor's writings on the subject of monogamy. See PRIMROSE, THE REV. DOCTOR.

Je-ron'i-mo, *or* Hī'ĕr-on'ȳ-mo. The principal character in an old play by Thomas Kyd, entitled "The Spanish Tragedy;" — used in the phrase, "Go by, Jeroniṁo," an expression made almost proverbial by the ridicule of contemporary writers. In the original, these words are spoken by Hieronymo, or Jeronimo, to himself, on finding his application to the king improper at the moment. Hence, probably, the word *go-by*, signifying a putting or thrusting aside without notice.

Jes'sā-mȳ Bride. A by-name given to Miss Mary Horneck, afterward Mrs. Gwyn. She was a contemporary and friend of Goldsmith, who is supposed to have been in love with her.

Jes'sĭ-cā. The beautiful daughter of Shylock, in Shakespeare's "Merchant of Venice." She is beloved by Lorenzo.

☞ "Jessica, though properly kept subordinate, is certainly —
'A most beautiful pagan, a most sweet Jew.'
She cannot be called a sketch; or, if a sketch, she is like one of those dashed off in glowing colours from the rainbow palette of a Rubens; she has a rich tint of Orientalism shed over her, worthy of her Eastern origin." *Mrs. Jameson.*

Jew, The Wandering. [Lat. *Judæus non Mortalis*, the undying Jew; Ger. *Der Ewiger Jude*, Fr. *Le Juif Errant*.] An imaginary personage, who owes his existence to a legend connected with the history of Christ's passion. As the Saviour was on the way to the place of execution, overcome with the weight of the cross, he wished to rest on a stone before the house of a Jew, whom the story calls *Ahasuerus*, who drove him away with curses. Jesus calmly replied, "Thou shalt wander on the earth till I return." The astonished Jew did not come to himself till the crowd had passed, and the streets were empty. Driven by fear and remorse, he has since wandered, according to the command of the Lord, from place to place, and has never yet been able to find a grave. According to another account, he was Pontius Pilate's porter, and his original name was *Cartaphilus*. Soon after the Saviour's crucifixion, he became converted, and took the name of *Joseph*. At the end of every hundred years, he falls into a fit or trance, upon which, when he recovers, he returns to the same state of youth he was in when our Saviour suffered, being about thirty years of age. He remembers all the circumstances of the death and resurrection of Christ; the saints that arose with him; the composing of the Apostles' Creed; and, the preaching and dispersions of the apostles themselves. In the fourteenth century, he was called *Isaac Lakedion*, or *Laquedem*; but the chronicles of that time make no mention of these periodical alternations of youth and age, though they still attribute to him perpetual life.

☞ Roger of Wendover, a monk of St. Albans (d. 1237), and Matthew Paris (d. 1259), a Benedictine monk of the Congregation of Clugny, and likewise of the monastery of St. Albans, give us the oldest traditions of the Wandering Jew. According to Menzel ("History of German Poetry"), the whole tradition is but an allegory, the Wandering Jew symbolising heathenism. M. Lacroix suggests that it represents the Hebrew race dispersed and wandering throughout the earth, but not destroyed. In Germany, the tradition of the Wandering Jew became connected with John Bultadœus, a real person. The story of this Jew was printed in 1602, and frequently afterward. He is said to have been seen at Antwerp in the thirteenth century, again in the fifteenth, and a third time in the sixteenth, with every appearance of age and decrepitude. His last recorded apparition was at Brussels, in April, 1774. Southey, in his poem of "The Curse of Kehama," and Croly, in his romance entitled "Salathiel," trace the course of the Wandering Jew, but in violation of the whole legend; and Eugene Sue adopted the name as the title of one of his most popular and most immoral novels ("Le Juif Errant"), though the Jew scarcely figures at all in the work.

☞ "Ahasuerus is the antitype of Faust. He shuns life, and seeks deliverance from its pains, while Faust seeks to eternise the moment." *Grässe, Trans.*

Coppet, ... in short, trudged and hurried hither and thither, inconstant as an *ignisfatuus*, and restless as the *Wandering Jew*. *Carlyle.*

Jewish Plā'to. A title bestowed upon Philo Judæus, the Alexandrian Jew and Platonist, who flourished in the first century of the Christian era.

Jewkes, Mrs. (jūks). A hateful character in Richardson's "Pamela."

Jez'e-bel. The wicked wife of Ahab, an infamous king of Israel. How she came to her end may be seen in

JIN 192 JOH

2 *Kings* ix. 30–37. The name is proverbially used to designate a showily dressed woman of frail morals or suspected respectability. It has been applied in this sense from the time of the Puritans.

O Philosophe-Sentimentalism, what hast thou to do with peace when thy mother's name is *Jezebel!* *Carlyle.*

Jingle, Mr. Alfred. An impudent, swindling stroller, in Dickens's "Pickwick Papers." He is represented as never speaking a connected sentence, but stringing together mere disjointed phrases, generally without verbs.

Jinnestan. See DJINNESTAN.

J. J. Initials used, particularly by writers of the last century, to designate Rousseau, the celebrated author of the "Confessions," whose Christian names were Jean Jacques, or John James.

Jōan. The name sometimes given to the wife of Punch. She is commonly called *Judy.*

I confess, that, were 'it safe to cherish such dreams at all, I should more enjoy the thought of remaining behind the curtain unseen, like the ingenious manager of Punch and his wife Joan, and enjoying the astonishment and conjectures of my audience. *Sir W. Scott.*

Jōan, Pope. A supposed individual of the female sex, who is placed by several chroniclers in the series of popes between Leo IV. and Benedict III., about 853–855, under the name of *John.* The subject of this scandalous story is said to have been a young woman of English parentage, educated at Cologne, who left her home in man's disguise, with her lover, a very learned man, and went to Athens, where she made great progress in profane law; afterward she went to Rome, where she became equally proficient in sacred learning, for which her reputation became so great, that, at the death of Leo, she was unanimously elected as his successor, under the general belief of her male sex. She, however, became pregnant, and one day, as she was proceeding to the Lateran Basilica, she was seized with the pains of child-labour, on the road between the Colosseum and the church of St. Clement; and there she died, and was buried without any honours, after a pontificate of two years, five months, and four days.

☞ The first to mention this delectable piece of scandal was Marianus Scotus, a monk of the abbey of Fulda, who died at Mainz in 1086; but the authenticity of the MS. attributed to him is very doubtful. The story is given more circumstantially by Martinus Polonus, a Cistercian monk, and confessor to Gregory X. It is also mentioned by Stephen de Bourbon, who wrote about 1225. "Until the Reformation," says Gibbon, "the tale was repeated and believed without offence." The learned Calvinist divine, David Blondel, demonstrated its historical groundlessness; yet attempts have occasionally been made, since his time, to maintain the truth of the tradition. Panvinius and other writers find the origin of the fable in the effeminacy or licentiousness of Pope John XII., who was killed in 964, while prosecuting an unlawful intrigue. There is an ancient miracleplay upon this subject, in German, entitled "The Canonisation of Pope Joan, 1480," which was widely diffused, and did much to shake the popular reverence for the Papal See.

Jo-cas'tă. [Gr. Ἰοκάστη.] (*Gr. & Rom. Myth.*) The mother of Œdipus, whom she married unknowingly, and to whom she bore Eteocles and Polynices.

Jockey of Norfolk. An epithet conferred upon Sir John, son of Sir Robert Howard, a close adherent to the house of York, and remarkable alike for the magnificence of his estate and for the high offices which he held. In 1485, he accompanied his master, Richard III., to the field of Bosworth, and, notwithstanding the celebrated and friendly warning,

"*Jockey of Norfolk,* be not too bold, For Dickon, thy master, is bought and sold,"

which was posted on his tent during the night before the battle, he entered into the fight, and paid the penalty of his fidelity with his life, being one of the slain on that well-contested day.

John. 1. A bastard brother of Don Pedro, in Shakespeare's "Much Ado about Nothing."

2. A Franciscan friar, in Shakespeare's "Romeo and Juliet."

☞ For the "Key to the Scheme of Pronunciation," with the accompanying Explanations,

John, Friar. See FRIAR JOHN.

John-a-dreams. A name apparently coined to suit a dreaming, stupid character, a "dreaming John," as it were.

                        Yet I,
A dull and muddy-mettled rascal, peak,
Like *John-a-dreams*, unpregnant of my cause,
And can say nothing.   *Shak.*

John Company. See COMPANY, JOHN.

Johnny Rebs. A sobriquet given by the soldiers of the United States army, in the time of the late Rebellion, to the "Confederate" soldiers. It is said to have originated in a taunting remark addressed to a rebel picket, to the effect that the Southern States relied on "John Bull" to help them gain their independence, and that the picket himself was no better than a "John Bull;" an accusation which he indignantly denied, saying that he would "as soon be called a 'nigger' as a 'Johnny Bull.'"

Jonathan. A son of Saul, king of Israel, famous for his tender friendship—"passing the love of women"—for David, whom Saul hated and persecuted. "The soul of Jonathan was knit with the soul of David, and Jonathan loved him as his own soul." (1 Sam. xviii. 1.)

Jonathan, Brother. See BROTHER JONATHAN.

Jones, Dā'vy. A familiar name among sailors for Death, formerly for the evil spirit who was supposed to preside over the demons of the sea. He was thought to be in all storms, and was sometimes seen of gigantic height, showing three rows of sharp teeth in his enormous mouth, opening great frightful eyes, and nostrils which emitted blue flames. The ocean is still termed by sailors, *Davy Jones's Locker*.

    The heads of Opposition, the Pitts and others of that country [England] ... wish dear Hanover safe enough (safe in *Davy Jones's* locker, if that would do); but are tired of subsidising, and fighting, and tumulting, all the world over, for that high end. *Carlyle.*

Jones, Tom. The hero of Fielding's novel entitled "The History of Tom Jones, a Foundling;" represented as a model of generosity, openness, and manly spirit, mingled with thoughtless dissipation.

    ☞ " Our immortal Fielding, was of the younger branch of the Earls of Denbigh, who drew their origin from the Counts of Hapsburg. ... Far different have been the fortunes of the English and German divisions of the family. ... The successors of Charles V. may disdain their brethren of England; but the romance of 'Tom Jones,' that exquisite picture of human manners, will outlive the palace of the Escurial and the imperial eagle of Austria."   *Gibbon.*

    ☞ "I cannot say that I think Mr. Jones a virtuous character; I cannot say but that I think Fielding's evident liking and admiration for Mr. Jones show that the great humourist's moral sense was blunted by his life, and that here in art and ethics there is a great error. ... A hero with a flawed reputation, a hero sponging for a guinea, a hero who cannot pay his landlady, and is obliged to let his honour out to hire, is absurd, and his claim to heroic rank untenable."
                              Thackeray.

Jörmungand (yör'mōon-gånd'). [Old Norse, *jörmun*, great, universal, and *gandr*, serpent.] (*Scand. Myth.*) A fearful serpent, the offspring of Loki, hurled down by the gods into the ocean that surrounds Midgard, where he is to remain until Ragnarök. He is represented by the poets as holding his tail in his mouth.

Josse, M. (mos'ē-ō' zhos). A jeweller in Molière's comedy, "L'Amour Médecin," whose advice to a friend who consults him is that of a man who wishes to dispose of his merchandise. The expression, "*Vous êtes orfèvre, M. Josse*," You are a jeweller, Mr. Josse, is proverbially applied, in France, to any one who seeks to advance his own interests at the expense of another.

Jötunheim (yö'tōon-hīm'). (*Scand. Myth.*) The abode of the Jötun, or Giants. See GIANTS, 2.

Jourdain, M. (mos'ē-ō' zhoor'dän', 62). The hero of Molière's comedy, "Le Bourgeois Gentilhomme;" represented as an elderly tradesman, who, having suddenly acquired immense riches, becomes desirous to emulate such as have been educated in the front ranks of society, in those accom-

and for the Remarks and Rules to which the numbers after certain words refer, see pp. xiv–xxxii.

plishments, whether mental or personal, which cannot be gracefully acquired after the early part of life is past.

The Arabs, under great emotional excitement, give their language a recognisable metre, and talk poetry as *M. Jourdain* talked prose [*i. e.*, without knowing it]. *Lewes.*

Journée des Dupes (zhooŕ'nȧ' düp, 34). See DAY OF DUPES.

Jove. See JUPITER.

Joyeuse, La (lȧ zhwŏ'yöz', 43). [Lat. *Gaudiosa.*] The sword of Charlemagne;—so called in the romances of chivalry. It bore the inscription, "*Decem præceptorum custos Carolus.*"

Joyeuse Garde, La (lȧ zhwŏ'yöz' gȧŕd). The residence of the famous Lancelot du Lac, commonly said to have been at Berwick-upon-Tweed. He having successfully defended the honour of Queen Guinever against Sir Mador (who had accused her of poisoning his brother), King Arthur, in gratitude to her champion, gave him the castle which had been the scene of the queen's vindication, and named it "La Joyeuse Garde" in memory of the happy event. See MADOR, SIR. [Written also Joyous Gard and Garde Joyesse.]

The *Garde Joyeuse*, amid the tale,
High reared its glittering head;
And Avalon's enchanted vale
In all its wonders spread. *Sir W. Scott.*

Juan, Don. See DON JUAN.

Judge Lynch. See LYNCH, JUDGE.

Judicious Hooker, The. See HOOKER, THE JUDICIOUS.

Judith. The heroine of a well-known book of the same name in the Apocrypha; a beautiful Jewess of Bethulia, who, to save her native town, undertook to assassinate Holofernes, general of Nebuchadnezzar, putting both her life and her chastity in jeopardy by venturing alone into his tent for this purpose. But she accomplished her object, and escaped with the head of Holofernes to Bethulia; whereupon her fellow-townsmen, inspired with a sudden enthusiasm, rushed out upon the enemy, and completely defeated them. The story, if not altogether fictitious, as many think it to be, is a legend founded upon some fact not mentioned by any historian.

Ju'dy (6). The wife of Punch, in the modern puppet-show of "Punch and Judy." See PUNCH.

Jug'gĕr-naut. [Sansk. *Jagannátha*, lord of the world.] (*Hindu Myth.*) A name of Vishnu, of whom an idol is kept in a temple at Jaggernaut, or Jaggernaut Puri, a town in Orissa. This idol is one of the chief objects of pilgrimage in India, and has acquired great notoriety in consequence of the fanatical practice, formerly very prevalent among Hindu believers, of throwing themselves under the wheels of the lofty chariot — sixty feet high — in which it is carried in procession, in the hope of attaining eternal bliss by such a sacrifice of their lives. [Written also Jaggernaut.]

Julia. The name of a lady beloved by Proteus, in Shakespeare's "Two Gentlemen of Verona."

Julie (zhü'le', 34). The heroine of Molière's comedy, "Monsieur de Pourceaugnac."

Ju'li-et (6). 1. A lady, in Shakespeare's "Measure for Measure," beloved by Claudio.

2. The heroine of Shakespeare's tragedy of "Romeo and Juliet."

☞ "Juliet is a child whose intoxication in loving and being loved whirls away the little reason she may have possessed. It is impossible, in my opinion, to place her among the great female characters of Shakespeare's creation." *Hallam.* "All Shakespeare's women, being essentially women, either love, or have loved, or are capable of loving; but Juliet is love itself. The passion is her state of being, and out of it she has no existence. It is the soul within her soul; the pulse within her heart; the life-blood along her veins, 'blending with every atom of her frame.' The love that is so chaste and dignified in Portia; so airy-delicate and fearless in Miranda; so sweetly confiding in Perdita; so playfully fond in Rosalind; so constant in Imogen; so devoted in Desdemona; so fervent in Helen; so tender in Viola, — is each and all of these in Juliet." *Mrs. Jameson.*

The hyperbole of *Juliet* seemed to be verified with respect to them. "Upon their brows shame was ashamed to sit." *Macaulay.*

☞ For the "Key to the Scheme of Pronunciation," with the accompanying Explanations,

June, Jennie. A pseudonym of Mrs. J. C. Croly, an American authoress of the present day.

Ju'ni-us (*or* jūn'yus, 6). A celebrated pseudonym, under which a series of remarkable political letters were published at intervals from 1769 to 1772, in the "Public Advertiser," then the most popular newspaper in Great Britain.

☞ In these letters, the writer who concealed himself under this signature attacked all the public characters of the day connected with the government, and did not spare even royalty itself. Every effort that could be devised by the government, or prompted by private indignation, was made to discover their author, but in vain. "It is not in the nature of things," he writes to his publisher, "that you or any body else should know me unless I make myself known: all arts, or inquiries, or rewards, would be ineffectual." In another place he remarks, "I am the sole depositary of my secret, and it shall die with me." Many conjectures, however, have been started on the subject of this great puzzle; and Burke, William Gerard Hamilton (commonly called "Single-speech Hamilton"), John Wilkes, Lord Chatham, Mr. Dunning (afterward Lord Ashburton), Lord George Sackville (afterward Lord Germain), Serjeant Adair, the Rev. J. Rosenhagen, John Roberts, Charles Lloyd, Samuel Dyer, General Charles Lee, Hugh Boyd, Colonel Isaac Barre, Sir Philip Francis, and many other eminent names, have all been identified by different inquirers with Junius. The evidence which has been presented to prove that Sir Philip Francis was the author of these memorable philippics, though entirely circumstantial, is very strong. Macaulay thinks it sufficient "to support a verdict in a civil, nay, in a criminal proceeding." For the whole question of the authorship of "Junius," the inquirer will do well to consult the articles that have appeared on this subject in "Notes and Queries," and in the "Athenæum" since 1848. See also JUNIUS in Allibone's "Dictionary of Authors."

This arch intriguer, whom, to use an expression of *Junius*, treachery itself could not trust, was at one moment nearly caught in his own toils. *Sir W. Scott.*

Ju'no. (*Gr. & Rom. Myth.*) The daughter of Saturn and Ops, the sister and wife of Jupiter, the queen of heaven, and the guardian deity of women, especially married women.

He, in delight . . .
Smiled with superior love; as Jupiter
On *Juno* smiles, when he impregns the clouds
That shed May flowers. *Milton.*

Junto. (*Eng. Hist.*) A small knot of distinguished men in the time of William III. (1690), who, under this name, exercised over the Whig body, by their counsel during twenty troubled years, an authority of which, says Macaulay, there is perhaps no parallel in history, ancient or modern. Russell, Lord-keeper Somers, and Charles Montague were prominent members of it.

Ju'pĭ-tĕr. [Lat., a contraction of *Diovis* or *Dies* (= *divum*, heaven) *pater*; *i. e.*, the father of heaven, or heavenly father.] (*Gr. & Rom. Myth.*) A son of Saturn and Ops, brother and husband of Juno, the father and king of gods and men, and the supreme ruler of the universe. As the god of heaven, he had all power of the phenomena of the skies; hence his numerous epithets, such as *Pluvius* (the rain-giver), *Tonans* (the thunderer), *Fulminator* (the lightning-wielder), and the like. [Called also *Jove* and *Zeus*.]

Ju'pĭ-tĕr Car'lyle. A sobriquet given to the Rev. Alexander Carlyle (1722-1805), minister of Inveresk, in Scotland, remarkable for his magnificent head, which was considered worthy of being a model for a Jupiter Tonans.

☞ "The grandest demigod I ever saw was Dr. Carlyle, minister of Musselburgh, commonly called Jupiter Carlyle, for having sat more than once for the king of gods and men to Gavin Hamilton." *Sir W. Scott.*

Ju'pĭ-tĕr Scā'pin. A nickname given by the Abbé de Pradt to Napoleon Bonaparte, on account of the mixture in his character of greatness and goodness with irregularity of imagination and a disposition to artifice which sometimes, as in his Egyptian campaign, led to conduct half impious, half childish. See SCAPIN.

Jŭ-tur'nă. The sister of King Turnus; changed into a fountain of the same name, the waters of which were used in the sacrifices of Vesta. See TURNUS.

K.

Kaf, Mount. See MOUNT CAF.

Kāil'yāl. The heroine of Southey's poem, "The Curse of Kehama."

Kāma (kä'mä), or **Kāmadeva** (kä-mä-dā'vä). (*Hindu Myth.*) The god of love. He is a favourite theme of description and allusion in Sanskrit poetry. His power is so much exalted that even the god Brahma is said to succumb to it. He is described or represented as riding on a parrot or a sparrow, — the symbol of voluptuousness, — and holding in his hands a bow of sugar-cane strung with bees, besides five arrows, each tipped with the bloom of a flower supposed to conquer one of the senses.

Katherine. A lady attending on the princess of France, in Shakespeare's "Love's Labour's Lost."

Kay, Sir. A foster-brother of King Arthur, and a rude and boastful knight of the Round Table. He was the butt of Arthur's court. He is generally made by the romancers the first to attempt an offered adventure, in which he never succeeds, and his failure in which acts as a foil to the brilliant achievement of some more fortunate and deserving, and less boastful, knight. [Written also Q u e u x.]

Ke-hā'mä. A Hindoo rajah, who obtains and sports with supernatural power. His adventures are related in Southey's poem entitled "The Curse of Kehama."

Keith, Wise Wife of. See WISE WIFE OF KEITH.

Kemp'fer-häu'ṣen (-zn). A name assumed by Robert Pearce Gillies, a contributor to "Blackwood's Magazine," and one of the interlocutors in the "Noctes Ambrosianæ" of that work.

Ken'nä-quhair (-kwâr). [Scot., Don't-know-where. Comp. Ger. *Weissnichtwo.*] A Scottish name for any imaginary locality.

It would be a misapprehension to suppose, because Melrose may in general pass for *Kennaquhair*, or because it agrees with some of the "Monastery" in the circumstances of the drawbridge, the mill-dam, and other points of resemblance, that therefore an accurate or perfect local similitude is to be found in all the particulars of the picture. *Sir W. Scott.*

Kent, Holy Maid of, or **Nun of.** See HOLY MAID OF KENT.

Kērr, Ōr'pheûs C. (4). [That is, Office-seeker.] The *nom de plume* of Robert H. Newell, a humourous and popular American writer of the present day.

Ketch, Jack. A hangman or executioner; — so called in England, from one John Ketch, a wretch who lived in the time of James II., and made himself universally odious by the butchery of many brave and noble victims, particularly those sentenced to death by the infamous Jeffreys during the "Bloody Assizes." The name is thought by some to be derived from Richard Jacquett, who held the manor of Tyburn, near London, where criminals were formerly executed.

Ket'tle-drum'mle, Gabriel (-drum'-ml). A covenanting preacher in Sir Walter Scott's "Old Mortality."

Key of Christendom. A name formerly given to Buda, the capital of Hungary, on account of its political importance, its situation on the Danube, and its proximity to the Ottoman empire. It was twice taken by the Turks in the sixteenth century, but was finally wrested from them in the year 1686.

Key of Russia. An appellation popularly given to Smolensk, a fortified city of Russia, on the Dnieper, celebrated for its resistance to the French in 1812.

Key of the Gulf. A name often given to the island of Cuba, from its commanding position at the entrance of the Gulf of Mexico.

Key of the Mediterranean. A name

☞ For the "Key to the Scheme of Pronunciation," with the accompanying Explanations,

frequently given to the fortress of Gibraltar, which to some extent commands the entrance to the Mediterranean Sea from the Atlantic.

Key-stone State. The State of Pennsylvania;—so called from its having been the central State of the Union at the time of the formation of the Constitution. If the names of the

thirteen original States are arranged in the form of an arch, Pennsylvania will occupy the place of the keystone, as in the above cut.

Kil'man-segg, Miss. The heroine of "A Golden Legend" by Thomas Hood; an heiress with great expectations and an artificial leg of solid gold.

King and Cobbler. King Henry VIII. and a certain merry London cobbler, who form the subject of one of the many popular tales in which the sovereign is represented as visiting the humble subject in disguise.

King Ar'thur. A famous king of Britain, supposed to have flourished at the time of the Saxon invasion, and to have died at Glastonbury, in the year 542, from wounds received on the fatal battle-field of Camlan, which is thought to be Camelford, near Tintagel, in Cornwall. His true history has been overlaid with so many absurd fictions by the monkish chroniclers and mediæval poets and romancers, that many have erroneously regarded him as altogether a mythical personage. The usual residence of King Arthur was said to be at Carleon, on the Usk, in Wales, where, with his beautiful wife Guinever, he lived in splendid state, surrounded by hundreds of knights and beautiful ladies, who served as patterns of valour, breeding, and grace to all the world. From his court, knights went out to all countries, to protect women, chastise oppressors, liberate the enchanted, enchain giants and malicious dwarfs, and engage in other chivalrous adventures. A popular traditional belief was long entertained among the Britons that Arthur was not dead, but had been carried off to be healed of his wounds in fairy-land, and that he would reappear to avenge his countrymen, and resume the sovereignty of Britain. This legend was proverbially referred to in the Middle Ages, in speaking of those who indulged vain hopes or cherished absurd expectations. According to another account, Arthur was buried by his sister, the fairy Morgana, in the vale of Avalon, fifteen feet deep, and his tomb bore this inscription,—

"Hic jacet Arthurus, rex quondam, rexque futurus."

Here Arthur lies, king once, and king to be.

Giraldus Cambrensis states, that, in the reign of Henry II., a leaden cross bearing the inscription, " *Hic jacet sepultus inclytus Rex Arthurus in insulâ Avalloniâ,*" Here in the island of Avalon the illustrious King Arthur is buried, was found in the cemetery of Glastonbury Abbey, under a stone seven feet below the surface; and that, nine feet below this, was found an oaken coffin containing bones and dust. See EXCALIBAR, GUINEVER, IGERNA, MODRED, RON, ROUND TABLE, UTHER.

The feats of *Arthur* and his knightly peers;
Of *Arthur*, who, to upper light restored,
   With that terrific sword
Which yet he wields in subterranean war,
Shall lift his country's fame above the polar
   star!   *Wordsworth.*

King Bomba. See BOMBA.

King Cam-by'sēṣ. The hero of "A Lamentable Tragedy" of the same name, by Thomas Preston, an elder contemporary of Shakespeare; a ranting character known to modern readers by Falstaff's allusion to him in Shakespeare's "1 Henry IV." (a. ii., sc. 4),— "Give me a cup of sack to make mine eyes look red; for I must speak in passion, and I will do it in King Cambyses' vein."

"How!" said the smith, in *King Cambyses'*

vein: "are we commanded to stand and deliver on the king's highway?" *Sir W. Scott.*
King Cambyses' vein is, after all, but a worthless one; no vein for a wise man. *Carlyle.*

King Cole. A legendary king of Britain, who reigned, as the old chronicles inform us, in the third century after Christ. According to Robert of Gloucester, he was the father of the celebrated St. Helena, and the successor of Asclepiad. He is further relegated to the realms of fable by the rhyme that sings,—

"Old *King Cole*
Was a merry old soul,
And a merry old soul was he."

See Halliwell's "Nursery Rhymes of England," where much curious information in regard to this celebrated personage may be found.

The venerable *King Cole* would find few subjects here to acknowledge his monarchy of mirth. *E. P. Whipple.*

King Cotton. A popular personification of the great staple production of the Southern States of the American Union. The supremacy of cotton seems to have been first asserted by Mr. James H. Hammond, of South Carolina, in a speech delivered by him in the senate of the United States, on the 4th of March, 1858, from which the following is an extract:—

"No: you dare not make war upon cotton. No power on earth dares to make war upon it. *Cotton is king.* Until lately, the Bank of England was king; but she tried to put her screws, as usual, the fall before the last, on the cotton crop, and was utterly vanquished. The last power has been conquered. Who can doubt, that has looked at recent events, that cotton is supreme?"

When ... the pedigree of *King Cotton* is traced, he is found to be the lineal child of the Tariff; called into being by a specific duty; reared by a tax laid upon the manufacturing industry of the North, to create the culture of the raw material in the South. *E. Everett.*

King Es'tēr-mēre. The hero of an ancient and beautiful legend, which, according to Bishop Percy, would seem to have been written while a great part of Spain was in the hands of the Saracens or Moors, whose empire was not fully extinguished before the year 1491. Sir Walter Scott suggests that an old romance, entitled "How the King of Estmureland married the daughter of the King of Westmureland," may have been the origin of the legend.

King Francooni (fron'ko'ne', 62). A nickname given to Joachim Murat (1767-1815), a famous French general, from a celebrated mountebank of that name, on account of his fantastic love of finery in dress. See HANDSOME SWORDSMAN.

King Goldemar. See GOLDEMAR, KING.

King Günther. See GÜNTHER, KING.

King Horn. The hero and title of a French metrical romance, the work of a poet who calls himself "Mestre Thomas," held by some to be a composition of the latter part of the twelfth century, and the original of the English "Horne Childe," or "Geste of Kyng Horn." By others, the English poem is regarded as the earlier of the two. Bishop Percy ascribed the English "King Horn" to so early a date as "within a century after the Conquest," although, in its present form, it is probably not older than the latter part of the thirteenth century.

King Log. A character in a celebrated fable of Æsop, which relates that the frogs, grown weary of living without government. petitioned Jupiter for a king, and that, in response to their request, he threw down a log among them for their ruler. The fable adds that the frogs, though at first terrified by the sudden appearance of their king, on becoming familiarised to his presence, and learning his true character, experienced a complete change of feeling, their dread being turned into the utmost contempt. They therefore entreated Jupiter for another king; whereupon he sent them a stork,— or, as some say, a serpent,— who immediately began to devour them with unappeasable voracity. Finding that neither their liberty, property, nor lives were secure under such a ruler, they sent yet once more to Jupiter for another king; but instead

---

☞ For the "Key to the Scheme of Pronunciation," with the accompanying Explanations,

of giving them one, he returned this answer merely: "They that will not be contented when they are well, must be patient when things go amiss."

> So, when Jove's block descended from on high, . . .
> Loud thunder to its bottom shook the bog,
> And the hoarse nation croaked, "God save King Log!" *Pope*.

> I do not find throughout the whole of it [Wouter Van Twiller's reign] a single instance of any offender being brought to punishment,—a most indubitable sign of a merciful governor, and a case unparalleled, excepting in the reign of the illustrious *King Log*, from whom, it is hinted, the renowned Van Twiller was a lineal descendant. *W. Irving*.

King-maker, The. A title popularly conferred upon Richard Nevil, Earl of Warwick (d. 1471), who was chiefly instrumental in deposing King Henry VI., and raising the Duke of York to the throne as Edward IV., and who afterward put Edward to flight, and restored the crown to Henry.

> Thus, centuries after feudal times are past, we find warriors still gathering under the old castle-walls, and commanded by a feudal lord, just as in the days of the *King-maker*, who, no doubt, often mustered his retainers in the same market-place where I beheld this modern regiment. *Hawthorne*.

King Nibelung (ne'bă-lŏong). A king of the Nibelungen, a mythical Burgundian tribe, who give name to the great mediæval epic of Germany, the "Nibelungen Lied." He bequeathed to his two sons a hoard or treasure beyond all price or computation, and incapable of diminution, which was won by Siegfried, who made war upon the Nibelungen and conquered them. See SIEGFRIED.

> Here is learning: an irregular treasury, if you will, but inexhaustible as the hoard of *King Nibelung*, which twelve waggons in twelve days, at the rate of three journeys a day, could not carry off. *Carlyle*.

King No'del. The name of the lion in the old German animal-epos entitled "Reinecke Fuchs." See RENARD.

King of Bark. A sobriquet given by the Swedish peasants of his day to Christopher III. (d. 1448), king of Denmark, Sweden, and Norway, on account of their having had to use birch-bark mixed with meal, in a time of scarcity. Michelet says that Christopher himself was obliged to subsist temporarily on the bark of a tree, and derived the nickname from this circumstance.

King of Băth (2). A title bestowed upon Richard Nash (1674–1761), commonly called "Beau Nash," a celebrated master of the ceremonies, or president over amusements, at Bath, England. His reign continued, with undiminished splendour, for fifteen years.

King of Beggars. A sobriquet given to Bampfylde Moore Carew, a noted English vagabond, who died in 1758. An "Apology" for his life was written by Robert Goadby (8vo, London, 1745).

King of Brave Men. [Fr. *Roi des Braves*.] A surname or title given by the troops under his command to Henry IV. (1553–1610), a valiant and successful general.

King of Cots'wŏuld. Grey Brydges, Lord Chandos (d. 1621):— so called from his magnificent style of living, and his numerous attendants. *Cotswould*, or *Cotswold*, is the name of a range of hills in Gloucestershire, in the neighbourhood of Sudley Castle, his lordship's residence.

King of England's Viceroy. A name given by the French, in derision, to Louis XVIII. (1755–1824), on account of his manifestations of gratitude to the government of Great Britain for the assistance he had received from it in recovering the throne of his ancestors.

King of Feuilletons (fō-y''tŏⁿ', 43, 62). [Fr. *Le Roi des Feuilletons*.] A sobriquet given to Jules Gabriel Janin (b. 1804), a clever and extremely popular French journalist, who for many years was connected with the "Journal des Débats" as a writer for the "*feuilleton*," or that part of the paper devoted to light literature and criticism, it being the foot of the page, and separated from the upper portion by a heavy line.

King of Kings. [Gr. Βασιλεὺς Βασιλέων.] 1. A title given to Christ in *Rev.* xvii. 14.

and for the Remarks and Rules to which the numbers after certain words refer, see pp. xiv–xxxii.

2. A title given to Artaxerxes, or Ardishir (d. 241), the first Sassanide king of Persia.

King of Men. 1. A title given by Homer, in the "Iliad," to Agamemnon, king of Mycenæ.

<blockquote>She, too, [Electra,] though a Grecian woman, and the daughter of the *King of Men*, yet wept sometimes, and hid her face in her robe. De Quincey.</blockquote>

2. The same title is given to Jupiter and to Odin. See JUPITER and ODIN.

King of Painters. A title assumed by Parrhasius of Ephesus, a celebrated painter of antiquity, and the contemporary of Zeuxis. According to Plutarch, he was accustomed to dress himself in a purple robe, and wear a crown of gold.

King of Preachers. [Fr. *Le Roi des Prédicateurs.*] An epithet conferred upon Louis Bourdaloue (1632-1704), a noted French preacher.

King of Reptiles. [Fr. *Le Roi des Reptiles.*] A nickname given to Bernard Germain Étienne de la Ville, Count Lacépède (1758-1825), on account of his researches in natural history, and also on account of the ready eloquence with which he justified the arbitrary measures of the Emperor Napoleon. He was the author of a work entitled "*Histoire des Reptiles.*"

King of Tars. The subject and title of an ancient English metrical romance. Tars is Thrace, or, according to some commentators, Tarsus.

King of Terrors. A common personification of death.

<blockquote>His confidence shall be rooted out of his tabernacle, and it shall bring him to the *King of Terrors*. Job xviii. 14.</blockquote>

King of the Border. A name given to Adam Scott of Tushielaw, a noted robber who infested the border territory of England and Scotland.

King of the Courts. [Lat. *Rex Judiciorum.*] An epithet conferred by Cicero upon Quintus Hortensius (d. B. C. 50), a distinguished Roman forensic orator.

King of the French. [Fr. *Le Roi des Français.*] The original style or title of the French kings, which was changed into that of "King of France" by Philip Augustus (1179-1223). On the 16th of Oct., 1789, the National Assembly decreed that the old style should be resumed by Louis XVI. In 1792, the monarchy was abolished, and the republic declared; but in 1814 the house of Bourbon was restored, and both Louis XVIII. and Charles X. assumed the title of "King of France." In 1830, the Revolution of July occurred, and soon after Louis Philippe was called to the throne as constitutional "King of the French," a title which he formally accepted on the 9th of August.

King of the Markets. [Fr. *Le Roi des Halles.*] A sobriquet conferred upon François de Vendôme Beaufort (1616-1669), grandson of Henry IV. He acquired this name from his popularity with the Parisians, his familiar manners, and the pleasure he took in using their language and slang.

King of the Romans. [Lat. *Rex Romanorum.*] A title assumed by the Emperor Henry II., previous to his coronation in 1014. He was the first reigning prince of Italy or Germany who bore it. In 1055, it was conferred upon the eldest son of Henry III., and afterward, for many years, was borne by the heirs of the emperors of Germany. Napoleon I. conferred the title of "King of Rome" upon his son, March 20, 1811.

King of Waters. A name given to the river Amazon.

King of Yvetot (ĕv'to'). [Fr. *Le Roi d' Yvetot.*] A title assumed by the lord of a little principality in France, named Yvetot, some time in the latter part of the eleventh century. In the sixteenth century, the title of king was changed to that of *prince souverain*, and, at a later day, the idea of sovereignty attached to this seigniory disappeared. Béranger has made of the King of Yvetot a model of a potentate, a good little king, not known in history, but happier than any monarch, having taken pleasure for his code. "Under this apologue," says Tissot, "Béranger has satirised the Great Emperor himself." The title is metaphorically applied to a ruler of large pretensions, but insignificant authority.

> There was a *King of Yvetot* once
> But little known in story;
> To bed betimes, and rising late,
> Sound sleeper without glory;
> With cotton night-cap, too, instead
> Of crown, would Jenny deck his head,
>   'T is said.
> Rat tat, rat tat, rat tat, rat tat,
> Oh, what a good little king was that!
>   Rat tat. *Béranger, Trans.*
>
> They would exchange Cæsar for Prusias, and Napoleon for the *King of Yvetot*.
>   *Victor Hugo, Trans.*

King Pe-cheûr'. [Fr. *pécheur*, a sinner.] Uncle of Perceval, and keeper of the sangreal and sacred lance, the guardianship of which was intrusted only to a descendant of Joseph of Arimathea, and on the sole condition of his leading a life of perfect purity in thought, word, and deed. Having one day so far forgotten the obligations of his sacred office as to look with unhallowed eye upon a young female pilgrim, whose robe was accidentally loosened as she knelt before him, his frailty was instantly punished by the sacred lance spontaneously falling upon him, and inflicting a deep and incurable wound.

King Pellenore. See PELLENORE.

King Pétaud (pâ'tō'). A French name occurring only in the phrase, "*Le cour de Roi Pétaud*," The court of King Pétaud. It derives its origin from an assembly of beggars, who formerly held meetings under the presidency of the most adroit, or the poorest, among them, who took the title of King Pétaud (from the Latin *petere*, to beg). The phrase "the court of King Pétaud" denotes a place of confusion, where every thing is out of order, where every body is master.

King Pym. A sobriquet given, on account of his great popularity and his political influence, to John Pym (1584–1643), leader of the English house of commons during the struggle preceding the parliamentary wars. He was originally so called by the royalists, in derision.

King Ryence. See RYENCE, KING.

Kings, The Do-nothing. See FAINÉANTS, LES ROIS.

King Sacripant. See SACRIPANT, KING.

King Serpent. See KING LOG.

> It might have been as well expected that the frogs in the fable would, in case of invasion, have risen in a mass to defend *King Serpent*.
>   *Sir W. Scott.*

Kings of Brentford, The Two. See BRENTFORD, THE TWO KINGS OF.

Kings of Cologne, The Three. See COLOGNE, THE THREE KINGS OF.

King Stork. See KING LOG.

Kiñk'el, Mme. A pseudonym adopted by Miss Elizabeth Sara Sheppard, an English novelist (d. 1862), author of "Charles Auchester," "Counterparts," &c.

Kin'mont Willie. William Armstrong, of Kinmonth, a notorious freebooter of the latter part of the sixteenth century, and the hero of a spirited and famous Scottish ballad.

Kirke, Edmund (4). The literary name of James Roberts Gilmore, an American writer, author of "Among the Pines," "My Southern Friends," &c.

Kirke's Lambs. A name given to the soldiers of Colonel Percy Kirke, an officer in the English army in the time of James II., on account of their ferocity and the barbarities which they committed.

Kiss of Lamourette. See LAMOURETTE'S KISS.

Kitchen Cabinet. A name sportively given, in the United States, to Francis P. Blair and Amos Kendall, by the opponents of President Jackson's administration. Blair was the editor of "The Globe," the organ of the president, and Kendall was one of the principal contributors to the paper. As it was necessary for Jackson to consult frequently with these gentlemen, and as, to avoid observation, they were accustomed, when they called upon him, to go in by a back door, the Whig party styled them, in

---

and for the Remarks and Rules to which the numbers after certain words refer, see pp. xiv–xxxii.

derision, the "Kitchen Cabinet," alleging that it was by their advice that the president removed so many Whigs from office and put Democrats in their place.

Kite, Sergeant. A prominent character in Farquhar's comedy of "The Recruiting Officer." He is an original and admirable picture of low life and humour.

Kite'ly. The name of a rich city merchant, extremely jealous of his wife, in Ben Jonson's comedy of "Every Man in his Humour."

Klabotermann (klä-bo'tĕr-män). A ship kobold of the Baltic, who is sometimes heard, but rarely seen. He helps sailors at their work, and beats them with a rope's-end, when needful. He appears only to doomed vessels, sitting on the bowsprit of a phantom-ship called "Carmilhan," smoking a short pipe, dressed in yellow sailor's clothes, and wearing a night-cap. [Written also Klabautermann.]

Klaus, Peter (klŏẃss). The hero of an old popular tradition of Germany, — the prototype of Rip Van Winkle, — represented as a goat-herd from Sittendorf, who, one day leading his herd to pasture on the Kyffhäuser, was accosted by a young man, who silently beckoned him to follow. The goat-herd, obeying the direction, was led into a deep dell enclosed by craggy precipices, where he found twelve knightly personages playing at skittles, no one of whom uttered a word. Gazing around him, he observed a can of wine which exhaled a delicious fragrance. Drinking from it, he felt inspired with new life, but at length was overpowered by sleep. When he awoke, he found himself again on the plain where his goats were accustomed to rest. But, rubbing his eyes, he could see neither dog nor goats; he was astonished at the height of the grass, and at trees which he had never before observed. Descending the mountain and entering the village, he found, to his consternation, that every thing in the place wore an altered look; most of the people were strangers to him; the few acquaintances he met seemed to have grown suddenly old; and only at last by mutual inquiries was the truth elicited that he had been asleep for twenty years. The story is related in Otmar's "Volcks-Sagen" (Traditions of the Harz), Bremen, 1800. See EPIMENIDES, SLEEPING BEAUTY IN THE WOOD, and WINKLE, RIP VAN.

Your Epimenides, your somnolent *Peter Klaus*, since named "Rip Van Winkle." *Carlyle.*

Knick'er-bock'er, Diē'drich (de'-drik nik'ĕr-bok'ĕr). The imaginary author of a humourous fictitious "History of New York," written by Washington Irving.

Knight of La Mancha. See DON QUIXOTE.

Knight of the Sorrowful Countenance. [Also *Knight of the Woful Countenance*, or *Knight of the Rueful Countenance*.] An appellation given to Don Quixote. See DON QUIXOTE.

Know-nothings. A name popularly given, in the United States, to a short-lived party of "Native Americans," a secret political order, which sprang up in 1853, and into which no members were admitted whose grandfathers were not natives of the country. To all questions regarding the movements of the organisation, the prescribed reply was, "I don't know;" hence the nickname. The cardinal principles of the party were, the repeal or radical modification of the naturalisation laws; the ineligibility to public office of any but native Americans; a pure American common-school system; and opposition to Catholicism. The party split on the slavery question, and became divided into "North Americans" and "South Americans." See HINDOOS and SAM.

Kriemhilt. See CHRIEMHILD.

Kriss Kringle (kring'gl), *or* **Christ Kinkle** (kingk'l). [From Ger. *Kristkindlein*, Christ-child.] A term somewhat vaguely used in the United States, — where German and Dutch customs prevail, — both for Christ in his boyhood and for St.

☞ For the "Key to the Scheme of Pronunciation," with the accompanying Explanations,

Nicholas. It generally means the latter, who, under the influence of the former, is presumed to issue his rewards to good children, on the vigil of his festival, "Christ Kinkle eve," disguised in a fur cap and strange apparel, with a capacious bag before him from which to distribute his gifts. Under the name *Pelznichel* (*pelz*, fur), in Germany, he is the terror of the young at that season, as he is presumed to have heard all about them from the omniscient Christ-child. He is the *Mumbo Jumbo* of Teutonic nations. By the little children he is often propitiated as follows:—

"Christkindchen komm;
Mach mich fromm;
Dus ich zu dir in Kimmel komm."

Christ-child come; make me devout; that I may come to thee in heaven. On Christmas eve, the young folks hang up their stockings in their chambers in expectation of being held in remembrance by the same mysterious stranger. [Written also Criss Kringle and Criss Cringle.]

Kuvera (koo-vä'rä). [Sansk., having a wretched body.] (*Hindu Myth.*) The god of riches, represented as frightfully deformed, and as riding in a car drawn by hobgoblins.

L.

Labe, Queen. See QUEEN LABE.

Lach'e-sis. [Gr. Λάχεσις.] (*Gr. & Rom. Myth.*) One of the three Fates; the one that spun the thread of life. See PARCÆ.

Lȧ-co'ni-ȧ. A name originally given to a tract of country bounded by the Merrimack, the Kennebec, the ocean, and the "River of Canada," included in a royal grant to Ferdinando Gorges and John Mason.

Ladies' Peace. [Fr. *La Paix des Dames.*] (*Fr. Hist.*) The treaty of peace concluded at Cambrai, in 1529, between Francis I. of France, and Charles V., emperor of Germany. It was so called because it was chiefly negotiated by Louise of Savoy, mother to Francis, and Margaret, duchess-dowager of Savoy, the emperor's aunt.

Lady Bountiful. A character in Farquhar's "Beaux' Stratagem;" a benevolent old country gentlewoman who goes about curing all sorts of distempers.

> To sum up the whole, the dame ... being a sort of *Lady Bountiful* in her way, ... was proud of the skill by which she had averted the probable attacks of hereditary malady, so inveterate in the family of Bridgenorth.
> *Sir W. Scott.*

> He [Southey] conceives that ... he [the magistrate] ought to be a perfect jack-of-all-trades, — architect, engineer, schoolmaster, merchant, theologian, a *Lady Bountiful* in every parish, a Paul Pry in every house, spying, eavesdropping, relieving, admonishing, spending our money for us, choosing our opinions for us. *Macaulay.*

Lady of Avenel, The White. See WHITE LADY OF AVENEL.

Lady of England. A title conferred upon Matilda, daughter of Henry I. of England, and wife of Geoffrey Plantagenet, by a council held at Winchester, April 7, 1141.

Lady of Shȧ-lott'. A maiden of gentle birth and exquisite beauty, who fell in love with Lancelot du Lac, and died on finding her passion unrequited and altogether hopeless. Tennyson has made her story the subject of one of the most beautiful of his minor poems.

Lady of the Lake. 1. A name given to Vivian, mistress of the enchanter Merlin. She had a palace situated in the midst of an imaginary lake, — like that often seen by the traveller across tropical deserts, — whose deluding semblance served as a barrier to her residence. Here she dwelt, surrounded by a splendid court of knights and damsels, and attended by a numerous retinue.

2. The title of a poem by Sir Walter Scott, and a name given to its heroine, Ellen, the daughter of Douglas, the former favourite of King James, but now banished, disgraced, and living in a secret retreat near Loch Katrine.

Lady of the Sun. A name given to Alice Perrers (or Pierce), a mistress of Edward III. of England, and a married woman of great beauty, who had been lady of the bed-chamber to Queen Philippa. Although Edward lavished upon her both honours and riches, yet at his death she stole his jewels, taking even the rings from his fingers.

Lady of Threadneedle Street. See OLD LADY OF THREADNEEDLE STREET.

Lady Touchwood. See TOUCHWOOD, LADY.

Lȧ-ẽr'tē̤ṣ (4). Son to Polonius, and brother to Ophelia, in Shakespeare's tragedy of "Hamlet."

Lȧ-feū'. An old lord, in Shakespeare's "All 's Well that Ends Well."

Lȧ-gā'do. The name of the capital city of Balnibarbi, a continent subject to the king of Laputa. (See GULLIVER, LEMUEL.) Lagado is celebrated for its grand academy of projectors, who try to extract sunbeams from cucumbers, to calcine ice into gunpowder, &c. In the description of this fancied academy, Swift ridicules

---

☞ For the "Key to the Scheme of Pronunciation," with the accompanying Explanations,

the speculative philosophers and the false and chimerical pretenders to science who were so common in his day.

Lā'i-us (20). [Gr. Λάιος.] (*Gr. & Rom. Myth.*) A king of Thebes, and the father of Œdipus, by whom he was unwittingly killed.

Lă-ke'di-ŏn, Isaac. See JEW, THE WANDERING.

Lake Poets, Lake School, Lakers, or **Lakists.** A nickname given by the British critics, near the beginning of the present century, to "a certain brotherhood of poets" — to use the language of the "Edinburgh Review," vol. xi., p. 214 — who "haunted for some years about the lakes of Cumberland," and who were erroneously thought to have united on some settled theory or principles of composition and style. Wordsworth, Southey, and Coleridge were regarded as the chief representatives of this so-called school, but Lamb, Lloyd, and Wilson were also included under the same designation.

☞ "The author who is now before us [Southey] belongs to a *sect* of poets that has established itself in this country within these ten or twelve years, and is looked upon, we believe, as one of its chief champions and apostles. The peculiar doctrines of this sect it would not, perhaps, be very easy to explain; but that they are *dissenters* from the established systems in poetry and criticism is admitted, and proved, indeed, by the whole tenor of their compositions." . . . "The productions of this school . . . cannot be better characterised than by an enumeration of the sources from which their materials have been derived. The greatest part of them, we apprehend, will be found to be composed of the following elements: 1. The anti-social principles and distempered sensibility of Rousseau; his discontent with the present constitution of society; his paradoxical morality; and his perpetual hankerings after some unattainable state of voluptuous virtue and perfection. 2. The simplicity and energy (*horresco referens*) of Kotzebue and Schiller. 3. The homeliness and harshness of some of Cowper's language and versification, interchanged occasionally with the *innocence* of Ambrose Philips, or the quaintness of Quarles and Dr. Donne. From the diligent study of these few originals, we have no doubt that an entire art of poetry may be collected, by the assistance of which the very *gentlest* of our readers may soon be qualified to compose a poem as correctly versified as 'Thalaba,' and to deal out sentiment and description with all the sweetness of Lamb, and all the magnificence of Coleridge." *Edinburgh Rev., vol. i.*

☞ "When, some years ago, a gentleman [Mr. Jeffrey], the chief writer and conductor of a celebrated review [the 'Edinburgh Review'] distinguished by its hostility to Mr. Southey, spent a day or two at Keswick [Mr. Southey's place of residence], he was circumstantially informed by what series of accidents it had happened that Mr. Wordsworth, Mr. Southey, and I had become neighbours; and how utterly groundless was the supposition that we considered ourselves as belonging to any common school but that of good sense, confirmed by the long-established models of the best times of Greece, Rome, Italy, and England, and still more groundless the notion that Mr. Southey (for, as to myself, I have published so little, and that little of so little importance, as to make it almost ludicrous to mention my name at all) could have been concerned in the formation of a poetic sect with Mr. Wordsworth, when so many of his works had been published, not only previously to any acquaintance between them, but before Mr. Wordsworth himself had written any thing but in a diction ornate and uniformly sustained; when, too, the slightest examination will make it evident that between those and the after-writings of Mr. Southey there exists no other difference than that of a progressive degree of excellence, from progressive development of power, and progressive facility from habit and increase of experience. Yet, among the first articles which this man wrote after his return from Keswick, we were characterised as 'the school of whining and hypochondriacal poets that haunt the Lakes.'" *Coleridge.*

Lake State. A name popularly given to the State of Michigan, which borders upon the four lakes, Superior, Michigan, Huron, and Erie.

Laks'mî. (*Hindu Myth.*) The consort of Vishnu, and the goddess of beauty, grace, riches, and pleasure. She is a favourite subject of Indian painting and poetry, and is pictured as a being of transcendent loveliness, yet of a dark blue colour.

Lăl'lă Rōōkh. The title of a poem by Moore, and the name of its heroine, the daughter of the great Aurengzebe. She is betrothed to the young king of Bucharia, and sets forth with a splendid train of attendants, to meet him in the delightful valley of Cashmere. To amuse the languor, or divert the impatience, of the royal bride, in the noontide and night halts of her luxurious progress, a young Cashmerian poet had been sent by the gallantry of the bridegroom, and, on these occasions, he recites the several tales that make up the bulk of the poem. With him she falls desperately in love, and by the time she enters the lovely vale of Cashmere, and sees the glittering palaces and towers prepared for her reception, she feels that she would joyfully forego all this pomp and splendour, and fly to the desert with the youthful bard whom she adores. He, however, has now disappeared from her side, and she is supported, with fainting heart and downcast eye, into the presence of her tyrant; when a well-known voice bids her be of good cheer, and, looking up, she sees her beloved poet in the prince himself, who had assumed this gallant disguise, and won her affections, without any aid from his rank or her engagements.

Lam'bro. The piratical father of Haidee, in Byron's "Don Juan;" considered by Coleridge to be the finest of all Byron's characters.

Lame and Unstable Peace. [Fr. *Paix Boiteuse et Mal-assise.*] (*Fr. Hist.*) A name given to a treaty of peace, of short duration, concluded with the Calvinists, in 1568, in the name of Charles IX., by Biron, who was lame. [Called also *Ill-grounded Peace* and *Patched-up Peace.*]

Lā'mi-ā. [Gr. Λαμία.] (*Gr. & Rom. Myth.*) A female phantom, whose name was used as a bugbear to frighten children. According to tradition, she was a Libyan queen, a daughter of Belus, of great beauty, and beloved by Jupiter, for which reason the jealous Juno robbed her of her children. Lamia, filled with revenge and despair, and unable to injure Juno, robbed others of their children, whom she afterward murdered. Her face became fearfully distorted and ugly by indulgence in such savage cruelty, and Jupiter invested her with still greater terror by giving her the power of taking out her eyes and putting them in again at will. Lamia is the subject and title of an admired poem by Keats.

☞ In a later age, a belief sprang up in a plurality of Lamiæ, handsome spectres, who, by voluptuous artifices, enticed young men to them, in order to feast upon their flesh and blood.

Lam'mĭ-kin. The subject of a well-known Scottish ballad.

☞ "The hero, if such a term is applicable to the blood-thirsty mason, has been celebrated under the names of Lammikin, Lamkin, Linkin, Belinkin, Bold Rankin, and Balcanqual, and has become, through the medium of injudicious servants, the prime terror of the Scottish nursery. Like most such ogres, he is a myth; at least, I have never seen any satisfactory attempt at his identification, nor has any one discovered the locality of the castle which he built and baptised with blood."
Aytoun.

Lamourette's Kiss (lȧ'moo'ret'). [Fr. *Le Baiser de Lamourette.*] (*Fr. Hist.*) A name derisively given to a sudden reconciliation of the different factions of the Legislative Assembly, which had previously been bitterly hostile to each other. It was brought about, on the 7th of July, 1792, by an eloquent appeal of the Abbé Lamourette, constitutional bishop of Lyons, — whose name signifies *the sweetheart,* — but was of very brief duration. [Called also *La Réconciliation Normande,* or *The Norman Reconciliation,* from the country of the bishop.]

☞ "The deputies of every faction, Royalist, Constitutionalist, Girondist, Jacobin, and Orleanist, rushed into each other's arms, and mixed tears with the solemn oaths by which they renounced the innovations supposed to be imputed to them. The king was sent for to enjoy this spectacle of concord, so strangely and so unexpectedly renewed. But the feeling, though strong, — and it might be with many overpowering for the moment, — was but like oil spilt on the raging sea, or rather like a shot fired across

☞ For the "Key to the Scheme of Pronunciation," with the accompanying Explanations,

the waves of a torrent, which, though it counteracts them by its momentary impulse, cannot for a second alter their course. The factions, like Le Sage's demons, detested each other the more for having been compelled to embrace."
Sir W. Scott.

Lăn′ce-lŏt du Lăc, *or* **Lancelot of the Lake.** The son of King Ban of Brittany, and one of the most famous knights of the Round Table; equally remarkable for his gallantry and good-nature. He was the hero of a celebrated romance of chivalry, written in Latin by an unknown author, and translated by Walter Mapes, in the twelfth century. He received the appellation of " du Lac " from having been educated at the court of Vivian, mistress of the enchanter Merlin, and better known as the Lady of the Lake. Lancelot was celebrated for his amours with Guinever, the wife of his friend and sovereign, King Arthur, and for the exploits he undertook for her sake, which involved him in a long and cruel war with Arthur. Toward the close of his life, he became a hermit.

☞ "Thou . . . wert never matched of none earthly knight's hands; and thou wert the curtiest knight that ever bare shield; and thou wert the truest friend to thy lover that ever bestrode horse; and thou wert the truest lover, of a sinful man, that ever loved woman; and thou wert the kindest man that ever struck with sword; and thou wert the goodliest person that ever came among press of knights; and thou wert the meekest man and the gentlest that ever ate in hall among ladies; and thou wert the sternest knight to thy mortal foe that ever put spear in the rest." *Morte d'Arthur.*

Land of Beu′lăh. In Bunyan's allegory, " The Pilgrim's Progress," a land of rest and quiet (symbolising the Christian's peace of mind), represented as lying upon the hither side of the river of Death. In it the pilgrims tarry till their summons comes to cross the stream, and enter the Celestial City. The name occurs in *Isa.* lxii. 4.

☞ " After this, I beheld until they came unto the land of Beulah, where the sun shineth night and day. Here, because they were weary, they betook themselves awhile to rest. But a little while soon refreshed them here; for the bells did so ring, and the trumpets continually sounded so melodiously, that they could not sleep, and yet they received as much refreshing as if they had slept their sleep over so soundly. Here also all the noise of them that walked the streets was, More pilgrims are come to town! And another would answer, saying, And so many went over the water, and were let in at the golden gates to-day! In this land they heard nothing, saw nothing, smelt nothing, tasted nothing, that was offensive to their stomach or mind; only when they tasted of the water of the river over which they were to go, they thought that it tasted a little bitterish to the palate; but it proved sweet when it was down."

Land of Bondage. A name given in the Bible to Egypt. The Israelites, during the first part of their sojourn in that country, were treated with great kindness, and increased in numbers and prosperity; but at length " there arose up a new king over Egypt, which knew not Joseph," and who adopted a subtle system to afflict and reduce them by making them perform forced labour, and soon afterward by killing their male children. This oppression led to the exodus, the forty years' wandering in the wilderness, and the subsequent conquest and occupation of the land of Canaan.

Land of Cakes. A name sometimes given to Scotland, because oatmeal cakes are a common national article of food, particularly among the poorer classes.

Hear, *Land o' Cakes* and brither Scots,
Frae Maidenkirk to John o' Groats,
If there 's a hole in a' your coats,
    I rede ye tent it:
A chiel 's amang you takin' notes,
    And, faith, he 'll prent it. *Burns.*

The lady loves, and admires, and worships every thing Scottish; the gentleman looks down on the *Land of Cakes* like a superior intelligence. *Blackwood's Mag.*

Land of Nod. The state or condition of sleep, conceived of as a country which people visit in their dreams.

☞ This figure is evidently borrowed from the use of the English word *nod*, as denoting the motion of the head in drowsiness. But it was also, most probably, at first employed as containing a ludicrous allusion to the language of Scripture

In regard to the conduct of the first murderer: "And Cain went out from the presence of the Lord, and dwelt in the land of Nod." (*Gen.* iv. 16.)

"And d'ye ken, lass," said Madge, "there's queer things chanced since ye hae been in the *Land of Nod?*" *Sir W. Scott.*

Land of Promise. See PROMISED LAND.

Land of Steady Habits. A name by which the State of Connecticut is sometimes designated, in allusion to the settled usages and staid deportment of its inhabitants.

Land of Wisdom. [Fr. *La Pays de Sapience.*] A name given to Normandy, in France, because of the wise customs which have prevailed there, and also because of the skill and judgment of the people in matters of jurisprudence.

Lane, Wyc'liffe. A pseudonym of Mrs. E. Jenings, a writer of the present day.

Lang'stäff, Läun'ce-lŏt (2). A pseudonym under which "Salmagundi" was jointly published by Washington Irving, William Irving, and James K. Paulding.

Languish, Miss Lydia. The heroine of Sheridan's comedy of "The Rivals;" distinguished for the extravagance of her romantic notions.

Let not those, however, who enter into a union for life without those embarrassments which delight a ... *Lydia Languish*, and which are perhaps necessary to excite an enthusiastic passion in breasts more firm than theirs, augur worse of their future happiness, because their own alliance is formed under calmer auspices. *Sir W. Scott.*

Lanternois, L'Île des (lěl dü lŏn'těr'nä', 62). See ISLAND OF LANTERNS.

Lȧ-oc'ŏ-ŏn. [Gr. Λαοκόων.] (*Gr. & Rom. Myth.*) A son of Priam and Hecuba, and a priest of Apollo, or, as some say, of Neptune. He opposed the reception of the Wooden Horse into Troy, thinking it some artifice of the deceitful Greeks. He and his two sons were killed by two monstrous serpents which came from the sea; but the reason of their being made to suffer this horrible fate is differently stated. The serpents first entwined the boys, and, when their father attempted to rescue them, they involved and crushed him also in their coils. The death of Laocoon is the subject of one of the most magnificent and celebrated works of ancient sculpture still in existence; it was discovered in 1506 at Rome, and is now preserved in the Vatican.

Lȧ-od'ȧ-mi'ȧ. [Gr. Λαοδάμεια.] (*Gr. & Rom. Myth.*) The wife of Protesilaus, whom she followed to the under-world, after his death at the hands of Hector. Wordsworth has made this myth the subject of his exquisite poem entitled "Laodamia." See PROTESILAUS.

Lȧ-om'e-dŏn. [Gr. Λαομέδων.] (*Gr. & Rom. Myth.*) A king of Troy, son of Ilus and Eurydice, and the father of Priam, Ganymede, and Tithonus. With the assistance of Apollo and Neptune, he built the walls of Troy; but, when the work was done, he refused to pay the reward which he had promised for the labour, and expelled them from his dominions. Hereupon Neptune sent a sea-monster to ravage the country; and in compliance with the command of an oracle, a maiden, chosen by lot, was from time to time sacrificed to propitiate it. On one occasion, Laomedon's own daughter Hesione was the victim selected; but Hercules saved her on receiving a certain solemn promise from her father, which not being fulfilled, Hercules killed him.

Lap'ï-thæ. [Gr. Λαπίθαι.] (*Gr. & Rom. Myth.*) Monstrous giants inhabiting the mountains of Thessaly. At the marriage of their king, Pirithous, they fought with the Centaurs and vanquished them, but were afterward themselves overcome by Hercules.

Lȧ-pu'tȧ. The name of a flying island described by Swift in his imaginary "Travels" of Lemuel Gulliver. It is said to be "exactly circular, its diameter 7837 yards, or about four miles and a half, and [it] consequently contains ten thousand acres." The inhabitants are chiefly speculative philosophers, devoted to mathematics and music; and such is their habitual absent-mindedness, that they are compelled to employ attendants — called "flappers" — to rouse them from their profound meditations, when necessary, by striking them gently on the mouth and ears with a peculiar instrument consisting of a blown bladder with a few pebbles in it, fastened on the end of a stick, like the swiple of a flail. See LAGADO.

Thou art an unfortunate philosopher of Laputa, who has lost his flapper in the throng.
Sir W. Scott.

Strange it is, that, whilst all biographers have worked with so much zeal upon the most barren dates or most baseless traditions in the great poet's life, realising in a manner the dreams of Laputa, and endeavouring to extract sunbeams from cucumbers, such a story with regard to such an event . . . should formerly have been dismissed without notice of any kind.
De Quincey.

So materialising is the spirit of the age, that the extended study of physical and mechanical science seems likely, one of these days, to convert our island into a Laputa. *Keightley.*

Lā'rā. The hero of Byron's poem of the same name; represented as a chief long absent from his own domain, who returns at length, attended by a single page. Dark hints and surmises are thrown out against him by a noble whom he encounters at a banquet, and who seems to be possessed of some knowledge of the manner in which Lara's time has been occupied during his prolonged absence. This knight disappears most opportunely for the reputation of Lara, when he should have come forward to substantiate the charges against him, and is never heard of after. A peasant, however, is witness to the concealment of a corpse on the same night, and the reader is left to draw his own conclusions.

Lā'rēṣ. [Lat., pl. of *lar*, a word of Etruscan origin, signifying *lord*, *king*, or *hero*.] (*Rom. Myth.*) Tutelary deities of particular localities. They were of two classes: 1. The domestic *lares*, or household gods, whose images were kept on the hearth in a little shrine, or in a small chapel, and who were regarded as disembodied and guardian spirits of virtuous ancestors; 2. The public *lares*, protectors of streets, highways, cross-roads, &c. [Written also, in an Anglicised form, L a r s.]

La Rōçhe. A Protestant clergyman, whose story — written by Henry Mackenzie — is told in "The Mirror."

Lar'væ. (*Rom. Myth.*) The same as *Lemures*. See LEMURES.

Last Man. An appellation given, by the parliamentary party in England, to Charles I. (1600-1649), he being, in their expectation, the last monarch who would ever sit on the British throne.

He did not consider himself as free in conscience to join with any party which might be likely ultimately to acknowledge the interest of Charles Stuart, the son of the "*Last Man*," as Charles I. was familiarly and irreverently termed by them in their common discourse, as well as in their more elaborate predications and harangues.
Sir W. Scott.

Last of the Fathers. A title given by some Roman Catholic writers to St. Bernard (1091-1153), one of the most influential theologians and voluminous writers of the Middle Ages.

Last of the Goths. Roderick, the thirty-fourth and last of the Visigothic line of kings, who filled the throne of Spain from 414 to 711.

Last of the Greeks. [Lat. *Ultimus Græcorum*, Gr. Ὕστατος Ἑλλήνων.] An appellation conferred upon Philopœmen (B. C. 253-183), a native of Arcadia, and the last really great and successful military leader of the ancient Greeks.

☞ "One of the Romans, to praise him, called him the Last of the Greeks, as if after him Greece had produced no great man, nor one who deserved the name of Greek." *Plutarch, Trans.*

Last of the Knights. A title bestowed upon Maximilian I. (1459-1519), emperor of Germany.

"The *Last of the Knights*," with his wild effrontery and spirited chamois-hunting, might be despised by the Italians as "Massimiliano Pochi Danari [Maximilian the Penniless];" but he was beloved by the Austrians as "Our Max." *Longe.*

Last of the Mo-hī'cans. The hero of Cooper's novel of the same name, by which title the Indian chief Uncas is designated.

Last of the Romans. [Lat. *Ultimus Romanorum.*] 1. An epithet applied to the Roman general Aëtius, by Procopius. When the invasion of Attila took place in A. D. 450, Aëtius, with the help of Theodoric, arrested it first by the relief of Orleans, and then by the victory of Châlons. With his death, which occurred in 454, the last support of the empire fell.

2. A name given by Marcus Junius Brutus to his fellow-conspirator, Caius Cassius Longinus (d. B. C. 42), one of the murderers of Julius Cæsar, and one of the best generals of his age.

3. [Fr. *Le Dernier des Romains.*] A title bestowed upon François Joseph Terasse Desbillons (1751-1789), a celebrated Jesuit, on account of the elegance and purity of his Latin style.

Last of the Troubadours. A name given by his admirers to Jacques Jasmin (1798-1864), a native of Gascony, and the most eminent modern patois poet of France.

Lā-ti'nus. A son of Faunus, and king of the Laurentians, a people of Latium, in Italy. When Æneas first arrived in Latium, Latinus opposed him; but he afterward formed an alliance with him, and gave him his daughter Lavinia in marriage.

Latin War. (*Ger. Hist.*) An insurrection of the peasantry in Salzburg, in 1523, occasioned by the unpopularity of an archbishop. It was quickly suppressed.

Lā-to'nā. [Gr. Λητώ, Doric, Λατώ, Æolic, Λατών.] (*Gr. & Rom. Myth.*) Daughter of Cœus, a Titan, and Phœbe, and by Jupiter the mother of Apollo and Diana, to whom she gave birth on the island of Delos. (See DELOS.) Ovid ("Met." vi., fab. iv.) relates a story of some clowns of Lycia who insulted Latona as she knelt with the infant deities in arms to quench her thirst at a small lake, and who were in consequence changed into frogs.

I did but prompt the age to quit their clogs
By the known rules of ancient liberty,
When straight a barbarous noise environs me
Of owls and cuckoos, asses, apes, and dogs:
As when those hinds that were transformed to frogs

Railed at *Latona's* twin-born progeny,
Which after held the sun and moon in fee.
Milton.

Laughing Philosopher. Democritus of Abdera, a celebrated philosopher of antiquity, contemporary with Socrates; — so called because he always made a jest of man's follies and sorrows, his feeble struggles and evanescent works. He is usually contrasted with Heraclitus, "The Weeping Philosopher." See WEEPING PHILOSOPHER.

Lâunçe. An awkward and silly servant of Proteus, in Shakespeare's "Two Gentlemen of Verona."

Lâun'fâl, Sir. One of the knights of the Round Table, the subject of a metrical romance composed by Thomas Chestre, in the reign of Henry VI. The name has also been adopted as the title of a poem by James Russell Lowell, entitled "The Vision of Sir Launfal."

Laura (*It. pron.* lŏw'rȧ). The Christian name of an Avignonese lady, young, but already married, for whom, in the year 1327, the poet Petrarch conceived a strong though Platonic affection, which exercised a powerful influence over his life, and ended only with his death. He sung her praises in "rime," or sonnets and canzoni, which have immortalised not only her name, but his own.

Laurence, Friar. See FRIAR LAURENCE.

Lā-vin'i-ā. 1. A daughter of Latinus, and the second wife of Æneas. She had previously been betrothed to Turnus. See LATINUS and CREUSA.

Sad task! yet argument
Not less but more heroic than the ... rage
Of Turnus for *Lavinia* disespoused. *Milton.*

2. The heroine of a tale introduced by Thomson, in his "Seasons," into the poem on "Autumn." See PALEMON.

Law's Bubble. A name given to a delusive speculation projected by John Law (1671-1729), a celebrated financier, and a native of Edinburgh. In 1716, he established a bank in France, by royal authority, composed of 1200 shares of 3000 livres each, which soon bore a premium. This bank became the office for all public receipts, and there was annexed to it a Mississippi company, which had grants of land in Louisiana, and was expected to realise immense sums by planting and commerce. In 1718, it was declared a royal bank, and its shares rose to twenty times their original value, so that, in 1719, they were worth more than eighty times the amount of all the current specie in France. In 1720, the shares sunk as rapidly as they had risen, nearly overthrowing the French government, and occasioning great and wide-spread financial distress and bankruptcy.

Laz'a-rus. A poor leper, who, in the parable of our Lord (*Luke* xvi.), implored in vain the pity of a rich man; but after the death of both, Lazarus went to heaven, and the rich man to hell, where he in turn vainly implored help from Lazarus.

☞ This is the only case in the New Testament where a proper name occurs in a parable. The use of the word *lazzaro* applied to a leper, and of the words *lazaretto* and *lazar-house* for leper hospitals, and of *lazzaroni* for beggars, shows the influence which this parable has had upon the mind of Christendom.

Lazy, Lawrence. The hero of a popular "history," or romance, of ancient date, "containing his Birth and slothful breeding; how he served the Schoolmaster, his Wife, the Squire's Cook, and the Farmer, which, by the laws of Lubberland, was accounted High Treason; his Arraignment and Trial, and happy deliverance from the many treasons laid to his charge."

League, The. [Fr. *La Ligue*.] (*Fr. Hist.*) A political coalition organised in 1576 by the Roman Catholics of France, to prevent the accession of Henry IV., who was then of the reformed religion. [Called also *The Holy League* (Fr. *La Sainte Ligue*), and *The Holy Union* (Fr. *La Sainte Union*).]

League and Covenant, Solemn. See SOLEMN LEAGUE AND COVENANT.

League of God's House. [Fr. *Ligue de la Maison de Dieu*.] (*Swiss Hist.*) A celebrated combination formed by the Grisons in 1400, for the purpose of resisting domestic tyranny. [Called also *Caddee*.]

League of the Public Good. [Fr. *Ligue du Bien Public*.] (*Fr. Hist.*) An alliance, in 1464, between the dukes of Burgundy, Brittany, and Bourgogne, and other French princes, against Louis XI.

Leander. [Gr. Λείανδρος.] A youth of Abydos, famous for his love for Hero, a priestess of Sestos, to visit whom he nightly swam across the Hellespont. See HERO.

Léandre (lā'ŏn'dr, 62, 64, 103). A lover in Molière's "L'Etourdi."

Lear. A fabulous or legendary king of Britain, and the hero of Shakespeare's tragedy of the same name. He is represented as a fond father, duped, in his old age, by hypocritical professions of love and duty on the part of two daughters (Goneril and Regan), to disinherit the third (Cordelia), who had before been deservedly more dear to him, and to divide his kingdom between her sisters, who, by their perfidious and cruel conduct, soon drive the poor old king mad. After his misery has reached its highest pitch, he is found by the daughter whom he has so deeply injured; and, through her tender care, he revives and recollects her. She endeavours to reinstate him upon his throne, but fails in her attempt, and is hanged in prison, where her brokenhearted father dies lamenting over her.

Learned Blacksmith. An epithet sometimes applied to Elihu Burritt (b. 1811), who began life as a blacksmith, and afterward distinguished himself as a linguist.

Learned Tailor. A title sometimes bestowed upon Henry Wild, a native of Norwich, England, where he was born about the year 1684. He was in early life a tailor, and, while working at his trade, mastered the Latin, Greek, Hebrew, Chaldaic, Syr-

and for the Remarks and Rules to which the numbers after certain words refer, see pp. xiv-xxxii.

iac, Arabic, and Persian languages. [Called also *The Arabian Tailor*.]

Leatherstocking, Natty. A sobriquet given to Natty, or Nathaniel, Bumppo, a celebrated character in Cooper's novel of "The Pioneers." He re-appears and closes his career in "The Prairie."

> "Leatherstocking stands half-way between savage and civilised life; he has the freshness of nature, and the first-fruits of Christianity, the seed dropped into vigorous soil. These are the elements of one of the most original characters in fiction, in whom Cooper has transplanted all the chivalry, ever feigned or practised in the Middle Ages, to the rivers, woods, and forests of the unbroken New World."
> *Duyckinck.*
>
> One *Natty Leatherstocking*, one melodious synopsis of man and nature in the West.
> *Carlyle.*

Le Beau. A courtier, in Shakespeare's "As You Like It."

Le'da. [Gr. Λήδα.] (*Gr. & Rom. Myth.*) The daughter of Thestius, and the wife of Tyndareus. Jupiter falling in love with her, and visiting her in the form of a swan, she bore two eggs, from one of which came forth Pollux and Helen, and from the other Castor and Clytemnestra.

Led'dy Grip'py. The name of the heroine in "The Entail," a novel by Galt.

> A decreet o' court, Jamie, as *Leddie Grippy* would have said. \ *Prof. J. Wilson.*

Le Fevre (lụ fev'r, 64). The name of a poor lieutenant, whose story is related in Sterne's "Life and Opinions of Tristram Shandy."

Legion. The name assumed by the demoniac, or the unclean spirit, spoken of in *Mark* v.: "My name is Legion; for we are many." The term implies the presence of a superior power, in addition to subordinate ones.

Legion, The Thundering. See THUNDERING LEGION.

Leg-of-Mutton School. A name given to those poetasters, who, attaching themselves as parasites and dependents to persons of wealth and station, endeavour to pay for good dinners and sumptuous entertainment by servile flattery of their patron, and profuse laudation of him and his, the "leg of mutton" being supposed to typify the source of their inspiration, which is chiefly gustatory. The phrase was first used by Lockhart, in a review of a ridiculous poem entitled "Fleurs, a Poem in Four Books," the author of which is not named. Fleurs Castle was the seat of the Duke of Roxburghe, whose mutton and hospitality the rhymster appears to have shared, greatly to his delectation.

> "The chief constellations in this poetical firmament consist of led captains and clerical hangers-on, whose pleasure and whose business it is to celebrate in tuneful verse the virtues of some angelic patron, who keeps a good table, and has interest with the archbishop, or the India House. Verily, they have their reward. The anticipated living falls vacant in due time, the son gets a pair of colours, or is sent out as a cadet, or the happy author succeeds in dining five times a week on hock and venison, at the small expense of acting as toad-eater to the whole family, from my lord to the butler inclusive. It is owing to the modesty, certainly not to the numerical deficiency, of this class of writers, that they have hitherto obtained no specific distinction among the authors of the present day. We think it incumbent on us to remedy this defect; and, in the baptismal font of this our magazine, we declare, that in the poetical nomenclature they shall in future be known by the style and title of *The Leg-of-Mutton School*." . . . "He [the bard of Fleurs abovementioned] is marked by a more than usual portion of the qualities characteristic of the *Leg-of-Mutton School;* by all their vulgar ignorance, by more than all their clumsy servility, their fawning adulation of wealth and title, their hankering after the flesh-pots, and by all the symptoms of an utter incapacity to stand straight in the presence of a great man."
> Z. (*J. G. Lockhart*), *Blackwood's Mag. vol. ix.*

Le-gree'. A slave-dealer, in Mrs. Stowe's novel, "Uncle Tom's Cabin;" a hideous exhibition of the brutalising influence of slavery.

Lēigh, Au-ro'rạ (lee). The heroine of Mrs. Browning's poem of the same name; "the representative of the spiritual and æsthetic spirit of the age, through whom are exemplified the noble ends and the high office of true art."

Lei'lă. The name of the heroine in Byron's poem of "The Giaour;" a beautiful slave-girl who suffers death for love of her paramour, a young "infidel."

Leilah. See MEJNOUN.

L. E. L. The initials and literary signature of Letitia Elizabeth Landon (afterward Mrs. Maclean, 1802-1838), a well-known English poetess.

Lélie (lă'le'). An inconsequential, light-headed, gentleman-like coxcomb, in Molière's "L'Étourdi."

Lem'u-rēṣ. (*Rom. Myth.*) Spirits of the dead thought to wander about at night, like ghosts, and to torment and frighten the living.

☞ Milton Anglicises the word in its pronunciation, making it consist of two syllables instead of three.

"In consecrated earth,
And on the holy hearth,
The Lars and *Lemures* moan with midnight plaint." *Ode on the Nativity.*

Le-nore'. 1. The heroine of a popular ballad, composed by Gottfried August Bürger (1748-1794), the German lyric poet. The subject of this ballad is an old tradition, which recounts the ride of a spectral lover, who reappears to his mistress after death, and carries her on horseback behind him, "a fiction not less remarkable for its extensive geographical dissemination, than for its bold imaginative character."

☞ Bürger is said to have borrowed the subject of his poem from an old English ballad entitled " The Suffolk Miracle, or a Relation of a Young Man, who, a month after his death, appeared to his sweetheart, and carried her on horseback behind him forty miles in two hours, and was never seen afterward but in her grave." Bürger, however, contradicted this assertion, and declared that an old Low Dutch ballad furnished him with the idea of Lenore. The traditions probably both have a common origin.

2. The angelic name of "a rare and radiant maiden" mentioned in Poe's mystical ballad entitled "The Raven."

Le'o-nă'to. Governor of Messina, in Shakespeare's "Much Ado about Nothing."

Le-on'ĭ-dăṣ of Modern Greece. A title given to Marco Bozzaris, a Greek patriot, and an heroic soldier, who distinguished himself in the early part of the modern Grecian War of Independence, particularly by a successful attack with 1200 men upon the van of the Turco-Albanian army, 4000 strong, at Kerpenisi, on the 20th of August, 1823. In this engagement, Bozzaris lost his life.

Le-on'ĭ-dăṣ We'dell (vā'del, 68). A name given by Frederick the Great to General C. H. Wedell (1712-1782), an officer in the Prussian service, on account of his heroic defence of the Elbe at Teinitz, on the 19th of November, 1744.

Le'o-nĭne. A servant to Dionyza, in Shakespeare's "Pericles."

Le'on-noys'. A fabulous country, formerly contiguous to Cornwall, though it has long since disappeared, and is said to be now more than forty fathoms under water. It is often mentioned in the old romances of chivalry. [Written also L e o n a i s, L i o n e s s e, L y o n n e s s e.]

☞ The Lyones or Leonnoys, where Sir Tristram was born (see TRISTRAM, SIR), is Léonnois in Brittany.

For Arthur, when none knew from whence he came,
Long ere the people chose him for their king,
Roving the trackless realms of *Lyonnesse*,
Had found a glen, gray bowlder, and black tarn. *Tennyson.*

Le-on'tĕṣ. King of Sicilia, in Shakespeare's "Winter's Tale."

☞ "Jealousy is a vice of the mind, a culpable tendency of the temper, having certain well-known and well-defined effects and concomitants, all of which are visible in Leontes, . . . such as, first, an excitability by the most inadequate causes, and an eagerness to snatch at proofs; secondly, a grossness of conception, and a disposition to degrade the object of the passion by sensual fancies and images; thirdly, a sense of shame of his own feelings, exhibited in a solitary moodiness of humour, and yet, from the violence of the passion, forced to utter itself, and therefore catching occasions to ease the mind by ambiguities, equivoques, by talking to those who cannot,

and for the Remarks and Rules to which the numbers after certain words refer, see pp. xiv-xxxii.

and who are known not to be able to, understand what is said to them, — in short, by soliloquy in the form of dialogue, and hence, a confused, broken, and fragmentary manner; fourthly, a dread of vulgar ridicule, as distinct from a high sense of honour, or a mistaken sense of duty; and lastly, and immediately consequent on this, a spirit of selfish vindictiveness." *Coleridge.*

Les'bĭ-ă. A name given by Catullus (b. B. C. 87) to his favourite Clodia, whose praises he celebrates in a number of amatory poems.

Lo'the. [Gr. Λήθη, forgetfulness.] (*Gr. & Rom. Myth.*) A river in Hades, the waters of which caused those who drank it entirely to forget the past.

Far off from these, a slow and silent stream,
Lethe, the river of oblivion, rolls
Her watery labyrinth: whereof whoso drinks
Straightway his former sense and being forgets, —
Forgets both joy and grief, pleasure and pain.
Milton.

Le'to. [Gr. Λητώ.] (*Myth.*) The Greek name of *Latona.* See LATONA.

Leu'co-the'ă. [Gr. Λευκοθέη.] (*Gr. & Rom. Myth.*) 1. A name given to Ino, after she was received among the sea-gods. See INO.
2. One of the Sirens. See SIRENS.

Le-vā'nă. [Lat., from *levare*, to raise.] (*Rom. Myth.*) The name of the goddess that protected new-born infants when they were taken up from the ground. Richter used the name as the title of an educational work which he wrote, and which has been translated into English.

Leviathian of Literature. An appellation very generally conferred upon Dr. Samuel Johnson (1709–1784), the eminent writer and critic.

Lewis, Monk. See MONK LEWIS.

Lī'bĕr. (*Rom. Myth.*) An old Italian deity, who presided over the cultivation of the vine, and fertility of the fields. By the later Latin writers, the name is used as a synonym of *Bacchus.*

Liberation, War of. See WAR OF LIBERATION.

Liberator, The. 1. [Sp. *El Libertador.*] A surname given by the Peruvians, in 1823, to Simon Bolivar (1785–1831), who established the independence of Peru, and also of the other Spanish colonies of South America.
2. A surname given to Daniel O'Connell (1775–1847), a celebrated Irish political agitator, on account of his endeavours — which were, after all, unsuccessful — to bring about a repeal of the Articles of Union between Great Britain and Ireland.

Lĭ-ġe'ă, } (20). [Gr. Λίγεια.] (*Gr.*
Lĭ-ġe'ĭ-ă, } *& Rom. Myth.*) One of the Sirens; also, a nymph.

By ... fair *Ligea's* golden comb,
Wherewith she sits on diamond rocks,
Sleeking her soft alluring locks. *Milton.*

Light-horse Harry. A sobriquet popularly conferred upon General Henry Lee (1756–1818), a gallant American cavalry officer in the war of the Revolution, in allusion to his rapid and daring movements in battle, particularly during the campaign in the Carolinas.

Lĭl'ĭth, or Lĭ'lĭs. In the popular belief of the Hebrews, a female spectre in the shape of a finely dressed woman, who lies in wait for, and kills, children. The old Rabbins turned Lilith into a wife of Adam, on whom he begot demons, and who still has power to lie with men, and to kill children, who are not protected by amulets, with which the Jews of a yet later period supply themselves as a protection against her. Burton, in his "Anatomy of Melancholy," tells us, "The Talmudists say that Adam had a wife called Lilis before he married Eve, and of her he begat nothing but devils." Heber says, " To revenge his deserting her for an earthly rival, she is supposed to hover round the habitation of new-married persons, showering down imprecations on their heads. The attendants on the bride spend the night in going round the house and uttering loud screams to frighten her away." A commentator on Skinner's " Etymologicon Linguæ Anglicanæ," quoted in the " Encyclopædia Metropolitana," says that the English word *lullaby* is derived from *Lilla, abi!* (Begone, Lilith!) In the demonology of the Middle Ages, Lilis was a famous witch, and is introduced as such in the Walpurgis-night scene in Goethe's "Faust."

Lil'li-put. An imaginary country described as peopled by a very diminutive race of men, in Swift's satirical romance entitled "Travels into several Remote Nations of the World, by Lemuel Gulliver." The voyage to Lilliput is for the most part a satire on the manners and usages of the court of George I.

There is no end to the variety of these small missiles of malice with which the Gullivers of the world of literature are assailed by the Lilliputians around them.   *T. Moore.*

Lim'bo, or **Lim'bus.** [Lat., *limbus*, a border.] A region supposed by some of the old scholastic theologians to lie on the edge or confines of hell. Here, it was thought, the souls of just men, not admitted into heaven or into Purgatory, remained to await the general resurrection. Such were the patriarchs and other pious ancients who died before the birth of Christ. Hence, the limbo was called *Limbus Patrum*. According to some of the schoolmen, there was also a *Limbus Puerorum*, or *Infantum*, a similar place allotted to the souls of infants dying unbaptised. To these were added, in the popular opinion, a *Limbus Fatuorum*, or Fools' Paradise, the receptacle of all vanity and nonsense. Of this superstitious belief Milton has made use in his "Paradise Lost." (See Book III. v. 440–497.) Dante has placed his limbo, in which the distinguished spirits of antiquity are confined, in the outermost of the circles of his hell.

Limonadière, La Muse. See MUSE LIMONADIÈRE, LA.

Limp. A Jacobite sign in the time of William III., which consisted in the zealots for hereditary right limping about at night and drinking. Those in the secret knew that the word "Limp" was formed from the initials of august names, and that the loyalist, when he drank his wine and punch, was taking off his bumper to Louis, James, Mary, and the Prince.

Lin-dab'rĭ-dēṣ. A celebrated heroine in the romance called "The Mirror of Knighthood." From the great celebrity of this lady, occasioned by the popularity of the romance, her name was commonly used for a mistress.

I value Tony Foster's wrath no more than a shelled pea-cod; and I will visit his Lindabrides, by Saint George, be he willing or no!   *Sir W. Scott.*

Lin'dŏr. A poetical name formerly in use for a swain or gallant.

A truce, dear Fergus! spare us those most tedious and insipid persons of all Arcadia. Do not, for heaven's sake, bring down Corydon and Lindor upon us.   Sir W. Scott.

I have listened to you when you spoke en bergère,—nay, my complaisance has been so great as to answer you en bergère,—for I do not think any thing except ridicule can come of dialogues betwixt Lindor and Jeanneton.
          Sir W. Scott.

Li'nus. [Gr. Λίνος.] (*Gr. & Rom. Myth.*) 1. The son of Apollo and an Argive princess; torn to pieces by dogs.

2. The son of Apollo and Terpsichore, and the instructor of Orpheus and Hercules, the latter of whom killed him by a blow with a lyre.

Lionesse. See LEONNOYS.

Lion of God. A title conferred upon Ali (597–660), son of Abu Taleb, the uncle of Mahomet. He was distinguished for his eloquence and valour in defence of Islamism.

Lion of the North. A title bestowed upon Gustavus Adolphus (1594–1632), king of Sweden, and the bulwark of the Protestant faith during the Thirty Years' War.

That great leader, captain, and king, the Lion of the North, . . . had a way of winning battles, taking towns, overrunning countries, and levying contributions, which made his service irresistibly delectable to all true-bred cavaliers who follow the noble profession of arms.   Sir W. Scott.

His task at this battle of Lutzen seems to have been a very easy one, simply to see the Lion of the North brought down, not by a cannon-shot, as is generally believed, but by a traitorous pistol-bullet.   Carlyle.

Lion of the Sea. [Port. *Leão do Mar.*] 'A name formerly given to the Cape of Good Hope.

Lis'mă-hā'go, Captain. A superannuated officer on half-pay, who figures in Smollett's "Expedition of Humphry Clinker" as the favoured suitor of Miss Tabitha Bramble. He is described as a hard-featured and forbidding Scotchman, of the most singular dress and manners, self-conceited, pedantic, rude, and disputatious, with a jealous sense of honour, and strong national pride.

☞ "Lismahago is the flower of the flock. His tenaciousness in argument is not so delightful as the relaxation of his logical severity when he finds his fortune mellowing in the wintry smiles of Mrs. Tabitha Bramble. This is the best-preserved and most severe of all Smollett's characters. The resemblance to 'Don Quixote' is only just enough to make it interesting to the critical reader without giving offence to any body else."
Hazlitt.

In quoting these ancient authorities, I must not forget the more modern sketch of a Scottish soldier of the old fashion, by a masterhand, in the character of *Lismahago*, since the existence of that doughty captain alone must deprive the present author of all claim to originality. *Sir W. Scott.*

Little, Thomas. A pseudonym — intended as a playful allusion to his diminutive stature — under which Thomas Moore, in 1808, published a volume of amatory poems.

Little Comedy. A name familiarly given to Miss Catharine Horneck, — afterward Mrs. Bunbury, — an acquaintance and friend of Goldsmith. The sobriquet was probably thought to be indicative of her disposition. She is described as being intelligent, sprightly, and agreeable, as well as very beautiful.

Little Corporal. [Fr. *Le Petit Caporal.*] A familiar appellation jocosely conferred upon *General* Bonaparte, immediately after the battle of Lodi (1796), by the soldiers under his command, on account of his juvenile appearance and surpassing bravery. Ever afterward, even as First Consul and as emperor, he was popularly known by this honorary and affectionate title.

Little Dauphin. [Fr. *Le Petit Dauphin.*] (*Fr. Hist.*) A name given to the Duke de Bourgogne, eldest son of Louis the Dauphin (commonly called the Great Dauphin), who was the son of Louis XIV.

Little-endians. See BIG-ENDIANS, THE.

Little England. A name popularly given to Barbadoes by the inhabitants.

Little Giant. A popular sobriquet conferred upon Stephen A. Douglas, a distinguished American statesman (1813-1861), in allusion to the disparity between his physical and his intellectual proportions.

Little John. A celebrated follower of the still more celebrated English outlaw, Robin Hood. His surname is traditionally said to have been Nailor. See ROBIN HOOD.

☞ "It is certain that another of the Sherwood heroes has imprinted his name upon our family nomenclature in the shape of Littlejohn." *Lower.*

In this our spacious isle, I think there is not one
But he hath heard some talk of him and Little John. *Drayton.*

A squat, broad, *Little-John* sort of figure, leaning on a quarter-staff, and wearing a jerkin, which . . . had once been of the Lincoln green. *Sir W. Scott.*

Little-John, Hugh. The designation given by Sir Walter Scott to his grandson, John Hugh Lockhart, to whom he addressed the "Tales of a Grandfather."

Little Magician. A sobriquet conferred upon Martin Van Buren (1782-1862), President of the United States from 1837 to 1841, in allusion to his supposed political sagacity and talents.

Little Marlborough (mawl'bŭr-o). A sobriquet given to Count von Schwerin (1684-1757), a Prussian field-marshal, and a companion-in-arms of the Duke of Marlborough.

The *Little Marlborough* — so they call him (for he was at Blenheim, and has abrupt, hot ways) — will not participate in Prince Karl's consolatory visit, then! *Carlyle.*

Little Master. A title given to Hans Sebald Beham, a very celebrated painter and engraver of the sixteenth century, on account of the extreme smallness of his prints. The name was also given to other artists of the same century.

Little Nell. A child, in Dickens's novel of "The Old Curiosity Shop;" distinguished for the celestial purity of her character, though living amid scenes of selfishness and shame, of passion and crime.

Little Paris. A name given to the city of Milan, in Italy, from its re-

☞ For the "Key to the Scheme of Pronunciation," with the accompanying Explanatory,

semblance, in point of gayety, to the French capital.

Little Parliament. The same as *Barebone's Parliament*. See BAREBONE'S PARLIAMENT.

Little Ped'dling-tŏn. An imaginary locality in which humbug, quackery, cant, puffery, affectation, unmitigated selfishness, and other social vices abound. It is described in a work of the same name, written by John Poole, — a good-natured and amusing satire on the present condition of literature, art, criticism, and social intercourse.

> The would-be founder of a great slave empire [Jefferson Davis] could now hardly lead the debates of *Little Peddlington*.
> *Boston Evening Transcript*, May 1, 1865.

Little Queen. A sobriquet given to Isabella of Valois (1387-1410), who married Richard II., king of England, when but eight years old, and was left a widow when but thirteen.

Little Red Riding-hood. [Fr. *Chaperon Rouge*, Ger. *Rothkäppchen*.] The heroine of a well-known nursery tale, which relates her encounter with a wolf in a forest, the arts by which he deceived her, and her tragical end. Grimm derives the story from a tradition current in the region bordering upon the river Main, in Germany. The legend is, however, widely disseminated. In the Swedish variation of the story, Little Riding-hood takes refuge in a tree, the wolf meanwhile gnawing away at the roots, when her lover, alarmed by her cries, comes up just in time to see the tree fall and his mistress crushed beneath it.

> No man, whatever his sensibility may be, is ever affected by " Hamlet " or " Lear " as a little girl is affected by the story of poor *Red Riding-hood*. *Macaulay*.

Little Rhody. See RHODY, LITTLE.

Little Whig. A sobriquet given to Anne, Countess of Sunderland, second daughter of the great Duke of Marlborough. She is described as "rather *petite* in person;" and it is said that she "did not disdain the appellation conferred upon her, at a time when every thing bore the ensigns of party of one kind or other." She died April 15, 1716.

Loathly Lady. A hideous creature whom Sir Gawain takes to be his wife, when no one else would have her, and who becomes a beautiful woman on the moment of being married to him, having previously been under the power of a malignant enchanter. The story forms the subject of an old ballad entitled "The Marriage of Sir Gawain," and occurs under other forms in our early literature. See GAWAIN, SIR.

> The walls of the apartment were partly clothed with grim old tapestry representing the memorable story of Sir Gawain's wedding, in which full justice was done to the ugliness of the *Loathly Lady*; although, to judge from his own looks, the gentle knight had less reason to be disgusted with the inatch on account of disparity of outward favour than the romancer has given us to understand.
> *Sir W. Scott.*

Lo-chī'el. Sir Evan Cameron (d. 1719), of Lochiel, surnamed "The Black," the ruler of the Camerons, who in personal qualities has been described as unrivalled among the Celtic princes; "a gracious master, a trusty ally, a terrible enemy." He figured largely in the wars of the Highlands, but ultimately took the oaths to the government of William III. His grandson, Donald Cameron (d. 1748), was sometimes called "The Gentle Lochiel."

> *Lochiel, Lochiel*, beware of the day When the Lowlands shall meet thee in battle-array. *Campbell.*

Loch'in-var'. The hero of a ballad by Sir Walter Scott, sung by the fair Lady Heron, in "Marmion." Appearing suddenly at Netherby Hall, where his sweetheart is to be sacrificed in marriage to

> "a laggard in love, and a dastard in war,"

he persuades her to join with him in one last dance, and, on reaching the hall-door, where his horse is standing, whispers in her ear, swings her to the croup, and, springing into the saddle, carries her off before the eyes of the astonished bridegroom and his friends, who pursue them without success.

> And so I come, — like *Lochinvar*, to tread a single measure,
> To purchase with a loaf of bread a sugar-plum of pleasure. *Holmes.*

Lock'it. A character in Gay's "Beg-

gar's Opera." The quarrel between Peachum and Lockit was an allusion to a personal collision between Walpole and his colleague, Lord Townshend. See PEACHUM.

When you peered at the misty prisoner in the dock, you were always reminded of Captain Macheath in his cell, when the inhuman Mr. Lockit wouldn't allow him any more candles, and threatened to clap on extra fetters in default of an immediate supply on the captain's part of "garnish," or jail-fees. Sala.

Locks'ley. An outlawed archer, in Sir Walter Scott's novel of "Ivanhoe." Under this name the author has represented Robin Hood, who, according to ballad authority, sometimes assumed it when in disguise. It is said to have been the name of the village where he was born.

Lo'co-Fo'cŏs. A nickname formerly given to adherents of the Democratic party in the United States. It originated in 1834, from an incident that occurred at a meeting in Tammany Hall, New York. There being a great diversity of sentiment among those who were present, a scene of confusion and tumult took place, during which the chairman left his seat, and the gas-lights were extinguished, with a view to break up the meeting. But the opposite faction produced loco-foco matches and candles, relighted the hall, continued the meeting, and accomplished their object.

Lo-crine'. A son of Brutus, a fabulous king of ancient Britain. By his father's death, he became king of Loegria, or England. See SABRINA.

Lod'o-vi'co. A Venetian, kinsman to Brabantio, in Shakespeare's tragedy of "Othello."

Loe'grĭ-ȧ (lē'grĭ-ȧ). In the romances of chivalry, and among the fabulous historians, an old name for the part of Britain occupied by the Saxons. It is said to be of Welsh origin.

Lo'gis-til'lȧ. A fairy in Ariosto's "Orlando Furioso;" a sister of Alcina and Morgana. She teaches Ruggiero how to master the hippogriff, and gives Astolpho a book and a horn of wonderful power.

Lo'gres. Another form of *Loegria*, an old name for England, in the romances of chivalry. [Written also L o g r i s.]

*Fairer than feigned of old, or fabled since,
Of fairy damsels, met in forest wide
By knights of Logres or of Lyones. Milton.*

Loki (lo'kee). [Old Norse *locka*, to tempt.] (*Scand. Myth.*) A sort of Eddaic Satan; a demigod descended from the Giants, but admitted among the gods, mingling freely with them as an associate and equal, yet essentially opposed to them, being full of all manner of guile and artifice, and often bringing them into perilous plights, from which however, he again extricates them by his cunning. He treacherously contrived the death of Baldur (see BALDUR), and was, in consequence, made to suffer the most terrible punishment, being bound with the intestines of his sons to a sharp subterranean rock, where two enormous serpents continually drop torturing venom on his limbs. His personal appearance is described as very beautiful. He is often called *Asa-Loki*, to distinguish him from his kinsman, *Utgard-Loki*; but the two are sometimes confounded. See UTGARD-LOKI. [Written also L o k, L o k e.]

Lol'li-us. A mysterious author often referred to by the writers of the Middle Ages; but so vain have been the attempts to discover and identify him, that he must be regarded as the *ignis-fatuus* of antiquaries. "Of Lollius," says one of these unhappy and baffled investigators, "it will become every one to speak with deference." According to Coleridge, "Lollius, if a writer of that name existed at all, was a somewhat somewhere." Dryden calls him "a Lombard."

Lone-Star State. The State of Texas; — so called from the device on its coat of arms.

Long, Tom. The hero of an old popular tale entitled "The Merry Conceits of Tom Long, the Carrier, being many pleasant Passages and mad Pranks which he observed in his travels."

Lon'gȧ-ville. A lord attending on the king of Navarre, in Shakespeare's "Love's Labour's Lost."

☞ For the "Key to the Scheme of Pronunciation," with the accompanying Explanations.

Lon'gl-us. A name given in the Middle Ages to the knight, or soldier, who pierced the side of the Saviour with his sword, to ascertain if he were dead.

Long Meg of Westminster. A "lusty, bouncing romp" and procuress of the sixteenth century, whose "Life and Pranks" were "imprinted at London," in 1582, and subsequently. She is often alluded to by the older English writers.

Long Parliament. (*Eng. Hist.*) The name which is commonly used by historians to designate the celebrated parliament which assembled November 3, 1640, and was dissolved by Cromwell, April 20, 1653.

Long Peter. [D. *Lange Peter*, It. *Pietro Lungo*, Fr. *Long Pierre*.] A sobriquet given to the eminent Flemish painter, Peter Aartsen (1507–1573), on account of his tallness.

Long Scribe. A sobriquet given to Vincent Dowling (d. 1852), an eminent British sportsman, and an infallible authority on all matters connected with field or other sports. He was remarkable for his great height.

Long Tom Coffin. A character in Cooper's novel, "The Pilot;" "probably the most widely known sailor character in existence. He is an example of the heroic in action, like Leatherstocking, losing not a whit of his individuality in his nobleness of soul."

Long Tom Coffin himself will be for fetching me, with a shroud in one hand, and a deadlight in the other. Hood.

Lor-brul'grud. The metropolis of the imaginary country of Brobdingnag, visited by Gulliver. The word is humourously said to mean, "Pride of the Universe."

Lord Bēi'çhăn. The title of an old ballad of which there are many versions, Scottish and English, and the name given to the hero, who is said to have been Gilbert Becket, father of the renowned St. Thomas of Canterbury. [Called also *Lord Bateman*.]

Lord Burleigh (bŭr'lĭ). The name of a character in Mr. Puff's tragedy of the "Spanish Armada," in Sheridan's farce of "The Critic." He says nothing, being a minister "with the whole affairs of the nation on his head," and therefore having no time to talk; but he comes forward upon the stage, and shakes his head extravagantly, — an action which is thus explained by Mr. Puff: "By that shake of the head, he gave you to understand, that, even though they had more justice in their cause, and wisdom in their measures, yet, if there was not a greater spirit shown on the part of the people, the country would at last fall a sacrifice to the hostile ambition of the Spanish monarchy."

If her looks express all this, my dear Tinto, replied I, interrupting him, your pencil rivals the dramatic art of Mr. Puff, who crammed a whole complicated sentence into the expressive shake of Lord Burleigh's head. Sir W. Scott.

There are no such soliloquies in nature, it is true; but, unless they were received as a conventional medium of communication betwixt the poet and the audience, we should reduce dramatic authors to the recipe of Master Puff, who makes Lord Burleigh intimate a long train of political reasoning to the audience, by one comprehensive shake of his noddle. Sir W. Scott.

The Provost answered with another sagacious shake of the head, that would have done honour to Lord Burleigh. Sir W. Scott.

Lord Fanny. A sobriquet conferred upon Lord Hervey, a foppish and effeminate English nobleman of the eighteenth century. He was in the habit of painting his face to conceal its ghastly paleness. See SPORUS.

☞ "The modern *Fanny* is apparently of the days of Anne, coming into notice with the beautiful Lady Fanny Shirley, who made it a great favourite, and almost a proverb for prettiness and simplicity. so that the wits of George II.'s time called John, Lord Hervey, 'Lord Fanny,' for his effeminacy." Yonge.

Rake from each ancient dunghill every pearl, Consult Lord Fanny and confide in Curll. Byron.

Lord Foppington. See FOPPINGTON, LORD.

Lord Gawkey. A nickname given to Richard Grenville, Lord Temple (1711–1770), in the pasquinades of his time.

Lord Harry. A vulgar name for the Devil. See OLD HARRY.

By the *Lord Harry*, he says true: fighting is meat, drink, and cloth to him. *Congreve.*

Lord Lóv'el. The hero of an ancient and well-known Scottish ballad.

Lord of Crazy Castle. A sobriquet of John Hall Stevenson (1718–1785), author of some clever, but licentious poems, called "Crazy Tales." His residence was at Skelton Castle,—nicknamed "Crazy Castle,"—an ancient and ruinous mansion near Guisborough.

His [Sterne's] conversation was animated and witty, but Johnson complained that it was marked by license better suiting the company of the *Lord of Crazy Castle* than of the Great Moralist. *Sir W. Scott.*

Lord of the Isles. A title assumed by Donald, a chief of Islay, who, in 1346, reduced the whole of the Hebrides, or Western Isles, under his authority. It was also borne by his successors.

Lord Ogleby. See OGLEBY, LORD.

Lord Peter. A humourous designation of the Pope in Arbuthnot's "History of John Bull."

Lords of Little Egypt. A title assumed by the leaders or chiefs of a horde of gypsies, who entered Hungary and Bohemia from the East, giving themselves out as Christian pilgrims.

Of the kingly demeanour and personal achievements of old Will Fow [a gypsy chief in Scotland], many curious particulars are related. He never forgot his high descent from the *Lords of Little Egypt*.
Blackwood's Mag.

Lord Strutt. Charles II. of Spain;—so called in Arbuthnot's satire entitled "The History of John Bull."

Every body must remember . . . the paroxysm of rage into which poor old *Lord Strutt* fell, on hearing that his runaway servant Nick Frog, his clothier John Bull, and his old enemy Lewis Baboon, had come with quadrants, poles, and ink-horns to survey his estate, and to draw his will for him.
Macaulay.

Lo-ren'zo. 1. A young man in love with Jessica, Shylock's daughter, in Shakespeare's "Merchant of Venice."

2. The name of a character in Young's "Night Thoughts," represented as a person of a thoroughly debauched and reprobate life, and by some supposed to be the portrait of the poet's own son, but probably nothing more than an embodiment of imaginary atheism and unavailing remorse and despair.

Lŏr're-quer, Harry. The hero of a novel of the same name by Charles James Lever (b. 1806); also, a pseudonym of the author.

Lo-san'tĭ-ville. [That is, L, the river Licking, *os* (Lat.), the mouth, *anti*, opposite to, *ville*, a town or city: the town opposite the mouth of the Licking.] The original name of the city of Cincinnati, Ohio.

Lo-thā'ri-o (9). One of the *dramatis personæ* in Rowe's tragedy, "The Fair Penitent." His character is that of a libertine and a seducer, and has served as the prototype of that of many dramatic and romance heroes.

Is this that haughty gallant, gay *Lothario?*
Rowe.

Shorn of their plumes, our moon-struck sonneteers
Would seem but jackdaws croaking to the spheres;
Our gay *Lotharios*, with their Byron curls,
Would pine like oysters cheated of their pearls. *Holmes.*

Lovel, Lord. See LORD LOVEL.

Lóve'làce. The hero of Richardson's novel, "The History of Clarissa Harlowe," represented as an unscrupulous voluptuary, who has devoted his life and his talents to the subversion of female virtue. He is, perhaps, the most finished picture of a self-possessed and insinuating libertine ever drawn. The character is an expansion of that of Lothario in Rowe's "Fair Penitent." See HARLOWE, CLARISSA.

The eternal laws of poetry regained their power, and the temporary fashions which had superseded those laws went after the wig of *Lovelace* and the hoop of Clarissa.
Macaulay.

Lover's Leap. The promontory from which Sappho is said to have thrown herself into the sea; Leucate, on the south-western extremity of Leucas, now Santa Maura.

Lovers' War. [Fr. *Guerre des Amoureux.*] (*Fr. Hist.*) A name given to a civil war in the year 1580, during the reign of Henry V. It was so called because it arose from the jeal-

---

☞ For the "Key to the Scheme of Pronunciation," with the accompanying Explanations,

ousies and rivalries of the leaders, who were invited to meet at the palace of the queen-mother.

Low-heels. See HIGH-HEELS.

Loys, Le Capitaine. See CAPTAIN LOYS.

Lreux (lroo). King Arthur's seneschal, introduced in romances of the Round Table, and always represented as a detractor, a coward, and a boaster.

Lubberland. The same as *Cockagne*, for which name it was substituted by the English poets of the sixteenth century. Hence, also, a burlesque name anciently applied to London. See COCKAGNE.

But the idea which Siéyès entertained of lodging the executive government in a Grand Elector, who was to be a very model of a king of *Lubberland*, was the ruin of his plan.
Sir W. Scott.

Black Forests and the glories of *Lubberland*, sensuality and horror, the spectre-nun and charmed moonshine, shall not be wanting.
Carlyle.

Lu-cas'tă. A poetical name under which Richard Lovelace (1618–1658) celebrated the praises of "the lady of his love," whom he usually called *Lux Casta*. Antony Wood says that she was "a gentlewoman of great beauty and fortune, named Lucy Sacheverell;" but W. C. Hazlitt, the latest editor of Lovelace's works (London, 1864), thinks the statement "may reasonably be doubted."

Luce. Servant to Adriana, in Shakespeare's "Comedy of Errors."

Lu-cen'ti-o. Son to Vincentio, in Shakespeare's "Taming of the Shrew."

Lu-cet'tă. The name of a waiting-woman to Julia, in Shakespeare's "Two Gentlemen of Verona."

Lu'ci-ā'nă. Sister-in-law to Antipholus of Ephesus, in Shakespeare's "Comedy of Errors."

Lu-cĭ-fẽr. One of the names of the Devil, being applied to him from an allegorical interpretation by the Church fathers of a passage in *Isaiah* (xiv. 12), in which the king of Babylon is likened to the morning star. Wierus makes him the highest officer of justice in the infernal court or empire.

☞ "Lucifer is, in fact, no profane or Satanic title. It is the Latin *Luciferus*, the light-bringer, the morning star, equivalent to the Greek φωσφόρος, and was a Christian name in early times, borne even by one of the popes. It only acquired its present association from the apostrophe of the ruined king of Babylon, in Isaiah, as a fallen star: 'How art thou fallen from heaven, O Lucifer, son of the morning!' Thence, as this destruction was assuredly a type of the fall of Satan, Milton took Lucifer as the title of his demon of pride, and this name of the pure, pale herald of daylight has become hateful to Christian ears."
Yonge.

Lu-ci'nă. [Lat., from *lux*, light, because she brings to light.] (*Rom. Myth.*) The goddess of childbirth, a daughter of Jupiter and Juno.

Lu'ci-o. A fantastic, in Shakespeare's tragedy, "Measure for Measure," who, without being absolutely depraved or intentionally bad, has become, through want of consideration, both vicious and dissolute.

The Introductory Epistle is written, in *Lucio's* phrase, "according to the trick," and would never have appeared had the writer meditated making his avowal of the work.
Sir W. Scott.

Mr. Hunt treats the whole matter a little too much in the easy style of *Lucio*. *Macaulay*.

Lud. A mythic king of Britain, said to have given his name to London.

The famous Cassibelan, who was once at point
(O giglot Fortune!) to Master Cæsar's sword,
Made *Lud's* town with rejoicing bright,
And Britons strut with courage. *Shak.*

Lud, General. A name of great terror given to the feigned leader of bands of distressed and riotous artisans in the manufacturing districts of England, who, in 1811, endeavoured to prevent the introduction of power-looms, — that is, looms worked by machinery, — which they thought would lessen the amount of manual labour. In 1816, they re-appeared, but were put down, after a short and sharp riot in London, by the police and military. The real leaders appeared in women's clothes, and were called "Lud's wives."

☞ Above thirty years before this time [1811], an imbecile named Ned Lud, living in a village in Leicestershire, was tormented by the boys in the streets, to

his perpetual irritation. One day, in a great passion, he pursued one of the boys into a house, and, being unable to find him, he broke two stocking-frames. His name was now either taken by those who broke frames, or was given to them. When frames were broken, Lud had been there; and the abettors were called Luddites."
H. Martineau.

Ludwig der Springer (lōōt'vĭk dĕr spring'ĕr). [Ger., Louis the leaper.] A name popularly given in Germany to a margrave of Thuringia, born in 1042. There is a tradition of his having become attached to the Palsgravine Adelheid of Saxony, whose husband, Frederick III., he killed, and then married her. For this he was imprisoned in the castle of Giebichenstein, near Halle, and escaped by a bold leap into the Saale.

One of their sisters, too, [sisters of the margraves of Brandenburg in the eleventh century,] had a strange adventure with "*Ludwig the Springer*,"— romantic, mythic man, famous in the German world, over whom my readers and I must not pause at this time.
Carlyle.

Lugg'năgg. The name of an imaginary island about a hundred leagues south-east of Japan, mentioned in Swift's fictitious "Travels" of Lemuel Gulliver. In the account of this country and its inhabitants, we are shown how miserable would be the consequence of human beings' receiving a privilege of eternal life, unaccompanied by corresponding health, strength, and intellect.

Lumber State. A popular designation for the State of Maine, the inhabitants of which are largely engaged in the business of cutting and rafting lumber, or of converting it into boards, shingles, scantlings, and the like.

Lump'kin, Tony. A young, clownish country squire, the foolish son of a foolish mother, in Goldsmith's comedy, "She Stoops to Conquer."

☞ "He is in his own sex what a hoiden is in the other. He is that vulgar nickname, a *hobbetyhoy*, dramatised; forward and sheepish, mischievous and idle, cunning and stupid, with the vices of the man and the follies of the boy; fond of low company, and giving himself all the airs of consequence of the young squire."
Hazlitt.

You ask me for the plan. I have no plan. I had no plan; but I had, or have, materials; though, if, like *Tony Lumpkin*, "I am to be snubbed so when I am in spirits," the poem will be naught, and the poet turn serious again.
Byron.

Nature had formed honest Meg for such encounters; and as her noble soul delighted in them, so her outward properties were in what *Tony Lumpkin* calls "a concatenation accordingly."
Sir W. Scott.

I feel as *Tony Lumpkin* felt, who never had the least difficulty in reading the outside of his letters, but who found it very hard work to decipher the inside.
A. K. H. Boyd.

Lun. A feigned name of John Rich (d. 1761), a celebrated English actor. When young, he attracted general admiration by his performance of Harlequin, and received frequent tributes of applause from contemporary critics.

When *Lun* appeared, with matchless art and whim.
Garrick.

Lu'nă. (*Rom. Myth.*) The goddess of the moon; a name of Diana.

Lu-pēr'cus (4). [Lat., from *lupus*, a wolf.] (*Rom. Myth.*) A god of the old Romans, sometimes identified with the Grecian *Pan*. He was worshipped by shepherds as the protector of flocks against wolves. His priests were called "Luperci," and his festivals "Lupercalia."

Lu'sig-năn. A prominent character in Aaron Hill's tragedy of "Zara;" the "last of the blood of the Christian kings of Jerusalem."

His head, which was a fine one, bore some resemblance to that of Garrick in the character of *Lusignan*.
Sir W. Scott.

Lu'si-tā'ni-ă. The ancient Latin name of Portugal; often used in modern poetry.

Woe to the conquering, not the conquered, host,
Since baffled Triumph droops on *Lusitania's* coast.
Byron.

Lu'sus. A mythical hero, fabled to have visited Portugal in company with Ulysses, and to have founded Lisbon under the name of Ulyssopolis.

Lu-te'ti-a (-te'shĭ-ă). The ancient Latin name of Paris.

Luz. A name given by the old Jewish Rabbins to an imaginary little bone which they believed to exist at the base of the spinal column, and to be incapable of destruction. To its ever-living power, fermented by a kind of dew from heaven, they ascribed the resurrection of the dead.

☞ "Hadrian (whose bones may they be ground, and his name blotted out!) asked R. Joshua Ben Hananiah, 'How doth a man revive again in the world to come?' He answered and said, 'From Luz, in the backbone.' Saith he to him, 'Demonstrate this to me.' Then he took Luz, a little bone out of the backbone, and put it in water, and it was not steeped; he put it in the fire, and it was not burned; he brought it to the mill, and that could not grind it; he laid it on the anvil, and knocked it with a hammer, but the anvil was cleft, and the hammer broken." *Lightfoot.*

Ly̆-cā'ŏn. [Gr. Λυκάων.] (*Gr. & Rom. Myth.*) A king of Arcadia whom Juno turned into a wolf because he defiled his altar with human sacrifices. He was the father of Callisto.

Ly̆-ehŏr'ĭ-dặ. A nurse, in Shakespeare's "Pericles."

Lyç'ĭ-dặs. 1. A shepherd in the third Eclogue of Virgil.
2. A poetical name under which Milton, in a celebrated monody, bewails the death of his friend Edward King, fellow of Christ College, Cambridge, who was drowned on his passage from Chester to Ireland, August 10, 1637.

Lyç'o-me'dēṣ. [Gr. Λυκομήδης.] (*Gr. & Rom. Myth.*) A king of the island of Scyros, with whom Achilles concealed himself for some time, disguised in female apparel, to avoid going to the Trojan war.

Ly̆'cus. [Gr. Λύκος.] (*Gr. & Rom. Myth.*) A king of Thebes, in Bœotia, and the husband of Antiope, whom he divorced because she was pregnant by Jupiter. He then married Dirce, who treated Antiope with great cruelty; but the children of the latter, when they were grown up, avenged their mother on both Dirce and Lycus. See DIRCE.

Lying Dick. See TALBOT, LYING DICK.

Lyn'ceŭs. [Gr. Λυγκεύς.] (*Gr. & Rom. Myth.*) 1. One of the Argonauts, famed for the sharpness of his sight.
2. A son of Ægyptus, and the husband of Hypermnestra. See DANAIDES.

Lynch, Judge. In America, a personification of violent and illegal justice, or of mob-law. The name is usually alleged to be derived from one Lynch, who lived in what is now the Piedmont district of Virginia at the time when that district was the western frontier of the State, and when, on account of the distance from the courts of law, it was customary to refer the adjustment of disputes to men of known character and judgment in the neighbourhood. This man became so prominent by reason of the wisdom and impartiality of his decisions that he was known throughout the country as "Judge Lynch." Criminals were brought before him to receive their sentence, which was perhaps administered with some severity. At present, the term Lynch-law is synonymous with mobocracy. By some, the term is said to be derived from one James Lynch Fitz-Stephen, a merchant of Galway, and in 1526 its mayor. His son having been convicted of murder, he, Brutus-like, sentenced him to death, and, fearing a rescue, caused him to be brought home and hanged before his own door. These explanations cannot be regarded as conclusive, or even tolerably well authenticated. A more probable solution is to be found, perhaps, in the Provincial English word *linch*, to beat or maltreat. If this were admitted, Lynch-law would then be simply equivalent to "club-law."

Ly'on-nesse'. Another form of *Leonnoys*. See LEONNOYS.

Lyric Muse. A title awarded to Corinna, a poetess of Tanagra, in Bœotia, contemporary with Pindar, whom she is said to have conquered five times in musical contests.

Ly̆-san'dẽr. A character in love with Hermia, in Shakespeare's "Midsummer-Night's Dream."

M.

Mab. [Erse *Meabhdh*, said to have been originally the name of a great Irish princess.] The name given by the English poets of the fifteenth and succeeding centuries to the imaginary queen of the fairies. Shakespeare has given a famous description of Queen Mab in "Romeo and Juliet," a. i., sc. 4.

> *Mab*, the mistress fairy,
> That doth nightly rob the dairy,
> And can hurt or help the churning
> As she please, without discerning;
> She that pinches country wenches
> If they rub not clean their benches,
> But if so they chance to feast her,
> In a shoe she drops a tester. *Ben Jonson.*

> If ye will with *Mab* find grace,
> Set each platter in its place;
> Rake the fire up and get
> Water in ere sun be set;
> Sweep your house; who doth not so,
> *Mab* will pinch her by the toe. *Herrick.*

Ma-câire′, Robert (*Fr. pron.* ro′bêř mȧ′kêř′, 64). The name of a character in a large number of French plays, particularly two, entitled "Chien de Montargis" and "Chien d'Aubry;" applied to any audacious criminal. Macaire was a real person, a French knight of the time of Charles V., but his Christian name was Richard, not Robert. He is traditionally said to have assassinated Aubry de Montdidier, one of his companions-in-arms, in the forest of Bondy, in the year 1371. As the dog of the murdered man displayed the most unappeasable enmity towards Macaire, the latter was arrested on suspicion, and required to fight a judicial combat with the animal. The result was fatal to the murderer, and he died confessing his guilt. The character of Macaire has been a favourite one upon the Parisian stage, and hence the name is sometimes used as a sportive designation of the French people generally.

Mac-beth′. An ancient king of Scotland, immortalised by being the hero of Shakespeare's tragedy of the same name. See DUNCAN.

Mac-beth′, Lady. The chief female character in Shakespeare's tragedy of "Macbeth."

☞ "In the mind of Lady Macbeth, ambition is represented as the ruling motive, — an intense, overmastering passion, which is gratified at the expense of every just and generous principle, and every feminine feeling. In the pursuit of her object, she is cruel, treacherous, and daring. She is doubly, trebly dyed in guilt and blood; for the murder she instigates is rendered more frightful by disloyalty and ingratitude, and by the violation of all the most sacred claims of kindred and hospitality. When her husband's more kindly nature shrinks from the perpetration of the deed of horror, she, like an evil genius, whispers him on to his damnation. . . . Lady Macbeth's amazing power of intellect, her inexorable determination of purpose, her superhuman strength of nerve, render her as fearful in herself as her deeds are hateful; yet she is not a mere monster of depravity, with whom we have nothing in common, nor a meteor, whose destroying path we watch in ignorant affright and amaze. She is a terrible impersonation of evil passions and mighty powers, never so far removed from our own nature as to be cast beyond the pale of our sympathies; for the woman herself remains a woman to the last, still linked with her sex and with humanity." *Mrs. Jameson.*

Mac′brĭ-ar, Ephraim. An enthusiast preacher in Scott's "Old Mortality."

McBride, Miss. A proud heiress with great expectations, whose history is related in a humourous and popular poem by John G. Saxe.

Mac-duff′. A Scottish thane, in Shakespeare's tragedy of "Macbeth."

McFin′gặl. The hero of Trumbull's Hudibrastic political poem of the same name; represented as a burly New England squire enlisted on the side of the Tory, or royalist, party of the American Revolution, and constantly engaged in controversy with Honorius, the champion of the Whigs, or rebels.

Mac Fleck′nŏe. [That is, Flecknoe's son.] The title of a poem by Dryden,

---

☞ For the "Key to the Scheme of Pronunciation," with the accompanying Explanations,

in which he lampoons Thomas Shadwell, a worthless contemporary poet and dramatist, who had repeatedly intimated his superiority to Dryden as a writer of plays. By "Mac Flecknoe," Shadwell is meant, though he is called, in the poem itself, by his real name only. The Flecknoe to whom the title alludes was a wretched poet, so distinguished for his bad verses that his name had become almost proverbial. Dryden describes him as an aged prince, who, for many years, had reigned

"without dispute,
Through all the realms of Nonsense, absolute."

Shadwell is represented as the adopted son of this venerable monarch, and is solemnly inaugurated as his successor on the throne of dulness.

McFlimsey, Flora. The heroine of "Nothing to Wear," a popular satirical poem by William Allen Butler (b. 1825), an American author.

Mac-greg'or. See ROB ROY.

Mā-chā'ŏn. [Gr. Μαχάων.] (*Gr. & Rom. Myth.*) A son of Æsculapius, and a surgeon of the Greeks before Troy, where he died.

Mac-hēath', Captain. A highwayman who is the hero of Gay's "Beggar's Opera."

I communicated this purpose, and recommended the old hag to poor Effie, by a letter, in which I recollect that I endeavoured to support the character of *Macheath* under condemnation,—a fine, gay, bold-faced ruffian, who is game to the last. *Sir W. Scott.*

He hears the sound of coaches and six, takes the road like *Macheath*, and makes society stand and deliver. *Thackeray.*

Mac-I'vŏr, Fĕr'gus (4). The chief of Glennaquoich, a prominent character in Scott's novel of "Waverley." [Called also *Vich Ian Vohr.*]

Mac-I'vŏr, Flora. The heroine of Scott's "Waverley;" sister to Fergus MacIvor.

Mā'cŏn, or **Măc'ŏn.** [It. *Macone*. "Evidently a corruption of *Mahomet* [or *Mahoun*]; for the Italians do not aspirate the *h*, they pronounce it like a *k*." *Ugo Foscolo.* See MAHOUN.] An old English form of *Mahomet*.

Praisèd, quoth he, be *Macon*, whom we serve.
Fairfax.

Mac-rab'in, Mark. A pseudonym under which a series of interesting "Recollections" by a Cameronian were contributed to "Blackwood's Magazine." The writer is believed to have been Allan Cunningham.

Mac-rab'in, Peter. An imaginary interlocutor in the "Noctes Ambrosianæ" of Wilson, Lockhart, and Maginn.

MacSycophant, Sir Pĕr'tĭ-nax (4). A noted character in Macklin's comedy of "The Way of the World."

McTab, The Honourable Miss Lucretia. A stiff maiden aunt in Colman's comedy, "The Poor Gentleman;" sister of one of the oldest barons in Scotland, and extremely proud of her noble birth, but reduced to dependence upon the husband of a deceased niece.

Mac-Turk', Captain Hec'tŏr. One of the Managing Committee at the Spa, in Scott's novel of "St. Ronan's Well;" characterised as "the man of Peace."

Mad Anthony. A sobriquet of Major-General Anthony Wayne (1745–1796), distinguished for his military skill and impetuous bravery in the war of the American Revolution.

Mad Cavalier. A sobriquet given to Prince Rupert of Bavaria (1619–1682), nephew of Charles I. of England, and a leader of that king's forces during the civil wars. He was remarkable for his rash courage and impetuosity, and his impatience of control and advice.

Madhava (mă-thā'vă). (*Hindu Myth.*) A name often given to *Vishnu*. See VISHNU.

Madman of Macedonia. An epithet sometimes applied to Alexander the Great (356–323 B. C.), king of Macedonia, whose extraordinary and uninterrupted military success created in him a thirst for universal dominion so insatiable that he is said to have wept because there were no more worlds than this for him to conquer.

Heroes are much the same, the point's agreed,
From *Macedonia's Madman* to the Swede.
Pope.

"A Nation which can fight," think the Gazetteers; "... and is led on by its king, too, who may prove, in his way, a very Charles XII., or small *Macedonia's Madman*, for aught one knows; " in which latter branch of their prognostic the Gazetteers were much out. *Carlyle.*

Madman of the North. Charles XII. of Sweden;—so called on account of the rashness and impetuosity of his character. He was born at Stockholm in 1682, and killed at the siege of Frederickshall, in 1718. His life was full of exciting adventures in war. He formed great plans for the aggrandisement of his kingdom, which he did not live to execute, and at his death, Sweden fell from the rank of a leading power.

Mā'dŏr, Sir. A Scottish knight with whom Lancelot du Lac engaged in single combat, in order to prove the innocence of Queen Guinever, falsely accused by Sir Mador of having poisoned his brother. The contest lasted from noon till evening, when Lancelot finally achieved a complete victory over his antagonist. See JOYEUSE GARDE, LA.

Mad Parliament. (*Eng. Hist.*) A name given by the old chroniclers to a parliament which assembled at Oxford on the 11th of June. 1258, and which, exasperated at the exorbitant demands for supplies made by the king, Henry III., to enable him to accomplish the conquest of Sicily, broke out into open revolt against the supremacy of the crown, which resulted in the appointment of twenty-four of their number, with the famous Simon de Montfort as president, to administer the government.

Mad Poet. 1. A name sometimes given to Nathaniel Lee (1657-1690), an English dramatic poet, who, in 1684, became insane, and was confined in Bedlam for four years.

2. A sobriquet applied to McDonald Clark (1798-1842), author of various fugitive poetical pieces in which there are some glimmerings of genius. He died in the Insane Asylum at Bloomingdale, New York.

Mæ-ce'nǎs (Caius Cilnius). A wealthy Roman nobleman (d. B. C.

8), a friend of Augustus, and a liberal patron of Virgil, Horace, Propertius, and other men of genius. The name is proverbially used to denote any munificent friend of literature.

Mæ-on'ī-dēṣ. [Gr. Μαιονίδης.] A poetical designation of Homer, who was born, according to some accounts, in Mæonia, a district of Eastern Lydia, in Asia Minor.

Those other two eqnalled with me in fate,
So were I equalled with them in renown,—
Blind Thamyris and blind *Mæonides.*
Milton.

Mā'gǎ. A popular sobriquet of "Blackwood's Magazine," the contributors to which have embraced many of the most eminent writers of Great Britain, including Wordsworth, Coleridge, Lamb, De Quincey, Landor, and others. The name is a contraction of the word *Magazine.*

On other occasions he was simllarly honoured, and was invariably mentioned with praise by Wilson, the presiding genius of *Maga.* *R. Shelton Mackenzie.*

Mā'gī, The Three. The "wise men from the East" who came to Jerusalem bringing gifts to the infant Jesus. (*Matt.* ii.) *Magi* (in the original Greek, μάγοι) is the Latin for "wise men," in the Vulgate translation of the Bible. The traditional names of the three Magi are Melchior, represented as an old man with a long beard, offering gold, in acknowledgment of the sovereignty of Christ; Jaspar, a beardless youth, who offers frankincense, in recognition of our Lord's divinity; and Balthazar, a black, or Moor, with a large spreading beard, who tenders myrrh, as a tribute to the Saviour's humanity. They are the patron saints of travellers. See COLOGNE, THE THREE KINGS OF.

☞ " Early did tradition fix the number at three, probably in allusion to the three races of men descended from the sons of Noah; and soon they were said to be descendants of the Mesopotamian prophet Balaam, from whom they derived the expectation of the star of Jacob. Their corpses were supposed to be at that storehouse of relics, Constantinople, whence the Empress Helena caused them to be transported to Milan. Frederick Barbarossa carried them to

Cologne, the place of their especial glory as the Three Kings of Cologne." *Yonge.*

Magician, Great. See GREAT MAGICIAN.

Magician, Little. See LITTLE MAGICIAN.

Magician of the North. [Ger. *Magus aus Norden.*] A title assumed by Johann Georg Hamann (1730–1788), a German writer of very original genius.

Maguelone, The Fair. See FAIR MAGUELONE.

Mahadeva (mă′hă-dā′vă). [Sansk., great god.] (*Hindu Myth.*) An appellation by which Siva is usually designated. See SIVA.

Mahadevî (mă′hă-dā′vee). [Sansk., great goddess.] (*Hindu Myth.*) Another name of Durga, the wife of Siva. See DURGA.

Mă-houn′, or **Mă′houn,**) [Old Fr.
Mă-hound′, or **Mă′hound.**) *Mahom.*]
Corrupted forms of the name *Mahomet*, used by our old writers.

And oftentimes by Termagaunt and *Mahound* swore. *Spenser.*

Of sundry faith together in that town, . . .
The greater, far, were votaries to *Mahoun*.
 Fairfax.

An antique flowered silk gown graced the extraordinary person to whom belonged this unparalleled *tête*, which her brother was wont to say was fitter for a turban for *Mahound* or Termagant, than a head-gear for a reasonable creature, or Christian gentlewoman.
 Sir W. Scott.

There was crying in Granada when the sun was going down,
Some calling on the Trinity, some calling on *Mahoun*. *Lockhart.*

Mahu (mă-hoo′, or mă′hoo). A fiend mentioned by Shakespeare, in the tragedy of "Lear," as the instigator of theft. See FLIBBERTIGIBBET, 1.

Mā′i-ă (20). [Gr. Μαῖα.] (*Gr. & Rom. Myth.*) A daughter of Atlas, and the mother of Mercury.

Maiden Queen. A name popularly given to Queen Elizabeth of England, who began to reign in 1558, at the age of twenty-five, and died unmarried in 1603, at the age of seventy. See VIRGIN QUEEN.

He merely asks whether, at that period, the *Maiden Queen* was red-painted on the nose, and white-painted on the cheeks, as her tirewomen — when, from spleen and wrinkles, she would no longer look in any glass — were wont to serve her. *Carlyle.*

Maiden Town. [Gael. *Magh-dun*, Brit. *Maidin*, Lat. *Castrum Puellarum.*] A name popularly given to Edinburgh, from a monkish fable or tradition that it was once the residence of the daughters of Pictish kings, who were sent to this stronghold for protection in times of war and trouble.

Your hands are weak with age, he said,
Your hearts are stout and true;
So bide ye in the *Maiden Town*,
While others fight for you. *Aytoun.*

Maid Mă′ri-ăn (9). A personage in the morris-dances, often dressed like a woman, and sometimes like a strumpet, and whose name is, therefore, used to describe women of an impudent or masculine character. Though the morris-dances were, as their name denotes, of Moorish origin, yet they were commonly adapted in England to the popular English story of Robin Hood, whose fair Matilda, or Marian, was the very person here originally represented. See ROBIN HOOD.

☞ Maid Marian, as Queen of May, has a golden crown upon her head, and in her left hand a red pink as an emblem of summer. Percy and Steevens agree in making Marian the mistress of Robin Hood. Douce, however, considers the character a dramatic fiction. "None of the materials that constitute the more authentic history of Robin Hood prove the existence of such a character in the shape of his mistress."

☞ "Probably the addition of the German diminutive *chen*, in French *on*, formed the name of

'A bonny fine maid, of noble degree,
 Maid Marian called by name.'

Very soon had her fame travelled abroad, for in 1332 the play of 'Robin et Marion' was performed by the students of Angers, one of them appearing as a *fillette déguisée;* the origin of *Marionettes*, puppets disguised to play the part of Maid Marian, is thus explained." *Yonge.*

Robin's mistress dear, his loved *Marion*,
Was sovereign of the woods, chief lady of the game;
Her clothes tucked to the knee, and daintybraided hair,
With bow and quiver armed. *Drayton.*

Maid of Anjou, Fair. See FAIR MAID OF ANJOU.

Maid of Băth (2). A name given to Miss Linley, a beautiful and accomplished singer, who became the wife

and for the Remarks and Rules to which the numbers after certain words refer, see pp. xiv-xxxii.

of Richard Brinsley Sheridan, the celebrated dramatist and statesman.

Maid of Kent, Fair. See FAIR MAID OF KENT.

Maid of Kent, Holy. See HOLY MAID OF KENT.

Maid of Norway. In Scottish history, a name given to Margaret, a grand-daughter of Alexander III., recognised as his successor by the states of Scotland, though a female, an infant, and a foreigner. She died, however, on her passage to Scotland, in 1290. Her father was Eric II., king of Norway, and her mother Margaret, only daughter of Alexander.

Maid of Ŏr'le-ăn§. A surname given to Joan of Arc, from her heroic defence of the city of Orleans. Having been taken captive by the English, she suffered martyrdom, being burned alive by order of the Earl of Warwick, on the 24th of May, 1431.

☞ "It was requisite that she should suffer; for had she not passed through the supreme trial and purification, dubious shadows would have remained among the rays that beam from her saintly head; she would not have dwelt in men's memory as the *Maid* of Orleans." *Michelet, Trans.*

Maid of Perth, Fair. See FAIR MAID OF PERTH.

Maid of Saragossa. An appellation bestowed upon Agustina Zaragoza, a young Spanish woman distinguished for her heroism during the defence of Saragossa in 1808–9. She first attracted notice by mounting a battery where her lover had fallen, and working a gun in his room. Byron has celebrated her in the first canto of his "Childe Harold."

Malagigi (mȧl-ȧ-je'jee). A celebrated hero in the romances and poems based upon the fabulous adventures of Charlemagne and his paladins. He is said to have been a cousin to Rinaldo, and a son of Beuves, or Buovo, of Aygremont. He was brought up by the fairy Orianda, and became a great enchanter.

Mal'ȧ-grī'dȧ. A nickname given by contemporary political opponents to Lord Shelburne (1737–1805), a zealous oppositionist during the administration of Lord North. Gabriel Malagrida (1689–1761) was an Italian Jesuit, and missionary to Brazil, who was accused of conspiring against the king of Portugal.

☞ "'Do you know,' said Goldsmith to his lordship, in the course of conversation, 'that I never could conceive why they call you Malagrida, for *Malagrida* was a very good sort of man.' This was too good a trip of the tongue for Beauclerc to let pass: he serves it up in his next letter to Lord Charlemont, as a specimen of a mode of turning a thought the wrong way, peculiar to the poet; he makes merry over it with his witty and sarcastic compeer, Horace Walpole, who pronounces it 'a picture of Goldsmith's whole life.' Dr. Johnson alone, when he hears it bandied about as Goldsmith's last blunder, growls forth a friendly defence: 'Sir,' said he, 'it was a mere blunder in emphasis. He meant to say, I wonder they should use Malagrida as a term of reproach.' Poor Goldsmith! On such points he was ever doomed to be misinterpreted." *W. Irving.*

Mal'ȧ-grow'thēr. 1. (Sir Muñ'go.) An old courtier in Sir Walter Scott's novel, "The Fortunes of Nigel." "He is a man of birth and talents, but naturally unamiable, and soured by misfortune, who now, mutilated by accident, and grown old, and deaf, and peevish, endeavours by the unsparing exercise of a malicious penetration and a caustic wit, under the protection of his bodily infirmities, to retaliate on an unfriendly world, and to reduce its happier inhabitants to a momentary level with himself."

2. (**Mal'ȧ-chī.**) A *nom de plume* used by Sir Walter Scott as the signature of several letters written by him to the Edinburgh "Weekly Journal" in 1826, in opposition to the proposition in the British parliament to restrict the circulation of bank-notes of less than five pounds value in Scotland.

☞ "These diatribes produced in Scotland a sensation not perhaps inferior to that of the Drapier's letters in Ireland; a greater one, certainly, than any political tract had excited in the British public at large since the appearance of Burke's 'Reflections on the French Revolution.'" *Lockhart.*

☞ For the "Key to the Scheme of Pronunciation," with the accompanying Explanations,

Mal'à-prop, Mrs. A character in Sheridan's comedy of "The Rivals," noted for her blunders in the use of words. The name is obviously derived from the French *mal à propos*, unapt, ill-timed.

☞ "Mrs. Malaprop's mistakes in what she herself calls 'orthodoxy' have been often objected to as improbable from a woman in her rank of life; but though some of them, it must be owned, are extravagant and farcical, they are almost all amusing; and the luckiness of her simile, 'as headstrong as an *allegory* on the banks of the Nile,' will be acknowledged as long as there are writers to be run away with by the wilfulness of this truly 'headstrong' species of composition." *T. Moore.*

The conclusion drawn was, that Childe Harold, Byron, and the Count in Beppo, are one and the same person, thereby making me turn out to be, as *Mrs. Malaprop* says, "like Cerberus, three gentlemen at once." *Byron.*

Mal-bec'co. A character in Spenser's "Faëry Queen" (B. III., c. 9, 10), designed to represent the self-inflicted torments endured by him

"Who dotes, yet doubts; suspects, yet fondly loves."

The sight could jealous pangs beguile,
And charm *Malbecco's* cares awhile.
Sir W. Scott.

Malcolm (măl'kum). A son of Duncan, in Shakespeare's tragedy of "Macbeth."

Malebolge (mă-lă-bol'jă). A name given by Dante to the eighth circle in his "Inferno," from the ten "evil" "*bolgi*," or pits, which it contains.

Mal-vo'li-o. Steward to Olivia, in Shakespeare's "Twelfth Night."

☞ "Malvolio is not essentially ludicrous. He becomes comic but by accident. He is cold, austere, repelling, but dignified, consistent, and, for what appears, rather of an overstretched morality. ... He is opposed to the proper *levities* of the piece, and falls in the unequal contest. Still his pride, or his gravity (call it which you will), is inherent, and native to the man, not mock or affected, which latter only are the fit objects to excite laughter. His quality is, at the best, unlovely, but neither buffoon nor contemptible. ... His dialect, on all occasions, is that of a gentleman and a man of education. We must not confound him with the eternal, old, low steward of comedy. He is master of the household to a great princess,— a dignity, probably, conferred upon him for other respects than age or length of service." *Charles Lamb.*

Four of the duke's friends, with the obedient start which poor *Malvolio* ascribes to his imaginary retinue, made out to lead the victor to his presence. *Sir W. Scott.*

Clearing his voice with a preliminary hem, he addressed his kinsman, checking, as *Malvolio* proposed to do when seated in his state, his familiar smile with an austere regard of control. *Sir W. Scott.*

We fools of fancy, who suffer ourselves, like *Malvolio*, to be cheated with our own visions, have, nevertheless, this advantage over the wise ones of the earth, that we have our whole stock of enjoyments under our own command, and can dish for ourselves an intellectual banquet with most moderate assistance from external objects. *Sir W. Scott.*

Mamamouchi (mä'mä'moo'she'). A knight of an imaginary order, of which M. Jourdain, in Molière's comedy, "Le Bourgeois Gentilhomme," is persuaded that the grand seignior has made him a member, and into which he is inducted by the ceremony of a mock installation.

All the women most devoutly swear,
Each would be rather a poor actress here,
Than to be made a *Mamamouchi* there.
Dryden.

Mambrino (măm-bre'no). A Moorish king, in the romantic poems of Bojardo and Ariosto, who was the possessor of an enchanted golden helmet, which rendered the wearer invulnerable, and which was the object of eager quest to the paladins of Charlemagne. This helmet was borne away by the knight Rinaldo. It owes its celebrity, in a great measure, to the mention which is made of it by Cervantes, in "Don Quixote," where the crazy knight of that name is represented as fully believing that he had found it in what was in reality nothing but a copper basin, highly polished, which a barber, on his way to bleed a patient, had put on his head to protect a new hat during a shower.

Like some enchanted *Mambrino's* helmet. *Carlyle.*

But the 'War' [between Charles VI., emperor of Germany, and Philip V., king of Spain, 1718-20], except that many men were killed in it, and much vain babble was uttered upon it, ranks otherwise with that of Don Quixote for conquest of the enchanted helmet of *Mambrino*, which, when looked into, proved to be a barber's basin. *Carlyle.*

Mă-mil'li-us. A young prince of Sicilia, in Shakespeare's "Winter's Tale."

---

and for the Remarks and Rules to which the numbers after certain words refer, see pp. xiv-xxxii.

Mam'mǒn. A Syriac word used in the Scriptures to signify either riches or the god of riches. By poetic license, Milton makes Mammon one of the fallen angels, and portrays his character in the following lines:—

*Mammon, the least erected spirit that fell
From heaven; for even in heaven his looks
  and thoughts
Were always downward bent; admiring more
The riches of heaven's pavement, trodden
  gold,
Than aught divine or holy else enjoyed
In vision beatific: by him first
Men, also, and by his suggestion taught,
Ransacked the centre, and with impious
  hands
Rifled the bowels of their mother earth
For treasures better hid.*   *Par. Lost, Bk. I.*

Wierus, in his account of the infernal court of Beëlzebub, makes Mammon its ambassador in England. Other medieval demonographers placed him at the head of the ninth rank of demons, of which they reckoned nine kinds.

Mammon, Cave of. See CAVE OF MAMMON.

Mam'mǒn, Sir Epicure. A worldly sensualist, in Ben Jonson's play, "The Alchymist."

Sir Epicure did not indulge in visions more magnificent and gigantic [than Bacon].
    Macaulay.

Manchester Massacre. See PETERLOO, FIELD OF.

Manchester Poet. An appellation given to Charles Swain (b. 1803), an English poet, and a native of Manchester.

Mandane (moⁿ/dân', 62). The heroine of Mme. Scudery's romance entitled "Artamanes, ou Le Grand Cyrus."

Mandricardo (mân-dre-kar'do). A Saracen warrior in Bojardo's "Orlando Innamorato," son of Agricane, and emperor of Tartary. He figures also in Ariosto's "Orlando Furioso" and other romantic poems and tales of the Carlovingian cycle.

Mā'nēṣ. [Lat., the good or benevolent ones.] (*Rom. Myth.*) The deified souls of the departed, worshipped with divine honours.

Man'fred. The hero of Byron's drama of the same name; represented as a being estranged from all human creatures, indifferent to all human sympathies, and dwelling in the magnificent solitude of the central Alps, where he holds communion only with the spirits he invokes by his sorceries, and with the fearful memory of the being he has loved and destroyed.

Man in Black. 1. A character in Goldsmith's "Citizen of the World," supposed to be, in its main features, a portrait of Goldsmith's father.

☞ "A most delightful compound is the 'Man in Black;' a rarity not to be met with often; a true oddity, with the tongue of Timon and the heart of Uncle Toby. He proclaims war against pauperism, yet he cannot say 'No' to a beggar. He ridicules generosity, yet would he share with the poor whatever he possessed."   *Henry Giles.*

2. The subject of a tale by Washington Irving.

Man in the Moon. A name popularly given to the dark lines and spots upon the surface of the moon which are visible to the naked eye, and which, when examined with a good telescope, are discovered to be the shadows of lunar mountains. It is one of the most popular, and perhaps one of the most ancient, superstitions in the world, that these lines and spots are the figure of a man leaning on a fork, on which he carries a bundle of thorns or brushwood, for stealing which on a Sunday he was confined in the moon. (See Shakespeare's "Midsummer-Night's Dream," a. iii., sc. 1, and "Tempest," a. ii., sc. 2.) The account given in Numbers xv. 32, *et seq.*, of a man who was stoned to death for gathering sticks upon the Sabbath-day, is undoubtedly the origin of this belief.

☞ To have a care "lest the chorle may fall out of the moon" appears from Chaucer's "Troilus and Cresseide" to have been a proverbial expression in his time. In the "Testament of Cresseide," describing the moon, he informs us that she had

"On her brest a chorle painted ful even
  Bearing a bush of thornès on his backe,
Which for his theft might climb no uer the
  heven."

With the Italians, Cain appears to have been the offender. Dante, in the twentieth canto of the "Inferno," describes

---

☞ For the "Key to the Scheme of Pronunciation," with the accompanying Explanations,

the moon by the periphrasis, "*Caino e le spine.*" The Jews have some Talmudical story that Jacob is in the moon, and they believe that his face is visible. For Oriental and other traditions, see Grimm, "Deutsche Mythologie," p. 679.

☞ "As for the forme of those spots, some of the vulgar thinke they represent *a man*, and the poets guess 't is *the boy Endymion*, whose company shee loves so well that she carries him with her; others will have it onely to be the face of a man, as the moon is usually pictured; but Albertus thinkes rather that it represents *a lyon*, with his tail toward the east and his head to the west; and some others have thought it to be very much like *a fox*; and certainly it is as much like a lyon as that in the zodiake, or as Ursa Major is like a beare."
Bp. Wilkins, Disc. of a New World.

Manly. One of the *dramatis personæ* in Wycherley's "Plain-dealer," described by the author as "of an honest, surly, nice humour, supposed first in the time of the Dutch War to have procured the command of a ship, out of honour, not interest, and choosing a sea-life only to avoid the world." Leigh Hunt characterises him as "a ferocious sensualist, who believed himself as great a rascal as he thought every body else."

Mă-nŏ'ă. A fabulous city of great size, wealth, and population, in El Dorado, on the west shore of Lake Parime, and at the mouth of a great river which empties into this lake. The houses were said to be covered with plates of gold.

☞ "This fable began to gain credit in 1534, and many were the stories invented by Juan Martinez, a Spaniard, who, among other things, asserted that he had lived a long time in the country, and that he left it by the permission of the chief who commanded it, and who was descended from the ancient Incas of Peru; that this same chief gave orders that he should be accompanied by Indians till he reached the Spanish frontiers; that they took care to lead him blindfold, lest he might observe the way by which to return; with several other things equally vague and foolish, but so as to induce, at first, many expeditions to this fair-reputed city at the expense of large sums of money and many lives." *Alcedo, Trans.*

Man of Bâth (2). A surname given to Ralph Allen, the friend of Pope, Warburton, and Fielding, celebrated in the well-known lines of the first:—
"Let humble Allen, with an awkward shame,
Do good by stealth, and blush to find it fame."

Man of Blood. An expression which occurs in the Old Testament (2 Sam. xvi. 7), in a marginal note explanatory of the context, and which refers in that place to King David. The application of the term to any man of violence is naturally suggested, and it would seem to have been employed by the Puritans in reference to Charles I. It was also popularly given to Thomas Simmons, an English murderer, executed at Hertford, March 7, 1808.

And the *Man of Blood* was there, with his long, essenced hair,
And Astley, and Sir Marmaduke, and Rupert of the Rhine. *Macaulay.*

Man of Destiny. An epithet conferred upon Napoleon Bonaparte, who believed himself to be a chosen instrument of Destiny, and that his actions were governed by some occult and supernatural influence.

The head of the royal house of Savoy . . . was to have the melancholy experience that he had encountered with the *Man of Destiny*, . . . who, for a time, had power, in the emphatic phrase of Scripture, "to bind kings with chains, and nobles with fetters of iron." *Sir W. Scott.*

Man of Feeling. The title of a novel, by Henry Mackenzie (1745–1831), designed to characterise the hero, Harley, and often applied to him as a descriptive epithet. It is also frequently used as a sobriquet to designate the author. See HARLEY.

The wonder rather is, that the *Man of Feeling* should never have been moved to mirth, than that Uncle Toby should have brushed away his tears with a laugh. *H. Martineau.*

Man of Ross. John Kyrle, a private gentleman of small fortune (1664–1754), who resided in the parish of Ross, county of Hereford, England, and who was distinguished for his benevolence and public spirit. Pope has immortalised him in his "Moral Essays," "Epistle Third," "On the Use of Riches." The title "Man of Ross" was given to him in his lifetime by a country friend; and Mr. Kyrle is said to have been highly pleased with the appellation.

> Richer than miser o'er his countless hoards,
> Nobler than kings, or king-polluted lords,
> Here dwelt the *Man of Ross!* O traveller,
> hear!
> Departed merit claims a reverent tear.
> *Coleridge.*

Man of Sin. A designation occurring in the New Testament (2 *Thess.* ii. 3), respecting the meaning of which commentators are at variance. Whitby says the Jewish nation is intended. Grotius affirms the reference to be to Caius Cæsar, or Caligula. Wetstein understands by it Titus and the Flavian house. Others, as Olshausen, suppose it to mean some one who has not yet appeared, in whom all the characteristics specified will be united. Roman Catholics apply the term to Antichrist, while most Protestants apply it to the Pope of Rome. The Fifth-Monarchy men called Cromwell the "Man of Sin."

> The zeal of your Majesty toward the house of God doth not slack or go backward, but is more and more kindled, manifesting itself abroad in the furthest parts of Christendom, by writing in defence of the truth, which hath given such a blow unto that *Man of Sin* as will not be healed. *Translators of the Bible.*

Man of the People. A title popularly given by his contemporaries and admirers to Charles James Fox (1749–1806), a celebrated English statesman.

Man of the Sea, Old. See OLD MAN OF THE SEA.

Man'tă-lī'nī. A cockney fop of extravagant habits, maintained by his wife, in Dickens's novel of "Nicholas Nickleby."

> Yet a gentleman of Mr. Charles Knight's taste and sympathetic appreciation of Shakespeare, editing his works in the middle of the nineteenth century, can perpetuate the *Mantalini*-ism of the tie-wig editors.
> *R. G. White.*

Mantuan Swan. A title given to the Latin poet Virgil, born at Mantua (70 B. C.), whose works have been more studied and admired, especially in the Middle Ages, than those of any other Latin author. He is distinguished for the exquisite smoothness and melodiousness of his versification.

> Ages elapsed ere Homer's lamp appeared,
> And ages ere the *Mantuan Swan* was heard;
> To carry Nature lengths unknown before,
> To give a Milton birth, asked ages more.
> *Cowper.*

Mar-cel'lă (*Sp. pron.* mar-thel'yä). The name of a fair shepherdess, whose story forms an episode in Cervantes's romance of "Don Quixote."

Mar-cel'lus. The name of an officer, in Shakespeare's tragedy of "Hamlet."

> The author of "Waverley" was, in this respect, as impassible to the critic as the ghost of Hamlet to the partisan of *Marcellus*.
> *Sir W. Scott.*

Marchioness, The. A poor, abused, half-starved girl, in Dickens's "Old Curiosity Shop;" the "small servant" to Sampson Brass. See BRASS, SAMPSON.

Mar-do'ni-us. The name of a captain, in Beaumont and Fletcher's play, "A King or No King."

Marfisa (mar-fe'sä). An Indian queen who figures in Bojardo's "Orlando Innamorato" and in Ariosto's "Orlando Furioso."

Mar-găr'e-lŏn. [Probably from Gr. μαργαρίτης, Lat. *margarita*, a pearl. The name is not classical, and was apparently coined to express "the pearl of knighthood."] A Trojan hero, of modern legendary history; called by Shakespeare ("Troilus and Cressida," a. v., sc. 5), "bastard," and described by him as performing deeds of prowess which seem to imply gigantic stature.

> "Bastard *Margarelon*
> Hath Doreus prisoner,
> And stands, Colossus-like, waving his beam
> Upon the pashèd corses of the kings."

Lydgate's "Boke of Troy" mentions him under the name of *Margariton*, and calls him a son of Priam. According to this author, he attacked Achilles, and fell by his hand.

Margaret. 1. The heroine of Goethe's "Faust." Faust meets her on her return from church, falls in love with her, and at last seduces her. Overcome with shame, Margaret destroys the infant to which she gives birth, and is in consequence condemned to death. Faust attempts to save her: gaining admission to the dungeon where she is immured, he finds her lying huddled on a bed of straw, singing wild snatches of ancient bal-

☞ For the "Key to the Scheme of Pronunciation," with the accompanying Explanations,

lads, her reason gone, her end approaching. For a long time he vainly strives to induce her to flee with him. At last the morning dawns, and Mephistopheles appears, grim and passionless, Faust is hurried off, and Margaret is left to her fate. The story of Margaret is original with Goethe, having little or no connection with the legends from which the main characters of the poem are drawn. [Called also *Gretchen*, a German diminutive of *Margaret*.]

☞ "Goethe is the only dramatic poet who has succeeded in giving to a simple, uncultured girl from the lower ranks of life a poetic interest. Gretchen is a perfect union of homely nature and poetic beauty. She says not a word that might not have been uttered by any girl of her class in any town in Germany; and yet, such is the exquisite art of the author, she acquires in our estimation an ideal import, and registers herself in the memory as one of the most remarkable portraits in the rich, wide gallery of dramatic art." *Christ. Examiner.* "Shakespeare himself has drawn no such portrait as that of Margaret; no such peculiar union of passion, simplicity, homeliness, and witchery. The poverty and inferior social position of Margaret are never lost sight of; she never becomes an abstraction; it is love alone which exalts her above her lowly station, and it is only *in* passion she is so exalted." *Lewes.*

2. The title of a strikingly original American romance, by the Reverend Sylvester Judd (1813-1853), and the name of its heroine.

Margutte (mȧr-gŏŏt′tä, 102). The name of a singular being, in Pulci's "Morgante Maggiore," who was desirous of becoming a giant, but repented, half-way, so that he only reached the height of ten feet. He is represented as an impudent, vulgar, low-minded fellow, without conscience, religion, humanity, or care for aught but the grossest indulgence of the senses, and as boasting of having no virtue but fidelity. His adventures — which form a mere episode in the poem — are conducted with a kind of straightforward wickedness which amuses from its very excess. At an inn, after eating all that is to be got, — his appetite is enormous, — and robbing the host, he sets fire to the house, and departs with Morgante, rejoicing greatly in his success, and carrying off every thing he can lay his hands upon. They go travelling on, and meet with various adventures. At last, one morning, Morgante, to play him a trick, draws off Margutte's boots while he is asleep, and hides them. Margutte looks for them, and at length perceives an ape, who is putting them on and drawing them off. The sight of the animal thus engaged so tickles Margutte's fancy that he laughs till he bursts.

Maria. 1. A lady attending on the princess of France, in Shakespeare's "Love's Labour's Lost."
2. Olivia's woman, in Shakespeare's "Twelfth Night."
3. A character in Sterne's "Sentimental Journey."

Mȧ′ri-an′ȧ (9). 1. A lady, in Shakespeare's "Measure for Measure," beloved by Angelo.

☞ "Shakespeare has given us in Mariana one of the most lovable and womanly of his feminine creations. We see little of her; indeed, she does not appear until the fourth act, in the first scene of which she says very little. In the last scene but eight words, and in the fifth act not a great deal. But the few touches of the master's hand make a charming picture. . . . Turn to the fifth act and hear her plead, — plead for the man [Angelo] whom she has loved through lonely years of wrong; the man whose life is justly forfeit for taking, as she thinks, the life of another, in a course of crime which involved a sin against her love. Timid and shrinking before, she does not now wait to be encouraged in her suit. She is instant and importunate. She does not reason or quibble with the duke; she begs, she implores, she kneels. . . . And does not her very prayer for Angelo make his crime seem more detestable, as well as her more lovable?" *R. G. White.*

2. A character in Shakespeare's "All 's Well that Ends Well."

Mȧ-rī′nȧ. Daughter of Pericles and Thaisa, in Shakespeare's play, "Pericles, Prince of Tyre."

Măr′ĭ-tor′nĕs. [Sp., bad woman. Comp. Old Fr. *Malitorne*.] A dwarfish, foul, ugly, lewd Asturian wench, who figures in Cervantes's "Don Quixote" as a servant at an inn. This inn the Don took for a castle, and imagined Maritornes to be the lord's daughter, and in love with himself.

<blockquote>
The <i>Maritornes</i> of the Saracen's Head, Newark, replied, Two women had passed that morning.   <i>Sir W. Scott.</i>

Had I used the privilege recommended to me by the reviewer, . . . I fear I should be considered as having fallen into the frenzy of him who discovered a beautiful <i>infanta</i> in the coarse skin of <i>Maritornes</i>, and "mistook her hair, which was as rough as a horse's mane, for soft flowing threads of curling gold."
    Dunlop.
</blockquote>

Mark, King. A fabulous king of Cornwall, husband of Isolde, and uncle of Tristram. See ISOLDE, TINTAGEL, and TRISTRAM, SIR.

Mark'ham, Mrs. A *nom de plume* adopted by Mrs. Elizabeth (Cartwright) Penrose, a popular English authoress of the present day.

Marlŏw, Sir Charles. A character in Goldsmith's comedy, "She Stoops to Conquer."

Marlŏw, Young. The hero of Goldsmith's comedy, "She Stoops to Conquer," distinguished for his excessive bashfulness before his mistress, and his easy familiarity with the chambermaid, who turns out to be his mistress in disguise.

Mar'mi-ŏn. The hero of Sir Walter Scott's poem of the same name; an English knight, valiant and sagacious, but profligate and unscrupulous, who meets with various adventures in Scotland, and finally falls upon the field of Flodden.

Marplot. 1. (Sir Martin.) The title, and the name of the hero, of an English comedy, — a translation of Molière's "L'Étourdi," — originally written by the Duke of Newcastle (Wm. Cavendish), and adapted for the stage by Dryden.

2. One of the *dramatis personæ* in Mrs. Centlivre's comedy of "The Busybody;" described as "a sort of silly fellow, cowardly, but very inquisitive to know every body's business."

Mar-Prelate, Martin. A name assumed by the author, or authors, of a series of powerf[ul] tracts, designed to scriptural character which were printed the reign of Queen [

The first of th[e] "An Epistle to the made its appearance in intense excitement. Waldgrave, who was in the publication of t[he] phlet, together with o tile to the Establis[h] obliged to flee with place to place, was o and his press at las great curiosity and in writings occasioned an anecdote furnished by a prohibition was issu should carry about wi Mar-Prelate tracts, o[r] ment, Robert, Earl of the queen, ' What, th[e] me?' drawing one of t his bosom, and present "Mar-Prelate controv[e] portant episode in th[e] tory of England, and Puritanism. Attempt been made to cast odi[um] tans by making them violent and abusive writings. Hopkins, i[n] the Puritans," defen[d] charge, declaring tha[t] way implicated in the thor, whoever he may a minister, was not e that is, in distinction and that he wrote fr[om] pendent point of view the Church and Sta[te] these violent attacks degree. The stricte[st] everywhere made to author. Four bishops country in search of Many persons were arr dealt with, on suspicio ery was ever made; remains a mystery. B him. " *Stat nominis u[mbra]*" ever, generally believ[ed] ductions proceeded, ei part, from John Pen who was executed Ma[y] ing written seditious queen. With Penry a Throckmorton, or T[h] Udall, and John Field,

Mars. (*Gr. & Ron[*] god of war, originall

For the "Key to the Scheme of Pronunciation," with the accompan

ral deity. As the reputed father of Romulus, he was held to be the progenitor of the Roman people, who paid him higher honours than any other god except Jupiter. He was identified, at a very early period, with the Greek *Ares*.

Marsh, The. [Fr. *Le Marais*.] (*Fr. Hist.*) A name given to "The Plain," or the lowest benches in the hall of the National Convention after the overthrow of the Girondists by the Jacobins. This part of the house was occupied by all the members of the convention who, though not belonging to "The Mountain," were yet meanly subservient to it. See MOUNTAIN, THE, and PLAIN, THE.

Marshal Forwards. [Ger. *Marschall Vorwärts*.] A title given by the Russians, in 1813, to Field-Marshal Lebrecht von Blücher (1742–1819), a distinguished general of Prussia, on account of the extraordinary celerity of his movements, and his peculiar manner of attack. From that time, it became his name of honour throughout all Europe.

Marsiglio (mar-seel'yo), *or* Mar-sil'i-us. A Saracen king who figures in the romantic poems of Italy. Having been defeated by Charlemagne, and condemned to pay him tribute, he plots with Gano (see GAN, *or* GANO) the destruction of Roland, or Orlando, who is to come, slenderly accompanied, to Roncesvalles, to receive the promised gifts and submission. Marsiglio accordingly advances, accompanied by 600,000 men, divided into three armies, which successively attack the paladin and his few troops, and completely overwhelm them. But their death is avenged by Rinaldo and Charlemagne, who now arrive on the scene, with a large force. Marsiglio is at length defeated; and Archbishop Turpin kindly performs the last office for him by tying him up to a carob-tree, — the same tree on which Judas Iscariot is said to have hanged himself, — under which he had planned his villany with Gano, who is also hanged, and drawn and quartered, amid the execrations of all who are present. See ROLAND. [Written also Marsirio and Marsirius.]

Mar'sȳ-ạs. [Gr. Μαρσύας.] (*Gr. & Rom. Myth.*) A famous Phrygian peasant, or, as some say, a satyr, who challenged Apollo to a trial of skill in music, and, being vanquished, was flayed alive for his presumption.

Marteau des Hérétiques, Le (lu mar'to' dā zā'rā'těk'). See HAMMER OF HERETICS.

Mar-Text, Sir Oliver. A vicar, in Shakespeare's "As You Like It."

Martha. A friend of Margaret, in Goethe's "Faust;" represented as making love to Mephistopheles with direct worldly shrewdness.

Marvel, Ik. A *nom de plume* of Donald G. Mitchell (b. 1822), a popular American writer of the present day.

Marvellous Boy. An epithet sometimes applied to Thomas Chatterton (1752–1770), whose precocious genius and early and tragical death made him one of the wonders of English literature. It originated with Wordsworth. See ROWLEY, THOMAS.

I thought of Chatterton, the *marvellous boy*,
The sleepless soul that perished in his pride.
Wordsworth.

Mascarille (mâs'kȧ'rē'y', 82). A valet in Molière's "L'Étourdi," "Le Dépit Amoureux," and "Les Précieuses Ridicules."

Mask, The Iron, *or* The Man with the Iron Mask. [Fr. *L'Homme au Masque de Fer*.] A name used to designate an unknown French prisoner, whose identity has never been satisfactorily established. He was carried, about the year 1679, with the greatest secrecy, to the castle of Pignerol, of which Saint Mars was governor. He wore, during the journey, a black mask, and orders were given to kill him if he discovered himself. In 1686, he was carried by Saint Mars to the isle of Sainte Marguerite; and, on the passage, the same precautions were observed as upon his first journey. Saint Mars, having been appointed governor of the Bastile in 1698, carried the prisoner with him (Sept. 18), but still masked.

There he remained till his death, on the 19th of Nov., 1703, treated with the utmost respect, but closely watched, and not permitted to take off his mask even before his physician. He was buried on the 20th of Nov., in the cemetery of St. Paul, under the name of Marchiali.

☞ Notwithstanding the appellation given him, the mask he wore was not of iron, but of black velvet, strengthened with whalebone, and secured behind the head with steel springs, or, as some assert, by means of a padlock. Many conjectures have been hazarded as to who this mysterious personage could have been. One opinion is, that he was a son of Anne of Austria, queen of Louis XIII., his father being Cardinal Mazarin (to whom that dowager queen was privately married), or the Duke of Buckingham. Others suppose him to have been a twin brother of Louis XIV., whose birth was concealed to prevent the civil dissensions in France which it might one day have caused. The latter view was adopted by Voltaire, in common with many others. Some Dutch writers assert that the prisoner was a young foreign nobleman, the chamberlain of Queen Anne, and the real father of Louis XIV. It has more recently been surmised that Fouquet was the mask; but M. Delort and the Right Honourable Agar Ellis (afterward Lord Dover) identify him with a Count Matthioli, a minister of Charles III., Duke of Mantua. This minister had been largely bribed by Louis XIV., and had pledged himself to urge the duke to give up to the French the fortress of Casale, which gave access to the whole of Lombardy. But Louis, finding that Matthioli was playing him false, lured him to the French frontier, and had him secretly arrested and imprisoned. Being a minister plenipotentiary at the time, his seizure was a flagrant violation of international law, which it was safer to be able to deny than to attempt to justify; and the denial once made, the honour of France was involved in upholding it. This opinion is the one generally received at the present day by those who have investigated the subject.

Mason and Dixon's Line. A name given to the southern boundary-line separating the free State of Pennsylvania from the former slave States of Maryland and Virginia. It lies in latitude 39° 43′ 26.3″, and was run — with the exception of about twenty-two miles — by Charles Ma-son and Jeremiah Dixon, two English mathematicians and surveyors, between Nov. 15, 1763, and Dec. 26, 1767. During the excited debate in congress, in 1820, on the question of excluding slavery from Missouri, the eccentric John Randolph of Roanoke made great use of this phrase, which was caught up and re-echoed by every newspaper in the land, and thus gained a proverbial celebrity which it still retains.

Massacre of St. Bartholomew. See BARTHOLOMEW'S DAY, ST.

Master, The. [Ger. *Der Meister.*] A title given to Goethe by his admirers.

I beseech you, Mr. Tickler, not to be so sarcastic on "*The Master.*" *Noctes Ambrosianæ.*

Master Adam. [Fr. *Maître Adam.*] The name under which the French poet Adam Billaut (1602–1662) is most familiarly known.

Master Humphrey. A character in Dickens's novel of "The Old Curiosity Shop;" a miserable old man, tottering on the verge of the grave, who has a mania for gambling.

Master Leonard. In the fantastic system of demonology received in the Middle Ages, a powerful devil in the infernal court. He was grand master of the sabbats, or nocturnal assemblies, in which demons and sorcerers were wont to celebrate their orgies. At these meetings, he presided in the favourite form of a three-horned goat with a black human countenance, and every guest did him homage. Stolen children were thought to be brought to him, to swear through their god-parents to renounce God, the Holy Virgin, and the Saints, and to be marked with one of his horns with a sign which they bore during their novitiate.

Master Matthew. A town gull in Ben Jonson's comedy of "Every Man in his Humour."

The folly of individuals led them, in those times, to assume or counterfeit the humours in real life, — an affectation which had become so general as to fall under the notice of the stage, and to produce a ridicule of the cheating humour, the bragging humour, the melancholy humour, the quarrelling humour, as in the characters of Nym, of Pistol, of Master Stephen, or *Master Matthew.*   *Edin. Rev.*

☞ For the "Key to the Scheme of Pronunciation," with the accompanying Explanations,

Master of Sentences. A title given to Peter Lombard (d. 1164), a native of Lombardy, and author of a book of "Sentences," collected from the fathers of the Church. This work acquired a high degree of celebrity in the Middle Ages.

> Matched against the master of "ologies," in our days, the most accomplished of Grecians is becoming what the *Master of Sentences* had become long since in competition with the political economist. *De Quincey.*

Master Stephen. The name of a country gull in Ben Jonson's comedy, "Every Man in his Humour."

Masters, The Four. See FOUR MASTERS, THE.

Maugis (mō'zhe'). One of Charlemagne's paladins. See MALAGIGI, the Italian form of the name.

Maul of Monks. [Lat. *Malleus Monachorum.*] A designation of Thomas Cromwell (1490–1540), an eminent English statesman and ecclesiastical reformer. In 1535, he was made visitor-general of English monasteries, which he shortly afterward suppressed in the most stern and summary manner.

Mau-so'lus. [Gr. Μαύσωλος.] A king of Caria, and husband of Artemisia, who raised a splendid tomb to his memory, called the Mausoleum, and accounted one of the Seven Wonders of the World.

Mawworm. A celebrated character in Bickerstaff's comedy of "The Hypocrite."

Max'i-min. A Roman tyrant in Dryden's play entitled "Tyrannic Love, or The Royal Martyr."

Mayeux (mä'e-ö', or mī'ö', 43). The name of a hunchback who figures prominently in numberless French caricatures and romances. The popularity of the character has made it the recognised type of a man dreadfully deformed, and vain and licentious, but brave and witty.

Maypole, The. A nickname given, by the English populace, to the Duchess of Kendal, mistress of George I., on account of her leanness and height.

Meal-tub Plot. (*Eng. Hist.*) A fictitious conspiracy against the Duke of York (afterward James II.), fabricated, in 1679, by one Dangerfield, and ascribed by him to the Presbyterians;—so called because the scheme of the pretended conspirators was concealed in a meal-tub in the house of his mistress, a Mrs. Cellier. Dangerfield secreted a bundle of seditious letters in the lodgings of Colonel Maunsell, and then gave notice to the revenue officers that they would find smuggled goods there. The papers having been proved to be forgeries, Dangerfield was committed to prison, whereupon he confessed that he had been hired by Roman Catholics to accuse of treason some of the most eminent Protestants opposed to the Duke of York's succession, particularly the Earls of Shaftesbury, Essex, and Halifax, the Countess of Powis, and Lord Castlemaine. He was condemned to a fine, the pillory, and a whipping, May 30, 1685, and died, two days afterward, of an injury received during the execution of his sentence.

Meaux, Eagle of. See EAGLE OF MEAUX.

Medamothi (m'dä'mo'te'). [Fr., from Gr. μηδαμόθι, nowhere, from μηδαμός, for μηδὲ ἁμός, not even one, none.] An island visited by Panurge and Pantagruel, in their search for the Oracle of the Holy Bottle.

Me-de'ä. [Gr. Μήδεια.] (*Gr. & Rom. Myth.*) A famous sorceress, daughter of Æetes, king of Colchis, and the wife of Jason, whom she assisted in obtaining the Golden Fleece, and then accompanied to Greece. Jason afterward repudiated her in order to marry Creusa, whereupon she killed the children she had borne him, and made away with her rival by sending her a poisoned robe or diadem. She finally became immortal, married Achilles in Elysium, and was honoured with divine worship. See ABSYRTUS.

Me-do'rä (9). The heroine of Byron's poem of "The Corsair."

Medoro (mā-do'ro). A character in Ariosto's romantic poem, "Orlando Furioso." See ORLANDO.

---

and for the Remarks and Rules to which the numbers after certain words refer, see pp. xiv–xxxii.

Me-du'să. [Gr. Μέδουσα.] (*Gr. & Rom. Myth.*) One of the Gorgons. Her head was cut off by Perseus, and presented to Minerva, who placed it on her ægis, where it turned into stone all who fixed their eyes upon it. See GORGONS and PERSEUS.

Me-gǣ'ră (9). [Gr. Μέγαιρα.] (*Gr. & Rom. Myth.*) One of the Furies. See FURIES.

Meg of Westminster, Long. See LONG MEG OF WESTMINSTER.

Mēi'kle-whăm, Mr. Sǎun'dẽrẓ (me'kl-). One of the Managing Committee at the Spa, in Scott's novel of " St. Ronan's Well; " "the man of Law."

Meister, Wilhelm (vĭl'helm mīs'tẽr, 42, 64, 68). The hero of Goethe's novel entitled "Wilhelm Meister's Apprenticeship."

☞ "The critic seeks a central point [to this romance], which, in truth, is hard to find. I should think a rich manifold life brought close to our eyes might suffice, without any determined moral tendency which could be reasoned upon. But, if this is insisted upon, it may perhaps be found in what Frederick, at the end, says to the hero, 'Thou seemest to me like Saul, the son of Kish, who went out to seek his father's asses, and found a kingdom!' For what does the whole say, but that man, despite all his follies and errors, led by a higher hand, reaches some higher aim at last?"
Goethe, Trans.

Mej'nŏun and Lēi'lăh. Pattern lovers among various Eastern nations, like "Pyramus and Thisbe" among the Greeks and Romans. [Written also M e j n u n.]

☞ "These personages are esteemed among the Arabians as the most beautiful, chaste, and impassioned of lovers, and their amours have been celebrated with all the charms of verse in every Oriental language. The Mohammedans regard them, and the poetical records of their love, in the same light as the 'Bridegroom and Spouse ' and the 'Song of Songs ' are regarded by the Jews."
D'Herbelot, Trans.

Me-lan'ti-us (mō-lan'shĭ-us). A brave, honest soldier, in Beaumont and Fletcher's play, " The Maid's Tragedy," who is incapable of suspecting evil till it becomes impossible to be ignorant of it, but is unshrinking punishing it.

Me-le'ă-gẽr. [Gr. Μελέαγρος.] (*Gr. & Rom. Myth.*) A son of Œneus. king of Calydon, a city of Ætoliaute Greece. He distinguished himself one of the Argonauts, and by his skill in throwing the javelin. The king, his father, having neglected to pay homage to Diana, the goddess sent a wild boar to lay waste the country; all the princes of the age assembled to hunt him down, but he was at last killed by Meleager. His mother — out of revenge for the death of her brothers, who had fallen in battle by his hand — caused his destruction by burning an extinguished brand, on the preservation of which his life depended.

Mel'e-sig'e-nĕṣ. [Gr. Μελησιγενής, from Μέλης, the river Meles, and γένειν, to beget.] An appellation sometimes given to Homer, on the supposition that he was born on the banks of the Meles, a river of Ionia, in Asia Minor, or that the river-god was his father.

Blind *Melesigenes*, thence Homer called, Whose poem Phœbus challenged for his own.
Milton.

Me-li'ă-dus. A prince of Léonnois, and a knight of the Round Table. He was the father of Sir Tristram. He is celebrated in a French mediæval romance, originally written by Rusticien de Pise, a more modern French compilation from which was printed at Paris in 1528.

Mel'ĭ-bœ'us. A shepherd in the first Eclogue of Virgil. The name is used by Chaucer in his prose composition entitled " The Tale of Melibeus," one of the " Canterbury Tales." He also writes it M e l i b e e.

Mel'ĭ-cẽr'tă, or **Mel'ĭ-cẽr'tēṣ** (4). [Gr. Μελικέρτης.] (*Gr. & Rom. Myth.*) A son of the Theban king Athamas by Ino. He was metamorphosed into a sea-god. See INO.

Me-lis'să. A beneficent fairy invented by the Italian poets; the protector of Bradamante and Ruggiero, in the " Orlando Furioso " of Ariosto. She is sometimes confounded with the fairy Melusina. The name, passing into French and English literature as a poetical title, has finally become a recognised Christian name.

Aellifluous Doctor. [Lat. *Doctor Mellifluus.*] An appellation given to St. Bernard, a celebrated and eloquent preacher and theologian of the twelfth century. His writings were termed by his admirers "a river of paradise."

Mel'mŏth, Coŭrt'ney. A pseudonym of Samuel Jackson Pratt (1749–1814), in his day a popular poet, and a voluminous writer both in prose and verse. He was originally a strolling player, next an itinerant lecturer, and finally a Bath book-seller.

Mel-pom'e-ne. [Gr. Μελπομένη.] (*Gr. & Rom. Myth.*) One of the Muses; the one who presided over tragedy. See MUSES.

Mel'ū-sī'nḝ. [Fr. *Mélusine.*] A daughter of the fairy Pressina, by Elénas, king of Albania; the most renowned of the French fairies. Her origin may be traced to the Teutonic "Amalaswinth." She was condemned to become every Saturday a serpent from the waist downward, as a punishment for having, by means of a charm, enclosed her father in a high mountain, in order to avenge an injury her mother had received from him. She married Raymond, Count of Poitiers, and, having been seen by him during her loathsome transformation,—in violation of his solemn promise never to visit her on a Saturday,—was immured in a subterranean dungeon of the castle of Lusignan. The traditions concerning Melusina were collected by Jean d'Arras, near the close of the fourteenth century.

☞ The Mélusine tradition lingers around the castle of Lusignan, near Poitiers, and to this day, at the fairs of that city, gingerbread cakes are sold with human head and serpent tail, and called *Mélusines.* A *cri de Mélusine* is a proverbial expression for a sudden scream, recalling that with which the unfortunate fair one discovered the indiscretion of her lord.

Mem'nŏn. [Gr. Μέμνων.] (*Gr. &*

Rom. Myth.) A son of Tithonus and Aurora, and king of Ethiopia. After the fall of Hector, he went to the assistance of his uncle Priam, with ten thousand men, and displayed great courage in the defence of Troy, but was at length slain by Ajax, or by Achilles, in single combat, whereupon he was changed into a bird by his mother, or, as some say, at her request.

☞ The colossal black statue of the Egyptian king Amenophis III., in the neighbourhood of Thebes, was called by the Greeks the statue of Memnon, and a sound like that of a breaking lute-string which it gave forth when struck by the first beams of the sun, they regarded as Memnon's greeting to his mother. The sound has been heard in modern times, and has been variously ascribed to the artifice of the priests who concealed themselves in a niche and with an iron rod struck the sonorous stone of which the statue is composed; to the passage of light draughts of air through the cracks; and to the sudden expansion of enclosed aqueous particles under the influence of the sun's rays.

As from æolian harps in the breath of dawn,
As from the *Memnon's* statue struck by the rosy finger of Aurora, unearthly music was around him, and lapped him into untried, balmy rest. *Carlyle.*

Soft as *Memnon's* harp at morning,
To the inward eye devout,
Touched with light by heavenly warning,
Your transporting chords ring out. *Keble.*

Me-nal'cạs. [Gr. Μενάλκας.] A shepherd in Theocritus and Virgil; hence any shepherd or rustic. Menalcas figures in Spenser's "Shepherd's Calendar" as the treacherous rival of Colin Clout.

Spend some months yet among the sheep-walks of Cumberland; learn all you can, from all the shepherds you can find,—from Thyrsis to *Menalcas.* *Sir E. Bulwer Lytton.*

Men'e-lā'us. [Gr. Μενέλαος.] (*Gr. & Rom. Myth.*) A son of Atreus, the brother of Agamemnon, and the husband of Helen, who eloped from him with Paris, and thus brought on the Trojan war. Menelaus took part in the contest, and behaved with great spirit and courage. See HELEN and PARIS.

Me-nœ'tēṣ. The pilot of the ship "Chimæra," which took part in the naval contest at Drepanum, in Sicily, where Æneas celebrated the first

and for the Remarks and Rules to which the numbers after certain words refer, see pp. xiv-xxxii.

anniversary of his father's death by various games and feats of skill. For his timidity in standing out from the shore, in order to avoid certain hidden rocks, and thereby allowing the "Chimæra" to be beaten, Gyas, the commander of the vessel, hurled him headlong into the sea, greatly to the amusement of the spectators.

Men'tọr. [Gr. Μέντωρ.] (*Gr. & Rom. Myth.*) A friend of Ulysses in Ithaca, whose form Minerva assumed, to give instructions to Ulysses's son Telemachus, whom she accompanied to Pylos and Lacedæmon.

With Friedrich Wilhelm, who is his second cousin (mother's grand-nephew, if the reader can count that), he [Leopold, prince of Anhalt-Dessau] is from of old on the best footing, and contrives to be his *Mentor* in many things beside war. *Carlyle.*

Me-phis'to. The same as *Mephistopheles.* See *infra.*

Meph'is-toph'e-lês. One of the seven chief devils in the old demonology, the second of the fallen archangels, and the most powerful of the infernal legions after Satan. He figures in the old legend of Dr. Faustus as the familiar spirit of that renowned magician, and, in former times, his name was commonly used as a term of jocular reproach. To modern readers he is chiefly known as the cold, scoffing, relentless fiend of Goethe's "Faust," and as the attendant demon in Marlowe's "Faustus." See FAUST.

☞ The name was formerly written *Mephostophilus* and *Mephostophilis*; the former spelling being that of Shakespeare (see "Merry Wives of Windsor," a. i., sc. 1), and the latter that adopted by Marlowe. The origin of the word is uncertain; various derivations have been proposed. By some it is thought to be derived from a Semitic tongue. (See Goethe's "Briefwechsel mit Zelter," v. 330.) Widman calls it a Persian name. But that etymology which refers it to the Greek μή, not, φώς, φωτός, light, and φίλος, loving, accords with the old orthography, and is the most plausible of all.

☞ "There is an awful melancholy about Marlowe's Mephistopheles, perhaps more expressive than the malignant mirth of that fiend in the renowned work of Goethe." *Hallam.*

☞ "Mephistopheles comes before us, not arrayed in the terrors of Cocytus and Phlegethon, but with natural indelible deformity of wickedness. He is the Devil, not of superstition, but of knowledge. Such a combination of perfect understanding with perfect selfishness, of logical life with moral death, so universal a denier both in heart and head, is undoubtedly a child of Darkness, an emissary of the primeval Nothing, and may stand in his merely spiritual deformity, at once potent, dangerous, and contemptible, as the best and only genuine Devil of these latter times." *Carlyle.*

Poets of the first order might safely write as desperately as *Mephistopheles* rode. *Macaulay.*

We have here [in the literature of the Restoration] Belial, not as when he inspired Ovid and Ariosto, "graceful and humane," but with the iron eye and cruel sneer of *Mephistopheles.* *Macaulay*

These are the fields of History which are to be, so soon as humanly possible, suppressed; which only *Mephistopheles*, or the Bad Genius of mankind, can contemplate with pleasure. *Carlyl*

Mẽr'cū-rỹ (4). [Lat. *Mercurius.*] (*Gr & Rom. Myth.*) The son of Jupiter and Maia, the messenger of the gods, particularly of Jupiter, the inventor of letters, the conductor of departed souls to the under-world, and the god of eloquence, commerce, thieves, and travellers.

Mer-cu'ti-o (mer-ku'shǐ-o). A friend to Romeo, in Shakespeare's tragedy of "Romeo and Juliet," and the portrait of a finished fine gentleman of his time.

☞ "Wit ever wakeful, fancy busy and procreative as an insect, courage, an easy mind, that, without cares of its own, is at once disposed to laugh away those of others, and yet to be interested in them, — these and all congenial qualities, melting into the common *copula* of them all, the man of rank and the gentleman, with all its excellences and all its weaknesses, constitute the character of Mercutio." *Coleridge.*

Mẽr'e-dith, Owen. A pseudonym adopted by Edward Robert Bulwer Lytton (b. 1831), a popular living English poet, and a lineal descendant of *Owen* Gwynnedd ap Griffith, king of North Wales, and of *Meredith* ap Tudor, great-grandfather of Henry VII. of England.

Mẽr'lin (4). A famous magician of alleged supernatural origin, contemporary with King Arthur, celebrated in the tales and romances of chivalry, in Spenser's "Faëry Queen," and in the romantic poems of Italy. He is said to have removed, by a wonderful machine of his own invention, the Giants'-dance, now called Stonehenge, from Ireland to Salisbury Plain in England, where part of it is still standing. The old legends recognise two persons of this name, one connected with the traditions of Scotland, the other with those of Wales; but the essential features of both are the same.

☞ The manner of Merlin's death is variously related. According to one account, he was enclosed in a hawthornbush by his mistress, the fairy Vivian (the Lady of the Lake), by means of a charm which he had communicated to her. Not believing in the spell, she tried it upon her lover, and found to her grief and astonishment that he could not be extricated from his thorny coverture.

Breugwain was there, and Sagramore,
And field-born *Merlin's* grammarye;
Of that famed wizard's mighty love,
Oh who could sing but he! *Sir W. Scott.*

He [Bacon] . . . knew, that, if his words sank deep into the minds of men, they would produce effects such as superstition had never ascribed to the incantations of *Merlin* and Michael Scott. *Macaulay.*

Mĕr'o-pe. [Gr. Μερόπη.] (*Gr. & Rom. Myth.*) 1. One of the Pleiades, whose star is dimmer than the rest, because she wedded Sisyphus, a mortal.
2. See ŒNOPION.

Mĕr'rĭ-lĭeṣ, Meg. A half-crazy gypsy, who is a prominent and celebrated character in Scott's novel of "Guy Mannering."

☞ "She is most akin to the witches of Macbeth, with some traits of the ancient sibyl ingrafted on the coarser stock of a gypsy of the last century. Though not absolutely in nature, however, she must be allowed to be a very imposing and emphatic personage, and to be mingled, both with the business and the scenery of the piece, with the greatest possible skill and effect." *Lord Jeffrey.*

Mĕr'rĭ-mạn, Mr. A name given to a zany, or attendant upon a mountebank at fairs, in market-places, and on village greens. It is, perhaps, of the same origin as Merry-andrew.

Merry-Andrew. A name given originally to Andrew Borde (1500-1549), a man of learning, and a noted itinerant physician, who, as Hearne tells us, frequented "markets and fairs, where a conflux of people used to get together, to whom he prescribed; and, to induce them to flock thither the more readily, he would make humourous speeches, couched in such language as caused mirth, and wonderfully propagated his fame." From him, any buffoon or zany, especially one who attends upon a mountebank or quack doctor, is called a Merry-andrew.

Merry England. A common designation of England, which is so called, not on account of the merry-makings of the inhabitants, but in the old sense of the word *merry*, that is, pleasant, agreeable. In this sense we speak of the "*merry* month of May;" and in this sense Wakefield and Carlisle were formerly termed *merry*, and Spenser spoke of "*merry* London," and Chaucer of a
"citee
That stood full *merry* upon a haven side."

Merry Monarch. A title by which King Charles II. of England (1630-1685) was in former times familiarly known.

Mersenne, The English. See ENGLISH MERSENNE.

Mĕr'ton, Tommy (-tn, 4). One of the principal characters in a very popular juvenile work written by Thomas Day (1748-1789), and entitled "The History of Sandford and Merton."

Me'rû (9). (*Hindu Myth.*) A sacred mountain, 80,000 leagues high, situated in the centre of the world. It is the abode of Indra, and abounds with every charm that can be imagined.

Merveilleuse (mêr'vŭl'yöz', 43). [Fr., wonderful.] The name of the sword of Doolin of Mayence. It was magically sharpened, and was so keen, that, when placed edge downward on a large tripod, its mere weight was sufficient to cut the tripod through. See DOOLIN OF MAYENCE.

Mes'o-po-tā'mĭ-ạ. A name popularly given by Londoners to the Warwick

and for the Remarks and Rules to which the numbers after certain words refer, see pp. xiv-xxxii.

and Eccleston Square districts in that city. [Called also *Cubitopolis*.]

Me'tis. [Gr. Μῆτις.] (*Gr. & Rom. Myth.*) A daughter of Oceanus and Tethys, the first wife of Jupiter, and the goddess of prudence.

Me-zen'ti-us (-shi-us). A tyrant of Cære, or Agylla, a city of Etruria. He was expelled by his subjects on account of his cruelties, and fled to Turnus, who employed him in his war against Æneas, by whom he was slain. Virgil calls him "a despiser of the gods."

Like *Mezentius* ... he [Bonaparte] ought to have acknowledged no other source of his authority [than his talents and his sword].
Sir W. Scott.

Mez'zo-rā'mi-ă (*It. pron.* med-zo-rä'-me-ä). The name of an imaginary country in the heart of the deserts of Africa, inaccessible except by one particular road, and unknown to the rest of the world. Gaudentio di Lucca, in the romance of that name, is represented as having visited it, and as residing there for twenty-five years. It is described as a terrestrial paradise, and its government, laws, and customs are highly commended. See GAUDENTIO DI LUCCA.

Mī-caw'bẽr, Mr. Wilkins. A prominent and celebrated character in Dickens's novel of "David Copperfield;" noted for his long speeches, ambitious style, love of letter-writing, alternate elevation and depression of spirits, hearty appetite, reckless improvidence, and everlasting troubles, and for his constantly "waiting for something to turn up."

☞ "There never was a Mr. Micawber in nature, exactly as he appears in the pages of Dickens; but Micawberism pervades nature through and through; and to have this quality from nature embodying the full essence of a thousand instances of it in one ideal monstrosity, is a feat of invention." *Masson.*

Who does not venerate the chief of that illustrious family, who, being stricken by misfortune, wisely and greatly turned his attention to "coals,"—the accomplished, the Epicurean, the dirty, the delightful *Micawber!*
Thackeray.

Mī'chă-el (*colloq.* mī'kel). The name of an archangel, mentioned in the Bible as having special charge of the Israelites as a nation (*Dan.* x. 13, 21), as disputing with Satan about the body of Moses (*Jude* 9), and as carrying on war, with the assistance of his angels, against Satan and his forces in the upper regions (*Rev.* xii. 7-9). Michael figures largely in Milton's "Paradise Lost," being sent with Gabriel to battle against Satan and his angels, and also with a band of cherubim, to Paradise, to dispossess Adam and Eve, and to foretell to them what should happen till the time of the coming of Christ.

Upwards of a century ... must elapse, ... and the Moloch of iniquity have his victims, and the *Michael* of justice his martyrs, before Tailors can be admitted to their true prerogatives of manhood, and this last wound of suffering humanity be closed. *Carlyle.*

Michael, Cousin. See COUSIN MICHAEL.

Mī'chă-el Ăn'ġe-lo of France. [Fr. *Michel-Ange de la France.*] An epithet given to Pierre Puget (1623–1694), a famous French statuary, painter, and architect, remarkable, like his illustrious namesake, for his enthusiasm and decision of character.

Mī'dăs. [Gr. Μίδας.] (*Gr. & Rom. Myth.*) A king of Phrygia, son of Gordius and Cybele. Bacchus gave him the power of turning whatever he touched into gold; but this proved to be very inconvenient, as it prevented him from eating and drinking, and he prayed that the gift might be revoked. At the command of the god, he washed in the Pactolus, the sands of which became in consequence mixed with gold. Another tradition is, that, in a musical contest between Pan and Apollo, he adjudged the victory to the former, and Apollo, in revenge, changed his ears into those of an ass. Midas tried to conceal them under his Phrygian cap, but they were discovered by his servant.

Middle Ages. A term applied, rather vaguely, to the great historic period between the times of classical antiquity and modern times, in which the feudal system was formed, chivalry rose, flourished, and declined, the Church extended its bounds and ac-

☞ For the "Key to the Scheme of Pronunciation," with the accompanying Explanations,

quired enormous wealth and power, and the nations of modern Europe had their origin and began to develop their respective political and social systems. "It is not possible," says Hallam, "to fix accurate limits to the Middle Ages. The ten centuries from the fifth to the fifteenth seem, in a general point of view, to constitute that period." The overthrow of the Western Roman Empire, in the year 476, is manifestly the termination of ancient history, and as the Reformation (which began in 1517) is the most convenient epoch from which to date the commencement of modern history, these events are pretty generally regarded as marking the beginning and close of the Middle Ages. [Called also, from the prevalent superstition and ignorance, the *Dark Ages*.]

Middle Kingdom. A translation of *Tchang-kooe*, a name given to China by the natives, from an idea that it is situated in the centre of the earth.

Middle States. A popular designation of the States of New York, New Jersey, Pennsylvania, Maryland, and Delaware, from their having been in reality, at the time of the formation of the Federal Constitution, the central States of the American Union. By some writers, Maryland is classed as a Southern, and not a Middle State.

Mid'gard. [That is, middle ward.] (*Scand. Myth.*) A name given to the earth, as being in the middle region between Asgard and Utgard.

Mid-Lothian, Heart of. See HEART OF MID-LOTHIAN.

Miggs, Miss. Mrs. Varden's maid, in Dickens's novel of "Barnaby Rudge."

☞ "She is an elderly maiden, who, by some strange neglect on the part of mankind, has been allowed to remain unmarried. This neglect might, in some small degree, be accounted for by the fact that her person and disposition came within the range of Mr. Tappertit's epithet of 'scraggy.' She had various ways of wreaking her hatred upon the other sex, the most cruel of which was in often honouring them with her company and discourse. . . . Dickens, in this charac-ter, well represents how such seemingly insignificant malignants as Miss Miggs can become the pest of families; and that, though full of weakness and malignity, they can be proud of their virtue and religion, and make slander the prominent element of their pious conversation." *E. P. Whipple.*

Overflowing with a humour as peculiar in its way as the humours of Andrew Fairservice, or a Protestant *Miss Miggs* (that impersonation of shrewish female service).
Lond. Athenæum.

Mignon (měn'yôn', 62). The name of a young Italian girl in Goethe's "Wilhelm Meister's Apprenticeship;" represented as beautiful and dwarfish, unaccountable, and full of sensibility, and secretly in love with Wilhelm, who is her protector, and who feels for her nothing but common kindness and compassion. She, at last, becomes insane, and dies the victim of her hopeless attachment.

☞ "This mysterious child, at first neglected by the reader, gradually forced on his attention, at length overpowers him with an emotion more deep and thrilling than any poet, since the days of Shakespeare, has succeeded in producing. The daughter of enthusiasm, rapture, passion, and despair, she is of earth, but not earthy. When she glides before us through the mazes of her fairy dance, or whirls her tambourine, and hurries round us like an antique Mænad, we could almost fancy her a spirit, so pure is she, so full of fervour, so disengaged from the clay of this world."
Carlyle.

Mil'an Decree. (*Fr. Hist.*) A decree of the Emperor Napoleon Bonaparte, dated at Milan on the 27th of December, 1807, which declared the whole British dominions to be in a state of blockade, and prohibited all countries from trading with each other in any articles of British produce or manufacture.

Mil'la-mănt, Mrs. A celebrated character in Congreve's comedy, "The Way of the World."

Benedick and Beatrice throw Mirabel and *Millamant* into the shade. *Macaulay.*

Mill-boy of the Slashes. A sobriquet conferred upon Henry Clay (1777-1852), a distinguished American orator and statesman, who was born in the neighbourhood of a place in Hanover County, Virginia, known as "the Slashes" (a local term for a low, swampy country), where there was a mill, to which he was often sent on errands when a boy.

Miller, Joe. See FATHER OF JESTS.

Mi′lo. [Gr. Μίλων.] An athlete of Crotona, famous for his extraordinary strength. In his old age, he attempted to rend the trunk of a tree which had been partially split open; but the wood closed upon his hands, and held him fast, in which state he was attacked and devoured by wolves.

He who of old would rend the oak
  Deemed not of the rebound;
Chained by the trunk he vainly broke,
  Alone, how looked he round!   *Byron.*

Mimir (me′mêr). (*Scand. Myth.*) The god of eloquence and wisdom. He was the guardian of a well in which wit and wisdom lay hidden, and of which he drank every morning from the horn Gjallar. Odin once drank from this fountain, and by doing so became the wisest of gods and men; but he purchased the privilege and distinction at the cost of one eye, which Mimir exacted from him. [Written also M i m e r.]

Mimung (me′mŏŏn). The name of a wonderful sword lent by Wittich to Siegfried. See SIEGFRIED.

Mĭ-nĕr′vȧ (4). (*Gr. & Rom. Myth.*) The goddess of wisdom, poetry, spinning, weaving, and the various arts and sciences. She was not born like others, but sprang forth fully armed from the brain of Jove.

Minerva Press. The name of a printing establishment in Leadenhall Street, London, from which, during the latter part of the last century and the early part of the present century, was issued a large number of mawkish and trashy, but very popular novels, which were widely distributed by means of the circulating libraries. Charles Lamb describes their heroes as "persons neither of this world, nor of any conceivable one; an endless string of activities without purpose, of purposes without a motive."

In this respect, Burns, though not perhaps absolutely a great poet, better manifested his capability, better proved the truth of his genius, than if he had, by his own strength kept the whole *Minerva Press* going to th end of his literary course.   *Carlyle*

Scarcely in the *Minerva Press* is there rec ord of such surprising, infinite, and inextri cable obstructions to a wedding or a doubl wedding.   *Carlyle*

Min′nȧ. One of the heroines in Scott' novel of "The Pirate;" sister t Brenda. She is distinguished by credulous simplicity and sober vanity and by talents, strong feelings, an high-minded enthusiasm.

Mi′nŏs. [Gr. Μίνως.] (*Gr. & Rom Myth.*) A son of Jupiter and Europa the brother of Rhadamanthus, an the father of Deucalion and Ariadne He was a king and lawgiver in Crete and so distinguished for his incor ruptible justice, that, after death, h was made supreme judge in the lowe world.

Min′o-tâur. [Lat. *Minotaurus*, Gr Μινώταυρος, bull of Minos.] (*Gr. & Rom. Myth.*) A celebrated monste with the head of a bull and the bod: of a man, the fruit of Pasiphaë's mos unnatural passion for a bull. He wa shut up in the Cretan labyrinth, an fed with young men and maiden whom Athens was obliged to suppl every year, until Theseus finall killed him with the help of Ariadne See ARIADNE and THESEUS.

Minstrel of the Border. A nam sometimes given to Sir Walter Scott See BORDER MINSTREL.

Once more by Newark's castle gate,
Long left without a warder,
I stood, looked, listened, and with thee,
Great *Minstrel of the Border*.   *Wordswort*

Mirabeau-Tonneau. See BARREL MIRABEAU.

Mĭr′ȧ-bel. 1. A travelled Monsieur i Beaumont and Fletcher's "Wild goose Chase;" represented as a grea defier of all ladies in the way of mar riage, and a very dissipated and licen tious fellow.

2. The name of two character in Farquhar's comedy, "The Incon stant,"— an old gentleman and hi son; the former of an odd compoun between the peevishness incident t his years and his fatherly fondnes for his son; the latter an incorrigibl debauchee.

He sat down at table with them, and they began to drink and indulge themselves in gross jokes, while, like *Mirabel*, . . . their prisoner had the heavy task of receiving their insolence as wit, answering their insults with good-humour, and withholding from them the opportunity which they sought of engaging him in a quarrel, that they might have a pretence for misusing him. *Sir W. Scott.*

Mir'a-bell. A character in Congreve's comedy, "The Way of the World."

Miraculous Child. [Fr. *L'Enfant du Miracle.*] An appellation popularly given to Henri Charles Ferdinand Marie Dieudonné d'Artois, Duc de Bordeaux, better known as the Comte de Chambord, and as the representative of the elder branch of the house of Bourbon, and of its claims to the throne of France. He was a posthumous child of the Duke of Berri, the second son of Charles X., having been born Sept. 29, 1820, nearly seven months after his father's death. As presumptive heir to the crown, his birth occasioned great rejoicing, and he was christened amid circumstances of unusual pomp, with water brought by M. de Châteaubriand from the river Jordan.

Mir'a-mont. An honest and testy old man, in Fletcher's comedy of "The Elder Brother," who admires learning without much more of it than enables him to sign his name.

Miranda. A daughter of the princely magician, Prospero, in Shakespeare's "Tempest;" brought up on a desert island, with the delicate spirit Ariel and the savage and deformed Caliban for her only attendants and acquaintances. Ferdinand, the son of the king of Naples, having been shipwrecked on the island, falls in love with her at once, but cannot obtain her father's consent to their union till he has proved the depth and sincerity of his affection by self-restraint, obedience, and the lowest menial services.

In her retired chamber, . . . she was in fancy . . . identifying herself with the simple yet noble-minded *Miranda*, in the isle of wonder and enchantment. *Sir W. Scott.*

Mir'za (4). An imaginary character, whose wonderful vision of the tide of time, the bridge of human life, and the illimitable ocean of eternity, studded with countless islands, the abodes of the blessed, forms the subject of a celebrated allegory in No. 159 of the "Spectator."

The massive and ancient bridge which stretches across the Clyde was now but dimly visible, and resembled that which *Mirza*, in his unequalled vision, has described as traversing the valley of Bagdad. *Sir W. Scott.*

Such strains of rapture as the genius played
In his still haunt on Bagdad's summit high;
He who stood visible to *Mirza's* eye,
Never before to human sight betrayed.
Lo! in the vale, the mists of evening spread!
The visionary arches are not there,
Nor the green islands, nor the shining seas.
Wordsworth.

Then is Monmouth Street a *Mirza's* hill, where, in motley vision, the whole pageant of existence passes awfully before us, with its wail and jubilee, mad loves and mad hatreds, church-bells and gallows-ropes, farce-tragedy, beast-godhood, — the Bedlam of creation.
Carlyle.

Vales, soft, Elysian,
Like those in the vision
Of *Mirza*, when, dreaming,
He saw the long hollow dell,
Touched by the prophet's spell,
Into an ocean swell,
With its isles teeming. *Whittier.*

Mississippi Bubble. See LAW'S BUBBLE.

Missouri Compromise. (*Amer. Hist.*) A name popularly given to an act of congress which was passed in 1820, and was intended to reconcile the two great sections that were struggling, the one to promote, the other to hinder, the extension of slavery. By this act it was determined that Missouri should be admitted into the Union as a slave-holding State, but that slavery should never be established in any State, to be formed in the future, lying to the north of lat. 36° 30'.

Mistress of the Seas. A name sometimes given to Great Britain, on account of her naval supremacy.

In the War of 1812, our navy, still in its infancy, . . . boldly entered the lists with the *Mistress of the Seas*, and bore away the palm from many a gallant encounter. *E. Everett.*

Mistress of the World. A common designation of ancient Rome, which was for centuries the grandest, richest, and most populous of European cities, and was regarded as the capital of a kind of universal empire.

Mistress Roper. See ROPER, MISTRESS.

---

and for the Remarks and Rules to which the numbers after certain words refer, see pp. xiv-xxxii.

Mite, Sir Matthew. A noted character in Foote's play of "The Nabob;" a returned East India merchant, represented as dissolute, ungenerous, tyrannical, ashamed of the humble friends of his youth, hating the aristocracy, yet childishly eager to be numbered amongst them, squandering his wealth on panderers and flatterers, tricking out his chairmen with the most costly hot-house flowers, and astounding the ignorant with jargon about rupees, lacs, and jaghires.

Sir John Malcolm gives us a letter worthy of *Sir Matthew Mite*, in which Clive orders "two hundred shirts, the best and finest that can be got for love or money." *Macaulay.*

Mith′räs. (*Per. Myth.*) One of the principal gods of the ancient Persians, a personification of the sun. He was regarded as a mediator between the two opposite deities, Ormuzd and Ahriman, or the principle of good and the principle of evil.

Mjölnir (m-yöl′nẽr, 46). [Probably from Old Norse *melja*, to pound, or *mala*, to grind. Comp. Eng. *mill*.] (*Scand. Myth.*) The name of Thor's celebrated hammer, — a type of the thunderbolt, — which, however far it might be cast, was never lost, as it always returned to his hand; and which, whenever he wished, became so small that he could put it in his pocket. This invaluable weapon was once stolen by the giant Thrym, who would not give it back unless he could have Freyja for a bride; but Thor disguised himself in the goddess's attire, and succeeded in recovering it, whereupon he killed Thrym and the whole giant tribe. See THOR.

Mne-mos′y̆-ne (ne-, 26). [Gr. Μνημοσύνη.] (*Gr. & Rom. Myth.*) The goddess of memory, and the mother of the Muses.

Mnes′theüs (nes′-, 26). [Gr. Μνησθεύς.] A Trojan, and a companion of Æneas in his voyage to Italy; the reputed progenitor of the family of the Memmii in Rome. At the funeral games by which Æneas celebrated the death of his father Anchises, Mnestheus took part in a naval contest, and, though not the victor, obtained a prize for skill and energy.

Modern Ar′is-toph′ȧ-nĕş. A name assumed by Samuel Foote (1720–1777), a celebrated English writer and actor of comedy. [Called also *English Aristophanes.*]

Modern Athens. 1. A name often given to Edinburgh, on account of its many noble literary institutions, the taste and culture of the people, the many distinguished men who have issued from it or resided in it, and the high character of its publications, and also on account of a marked resemblance to Athens in its topographical position and its general appearance.

2. The same epithet is applied to Boston, Massachusetts, a city remarkable for the high intellectual character of its citizens, and for its many excellent literary, scientific, and educational institutions and publications.

Modern Babylon. A name often given to the city of London, the largest city of modern, as Babylon was of ancient, times.

He [William Saurin] was well aware that he should disappear in the *Modern Babylon*, and . . . preferred to the lackeying of the English aristocracy the enjoyment of such provincial influence as may still be obtained in Ireland. *Sheil.*

Modern Mes′sȧ-lī′nȧ. An appellation conferred upon Catharine II. of Russia (1729–1796), who had great administrative talent, but whose character, like that of her ancient namesake, Valeria Messalina, was infamous on account of her licentiousness.

Modern Rabelais (răb′lā′). A title given, on account of his learning, wit, eloquence, eccentricity, and humour, to William Maginn (1794–1842), the most remarkable magazine writer of his time.

Mo′do. A fiend referred to by Shakespeare, in "Lear," as presiding over murders. See FLIBBERTIGIBBET, 1.

Mod′red, Sir. A knight of the Round Table, the rebellious nephew of King

☞ For the "Key to the Scheme of Pronunciation," with the accompanying Explanations,

Arthur, whose wife he seduced. He was slain in the battle of Camlan, in Cornwall. [Written also Medrod and Mordred.]

Mœ'ræ (9). [Gr. Μοῖραι.] (*Myth.*) The Greek name of the *Parcæ*, or Fates. See PARCÆ.

Mo-hā'dî, Imaum. A mysterious individual, of whom the Orientals believe that he is not dead, but is destined to return and combat Antichrist before the consummation of all things takes place.

"I am," replied the dwarf, with much assumed gravity and dignity, "the twelfth Imaum,—I am Mahommed *Mohadi*, the guide and the conductor of the faithful. An hundred horses stand ready saddled for me and my train at the Holy City, and as many at the City of Refuge." *Sir W. Scott.*

Mo'hawks, *or* **Mo'hocks.** See TITYRE TUS.

Mol-mu'ti-us, Dun-wăl'lo (mol-mu'shi-us). A legendary or mythical king of Britain; said to have established the Molmutine laws, by which the privilege of sanctuary was bestowed upon temples, cities, and the roads leading to them, and a like protection given even to ploughs.

Molmutius made our laws;
Who was the first of Britain which did put
His brows within a golden crown, and called
Himself a king. *Shak.*

Mo'loch. [Heb. *molech*, king.] (*Myth.*) The name of the chief god of the Phœnicians, frequently mentioned in Scripture as the god of the Ammonites. Human sacrifices, particularly of children, were offered at his shrine. Two fires were kindled before the image of the god, and through these the miserable victims were compelled to pass, while the priests, to drown their cries, made a deafening noise upon instruments of various kinds. It was chiefly in the valley of Tophet,—that is, the valley of "the sound of drums and cymbals,"—to the east of Jerusalem, that this brutal idolatry was perpetrated. Solomon built a temple to Moloch upon the Mount of Olives, and Manasseh long after imitated his impiety by making his son pass through the fire kindled in honour of this deity. In the fantastic demonological system of Wierus, Moloch is called prince of the realm of tears. Milton has described his character in the following lines:—

First *Moloch*, horrid king, besmeared with blood
Of human sacrifice and parents' tears;
Though, for the noise of drums and timbrels loud,
Their children's cries unheard, that passed through fire
To his grim idol. Him the Ammonite
Worshipped in Rabba and her watery plain,
In Argob and in Basan, to the stream
Of utmost Arnon. Nor content with such
Audacious neighbourhood, the wisest heart
Of Solomon he led, by fraud, to build
His temple right against the temple of God,
On that opprobrious hill; and made his grove,
The pleasant valley of Hinnom, Tophet thence
And black Gehenna called, the type of Hell.
Par. Lost, Bk. I.

The name has passed into common use as a designation of any dread and irresistible influence at whose shrine every thing must be offered up, even as the deluded father of old sacrificed his child to the terrible idol.

Mom'mur. The name of an imaginary city, where Oberon, king of the fairies, was once supposed to hold his court.

Mo'mus. [Gr. Μῶμος.] (*Gr. & Rom. Myth.*) The god of raillery and ridicule, said to be a son of Nox, or night.

Monarque, Le Grand. See GRAND MONARQUE, LE.

Mŏ-nim'i-ă. The heroine of Otway's tragedy of "The Orphan."

Dread o'er the scene the ghost of Hamlet stalks;
Othello rages; poor *Monimia* mourns,
And Belvidera pours her soul in love. *Thomson.*

Mon'I-plies, Richard. A servant of Nigel Olifaunt in Sir Walter Scott's novel, "The Fortunes of Nigel;" an honest, self-willed, conceited, pedantic Scotchman.

Mŏnk'barns. See OLDBUCK, JONATHAN.

Monk Lewis. Matthew Gregory Lewis (1773-1818) ;—so called from being the author of a celebrated novel entitled "The Monk."

Monk of Westminster. A designation sometimes given to Richard of Cirencester, or Ricardus Corinensis, an eminent monkish historian of the fourteenth century, of the Benedictine monastery of St. Peter, at Westminster.

Monster, The. A name popularly given to Renwick Williams, a wretch who prowled nightly through London, secretly armed with a sharp, double-edged knife, with which he shockingly wounded numbers of women whose respectable appearance attracted his attention. He was tried and convicted on a variety of these charges, July 8, 1790.

Monster, The Green-eyed. See GREEN-EYED MONSTER.

Mon'tā-gūe. The head of a noble house in Verona, at deadly enmity with the house of Capulet, in Shakespeare's tragedy of "Romeo and Juliet." See CAPULET, LADY.

Montesinos (mon-tā-se'nōs). [Sp., from *montesino*, bred or found in a forest or mountain, from *monte*, mountain, forest.] A legendary hero whose history and adventures are described in the ballads and romances of chivalry. Having received some cause of offence at the French court, he is said to have retired into Spain, where, from his fondness for wild and mountainous scenery, he acquired the name by which he became so celebrated, and which has been given to a cavern in the heart of La Mancha, supposed to have been inhabited by him. This cavern has been immortalised by Cervantes in his account of the visit of Don Quixote to the Cave of Montesinos. It is about sixty feet in depth. Entrance is much more easily effected at the present day than in Cervantes's time, and it is frequently resorted to by shepherds as a shelter from the cold and from storms. See DURANDARTE.

Monticello, Sage of. See SAGE OF MONTICELLO.

Montsalvage. See ST. GRAAL.

Monumental City. The city of Baltimore; — so called from the monuments which it contains.

What, under the circumstances, would not have been the fate of the *Monumental City*, of Harrisburg, of Philadelphia, of Washington, the capital of the Union, each and every one of which would have lain at the mercy of the enemy? *E. Everett.*

Mop'sus. [Gr. Μόψος.] A shepherd in Virgil's fifth Eclogue, who, with Menalcas, celebrates in amœbæan verse the funeral eulogium of Daphnis.

Mor'dred. A knight of the Round Table, distinguished for his treachery. See MODRED.

Moreno, Don Antonio (dŏn än-to'ne-o mo-rā'no). The name of a gentleman of Barcelona, who figures in Cervantes's "Don Quixote." He entertains the Don with mock-heroic hospitality.

More of More-Hall. See DRAGON OF WANTLEY.

Mor'gā-dôur, Sir. A knight of the Round Table, celebrated in the old romances of chivalry.

Morgaine la Fée (mor'gān' lä fā). A fairy, sister of King Arthur. She revealed to him the intrigues of Lancelot and Geneura. [Written also Morgana.] See FATA MORGANA.

You have had, I imagine, a happy journey through Fairy-land, — all full of heroic adventure, and high hope, and wild minstrel-like delusion, like the gardens of *Morgaine la Fée*. *Sir W. Scott.*

Mor'gan. A feigned name adopted by Belarius, a banished lord, in Shakespeare's "Cymbeline."

Morgante (mor-gän'tā). The hero of Pulci's romantic poem entitled "Morgante Maggiore." He is a ferocious pagan giant, whom Orlando attacks, conquers, and converts to Christianity. He becomes the fast friend of Orlando, and acquires great renown for his gentleness, generosity, kindness of heart, and chivalrous defence of ladies in distress. He dies of the bite of a crab, as if to show on what trivial chances depends the life of the strongest. See ORLANDO.

As for the giant *Morgante*, he always spoke very civil things of him; for, though he was one of that monstrous brood who over were intolerably proud and brutish, he still behaved himself like a civil and well-bred person. *Cervantes, Trans.*

Mor'gi-ā'nā. A female slave of Ali Baba in the story of the "Forty Thieves" in the "Arabian Nights' Entertainments."

He went to work in this preparatory lesson, not unlike *Morgiana*, . . . looking into all the

☞ For the "Key to the Scheme of Pronunciation," with the accompanying Explanations,

vessels ranged before him, one after another, to see what they contained. *Dickens.*

Mor'glăy. [Celt. *mor, mawr,* large, great, and *glaif,* a crooked sword. *Claymore,* or *glaymore,* is an inversion of the word.] The sword of Sir Bevis of Southampton ; so famous that it became a general name for a sword.

Morgue the Fay. See MORGAINE LA FÉE and FATA MORGANA.

Mor'hăult, Sir. A knight who makes a great figure in some of the romances of chivalry, particularly in that of "Meliadus." [Written also Moraunt, Marhous, Morhaus, Morholf, Morhoult.]

Mor'ley, Mrs. An assumed name under which Queen Anne corresponded with the Duchess of Marlborough. See FREEMAN, MRS.

Mor'mŏn. The last of a pretended line of Hebrew prophets, described as existing among a race of Israelites, principally the descendants of Joseph, son of the patriarch Jacob, who are fabled to have emigrated from Jerusalem to America about six hundred years before Christ. This imaginary prophet is said to have written the book called "The Book of Mormon," which contains doctrines upon which the "Mormons," or "Latter-day Saints," found their faith; but the real author was one Solomon Spalding (1761-1816), an inveterate scribbler, who had in early life been a clergyman. The work fell into the hands of Joseph Smith (1805-1844), who claimed it as a direct revelation to himself from heaven, and, taking it as his text and authority, began to preach the new gospel of "Mormonism."

Morning Star of the Reformation. A title often bestowed upon John Wycliffe (d. 1384), the first of the reformers.

☞ "When the lamentable ignorance and darkness of God's truth had overshadowed the whole earth, this man, Wycliffe, stepped forth like a valiant champion, unto whom it may justly be applied that is spoken in the book called Ecclesiasticus (chap. i. ver. 6), of one Simon, the son of Onias, 'Even as the morning star being in the middest of a cloud, and as the moon being full in her course, and as the bright beams of the sun,' so doth he shine and glister in the temple and church of God." *J. Foxe.*

Wycliffe will ever be remembered as a good and great man, an advocate of ecclesiastical independence, an unfailing foe to popish tyranny, a translator of Scripture into our mother tongue, and an industrious instructor of the people in their own rude but ripening dialect. May he not be justly styled the "*Morning Star of the Reformation?*" *Eadie.*

Mor'pheŭs (28). [Gr. Μορφεύς.] (*Gr. & Rom. Myth.*) The god of dreams, a son of Somnus, or sleep.

Mŏr'rĭce, Gĭl. The hero of a celebrated Scottish ballad; represented as the son of an earl, whose name is not mentioned, and the wife of Lord Barnard, a "bauld baron." On Gil Morrice's sending a message to his mother requesting her to come to him, and accompanying the message with a gay mantle of her own workmanship, by way of token, Lord Barnard, who had never seen him, supposed him to be a paramour of the baroness. He went out, therefore, in a great rage, to seek revenge, and finding Gil Morrice in the greenwood, slew him with his broadsword, stuck the bloody head upon a spear, and gave it to the meanest of his attendants to carry. On returning to the castle, where the lady was watching his coming "wi' meikle dule and doune," he upbraided her with her adulterous love.

"But when she looked on *Gil Morrice'* head,
  She never spake words but three:
'I never bare no child but ane,
  And ye've slain him cruellie.'"

☞ This pathetic tale suggested the plot of Home's tragedy of "Douglas." The word "Gil" is the same as "Childe" (pronounced *chĭld*), a title formerly prefixed to the surnames of the oldest sons of noble families, while they had not as yet succeeded to the titles of their ancestors, or gained new ones by their own prowess.

Morris, Peter. The pseudonymous author of a work entitled "Peter's Letters to his Kinsfolk," published in 1819, and written by John Gibson Lockhart. It gives graphic sketches of Scottish men and manners at that time.

Morę. [Lat.] (*Gr. & Rom. Myth.*) A deified personification of death, represented as the daughter of Erebus and Nox.

Mortality, Old. See OLD MORTALITY.

Morton. A retainer of the Earl of Northumberland, in the Second Part of Shakespeare's "King Henry IV."

Mo'rus Mul'ti-cáu'lis Mania. A wild, reckless spirit of speculation which seized upon people, even those of intelligence, in the United States, about the year 1835, and which led them to purchase and cultivate mulberry-trees at fabulous prices, with the view of rearing the silkworm. It soon died out, however, but not without great losses having been sustained by the deluded.

Mor'ven. A kingdom spoken of in the poems of Ossian, of which Fingal was the ruler, supposed to represent Argyleshire and the adjoining parts of the West Highlands, but of whose existence there is absolutely no evidence.

Moses. See PRIMROSE, MOSES.

Most Catholic Majesty. See CATHOLIC MAJESTY.

Most Christian Doctor. [Lat. *Doctor Christianissimus.*] 1. An epithet bestowed upon Jean de Gerson (1363–1429), one of the most eminent and learned divines of his age.
2. The same title was given to Nicolas de Cusa, Cuss, or Cusel (1401–1464), a celebrated German philosopher and cardinal.

Most Christian King, or **Majesty.** [Lat. *Christianissimus Rex.*] A name given by Pope Stephen III., in 755, to Pepin the Short of France, and by the council of Savonnières, in 859, to Charles the Bald; but it did not become the peculiar appellation of the sovereigns of that country until 1469, when Pope Paul II. conferred it upon Louis XI. It has been justly said that never was the name of Christian less deserved. His tyranny and oppressions obliged his subjects to enter into a league against him; and four thousand persons were executed publicly or privately in his merciless reign.

Most Faithful Majesty. A title given, in 1748, by Pope Benedict XIV., to John V., king of Portugal.

Most Learned of the Romans. [Lat. *Eruditissimus Romanorum.*] A title bestowed upon Marcus Terentius Varro (B. C. 116-27), on account of his vast and varied erudition in almost every department of literature. He was so called by Quintilian, by Cicero, and by St. Augustine. According to his own statement, he wrote four hundred and ninety books.

Most Methodical Doctor. [Lat. *Doctor Ordinatissimus.*] An honorary title given to John Bassol (d. 1347), a distinguished Scotch philosopher, and a disciple of Duns Scotus, on account of the clear and accurate manner in which he lectured and composed. His master greatly admired him, and used to say, "If only Bassol be present, I have a sufficient auditory."

Most Resolute Doctor. [Lat. *Doctor Resolutissimus.*] A name given to Durand de St. Pourçain (d. 1332), a member of the order of Dominicans, and a scholastic philosopher distinguished as an opponent of the realism of Scotus and his followers. His style is said to have been characterised by a singular energy, and freedom from all periphrasis and ambiguity.

Moth. 1. A page to Don Adriano de Armado, in Shakespeare's "Love's Labour's Lost."

☞ "To the stiff, weak, melancholy Armado is opposed the little Moth, who, light as his name, is all jest and playfulness, versatility and cunning."
Gervinus, Trans.

2. A fairy, in Shakespeare's "Midsummer-Night's Dream."

Mother Ann. A title conferred upon Ann Lee (1735–1784), the "spiritual mother" and leader of the society of Shakers, and the name by which she is familiarly known among the members of that sect. She is regarded as a second manifestation of the Christ under a female form, Jesus being the male manifestation.

☞ For the "Key to the Scheme of Pronunciation," with the accompanying Explanations,

Mother Bunch. 1. A celebrated ale-wife, apparently of the latter part of the sixteenth century, mentioned by Dekker in his "Satiromastix," 1602; and in 1604 was published "Pasquil's Jests, mixed with Mother Bunch's Merriments."

> Wit that shall make thy name to last,
> When Tarlton's jests are rotten,
> And George a-Green and *Mother Bunch*
> Shall all be quite forgotten.
> *Wit and Drollery*, 1682.

2. The subject of a book, formerly very popular, entitled "Mother Bunch's Closet newly broke open, containing Rare Secrets of Art and Nature, tried and experimented by Learned Philosophers, and recommended to all Ingenious Young Men and Maids, teaching them, in a Natural Way, how to get Good Wives and Husbands. By a Lover of Mirth and Hater of Treason. In Two Parts, London, 12°, 1760." The following extract from the work may serve as a specimen of its contents.

☞ "*A Way to tell who must be your Husband.* — Take a St. Thomas's onion, pare it, and lay it on a clean handkerchief under your pillow; put on a clean smock; and, as you lie down, lay your arms abroad, and say these words: —

> 'Good St. Thomas, do me right,
> And bring my love to me this night,
> That I may view him in the face,
> And in my arms may him embrace.'

Then, lying on thy back with thy arms abroad, go to sleep as soon as you can, and in your first sleep you shall dream of him who is to be your husband, and he will come and offer to kiss you; do not hinder him, but catch him in thy arms, and strive to hold him, for that is he. This I have tried, and it was proved true."

☞ "Now that we have fairly entered into the matrimonial chapter, we must needs speak of Mother Bunch; not the Mother Bunch whose fairy tales are repeated to the little ones, but she whose 'cabinet,' when broken open, reveals so many powerful love-spells. It is Mother Bunch who teaches the blooming damsel to recall the fickle lover, or to fix the wandering gaze of the cautious swain, attracted by her charms, yet scorning the fetters of the parson, and dreading the still more fearful vision of the churchwarden, the constable, the justice, the warrant, and the jail." *Qu. Rev.*

My thoughts naturally turned to Master B. My speculations about him were uneasy and manifold, — whether his Christian name was Benjamin, Bissextile (from his having been born in leap-year), Bartholomew, or Bill; ... whether he could possibly have been kith and kin to an illustrious lady who brightened my own childhood, and had come of the blood of the brilliant *Mother Bunch. Dickens.*

Mother Ca'rey (9). A name which occurs in the expression "Mother Carey's chickens," which is applied by sailors to the *Procellaria pelagica,* or stormy petrel, a small oceanic bird vulgarly supposed to be seen only before a storm, of which it is regarded as the harbinger. According to Yarrell, the distinguished ornithologist, "The name of 'Mother Carey's chickens' is said to have been originally bestowed upon the stormy petrel by Captain Carteret's sailors, probably from some celebrated ideal hag of that name." Others regard the words as a characteristic English corruption of "*Mater cara*" (that is, dear Mother), an affectionate appellation said to be given by Italian sailors to the Virgin Mary — the special patroness of mariners — for her kindness in sending these messengers to forewarn them of impending tempests; but this explanation is rather ingenious than probable. When it is snowing, Mother Carey is said by the sailors to be plucking her goose; and this has been supposed to be the comical and satirical form assumed by a myth of the old German mythology, that described the snow as the feathers falling from the bed of the goddess Holda, when she shook it in making it.

Among the unsolvable riddles which nature propounds to mankind, we may reckon the question, Who is *Mother Carey,* and where does she rear her chickens? *H. Bridge.*

Mother Company. See COMPANY, JOHN.

Mother Doug'lass. A famous procuress of the last century. Foote represents her in "The Minor," in the character of Mrs. Cole. She resided "at the north-east corner of Covent Garden," where she died June 10, 1761. Her house was superbly furnished, and decorated with expensive pictures by old masters.

I question whether the celebrated *Mother Douglass* herself could have made such a figure in an extemporaneous altercation. *Smollett.*

Mother Goose. 1. The feigned narrator of a celebrated volume of fairy tales ("Contes de ma Mère l'Oye"), written by Charles Perrault, and first published, under the name of his infant son, Perrault d'Armancourt, in 1697. Of the ten stories in this work, seven are to be found in the "Pentamerone."

2. The fictitious writer or compiler of the collection of ancient nursery rhymes known as "Mother Goose's Melodies."

☞ This "Mother Goose" is not an imaginary personage, as is commonly supposed. She belonged to a wealthy family in Boston, Massachusetts, where she was born, and resided for many years. Her eldest daughter, Elizabeth Goose, was married, by the celebrated Cotton Mather, on the 8th of June, 1715, to an enterprising and industrious printer by the name of Thomas Fleet, and, in due time, gave birth to a son. Mother Goose, like all good grandmothers, was in ecstasies at the event; her joy was unbounded; she spent her whole time in the nursery, and in wandering about the house, pouring forth, in not the most melodious strains, the songs and ditties which she had learned in her younger days, greatly to the annoyance of the whole neighbourhood, — to Fleet in particular, who was a man fond of quiet. It was in vain he exhausted his shafts of wit and ridicule, and every expedient he could devise. It was of no use; the old lady was not thus to be put down; so, like others similarly situated, he was obliged to submit. His shrewdness, however, did not forsake him: he conceived the idea of collecting the songs and ditties as they came from his good mother-in-law, and such as he could gather from other sources, and publishing them for the benefit of the world — not forgetting himself. This he did, and soon brought out a book, the earliest known edition of which bears the following title: "Songs for the Nursery; or, Mother Goose's Melodies for Children. Printed by T. Fleet, at his Printing-house, Pudding Lane [now Devonshire Street], 1719. Price, two coppers." The adoption of this title was in derision of his mother-in-law, and was perfectly characteristic of the man, as he was never known to spare his nearest friends in his raillery, or when he could excite laughter at their expense.

Mother Hubbard. The subject of an old and well-known nursery rhyme.

Mother Hubberd. The feigned narrator of Spenser's poem entitled "Mother Hubberd's Tale," which is a satire upon the common modes of rising in Church and State, and which purports to be one of several tales told to the author by his friends, to beguile a season of sickness.

Mother Nicneven. See NICNEVEN.

Mother of Cities. [Arab. *Amu al Balud.*] A title given by Orientals, on account of its antiquity, to Balkh, the capital city of the province of the same name (the ancient kingdom of Bactria), which is subordinate to the khanate of Bokhara.

Mother of Presidents. A name frequently given, in the United States, to the State of Virginia, which has furnished six presidents to the Union.

Mother of States. A name sometimes given to Virginia, the first settled of the thirteen States which united in the declaration of independence. From the large amount of territory originally included under this name have been formed the States of Kentucky, Ohio, Indiana, Illinois, and West Virginia.

Mother of the Camps. [Lat. *Mater Castrorum.*] A title given by the Roman legions in Gaul to Victoria, or Victorina, after the death of her son Victorinus (A. D. 268), one of the Thirty Tyrants. See THIRTY TYRANTS.

Mother of the Gods. See CYBELE.

Mother Shipton. The subject of a popular tale of ancient, but uncertain date, and of unknown authorship, entitled "The Strange and Wonderful History and Prophecies of Mother Shipton, plainly setting forth her birth, life, death, and burial."

Mouldy. A recruit, in the Second Part of Shakespeare's "King Henry IV."

Mound City. A name popularly given to St. Louis, Missouri, on account of the numerous artificial mounds in the neighbourhood of the site on which the city is built.

Mountain, The. [Fr. *La Montagne.*] A name given to the Jacobins, or

---

☞ For the "Key to the Scheme of Pronunciation," with the accompanying Explanations,

extreme democratic politicians, in the National Convention of France, from their occupying the highest benches. Of this formidable party, Collot d'Herbois, Danton, Marat, Robespierre, and St. Just were the principal members. Brissot first used the term in the Constitutional Assembly, in contrasting the Jacobins with the Aristocrats. The expression is still in use on the continent of Europe, as applied to the extreme radicals, or "the left."

Mount Badon. See BADON, MOUNT.

Mount Caf (käf). (*Mohammedan Myth.*) A fabulous mountain encircling the earth, — supposed to be a circular plain or flat disc, — as a ring encircles the finger. It is the home of giants and fairies, and rests upon the sacred stone Sakhrat. See SAKHRAT. [Written also Mount Kaf.]

Mount Meru. See MERU.

Muc′kle-back′it, Säun′dẽrs (muk′-l-). An old fisherman in Sir Walter Scott's novel of "The Antiquary."

Muc′kle-wrath, Hă-bak′kuk (muk′-l-rawth). A fanatic preacher in Scott's "Old Mortality."

Muggins. See HUGGINS AND MUGGINS.

Mul′cĭ-bẽr. [Lat.] (*Rom. Myth.*) A surname of Vulcan. For taking the part of Juno against Jupiter, in a quarrel between the two deities, the latter seized him by the leg and hurled him down from Olympus. He was a whole day in falling; but, in the evening, he came down in the island of Lemnos, where he was kindly received and taken care of. See VULCAN.

Nor was his name unheard or unadored
In ancient Greece; and in Ausonian land
Men called him *Mulciber;* and how he fell
From heaven they fabled, thrown by angry Jove
Sheer o'er the crystal battlements: from morn
To noon he fell, from noon to dewy eve,
A summer's day; and with the setting sun
Dropped from the zenith like a falling star,
On Lemnos, the Ægean isle. *Milton.*

Mŭl′lă. A poetical name given by Spenser to the Awbeg, — a tributary of the Blackwater, — in Ireland, near which he lived for many years.

As erst the bard by *Mulla's* silver stream,
Oft as he told of deadly dolorous plight,
Sighed as he sung, and did in tears indite.
Shenstone.

Mŭl′lẽr, Maud. The heroine of a ballad by Whittier, having this name for its title.

Mŭl′lion, Mor′de-câi (mul′yun). One of the interlocutors in the "Noctes Ambrosianæ" of Wilson, Lockhart, &c.; a purely imaginary character, designed to represent, very generally, the population of Glasgow and its vicinity. Wilson also used the name as a *nom de plume.*

Mum′bo Jum′bo. A strange bugbear, common to all the Mandingo towns, and resorted to by the negroes as a means of discipline.

☞ "On the 7th of December, 1795, I departed from Konjour, and slept at a village called Malla (or Mallaing); and, on the 8th, about noon, I arrived at Kalor, a considerable town, near the entrance into which I observed, hanging upon a tree, a sort of masquerade habit, made of the bark of trees, which I was told, on inquiry, belonged to Mumbo Jumbo. This is a strange bugbear, common to the Mandingo towns, and much employed by the pagan natives in keeping their women in subjection; for, as the Kaffirs are not restricted in the number of their wives, every one marries as many as he can conveniently maintain; and, as it frequently happens that the ladies do not agree among themselves, family quarrels sometimes rise to such a height, that the authority of the husband can no longer preserve peace in his household. In such cases, the interposition of Mumbo Jumbo is called in, and is always decisive. This strange minister of justice (who is supposed to be either the husband himself or some person instructed by him), disguised in the dress that has been mentioned, and armed with the rod of public authority, announces his coming by loud and dismal screams in the woods near the town. He begins the pantomime at the approach of night, and as soon as it is dark he enters the town. The ceremony commences with songs and dances, which continue till midnight, about which time Mumbo fixes on the offender. The unfortunate victim, being seized, is stripped, tied to a post, and severely scourged with Mumbo's rod, amidst the shouts and derision of the whole assembly. Daylight puts an end to the unseemly revel."
Mungo Park.

The grand question and hope, however, is,

Will not this feast of the Tuileries' *Mumbo Jumbo* be a sign, perhaps, that the guillotine is to abate? *Carlyle.*

Mun-chāu'sen (-sn). The putative author and hero of a book of travels filled with the most marvellous fictions, compiled from various sources, and first published in England, in 1785, by Rudolf Erich Gaspe, an expatriated German. The wit and humour of the work gave it great success. Several other editions soon appeared, and translations or imitations were brought out in German and other foreign languages. The name Munchausen is corrupted from that of Jerome Charles Frederick von Münchhausen (1720–1797), a German officer in the Russian service, who acquired a remarkable notoriety by relating the most ridiculously false and exaggerated tales of his adventures. He is said to have repeated the same stories so often, without the slightest variation in their most minute points, that he came at length really to believe even his most extravagant fictions, and was highly offended if any one presumed to doubt them. Yet there was nothing of the braggart about him, his whole demeanour being that of a quiet and modest gentleman. He must not be confounded, as is sometimes the case, with Gerlach Adolphus, Baron von Münchhausen (1688–1770), one of the founders of the University of Göttingen, and for many years a privy councillor of the Elector of Hanover, George II. of England.

Mun-dun'gus. A nickname — signifying *tobacco* — given by Sterne, in his "Sentimental Journey," to Doctor Samuel Sharp (d. 1778), an English tourist who travelled upon the continent at the same time as Sterne, and who published a cold, didactic account of what he had seen, disfigured by coarse libels upon the ladies of Italy. See SMELFUNGUS.

Munin (moo'nin). (*Scand. Myth.*) One of Odin's two ravens. See ODIN.

Muse Limonadière, La (lä müz le'mo'nä'de-êr', 34). [Fr., coffee-house muse.] A sobriquet given to Charlotte Bourette (1714–1784) a French poetess who kept a *café* which was frequented by all the wits of her time in Paris.

Muse of Greece. See ATTIC MUSE.

Muses. [Lat. *Musæ*, Gr. Μοῦσαι.] (*Gr. & Rom. Myth.*) Daughters of Jupiter and Mnemosyne, and goddesses who presided over the different kinds of poetry, and over music, dancing, and the other liberal arts. They were nine in number; namely, Clio, the muse of history; Melpomene, of tragedy; Thalia, of comedy; Euterpe, of music; Terpsichore, of dancing; Calliope, of epic poetry; Erato, of lyric and amatory poetry; Urania, of astronomy; Polyhymnia, or Polymnia, of singing and rhetoric.

Mu'sĭ-do'rạ (9). A beautiful young woman who forms the subject of an episode in the poem on "Summer" in Thomson's "Seasons."

☞ "Musidora was one of the fashionable poetical sobriquets of the last century." *Yonge.*

Muspel (moos'pel), *or* **Muspelheim** (moos'pel-him). (*Scand. Myth.*) A region of fire and heat, lying to the south of Ginnunga-gap. From it, at Ragnarök, Surtur will collect flames, and set fire to the universe.

Mutch. One of Robin Hood's band of outlaws. See ROBIN HOOD. [Written also M u c h , M i d g e.]

Mutual Admiration Society. [Fr. *Société d' Admiration Mutuelle.*] A nickname popularly given in Paris to the Société d'Observation Médicale. It is used in English, in a more general way, usually with reference to a circle or set of persons who are lavish of compliments on each other.

Who can tell what we owe to the *Mutual Admiration Society* of which Shakespeare, and Ben Jonson, and Beaumont and Fletcher were members? Or to that of which Addison and Steele formed the centre, and which gave us the "Spectator?" Or to that where Johnson, and Goldsmith, and Burke, and Reynolds, and Beauclerc, and Boswell, most admiring among all admirers, met together? . . . Wise ones are prouder of the title M. S. M. A. than of all their other honours put together. *Holmes.*

Myrrha (mĭr'rạ). The heroine of

Lord Byron's tragedy of "Sardanapalus."

Myrtle, Minnie. A pseudonym of Mrs. Anna C. Johnson, an American authoress of the present day.

Mystical Babylon. A name often opprobriously given by Protestants to Rome, or the Roman Catholic church, with reference to the language used by St. John, in the seventeenth and eighteenth chapters of the book of *Revelation*, where he prophetically foretells the downfall of some religious system or tenets, which he compares to Babylon, once the proudest and most powerful city in the world, but, in his time, fallen from its high and palmy state into a condition of utter ruin and desolation, through its luxury, licentiousness, and effeminacy.

---

and for the Remarks and Rules to which the numbers after certain words refer, see pp. xiv-xxxii.

N.

Naglfar (nä'gl-fär). [Old Norse *nagl*, a human nail, and *fara*, to go, to fare.] (*Scand. Myth.*) A ship constructed by the Giants out of dead men's nails. On board of it the Giants will embark, at Ragnarök, to give battle to the gods.

Nā'iădş. [Lat. *Naiades*, Gr. Ναϊάδες.] (*Gr. & Rom. Myth.*) Nymphs of lakes, streams, and fountains.

Nameless City. Ancient Rome; — so called because it had an elder and mysterious name, which it was death to pronounce. This name is said to have been *Valentia*, afterward translated into the Greek word Ῥώμη. Ῥώμη, as the Greek form of Rome, is first mentioned, among Grecian writers, by Aristotle or Theophrastus.

☞ "They [certain local names and nicknames] are all inferior, I think, to the one sacred and proverbial name which belonged to Rome. They take many words to convey one idea. In one word, the secret qualifying name of the ancient city, many ideas found expression, — *Valentia!*" *Dr. Doran.*

Namo (nä'mo'), or **Nā'mus.** A semi-mythical duke of Bavaria, who figures in old romances of chivalry as one of Charlemagne's Twelve Peers.

Nanna (nän'nä). (*Scand. Myth.*) The wife of Baldur, famed for her piety and constancy. When her husband died, she threw herself on the funeral pyre, and was buried with him.

Nantes, Edict of. See EDICT OF NANTES.

Napoleon of Mexico. A name given to Augusto Iturbide (1784–1824), emperor of Mexico, whose career in some respects bears a distant resemblance to that of Napoleon Bonaparte.

Napoleon of Peace. A name sometimes given to Louis Philippe, king of the French, in allusion to the great increase in wealth and the steady physical progress of the nation during his reign of eighteen years (1830–1848), — results which may be advantageously compared with those of the first empire. It is said that the king liked to be called by this appellation.

Nar-cis'sus. [Gr. Νάρκισσος.] (*Gr. & Rom. Myth.*) A son of Cephissus and the nymph Liriope. He was uncommonly beautiful, and, seeing his own image reflected in a fountain, became enamoured of it, thinking it to be the nymph of the place. As the shadow was unapproachable, he wasted away with desire, and was changed into a flower, which still bears his name. See ECHO.

Naströnd (nä'strönd, 46). [Old Norse *ná*, a corpse, and *strönd*, strand.] (*Scand. Myth.*) A noisome and horrible marsh in the under-world, where the impenitent will be punished in the future life.

Nathaniel, Sir. A grotesque curate in Shakespeare's "Love's Labour's Lost."

Nation of Gentlemen. A complimentary designation given to the people of Scotland by George IV., on occasion of a royal visit to that kingdom in 1822. He is said to have been much struck with the quiet and respectful demeanour of the multitude, which offered a strong contrast to the wild enthusiasm with which he was greeted at Dublin the year before.

Nation of Shop-keepers. A contemptuous appellation bestowed upon the English by Napoleon Bonaparte.

Ne-æ'ră (9). [Gr. Νέαιρα.] The name of a girl mentioned by the Latin poets Horace, Virgil, and Tibullus; sometimes also introduced into modern pastoral poetry as the name of a mistress or sweetheart.

To sport with Amaryllis in the shade,
Or with the tangles of *Neæra's* hair.
Milton.

Ne'me-ăn Lion. See HERCULES.

Nem'e-sis. [Gr. Νέμεσις.] (*Gr. & Rom. Myth.*) A daughter of Nox, or

☞ For the "Key to the Scheme of Pronunciation," with the accompanying Explanations,

of Erebus, originally a personification of conscience; afterward regarded as the awful and mysterious goddess of retribution, who avenges all wrong-doing, and punishes and humbles the proud and presumptuous in particular.

O thou, who never yet of human wrong
Left the unbalanced scale, great *Nemesis!*
Thou who didst call the Furies from the abyss,
And round Orestes bade them howl and hiss,
For that unnatural retribution, — just,
Had it been from hands less near, — in this,
Thy former realm, I call thee from the dust.
Byron.

Ne'op-tol'e-mus. [Gr. Νεοπτόλεμος.] (*Gr. & Rom. Myth.*) The son of Achilles. [Called also *Pyrrhus.*] See PYRRHUS.

Neph'e-lo-coc-cyg'i-ă. [Gr. Νεφελοκοκκυγία, cloud-cuckoo-town, from νεφέλη, cloud, and κόκκυξ, cuckoo.] A town built in the clouds by the cuckoos, in the "Birds" of Aristophanes, a comedy intended as a satire on Athenian frivolity and credulity, on that building of castles in the air, and that dreaming expectation of a life of luxury and ease, in which the great mass of the Athenian people of that day indulged. This imaginary city occupied the whole horizon, and was designed to cut off the gods from all connection with mankind, and even from the power of receiving sacrifices, so as to force them ultimately to surrender at discretion to the birds. The name occurs also in the "Veræ Historiæ" of Lucian, a romance written probably in the age of M. Aurelius Antoninus, and composed with the view of ridiculing the authors of extraordinary tales.

Without flying to *Nephelococcygia,* or to the court of Queen Mab, we can meet with sharpers, bullies, hard-hearted, impudent debauchees, and women worthy of such paramours.
Macaulay.

What you do
For bread, will taste of common grain, not grapes,
Although you have a vineyard in Champagne,
Much less in *Nephelococcygia,*
As mine was, peradventure.
Mrs. E. B. Browning.

Nep'tune (nep'ch'oon). [Lat. *Neptunus.*] (*Gr. & Rom. Myth.*) The god of the sea and of all other waters, the son of Saturn and Ops, the brother of Jupiter, and the husband of Amphitrite. He is represented with a trident in his hand.

Ne're-ids (9). [Lat. *Nereides,* Gr. Νηρεΐδες.] (*Gr. & Rom. Myth.*) Sea-nymphs, daughters of Nereus and Doris. They were fifty in number, and were regarded as nymphs of the Mediterranean, in distinction from the Oceanids, or nymphs of the great ocean.

Ne'reûs (9). [Gr. Νηρεύς.] (*Gr. & Rom. Myth.*) A sea-god, father of the Nereids; described as a wise and unerring old man, ruling over the Mediterranean, or, more particularly, the Ægean Sea.

Ne-ris'să. Portia's waiting-woman, in Shakespeare's "Merchant of Venice." See PORTIA.

☞ "Nerissa is . . . a clever, confidential waiting-woman, who has caught a little of her lady's elegance and romance; she affects to be lively and sententious, falls in love, and makes her favour conditional on the fortune of the caskets, and, in short, mimics her mistress with good emphasis and discretion."
Mrs. Jameson.

Nero of the North. A title given to Christian II. (1480–1559), king of Denmark and Sweden, and well merited by him on account of his ferocious cruelty.

Nes'sus. [Gr. Νεσσός.] (*Gr. & Rom. Myth.*) A famous Centaur, who, for offering violence to Dejanira, was slain by Hercules with a poisoned arrow, which afterward became the cause of Hercules's own death. See DEJANIRA.

Nes'tor. [Gr. Νέστωρ.] (*Gr. & Rom. Myth.*) A son of Neleus and Chloris, and king of Pylos in Triphylia. He took a prominent part in the Trojan war, acting as counsellor of the other Grecian chiefs, but was equally distinguished for his valour in the field of battle. Homer extols his wisdom, justice, bravery, and eloquence. He lived to so great an age that his advice and authority were deemed equal to those of the immortal gods.

New Albion. See ALBION, NEW.

New Am'ster-dăm. [D. *Nieuw Amsterdam.*] The original name of

and for the Remarks and Rules to which the numbers after certain words refer, see pp. xiv–xxxii.

the present city of New York; — given to it by the first settlers, who were Dutch.

New Atlantis. See ATLANTIS, THE NEW.

Newbury, Jack of. See JACK OF NEWBURY.

New Christians. A name given in Portugal, in the fifteenth century, to the Jews, who, yielding to compulsion, suffered themselves to be baptised *en masse*, but who in private remained faithful to their old religion, and continued scrupulously to observe the Mosaic ceremonies.

New'còme, Colonel. A prominent character in Thackeray's novel, "The Newcomes;" distinguished for the moral beauty of his life.

New'còme, Johnny. A nickname for any raw, unpractised youth or person, especially any very young officer in the army or navy of Great Britain.

"'A' comes o' taking folk on the right side, I trow," quoth Caleb to himself; "and I had ance the ill hap to be was but a *Johnnie Newcome* in our town, and the carle bore the family an ill-will ever since." *Sir W. Scott.*

New Con-nec'ti-cut (kon-net'tĭ-kut). A name formerly given to the Western Reserve. See WESTERN RESERVE.

New France. An old name of Canada, which was first settled and possessed by the French.

New Jerusalem. The name by which, among Christians, heaven, or the abode of the redeemed, is symbolised. The allusion is to the description contained in the twenty-first chapter of the book of *Revelation.*

Newland, Abraham. A name by which a Bank-of-England note was long known, owing to its being made payable to Mr. Newland, one of the governors. An old song, fifty or sixty years ago, ran thus: —

"For fashion and arts, should you seek foreign parts,
It matters not whenever you land,
Hebrew, Latin, or Greek, the same language they speak,
The language of *Abraham Newland.*
CHORUS.
Oh *Abraham Newland*, notified *Abraham Newland!*

With compliments crammed, you may dio and be damned,
If you haven't an *Abraham Newland.*"

New Moses. [Gr. Μωσῆς νέος.] A designation given, by the later Greek writers, to Anastasius, a presbyter and monk of Mount Sinai, who lived toward the end of the seventh century.

New Netherlands. The name originally given to the Dutch colony or settlements included within what is now the State of New York.

New Sweden, *or* **New Swede'land.** The name given to the territory between Virginia and New York, while it was in the possession of the Swedes, who founded a colony here in 1627. It was afterward claimed by the Dutch.

New World. A familiar name for the Western Hemisphere. By whom it was first employed is not known. But, from its obvious appropriateness, it must have been applied contemporaneously with the discovery. Upon the tomb of Columbus, Ferdinand ordered this inscription to be placed: —

"A Castilla y a Leon
Nuovo mondo dió Colon,"

that is, To Castile and to Leon, Columbus gave a New World.

Nibelung, King. See KING NIBELUNG.

Nibelungen. See KING NIBELUNG.

And now has begun, in Nanci, as in that doomed Hall of the *Nibelungen,* "a murder grim and great." *Carlyle.*

Nicholas, St. See ST. NICHOLAS.

Nick, Old. See OLD NICK.

Nickers. See TITYRE TUS.

Nick'ie-Ben. A familiar Scottish name for the Devil. (See Burns's "Address to the Deil.") *Ben* is a Scotch adverb, denoting toward, or into, the inner apartment of a house. It is used adjectively and metaphorically to denote intimacy, favour, or honour. See OLD NICK.

Nick'le-bỹ, Mrs. (nik'l-bī). The mother of Nicholas Nickleby, in Dickens's novel of this name; a widow lady of no force of character, chiefly remarkable on account of her habit of introducing, in conversation, topics wholly irrelevant to the subject under consideration, and of always declaring, when any thing unanticipated occurred, that she had expected it all along, and had prophesied to that precise effect on divers (unknown) occasions.

This is so thoroughly De-Quinceyish (like *Mrs. Nickleby* bringing in persons and things quite independent of the matter on the *tapis*), that of course I cannot complain of his thus writing "an infinite deal of nothing."
R. Shelton Mackenzie.

Nick'le-bў, Nicholas. The hero of Dickens's novel of the same name.

Nic'nev-en. A gigantic and malignant female spirit of the old popular Scottish mythology. The Scottish poet Dunbar has given a spirited description of this hag riding at the head of witches and fairies, sorceresses and elves, indifferently, upon the ghostly eve of All-hallow-mass. See his "Flyting of Dunbar and Kennedy."

Nicole (nē'kōl'). A female servant of M. Jourdain, in Molière's comedy, "Le Bourgeois Gentilhomme," who sees the folly of her master, and exposes it in a most natural and amusing manner.

Nidhögg (nēd'hög, 46). (*Scand. Myth.*) A terrible dragon who dwells in Naströnd, and continually gnaws the root of Yggdrasil, the mundane ash-tree.

Niflheim (nēf'l-hīm). [Old Norse *nifl*, cloud, mist, and *heimr*, home.] (*Scand. Myth.*) A region of eternal cold, fog, darkness, and horror, on the north of Ginnunga-gap. It consisted of nine worlds, reserved for those that died of disease, or old age, and was ruled over by Hela, or death. [Written also Niflheimr, Niffelbeim, Nifflehcim, and Niflhel.]

Nigel. See OLIFAUNT, NIGEL.

Nightmare of Europe. An appellation given to Napoleon Bonaparte, whose schemes of personal aggrandisement and whose stupendous military successes terrified, and, for a time, stupefied, the nations of Europe.

Nim'rod. A pseudonym of Charles James Apperley (d. 1843), an English writer on sporting subjects. He was for many years looked up to as the highest authority on all matters connected with the field, the road, or the turf.

Nine Gods. See NOVENSIDES.

Lars Porsena of Clusium,
By the *Nine Gods* he swore. *Macaulay.*

Nine Worthies. See WORTHIES, THE NINE.

Ni'nus. [Gr. Νῖνος.] (*Gr. & Rom. Myth.*) The son of Belus, the husband of Semiramis, and the reputed builder of Nineveh and founder of the Assyrian monarchy.

Ni'o-be. [Gr. Νιόβη.] (*Gr. & Rom. Myth.*) The daughter of Tantalus, and the wife of Amphion, king of Thebes. On the strength of her more numerous progeny, she set herself before Latona, and her six sons and six daughters were in consequence slain by Apollo and Diana, while the weeping Niobe was changed into a stone, and transported in a whirlwind to the top of Mount Sipylus, where she has ever since remained, her tears flowing unceasingly.

The *Niobe* of nations! there she stands,
Childless and crownless in her voiceless woe.
Byron (on Rome).

Nip, Number. See NUMBER NIP.

Nipper, Susan. An attendant upon Florence Dombey, in Dickens's novel of "Dombey and Son;" a spicy, though good-natured little body, sharp and biting, but affectionate and faithful.

Niquée (nē'kā'). A female character in the romance of "Amadis de Gaul." Her godmother, the fairy Zorphée, wishing to withdraw her from the incestuous love of her brother Anasterax, enchanted her, after having placed her upon a magnificent throne.

Ni'sus. [Gr. Νῖσος.] A Trojan youth who accompanied Æneas to Italy, after the fall of Troy, and who is celebrated for his devoted attachment to Euryalus. The two friends fought with great bravery against the Rutulians, but at last Nisus perished in attempting the rescue of his friend Euryalus, who had fallen into the enemy's hands.

Njörd (n-yörd, 46). (*Scand. Myth.*) The god of the winds, and especially of the north wind. [Written also N i ö r d.]

Nōakes, John o', *or* John a. A fictitious character made use of by lawyers in actions of ejectment, usually coupled with the name of *John*, or *Tom, Styles*. Many other names were also formerly used in these fictitious proceedings. John a Noakes and John a Styles being often employed in this way, they came to have the appearance and reputation of being very litigious characters. See DOE, JOHN, and STYLES, TOM. [Written also N o k e s.]

☞ "Originally the name [Noakes] was spelled Aten Oke and Atten Oke; afterward, when the preposition was contracted, the final N adhered (as in some other instances) to the name of the tree, giving us A - Noke, subsequently pluralised into Noakes. John-A-Noakes and his constant antagonist, John Atte Style, were formerly as well known in our law-courts as the redoubtable John Doe and Richard Roe of later times. Jack Noakes and Tom Styles — the phrase by which we designate the *ignobile vulgus* — are lineal descendants of those litigious parties. In the Middle Ages, the phrase John at Style was in common use, to designate a plebeian; and it still survives in the slightly altered form above given." *Lower.*

A litigated point, fairly hung up; — for instance, whether *John o' Nokes* his nose could stand in Tom o' Stiles his face, without a trespass or not. *Sterne.*

There is, in the present day, so little opportunity of a man of fortune and family rising to that eminence at the bar which is attained by adventurers who are as willing to plead for *John a Nokes* as for the first noble of the land, that I was early disgusted with practice. *Sir W. Scott.*

Nod, Land of. See LAND OF NOD.

Noddy, Tom. } A type of fools or
Noodle, Tom. } folly; a popular designation for any very foolish person.

Noll, Old. See OLD NOLL.

No-Popery Riots. (*Scot. Hist.*) A name given to riots at Edinburgh and Glasgow, Feb. 5, 1779; and in London, from June 2 to June 9, 1780.

The latter were occasioned by the zeal of Lord George Gordon, and 40,000 persons are said to have taken part in them. In the end, 210 of the rioters were killed, and 248 were wounded, of whom 75 died afterwards in the hospitals.

Norman Reconciliation. See LAMOURETTE'S KISS.

Nor'nă. A mysterious being of supernatural powers, in Scott's novel of "The Pirate."

☞ "The character of Norna is meant to be an instance of that singular kind of insanity, during which the patient, while she or he retains much subtlety and address for . . . imposing upon others, is still more ingenious in endeavouring to impose upon themselves." *Sir W. Scott.*

Norns. [Old Norse *Nornir*, pl. of *Norna*.] (*Scand. Myth.*) Three virgin goddesses who weave the woof of human destiny sitting by the Asgard root of the world-tree Yggdrasil, which they carefully tend. Their names are Urda (the past), Verdandi (the present), and Skulda (the future). The name is also given to subordinate beings, some good and some bad, of whom one is assigned to every person born into the world, and determines his fate.

North, Christopher, *or* **Kit.** A celebrated pseudonym adopted by Professor John Wilson (1785-1854) in connection with the famous series of dialogues first published in "Blackwood's Magazine" and entitled "Noctes Ambrosianæ," of which he was the chief author.

North Britain. A popular synonym of *Scotland*, which forms the northern part of the island of Britain, or Great Britain.

The reviewers of *North Britain*, in common with the other inhabitants of the Scottish metropolis, enjoy some advantages, unknown, it is believed, to their southern brethren. *Edin. Rev.*

Northern Apostle. See APOSTLE OF THE NORTH.

Northern Athens. A name given to the city of Edinburgh, from a fancied resemblance in its appearance to Athens, and in allusion also to its lit-

☞ For the "Key to the Scheme of Pronunciation," with the accompanying Explanations,

crary and scientific institutions. See MODERN ATHENS, 1.

Northern Bear. A popular designation of Russia.

For ourselves, we believe that in arranging the terms of peace he [the French emperor] was as little inclined to clip the claws of the *Northern Bear* as his ally. *Christ. Examiner.*

Northern Giant. A common designation of Russia, in allusion to the enormous size, the rapid growth, and the immense power and resources of that empire, which occupies the whole northern portion of the eastern hemisphere, from Norway to Behring's Strait, and a large adjoining region in North America.

It is no small delight to the lovers of truth, freedom, and England, to see that the *Northern Giant* has, by dint of too much *finesse*, suffered his once-willing prey to slip through his hands. *Edin. Rev.*

Northern Harlot, The Infamous. [Fr. *Infâme Catin du Nord.*] A name given to Elizabeth Petrowna (1709-1761), empress of Russia, infamous for her sensuality.

Northern He-rod'o-tus. A name given to Snorro Sturleson (1179-1241), a native of Iceland, famous as a poet, lawgiver, and historian. He lived many years at the courts of Norway and Sweden, and composed a general history of the North from the ancient songs of the skalds, and from other sources.

Northern Semiramis. See SEMIRAMIS OF THE NORTH.

North-west Territory. (*Amer. Hist.*) A region north-west of the Ohio River, bounded on the north by a line touching the southern boundary of lakes Erie and Michigan, and on the west by the Mississippi River. After the war of the Revolution, it was ceded to the federal government by the States owning or laying claim to it. A bill for its organisation was passed, in 1787, by the continental congress, which immediately began to exercise jurisdiction over the territory; but its full or complete organisation did not take place until 1799. See WESTERN RESERVE.

Nŏr'um-be'gä. A name formerly given to some now unknown subarctic portion of North America.

Now, from the north
Of *Norumbega*, and the Samoëd shore,
Bursting their brazen dungeon, armed with ice
And snow and hail, and stormy gust and flaw,
Boreas, and Cæcias, and Argestes loud,
And Thracias, rend the woods, and seas upturn. *Milton.*

Nor'val. The name of an aged peasant and his son, in Home's tragedy of "Douglas."

The reflection perhaps reminded him that he had better, like young *Norval's* father, "increase his store." *Dickens.*

Norway, Maid of. See MAID OF NORWAY.

Novalis (no-vä'lis). A pseudonym of Friedrich von Hardenberg (1772-1801), a distinguished German littérateur and poet.

No-ven'sĭ-dĕş, or **No-ven'sĭ-lĕş.** [Lat. *novus,* new, and *insidere,* to settle.] (*Rom. Myth.*) A name given by the ancient Romans to the new gods received from abroad, in distinction from the Indigetes, or native gods. Some have thought that the first part of the word was from *novem,* nine, and have asserted that the Novensides were nine gods to whom Jupiter gave permission to hurl his thunderbolts. But this opinion seems not to be supported by evidence.

Nox. [Lat:] (*Gr. & Rom. Myth.*) Goddess of night; one of the most ancient of the deities. By her brother Erebus, she became the mother of Æther (air) and Dies (day).

Nub'bleş, Kit (nub'blz). A character in Dickens's "Old Curiosity Shop."

Number Nip. The same as *Rübezahl,* the famous mountain goblin of Germany. His history is told by Musæus in his "Popular Tales." See RÜBEZAHL.

Nun of Kent. See HOLY MAID OF KENT.

Nu'ri-el (9). [Another form of *Uriel.* See URIEL.] In the Rabbinical mythology, the name of an angel who presided over hailstorms.

Nut-brown Maid. The subject of a celebrated English ballad of the same name, of uncertain date and origin;

and for the Remarks and Rules to which the numbers after certain words refer, see pp. xiv-xxxii.

a perfect female character, exposed, like Boccaccio's Griselda, to the severest trials, submitting without a murmur to unmerited cruelty, disarming a tormentor by gentleness and patience, and, finally, recompensed for her virtues by transports rendered more exquisite by her suffering.

☞ The most ancient form in which the ballad is now extant is in Arnold's "Chronicle," the earliest edition of which is thought to have been printed in 1502. It seems to have been long forgotten, but was at length brought to notice by Percy, who included it in his "Reliques of Ancient English Poetry." This ballad has been modernised by Prior, who entitled it "Henry and Emma," supposing it to have been founded on the history of Lord Clifford, the "Shepherd Lord." See SHEPHERD LORD.

Nutmeg State. A popular name, in America, for the State of Connecticut, the inhabitants of which have such a reputation for shrewdness that they have been jocosely accused, of palming off wooden nutmegs on unsuspecting purchasers, instead of the genuine article.

Nym. A follower of Falstaff, and an arrant rogue, in Shakespeare's "Merry Wives of Windsor."

☞ To *nim* is an old word, still common among thieves, meaning to pilfer, to steal.

The reader may expect me to explain the motives why I have so long persisted in disclaiming the works of which I am now writing. To this it would be difficult to give any other reply save that of Corporal *Nym*,—it was the author's humour or caprice for the time. *Sir W. Scott.*

Nymphs. [Lat. *Nymphæ*, Gr. Νύμφαι.] (*Gr. & Rom. Myth.*) Goddesses of an inferior rank, inhabiting the sea, rivers, lakes, fountains, woods, trees, mountains, &c., and having special names according to the nature of the place in which they dwell; as, Oceanids, Naiads, Dryads, Hamadryads, Oreads, &c.

☞ For the "Key to the Scheme of Pronunciation," with the accompanying Explanations,

O.

O-an'nĕṣ. (*Eastern Myth.*) A Babylonian god represented as a monster, half man and half fish. He lived amongst men during the daytime, instructing them in the use of letters, and in the arts and sciences; but at night he retired to the sea.

Obadiah. The name of a servant in Sterne's "Life and Opinions of Tristram Shandy, Gent."

Obermann (o'bĕr-mȧn). The title of a novel by Étienne Pivert de Sénancour (1770–1846), and the name of the hero, who is a personification of moral elevation unaccompanied by genius, a man of feeling tortured by the absence not only of the means of action, but of all stimulus to it.

Ŏ'bẹr-ŏn, or Ŏb'ẹr-ŏn. (*Fairy Myth.*) The king of the fairies. He is the elfin dwarf *Elberich*, or *Alberich*, whose name became *Alberon* or *Auberon* in French, and subsequently in English *Oberon*. He was represented as endowed with magical powers, and with the qualities of a good and upright monarch, rewarding those who practised truth and honesty, and punishing those who acted otherwise. He and Titania, his wife, are fabled to have inhabited India, and to have crossed the seas to Northern Europe to dance by the light of the moon. He is familiar to all readers of Shakespeare, and has been made the subject of a romantic poem by Wieland, having this name as its title.

"Nay, but I must see the riders," answered Wamba: "perhaps they are come from Fairyland with a message from King Oberon."
Sir W. Scott.

And play the graceless robber on
Your grave-eyed brother *Oberon*.
Leigh Hunt.

O-bī'dạh. The subject of an allegory by Dr. Johnson, in the "Rambler" (No. 65), which relates the adventures and misfortunes of a young man during the journey of a day, and is designed as a picture of human life.

O-bid'ī-cut. A fiend mentioned by Shakespeare ("Lear," a. iv., sc. 1) as provoking men to the gratification of lust. See FLIBBERTIGIBBET, 1.

O'Cataract, Jehu. A sobriquet given to John Neal (b. 1793), a versatile American author, on account of his impetuosity; adopted by him in some of his works as a pseudonym.

Occidente, Maria dell' (mä-re′ȧ del ot-che-den′tä, 102). A pseudonym adopted by Mrs. Maria (Gowen) Brooks (1795–1845), an American writer, whom Southey pronounced "the most impassioned and most imaginative of all poetesses." She is best known as the author of "Zophiel, or The Bride of Seven."

O-ce'ạ-nạ̇. The name of an imaginary country described by James Harrington (1611–1677) in a political romance bearing the same title, and illustrating the author's idea of a model commonwealth.

O-ce'ạ-nids. [Lat. *Oceanides*, Gr. Ὠκεανίδες.] (*Gr. & Rom. Myth.*) Nymphs of the ocean, said to be three thousand in number; daughters of Oceanus.

O-ce'ạ-nus. [Gr. Ὠκεανός.] (*Gr. & Rom. Myth.*) The god of the great salt river which, in the ancient cosmogony, was thought to encompass the whole earth. He was the son of Cœlus and Terra, the husband of Tethys, and the father of the rivers and ocean-nymphs.

O'ȼhil-tree, Ed'ĭe. An old wandering beggar, garrulous and kind-hearted, who performs a prominent part in Sir Walter Scott's novel of "The Antiquary."

O'Con'nell's Tail. A nickname given, in England, after the passage of the Reform Bill (in 1832), to a parliamentary body voting together under the leadership of Daniel O'Connell, the celebrated Irish agitator.

O'din. (*Scand. Myth.*) The supreme and omniscient ruler of the universe, the king of gods and men, and the reputed progenitor of the Scandinavian kings. He corresponds both to the *Jupiter* and the *Mars* of classical mythology. As god of war, he holds his court in Valhalla, surrounded by all brave warriors who have fallen in battle, and attended by two favourite wolves, to whom he gives his share of food; for he himself lives on wine alone. On his shoulders he carries two ravens, Hugin (mind) and Munin (memory), whom he despatches every day to bring him news of all that is doing throughout the world. He has three great treasures; namely, Sleipnir, an eight-footed horse of marvellous swiftness; Gungnir, a spear, which never fails to strike what it is aimed at; and Draupnir, a magic ring, which every ninth night drops eight other rings of equal value. At Ragnarök, Odin will be swallowed up by the wolf Fenrir. [Called also *Alfadur*, and by a great many other names.]

☞ The German tribes worshipped Odin under the name of *Woden*, or *Wuotan*. The fourth day of the week, Wednesday (*i. e.*, Woden's day), was sacred to him.

O-dŏh'ẽr-tў, Mor'gan, Sir. A pseudonym of Dr. William Maginn (1793–1842), a frequent contributor to "Blackwood's Magazine" and to "Fraser's Magazine," and an interlocutor in the "Noctes Ambrosianæ."

O'Dowd, Cornelius. The pseudonym of a writer in "Blackwood's Magazine;" generally believed to be Charles James Lever, the Irish novelist.

Odur (o'dōor). (*Scand. Myth.*) The name of Freyja's husband. He abandoned his wife on her loss of youth and beauty, and was punished by being changed into a statue. See FREYJA.

O-dys'seŭs. [Gr. 'Οδυσσεύς.] The Greek form of *Ulysses*. See ULYSSES.

Œd'ĭ-pus. [Gr. Οἰδίπους.] (*Gr. & Rom. Myth.*) A king of Thebes, the son of Laius and Jocasta. He solved the riddle of the Sphinx, unwittingly killed his own father and married his mother, who bore him four children. When the incest was discovered, Jocasta hung herself, and Œdipus went mad, and put out his own eyes. See SPHINX.

Œ'neŭs. [Gr. Οἰνεύς.] (*Gr. & Rom. Myth.*) A king of Calydon, in Ætolia, and the father of Meleager, Tydeus, Dejanira, &c. See MELEAGER.

Œ-no'ne. [Gr. Οἰνώνη.] (*Gr. & Rom. Myth.*) A Phrygian nymph beloved and married by Paris, who afterward deserted her for Helen. Tennyson has chosen Œnone as the subject of one of his minor poems. See PARIS.

Œ-no'pi-ŏn. [Gr. Οἰνοπίων.] (*Gr. & Rom. Myth.*) A king of Chios, and the father of Merope. The giant Orion was a suitor for the hand of Merope, but, as Œnopion constantly deferred their marriage, Orion once, when intoxicated, offered her violence. For this Œnopion blinded him, while asleep, and expelled him from the island. He afterward recovered his sight, and returned to Chios seeking revenge; but Œnopion was not to be found, his friends having concealed him. See ORION.

O'gier le Danois (lụ dăʹnäʹ). [It. *Uggero, Oggero, Oggieri*, Lat. *Ogerius*.] The hero of an ancient French romance, whose story is probably a contribution from the stores of Norman tradition, Holger, or Olger, Danske being the national hero of Denmark. He figures in Ariosto's "Orlando Furioso," and other romantic tales and poems.

☞ "According to some authorities, his surname was bestowed on him because he came from Denmark ; others say that he took it after having conquered that country ; while others again . . . say that Ogier was a Saracen who turned Christian, and as they wrote to him from home, *Tu es damné* [You are damned], for having changed his religion, the French barons called him in jest, Ogier *Damné*, and he himself insisted on being so called, when he was christened. This surname agrees with the assertion that he was condemned by Charlemagne." *Panizzi.* Keightley advances the opinion that Ogier is the Helgi of the Edda, and in this view Panizzi himself concurs.

O'gle-by, Lord (o'gl-bĭ). A superannuated peer who affects gayety and the graces of youth, but is withal kind-hearted and benevolent; a character in the comedy of the "Clandestine Marriage," by Garrick and the elder Colman.

O'Grōat', John (*or* **Johnny Grōat**). A name which occurs in the phrase "John O'Groat's House," used to designate an ancient building formerly situated on Duncansby Head, remarkable for being the most northerly point in Great Britain. John of Groat, or Groot, and his brothers, were originally from Holland, and are said to have settled here about 1489. According to tradition, the house was of an octagonal shape, being one room with eight windows and eight doors, to admit eight members of the family, the heads of eight different branches of it, to prevent their quarrels for precedence at table, which on a previous occasion had well-nigh proved fatal. Each came in, by this contrivance, at his own door, and all sat at an octagonal table, at which, of course, there was no chief place, or head.

> Hear, Land o' Cakes and brither Scots,
> Frae Maidenkirk to *John o' Groat's*,
> If there 's a hole in a' your coats,
>   I rede ye tent it;
> A chiel 's amang you takin' notes,
>   And, faith, he 'll prent it. *Burns.*

O-ġyġ'i-ặ. [Gr. Ὠγυγία.] (*Gr. & Rom. Myth.*) An island in the Mediterranean, or, according to some, in the great Western Ocean; the abode of Calypso. It presented such a scene of sylvan beauty as charmed even Mercury, one of the dwellers on Olympus. See CALYPSO.

Old Bags. A nickname given to John Scott, Lord Eldon (1751–1838), lord chancellor of England for twenty-five years. He was so very cautious of delivering a hasty judgment, that he always expressed his doubts, and was accustomed to take all the papers of complicated cases home with him in different bags; hence the name. According to another account, he was so called from the large and richly embroidered bag in which the great seal of England is carried — or supposed to be carried — before the lord chancellor when he proceeds to take his seat on the judicial bench or on the woolsack.

> You found them all in good savour? How does *Old Bags* look? And the worthy Doctor [Lord Sidmouth]? I hope years sit lightly on that lofty fabric. *Noctes Ambrosianæ.*

Old Bendy. A cant name for the Devil.

Old Bo'ġy̆. [Probably a corruption of *Bogu*, the Slavonic name of the Deity.] A nursery ghost or demon, whose name, like that of Lilith, was formerly used to frighten children. [Written also B o g e y.]

> This man ... has a friendly heart (although some wiseacres have painted him as black as *Bogey*), and you may trust what he says. *Thackeray.*

Ŏld'buck, Jonathan. A whimsical virtuoso, who gives name to Scott's novel of "The Antiquary." He is devoted to the study and accumulation of old coins and medals, and indeed every kind of Roman relics, and is sarcastic, irritable, and, from early disappointment in love, a misogynist, but humourous, kind-hearted, and faithful to his friends. [Called also *Monkbarns*.]

> ☞ "The character of Jonathan Oldbuck, in the 'Antiquary,' was partly founded on an old friend of my youth ...; but I thought I had so completely disguised the likeness, that it could not be recognised by any one now alive. I was mistaken. ... The reader is not to suppose, however, that my late respected friend resembled Mr. Oldbuck, either in his pedigree, or the history imputed to the ideal personage. ... An excellent temper, with a slight degree of subacid humour; learning, wit, and drollery, the more poignant that they were a little marked by the peculiarities of an old bachelor; a soundness of thought, rendered more forcible by an occasional quaintness of expression, — were, I conceive, the only qualities in which the creature of my imagination resembled my benevolent and excellent old friend." *Sir W. Scott.*

> How much good might we have done, if we had had the looking-over and methodising of the chaos in which Mr. *Oldbuck* found himself just at the moment, so agonising to the author, when he knows that the patience of his victim is oozing away, and fears it will be quite gone before he can lay his hand on the charm which is to fix him a hopeless listener! *Notes and Queries.*

---

and for the Remarks and Rules to which the numbers after certain words refer, see pp. xlv–xxxii.

Old Bullion. A sobriquet conferred on Colonel Thomas Hart Benton (1782-1858), a distinguished American statesman, on account of his advocacy of a gold and silver currency as the true remedy for the financial embarrassments in which the United States were involved, after the expiration of the charter of the national bank, and as the only proper medium for government disbursements and receipts.

Old Clootie. See AULD CLOOTIE.

Old Colony. A name popularly given to that portion of Massachusetts included within the original limits of the Plymouth colony, which was formed at an earlier date than the colony of Massachusetts Bay. In 1692, the two colonies were united in one province, bearing the name of the latter, and, at the formation of the Federal Union, became the State of Massachusetts.

Old Country. A term usually applied, in the United States, to the British Isles; sometimes restricted to Ireland.

Old Dessauer (des-sŏu'ẽr). A sobriquet given to Leopold, prince of Anhalt-Dessau (1676-1747), distinguished as the creator of the Prussian army. See MENTOR.

Old Dominion. A popular name for the State of Virginia. The origin of this term has been differently accounted for by different writers. The following explanation is the most plausible of all, and is probably the true one.

☞ "In Captain John Smith's 'History of Virginia,' edition of 1629, there is a map of the settlements of Virginia, which, at that time, included New England, as well as every other part of the British settlements in America. He there calls our present Virginia 'Ould Virginia,' — the word *old* being so spelt at that time, — in contradistinction to the New England colony, which is called 'New Virginia.' Here, then, we have the word 'ould,' the distinctive word of the title. Now, we know, that, from the settlement of the colony to the Revolution, every act of parliament, every letter of the king, to the governor, always designated Virginia as the 'Colony and *Dominion*' of Virginia. Here is found the other word; and the change in common talk from 'Ould Virginia' to 'Old Dominion' was easy, imperceptible, and almost inevitable." *Historical Magazine, iii.* 319.

What means the *Old Dominion?* Hath she forgot the day
When o'er her conquered valleys swept the Briton's steel array? *Whittier.*

Old Doû'ro (9). A sobriquet conferred upon the Duke of Wellington, on account of his passage of the Douro, May 11, 1809, by which he surprised Marshal Soult, and put him to flight.

Old Ebony. See EBONY.

Old Fox. [Fr. *Le Vieux Renard.*] A nickname given to Marshal Soult (1769-1851), by the soldiers under his command, on account of his remarkable strategic abilities and fertility of resources.

Old Gentleman. In some parts of England, a familiar name of the Devil.

Old Glory. A name popularly given, in the United States, to the national flag, — "the star-spangled banner."

Old Gobbo. See GOBBO, OLD.

Old Grimes. The subject of a popular ballad by Albert G. Greene (b. 1802), an American poet. The name seems to have originated with Crabbe. It is the title of one of his metrical tales.

Old Grog. A nickname given by the sailors in the British navy to Admiral Edward Vernon (1684-1757), on account of his wearing a grogram cloak in foul weather. They afterward transferred the abbreviated term *grog* to a mixture of rum, gin, or other spirituous liquor, with water, — a kind of beverage first introduced by the admiral on board ship.

Old Harry. A vulgar name for the Devil. [Called also *Lord Harry.*]

☞ It has been suggested ("Notes and Queries," xii. 229) that this appellation comes from the Scandinavian *Hari* or *Herra* (equivalent to the German *Herr*), names of Odin, who came in time (like the other deities of the Northern mythology) to be degraded from his rank of a god to that of a fiend or evil spirit. According to Henley, the hirsute honours of the Satan of the ancient religious stage procured him the name "Old Hairy," corrupted into "Old Harry."

Old Hickory. A sobriquet conferred upon General Andrew Jackson, in 1813, by the soldiers under his command.

☞ "The name of 'Old Hickory' was not an instantaneous inspiration, but a growth. First of all, the remark was made by some soldier, who was struck with his commander's pedestrian powers, that the general was 'tough.' Next it was observed . . . that he was 'tough as hickory.' Then he was *called* 'Hickory.' Lastly, the affectionate adjective 'old' was prefixed, and the general thenceforth rejoiced in the completed nickname, usually the first-won honour of a great commander." *Parton.* According to another account, the name sprung from his having, on one occasion, set his men an example of endurance by feeding on hickory-nuts, when destitute of supplies.

True, surely; as all observation and survey of mankind from China to Peru, from Nebuchadnezzar to *Old Hickory*, will testify!
Carlyle.

Old Humphrey. A pseudonym of George Mogridge (d. 1854), of London, author of numerous religious books and essays, intended especially for the young, which have enjoyed an extensive popularity.

Old Hunkers. A nickname applied to the ultra-conservative portion of the Democratic party in the United States, and especially in the State of New York. It is said to have been intended to indicate that those to whom it was given had an appetite for a large "hunk" of the spoils.

Old Ironsides. A title popularly conferred upon the United States frigate "Constitution," which was launched at Boston, Sept. 20, 1797, and is still (1865) in the service. She became greatly celebrated on account of the prominent part she took in the bombardment of Tripoli, in 1804, and for the gallantry displayed by her officers and men during the War of 1812.

☞ "In the course of two years and nine months [July, 1812, to March, 1815], this ship had been in three actions, had been twice critically chased, and had captured five vessels of war, two of which were frigates, and a third frigate-built. In all her service, . . . her good fortune was remarkable. She never was dismasted, never got ashore, and scarcely ever suffered any of the usual accidents of the sea. Though so often in battle, no very serious slaughter ever took place on board her. One of her commanders was wounded, and four of her lieutenants had been killed, two on her own decks, and two in the 'Intrepid;' but, on the whole, her entire career had been that of what is usually called 'a lucky ship.' Her fortune, however, may perhaps be explained in the simple fact, that she had always been well commanded. In her two last cruises, she had probably possessed as fine a crew as ever manned a frigate. They were principally from New England; and it has been said of them that they were almost qualified to fight the ship without her officers."
James Fenimore Cooper.

Old Lady of Threadneedle Street. A cant name in London for the Bank of England, which is situated in Threadneedle Street.

Old Man Eloquent. An expression made use of by Milton, in his tenth sonnet, in allusion to Isocrates, and very generally applied, in America, to John Quincy Adams (1767–1848), sixth president of the United States.

When that dishonest victory
At Chæronea, fatal to liberty,
Killed with report that *old man eloquent.*
Milton.

Old Man of the Mountain. [Arab. *Sheikh-al-Jebal.*] 1. An Eastern title first applied to the Imaum Hassan Ben-Sabbah-el-Homairi, who founded a formidable dynasty in Syria, A. D. 1090. He was the prince or chief of a sect of the Mohammedans, which in the West acquired the name of Assassins. His residence was in the mountain fastnesses of Syria. The name was also given to his seven successors. At the close of the twelfth century, the Mongols put an end to the dynasty.

2. A name popularly given, in the United States, to a remarkable natural formation on Profile Mountain, one of the mountains of the Franconia range, in New Hampshire. It consists of a projecting rock, elevated about 1000 feet above the plain, and, viewed at a certain angle, bears a wonderful resemblance to the human face.

Old Man of the Sea. In the "Arabian Nights' Entertainments," a monster encountered by Sindbad the

and for the Remarks and Rules to which the numbers after certain words refer, see pp. xiv–xxxii.

Sailor, in his fifth voyage. He managed to fasten himself upon the shoulders of Sindbad so firmly that he could not be dislodged by the utmost efforts of his unfortunate victim; but, after carrying him about for a long time, Sindbad at last succeeded in intoxicating him, and effected his escape. See SINDBAD THE SAILOR.

> He has powers of boring beyond ten of the dullest of all possible doctors, — stuck like a limpet to a rock, — a perfect double of the *Old Man of the Sea*, whom I take to have been the greatest bore on record. *Sir W. Scott.*

> It is quite cruel that a poet cannot wander through his regions of enchantment, without having a critic for ever, like the *Old Man of the Sea*, upon his back. *T. Moore.*

> In the life of Friedrich Wilhelm there is now to be discovered as little of human interest or pathos as could well be imagined of any life so near our own times. He is a horrible *Old Man of the Sea* for our Sindbad to carry. *Christ. Examiner.*

Old Mortality. A character and the title of a novel by Sir Walter Scott. The name is said to have been a sobriquet popularly conferred upon one Robert Patterson, the traditions concerning whom are related in the story, and who is described as a religious itinerant of the latter half of the last century, frequenting country church-yards, and the graves of the Covenanters, in the south of Scotland, and whose occupation consisted in clearing the moss from the gray tombstones, renewing with his chisel the half-defaced inscriptions, and repairing the emblems of death with which the monuments were adorned.

> Even Capefigue — whose business is to belittle all that is truly great, and especially to efface those names which are associated with human liberty, while, like another *Old Mortality*, he furbishes the tombstones of royal mistresses — is yet constrained to bear witness to the popularity and influence which Franklin achieved. *Charles Sumner.*

Old Nick. A vulgar and ancient name for the Devil, derived from that of the Neck, or Nikr, a dangerous water-demon of the Scandinavian popular mythology. "The British sailor," says Scott, "who fears nothing else, confesses his terrors for this terrible being, and believes him the author of almost all the various calamities to which the precarious life of a seaman is so continually exposed." Butler, the author of "Hudibras," erroneously derives the term from the name of Nicolò Macchiavelli.

Old Noll. An epithet contemptuously applied to Oliver Cromwell by his contemporaries.

> Nay, *Old Noll*, whose bones were dug up and hung in chains here at home, has not he, too, got to be a very respectable grim bronze-figure, of whom England seems proud rather than otherwise? *Carlyle.*

Old North State. A popular designation of the State of North Carolina.

Old One. See AULD ANE.

Old Public Functionary. A sobriquet sometimes given to James Buchanan, fifteenth president of the United States. He first applied the expression to himself, in his Annual Message to congress in the year 1859. Sometimes humourously abbreviated O. P. F.

> ☞ "This advice proceeds from the heart of an *old public functionary*, whose service commenced in the last generation, among the wise and conservative statesmen of that day, now nearly all passed away, and whose first and dearest earthly wish is to leave his country tranquil, prosperous, united, and powerful." *James Buchanan.*

Old Put. A nickname given, by the soldiers under his command, to Israel Putnam (1718-1790), a major-general in the war of the American Revolution.

Old Rowley. A nickname given to Charles II., who was famous for his amours. Old Rowley was a famous stallion in his majesty's stud.

> Moving back towards her couch, [she] asked, "Who is there?" "*Old Rowley* himself, madam," said the king, entering the apartment with his usual air of easy composure. *Sir W. Scott.*

Old Scratch. A jocular and ancient term for the Devil, supposed to be a corruption of *Skratti*, *Schrat*, or *Schratz*, a demon of the old Northern mythology.

Old Stars. A sobriquet given by the men of his command to General Ormsby McKnight Mitchel (1810-1862), of the American army, on account of his distinguished reputation and attainments as an astronomer.

Oldstyle, Jonathan. A *nom de plume* of Washington Irving, under which he contributed, in 1802, to the "Morning Chronicle," a democratic journal of New York city.

Old Waggon. A sobriquet often given, in America, to the frigate "United States," which was launched at Philadelphia in 1797, and was afterward rebuilt on the original model. She got her nickname, previously to the War of 1812, from her dull sailing qualities, which were subsequently very much improved.

Old World. A name popularly given to the Eastern Hemisphere after the discovery of America in 1492.

Ol'i-fȧunt, Nĭg'el. The hero of Sir Walter Scott's novel, "The Fortunes of Nigel." [Otherwise called *Lord Glenvarloch.*]

Olimpia (o-lĕm'pe-ȧ). The lady-love and wife of Bireno, in Ariosto's "Orlando Furioso;" represented as equally uncompromising in her love and in her hate.

Olindo (o-lĕn'do). The hero of a celebrated episode in Tasso's epic poem, "Jerusalem Delivered." See SOFRONIA.

Oliver. [It. *Olivieri, Oliviero, Uliviero, Ulivieri.*] 1. One of the Twelve Peers of Charlemagne. See ROWLAND. [Written also O l i v i e r.]
2. A son of Sir Rowland de Bois, in Shakespeare's "As You Like It."

O-liv'ĭ-ȧ. A rich countess, in Shakespeare's "Twelfth Night."

Ol'lȧ-pod, Cornet. A whimsical apothecary, in Colman's "Poor Gentleman," who is also a cornet in the Association Corps of Cavalry. He is noted for "his jumble of physic and shooting."

O-lym'pus. [Gr. Ὄλυμπος.] A mountain about 6000 feet high, between Macedonia and Thessaly, on the summit of which Vulcan was fabled to have built a walled town as a residence for Jupiter and the other heavenly gods, and a convenient place of assembly for the gods who dwelt on the earth and in the sea.

Omnibus Bill. A name popularly given, in America, to a compromise act originally introduced in the senate of the United States by Henry Clay, on the 29th of January, 1850, from the circumstance that several measures, entirely distinct in their object, were embodied in one bill. The most important stipulations of this act were those providing for the admission of California into the Union as a State with its anti-slavery constitution, for the admission of Utah and New Mexico as Territories with no mention of slavery, for the abolition of the slave-trade in the District of Columbia, and for the more certain rendition of fugitive slaves. The bill did not become a law in the form in which it was first presented, but the object aimed at by Mr. Clay was accomplished by the passage of separate acts.

Om'phȧ-le. [Gr. Ὀμφάλη.] (*Gr. & Rom. Myth.*) A queen of Lydia to whom Hercules was sold for three years for murdering Iphitus. The hero fell in love with her, and for a time led an effeminate life in her society, spinning wool, and wearing the garments of a woman, while Omphale donned his lion's skin.

Only, The. [Ger. *Der Einzige.*] A title affectionately applied by the Germans to their admired poet and romancist, Jean Paul Friedrich Richter (1763–1825), on account of the unique character of his writings and genius.

☞ "Not without reason have his panegyrists named him Jean Paul der Einzige, 'Jean Paul the Only:' in one sense or the other, either as praise or censure, his critics also must adopt this epithet; for surely, in the whole circle of literature we look in vain for his parallel." *Carlyle.*

Only Aretino, The. See ARETINO, THE ONLY.

O-phe'li-ȧ (*or* o-feel'yȧ). The heroine of Shakespeare's tragedy of "Hamlet." She is beloved by Hamlet, who, during his real or assumed madness, treats her with undeserved and angry violence, and who afterward, in a fit of inconsiderate rashness, kills her father, the old Polonius, by mistake. The terrible shock given to her mind

and for the Remarks and Rules to which the numbers after certain words refer, see pp. xiv-xxxii.

by these events completely shatters her intellect, and she comes to her death by accidental drowning.

O. P. Riot. [That is, Old Prices Riot.] The common designation of a popular disturbance which took place at the opening of the new Covent-Garden Theatre in London, on the 17th of September, 1809, and which grew out of an advance in the rates of admission. The play was "Macbeth," and, from the rising of the curtain until its fall, not a single word from the stage could be heard in any part of the house. The concurrence of the whole audience — many of them being persons well known and of some consideration in the city — gave a furious and determined party in the pit courage to proceed, and great damage was done in pit, boxes, and galleries. For many nights in succession, the audience, too strong to be controlled, continued their demand, and renewed their depredations, while the managers seemed, on their part, resolved not to give way; but in the end they yielded. This contest, which had continued for nearly three months, was terminated on the 10th of December.

Ops. (*Gr. & Rom. Myth.*) A goddess of plenty, fertility, and power, the wife of Saturn, and the patroness of husbandry; identical with *Cybele*, or *Rhea*.

Optic, Oliver. A pseudonym adopted by William T. Adams, an American writer of juvenile works.

Oracle, Sir. A name which occurs in Shakespeare's "Merchant of Venice" (a. i., sc. 1), in the expression, —

"I am Sir Oracle,
And, when I ope my lips, let no dog bark."

In the first folio, the words are, "I am, sir, an Oracle," which is probably the true reading.

Well, *Sir Oracle*, you that have laid so many schemes to supplant this she-wolf of Gaul, where are all your contrivances now?
Sir W. Scott.

Mouthy gentlemen are all *Sir Oracles*; and where they are, no dogs must bark nor violets be cried.
Sala.

Oracle of the Holy Bottle. See HOLY BOTTLE, ORACLE OF THE.

Orange-Peel. A nickname given by the Irish to Sir Robert Peel (1788–1850), at the time of his holding the office of Chief Secretary for Ireland (1812-1818), on account of the strong anti-Catholic spirit which he displayed, and which was characteristic of the Protestant association, called — after William III., Prince of Orange — the "Orange Society." In 1829, however, — his opinions on this subject having, in the mean time, undergone a great change, — he actually introduced into the house of commons a "Relief Bill," or "Emancipation Act" (10 Geo. IV. c. 7), granting certain political privileges to the Roman Catholics.

Orator Hen'ley. The name by which John Henley (1692-1756), a celebrated English lecturer, is generally known and referred to. He delivered lectures or orations on theology, politics, fashions, and matters in general, during a period of nearly thirty years, and was one of the celebrities of London. Pope calls him the "zany of his age;" and Hogarth has introduced him into many of his humourous delineations.

Or'cus. (*Rom. Myth.*) The lower world, the abode of the dead; also, the god of the lower world, Pluto; sometimes used by the poets as a name of Death.

Orderley, John. See AUDLEY, JOHN.

Ordinance of 1787. (*Amer. Hist.*) An act of congress for the government of "the territory north-west of the Ohio River." Article 6 was as follows: "There shall be neither slavery nor involuntary servitude in the said territory, otherwise than as in the punishment of crimes whereof the party shall have been duly convicted: Provided always, that, any person escaping into the same, from whom labour or service is lawfully claimed in any one of the original States, such fugitive may be lawfully reclaimed, and conveyed to the person claiming his or her labour or service as aforesaid."

O're-ads (9). [Lat. *Oreades*, Gr. 'Ορειάδες.] (*Gr. & Rom. Myth.*) Nymphs

---

☞ For the "Key to the Scheme of Pronunciation," with the accompanying Explanations,

of the mountains, and attendants on Diana.

O'Reil'ly, Private Miles. A pseudonym of Colonel Charles G. Halpine, under which he has published a volume of songs and speeches, professedly the production of an Irish private in the forty-seventh regiment of New York volunteers.

O-res'tēs. [Gr. 'Ορέστης.] (*Gr. & Rom. Myth.*) The son of Agamemnon and Clytemnestra, and the constant friend of Pylades. Having slain his mother and her paramour Ægisthus, because they had murdered his father, he became mad, and fled from land to land, vainly endeavouring to avoid the Furies, who pursued and tormented him. His sufferings were a favourite subject for representation with the tragic poets of Greece. See NEMESIS.

Orgoglio (or-gōl'yo). [It., pride, arrogance.] The name of a giant, in Spenser's "Faëry Queen," who defeats the Red-cross Knight in single combat, and imprisons him in a dungeon of his castle.

Orgon (or'gŏn', 62). A brother-in-law and a dupe of Tartuffe, in Molière's comedy of the latter name.

> ☞ "Nothing can be more happily conceived than the credulity of the honest Orgon and his more doting mother; it is that which we sometimes witness, incurable except by the evidence of the senses, and fighting every inch of ground against that." *Hallam.*

O'rĭ-ăn'ă (9). 1. In the romance of "Amadis de Gaul," a daughter of Lisuarte, an imaginary king of England. She is beloved by Amadis, and is represented as the fairest, gentlest, and most affable, courteous, and faithful woman in the world.

> For thou hast sung how he of Gaul,
> That Amadis so famed in hall,
> For *Oriana* foiled in fight
> The necromancer's felon might.
> *Sir W. Scott.*

2. The name was also given, in flattery, to Queen Elizabeth, in a set of madrigals published in 1601, to celebrate her beauty and chastity at sixty-eight.

3. Ben Jonson applied the name to Anne, queen of James I., quasi *Oriens Anna.*

Oriande (o're-ŏnd', 62). A fairy celebrated in the French romances of chivalry.

O-rin'dă, The Matchless, *or* **The Incomparable.** A poetical name given to Mrs. Katharine Phillips (1631–1664), a distinguished poetess of the period of the Restoration, highly popular among her contemporaries.

> It never did to pages wove
> For gay romaunt belong:
> It never dedicate did move,
> As Sacharissa, unto love, —
> *Orinda*, unto song.
> *Mrs. E. B. Browning.*

O-rī'ŏn. [Gr. 'Ωρίων.] (*Gr. & Rom. Myth.*) A mighty giant and hunter, famous for his beauty. He was blinded by Œnopion for ravishing Merope, and expelled from Chios; but, by following the sound of a Cyclops' hammer, he reached Lemnos, where he found Vulcan, who gave him Cedalion as a guide to the abode of the sun. Proceeding to the east, — as he had been commanded to do by an oracle, — and exposing his eyeballs to the rays of the rising sun, he recovered his lost sight. Orion was slain by Diana, or, as some say, by Jupiter, and placed among the stars, where he forms the most splendid of all the constellations, appearing as a giant wearing a lion's skin and a girdle, and wielding a club. See ŒNOPION.

> Down fell the red skin of the lion
> Into the river at his feet;
> His mighty club no longer beat
> The forehead of the Bull; but he
> Reeled as of yore beside the sea
> When, blinded by Œnopion,
> He sought the blacksmith at his forge,
> And, climbing up the narrow gorge,
> Fixed his blank eyes upon the sun.
> *Longfellow, The Occultation of Orion.*

Ŏr'ĭ-thy'ĭ-ă (20). [Gr. 'Ορείθυια.] (*Gr. & Rom. Myth.*) A daughter of Erechtheus, beloved by Boreas, who carried her off as she was wandering near the river Ilissus. See BOREAS.

Or-lan'do. [Otherwise called *Roland.*] 1. The name of a so-called nephew of Charlemagne, and the hero of the romantic tales and poems founded on the adventures of Charlemagne and his paladins, as Pulci's "Morgante Maggiore," Bojardo's "Orlando Innamorato," and Ariosto's "Orlando Furioso." He is the model of a true knight, — single-minded, generous, compassionate, and valiant. His death is courageous and pious: he thinks of the grief of his wife Aldabella, and the mourning of Charlemagne, and after recommending them to God, he embraces his famous sword Durandal, pressing it to his heart, and, comforted by an angel, fixes his eyes on heaven and expires. Many wonderful stories are told of his magical horn, called Olivant, which he won from a giant named Jatmund, or Jasmandus, and which was originally the property of Alexander the Great. It was of ivory, of immense size, — bigger than a massy beam, Cervantes says, — and endowed with such marvellous power that it might be heard to a distance of twenty miles. See MARSIGLIO, ROLAND, and DURANDAL.

☞ Bojardo took for his subject the fabulous wars of Charlemagne against the Saracens, the theme of many an old legend and romance; but he placed the scene in France, and under the walls of Paris, which he represents as besieged by two hosts of infidels, one under the command of Agramante, emperor of Africa, and the other led by Gradasso, king of Sericana. He adopted Orlando — the *Roland* of the French romances — for his hero; but, while others had represented him as the champion of Christendom, passionless and above frailty, Bojardo makes him fall in love with Angelica, a fascinating coquette, who had come all the way from farthest Asia to sow dissension among the Christians. Ariosto took up the subject as left to him by Bojardo, and making Angelica fall in love herself with Medoro, an obscure youthful squire, he represents Orlando as driven mad by jealousy and indignation; he continues in this state during the greater part of the poem, committing a thousand absurdities, until he is restored to reason by Astolfo, who brings back his wits in a phial from the moon.

Like that mirror of knightly virtue, the renowned paladin *Orlando*, he was more anxious to do great actions than to talk of them after they were done. *W. Irving.*

The clangour of his trumpet, like that of the ivory horn of the renowned paladin *Orlando*, when expiring on the glorious field of Roncesvalles, rang far and wide through the country, alarming the neighbours round, who hurried in amazement to the spot. *W. Irving.*

2. A son of Sir Rowland de Bois, in Shakespeare's comedy of "As You Like It."

Or′mŭzd, *or* Ŏr′o-mas̡′dēs̡. [Old Per. *ahurô-mazdaô*, the spiritual being who is the creator of all things.] (*Per. Myth.*) The name of the supreme deity of the ancient Persians, and of their descendants, the Parsees and Guebers. He is an embodiment of the principle of good, and was created by the will of the great eternal spirit, Zervan-Akharana, simultaneously with Ahriman, the principle of evil, with whom he is in perpetual conflict. Ormuzd is the creator of the earth, sun, moon, and stars, to each of which he originally assigned its proper place, and whose various movements he continues to regulate.

☞ According to the Persian myths, the world — which is to last 12,000 years, during which the war between the good and the evil principle is to go on increasing — is at length to be consumed, the evil principle exterminated, and a new world created in its room, over which Ormuzd is to reign as the supreme and sole monarch.

It seemed as if those two [Pitt and Fox] were the *Ormuzd* and Ahriman of political nature. *Carlyle.*

Ŏr′o-ŏn-dā′tēs̡. A prominent character in La Calprenède's romance, "Cassandra." He is the only son of a great king of Scythia, and falls in love with the fair Statira, widow of Alexander the Great, and daughter of Darius. After many adventures, full of difficulty and danger, he wins her hand.

I looked upon myself as a princess in some region of romance, who, being delivered from the power of a brutal giant or satyr by a generous *Oroondates*, was bound in gratitude, as well as by inclination, to yield up my affection to him without reserve. *Smollett.*

It was the love of Amadis and Oriana, of *Oroondates* and Statira; that love which required a sacrifice of every wish, hope, and feeling unconnected with itself. *Sir W. Scott.*

A creature so well educated, said the Duke, with the sense she is said to possess, would, rustic as she is, laugh at the assumed rants of *Oroondates*. *Sir W. Scott.*

Or′pheŭs. [Gr. Ὀρφεύς.] (*Gr. & Rom. Myth.*) A famous Argonaut, whose skill in music was so wonderful that he could make even trees and rocks follow him. He was the husband of Eurydice; after her death, he went to the lower world to recover her, and so charmed Pluto and Proserpine with the music of his lyre that they consented to let her go, provided he forbore to look behind him until he had gained the upper regions; but he forgot his promise, and looked back to see if Eurydice was following, when she vanished from his sight instantly and for ever.

But oh, sad virgin, that thy power
Might . . . bid the soul of *Orpheus* sing
Such notes as, warbled to the string,
Drew iron tears down Pluto's cheek,
And made hell grant what love did seek.
Milton.

Or'pheus of Highwaymen. A title popularly given to the poet Gay (1688-1732) on account of his "Beggar's Opera," a famous play, which, according to Sir John Fielding, was never represented "without creating an additional number of thieves."

Or-sī'no. Duke of Illyria, in Shakespeare's "Twelfth Night."

Or'son (ŏr'sn). [Fr. *ourson*, a little bear, *ours*, a bear, from Lat. *ursus*, It. *orso*.] One of the heroes in the old romance of "Valentine and Orson;" a twin, who, being adopted by a bear, grew up with bearish qualities. See VALENTINE.

Among the dapper royal gentlemen of the eighteenth century, what was to be done with such an *Orson* of a king [as Frederick William of Prussia]? *Carlyle.*

A large class of her fellow-countrymen, who, in their every word, avow themselves to be as senseless to the high principles on which America sprang, a nation, into life, as any *Orson* in her legislative halls. *Dickens.*

Orville, Lord. The hero of Miss Burney's novel of "Evelina," and the amiable and devoted lover of that young lady, whom he finally marries.

Os-băl'dis-tŏne, Rash'leigh (-lĭ). See RASHLEIGH.

O'Shan'tẽr, Tam. The title of a poem by Burns, and the name of its hero, a farmer, who, riding home very late and very drunk from Ayr, in a stormy night, had to pass by the kirk of Alloway, a place reputed to be a favourite haunt of the Devil and his friends and emissaries. On approaching the kirk, he perceived a light gleaming through the windows; but having got courageously drunk, he ventured on till he could look into the edifice, when he saw a dance of witches merrily footing it round their master, who was playing on the bagpipe to them. The dance grew so furious that they all stripped themselves of their upper garments, and kept at it in their shifts. One "winsome wench" happening unluckily to have a shift which was considerably too short to answer all the purposes of that useful article of dress, Tam was so tickled that he involuntarily roared out, "Weel done, Cuttysark," [Well done, Short-smock]; whereupon in an instant all was dark, and Tam, recollecting himself, turned and spurred his "gray mare, Meg," to the top of her speed, chased by the whole fiendish crew. It is a current belief that witches, or any evil spirits, have no power to follow a poor wight any further than the middle of the next running stream. Fortunately for Tam, the river Doon was near; for, notwithstanding the speed of his mare, by the time he had gained the middle of the arch of the bridge, and consequently the middle of the stream, the pursuing vengeful hags were so close at his heels that one of them, "Cutty-sark," actually sprang to seize him; but it was too late,—nothing was on her side of the stream but the mare's tail, which immediately gave way at her infernal gripe, as if blasted by a stroke of lightning; but the farmer was beyond her reach.

The number and nature of the "mosses and waters" which he had to cross in his peregrination was fully sufficient to . . . render his journey as toilsome and dangerous as *Tam O'Shanter's* celebrated retreat from Ayr.
Sir W. Scott.

O-sī'ris (9). [Gr. 'Οσιρις.] (*Myth.*) A great Egyptian divinity, the god of the sun, and the source of life and fruitfulness; regarded also as the god of the Nile. He was worshipped under the form of an ox.

☞ In the beginning, Osiris reigned over Egypt, and was greatly beloved; but

and for the Remarks and Rules to which the numbers after certain words refer, see pp. xiv-xxxii.

18

his envious brother Typhon formed a conspiracy to get rid of him. Making a handsome chest of the exact dimensions of Osiris, he produced it at a banquet at which Osiris was present, and promised to give it to whomsoever it would fit. All of the conspirators in turn lay down and tried it, but it suited none of them. At last Osiris got into it, when Typhon closed the lid, and threw the chest into the Nile. It floated down the river, and through the Tanaitic branch into the Mediterranean. The loss of the god was soon discovered, and his wife Isis immediately began to search for the body. At length she found it on the coast of Phœnicia, and took it back to Egypt, where she deposited it in an unfrequented spot; but Typhon discovered it, and cut it into fourteen pieces, distributing them among as many nomes, or districts. Isis was forced to make another search, and succeeded in finding thirteen of the pieces, but the remaining one had been eaten by the fishes of the Nile, and had to be replaced by one of wood. Temples were ultimately raised wherever a limb of the god had been found, and one of surpassing magnificence at Philæ, where the body was finally placed. During all this time Typhon had been undisputed monarch in Egypt, but he had not slain Horus, the son of Osiris and Isis, who had been concealed from his anger in the city of Butis. When Horus grew up and became strong, he left his concealment, proclaimed war upon his father's murderer, vanquished him in a series of battles, and finally slew him, and threw his carcass into Lake Sirbon.

Nor is *Osiris* seen
In Memphian grove or green,
 Trampling the unshowered grass with lowings loud:
Nor can he be at rest
Within his sacred chest;
 Naught but profoundest hell can be his shroud:
In vain with timbrelled anthems dark
The sable-stolèd sorcerers bear his worshipped ark. *Milton.*

Os'rick. A courtier, in Shakespeare's "Hamlet."

☞ "Osrick is a type of the euphuist, or affected courtier of Shakespeare's time, who was a hair-splitter in thought, and absurdly dainty and extravagant in expression." *R. G. White.*

Os'sa. [Gr. Ὄσσα.] A high mountain in Thessaly, near Pelion. The ancients placed the abode of the Giants and the Centaurs in the neighbourhood of these two mountains, and they feigned that the Giants piled Ossa upon Pelion in their attempts to scale heaven.

Os'siăn (osh'ăn). A fabulous Celtic warrior poet mentioned in Erse ballads and Highland traditions, and chiefly known from Macpherson's pretended "Poems of Ossian."

Ost-end' Manifesto. (*Amer. Hist.*) A name popularly given in America to a declaration by James Buchanan, minister to England, John Y. Mason, minister to France, and Pierre Soulé, minister to Spain, that Cuba must be acquired by the United States, as not only necessary to the political power of the Union, but especially indispensable to the welfare and security of the slave-holding portion of it. This declaration was in the form of a joint communication to the home government, and was dated at Aix-la-Chapelle on the 17th of October, 1857, though a preliminary conference of three days' duration had been held at Ostend in Belgium.

Os'wǎld. Steward to Goneril, in Shakespeare's tragedy of "Lear."

O-thel'lo. A Moor of Venice, in Shakespeare's play of the same name. He marries Desdemona, the daughter of a Venetian senator, and is led by his ensign, Iago, a consummate villain, to distrust her fidelity and virtue, and finally to kill her; not, however, in jealousy, properly speaking, but, as Coleridge says, "in a conviction forced upon him by the almost superhuman art of Iago, — such a conviction as any man would and must have entertained who had believed Iago's honesty, as Othello did."

Other One, The. [Fr. *L'Autre.*] An allusive sobriquet given to Napoleon Bonaparte by his partisans in France during his banishment to Elba. See VIOLET, CORPORAL.

Ot'nit. A fabulous emperor of the Lombards who figures in one of the most pleasing poems in the old German "Heldenbuch." By the help of the celebrated dwarf Elberich (see OBERON) he gains the daughter of the painim soldan of Syria for his wife.

☞ For the "Key to the Scheme of Pronunciation," with the accompanying Explanations,

O'Trig'ğer, Sir Lucius. An honest, fortune-hunting Hibernian in Sheridan's comedy of "The Rivals." He is noted for his love of fighting.

As *Sir Lucius O'Trigger* says, there was an air of success about Captain Cleveland, which was mighty provoking. *Sir W. Scott.*

Ot'u-el, Sir. A haughty and presumptuous Saracen, nephew to the famous Ferragus, or Ferracute. He was miraculously converted from paganism to Christianity, and married the daughter of Charlemagne.

Outis (ow'tis, or oo'tis). [Gr. οὖτις, nobody, from οὐ, not, and τις, any one.] An assumed name which Ulysses, in the "Odyssey," palms off as his real name upon Polyphemus, a Cyclops, whose single eye he destroys while the monster is stretched out on the ground in a drunken sleep.

All now looked on him [Robespierre] with fear, and none dared hope at the hands of the Dictator a better boon than that which is promised to *Outis*, that he should be the last devoured. *Sir W. Scott.*

Those feel it [poetry] most, and write it best, who forget that it is a work of art; ... who are too much frightened for Ulysses in the cave of Polyphemus to care whether the pun about *Outis* be good or bad. *Macaulay.*

Overdo, Justice. A prominent and celebrated character in Ben Jonson's "Bartholomew Fair."

"Your friend, here," said Claverhouse to the veteran, coolly, "is one of those scrupulous gentlemen who, like the madman in the play, will not tie his cravat without the warrant of Mr. *Justice Overdo.*" *Sir W. Scott.*

Overdone, Mistress. A bawd, in Shakespeare's "Measure for Measure."

Overreach, Sir Giles. A famous character in Massinger's comedy, "A New Way to pay Old Debts," intended to represent a real person, one Sir Giles Mompesson, a notorious usurer of the day, who was expelled the kingdom for his misdeeds. Overreach is a bold, unscrupulous oppressor, greedy of wealth, intensely passionate, and of inordinate pride and ambition.

The son was proud, not of his father's fame, but of his father's money, and withal not generous, nor exactly extravagant, but using money as power, — power that allowed him to insult an equal or to buy a slave. In a word, his nickname at school was "*Sir Giles Overreach.*" *Sir E. Bulwer Lytton.*

Ōw'aIn, Sir. An Irish knight of King Stephen's court, who is fabled to have entered and passed through St. Patrick's Purgatory by way of performing penance for having lived a life of violence and rapine. The legend of the descent of Owain, composed by Henry, an English Benedictine monk of the abbey of Saltrey, in 1153, first made known to the world the story of the Purgatory of St. Patrick. See ST. PATRICK'S PURGATORY.

Owle-glass, Tyll. [Ger. *Tyll Eulenspiegel*, from *eule*, owl, *spiegel*, glass; hence, Fr. *espiègle*, waggish, originally *ulespiègle.*] The hero of a "Volksbuch," or German popular comic tale, often alluded to by various old authors, which relates the freaks, pranks, drolleries, fortunes, and misfortunes, of a wandering mechanic, said to have been born in the village of Kneittingen, in Brunswick. The author of this work is supposed to have been Dr. Thomas Murner (1475 — about 1530), a Franciscan friar, and a prolific writer. Translations exist in English, French, Italian, and other languages. Our English version, entitled "The merrye jeste of a man that was called *Howle-glass*, and of many marveylous thinges and jestes that he did in his lyfe in Eastland," was "Imprinted at London in Tamestreete, at the Vintre, in Three Craned Warfe, by Wyllyam Copland." Another edition, in a modified form, appeared in 1720. The excellent edition by Kenneth R. H. Mackenzie (London, 1860), though in the main following the Low German original of 1519, is not a simple translation, but a collection or selection of Owle-glass stories made by a collation of several editions in the German, French, and Flemish languages, and including two or three tales wholly his own. [Written also Howle-glass, Owle-Spiegel, and Ulen-Spiegel.]

☞ "We may say that to few mortals has it been granted to earn such a place in universal history as Tyll Eulenspiegel. Now, after five centuries, Tyll's native village is pointed out with pride to the

traveller; and his tombstone — with a sculptured pun on his name, an owl, namely, and a glass — still stands, or pretends to stand, 'at Möllen, near Lübeck,' where, since 1350, his once nimble bones have been at rest." *Carlyle.*
"The inhabitants of Damme, in Belgium, also boast of having his bones in their church-yard, and place his death in 1301, so that several critics regard Eulenspiegel as an altogether imaginary person, a mere *nominis umbra* affixed to a cycle of mediæval tricks and adventures. The opinion, however, considered most probable is, that Eulenspiegel is not a myth, but that there were two historical individuals of that name, father and son, of whom the former died at Damme, and the latter at Möllu." *Chambers.*

Ox, Dumb, *or* **Mute.** See DUMB OX.

☞ For the "Key to the Scheme of Pronunciation," with the accompanying Explanations,

P.

Pacification of Ghent. (*Hist.*) The name given to a compact entered into by the north and south provinces of the Netherlands to resist the tyranny of Spain. It was signed at Ghent, November 8, 1576.

Pac'o-let. A dwarf in the old romance of "Valentine and Orson," "full of great sense and subtle ingenuity," who owned an enchanted steed, made of wood, which is often alluded to by early writers. The name of Pacolet was borrowed by Steele for his familiar spirit in the "Tatler." The French have a proverb, "It is the horse of Pacolet;" that is, it is one who goes extremely quick.

<small>Here is a letter, she said, ... which ... might, perhaps, never have reached your hands, had it not fallen into the possession of a certain *Pacolet*, or enchanted dwarf, whom, like all distressed damsels of romance, I retain in my secret service. *Sir W. Scott.*</small>

Pac-to′lus. [Gr. Πακτωλός.] The ancient name of a river of Lydia, Asia Minor, which was said to flow over golden sands. It is now the Bagouly. See MIDAS.

Pad′ȧ-lŏn. (*Hindu Myth.*) The under-world, the abode of departed spirits; thought to be of an octagonal shape, and to have its eight gateways guarded by as many gods.

Pæ′ŏn. [Gr. Παιών.] (*Gr. & Rom. Myth.*) The physician of the gods; the god of medicine; — used sometimes as a surname of *Æsculapius*. See ÆSCULAPIUS. [Written also P æ a n.]

Page, Anne. A young woman, in Shakespeare's "Merry Wives of Windsor," in love with Fenton.

Page, Mr. A gentleman living at Windsor, in Shakespeare's "Merry Wives of Windsor;" distinguished for his uxoriousness.

Page, Mrs. A gentlewoman, in Shakespeare's "Merry Wives of Windsor," with whom Sir John Falstaff is in love, and who joins with Mrs. Ford in a plot to dupe and disgrace him.

Page, William. A school-boy in Shakespeare's "Merry Wives of Windsor;" a son of the Mr. Page who figures in the same play.

Painter of the Graces. An epithet applied by his contemporaries to Andrea Appiani (1754–1817), an Italian painter celebrated for his beautiful frescoes.

Paix des Dames (pā dä däm). See LADIES' PEACE.

Paix Fourrée (pā foo′rā′). See PATCHED-UP PEACE.

Pȧ-læ′mŏn. [Gr. Παλαίμων.] 1. (*Gr. & Rom. Myth.*) A sea-god friendly to the shipwrecked; — a surname of *Melicertes*, the son of Ino. See MELICERTES.

2. A shepherd in Virgil's third Eclogue. He is chosen umpire in a musical contest between Damœtas and Menalcas, but, after hearing them, declares his inability to decide such an important controversy.

Pal′ȧ-me′dĕṣ. [Gr. Παλαμήδης.] (*Gr. & Rom. Myth.*) A son of Nauplius, king of Eubœa, and of Clymene, his wife. He was celebrated for his inventive genius, and is said to have been the first who made measures, scales, dice, &c. Hence the name is sometimes used as an appellation of any ingenious man. When Ulysses, to avoid going to the Trojan war, feigned madness, and ploughed up the sea-shore, sowing it with salt, Palamedes discovered the deception by placing Ulysses' son Telemachus in the way, which compelled him to turn the plough aside, that he might not hurt the boy. For this Ulysses hated and persecuted Palamedes, and at last caused his destruction; though, as to the way in which this was effected, accounts differ.

<small>and for the Remarks and Rules to which the numbers after certain words refer, see pp. xiv–xxxii.</small>

Pal'ā-me'dēs, Sir. A gallant Saracen knight, the unfortunate and despairing adorer of Isolde, overcome in single combat by Sir Tristram, his successful rival, who converted him to Christianity, had him baptised, and became his godfather.

Păl'ā-mŏn. A character in the "Knight's Tale" in Chaucer's "Canterbury Tales." This poem is an imitation of one by Boccaccio, entitled "Le Teseide." Dryden made a spirited version of Chaucer's poem, which he published under the name of "Palamon and Arcite." The plot turns upon the love of these two youths for a beautiful lady named Emilia. In the conclusion, Palamon, after many troubles, obtains her; while Arcite, who had taken advantage of Palamon's friendship, is killed.

Pale, The. (*Irish Hist.*) That portion of the kingdom of Ireland over which the English rule and English law were acknowledged after the invasion of 1172. It may be considered, in a general way, as comprising the counties of Dublin, Meath, Carlow, Kilkenny, and Louth, though the limits of the district varied at different times. According to Knight, it originally comprised all the eastern coast of Ireland from Dundalk Bay to Waterford harbour, and extended some forty or fifty miles inland. It was so called because the conquerors, in fear of the half-subdued natives, "enclosed and *impaled* themselves, as it were, within certain lists and territories." [Called also *The English Pale.*]

Pă-le'mŏn. 1. A character in Falconer's "Shipwreck," in love with the daughter of Albert, the commander.

2. The hero of an episode in Thomson's "Seasons" ("Autumn"); represented as "the pride of swains," and the owner of harvest-fields, in which "the lovely young Lavinia" coming to glean, Palemon falls in love with her, and woves and wins her.

The composition and harmony of the work [Southey's "Thalaba"], accordingly, is much like the pattern of that patchwork drapery that is sometimes to be met with in the mansions of the industrious, where a blue tree overshadows a shell-fish, and a gigantic butterfly seems ready to swallow up *Palemon* and Lavinia.
Jeffrey.

Pā'lēṣ. (*Rom. Myth.*) The tutelary deity of shepherds, flocks, and cattle; worshipped with great solemnity among the Romans.

Pomona loves the orchard,
And Liber loves the vine,
And *Pales* loves the straw-built shed
Warm with the breath of kine.
Macaulay.

Păl'ĭ-nu'rus. [Gr. Παλίνουρος.] The pilot of Æneas, in Virgil's "Æneid," who fell asleep at the helm, and tumbled into the sea when off the coast of Lucania, whence the name of the promontory near the spot. [Written also poetically, and in an Anglicised form, P a l i n u r e.]

More had she spoke, but yawned. All nature nods;
What mortal can resist the yawn of gods? . . .
Wide, and more wide, it spreads o'er all the realm;
Even *Palinurus* nodded at the helm. *Pope.*

Ills [Frederick the Great's] *Palinurus* and chief counsellor, at present and afterward, is a Count von Brühl, . . . a cunning little wretch, they say, and of daft tongue, but surely among the unwisest of all the sons of Adam in that day, and such a *Palinurus* as seldom steered before. *Carlyle.*

Păl'lē-dine of England. The hero of an old "Famous, Pleasant, and Delightful History," formerly very popular. It was translated from the French, and was originally published in 1586.

Pal-lā'di-um. [Gr. Παλλάδιον.] (*Gr. & Rom. Myth.*) A famous statue of Pallas, or Minerva, said to have fallen from heaven upon the plain of Troy. On its preservation the safety of Troy depended; and it was therefore stolen by Ulysses and Diomed.

Pal'lăs. [Gr. Παλλάς.] (*Gr. & Rom. Myth.*) A surname of *Minerva*. See MINERVA.

Can tyrants but by tyrants conquered be,
And Freedom find no champion and no child,
Such as Columbia saw arise, when she
Sprang forth a *Pallas*, armed and undefiled?
Byron.

Păl'mer-in. The hero of several famous old romances of chivalry, particularly the two entitled "Palmerin de Oliva" and "Palmerin of England."

☞ For the "Key to the Scheme of Pronunciation," with the accompanying Explanations,

But, believe me, though to be an absolute *Palmerin* of England is not in my nature, no son ever loved a mother more dearly, or would do more to oblige her. *Sir W. Scott.*

Palmetto State. The State of South Carolina;—so called from the arms of the State, which contain a palmetto-tree.

Pam. A familiar diminutive or contraction of *Palmerston*, the titular name of Henry John Temple (b. 1784), a distinguished English statesman, minister, and diplomatist, and a viscount of the Irish peerage.

Pă-me′lă. The title of a celebrated novel by Richardson, and the name (adopted by him from Sir Philip Sidney's "Arcadia") of its heroine, a simple and innocent country-girl, whose virtue a dissolute master assails by violence, as well as all the milder means of seduction, but who conquers him at last, by persevering in the paths of rectitude, and is rewarded by being raised to the station of his wife, the lawful participator in his rank and fortune.

☞ "Although some objection may be made to the deductions which the author desired and expected should be drawn from the story of Pamola, yet the pure and modest character of the English maiden is so well maintained during the work; her sorrows and afflictions are borne with so much meekness; her little intervals of hope or comparative tranquillity break in on her troubles so much like the specks of blue sky through a cloudy atmosphere, that the whole recollection is soothing, tranquillising, and doubtless edifying." *Sir W. Scott.*

☞ "She told me that . . . they had a daughter of a very strange name, Paměla or l'aměla; some pronounce it one way, and some the other."
Fielding, Joseph Andrews.

Pan. [Gr. Πάν, probably connected with παω, Lat. *pasco*, to feed, to pasture; but thought by some to be the same as τὸ πᾶν, the whole, the universe.] (*Gr. & Rom. Myth.*) The son of Mercury and Penelope, and the god of woods, shepherds, and huntsmen; represented as a grim, shaggy being, with horns, pointed ears, a crooked nose, a tail, and goat's feet. He was fond of music, and possessed prophetic powers. He had a terrific voice, and sometimes appeared unexpectedly to travellers, whom he startled with a sudden awe or terror. It was a current belief among the early Christians, that, at the moment of our Saviour's crucifixion, a deep groan, heard all through the Grecian isles, told that the great Pan was dead, and all the gods of Olympus dethroned. See SYRINX.

Airs, vernal airs,
Breathing the smell of field and grove, attune
The trembling leaves; while universal *Pan*,
Knit with the Graces and the Hours in dance,
Led on the eternal spring. *Milton.*

The lonely mountains o'er,
And the resounding shore,
A voice of weeping heard and loud lament;
From haunted spring and dale,
Edged with poplar pale,
The parting genius is with sighing sent;
With flower-inwoven tresses torn,
The nymphs in twilight shade of tangled
thickets mourn. *Milton.*

Pan′dă-rus. [Gr. Πάνδαρος.] A son of Lycaon, and leader of the Lycians in the Trojan war, celebrated by Homer in the "Iliad." In mediæval romances, and by Chaucer in "Troilus and Cresseide," and Shakespeare in "Troilus and Cressida," he is represented as procuring for Troilus the love and good graces of Chryseis; hence the word *pander* (formerly written *pandar*) is used to denote a pimp, or procurer.

Pan′de-mo′ni-um. [Gr. πᾶς, πᾶν, all, and δαίμων, a demon.] A name given by Milton to
"The high capital
Of Satan and his peers."
(*Par. Lost, Bk. I.*)

Pan-do′ră (9). [Gr. Πανδώρα, the all-endowed.] (*Gr. & Rom. Myth.*) The first mortal woman; made by Vulcan, at the command of Jupiter. She was very beautiful, and all the gods made her presents, that she might win the heart of Prometheus, to whom Jove sent her, designing, that, by her charms, miseries of every kind should be brought upon men, as a punishment for the crime of Prometheus in stealing fire from heaven. Prometheus, however, would not receive her; and Mercury accordingly took her to Epimetheus, who had less wisdom, and was captivated by her loveliness. A later form of the tradition says that Jupiter gave her a box filled with winged blessings, which would have been preserved for the human race, had not curiosity tempted her to open it, when all flew out, except Hope.

> In naked beauty more adorned,
> More lovely, than *Pandora*, whom the gods
> Endowed with all their gifts; and obl' too like
> In sad event, when to the unwiser son
> Of Japhet brought by Hermes, she ensnared
> Mankind with her fair looks, to be avenged
> On him who had stole Jove's authentic fire.
> *Milton.*

Pan'gloss. [Gr. πᾶν, all, and γλῶσσα, tongue.] 1. An optimist philosopher in Voltaire's "Candide."
2. A noted pedant in Colman's play entitled "The Heir at Law;" poor, but proud of being an LL.D., and, moreover, an *A.S.S.* (*Artium Societatis Socius*).

Pan-handle, The. A fanciful and cant name given, from its form, to the most northerly portion of the State of West Virginia, — a long, narrow projection between the Ohio River and the western boundary of Pennsylvania.

Pan-jan'drum, The Grand. A sort of mythical nonentity invented by Foote, the comic dramatist. The name occurs in a farrago of utter nonsense, of about a dozen lines in length, which he wrote on a wager, to test the memory of a person who boasted of the wonderful retentiveness of this faculty in himself, and who agreed to get Foote's galimatias by heart in twelve minutes, and repeat it without making the slightest mistake. It is said that Foote won the wager.

> He was the great *Panjandrum* of the place. Calais, in fact, centred in Dessein.
> *Percy Fitzgerald.*

> So, said Charles, there were at the marriage the Picanninies, and the Joblillies, but not *The Grand Panjandrum* himself. *Yonge.*

Pan'o-pæ'ē, or Pan'o-pe. [Gr. Πανόπη.] (*Gr. & Rom. Myth.*) A sea-nymph, one of the Nereids.

> The air was calm, and on the level brine
> Sleek *Panope* with all her sisters played.
> *Milton.*

Pantagruel (pan-tag'roo-el; *Fr. pron.* pŏⁿ'tȧ'grü'el', 34, 62). One of the principal characters in Rabelais' celebrated satirical romance of the same name; represented as a gigantic personage, beneath whose tongue a whole army takes shelter from rain; in whose mouth and throat are cities which contain an immense population, &c. Pantagruel is a virtuous prince, devout, and severe in his morals; yet he takes for his favourite the licentious, intemperate, cowardly rogue, Panurge. Born in the midst of a drought, when all the moisture of the earth was a salt perspiration, he is named Pantagruel, by the combination of a Greek word (πάντα) and an Arabic word, to signify "All-thirsty." See BADEBEC, PANURGE.

> Old Chaucer doth of Thopas tell;
> Mad Rabelais of *Pantagruel*. *Drayton.*

> He fair besought the ferryman of hell
> That he might drink to dead *Pantagruel*.
> *Bp. Hall.*

Pantagruélion (pan'tȧ-groo-e'll-ŏn; *Fr. pron.* pŏⁿ'tȧ'grü'ȧ'le-ôⁿ'). The name of an herb mentioned in Rabelais' romance of "Pantagruel," and supposed to mean *hemp*, and to bear a reference to the persecution of the Protestants.

Pan'tȧ-loon'. [Fr. *Pantalon*, It. *Pantalone*, from *Pantaleone* (Gr. Πανταλέων, all or entirely lion, a Greek personal name), the patron saint of Venice, and hence a baptismal name very frequent among the Venetians, and applied to them in derision by the other Italians. Some, however, derive the name from the Italian words *pianta-leone*, that is, the "lion-planter," the lion of St. Mark being the standard of the Venetian republic. (See Byron's "Childe Harold," canto iv.)] One of the chief characters in the modern Christmas pantomime; usually represented as a feeble-minded old man, the butt of the clown, and yet the aider and abettor of his comic villany. In the original Italian pantomime, he was a Venetian burgher, dressed in close breeches and stockings that were all of a piece.

Panurge (pȧ-nurj'; *Fr. pron.* pȧ'-nürzh', 34). A celebrated character in Rabelais' "Pantagruel," and the real hero of the story; represented as an arrant rogue, crafty and versatile in the extreme, a drunkard, a coward, and a libertine.

☞ Learned in the highest degree, this eccentric person is a kind of spoiled child, and, on that account, the privileged jester of Pantagruel and his friends. He is described as of middle stature, with an aquiline nose, handsome to look upon, and subject to a disease called "want of money." The great object of his life, previous to his acquaintance with Pantagruel, was the performance of countless malicious practical jokes, with the materials for which his numerous pockets are armed. In one he has little horns full of fleas, which he amuses himself by blowing upon the necks of the ladies in church; in another he has a store of hooks, that he may fasten people's dresses together; in the third a bottle of oil, that he may soil handsome suits; in another an itching powder; and so on. These are no very amiable qualities, but, nevertheless, the reader always has an affection for Panurge. In the third book, Pantagruel is represented as making Panurge governor of Salmagondin, in which capacity he soon contrives to waste his revenue. For immersing himself in debt, he has to endure the reproaches of his master; and his defence, in which he sets up a eulogy of indebtedness, is a masterpiece of pompous burlesque. Pantagruel is not convinced by the eloquent harangue of his favourite, but discharges his debts; whereupon Panurge takes a new freak into his head, for he attires himself in a coarse gown, and attaches a pair of spectacles to his cap, declaring it is his resolution to take to himself a wife. An uneasy doubt as to whether his entrance into married life will insure felicity is the foundation of all the humour and satire of the book. Every mode of divination into future events is tried, a member of every conceivable calling is consulted. The theologian, the lawyer, the physician, and sceptical philosopher, the poet, the idiot, the sibyl, — all are asked for counsel, besides a recurrence to dreams, and a search for oracular answers, according to the old superstition, in the works of Virgil. All the oracles unite in giving answers which, in the opinion of disinterested friends, are plain dissuasives from matrimony; while Panurge, whose heart is bent on a wife, displays the most vexing ingenuity in torturing them to mean the reverse. The last person of whom he asks advice puts into his hands an empty bottle, which Panurge interprets to imply that he should undertake a voyage for the purpose of obtaining a response from the oracle of the Holy Bottle. The fourth and fifth books are occupied with the expedition of Panurge, accompanied by Pantagruel, in quest of the oracle. This voyage is said to signify a departure from the world of error to search after truth, which the author places in a bottle, in consequence of the proverbial effects of intoxication ("*in vino veritas*"). See HOLY BOTTLE, ORACLE OF THE.

☞ "All Rabelais' personages are phantasmagoric allegories, but Panurge above all. He is, throughout, the πανουργία, — the wisdom, that is, the cunning, of the human animal, — the understanding, as the faculty of means to purposes without ultimate ends, in the most comprehensive sense, and including art, sensuous fancy, and all the passions of the understanding." *Coleridge.*

Panza, Sancho (sank'o pan'zạ; *Sp. pron.* sän'cho pän'thä). [Sp., from *zancas,* spindle-shanks, and *panza,* paunch.] The esquire of Don Quixote, in Cervantes's famous novel of this name; a short, pot-bellied peasant, with small legs. He is a type of vulgar common sense without imagination. See DON QUIXOTE and BARATARIA.

☞ "At first he is introduced as the opposite of Don Quixote, and used merely to bring out his master's peculiarities in a more striking relief. It is not until we have gone through nearly half of the First Part that he utters one of those proverbs which form afterward the staple of his conversation and humour; and it is not till the opening of the Second Part, and, indeed, not till he comes forth, in all his mingled shrewdness and credulity, as governor of Barataria, that his character is quite developed and completed to the full measure of its grotesque yet congruous proportions." *Ticknor.*

Sleep, says *Sancho Panza,* covers a man all over like a mantle of comfort; but rising before daylight envelops the entire being in petty misery. *A. K. H. Boyd.*

Panza, Teresa (te-re'zạ pan'zạ; *Sp. pron.* tā-rā'zä pän'thä). A character in Cervantes's "Don Quixote;" the wife of Sancho Panza.

Paper King. A name formerly popularly given to John Law (1671-1729), the celebrated financial projector. See LAW'S BUBBLE.

☞ "The basis of Law's project was the idea that paper money may be multiplied to any extent, provided there be security in fixed stock; while the truth is, if tho bulk of a currency is increased beyond the actual wants of commerce, all its parts, or separate coins and notes, must depreciate in proportion." *Rich.*

Paradise of Fools. See LIMBO.

Par'cæ. (*Rom. Myth.*) Three daughters of Nox and Erebus; all-powerful goddesses who presided over the destiny of man. Their names were Clotho, who was supposed to hold the distaff or spindle; Lachesis, who was sometimes said to draw out the thread of human life; and Atropos, who cut it off.

Paribanou (pä-re-bȧ'noo). [Per., female fairy.] A fairy in the story of "Prince Ahmed," in the "Arabian Nights' Entertainments." [Written also Pori Banou.]

His [Bacon's] understanding resembled the tent which the fairy *Paribanou* gave to Prince Ahmed. Fold it, and it seemed a toy for the hand of a lady; spread it, and the armies of powerful sultans might repose beneath its shade. *Macaulay.*

Păr'ĭ-del. A fickle and inconstant libertine in Spenser's "Faëry Queen."

Nor durst light *Paridel* advance,
Bold as he was, a looser glance.
Sir W. Scott.

Păr'is (*classical pron.* pā'ris). [Gr. Πάρις.] 1. (*Gr. & Rom. Myth.*) A son of Priam and Hecuba, distinguished for his beauty. His mother, having had an ominous dream, exposed him, as soon as he was born, on Mount Ida; but he was found by a shepherd, who reared him. When he had grown up, he married Œnone, daughter of the river-god Cebren. A dispute having arisen between Juno, Minerva, and Venus as to which of them was the handsomest, Paris was chosen umpire, and decided in favour of Venus, who had promised him Helen, the handsomest woman in the world. By running away with her, he caused the Trojan war, in which he was mortally wounded by the arrow of Philoctetes. In his dying moments, his love for his first wife, the long-abandoned Œnone, returned; but she, remembering her wrongs, would at first have nothing to do with him. Soon, however, repenting of her unkindness, she hastened after him with remedies; but it was too late, and, in her grief, she hung herself.

2. A young nobleman, kinsman to Escalus, Prince of Verona, in Shakespeare's tragedy of "Romeo and Juliet.

Păr'ĭ-sĭ-nặ. The heroine of Byron's poem of the same name. She had been betrothed to Hugo, the natural son of Azo, Prince of Este. Azo saw and coveted her beauty; and, reproaching his son for the stain of his birth, which, he said, rendered him unworthy the possession of so rich a treasure, he himself wedded her. The unhappy lovers could not control the passion, which was innocent and praiseworthy in its commencement, but which a change of circumstances had rendered criminal. Their incestuous love being discovered, Hugo is executed; but the poem leaves the fate of Parisina doubtful.

Păr'ĭs-me'nos. The hero of a continuation or "second part" of the history of Parismus. It records his "adventurous travels and noble chivalry, with his love to the fair Princess Angelica, the Lady of the Golden Tower;" and it was first published in 1598.

Pặ-rĭs'mus. A "valiant and renowned prince of Bohemia," the hero of an old romance, or "history," formerly very popular. It contains an account of "his noble battles against the Persians, his love to Laurana, the king's daughter of Thessaly, and his strange adventures in the Desolate Island." It was written by Emanuel Foord, and was first published in 1598.

Păr'ĭ-zāde. A princess whose adventures in search of the Talking Bird, the Singing Tree, and the Yellow Water, are related in the "Story of the Sisters who envied their younger Sister," in the "Arabian Nights' Entertainments." Of these curiosities, the first was a bird, which could not only talk and reason like human beings, but could call all the singing-birds in his neighbourhood to come and join in his song; the second was a tree, of which the leaves were so

---

☞ For the "Key to the Scheme of Pronunciation," with the accompanying Explanations,

many mouths, that formed a most harmonious concert; the third was a kind of water, a small quantity of which, being put into a basin, would fill it, and form a beautiful fountain, which would continually play without overflowing. Parizade, or Parizadeh, — the *Parisatis* of the Greeks, — signifies *born of a fairy*.

In truth, much of Bacon's life was passed in a visionary world . . . amidst buildings more sumptuous than the palace of Aladdin, fountains more wonderful than the golden water of *Parizade*. *Macaulay.*

Par'ley, Peter. An assumed name under which Samuel Griswold Goodrich (1793–1860), an American writer, published a series of very popular books for the young.

Parliament, Addle. See ADDLE PARLIAMENT.

Parliament, Barebone's. See BAREBONE'S PARLIAMENT.

Parliament, Devils'. See DEVILS' PARLIAMENT.

Parliament, Drunken. See DRUNKEN PARLIAMENT.

Parliament, Long. See LONG PARLIAMENT.

Parliament, Mad. See MAD PARLIAMENT.

Parliament, Rump. See RUMP PARLIAMENT.

Parliament, Unlearned. See PARLIAMENT OF DUNCES.

Parliament, Useless. See USELESS PARLIAMENT.

Parliament, Wonderful. See WONDERFUL PARLIAMENT.

Parliament of Dunces. [Lat. *Parliamentum Indoctorum.*] (*Eng. Hist.*) A name given to a Parliament convened by Henry IV. at Coventry, in Warwickshire (1404), because lawyers were excluded from it.

Par-nas'sus. [Gr. Παρνασός, or Παρνασσός.] A lofty mountain of Phocis in Greece, sacred to Apollo and the Muses. At its base were the Castalian spring and the city of Delphi.

Pa̤-rol'lĕs. A boastful and cowardly follower of Bertram in Shakespeare's "All 's Well that Ends Well;" so consummate in baseness, that we regard him with contemptuous complacency: "he hath outvillained villany so far, that the rarity redeems him."

☞ "The braggart Parolles, whose name signifies *words*, as though he spoke nothing else, scarcely utters a sentence that is not rich with ideas; yet his weakness and self-committals hang over them all like a sneaking infection, and hinder our laughter from becoming respectful. The scene in which he is taken blindfold among his old acquaintances, and so led to vilify their characters under the impression that he is gratifying their enemies, is almost as good as the screen scene in the 'School for Scandal.'"
Leigh Hunt.

Rust, sword; cool, blushes; and, *Parolles*, live
Safest in shame; being fooled, by fooling thrive. *Shak.*

There was *Parolles*, too, the legal bully.
Byron.

He [Dr. Samuel Parr] was a mere *Parolles* in a pedagogue's wig. *Noctes Ambrosianæ.*

Parricide, The Beautiful. See BEAUTIFUL PARRICIDE.

Parsons' Emperor. [Ger. *Pfaffen-Kaiser.*] A nickname given to Charles IV. of Moravia, who, at the instigation of the pope, — Clement VI., — was set up as a competitor of Louis IV., the actual reigning emperor of Germany.

Par-the'ni-ă. The mistress of Argalus, in Sir Philip Sidney's "Arcadia."

She thought . . . that Alice gave him a little more encouragement than *Parthenia* would have afforded to any such Jack-a-dandy, in the absence of Argalus.
Sir W. Scott.

Par-then'o-pe. [Gr. Παρθενόπη.] (*Gr. & Rom. Myth.*) One of the three Sirens. She became enamoured of Ulysses, and, in her grief at not winning him, threw herself into the sea, and was cast up on the shore where Naples afterward stood, for which reason that city was originally called by her name.

Par'ting-tŏn, Mrs. An imaginary old lady whose laughable sayings have been recorded by the American humourist, B. P. Shillaber. She is distinguished, like Smollett's Tabitha Bramble and Sheridan's Mrs. Malaprop, for her amusing affectation and misuse of learned words.

☞ The *name* of this character seems to have been suggested by the following anecdote which Sydney Smith related in a speech delivered by him at Taunton (Eng.), in 1831, and which has become somewhat celebrated: "I do not mean to be disrespectful; but the attempt of the Lords to stop the progress of reform reminds me very forcibly of the great storm of Sidmouth, and the conduct of the excellent Mrs. Partington on that occasion. In the winter of 1824, there set in a great flood upon that town; the tide rose to an incredible height, the waves rushed in upon the houses, and every thing was threatened with destruction. In the midst of this sublime storm, Dame Partington, who lived upon the beach, was seen at the door of her house, with mop and pattens, trundling her mop, and squeezing out the sea-water, and vigorously pushing away the Atlantic Ocean. The Atlantic was roused. Mrs. Partington's spirit was up. But I need not tell you that the contest was unequal. The Atlantic Ocean beat Mrs. Partington. She was excellent at a slop or a puddle, but she should not have meddled with a tempest."

Partridge. The attendant of Tom Jones, in Fielding's novel, "The History of Tom Jones, a Foundling;" noted for his fidelity, shrewdness, and child-like simplicity.

Parvati (par-vä'tee). [Sansk., mountain-born.] (*Hindu Myth.*) The daughter of the mountain Himalaya; one of the names by which the goddess Durga is usually called. See DURGA.

Pâ-siph'ä-e. [Gr. Πασιφάη.] (*Gr. & Rom. Myth.*) A daughter of Helios, or Sol (the sun), and Perse; sister of Circe, wife of Minos, and mother of Phædra, Ariadne, and Androgeus, and also of the Minotaur by a beautiful bull, for which Venus, out of hatred, had inspired her with a violent passion. See MINOTAUR.

Pas'quin (pas'kwin). [It. *Pasquino.*]
1. A Roman cobbler of the latter half of the fifteenth century, whose shop stood in the immediate neighbourhood of the Braschi palace, near the Piazza Navona. Pasquin was notorious for making caustic remarks, and by degrees every bitter saying current in the city became attributed to him or his workmen. After his death, a mutilated statue, which had long lain half imbedded in the ground near his shop, was dug out and set up in the vicinity, upon which the populace declared that the cobbler had come to life again, and called the torso by his name. Thenceforth a custom arose of attaching to it stinging epigrams or satirical verses, often directed against the pope and cardinals, and other persons in high public station. No prohibitions or penalties could put a stop to the practice; and even now, after the lapse of more than four centuries, the statue pursues his ancient calling with undiminished vigour.

2. (Tony, *or* Antony.) A *nom de plume* of John Williams, author of loads of writing in prose and verse. See DELLA CRUSCANS.

Passamonte, Gines de. See GINES DE PASSAMONTE.

Pâsse'treûl. The name of Sir Tristram's horse. See TRISTRAM, SIR.

Patched-up Peace. [Fr. *La Paix Fourrée.*] (*Fr. Hist.*) 1. The name given to a treaty of peace between the Duke of Orleans and John of Burgundy, in 1409.
2. [Called also *Ill-grounded Peace* and *Lame and Unstable Peace.*] The name of a treaty between Charles IX. and the Huguenots, concluded at Longjumeau, in 1568. It was so called because it was made very suddenly, and because neither of the parties to it had any confidence in the other.

Patelin (pät'län', 62). The hero of an ancient French comedy, entitled "L'Avocat Patelin," reproduced by Brueys, in 1706. By his address and cunning he succeeds in obtaining six ells of cloth from a merchant. The name has passed into popular use to designate a subtle and crafty man, who, by flattery and insinuating arts, entices others to the accomplishment of his designs.

Path-finder, The. A title popularly given to Major-General John Charles Fremont (b. 1813), who conducted four exploring expeditions across the Rocky Mountains.

Patient Griselda, *or* **Grissell.** See GRISELDA, THE PATIENT.

Patient Helena. See HELENA, THE PATIENT.

Patriarch of Dorchester. An appellation given to John White, of Dorchester, England, a puritan divine, highly esteemed for his eloquence and piety. He died in 1648, aged 74.

Pạ-tro'clus. [Gr. Πάτροκλος.] (*Gr. & Rom. Myth.*) One of the Grecian chiefs in the Trojan war, and the constant companion and friend of Achilles. He one day put on the armour of Achilles, and slew many of the Trojans; but, being struck by Apollo, he became senseless, and in that state was killed by Euphorbus and Hector. See HECTOR.

Pat'tie-son, Peter (-sn). An imaginary assistant teacher at Gandercleuch, and the feigned author of Scott's "Tales of My Landlord," which were represented as having been published posthumously by his pedagogue superior, Jedediah Cleishbotham.

Paul. See VIRGINIE.

Pāu-lī'nạ. Wife of Antigonus, in Shakespeare's "Winter's Tale."

☞ "She is a character strongly drawn from real and common life, — a clever, generous, strong-minded, warm-hearted woman, fearless in asserting the truth, firm in her sense of right, enthusiastic in all her affections; quick in thought, resolute in word, and energetic in action; but heedless, hot-tempered, impatient; loud, bold, voluble, and turbulent of tongue; regardless of the feelings of those for whom she would sacrifice her life, and injuring, from excess of zeal, those whom she most wishes to serve." *Mrs. Jameson.*

Pạ-vo'ni-ạ. A name given in ancient maps to a tract of country extending from about Hoboken to Amboy, in what is now the State of New Jersey.

Pax. (*Rom. Myth.*) A deified personification of peace; the same as the *Irene* of the Greeks.

Pays de Sapience. See LAND OF WISDOM.

Pēach'um. A character in Gay's "Beggar's Opera," represented as a pimp and a receiver of stolen property, and as making his house a resort for thieves, pickpockets, and villains of all sorts. See LOCKIT.

No *Peachum* it is, or young Lockit,
That rifles my fob with a snatch;
Alas! I must pick my own pocket,
And make gravy-soup of my watch.
Hood.

Pēach'um, Mrs. A character in Gay's "Beggar's Opera;" wife of Peachum. See *supra.*

☞ The authors of this scheme [the Kansas usurpation] have scarcely shown the ordinary cunning of rogues, which conceals its ulterior purposes. Disdaining the advice of *Mrs. Peachum* to her daughter Polly, to be "somewhat nice" in her deviations from virtue, they have advanced bravely and flagrantly to their nefarious object. *Atlantic Monthly.*

Pēach'um, Polly. A celebrated character in Gay's "Beggar's Opera;" daughter of Peachum. She is represented as having great beauty, and as preserving, unspotted, the purity of her character, though living among the basest persons.

Peasant Bard. A descriptive epithet conferred upon Robert Burns, the great lyric poet of Scotland.

Peasant of the Danube. A title given to Louis Legendre (1756–1797), member of the French National Convention, who took an active part in all the events of the Revolution. His wild eloquence was the occasion of this surname being given him.

Peasant Poet of Northamptonshire. A name given to John Clare (1793–1864), an English poet of humble origin, whose remarkable powers of description brought him into public notice and secured the public favour.

☞ "The instance before us is, perhaps, one of the most striking of patient and persevering talent existing and enduring in the most forlorn and seemingly hopeless condition that literature has at any time exhibited." *Lond. Qu. Rev.*

Peasants' War. [Ger. *Bauern Krieg.*] (*Ger. Hist.*) The name given to a revolt of the German peasantry in Swabia and Franconia, and subsequently in Saxony, Thuringia, and Alsace, occasioned by the increasing oppression and cruelty of the nobles and clergy. It broke out several different times, from about 1500 to 1525, in which latter year it was finally terminated, after upwards of 150,000 lives had been lost. The defeated insurgents not only failed to obtain relief from their feudal burdens, but their lot became in many respects harder than before.

Pecksniff. A hypocrite in Dickens's "Martin Chuzzlewit," "so thoroughly impregnated with the spirit of falsehood that he is moral even in drunkenness, and canting even in shame and discovery."

Pedro, Don. See DON PEDRO.

Pee'bles, Peter (pe'blz). A character in Sir Walter Scott's novel of "Redgauntlet;" represented as vain, litigious, hard-hearted, credulous, a liar, a drunkard, and a pauper.

In one point of view, there is nothing more Hogarthian comic than this long *Peter-Peebles* "ganging plea" of "Marquis Mirabeau *versus* Nature and others;" yet, in a deeper point of view, it is but too serious. *Carlyle.*

Peelers. The uniformed constabulary of Ireland appointed under the "Peace Preservation Act" of 1814, proposed by Sir Robert Peel. The name was subsequently given to the new police of England, who were, also, vulgarly called "Bobbies," after Sir Robert.

Peeping Tom of Cóv'en-trý. An epithet given to a person of ungovernable inquisitiveness.

☞ "The Countess Godiva, bearing an extraordinary affection to this place [Coventry], often and earnestly besought her husband [Leofric, Earl of Mercia], that, for the love of God and the blessed Virgin, he would free it from that grievous servitude whereunto it was subject; but he, rebuking her for importuning him in a matter so inconsistent with his profit, commanded that she should thenceforth forbear to move therein; yet she, out of her womanish pertinacity, continued to solicit him; insomuch that he told her [A. D. 1057] if she would ride on horseback, naked, from one end of the town to the other, in the sight of all the people, he would grant her request. Whereunto she answered, 'But will you give me leave so to do?' And he replying, 'Yes,' the noble lady, upon an appointed day, got on horseback, naked, with her hair loose, so that it covered all her body but her legs, and thus performing the journey, returned with joy to her husband, who therefore granted to the inhabitants a charter of freedom, which immunity I rather conceive to have been a kind of manumission from some ... servile tenure, whereby they then held what they had under this great earl, than only a freedom from all manner of toll, except horses, as Knighton affirms." *Dugdale.* It is said by Rapin, that the countess, previous to her riding, commanded all persons to keep within doors and from their windows on pain of death; but, notwithstanding this severe penalty, there was one person who could not forbear giving a look, out of curiosity; but it cost him his life. From this circumstance originated the familiar epithet of "Peeping Tom of Coventry." To commemorate the event, the mayor and corporation periodically walk in procession through the town, accompanied by a female on horseback, clad in a linen dress closely fitted to her limbs. A figure, commemorative of the peeper, has long been preserved in Coventry, and is now inserted in the niche of a new house communicating with the High Street. Tennyson has versified the story of the Countess and Peeping Tom in his poem entitled "Godiva."

Peers, The Twelve. See TWELVE PEERS.

Peg-a-Lantern. Another name for Will-with-the-Wisp, or Jack-with-the-Lantern.

Peg-a-Ram'sey. The heroine of an old song, having this name for its title, which is alluded to in Shakespeare's "Twelfth Night," a. ii., sc. 3. Percy says it was an indecent ballad. [Written also P e g g y R a m s e y.]

He [James I.] had been much struck with the beauty and embarrassment of the pretty *Peg-a-Ramsey*, as he called her, when he first saw her. *Sir W. Scott.*

Peg'ạ-sus. [Gr. Πήγασος.] (*Gr. & Rom. Myth.*) A winged horse which sprung from the blood of Medusa, and belonged to Apollo and the Muses. From a stroke of his hoof the fountain Hippocrene burst forth on Mount Helicon. He was caught by Bellerophon, who destroyed the Chimæra with his aid. But when Bellerophon attempted to ride to heaven on his back, he threw him off, and ascended alone to the skies, where he was changed into a constellation.

Pe'leũs. [Gr. Πηλεύς.] (*Gr. & Rom. Myth.*) A king of Thessaly, son of

Æacus, husband of Thetis, father of Achilles, and a sharer in the Argonautic expedition.

Pe-li'dēṣ. [Gr. Πηλείδης.] (*Gr. & Rom. Myth.*) A patronymic of Achilles, the son of Peleus.

Pe'li-ŏn. [Gr. Πήλιον.] A high mountain in Thessaly. See OSSA.

Pel'le-ạs, Sir. A very valorous knight of Arthur's Round Table. In "The Faëry Queen," he is one of those who pursue "the blatant beast," when, after having been conquered and chained up by Sir Calidore, it breaks its iron chain, and again ranges through the world.

Fairy damsels, met in forests wide
By knights of Logres, or of Lyones,
Lancelot, or *Pelleas*, or Pellenore. *Milton.*

Pel'le-nore, King. A celebrated character in the old romance of "Morte d'Arthur."

Pe'lops. [Gr. Πέλωψ.] (*Gr. & Rom. Myth.*) A Phrygian prince, grandson of Jupiter, and son of Tantalus. He was slain, and served up before the gods by his own father, who wished to test their omniscience. They were not deceived, however, and would not touch the horrible food; but Ceres, absorbed in grief for the loss of Proserpine, tasted of the shoulder before she discovered what it was. Jupiter restored Pelops to life, and replaced his shoulder with one of ivory.

Pe-nā'tēṣ. (*Rom. Myth.*) Guardian deities of the household, and of the State regarded as a larger household formed by the union of many smaller ones. They were similar to, or identical with, the Lares. See LARES.

Pen-den'nis, Arthur. The hero of Thackeray's satirical romance entitled "The History of Pendennis, his Fortunes and Misfortunes;" a young man of warm feelings and lively intellect, self-conceited and selfish, with no attractive points of character but a sense of honour and a capacity for love.

Pen-den'nis, Major. A gentlemanlike parasite, or rather tuft-hunter, in Thackeray's "History of Pendennis," who fawns upon his patrons for the sake of being received into their society.

Pen-drag'ŏn. A son of Constans, and his successor on the throne of Britain, according to legendary historians; also, a surname given, after the death of this king, to Uther, another son of Constans, and the father of King Arthur. See CONSTANS and UTHER.

For once I read
That stout *Pendragon* in his litter sick
Came to the field and vanquished his foes.
Shak.

Pe-nel'o-pe. [Gr. Πηνελόπη.] (*Gr. & Rom. Myth.*) A celebrated Grecian princess, wife of Ulysses, and mother of Telemachus, famed for her chastity and constancy during the long absence of her husband. Being greatly annoyed by many importunate suitors, she put them off for a time by declaring that she could not decide between them until she had finished weaving a shroud for her aged father-in-law; and, to protract the time, she pulled out by night what she had woven during the day. The stratagem was at length discovered; but Ulysses happened to return in season to prevent the unpleasant consequences that might otherwise have ensued.

Peninsular State. The State of Florida;—popularly so called from its shape.

Peninsular War. (*Hist.*) The name given to the war carried on in Portugal and Spain by the English forces under Sir Arthur Wellesley against the invading armies of Napoleon I., between 1808 and 1812.

Pennsylvania Farmer. A surname given to John Dickinson (1732–1808), an American statesman and author, and a citizen of Pennsylvania. In the year 1768, he published his "Letters from a Pennsylvania Farmer to the Inhabitants of the British Colonies." These were republished in London, with a preface by Dr. Franklin, and were subsequently translated into French, and published in Paris.

Pen-tap'o-lin (*Sp. pron.* pen-tä-po-leen'). The leader of one of two vast hostile armies into which the

and for the Remarks and Rules to which the numbers after certain words refer, see pp. xiv-xxxii.

distempered imagination of Don Quixote (see DON QUIXOTE) transformed two large flocks of sheep, which, from a distance, he saw approaching each other on a wide and dusty plain. This phantom warrior, according to the veracious Don, was the Christian king of the Garamantians, surnamed "Of the Naked Arm," because he always entered into battle with his right arm bare. His beautiful daughter had been demanded in marriage by Alifanfaron, emperor of the great isle of Taprobana, who was a strong pagan. But as Pentapolin would not accept such a misbeliever for a son-in-law, Alifanfaron resolved to win the lady by means of the sword; and the armies of the hostile chiefs were upon the point of engaging each other when the Don descried them.

Not Sancho, when his master interrupted his account of the combatants of *Pentapolin* with the naked arm to advance in person to the charge of the flock of sheep, stood more confounded than Oldbuck at this sudden escapade of his nephew. *Sir W. Scott.*

Pen-thes'ĭ-le'ă. [Gr. Πενθεσίλεια.] (*Gr. & Rom. Myth.*) A queen of the Amazons, who fought against the Greeks during the Trojan war, and was slain by Achilles.

Had I not unfortunately, by the earnestness of my description, awakened the jealousy of his *Penthesilea* of a countess, he had forgotten the crusade and all belonging to it. *Sir W. Scott.*

Pen'theŭs. [Gr. Πενθεύς.] (*Gr. & Rom. Myth.*) A king of Thebes, who, for treating with contempt the rites of Bacchus, was torn in pieces by his mother and aunts, they being at the time under the influence of the god.

A man hunted by the devils that dwell unchained within himself; like *Pentheus* by the Mænads; like Actæon by his own dogs. *Carlyle.*

People, Man of the. See MAN OF THE PEOPLE.

Pepper, K. N. [That is, Cayenne Pepper.] A *nom de plume* of James M. Morris, a humourous American writer of the present day.

Pērce'fŏr-est (4). The title of an old romance of chivalry, and the name of its hero, a knight of the Round Table. An analysis of the romance is given in Dunlop's "History of Fiction."

Pēr'ce-vąl (4). The hero of an old romance of chivalry of the same name, celebrated for his adventures in search of the sangreal.

Pēr'cĭ-net (4). See GRACIOSA.

Pēr'dĭ-tă (4). 1. Daughter of Leontes, king of Sicilia, and of Hermione, his queen, in Shakespeare's "Winter's Tale;" in love with Florizel.

☞ "The qualities which impart to Perdita her distinct individuality are the beautiful combination of the pastoral with the elegant, of simplicity with elevation, of spirit with sweetness." *Mrs. Jameson.*

2. Under this name the beautiful and unfortunate Mrs. Mary (Darby) Robinson (1758–1800), who fell a victim to the licentiousness of the Prince of Wales,—afterward George IV.,—was known at the time of her connection with him. She first attracted his attention while playing the part of Perdita in the "Winter's Tale." The prince was nicknamed Florizel.

Père de la Pensée (pêr du lä pŏn'-sā', 62). See FATHER THOUGHTFUL.

Père Duchesne, Le (lụ pêr dü'shăn', 34). A by-name given to Jacques René Hébert (1755–1794), a brutal and profligate Jacobin leader of the French Revolution, from the name of a newspaper which he edited.

Perez, Michael. See COPPER CAPTAIN.

Peri Banou. See PARIBANOU.

Pe'rĭ-ŏn of Gaul (9). A king of Wales (Gaula) in the old romance of "Amadis de Gaul." See AMADIS DE GAUL.

Pernelle, Mme. (mă'dăm' pĕr'nel'). A scolding old grandmother in Molière's "Tartuffe."

Pēr'o-nel'lă. [Fr. *Péronelle*, a corruption of *Pétronelle*, from *Pierre*, Peter. *Pétronelle* was a character in the ancient mysteries.] The subject of a fairy tale, represented as a pretty country lass, who, at the offer of a fairy, changes place with an old and decrepit queen, and receives the homage paid to rank and wealth, but af-

☞ For the "Key to the Scheme of Pronunciation," with the accompanying Explanations,

terward gladly resumes her beauty and rags.

Perpetual Edict. [Lat. *Edictum Perpetuum.*] (*Rom. Hist.*) A decree issued by the emperor Ælius Hadrianus (76-138), promulgating and embodying a fixed code of laws, which was drawn up by the jurist Salvius Julianus.

Perrin, Dandin. See DANDIN, PERRIN.

Per-seph'o-ne. [Gr. Περσεφόνη.] (*Myth.*) The Greek name of *Proserpine*. See PROSERPINE.

Pĕr'seŭs (4). [Gr. Περσεύς.] (*Gr. & Rom. Myth.*) The son of Jupiter and Danaë, who, being furnished by Mercury with a sickle-shaped sword, by Minerva with a mirror, and by the nymphs with winged sandals, a bag, and a helmet of invisibility, vanquished the Gorgons (see GORGONS), and armed himself with Medusa's head, by means of which he turned into stone the sea-monster to whom Andromeda was exposed, besides performing many other exploits. After death, he was placed among the stars as a constellation.

Persian Anacreon. See ANACREON OF PERSIA.

Perth, Fair Maid of. See FAIR MAID OF PERTH.

Pétaud. See KING PÉTAUD.

Peter. 1. (Lord.) The name by which Swift designates the pope in his "Tale of a Tub."
2. See MORRIS, PETER.

Pe'tĕr-loo, Field of. A name popularly given in England to the scene of an attack made by the military, acting under the orders of the magistrates, upon a reform meeting, held in St. Peter's Field, at Manchester, on the 16th of August, 1819, which was attended by 60,000 persons, of whom only eight were killed, though many were wounded; a word formed in burlesque imitation of *Waterloo*.

Battles and bloodshed, September Massacres, Bridges of Lodi, retreats of Moscow, Waterloos, *Peterloos*, ten-pound franchises, tar-barrels, and guillotines. *Carlyle.*

Peter the Wild Boy. See WILD BOY, THE.

Pe'to. A companion of Sir John Falstaff, in the First and Second Parts of Shakespeare's "King Henry IV."

Petrified City. A name given to Ishmonie, in Upper Egypt, on account of a great number of statues of men, women, children, and animals, which are said to be seen there at this day, and which, according to the popular superstition, were once animated beings, but were miraculously changed into stone in all the various postures and attitudes which were assumed by them at the instant of their supposed transubstantiation. Allusions to this city occur in several English writers. The story is said to have been first mentioned by Kircher, in his "Mundus Subterraneus."

Pe-trû'chi-o. A gentleman of Verona, in Shakespeare's "Taming of the Shrew."

☞ "Petruchio is a madman in his senses, a very honest fellow, who hardly speaks a word of truth, and succeeds in all his tricks and impostures. He acts his assumed character to the life, with the most fantastical extravagance, with untired animal spirits, and without a particle of ill-humour from beginning to end." *Hazlitt.* "He is a fine, hearty compound of bodily and mental vigour, adorned by wit, spirits, and good-nature." *Leigh Hunt.*

Phæ'drą. [Gr. Φαίδρα.] (*Gr. & Rom. Myth.*) A daughter of Minos, king of Crete, a sister of Ariadne, and the wife of Theseus. See HIPPOLYTUS.

Phā'e-tŏn. [Gr. Φαέθων, the shining.] (*Gr. & Rom. Myth.*) A son of Helios, or Sol (the sun), and Clymene, who asked and obtained leave to drive his father's chariot for one day, as a proof of his divine descent. Losing control of the steeds, he set the world on fire, and was punished for his presumption by being struck with a thunderbolt and thrown into the river Eridanus, or Po. [Written also P h a ë t h o n.]

Gallop apace, you fiery-footed steeds,
Towards Phœbus' mansion; such a waggoner
As *Phaëton* would whip you to the west,
And bring in cloudy night immediately. *Shak.*

Phăr'ą-mŏnd. A king of the Franks, and a knight of the Round Table, who visited King Arthur's court *incognito*, to obtain, by his prowess and exploits, a seat at this renowned board.

Phe′be. A shepherdess, in Shakespeare's "As You Like It."

Phi-lā′ri-o (9). An Italian, and a friend to Posthumus, in Shakespeare's play of "Cymbeline."

Phi-le′mŏn. [Gr. Φιλήμων.] (*Gr. & Rom. Myth.*) A pious rustic, husband of Baucis. See BAUCIS.

Philinte (fe′lănt′, 62). A character in Molière's comedy of "The Misanthrope."

Phi-lis′I-dĕs. One of the poetical names of Sir Philip Sidney; formed from portions of the two names *Philip* and *Sidney*, with a Latin termination added. It was invented by himself, and occurs in the "Arcadia."

He knows the grace of that new elegance
Which sweet *Philisides* fetched of late from
France. *Bp. Hall.*

Phil′oc-te′tēs. [Gr. Φιλοκτήτης.] (*Gr. & Rom. Myth.*) A son of Pœas, and one of the Argonauts. He was present at the death of Hercules, and received from him certain arrows which had been dipped in the gall of the Lernæan hydra. (See HERCULES.) On his journey to Troy, he was wounded in the foot by one of these arrows, — or, according to some accounts, by a water-snake, — and, as the wound ulcerated and became excruciatingly painful, his companions treacherously left him on the solitary island of Lemnos. In the tenth year of the war, however, an oracle declared, that Troy could not be taken without the arrows of Hercules; and Philoctetes, yielding to the solicitation of Ulysses and Diomed, repaired to Troy, and made use of them, distinguishing himself by his valour and dexterity.

How changed for Marat, lifted from his dark cellar into this luminous "peculiar tribune!" All dogs have their day; even rabid dogs. Sorrowful, incurable *Philoctetes* Marat, without whom Troy cannot be taken! *Carlyle.*

Phil′o-me′lă. [Gr. Φιλομήλα.] (*Gr. & Rom. Myth.*) A daughter of Pandion, king of Athens, changed into a nightingale.

Philosopher, The. 1. A common designation of the Roman emperor Marcus Aurelius Antoninus. The epithet *Verissimus* — "The Philosopher" — was applied to him by Justin Martyr, and is that by which he has been commonly distinguished from that period to the present, although no such title was ever publicly or formally conferred.

2. A surname given to Leo VI. (867-911), emperor of the East, probably on account of his writings, for his conduct gave him no claims to the appellation.

3. An appellation bestowed upon Porphyry (223-304), an acute and learned Neoplatonist, and an earnest opponent of Christianity.

Philosopher of Fēr′neỹ (or fĕr′nā′). Voltaire is sometimes so called from his chateau of Ferney, near Geneva, where he spent the last twenty years of his life.

This, and several subsequent appeals of the same sort, are among the best points in the conduct of the "*Philosopher of Ferney.*" *W. Spalding.*

Philosopher of Malmesbury (mămz′bĕr-rĭ). A name often given to Thomas Hobbes, who was born at Malmesbury in 1588, and who is celebrated as the first English psychologist, and the first great English writer on the science of government. His, says Mill, was "a great name in philosophy, on account both of the value of what he taught, and the extraordinary impulse which he communicated to the spirit of free inquiry in Europe."

Philosopher of Sans-Souci (sŏⁿ soo′se′, 62). A name given to Frederick the Great (1712-1786), who was a disciple of Voltaire, and the author of a book entitled "Anti-Machiavel," as well as several other political-philosophical works.

Philosopher of the Unknown. [Fr. *Le Philosophe Inconnu.*] The self-assumed appellation of Louis Claude de Saint Martin (1743-1803), a French mystic.

Philosopher of Wim′ble-dŏn (-bl-). A designation of John Horne Tooke

☞ For the "Key to the Scheme of Pronunciation," with the accompanying Explanations,

(1736–1812), a noted English grammarian, philologist, and politician, who resided at Wimbledon, a parish in the vicinity of London.

Phil'os-trāte. Master of the revels to Theseus, in Shakespeare's "Midsummer-Night's Dream."

Phi'neūs. [Gr. Φινεύς.] (*Gr. & Rom. Myth.*) A blind king of Thrace, who possessed the gift of prophecy. He was tormented by the Harpies for his cruelty toward his sons, whom he deprived of sight in consequence of a false accusation made against them by their mother-in-law, who charged them with having behaved improperly to her. Whenever Phineus wanted to eat, the Harpies came, and took away or devoured a portion of his food, and defiled the rest.

Phiz. A pseudonym adopted by Hablot K. Browne, an English comic draughtsman, who designed the illustrations in the first edition of Dickens's "Pickwick Papers."

Phleg'e-thǒn. [Gr. Φλεγέθων, burning, flaming.] (*Gr. & Rom. Myth.*) A river in Hades which rolled with waves of fire instead of water. Nothing grew on its scorched and desolate shores.

> Fierce *Phlegethon*,
> Whose waves of torrent fire inflame with rage.
> *Milton.*

Phle'gy̆-ǎs. [Gr. Φλεγύας.] (*Gr. & Rom. Myth.*) The son of Mars, the king of the Lapithæ, and the father of Ixion and Coronis. For his impiety in plundering and burning the temple of Apollo at Delphi, he was placed in hell, where a huge stone was suspended over his head, which kept him in a state of continual alarm.

Phœ'be. [Gr. Φοίβη.] (*Gr. & Rom. Myth.*) The goddess of the moon, and sister of Phœbus; a name of Diana. See DIANA.

Phœ'bus. [Gr. Φοίβος, the radiant.] (*Gr. & Rom. Myth.*) A poetical name of Apollo, considered as the sun-god. See APOLLO.

Phœ'nix. [Gr. Φοῖνιξ.] (*Gr. & Rom. Myth.*) A bird said to visit Heliopolis, in Egypt, once in every 500 years; according to another and the more popular account, it lived 500 years, and, when about to die, made a nest in Arabia, and burned itself to ashes, from which a young phœnix arose.

Phœ'nix, John, Gentleman. A pseudonym of Captain George Horatio Derby (d. 1861), a humourous and popular American writer.

Phoo'kă or Poo'kă. [Probably the same as the English *Puck*.] (*Fairy Myth.*) Among the Irish, a spirit of diabolical disposition. He sometimes appears as an eagle or a black horse, and hurries to destruction the person he gets possession of.

Phor'cus. [Gr. Φόρκος.] (*Gr. & Rom. Myth.*) A son of Neptune, and father of Medusa and the other Gorgons. After death, he was changed into a sea-god. [Written also **P h o r c y s.**]

Phor'mi-o. A parasite in Terence's comedy of the same name; an accommodating gentleman who reconciles all parties.

Phyl'lis. [Gr. Φυλλίς.] 1. (*Gr. & Rom. Myth.*) A daughter of King Sithon of Thrace, who hung herself, thinking that she was deserted by her lover, and was changed by the gods into an almond-tree.

2. A country girl in Virgil's third and fifth Eclogues; hence, a rustic maiden in general.

> At their savory dinner set
> Of herbs, and other country messes,
> Which the neat-handed *Phyllis* dresses.
> *Milton.*

Pickelherringe (pik'el-her'ring-ǎ). The popular name of a buffoon among the Dutch. See HANSWURST. [Called *Picklehäring* by the Germans.]

☞ Sir F. Palgrave conjectures, that the term may have been originally Picklehärin, *i. e.*, the hairy sprite, answering to Ben Jonson's Puck-hairy; and that he may have worn a rough garment of hair or leaves, like the Scottish Brownie and other similar beings.

Pickle, Pĕr'e-grĭne. The hero of Smollett's novel, "The Adventures of Peregrine Pickle."

☞ "The savage and ferocious Pickle, ... besides his gross and base brutality, besides his ingratitude to his uncle, and

and for the Remarks and Rules to which the numbers after certain words refer, see pp. xiv–xxxii.

the savage propensity which he shows in the pleasure he takes to torment others by practical jokes, resembling those of a fiend in glee, exhibits a low and ungentlemanlike tone of thinking, only one degree higher than that of Roderick Random. ... We certainly sympathise very little in the distress of Pickle, brought on by his own profligate profusion and enhanced by his insolent misanthropy. We are only surprised that his predominating arrogance does not weary out the benevolence of Hatchway and Pipes, and scarce think the ruined spendthrift deserves their persevering and faithful attachment." *Sir W. Scott.*

Pick′wick, Samuel. The hero of Dickens's "Pickwick Papers;" distinguished for his genial goodness and his unsophisticated simplicity. He is represented as the founder of a club called after his own name, in company with other members of which, who are under his care and guidance, he travels over England, meeting with many laughable adventures. The expression, "a Pickwickian sense," which has passed into common speech as denoting a merely technical or constructive sense, refers to a quarrel at a meeting of the club, in which Mr. Pickwick accused Mr. Blotton of acting in a "vile and calumnious" manner, whereupon the latter retorted by calling Mr. Pickwick "a humbug;" but, it finally being made to appear that they both used the offensive words not in a common, but in a parliamentary sense, and that each personally entertained "the highest regard and esteem" for the other, the difficulty was readily settled, and the gentlemen expressed themselves mutually satisfied with the explanations which had been made.

☞ "This name [Pickwick] is no fabrication of our great novelist; and, indeed, very few of his names, however happy, however ludicrous, are so. I have noticed a large proportion of them on actual sign-boards in his own native county of Kent. At Folkestone there is, or at least there recently was, a veritable Mark Tapley, — one, too, who had been to America." ' *Lower.*

Lawyers and politicians daily abuse each other in a *Pickwickian* sense. *Bowditch.*

Picrochole (pĕk′ro′kōl′). [Fr., from Gr. πικρός, bitter, and χολή, choler, bile, or gall.] The name of a character in Rabelais' "Gargantua," celebrated for his thirst of empire, and his vast projects. By some, Charles V. of Spain is supposed to be satirised under this name.

Pi′cus. (*Rom. Myth.*) A king of Latium, son of Saturn and father of Faunus; turned by Circe, whose love he had slighted, into a woodpecker.

Pied Piper of Ham′e-lin. [Lat. *Tibicen Omnicolor.*] The hero of an old and celebrated German legend, related in Verstegan's "Restitution of Decayed Intelligence" (London, 1634), of which narrative Robert Browning, in his poem entitled "The Pied Piper," has given an extended metrical version. The legend recounts how a certain musician, dressed in a fantastical coat, came into the town of Hamel, in the country of Brunswick, and offered, for a sum of money, to rid the town of the rats by which it was infested; and how, having executed his task, and the promised reward having been withheld, he in revenge blew again his pipe, and, by the magic of its tones, drew the children of the town, to the number of a hundred and thirty, to a cavern in the side of a hill, which, immediately upon their entrance, closed and shut them in for ever. Erichius wrote a work, entitled "Exodus Hamelensis," expressly on the subject, in which he maintained the historical authenticity of the story; and Martin Schoock wrote another, "Fabula Hamelensis," in which he took the opposite ground. According to Verstegan, the "exodus" took place on the 22d of July, 1376; but the date commonly given is June 26, 1284. Harenberg maintains, according to Zedler, that a number of Hamelin children, who were carried away captive in a contest with the Bishop of Minden (Conrad II.), never returned to their native land, and so gave occasion for the tradition that they had been swallowed up alive.

☞ It has been remarked that the

☞ For the "Key to the Scheme of Pronunciation," with the accompanying Explanations,

German *pfeiffen*, to pipe, means, also, to decoy, to allure, to entice, to inveigle, and that this, perhaps, is the origin of the Hamelin myth so far as relates to the children's being spirited away by a piper. As all the mischief came from not paying the Tibicen Omnicolor his just dues, we have a curious illustration of our proverbial expression, "Pay the Piper," which may, indeed, have sprung from this story.

> This is that despotism which poets have celebrated in the *Pied Piper of Hamelin*, whose music drew like the power of gravitation,—drew soldiers and priests, traders and feasters, women and boys, rats and mice.
> *Emerson.*

> I rather think Petrarch was the first choragus of that sentimental dance which so long led young folks away from the realities of life, like the *Piper of Hamelin*. *Lowell.*

Pī-ĕr'ĭ-dĕṣ. [Gr. Πιερίδες.] (*Gr. & Rom. Myth.*) 1. A name given to the Muses, from Pieria, a fountain near Mount Olympus.

2. Daughters of Pierus, whom the Muses changed into magpies for challenging them to sing.

Pierre (peer; *Fr. pron.* pĕ-ĕr'). A conspirator in Otway's tragedy of "Venice Preserved," impelled to treason by a mixture of patriotism and misanthropy. See JAFFIER.

> Ours is a trophy which will not decay
> With the Rialto; Shylock, and the Moor,
> And *Pierre*, cannot be swept or worn away.
> *Byron.*

Pierrot (pē-ĕr'o'). [Fr., little Peter, from *Pierre*, Peter.] A jesting character in pantomime, who takes the part of a simple valet, wearing white pantaloons, and a large white jacket with a row of big buttons in front, and who often paints his face white.

Pī'gro-grom'ĭ-tus. A name occurring in Shakespeare's comedy of "Twelfth Night." Who or what is meant by it, is not known. Sir Andrew Ague-cheek merely alludes to it as having been used by Olivia's clown upon an occasion of mirth and jesting, so that, in all likelihood, it was not intended to be taken seriously as a genuine name.

> In sooth, thou wast in very gracious fooling last night, when thou spokest of *Pigrogromitus*, of the Vapians passing the equinoctial of Queubus; 't was very good, i' faith. *Shak.*

Pig-wig'gin. The name of a doughty elf, whose amours with Queen Mab, and furious combat with the jealous Oberon, are related in Drayton's "Nymphidia."

> The same genius which now busies us with their concerns might have excited an equal interest for the adventures of Oberon and *Pigwiggin*. *Jeffrey.*

Pillar of Doctors. [Fr. *La Colonne des Docteurs.*] An honorary appellation given by his admirers to William de Champeaux, a celebrated French philosopher and theologian of the twelfth century.

Pillars of Hēr'cu-lēṣ. [Lat. *Columnæ Herculis*, Gr. Ἡράκλειαι στῆλαι.] A name given by the old Greeks and Romans to two mountains on opposite sides of the strait connecting the Mediterranean Sea with the Atlantic Ocean. These mountains — anciently called Calpe and Abyla — were situated, the former in Europe, and the latter in Africa. Their modern names are, respectively, the Rock of Gibraltar, and Jebel Zatout, or Apes' Hill. The classical appellation of the Pillars of Hercules was given to them in consequence of a fiction that Hercules, in his travels to find the oxen of Geryon, raised these two mountains as monuments of his journey, and placed on them the inscription, "*Ne plus ultra*," importing that they marked the utmost limits of the habitable world in that direction. The Pillars of Hercules long remained deeply fixed in the Greek mind as a terminus of human adventure and aspiration.

> Perhaps the strongest circumstance of the whole was, that the old dethroned king of Spain, and his consort, undertook a journey, for the purpose of carrying their personal congratulations on the birth of an heir, to one who had deposed, and was detaining in prison, their own lineage, and had laid Spain, their native dominions, in blood, from the Pyrenees to the *Pillars of Hercules*. *Sir W. Scott.*

Pinch. A schoolmaster and conjurer in Shakespeare's "Comedy of Errors."

Pinch, Tom. A character in Dickens's "Martin Chuzzlewit," distinguished by his guilelessness, his oddity, his excessive modesty, and his exhaustless goodness of heart.

Pinchwife, Mr. A prominent character in Wycherley's comedy of "The Country Wife."

---

and for the Remarks and Rules to which the numbers after certain words refer, see pp. xiv-xxxii.

She [Lady Drogheda] well knew in what esteem conjugal fidelity was held among the fine gentlemen there, and watched her town husband as assiduously as *Mr. Pinchwife* watched his country wife. *Macaulay.*

Pinchwife, Mrs. The heroine of Wycherley's "Country Wife." See AGNES, 1.

Pindar, Peter. A pseudonym adopted by Dr. John Wolcott (1738-1819). In his first publication, "Lyric Odes to the Royal Academicians for 1782," he styles himself " a distant relation of the poet of Thebes."

Pindar of Wakefield. See GEORGE A-GREEN.

Pine-tree State. A popular name of the State of Maine, the central and northern portions of which are covered with extensive pine forests.

Pip. [A childish corruption of *Philip Pirrip.*] A by-name of the hero of Dickens's novel of " Great Expectations."

Piper, Tom. One of the characters making up a morris-dance.

So have I seen
Tom Piper stand upon our village green,
Backed with the May-pole, while a gentle crew,
In gentle motion, circularly threw
Themselves about him. *Wm. Browne.*

Piper of Hamelin, The Pied. See PIED PIPER OF HAMELIN.

Pipes, Tom. The name of a character in Smollett's "Adventures of Peregrine Pickle;" celebrated for his taciturnity, and represented as a retired boatswain's mate, living with the eccentric Commodore Trunnion to keep the servants in order.

One wonders, Were *Pipes* and Hatchway there in [Commodore] Martin's squadron? In what station Commodore Trunnion did then serve in the British Navy ? *Carlyle.*

Pī-rĭth'o-us. [Gr. Πειρίθοος.] (*Gr. & Rom. Myth.*) A son of Ixion, and a king of the Lapithæ. His friendship for Theseus, king of Athens, was proverbial. After the death of Hippodamia, he descended, in company with Theseus, to the infernal regions, to carry away Proserpine; but Pluto, who was advised of their intention, bound Pirithous to his father's wheel (see IXION), and Theseus to a monstrous stone.

Pī-sä'nĭ-o. A servant to Posthumus, in Shakespeare's "Cymbeline." He is distinguished for faithful attachment to Imogen, his master's wife.

Pistol, Ancient. A follower of Falstaff, in Shakespeare's "Merry Wives of Windsor," and in the Second Part of "King Henry the Fourth." He is a bully and a swaggerer by profession.

☞ Perhaps from *pistolfo*, explained by Florio as "a roguing beggar, a cantler, an upright man that liveth by cozenage." *Halliwell.*

In this mood, if any one endeavoured to bring Sir Arthur down to the regions of common life, his replies were in the vein of *Ancient Pistol :*—

"A fico for the world, and worldlings base !
I speak of Africa and golden joys!"
Sir W. Scott.

I only say, that I read from habit and from indolence, not from real interest; that, like *Ancient Pistol* devouring his leek, I read and swear till I get to the end of the narrative.
Sir W. Scott.

Plagiary, Sir Fretful. A character in Sheridan's play, "The Critic," designed, it is said, for Richard Cumberland (1732-1811), an English dramatic writer, noted for his vanity and irritability.

He has, therefore, no reason to complain; and I dare say, that, like *Sir Fretful Plagiary*, he is rather pleased than otherwise. *Byron.*

Plain, The. [Fr. *La Plaine.*] (*Fr. Hist.*) A name given to that part of the benches, in the National Convention, occupied by the Girondists, or the more moderate among the deputies; hence, these deputies themselves. The Plain succumbed in the contest with "The Mountain." See MOUNTAIN, THE, and MARSH, THE.

Plain and Perspicuous Doctor. [Lat. *Doctor Planus et Perspicuus,* or *Conspicuus.*] An honorary title bestowed upon Walter Burleigh (1275-1357), a famous scholastic, by his admiring contemporaries. He is said to have combated the opinions of Duns Scotus with great vigour.

Platonic Puritan. An appellation given to John Howe (1630-1706), a distinguished Non-conformist divine, and a man of great general learning. His writings are distinguished for their originality, profundity, and philosophical calmness and comprehensiveness.

☞ For the "Key to the Scheme of Pronunciation," with the accompanying Explanations,

Plē′iad, The. A title given, in allusion to the seven stars of this name, to a group or *réunion* of seven celebrated persons.
1. THE PHILOSOPHICAL PLEIAD. See SEVEN WISE MEN OF GREECE.
2. THE FIRST LITERARY PLEIAD, or PLEIAD OF ALEXANDRIA, was instituted by Ptolemy Philadelphus, and composed of the contemporary poets, Callimachus, Apollonius of Rhodes, Aratus, Homer the younger, Lycophron, Nicander, and Theocritus.
3. THE LITERARY PLEIAD OF CHARLEMAGNE was a sort of academy founded by that monarch, in which Alcuin was called *Albinus;* Angilbert, *Homer;* Adelard, *Augustine;* Riculfe, *Damœtas;* and Charlemagne himself, *David.* Varnefrid and one other completed the Pleiad.
4. A literary school in France, in the sixteenth century, of which Ronsard was the head, and six of his admirers the remaining members; namely, the poets Joachim du Bellay, Antoine de Baïf, Amadis Jamyn, Belleau, Jodelle, and Ponthus de Thiard. They were at first called *La Brigade.*

Ple′i-a-dēş (ple′yạ-dĕz, 20). [Gr. Πλειάδες.] (*Gr. & Rom. Myth.*) Seven daughters of Atlas and Pleione, named Electra, Alcyone, Celæno, Maia, Sterope, Taygete, and Merope. Their history is differently related, but all authorities agree that they were transformed into the constellation which bears their name. Only six of these stars are visible to the naked eye; and the ancients believed that the seventh (Merope) hid herself from shame, she alone having married a mortal, while her sisters were the wives of gods.

Plĕy′dell, Mr. Páu′lus. A shrewd and witty lawyer in Scott's novel of "Guy Mannering."

Did the old gentleman who drawls about the boozing buffoonery of the "Noctes" ever hear of a celebrated lawyer, one *Pleydell*, who, in his leisure hours, was strenuously addicted to High Jinks? *Noctes Ambrosianæ.*

Pliant, Sir Paul. An uxorious, foolish old knight, in Congreve's comedy of "The Double Dealer."

Of what consequence is it to Virtue, or how is she at all concerned about it, . . . who is the father of Lord Froth's or *Sir Paul Pliant's* children? *Charles Lamb.*

Plon-plon, Prince (plŏn′plŏn′, 62). A nickname given to Prince Napoleon Joseph Charles Bonaparte, son of Jerome Bonaparte by his second wife, the Princess Frederica Catherine of Würtemberg.

Ploughman, Piĕrs. The hero of a celebrated satirical poem ("The Vision of Piers Ploughman") of the fourteenth century, of which Robert Langland (or Langlande) is the reputed author. Piers is represented as falling asleep on the Malvern Hills, in Worcestershire, and as having a series of dreams. In describing these, he exposes the corruptions of society, and particularly the dissoluteness and avarice of the religious orders, with great humour and fancy, but considerable bitterness. An imitation of the "Vision," called "Piers Ploughman's Creed," appears to have been written about the end of the fourteenth century. It is an exposition of the impediments and temptations which beset this mortal life. The method, like that of Bunyan's "Pilgrim's Progress," is allegorical, but the spirit of the poetry is not so much picturesque as satirical.

Plu′to. [Gr. Πλούτων.] (*Gr. & Rom. Myth.*) A son of Saturn and Ops, brother of Jupiter and Neptune, husband of Proserpine, and the inexorable king of the under-world. See PROSERPINE. [Called also *Dis.*]

Plu′tus. [Gr. Πλοῦτος.] (*Gr. & Rom. Myth.*) The god of riches; a son of Iasius, or Iasion, and Ceres.

Plym′ley, Peter. A pseudonym under which Sydney Smith (1771–1845), published a powerful political tract, entitled "Letters on the Subject of the Catholics, to my Brother Abraham, who lives in the Country."

Pochi Danari (po′kee dä-nä′ree). [It., the penniless.] A sobriquet given by the Italians to Maximilian I. (1459-1519), emperor of Germany.

Poet of Poets. A name often given to Shelley (1792-1822), who is preeminent among modern writers for the compass of his imagination and the peculiar graces of his style. Macaulay says that the words "bard" and "inspiration," generally so unmeaning when applied to modern poets, have a special significance when applied to Shelley.

Poets' Corner. An angle in the south transept of Westminster Abbey, London; — popularly so called from the fact that it contains the tombs of Chaucer, Spenser, and other eminent English poets, and memorial tablets, busts, statues, or monuments, to many who are buried in other places.

Poet Squab. A nickname given by Lord Rochester to Dryden, on account of his corpulence in later life.

Poins. A companion of Sir John Falstaff in the two parts of Shakespeare's "King Henry IV." [Written also Poyns.]

We were still further removed from the days of "the mad prince and *Poins.*"
Sir W. Scott.

The chronicles of that day contain accounts of many a mad prank which he [Lord Warwick, Addison's step-son] played, as we have legends of a still earlier date of the lawless freaks of the wild prince and *Poyns.*
Thackeray.

Polish Bāy'ạrd. A name given to Prince Joseph Poniatowski (1763–1814), a Polish general of distinguished bravery.

Polish Bȳ'rọn (9). A name which has been very generally given to the Polish poet, Adam Mickiewicz (1798–1855). It has been said to convey "as correct a notion of the nature and the extent of his genius as any single epithet could possibly do."

Polish Franklin. An epithet conferred upon Thaddeus Czacki (1765–1813), a distinguished counsellor, philosopher, and historian of Poland.

Polish Vol-tâire'. A name popularly given to Ignatius Krasicki (1774–1801), one of the most distinguished literary men of Poland, and author of a great number of works in prose and verse.

Polixène (po'lĕk'sän'). An assumed name, adopted, instead of her baptismal one of *Madelon*, by a female character in Molière's famous comedy, "Les Précieuses Ridicules."

Po-lix'e-nēs. King of Bohemia, in Shakspeare's "Winter's Tale."

Pol'lux. A famous pugilist, the twin brother of Castor. See CASTOR.

Po-lo'ni-us. Lord chamberlain to the king of Denmark, in Shakespeare's tragedy of "Hamlet."

☞ "Polonius ... is the personified memory of wisdom no longer actually possessed. This admirable character is always misrepresented on the stage. Shakespeare never intended to exhibit him as a buffoon; for, although it was natural that Hamlet — a young man of fire and genius, detesting formality, and disliking Polonius on political grounds, as imagining that he had assisted him in his usurpation — should express himself satirically, yet this must not be taken as exactly the poet's conception of him. In Polonius, a certain induration of character had arisen from long habits of business; but take his advice to Laertes, and Ophelia's reverence for his memory, and we shall see that he was meant to be represented as a statesman somewhat past his faculties, — his recollections of life all full of wisdom, and showing a knowledge of human nature, whilst what immediately takes place before him, and escapes from him, is indicative of weakness. . . . In the great, ever-recurring dangers and duties of life, — where to distinguish the fit objects for the application of the maxims collected by the experience of a long life requires no fineness of tact, as in the admonitions to his son and daughter, — Polonius is uniformly made respectable."
Coleridge.

Po-lyd'ạ-mạs. [Gr. Πολυδάμας.] A Grecian athlete, famous for his immense size and strength. Many marvellous stories are related of him, as that, when unarmed, he killed a huge and fierce lion, stopped a chariot in full career, lifted a mad bull, and the like. He is said to have met his death in attempting to stop or to sustain a falling rock.

Pol'ȳ-deu'cēs. [Gr. Πολυδευκής.] (*Gr. & Rom. Myth.*) The Greek form of *Pollux.* See POLLUX.

Pol'ȳ-dore. [Lat. *Polydorus,* Gr. Πολύδωρος.] 1. (*Gr. & Rom. Myth.*) The youngest son of Priam and Hecuba; he was killed for his riches by Polymnestor, king of Thrace, who had been intrusted with the care of him.

2. A feigned name assumed by Guiderius, in Shakespeare's "Cymbeline."

Pol'ȳ-hym'ni-ạ̈, *or* **Po-lym'ni-ạ̈**. [Gr. Πολύμνια.] (*Gr. & Rom. Myth.*) One of the Muses; the one who presided over rhetoric and singing. She was reputed to be the inventress of the lyre.

Pol'ȳ-ni'cēṣ. [Gr. Πολυνείκης.] (*Gr. & Rom. Myth.*) Son of Œdipus and Jocasta, and brother of Eteocles. See ETEOCLES and SEVEN AGAINST THEBES.

Pol'ȳ-phe'mus. [Gr. Πολύφημος.] (*Gr. & Rom. Myth.*) A son of Neptune, and one of the Cyclops, who dwelt in Sicily. He was a cruel monster, of immense size and strength, and had but one eye, which was in the middle of his forehead. When Ulysses landed in Sicily, he, with twelve of his companions, got caught in the cave of Polyphemus, and six of the number were eaten by the tremendous cannibal. The rest were in expectation of the same fate, but their cunning leader enabled them to escape, by contriving to intoxicate Polyphemus, and then destroying his single eye with a fire-brand. [Written also poetically, and in an Anglicised form, Polypheme.]

Po-mo'nạ̈. [Lat., cognate with *pomum*, fruit.] (*Rom. Myth.*) The goddess of fruit and fruit-trees. See VERTUMNUS.

Pom'pey. The name of a clown, in Shakespeare's "Measure for Measure."

Ponocrates (po-nok'rȧ-tĕz; *Fr. pron.* po'nok'rȧ-tess'). The name of Gargantua's tutor, in Rabelais' famous romance.

Pons As'ĭ-no'rum. [Lat., Bridge of Asses.] A name given to the famous forty-seventh proposition of the first book of Euclid's "Elements," from the circumstance that tyros usually find much difficulty in getting over it.

Poor Richard. The feigned author of a series of Almanacs (commenced in 1732, and continued for twenty-five years), really written by Benjamin Franklin, and distinguished for their inculcation of the prudential virtues, as temperance, frugality, order, justice, cleanliness, chastity, and the like, by means of maxims or precepts, which, it has been said, "are as valuable as any thing that has descended from Pythagoras." See SAUNDERS, RICHARD.

<small>Few of the many wise apothegms which have been uttered, from the time of the Seven Sages of Greece to that of *Poor Richard*, have prevented a single foolish action. *Macaulay*.</small>

Poor Robin. The imaginary author of a celebrated series of Almanacs first published in 1661 or 1662, and said to have originated with Robert Herrick, the poet. Other books were also published under the same name, as "Poor Robin's Visions," "Poor Robin's Pathway to Knowledge," &c.

Pope Joan. See JOAN, POPE.

Pope of Philosophy. An appellation conferred upon Aristotle (B. C. 384–322), in modern times, on account of the boundless reverence paid to his name, the infallibility ascribed to his teaching, and the despotic influence which his system of thought exercised upon the strongest minds of Europe for centuries.

Popish Plot. (*Eng. Hist.*) The name given to an imaginary plot on the part of the Roman Catholics in the time of Charles II., to massacre the Protestants, burn the city of London, and assassinate the king. The fiction was devised by one Titus Oates, an unprincipled and vagabond adventurer, who had been successively an Anabaptist minister, a clergyman of the Established Church, and a Roman Catholic. By the aid of suborned witnesses, he procured the judicial murder of many innocent persons; but a violent reaction at last set in, and he was tried, convicted of perjury, pilloried, whipped, and imprisoned.

Poplar, Anthony. A name assumed by the editor of the "Dublin University Magazine," when it was first started.

---

and for the Remarks and Rules to which the numbers after certain words refer, see pp. xlv–xxxii.

Porcupine, Peter. A pseudonym adopted by William Cobbett (1762–1835), a voluminous political writer. In 1796, he established in Philadelphia "Peter Porcupine's Gazette." An edition of the Porcupine Papers, in 12 vols., was published in London in 1801.

Pŏrk-op′o-lis. [Eng. *pork*, and Gr. πόλις, city.] A jocular nickname for the city of Cincinnati, which is one of the greatest markets for pork in America.

Pŏr′rex. See FERREX.

Por′se-nȧ, *or* **Pŏr-sen′nȧ, Larṣ.** A legendary king of Etruria, who made war on Rome on account of the banishment of the Tarquins from that city. Macaulay has made him the subject of one of the most magnificent of his "Lays of Ancient Rome."

Porte-Crayon. A pseudonym of David H. Strother, author of an interesting series of illustrated papers published in "Harper's Magazine."

Por′ti-ȧ (pōr′shĭ-ȧ, *or* pōr′shĭ-ȧ). A rich heiress, in Shakespeare's "Merchant of Venice." She is in love with Bassanio; but her choice of a husband is restrained by a whim of her deceased father, who deposited her picture in one of three locked caskets, of gold, silver, and lead, respectively, with the testamentary proviso that her hand and fortune were to be bestowed upon that suitor only who should guess which of the caskets contained her likeness. Foreign princes, who come to try their luck, select the golden and silver chests, which contain nothing but a death's-head and a fool's head, with scrolls bearing mocking mottoes; but Bassanio fortunately chooses the "meagre lead," and wins his mistress. Soon after, his friend Antonio, a wealthy merchant, having thoughtlessly signed a bond in favour of Shylock, a Jewish usurer, by which he agreed to forfeit a pound of flesh in case of failure to repay in a stipulated time a sum of money which he had borrowed, and being unable, from a concurrence of unfortunate circumstances, to meet the obligation, Portia, in the disguise of a "young doctor of Rome," and under the assumed name of Balthazar, manages to have the case tried before herself, and at last gives judgment against the Jew. Bassanio urges her to accept of three thousand ducats — the sum due to Shylock from Antonio — by way of remuneration; but she begs for a ring that she had once given him, and which he had sworn never to sell, or give away, or lose. He begs to be excused from parting with it, but is finally over-persuaded, and lets her have it. This incident furnishes the occasion for a simulated quarrel between Bassanio and Portia when they meet at Portia's house in Belmont. The story of the bond is of Eastern origin.

Portuguese Ȧ-pol′lo. A title bestowed upon Luis Camoens (1527–1579), the great national poet of Portugal. See APOLLO.

Portuguese Liv′y. An appellation conferred upon João de Barros (1496–1570), the most distinguished of Portuguese historians. His style is greatly admired.

Portuguese Mars. A title of Affonso de Alboquerque (1452–1515), viceroy of India, and a man of extraordinary wisdom and enterprise, who, in 1503, took possession of Goa, which he made the centre of Portuguese power and commerce in Asia, and subdued the whole of Malabar, Ceylon, the Sunda Isles, and the peninsula of Malacca.

Portuguese Nos′trȧ-dā′mus. A surname of Gonçalo Annes Bandarra (d. 1556), a poet-cobbler, whose writings were suppressed by the Inquisition.

Portuguese Nun. Mariana Alcaforada (d. about 1700), a Portuguese lady who addressed a series of famous letters to the Chevalier de Chamilly, with whom she was deeply in love, though he did not reciprocate her passion. She derived the sobriquet from her supposed connection with a convent.

Portuguese Tī′ti-ȧn (tish′ĭ-ȧn). A title given to Alonzo Sanches Coello

☞ For the "Key to the Scheme of Pronunciation," with the accompanying Explanations,

(1515-1590), a Portuguese painter whose style is thought to resemble that of the illustrious Italian painter, Vecellio Tiziano, or Titian.

Pŏr-tu'nus (6). [Lat., from *portus*, a harbour.] (*Rom. Myth.*) The protecting god of harbours.

Po-sei'dŏn. [Gr. Ποσειδῶν.] (*Myth.*) The Greek name of *Neptune*. See NEPTUNE.

Pŏst'hu-mus, Le'o-nā'tus. Husband to Imogen, in Shakespeare's "Cymbeline." He is distinguished for his rash but unsuccessful plotting of his wife's death as a punishment of her supposed infidelity to him.

Potage, Jean (zhŏⁿ po'tăzh', 62). A grotesque character on the French stage. See HANSWURST.

Pounce, Mr. Peter. A character in Fielding's novel, "The Adventures of Joseph Andrews." See ADAMS, PARSON ABRAHAM.

Poundtext, Peter. An "indulged pastor" with the Covenanters' army, in Sir Walter Scott's "Old Mortality."

Pourceaugnac M. de (mos'e-ö' dü poor'sŏn'yak', 43, 78). The hero of Molière's comedy of the same name; a pompous country gentleman who comes to Paris to marry Julie, — the heroine of the piece, — the authority of her father having destined her hand to him. But Julie has a lover, and this lover plays off so many tricks and mystifications upon the provincial suitor that he finally relinquishes his suit in despair.

Pŏw'ell, Mary. A pseudonym of Mrs. Richard Rathbone, a writer of the present day.

Poy'nings' Law. (*Irish Hist.*) A law passed by a parliament summoned to meet at Drógheda, by Sir Edward Poynings, governor of Ireland in the time of Henry VII. This memorable statute established the authority of the English government in Ireland.

P. P., Clerk of this Parish. The feigned author of a humourous and celebrated volume of Memoirs really written by Arbuthnot, in ridicule of Burnet's "History of My Own Times." The following extract will give an idea of this famous work:—

"In the name of the Lord, Amen. I, P. P., Clerk of this Parish, by the grace of God write this history. . . . Even when I was at school my mistress did ever extol me above the rest of the youth, in that I had a laudable voice. And it was furthermore observed that I took a kindly affection unto that black letter in which our Bibles are printed. Yea, often did I exercise myself in singing goodly ballads, such as 'The Lady and Death,' 'The Children in the Wood,' and 'Chevy Chase;' and not, like other children, in lewd and trivial ditties. Moreover, while I was a boy, I always ventured to lead the psalm next after Master William Harris, my predecessor, who (it must be confessed to the glory of God) was a most excellent parish clerk in that his day. . . . Ever since I arrived at the age of discretion, I had a call to take upon me the function of a parish clerk; and to that end it seemed to me meet and profitable to associate myself with the parish clerks of this land,—such, I mean, as were right worthy in their calling, and of becoming gravity. Now it came to pass that I was born in the year of our Lord, Anno Domini, 1655, the year wherein our worthy benefactor Esquire Bret did add one bell to the ring of this parish. So that it hath been wittily said, that 'one and the same day did give to this our church two rare gifts,—its great bell, and its clerk.'"

Those who were placed around it [a dinner-table] had those feelings of awe with which *P. P., Clerk of the Parish*, described himself oppressed, when he first uplifted the psalm in presence of those persons of high worship, the wise Mr. Justice Freeman, the good Lady Jones, and the great Sir Thomas Truby.
Sir W. Scott.

The example of the famous "*P. P., Clerk of this Parish*," was never more faithfully followed. *Hawthorne.*

Interspersed also are long, purely autobiographical delineations, yet without connection, without recognisable coherence; so unimportant, so superfluously minute, they almost remind us of "*P. P., Clerk of this Parish.*" *Carlyle.*

Pragmatic Sanction. (*Hist.*) A decree by which, in the year 1713, Charles VI., emperor of Germany, and the last descendant in the male line of the house of Austria, settled his dominions on his daughter, the Archduchess Maria Theresa, wife of Francis of Lorraine. Her succession was guaranteed by Great Britain,

France, the States General, and most of the European powers, and she ascended the throne in October, 1740; but a general European war was the result.

☞ The term "Pragmatic Sanction" is sometimes applied to other solemn ordinances or decrees relating either to Church or State affairs; but that by which the empire of Germany was settled in the house of Austria is the most celebrated of all.

Prairie State. A name popularly given to Illinois, in allusion to the wide-spread and beautiful prairies which form a striking feature of the scenery of the State.

Prasildo (prä-zĕl′do). A nobleman of Babylon, in Bojardo's "Orlando Innamorato," noted for his devoted friendship for Iroldo, with whose wife, Tisbina, he falls violently in love. Being overheard by her and her husband threatening to kill himself, the lady, hoping to divert him from his passion by time and absence, promises to return it on condition of his performing a distant and perilous adventure. He performs the adventure; and the husband and wife, supposing that there is no other way of her escaping the consequences, resolve to take poison; after which the lady goes to Prasildo's house, and informs him of their having done so. Prasildo resolves to die with them; but hearing, in the mean time, that the apothecary had given them a drink that was harmless, he goes and tells them of their good fortune; upon which the husband is so struck with his generosity, that he voluntarily quits Babylon for life, and the lady marries the lover. The new husband subsequently hears that his friend's life is in danger, and quits the wife to go and deliver him from it at the risk of his own.

Preacher, The. A title sometimes given to Solomon, "the son of David, king in Jerusalem," and author of the book of "Ecclesiastes," — a word which signifies *preacher*.

Thus saith *The Preacher*: "Naught beneath the sun
Is new;" yet still from change to change we run. *Byron.*

Precht, Frau (frŏw prekt). See BERTHA, FRAU.

Précieuses Ridicules, Les (lä prā′-sē-ŭz′ re/de/kül′, 34, 43). The title of a comedy by Molière (1622–1673), and a name given to its heroines, Aminte and Polixène, who represent a class of women among Molière's contemporaries remarkable for their affectation of extreme politeness, their high-flown sentiments, their metaphysical conceits, and their euphuistic style of speaking and writing.

☞ It has been customary to say that Molière's charming satire was aimed at the Hôtel de Rambouillet, a famous coterie of the most accomplished and illustrious wits, critics, scholars, and poets, of both sexes, to be found in Paris during the seventeenth century; but the notion has been shown to be utterly groundless. In its original acceptation, the word *précieuse* was an honourable designation, signifying a woman who, to grace and dignity of manner, added elegance and culture of mind. It was therefore applied with perfect propriety to the brilliant and cultivated ladies of the Rambouillet circle. But, in the course of time, grotesque imitations of the manners and style of the Hôtel became prevalent both in Paris and the provinces, and the epithet consequently took on a tinge of reproach or contempt.

Prĕs′ter John. [That is, the Priest, or the Presbyter, John.] The name given, in the Middle Ages, to a supposed Christian sovereign and priest in the interior of Asia, whose dominions were variously placed. The story is said to have originated in the fact that the Nestorian missionaries, in the eleventh or twelfth century, penetrated into Eastern Asia, and converted Ung (or Ungh Khan), the chief of the Kerait, or Krit, Tartars. This name they corrupted or translated into Prester John, *Ung* being turned into "Jachanan," or "John," and *Khan* being rendered by "Priest." His fame spread to Europe, and not only furnished the material of numberless mediæval legends, but supplied the occasion of several missionary expeditions to the East.

I will go on the lightest errand now to the Antipodes that you can devise to send me on; I will fetch you a tooth-picker now from the furthest inch of Asia; bring you the length of *Prester John's* foot; fetch you a hair of the great Cham's beard; do you any embassage to the Pygmies, — rather than hold three words' conference with this harpy. *Shak.*

Pres'to. [It. and Sp., quick, nimble, swift, from Lat. *præstus*, ready.] A name given to Swift by the Duchess of Shrewsbury, who, being a foreigner, could not remember the English word *swift*. The sobriquet is frequently used in Swift's "Journal to Stella." See STELLA.

Pretenders, The. James Francis Edward Stuart, son of James II., and Charles Edward Stuart, grandson of James II.; called respectively, the Elder and the Younger Pretender. By the forced abdication and flight of James II., in 1688, the crown of England passed to William, Prince of Orange (who was the son of Mary, daughter of Charles I.), and to Mary, his wife (who was the daughter of James II., and consequently cousin to William). The Acts of Settlement passed in the reign of William III. (A. D. 1701 and 1708) secured the succession of the house of Hanover to the English throne. The Elder Pretender made some vain attempts to recover the kingdom, but surrendered his claims, in 1743, to his son, Charles Edward, the Younger Pretender, who, in the following year, invaded Great Britain from France, and fought gallantly for the throne of his ancestors, but was signally defeated at Culloden, in 1746, and compelled to escape to the Continent.

Prettyman, Prince. See PRINCE PRETTYMAN.

Pri'ăm. [Lat. *Priamus*, Gr. Πρίαμος.] (*Gr. & Rom. Myth.*) A son of Laomedon, and the last king of Troy; husband of Hecuba, and father of Hector, Helenus, Paris, Deiphobus, Polyxena, Troilus, Cassandra, &c. He was slain by Pyrrhus, the son of Achilles, the same night on which Troy was taken by the Greeks.

Pri'ă-pus. [Gr. Πρίαπος.] (*Gr. & Rom. Myth.*) The god of procreation in general, or a deified personification of the fructifying principle in nature. He was worshipped particularly as the god of gardens and vineyards, and of whatever pertains to agriculture. He is variously described as the son of Adonis and Venus, of Bacchus and Venus, and of Mercury and Chione.

Pride's Purge. (*Eng. Hist.*) A name given to a violent invasion of parliamentary rights, in 1649, by Colonel Pride, who, at the head of two regiments, surrounded the house of commons, and seized in the passage forty-one members of the Presbyterian party, whom he confined. Above one hundred and sixty others were excluded, and none admitted but the most furious and determined of the Independents. These privileged members were called "The Rump."

Prid'win. The name of Arthur's shield, on which the picture of the blessed Virgin Mary was painted, in order to put him frequently in mind of her. [Written also P r i w e n.]

The temper of his sword, the tried Excalibor,
The bigness and the length of Rone, his
noble spear,
With *Pridwin,* his great shield, and what the
proof could bear. *Drayton.*

Primrose, George. A character in Goldsmith's "Vicar of Wakefield," who went to Amsterdam to teach Dutchmen English, without recollecting, until he landed, that he should first know something of Dutch himself.

Primrose, Moses. A character in Goldsmith's "Vicar of Wakefield;" celebrated for his quiet pedantry and blundering simplicity, and especially for having bartered away a good horse for a gross of worthless green spectacles with tortoise-shell rims and shagreen cases.

As for myself, I expect to rival honest *Primrose's* son *Moses* in his great bargain of the green spectacles. *W. Irving.*

Primrose, Mrs. Deborah. The wife of the vicar, in Goldsmith's novel, "The Vicar of Wakefield." She is distinguished for her boasted skill in housewifery, her motherly vanity, her pride in her husband, and her desire to appear genteel.

Thackeray's works, like *Mrs. Primrose's* "wedding gown," wear well, though they may not at once captivate the fancy.
Christ. Examiner.

and for the Remarks and Rules to which the numbers after certain words refer, see pp. xlv-xxxii.

Primrose, Olivia. A lovely and beloved child of Doctor Primrose, in Goldsmith's "Vicar of Wakefield."

Primrose, Sophia. A beautiful daughter of Doctor Primrose, in "The Vicar of Wakefield."

Primrose, The Rev. Doctor. The vicar, in Goldsmith's "Vicar of Wakefield;" celebrated for the simplicity of his character, and for his support of the Whistonian theory in regard to marriage, that it is unlawful for a priest of the Church of England, after the death of his first wife, to take a second. His weaknesses, however, it has been well said, "only serve to endear him more closely to his readers; and when distress falls upon the virtuous household, the noble fortitude and resignation of the principal sufferer, and the efficacy of his example, form one of the most affecting and even sublime moral pictures."

☞ "What reader is there in the civilised world who is not the better for the story of the washes which the worthy Doctor Primrose demolished so deliberately with the poker; for the knowledge of the guinea which the Miss Primroses kept unchanged in their pockets; the adventure of the picture of the vicar's family, which could not be got into the house, and that of the Flamborough family, all painted with oranges in their hands; or for the story of the case of green spectacles and the cosmogony?" *Hazlitt.*

The Colonel bowed and smiled with very pleasant good-nature at our plaudits. It was like *Doctor Primrose* preaching his sermon in the prison. There was something touching in the *naïveté* and kindness of the placid and simple gentleman. *Thackeray.*

Prince Ah'med. A character in the "Arabian Nights' Entertainments," in the story of "Prince Ahmed and the fairy Paribanou." He purchases in Samarcand an artificial apple, the smell of which has power to cure all kinds of disorders. See PARIBANOU.

It proves only this; that laws have no magical or supernatural virtue; that laws do not act like . . . *Prince Ahmed's* apple. *Macaulay.*

Prince Alasnam. See ALASNAM.

Prince Beder. See QUEEN LABE.

Prince Cam′ḁ-ral′zā-măn. A character in the "Arabian Nights' Entertainments," in the story of "Prince Camaralzaman and the Princess Badoura."

As for Colonel Thomas Newcome and his niece, they fell in love with each other instantaneously, like *Prince Camaralzaman* and the princess of China. *Thackeray.*

Prince Cherry. [Fr. *Le Prince Chéri*, Prince Beloved.] The hero of a nursery story, originally written in French by Mme. D'Aunoy. He is represented as the sovereign of a great empire, who, for his cruelty and other vices, was transformed by a kind guardian fairy into a frightful monster, until he had learned to conquer his evil passions, and had proved himself worthy to wear his crown again.

Prince Hôus′sāin. A character in the story of "Prince Ahmed and the fairy Paribanou," in the "Arabian Nights' Entertainments;" the eldest brother of Prince Ahmed. He possessed a piece of carpeting of very indifferent appearance, but of such a wonderful quality that any one who simply sat on it could be transported in an instant whithersoever he desired.

Whether the rapid pace at which the fancy moveth in such exercitations, where the wish of the penman is to him like *Prince Houssain's* tapestry, in the Eastern fable, be the chief source of peril, — . . . this question belongeth not to me. *Sir W. Scott.*

He [Prince Le Boo] had lost all usual marks for comparing difficult and easy; and, if *Prince Houssain's* flying tapestry or Astolpho's hippogriff had been shown, he would have judged of them by the ordinary rules of convenience, and preferred a snug corner in a well-hung chariot. *Sir W. Scott.*

Prince of Artists. A title often given by the Germans to Albert Dürer (1471-1528), a celebrated painter, sculptor, and engraver. He is said to have invented the art of etching, and he carried wood-engraving to a degree of excellence that has hardly been surpassed.

Prince of Coxcombs. A sobriquet given to Charles Joseph, Prince de Ligne (1735-1814).

Prince of Darkness. A title often given to Satan.

The *Prince of Darkness* is a gentleman. *Shak.*

He was treated as one who, having sinned

☞ For the "Key to the Scheme of Pronunciation," with the accompanying Explanations,

against light, was, therefore, deservedly left a prey to the *Prince of Darkness. Sir W. Scott.*

Prince of Destruction. A name conferred upon Tamerlane, or Timour (1335-1405), one of the most celebrated of Oriental conquerors, who overran Persia, Tartary, and Hindostan, his conquests extending from the Volga to the Persian Gulf, and from the Ganges to the Archipelago. He was only prevented by the want of shipping from crossing into Europe. He died just as he was making vast preparations for the invasion of China. No conquests were ever attended with greater cruelty, devastation, and waste of life.

Prince of Grammarians. 1. See CORYPHÆUS OF GRAMMARIANS.
2. Apollonius of Alexandria (d. n. c. 240), denominated by Priscian, "Grammaticorum Princeps." He was the first who reduced grammar to a system.

Prince of Liars. An epithet applied to Ferdinand Mendez Pinto, a celebrated Portuguese traveller of the sixteenth century. He published an account of his travels, full of extravagant fictions, which have caused him to be classed with Munchausen. The epithet was originally conferred upon him by Cervantes.

Prince of Peace. A title often given to the Saviour, who came "not to destroy men's lives, but to save them," and who proclaimed, "Blessed are the peace-makers; for they shall be called the children of God." See *Isa.* ix. 6.

Prince of Physicians. A title given to Avicenna (980-1037), a famous Arabian philosopher and physician. His system, a kind of logical alchemy, was founded on the supposition that the operations of nature are in perfect correlation with those of the human spirit.

Prince of Poets. A name sometimes given to Edmund Spenser (1553-1598), the admired author of the "Faëry Queen." He is so termed in the inscription on his monument in Westminster Abbey; and though, at the present day, the fitness of the appellation may be doubted, it is thought by some that "his poetry is the most poetical of all poetry."

Prince of Spanish Poetry. A name often applied to Garcilaso de la Vega (1503-1536), a celebrated Spanish poet, for whom his countrymen express an admiration such as they give to none of his predecessors, and to few of those who have lived since his time. It occurs repeatedly in Cervantes.

☞ "This title, which can be traced back to Herrera, and has been continued down to our own times, has, perhaps, rarely been taken literally." *Ticknor.*

Prince of the Apostles. An honorary title bestowed upon St. Peter, from the supposed pre-eminence ascribed to him in *Matt.* xvi. 18, 19, — upon which verses the claims of the Roman Catholic church are founded. In the plural, the expression is applied to St. Peter and St. Paul.

The Irish, regardless of the true history of Patricius, want to make St. Patrick a namesake of St. Peter, and make all their Paddies own not only their national apostle, but the *Prince of Apostles,* for their patrons. *Yonge.*

Prince of the Ode. A title given to Pierre de Ronsard (1524-1585), a celebrated French lyric poet.

Prince of the Peace. A title given, in 1795, by Charles IV. of Spain to his prime minister, Don Manuel de Godoy (1767-1851), on account of his separating Spain from England, and forming an offensive and defensive alliance with France, the same year, after having previously declared war against the latter country.

Prince of the Power of the Air. A name given to Satan in *Eph.* ii. 2: "Wherein in time past ye walked according to the course of this world, according to the prince of the power of the air, the spirit that now worketh in the children of disobedience."

Prince of the Sonnet. A title bestowed upon Joachim du Bellay (1524-1560), a distinguished French poet.

Prince Prettyman. A character in the Duke of Buckingham's farce,

"The Rehearsal," in love with Cloris. He figures sometimes as a fisher's son, sometimes as a prince, much to his own distress. He is said to have been intended as a parody upon the character of Leonidas in Dryden's "Marriage à-la-Mode."

Prince Prettyman, now a prince, and now a fisher's son, had not a more awkward sense of his degradation. — *Sir W. Scott.*

Princess Fair-Star. [Fr. *La Princesse Belle-Étoile.*] The lady-love of Prince Cherry. See PRINCE CHERRY.

Prince Vol'sci-us. A military hero in Buckingham's play, "The Rehearsal." He falls in love with a fair damsel named Parthenope, and disputes with Prince Prettyman about her, maintaining her superiority to Cloris, the latter's sweetheart.

Unlikely as it all was, I could not help suspecting from the beginning that there was a girl in the case. Why, this is worse than *Prince Volscius* in love! — *Sir W. Scott.*

Prisoner of Chil'lŏn (*Fr. pron.* shē'-yŏn', 62, 82). An appellation sometimes given to François de Bonnivard (1496-1570), a Frenchman residing in Geneva, who made himself obnoxious to Charles III., duke of Savoy, — who had become in a manner master of Geneva, — and was immured by him for six years in a dungeon of the Château-de-Chillon, a fortified castle at the eastern end of the Lake of Geneva. At the expiration of that time, he was released by the Bernese, who were at war with Savoy, and had gained possession of the fortress. On the fact of Bonnivard's imprisonment here, and on certain traditions of the residents in the vicinity, Byron founded his affecting narrative poem of "The Prisoner of Chillon;" but the additional circumstance of two brothers of Bonnivard having been imprisoned with him, and dying in consequence of their confinement and sufferings, has no foundation except in the imagination of the poet, and was probably suggested by Dante's Count Ugolino and his two sons. See UGOLINO.

Priuli (pre-oo'lee). A character in Otway's tragedy of "Venice Preserved;" noted for his pride, and his harsh, unnatural cruelty to his daughter.

Priwen. See PRIDWIN.

Pro'cris. [Gr. Πρόκρις.] (*Gr. & Rom. Myth.*) A daughter of Erechtheus, king of Athens, and wife of Cephalus, who shot her in a wood, having mistaken her for a wild beast. She was turned into a star by Jupiter.

Pro-crus'tēṣ. [Gr. Προκρούστης, the stretcher.] (*Gr. & Rom. Myth.*) The surname of a noted highwayman of Attica, named Polypemon, or Damastes. He used to tie travellers who fell into his hands upon a bed, and accommodate them to the length of it by stretching or lopping off their limbs, as the case required.

Profound Doctor. [Lat. *Doctor Profundus.*] 1. A title given to Thomas Bradwardine (d. 1349), archbishop of Canterbury, and one of the most distinguished and learned of the English schoolmen.

2. An appellation of Richard Middleton (d. 1304), an English scholastic divine. See SOLID DOCTOR.

Prog'ne. [Gr. Πρόκνη.] (*Gr. & Rom. Myth.*) The daughter of the Athenian king Pandion, the sister of Philomela, and the wife of Tereus; changed into a swallow by the gods. See TEREUS.

Pro-me'theûs (28). [Gr. Προμηθεύς.] (*Gr. & Rom. Myth.*) A son of Iapetus and Clymene, the brother of Epimetheus, and the father of Deucalion. He made men of clay, and animated them by means of fire which he stole from heaven; for this he was chained by Jupiter to Mount Caucasus, where an eagle, or, as some say, a vulture, preyed by day upon his liver, which grew again by night. See PANDORA.

Like the thief of fire from heaven
Wilt thou withstand the shock,
And share with him, the unforgiven,
His vulture and his rock.
Byron, Ode to Napoleon.

Promised Land. A name often given to Canaan, or that portion of Palestine lying west of the river Jordan, which was repeatedly promised

☞ For the "Key to the Scheme of Pronunciation," with the accompanying Explanations,

by Jehovah to the patriarchs Abraham, Isaac, and Jacob. See *Gen.* xii. 7, xiii. 15, xxviii. 13, xxxv. 12.

Prophet of the Syrians. A title given to Ephraem Syrus (d. 378), a celebrated father of the Church of the Antiochian school.

Pros'ĕr-pĭne. [Lat. *Proserpina*, Gr. Περσεφόνη.] (*Gr. & Rom. Myth.*) The daughter of Jupiter and Ceres, and wife of Pluto, who carried her off to the under-world as she was gathering flowers in Sicily. See PLUTO.

> Forgive, if somewhile I forget,
> In woe to come, the present bliss;
> As frighted *Proserpine* let fall
> Her flowers at sight of Dis. *Hood.*

Prosperity Rob'in-son (-sn). A nickname given to Frederick Robinson (afterwards Viscount Goderich and Earl of Ripon), chancellor of the exchequer in 1823. Just before the commercial crisis which occurred in 1825, he boasted of the great prosperity of the country, derived, he said, from the vast number of joint-stock companies, which, he argued, showed a superabundance of wealth. The general financial distress and ruin which occurred shortly after, and which amounted almost to national bankruptcy, proved the fallacy of the chancellor's opinion; whereupon Cobbett gave him the sobriquet of "Prosperity Robinson." [Called also *Goosey Goderich.*]

Pros'pe-ro. One of the principal characters in Shakespeare's "Tempest." Prospero is the rightful duke of Milan, who, having been dispossessed of his dukedom by his brother Antonio and the king of Naples, is carried to sea, and there set adrift with his daughter Miranda, in a "rotten carcass of a boat." He fortunately reaches an uninhabited island, where he betakes himself to the practice of magic (an art which he had studied in Milan); and, having raised a tempest, in which Antonio, the king of Naples, and others, are completely shipwrecked upon the island, he secretly subjects them to many discomforts by way of punishment, but finally discovers himself, forgives his brother and the king, and provides for their safe and speedy return, with that of their followers, accompanying them himself, with his daughter, of whom Ferdinand, the king's son, has already become enamoured. This done, Prospero renounces his magic arts.

☞ "Prospero, with his magical powers, his superhuman wisdom, his moral worth and grandeur, and his kingly dignity, is one of the most sublime visions that ever swept, with ample robes, pale brow, and sceptred hand, before the eye of fancy. He controls the invisible world, and works through the agency of spirits, not by any evil and forbidden compact, but solely by superior might of intellect, by potent spells gathered from the lore of ages, and abjured when he mingles again as a man with his fellow-men. He is as distinct a being from the necromancers and astrologers celebrated in Shakespeare's age as can well be imagined; and all the wizards of poetry and fiction, even Faust and St. Leon, sink into commonplaces before the princely, the philosophic, the benevolent Prospero." *Mrs. Jameson.*

Although he [Maturin] has threatened, like *Prospero*, to break his wand, we have done our poor endeavour to save his book from being burned. *Sir W. Scott.*

His existence was a bright, soft element of joy, out of which, as in *Prospero's* island, wonder after wonder bodied itself forth, to teach by charming. *Carlyle.*

Pro-tes'ĭ-lā'us. [Gr. Πρωτεσίλαος.] (*Gr. & Rom. Myth.*) A son of Iphicles, and the husband of Laodamia. He went to the siege of Troy, and was the first who landed, but fell by the hand of Hector. His dead body being sent home to Laodamia, she prayed to be allowed to converse with him for three hours only. Her prayer was granted, Mercury conducted Protesilaus to the upper world, and, when he died a second time, Laodamia expired with him.

Protestant Duke. A name given by his contemporary admirers to James, Duke of Monmouth (1619–1685), a natural son of Charles II. Though brought up as a Catholic, he embraced Protestantism, and became the idol of the English people, — especially of the Non-conformists, — and a formidable rival of the Duke of York (afterward James II.), whose

Catholicism and arbitrary disposition rendered him very unpopular.

Protestant Pope. An appellation conferred upon Pope Clement XIV. (Gian Vincenzo Ganganelli, 1705–1774), a pontiff distinguished for his enlightened and liberal policy, and for his Bull suppressing the Jesuits.

Pro'teūs (28). [Gr. Πρωτεύς.] 1. (*Gr. & Rom. Myth.*) A sea-god, son of Oceanus and Tethys, residing usually in the Carpathian Sea, between Rhodes and Crete. He possessed the gift of prophecy, and also the power of changing himself into different shapes.

> He [Voltaire] was all fire and fickleness; a child,
> Most mutable in wishes, but in mind
> A wit as various, — gay, grave, sage, or wild, —
> Historian, bard, philosopher, combined;
> He multiplied himself among mankind,
> The *Proteus* of their talents. *Byron.*

2. One of the "Two Gentlemen of Verona," in Shakespeare's play of that name.

Proud Duke. A name proverbially given to Charles Seymour, Duke of Somerset, who died on the 12th of August, 1748, and who was noted for his boundless pride, and the fantastic exhibitions which he used to make of his title and station. It is said that he would never suffer any of his children to sit in his presence, and that to his servants he deigned to speak only by signs.

Proud'fute, Oliver. A boasting bonnet-maker, in Sir Walter Scott's "Fair Maid of Perth."

Prudhomme, M. (mos'e-ō' prü'dōm', 34, 43). A character created by Henry Monier; a professor of penmanship, sworn appraiser, &c.

Prudoterie, Mme. de la (prü'dōt're', 34). A character in Molière's comedy of "George Dandin."

Pry, Paul. The title of a well-known comedy by John Poole, and the name of its principal character, "one of those idle, meddling fellows, who, having no employment themselves, are perpetually interfering in other people's affairs."

> He [Boswell] was a slave proud of his servitude, a *Paul Pry*, convinced that his own curiosity and garrulity were virtues. *Macaulay.*

Prynne, Hester. A character in Hawthorne's romance, "The Scarlet Letter," whose singular punishment gives name to the story.

Psy'çhe (si'ke, 26). [Gr. ψυχή, breath, spirit, soul.] (*Gr. & Rom. Myth.*) A beautiful maiden beloved by Cupid, who visited her only in the night, and warned her not to seek to know who he was. She violated the injunction, and happening to let a drop of hot oil from the lamp she had lighted fall upon his shoulder, he awoke, upbraided her for her mistrust, and vanished. He finally forgave her, however, and they were united in immortal wedlock.

Public Good, League of the. See LEAGUE OF THE PUBLIC GOOD.

Pub'li-us. A *nom de plume* under which Alexander Hamilton (1757–1804) wrote his celebrated contributions to "The Federalist."

Pu-celle', La (*Fr. pron.* pü'sel', 34). [Fr., the Maid.] A surname given to the celebrated Joan of Arc (1410–1431). See MAID OF ORLEANS.

Puck. Originally, the name of a fiend; subsequently, the name for that "merry wanderer of the night," styled also *Robin Goodfellow*, who plays so conspicuous a part in Shakespeare's "Midsummer-Night's Dream." *Pug*, in Ben Jonson's play called "The Devil is an Ass," is evidently the same person, though Jonson makes him a goblin or fiend, and not a fairy. See GOODFELLOW, ROBIN.

> ☞ "In truth, it is first in Shakespeare that we find Puck confounded with the house spirit, and having those traits of character which are now regarded as his very essence, and have caused his name Pug to be given to the agile, mischievous monkey, and to a kind of little dog." *Keightley.*

> ☞ "Who that has read the play ['A Midsummer Night's Dream'] (and who has not?) cannot call the urchin before his mind's eye as instantly as Oberon commanded his real presence, — a rough,

---

☞ For the "Key to the Scheme of Pronunciation," with the accompanying Explanations,

knurly-limbed, faun-faced, shock-pated little fellow, a very Shetlander among the gossamer-winged, dainty-limbed shapes around him, and strong enough to knock all their heads together for his elvish sport?" *R. G. White.*

The mirth of Swift is the mirth of Mephistopheles; the mirth of Voltaire is the mirth of *Puck*. *Macaulay.*

Pudding, Jack. A zany; a Merry-andrew; a buffoon; a clown. See HANSWURST.

☞ "A buffoon is called by every nation by the name of the dish they like best; in French, Jean Potage, and in English, *Jack Pudding.*" *Guardian.*

Ills [Addison's] tone is never that either of a *Jack Pudding* or of a cynic. *Macaulay.*

Puff. A bold and impudent literary quack, who figures in Sheridan's farce of "The Critic."

Perhaps not,—but what then? I may have seen her picture, as *Puff* says, ... or fallen in love with her from rumour. *Sir W. Scott.*

Mrs. Radcliffe is, indeed, too lavish of her landscapes, and her readers have frequent occasion to lament that she did not follow the example of Mr. *Puff* in the play,—"I open with a clock striking, to beget an awful attention in the audience; it also marks the time, which is four o'clock in the morning, and saves a description of the rising sun, and a great deal about gilding the eastern hemisphere." *Dunlop.*

Pum'ble-chook, Uncle. A character in Dickens's "Great Expectations," who bullied Pip—the hero of the story—when he was a poor boy, and fawned on him when he had a prospect of becoming rich. He is noted for saying, "Might I, Mr. Pip, —May I,—" (*scilicet*, shake hands).

Punch, *or* **Pǔnch'ĭ-nel'lo.** A humourous character in a species of puppet-show exhibited on the Italian stage and in the streets of European cities. In person he is short and fat, with an enormous hump on his back, a wide mouth, long chin, and hooked nose. His dress consists of wide drawers of white woollen, and a large upper garment of the same material, with wide sleeves, fastened with a black leather belt or hair cord. This upper garment is sprinkled over with hearts of red cloth, and is trimmed round the bottom with a fringe. Around his neck he wears a linen ruffle, and on his head a tall, three-pointed cap terminating in a red tuft. The modern puppet-show of "Punch and Judy" embodies a domestic tragedy, followed by a supernatural retribution, the whole of which is treated in a broadly farcical manner.

☞ The name Punch, or Punchinello, is supposed to be a corruption of *Policinello*, or *Pulcinello*, which, in turn, according to Gallani in his "Vocabolario del Dialetto Napoletano," was derived from *Puccio d'Aniello*, a peasant, whose humourous eccentricities were, in the seventeenth century, transferred to the Neapolitan stage, where he has continued to be the medium of local and political satire, and a favourite conventional character in the Italian exhibitions of *fantoccini*, or puppet-shows.

Pure, Simon. The name of a Pennsylvania Quaker in Mrs. Centlivre's comedy, "A Bold Stroke for a Wife." Being about to visit London to attend the quarterly meeting of his sect, his friend, Aminadab Holdfast, sends a letter of recommendation and introduction to another Quaker, Obadiah Prim, a rigid and stern man, who is guardian of Anne Lovely, a young lady worth £30,000. Colonel Feignwell, another character in the same play, who is enamoured of Miss Lovely and her handsome fortune, availing himself of an accidental discovery of Holdfast's letter and of its contents, succeeds in passing himself off on Prim as his expected visitor. The real Simon Pure, calling at Prim's house, is treated as an impostor, and is obliged to depart in order to hunt up witnesses who can testify to his identity. Meantime, Feignwell succeeds in getting from Prim a written and unconditional consent to his marriage with Anne. No sooner has he obtained possession of the document, than Simon Pure re-appears with his witnesses, and Prim discovers the trick that has been put upon him.

I believe that many who took the trouble of thinking upon the subject were rather of the opinion that my ingenious friend was the true, and not the fictitious, *Simon Pure*. *Sir W. Scott.*

Purgatory, St. Patrick's. See ST. PATRICK'S PURGATORY.

---

and for the Remarks and Rules to which the numbers after certain words refer, see pp. xiv-xxxii.

Puritan, The Platonic. See PLATONIC PURITAN.

Puritan City. A by-name sometimes given to the city of Boston, Massachusetts, in allusion to the character of its founders and inhabitants.

Purple Island. The subject and title of a long and grotesque allegorical poem by Phineas Fletcher, published in 1633; the Purple Island representing the human body, and the poem being in great part a system of anatomy.

Puss in Boots. [Fr. *Le Chat Botté*.] The hero of an old and popular nursery tale of the same name, written by Perrault; a marvellously accomplished cat, who, by his ready wit and ingenious tricks, secures a fortune and a royal consort for his master, a penniless young miller, who passes under the name of the Marquis of Carabas. This story is taken from the first of the eleventh night of Straparola, where the cat of Constantine procures his master a fine castle and the heiress of a king. The Germans and the Scandinavians have a nursery tale very similar to this. See CARABAS, MARQUIS OF.

Like *Puss in Boots*, after the nuptials of his master, Jackeymo only now caught minnows and sticklebacks for his own amusement. *Sir E. Bulwer Lytton.*

Pyg-mā'li-ŏn. [Gr. Πυγμαλίων.] (*Gr. & Rom. Myth.*) 1. A grandson of Agenor. He made a beautiful statue, which he fell so deeply in love with, that Venus, at his earnest petition gave it life.

2. A son of Belus, and king of Tyre, who slew his brother-in-law, Sichæus, — the husband of Dido, — for his riches.

Pygmies. [Lat. *Pygmæi*, Gr. Πυγμαῖοι.] (*Gr. & Rom. Myth.*) A nation of dwarfs, only a span high, who dwelt on the banks of the upper Nile. They were warred on and defeated every spring by the cranes.

Pў-lā'dĕṣ. [Gr. Πυλάδης.] (*Gr. &*
Rom. Myth.) A friend of Orestes, celebrated for the constancy of his affection. See ORESTES.

You seem to have conceived, my lord, that you and I were *Pylades* and *Orestes*, — a second edition of Damon and Pythias, — Theseus and Pirithous, at the least. You are mistaken. *Sir W. Scott.*

Pȳr'ȧ-mus. [Gr. Πύραμος.] (*Gr. & Rom. Myth.*) The lover of Thisbe, who, on account of her supposed death, stabbed himself under a mulberry-tree. Thisbe, afterward, finding the body of her lover, killed herself on the same spot with the same weapon; and the fruit of the mulberry has ever since been as red as blood. See THISBE.

☞ In Shakespeare's "Midsummer-Night's Dream," he is introduced as one of the characters in a burlesque interlude.

Pȳr'go-pol'ĭ-ni'cēṣ (4). [Lat., tower-town-taker, from Gr. πύργος, tower, πόλις, city, town, and νικᾶν, to conquer, vanquish, νικητής, a victor.] The name of the hero — an extravagant blusterer — in Plautus's "Miles Gloriosus."

If he [the modern reader] knows nothing of *Pyrgopolinices* and Thraso, he is familiar with Bobadil and Bessus, and Pistol and Parolles. If he is shut out from Nephelococcygia, he may take refuge in Lilliput. *Macaulay.*

Pȳr'rhȧ (pĭr'rȧ). [Gr. Πύρρα.] (*Gr. & Rom. Myth.*) A daughter of Epimetheus, and wife of her cousin Deucalion. See DEUCALION.

Pȳr'rhus (pĭr'rus). [Gr. Πύρρος.] (*Gr. & Rom. Myth.*) A son of Achilles and Deïdamia, remarkable for his cruelty at the siege of Troy. He was slain at Delphi, at the request of his own wife, by Orestes. [Called also *Neoptolemus*.]

Pȳth'ĭ-ȧs. A friend of Damon. See DAMON, 1.

Pȳ'thŏn. [Gr. Πύθων.] (*Gr. & Rom. Myth.*) A huge serpent engendered from the mud of the deluge of Deucalion, and slain near Delphi by Apollo, who, in memory thereof, instituted the Pythian games.

Q.

Quadrangle, *or* **Quadrilateral, The.** A name given to four strong Austrian fortresses in northern Italy, which mutually support each other, and form a barrier that divides the north plain of the Po into two sections. These fortresses are, 1. Peschiera, on an island in the Mincio, near the lake of Garda; 2. Mantua, on the Mincio; 3. Verona; and 4. Legnago; — the last two on the Adige.

Quadruple Alliance. (*Hist.*) An alliance between Great Britain, France, the emperor of Germany (Charles VI.), and the United Provinces of Holland, for the purpose of guaranteeing the succession of the reigning families in Great Britain and France, and settling the partition of the Spanish monarchy. It was originated by Great Britain and France, and was signed at Paris, July 7, 1718. The emperor acceded to it on the 22d of the same month, and the United Provinces on the 8th of February, 1719.

Quaker City. A popular name of Philadelphia, which was planned and settled by William Penn, accompanied by a colony of English Friends.

Quaker Poet. 1. A common designation of Bernard Barton (1784–1849), an English poet of some note, and a member of the society of Friends.
2. A name often given to John Greenleaf Whittier (b. 1807), a member of the society of Friends, and an eminent and peculiarly national American poet.

Quarll, Philip. The hero of a work entitled "The Hermit, or The Sufferings and Adventures of Philip Quarll, an Englishman." The story is an imitation of "Robinson Crusoe," with the substitution of an affectionate ape or chimpanzee for Man Friday. The book was first published in 1727, and has been frequently reprinted.

Quăsh'ee (kwŏsh'ee). A cant name given to any negro, or to the negro race; — said to be derived from Quassi, or Quasha, a black man of Surinam, by whom the medicinal virtues of one species of the quassia plant were made known to the Swedish naturalist Rolander, about the middle of the last century.

Quasimodo (kü-ä'ze'mo'do', 34). [Fr.] A foundling adopted by Frollo, in Victor Hugo's "Notre-Dame de Paris;" a man of great strength, but a complete monster of deformity, without one redeeming grace. The name is used popularly and generically to designate any hideously deformed man.

Quatre-Filz-Aymon, Les (lä kä'tr-fĕz-ä'mōⁿ'). See AYMON.

Queen City. A popular name of Cincinnati; — given to it when it was the undisputed commercial metropolis of the West. See QUEEN OF THE WEST.

Queen City of the Lakes. A name sometimes given to the city of Buffalo, New York, from its position and importance.

Queen Lâbe. A magic queen, ruling over the City of Enchantments, in the story of "Beder, Prince of Persia," in the "Arabian Nights' Entertainments." By her diabolic art, she transforms men into horses, mules, and other animals. Beder marries her, defeats her plots against him, turns her into a mare, and takes her to a distance; there she is restored to her own shape, and, by the assistance of her mother, turns the tables upon the young prince, and changes him into an owl; but, after some adventures, he escapes their vengeance.

☞ "Queen Labe, with her lovers turned into various animals, reminds one strongly of the Homeric Circe; and I think it not at all impossible that Grecian fable may have penetrated into Persia." *Keightley.*

Queen of Cities. One of the names popularly given to Rome. See SEVEN-HILLED CITY.

Queen of Hearts. Elizabeth, the daughter of James I., and the unfortunate queen of Bohemia. So engaging was her behaviour, that in the Low Countries she was called the Queen of Hearts. When her fortunes were at the lowest ebb, she never departed from her dignity; and poverty and distress seemed to have no other effect upon her than to render her more an object of admiration than before.

Queen of Queens. A title given by Antony to Cleopatra (B. C. 69–30), the last sovereign of the dynasty of the Ptolemies in Egypt.

Queen of Tears. A name given to Mary of Modena, the second wife of James II. of England. "Her eyes," says Noble, "became eternal fountains of sorrow for that crown her own ill policy contributed to lose."

Queen of the Antilles (an-teelz'). An appellation sometimes given to Cuba, which, from its great size, its rich natural productions, its fine harbours, its varied and beautiful scenery, and its commanding geographical position, ranks first among all the islands of the West Indian group.

Queen of the East. 1. A title assumed by Zenobia, queen of Palmyra, on the death of her husband Odenatus (A. D. 267).

2. A name given to Antioch, the ancient capital of Syria, the residence of the Macedonian kings and the Roman governors, and long celebrated as one of the first cities of the East.

3. In modern times, a name sometimes given to Batavia, in Java, capital of the Dutch possessions in the East.

Queen of the Eastern Archipelago. A popular appellation of Java, one of the most beautiful and fertile islands of the East Indian group, and commercially the most important of them all.

Queen of the North. A name sometimes given to Edinburgh, the capital of Scotland.

Queen of the West. A name sometimes given to Cincinnati. See QUEEN CITY.

And this Song of the Vine,
This greeting of mine,
The winds and the birds shall deliver
To the *Queen of the West*,
In her garlands dressed,
On the banks of the Beautiful River.
Longfellow.

Queen Scheherezade. See SCHEHEREZADE, QUEEN.

Quern-biter (kwĕrn'bĭt'ẽr, 4). A famous sword of Hako I. of Norway, surnamed "The Good."

Quern-biter of Hakon the Good,
Wherewith at a stroke he hewed
The millstone through and through,
And Foot-breadth of Thoralf the Strong,
Were neither so broad nor so long,
Nor so true. *Longfellow.*

Que-u'bus, Equinoctial of. An expression which occurs in Shakespeare's "Twelfth Night" (a. ii., sc. 3); but what is meant by it is not known. Leigh Hunt says, "some glorious torrid zone lying beyond three o'clock in the morning." See PIGROGROMITUS.

Queux. See KAY, SIR.

Quickly, Mrs. 1. A servant to Dr. Caius, in Shakespeare's "Merry Wives of Windsor."

The controversy has been maintained with great warmth; we leave it with the prudent resolution of *Dame Quickly*, "We will not burn our fingers, and need not, indeed, la!" *Edin. Rev.*

2. The hostess of a tavern in Eastcheap, in the First and Second Parts of Shakespeare's "King Henry the Fourth."

Shakespeare knew innumerable things; what men are, and what the world is, and what men aim at there, from the *Dame Quickly* of modern Eastcheap to the Cæsar of ancient Rome. *Carlyle.*

Quilp. A hideous dwarf, full of ferocity and cunning, in Dickens's "Old Curiosity Shop."

Quince, Peter. A carpenter, in Shakespeare's "Midsummer-Night's Dream."

This is indeed "very tragical mirth," as Peter Quince's play-bill has it; and we would

☞ For the "Key to the Scheme of Pronunciation," with the accompanying Explanations,

not advise any person who reads for amusement to venture on it as long as he can procure a volume of the Statutes at Large.
Macaulay.

Quintessence, Queen (kwint′essenss; *Fr. pron.* kän′tes′sŏⁿss′, 62). A character in Rabelais' romance of "Pantagruel;" represented as ruling over the kingdom of Entéléchie. See ENTÉLÉCHIE.

Quin′tus Fixlein. The title of a romance by Jean Paul Friedrich Richter, and the name of its principal character.

Francia, like *Quintus Fixlein*, had "perennial fire-proof joys, namely, employments.".
Carlyle.

Qui-ri′nus. [Lat., from *quiris*, or *curis*, a Sabine word signifying *a spearman*.] (*Rom. Myth.*) A name given, after his deification, to Romulus, the reputed founder of Rome. See ROMULUS.

Quisada (ke-sä′thä, 56). The same as *Don Quixote,* of which name two derivations are given. See DON QUIXOTE.

Nevertheless, noble R——, come in, and take your seat here, between Armado and *Quisada;* for, in true courtesy, in gravity, in fantastic smiling to thyself, in courteous smiling upon others, in the goodly ornature of well-apparelled speech, and the commendation of wise sentences, thou art nothing inferior to those accomplished Dons of Spain.
Charles Lamb.

Quixote, Don. See DON QUIXOTE.

Quix′ọte of the North. An appellation sometimes bestowed upon Charles XII. of Sweden (1682–1718), on account of the rash impetuosity of his character. See MADMAN OF THE NORTH.

Quo′tem, Caleb. A parish clerk, and a Jack-at-all-trades, in Colman's play entitled "The Review, or The Wags of Windsor."

I had sworn to be there, and I determined to keep my oath, and, like *Caleb Quotem*, to "have a place at the review." *W. Irving.*

R.

Rabelais, The English. See ENGLISH RABELAIS.

Rabelais, The Modern. See MODERN RABELAIS.

Rabicano (rä-be-kä′no). The name of Argalia's steed in Bojardo's "Orlando Innamorato."

Rā′bў, Aurora. A character in the fifteenth and sixteenth cantos of Byron's "Don Juan."

Rack′rent, Sir Con′dў. A character in Miss Edgeworth's novel, "Castle Rackrent.

Like *Sir Condy Rackrent* in the tale, she [Madame d'Arblay] survived her own wake, and overheard the judgment of posterity.
Macaulay.

Ragnarŏk (rȧg′nȧ-rök, 46). [Old Norse *Ragnarökr*, twilight of the gods.] (*Scand. Myth.*) The "last day," the period of the destruction of the universe, when the whole creation, mankind, giants, and gods, are to perish in a shower of fire and blood. Vidar and Vali alone will survive the general conflagration, and will reconstruct the universe on an imperishable basis. [Written also **Ragnaröck.**]

Belleisle — little as Belleisle dreamt of it, in these high enterprises — was ushering in a *Ragnarök*, or Twilight of the Gods, which, as "French Revolution, or Apotheosis of Sansculottism," is now well known. *Carlyle.*

Railroad City. Indianapolis, the capital of the State of Indiana, is sometimes called by this name, as being the terminus of various railroads.

Rail-Splitter, The. A popular designation of Abraham Lincoln (1809–1865), the sixteenth president of the United States, who is said to have supported himself for one winter, in early life, by splitting rails for a farmer.

Railway King, The. A title popularly given in England to Mr. George Hudson (b. 1800), of York, one of the most daring and celebrated speculators of modern times. He is said to have made, in one instance, £100,000 in one day. Since 1859, he has resided on the Continent, in comparatively narrow circumstances.

☞ " In 1839 he became chairman of the York and North Midland Corporation, and, by his indefatigable industry and his shrewdness in matters of business, he soon gained an important and influential position as a railway-man. The shares in all the lines of which he was chairman went to a premium; large dividends were declared; share-holders and directors recognised his power, — and thus he shortly found himself at the head of six hundred miles of railways, and of numerous new projects by means of which paper wealth could he created, as it were, at pleasure. He held in his own hands almost the entire administrative power of the companies over which he presided; he was chairman, board, manager, and all. He was voted praises, testimonials, and surplus shares alike liberally; and scarcely a word against him could find a hearing. He was equally popular outside the circle of railway proprietors. His entertainments were crowded; and he went his round of visits among the peerage like any prince. Of course, Mr. Hudson was a great authority on railway questions in parliament, to which the burgesses of Sunderland had sent him. In the session of 1845, when he was at the height of his power, it was triumphantly said of him, that 'he walked quietly through parliament with some sixteen railway bills under his arm.' But his reign was drawing rapidly to a close. The railway mania of 1845 was followed by a sudden reaction. Shares went down faster than they had gone up; the holders of them hastened to sell, in order to avoid payment of the calls; and the fortunes of many were utterly wrecked. The stockholders were all grievously enraged, and looked about them for a victim. At a railway meeting in York, some pertinent questions were put to the Railway King. His replies were not satisfactory, and the questions were pushed home. Mr. Hudson became confused. A committee of investigation was appointed, and the gilded idol of the railway world was straightway dethroned. A howl of execration arose from his deluded followers; and those who had bowed the lowest before him during his brief reign, hissed the loudest when he fell." *Smiles.*

Ralph. 1. An Independent clerk, the

[☞ For the "Key to the Scheme of Pronunciation," with the accompanying Explanations,

attendant of Hudibras, in Butler's celebrated burlesque poem. See HUDIBRAS. [Called also *Ralpho*.]

> Yet he [Johnson] was himself under the tyranny of scruples as unreasonable as those of . . . Ralpho. *Macaulay*.

2. The name of a spirit formerly supposed to haunt printing-houses.

Raminagrobis (rä'me-nä'gro'be'). The name of one of the characters in Rabelais' romance of "Pantagruel;" described as an old French poet who was almost at death's-door. He is said to have been intended for Crétin, an author of high repute in his own day, though utterly neglected by posterity.

Ramsbottom, Mrs. The imaginary author of a celebrated series of letters which appeared in the "John Bull," a London newspaper, commenced in 1820. These letters were written by the editor, Theodore Hook, who, following the example of Smollett's Winifred Jenkins, managed by bad spelling to excite the merriment usually elicited by humourous writing.

Random, Rod'ĕr-ick. The title of a novel by Smollett, and the name of its hero, a young Scotsman in quest of fortune, who at one time revels in prosperity, and at another is plunged into utter destitution. Although he is represented as having a dash of generosity and good-humour in his character, he is equally conspicuous for reckless libertinism and mischief, — more prone to selfishness and revenge than disposed to friendship or gratitude. He borrows the money, and wears the clothes, of his simple and kind-hearted adherent, Strap, by whom he is rescued from starving, and whom he rewards by squandering his substance, receiving his attendance as a servant, and beating him when the dice run against him.

Ranger. 1. A young gentleman of the town, in Wycherley's comedy of "Love in a Wood."
2. The leading character in Hoadley's comedy of "The Suspicious Husband."

Ra'phȧ-el (*colloq.* rā'fel). [Heb., remedy or physic of God, in allusion to the cures he performed on Sara and Tobit.] The name of an angel mentioned in the Apocryphal book of *Tobit* as travelling with Tobias into Media and back again, and instructing him how to marry Sara, and how to drive away the wicked spirit. Milton calls him "the sociable spirit," and "the affable archangel," and represents him as sent by God to Adam "to admonish him of his obedience, of his free estate, of his enemy near at hand, who he is, and why his enemy, and whatever else may avail Adam to know." See ASMODEUS.

Răph'ȧ-el of Cats. An epithet bestowed upon Godefroi Mind (1768–1814), a Swiss painter, famous for his skill in painting cats.

Rare Ben Jonson. A famous appellation conferred upon Ben Jonson (1574–1637), the dramatic poet. It is said, that, soon after his death, a subscription was commenced for the purpose of erecting a monument to his memory; but, the undertaking having advanced slowly, an eccentric Oxfordshire squire took the opportunity, on passing one day through Westminster Abbey, to secure at least an epitaph for the poet, by giving a mason 18*d.* to cut, on the stone which covered the grave, the words, "O rare Ben Jonson."

Rash'leigh (rash'li). A hypocritical and accomplished villain in Sir Walter Scott's novel of "Rob Roy;" one of the Obaldistone family.

Rä'si-el. The name of an angel spoken of in the Talmud as the tutor of Adam.

Ras'se-lȧs. The title of a celebrated romance by Dr. Johnson, and the name of its hero, an imaginary prince of Abyssinia.

Ratt'lin, Jack. A celebrated naval character in Smollett's "Adventures of Roderick Random."

Rä'veng-wŏŏd. The hero of Sir Walter Scott's novel of "The Bride of Lammermoor;" a Scottish royalist, intrepid, haughty, and revengeful.

Rawhead. In the popular superstition of former days, the name of a spectre or bugbear. [Called also *Rawhead-and-bloody-bones.*]

Servants awe children, and keep them in subjection, by telling them of *Rawhead-and-bloody-bones*. *Locke.*

In short, he became the bugbear of every house; and was as effectual in frightening little children into obedience and hysterics as the redoubtable *Rawhead-and-bloody-bones* himself. *W. Irving.*

Reason, Goddess of. A personification of those intellectual powers which distinguish man from the rest of the animal creation; deified in 1793 by the revolutionists of France, and substituted as an object of worship for the divine beings of the Christian faith. It was decreed that the metropolitan church of Notre-Dame should be converted into a Temple of Reason; and a festival was instituted for the first day of each decade, to supersede the Catholic ceremonies of Sunday. The first festival of this sort was held with great pomp on the 10th of November. A young woman, the wife of Momoro, a well-known printer, represented the Goddess of Reason. She was dressed in white drapery; an azure mantle hung from her shoulders; and her flowing hair was surmounted with the cap of liberty. She sat upon an antique seat, entwined with ivy, and borne by four citizens. Young girls dressed in white, and crowned with roses, preceded and followed her. The services of the occasion consisted of speeches, processions, and patriotic hymns.

Rebecca. A name assumed by the leader of the Rebeccaites, a band of Welsh rioters, who, in 1843, exasperated by the heavy and vexatious tolls to which they were subjected, undertook to demolish the gates and toll-houses upon the turnpikes in the rural districts of Pembrokeshire and Caermarthenshire, and who afterward committed various excesses throughout the mining and manufacturing districts of the principality. The crusade had begun as early as 1830, but did not assume the shape of a system and organisation until 1843. The name was derived from a strange and preposterous application of the following passage in Genesis (xxiv. 60):—"And they blessed Rebekah, and said unto her, . . . let thy seed possess the gate of those which hate them." The captain of the rioters disguised himself in female apparel, as did his body-guard, who were called his daughters. Their marches and attacks were always made by night. The insurrection was ultimately suppressed by the police and the military.

Rebecca the Jewess. A meek but high-souled Hebrew maiden in Sir Walter Scott's novel of "Ivanhoe," and the actual heroine of the story. See ROWENA.

Réconciliation Normande, La (lȧ rā/kŏnⁿ/sė/lė-ȧ/sė-ȯnⁿ/ nor/mȯnd/, 62). [Fr., the Norman, or feigned, reconciliation.] (*Fr. Hist.*) A name given to a sudden and brief restoration of harmony which was effected in the distracted Legislative Assembly, on the 7th of July, 1792, by the Abbé Lamourette, a native of Normandy. [Called also *Le Baiser de Lamourette.*] See LAMOURETTE'S KISS.

Red-coats. The name given by the Americans, in the Revolutionary War, to the British soldiery, in allusion to their scarlet uniform.

Red-cross Knight. A prominent character in Spenser's "Faëry Queen." To him was assigned the adventure of slaying a dragon, by which the kingdom of Una's father was laid waste, and his person endangered. Una herself had gone to the court of the fairy queen to solicit a champion, and, at the commencement of the poem, is represented as accompanying the knight upon his expedition. After various vicissitudes of fortune, the dragon is at last met and completely destroyed; when the knight marries Una, and departs to engage in other adventures assigned him by the fairy queen.

☞ The Red-cross Knight is St. George, the patron saint of England, and, in the obvious and general interpretation, typifies Holiness, or the perfection of the spiritual man in religion; but, in a political and particular sense, his adventures are intended to shadow forth the history of the Church of England.

☞ For the "Key to the Scheme of Pronunciation," with the accompanying Explanations,

Like the *Red-cross Knight*, they urge their way,
To lead in memorable triumph home
Truth,—their Immortal Una. *Wordsworth.*

Redeemed Captive. An appellation given to the Rev. John Williams (1644–1729), a New England clergyman who was made prisoner by the French and Indians in 1704, and obtained his freedom in 1706. He published a narrative of his experiences under the title of "The Redeemed Captive."

Red'gäunt'let, Sir Edward Hugh. One of the principal characters in Sir Walter Scott's novel of the same name; a political enthusiast and Jacobite, who scruples at no means of upholding the cause of the Pretender, and finally accompanies him into exile. He is represented as possessing the power of contorting his brow into a terrific frown, which made distinctly visible the figure of a horseshoe, the fatal mark of his race.

Red Man. [Fr. *Homme Rouge.*] 1. In the popular superstition of France, and especially of Brittany, a demon of tempests, who commands the elements, and precipitates into the waves the voyager who seeks to molest the solitude which he loves. It is said to be a popular belief in France, that a mysterious little Red Man appeared to Napoleon, and foretold his reverses.
2. A name given, on account of his copper-coloured skin, to the American Indian.

Red Republicans. See REPUBLICANS, RED.

Red Riding-hood. See LITTLE RED RIDING-HOOD.

Red Rose. A popular designation of the house of Lancaster, from its emblem, a red rose.

Reekie, Auld. See AULD REEKIE.

Re'găn. An unnatural daughter of Lear, in Shakespeare's tragedy of that name. See LEAR.
"Father! madam," said the stranger; "they think no more of their father than *Regan* or Goneril." *Sir W. Scott.*

Regno (răn'yo, 78). [It., kingdom.] A name given to Naples by way of distinction among the Italian States. Are our wiser heads leaning towards alliance with the Pope and the *Regno*, or are they inclining their ears to the orators of France and Milan? *Mrs. Lewes ("George Eliot").*

Reign of Terror. (*Fr. Hist.*) A term applied to a period of anarchy, bloodshed, and confiscation, in the time of the first Revolution, during which the country was under the sway of the actual terror inspired by the ferocious measures of its governors, on which they depended for the support of their authority. It began after the fall of the Girondists, May 31, 1793, and extended to the overthrow of Robespierre and his accomplices, July 27, 1794. Thousands of persons were put to death during this short time.

Re'mus. In Roman legendary history, the twin brother of Romulus, by whom he was killed for leaping in scorn over the walls of Rome, when they were building.

Ren'ard. A name given to a fox in fables or familiar tales and in poetry. It is derived from the celebrated German beast-epic ("Thier-epos") entitled "Reinecke Fuchs," or "Reinhard Fuchs," which is a satire on the state of society in Germany during the Middle Ages and the feudal *régime*, originated at an unknown period among the Frankish tribes, and first made known through the medium of a Low German version in the fifteenth century. Written also Reynard.]

☞ This remarkable poem contains a humourous account of the adventures of Renard the Fox at the court of King Nodel (the lion); and it exhibits the cunning of the former, the means which he adopted to rebut the charges made against him, and the hypocrisy and lies by which he contrived to gain the favour of his sovereign, who loaded him with honours. The plot turns chiefly on the long struggle between Renard and his uncle Isengrin, the wolf, who typifies the feudal baron, as Renard does the Church. Renard is swayed by a constant impulse to deceive and victimise every body, whether friend or foe, but especially Iseugrin; and, though the latter frequently reduces him to the greatest straits, he generally gets the better of it in the end.

Renault (re-nō'). An aged, sanguinary, and lustful conspirator in Otway's "Venice Preserved."

Each man indulges in his peculiar propensities. "Shed blood enough," cries old *Renault*. "Be just, be humane, be merciful," says Dusha. *Sheil.*

René (ry-nā', 31). The title of a romance by François René, Viscount de Châteaubriand (1768-1848), and the name of its hero, a man in whom social inaction, blended with a proud scorn resulting from a consciousness of superior genius, has produced a peculiar and morbid bitterness of spirit.

Ren'tow-el, Mr. Jabesh. A "precious" covenanting preacher mentioned in Sir Walter Scott's novel of "Waverley." See GOWKTHRAPPLE, MAISTER.

Republic, Heir of the. See HEIR OF THE REPUBLIC.

Republican Queen. An appellation given to Sophie Charlotte, wife of Frederick I., king of Prussia, "a famed queen and lady in her day."

Republicans, Black. A nickname given by the pro-slavery or "conservative" party in the United States to the members of the "Republican" party, which was organised to prevent the introduction of slavery into the national Territories, and to confine it to the States, where it had an acknowledged legal existence.

Republicans, Red. A sobriquet given by the French to those who are bent upon maintaining extreme republican doctrines, even at the expense of blood.

Resolute, The. A surname assumed by John Florio (d. 1625), the philologist and lexicographer. Shakespeare ridiculed him in the character of Holofernes, the pedantic schoolmaster in "Love's Labour's Lost," and in the character of Don Adriano de Armado, the vapouring and ridiculous Spaniard, in the same play. See *infra*, 1.

Resolute Doctor. 1. An appellation given to Durand, or Durandus, a scholastic philosopher of the Middle Ages. "Resolute" is here used in the sense of resolving, explaining, or interpreting. See MOST RESOLUTE DOCTOR.

2. A title bestowed upon John Baconthorp, Bacondorp, or Bacon (d. 1346), a distinguished mediæval schoolman, on account of the readiness and skill with which he decided controverted questions.

Restitution, Edict of. See EDICT OF RESTITUTION.

Restorer of Parnassus. [Sp. *Restaurador del Parnaso.*] A title given by his admiring countrymen to Don Juan Melendez Valdes (1754-1817), a very distinguished Spanish poet, who has had great influence on the literature of his country.

Review, Breeches. See BREECHES REVIEW.

Review, My Grandmother's. See GRANDMOTHER'S REVIEW, MY.

Rey-nal'do. A servant to Polonius, in Shakespeare's "Hamlet."

Rëyn'ard. See RENARD.

Rhad'ā-man'thus (rad'-). [Gr. 'Ραδάμανθος.] (*Gr. & Rom. Myth.*) A son of Jupiter and Europa, brother of Minos, and king of Lycia. He was so renowned for his justice and equity, that, after death, he was made one of the three judges in the underworld.

Rhe'ā (re'ā). [Gr. 'Ρεία, 'Ρέα.] (*Gr. & Rom. Myth.*) Another name for *Cybele.* See CYBELE.

Rhe'sus (re'-). [Gr. 'Ρῆσος.] (*Gr. & Rom. Myth.*) A warlike king of Thrace, who marched to the assistance of Priam when the Trojan war broke out, but was robbed of his horses and killed, on the night of his arrival, by Diomed and Ulysses, who wished to prevent the fulfilment of a prophecy that Troy should never be taken, if the horses of Rhesus drank the waters of Xanthus and grazed on the Trojan plains.

Rho'dy, Little (ro'dÿ). A popular designation of Rhode Island, the smallest of the United States.

Ricciardetto (rēt-chaŕ-det'to, 102). A son of Aymon, and brother of Bradamante, in Ariosto's "Orlando Furioso."

Rig'dum Fun'nĭ-dos. 1. A char-

For the "Key to the Scheme of Pronunciation," with the accompanying Explanations,

actor in Henry Carey's play entitled "Chrononhotonthologos."

2. A nickname given by Sir Walter Scott to John Ballantyne (1776-1821), his friend and partner in the publishing house of "John Ballantyne & Company." Lockhart says of him: "He was a quick, active, intrepid little fellow; and in society so very lively and amusing, so full of fun and merriment, such a thoroughly light-hearted droll, all over quaintness and humourous mimicry, and moreover such a keen and skilful devotee to all manner of field-sports, from fox-hunting to badger-baiting inclusive, that it was no wonder he should have made a favourable impression on Scott." See ALDIBORONTEPHOSCOPHORNIO.

Rigolette (re′go′let′). The name of a female character in Eugene Sue's "Mysteries of Paris." It has acquired a proverbial currency, and is used as a synonym of *grisette*.

Rim′mŏn. (*Myth.*) A god of the Syrians, generally thought to have been the same as *Baäl*. See BAÄL.

Him followed *Rimmon*, whose delightful seat
Was fair Damascus, on the fertile banks
Of Abbana and Pharphar, lucid streams.
Milton.

Rinaldo (re-năl′do). [Fr. *Renaud*, Lat. *Rinaldus*, *Reginaldus*.] 1. A famous warrior, violent, headstrong, and unscrupulous, but of great gallantry, ingenuity, and generosity, in Tasso's "Gerusalemme Liberata," Pulci's "Morgante Maggiore," Bojardo's "Orlando Innamorato," Ariosto's "Orlando Furioso," and other romantic tales of Italy and France. He was a son of the great Duke Aymon, and cousin to Orlando, and one of the most renowned of Charlemagne's paladins. Having, in a transport of rage, killed Charlemagne's nephew Berthelot by a blow with a chess-board, he was, with all his family except his father, banished and outlawed. After various adventures and disasters, he went to the Holy Land, and, on his return, succeeded in making peace with the emperor. Angelica, the lovely infidel princess, fell madly in love with him; but he could not endure her, and, while kings and nations were warring only for her, he turned a deaf ear to her prayers, and left her to deplore her unrequited love. See ANGELICA, ARMIDA.

We stare at a dragoon who has killed three French cuirassiers as a prodigy; yet we read, without the least disgust, how Godfrey slew his thousands, and *Rinaldo* his ten thousands.
Macaulay.

2. Steward to the Countess of Rousillon, in Shakespeare's "All 's Well that Ends Well."

Ringing Island. A name given to England, on account of the music of its many bells.

☞ "From very early ages, England has been famous for its bells; so much so, that Britain was known even in Saxon times as 'The Ringing Island.'" *Lower.*

Rippach, Hans von. See HANS VON RIPPACH.

Rip Van Winkle. See WINKLE, RIP VAN.

Riquet with the Tuft (re′kă). [Fr. *Riquet à la Houppe.*] A prince of surpassing ugliness, but of great wit and good sense, upon whom a fairy bestowed the power of communicating these gifts to the person he should love best. Becoming enamoured of a very beautiful but excessively stupid princess of a neighbouring country, he makes her, by the exercise of his power, altogether clever and charming; while she, in return, and by the exercise of a like power bestowed upon her by the same fairy, makes him become the handsomest man in the world.

Robber Synod. [Gr. Σύνοδος ληστρικἠ.] (*Ecclesiastical Hist.*) A name given by the Greeks to a council convoked at Ephesus, by the emperor Theodosius, in the year 449. The name was intended to signify that every thing was carried in it by fraud and violence;' but, as has been justly said, it would be equally applicable to many councils of subsequent times.

Robert the Devil. [Fr. *Robert le Diable.*] 1. The hero of an old French metrical romance of the thirteenth century, the same as Robert, first Duke of Normandy, who became an early object of legendary scandal. Having been given over to the Devil before birth, he ran a career of cruelties and crimes unparalleled, till he was miraculously reclaimed, whereupon he did penance by living among the dogs, became an exemplary Christian, and married the emperor's daughter. It is thought in Normandy that his wandering ghost is doomed to expiate his crimes until the day of judgment. In the fourteenth century, the romance above mentioned was turned into prose, and of the prose story two translations were made into English. There was also a miracle play on the same subject. The opera of "Robert le Diable" was composed by Meyerbeer, in 1826.

2. The same name was popularly given to Robert François Damiens (1714-1757), noted for his attempt to assassinate Louis XV.

Robin Bluestring. A nickname given to Sir Robert Walpole (1676-1745), by contemporary political opponents, in allusion to his blue ribbon as a knight of the Garter.

Robin des Bois (ro'băn'dă bwŏ, 62). [Fr.] In Germany, a mysterious hunter of the forest. (See FREISCHÜTZ.) Robin des Bois occurs in one of Eugene Sue's novels "as a well-known mythical character whose name is employed by French mothers to frighten their children."

Robin Goodfellow. See GOODFELLOW, ROBIN.

Robin Gray. See GRAY, AULD ROBIN.

Robin Hood. A famous English outlaw, whose exploits are the subject of many old ballads and traditionary stories, but of whose actual existence little or no evidence can be discovered. Various periods, ranging from the time of Richard I. to near the end of the reign of Edward II., have been assigned as the age in which he lived. He is usually described as a yeoman, and his chief residence is said to have been the forest of Sherwood, in Nottinghamshire. Of his followers, the most noted are Little John; his chaplain, Friar Tuck; and his paramour, named Marian. All the popular legends extol his personal courage, his generosity, his humanity, and his skill in archery. His conduct in many respects resembled that of a feudal lord. He robbed the rich only, and gave freely to the poor, protecting the needy, and also the fair sex, whose wrongs he undertook to avenge. He was particularly fond of pillaging prelates.

☞ The principal incidents of his history are to be found in Stow, and in Ritson's "Robin Hood, a Collection of all the Ancient Poems, Songs, and Ballads now extant, relating to that celebrated English Outlaw," 8vo, London, 1795. Prefixed to this collection are "Historical Anecdotes" of the life of Robin Hood, an accumulation of all the notices respecting the outlaw that the compiler's reading had discovered in manuscripts or printed books. Various and widely different hypotheses have been advanced concerning Robin Hood, and his claim to be considered a real historical personage. These are well stated, and are investigated with entire candour and much acuteness of criticism, in the elaborate Introduction to the fifth volume of the "English and Scottish Ballads," edited by Professor Francis J. Child (Boston, U. S., 1857).

But chief, beside the butts, there stand
Bold *Robin Hood* and all his band, —
Friar Tuck, with quarter-staff and cowl,
Old Scathelocke, with his surly scowl,
Maid Marian, fair as ivory bone,
Scarlet, and Mutch, and Little John.
  Sir W. Scott.

The Duke of Marlborough, the Duke of Cumberland, the Marquis of Granby, have flourished upon sign-posts, and have faded there; so have their compeers, Prince Eugene and Prince Ferdinand. Rodney and Nelson are fading, and the time is not far distant when Wellington also will have had his day. But while England shall be England, *Robin Hood* will be a popular name. *Southey.*

Rob'in-son, Jack (-sn). A name used in the phrase, "Before one could say Jack Robinson," — a saying to express a very short time; said by Grose to have originated from a very volatile gentleman of that appellation who would call on his neighbours and be gone before his name could be announced. The following lines "from an old play" are elsewhere given as the original phrase: —

"A warke it ys as easie to be doone,
As tys to saye, *Jacke! robys on.*"

☞ For the "Key to the Scheme of Pronunciation," with the accompanying Explanations,

The expression has been erroneously connected with one John Robinson (1727-1802), of Appleby, Westmoreland, who, in a surprisingly short time, rose from obscurity to wealth and power, becoming an influential member of parliament, secretary to the treasury, surveyor-general of His Majesty's woods and forests, &c.

An operation in comparison to the celerity of which a pig's whisper is an age, and the pronunciation of the mystic words "*Jack Robinson*" a life-long task. *Sala.*

Robinson, Prosperity. See PROSPERITY ROBINSON.

Robinson Crusoe. See CRUSOE, ROBINSON.

Robin the Devil. [Fr. *Robert le Diable.*] Robert, the first Duke of Normandy; — so surnamed "for his monstrous birth and behaviour." See ROBERT THE DEVIL.

Rob Roy. [That is, Robert the Red.] A nickname popularly given to a celebrated Highland freebooter, whose true name was Robert Macgregor, but who assumed that of Campbell, on account of the outlawry of the clan Macgregor by the Scottish parliament, in 1662. He is the hero of Sir Walter Scott's novel entitled "Rob Roy."

A famous man is Robin Hood,
The English ballad-singer's joy!
And Scotland has a thief as good,
An outlaw of as daring mood;
She has her brave *Rob Roy!*
Wordsworth.

Brilliant and handsome though Peschiera be, Lord L'Estrange, like *Rob Roy* Macgregor, is "on his native heath," and has the decided advantage over the foreigner.
Sir E. Bulwer Lytton.

Rod/ĕr-ī'go. A Venetian gentleman, in Shakespeare's tragedy of "Othello;" represented as the dupe of Iago.

Rod'o-mŏnt, or **Rodomonte** (rŏd-o-mŏn'tā). [That is, one who rolls away mountains, from Prov. It. *rodare*, to roll away or forward, from Lat. *rota*, a wheel, and It. *monte*, Lat. *mons*, a mountain.] A famous Moorish hero in Bojardo's "Orlando Innamorato" and Ariosto's "Orlando Furioso;" represented as a king of Algiers, and the bravest, fiercest, and wildest of all warriors. His name is generally used to stigmatise a boaster, and from it we derive the word *rodomontade.*

He vapoured; but, being pretty sharply admonished, he quickly became mild and calm, — a posture ill becoming such a *Rodomont.*
Sir T. Herbert.

Roe, Richard. A merely nominal defendant in actions of ejectment; usually coupled with the name of *John Doe.* See DOE, JOHN.

We need hardly say, therefore, that, in the present instance, M. Périer is merely a *Richard Roe,* — that his name is used for the sole purpose of bringing Macchiavelli into court, — and that he will not be mentioned in any subsequent stage of the proceedings.
Macaulay.

Ro-ġe'ro (9). 1. See RUGGIERO.
2. A gentleman of Sicilia, in Shakespeare's "Winter's Tale."

Rois Fainéants, Les. See FAINÉANTS, LES ROIS.

Roister Doister, Ralph. The subject and the title of the earliest English comedy, the production of Nicholas Udall, in the sixteenth century.

Ro'lănd. One of the Twelve Peers of Charlemagne, and his supposed nephew, warden of the marches of Brittany, and the hero of many a romantic tale. He is said to have been killed in 778, at Roncesvalles, or Roncesveaux, where the rear of Charlemagne's army was cut off by some revolted Gascons on its return from a successful expedition into Spain, — a circumstance which has been magnified by poets and romancers into a "dolorous rout" of Charlemagne "with all his peerage." See ORLANDO and ROWLAND. [Written also R o w l a n d and O r l a n d o.]

☞ According to Pulci, Charlemagne's warriors were decoyed into the pass of Roncesvalles, where they were set upon by three armies of the Saracens, while Charlemagne himself remained at St. Jean Pied de Port, a few miles distant, whither he had come to receive promised tribute from Marsiglio, or Marsilius, the Saracen king. The French knights performed prodigies of valour, but the battle went against them. Roland was accidentally, but fatally, wounded by his friend Oliver, who had himself received a death-blow, and was blinded with his own blood. Roland now sounded his marvellous horn, which was to give Charlemagne notice of his peril, and with such force, that, at the third blast, it broke in two. Over all the noise of the battle, the horn was heard as if it had been a voice from the other world. Birds fell dead at the sound, and the whole Saracen army drew back in terror, while Charlemagne heard it at St. Jean Pied de Port, and understood at once that he was the victim of treachery. It is also recorded that Roland, wishing to prevent his wonderful sword Durandal (see DURANDAL) from falling into the hands of the enemy, smote it upon a rock near him, making a monstrous fissure therein (the celebrated "Brèche de Roland," a deep defile in the crest of the Pyrenees from 200 to 300 feet in width, between precipitous rocks rising to a height of from 800 to 600 feet), while the sword remained uninjured. See MARSIGLIO.

> Oh for one blast of that dread horn,
> On Fontarabian echoes borne,
> Which to King Charles did come,
> When *Roland* brave, and Olivier,
> And every paladin and peer,
> On Roncesvalles died!   *Sir W. Scott.*

> Then would I seek the Pyrenean breach
> Which *Roland* clove with huge two-handed sway,
> And to the enormous labour left his name,
> Where unremitting frosts the rocky crescent bleach.   *Wordsworth.*

Roland of the Army. [Fr. *Roland d'Armée.*] A sobriquet of Louis Vincent Joseph Le Blond, Comte de Saint Hilaire (1766–1809), a French general distinguished for his valiant and chivalrous conduct.

Roman Á-chillēs. A surname of Sicinius Dentatus (405 B. C.), bestowed upon him on account of his bravery.

Ro'me-o. In Shakespeare's tragedy of "Romeo and Juliet," a son of Montague, in love with Juliet, the daughter of Capulet. Between the two houses of Montague and Capulet there existed a deadly feud.

Rom'u-lus. In the legendary history of Rome, the son of Mars and a vestal named Silvia. He was thrown into the Tiber, together with his twin brother Remus, by his uncle, but was washed ashore, suckled by a she-wolf, found and adopted by a shepherd, and finally became the founder and first king of Rome. After a reign of thirty-seven years, he was suddenly carried off to heaven by his father Mars, as he was reviewing the people near the marsh of Capra, and was thenceforth worshipped under the name of *Quirinus*. Another form of the tradition represents Romulus as a tyrant, and relates that the senators, discontented with his oppressive rule, murdered him during the darkness of a tempest, cut up his body, and carried home the mangled pieces under their robes.

Ron. The name of Arthur's lance, which was "hard, broad, and fit for slaughter." See PRIDWIN. [Written also R o n e.]

Roncesvalles, Battle of (ron'se-val'les, *or* rōn-thes-väl'yes). See ROLAND, MARSIGLIO.

Rondibilis (ron-dib'I-lis; *Fr. pron.* rōn'de'be'le', 62). A physician consulted by Panurge, in Rabelais' romance of "Pantagruel." See PANURGE.

Ropemaker, The Beautiful. [Fr. *La Belle Cordière.*] A sobriquet given to Louise Labé (1526–1566), a French poetess who wrote in three different languages, and who was distinguished for her extraordinary courage at the siege of Perpignan. She married Ennemond Perrin, a rich merchant, and a rope manufacturer.

Rōp'ēr, Mistress. A cant name given in the British navy to the "Royal Marines."

Roque Guinart (ro'kä ḡe-nart'). A famous freebooter introduced by Cervantes into "Don Quixote." His true name was Pedro Rocha Guinarda, and he was one of the principal leaders of a great band of robbers who levied shameful contributions all over the mountainous districts of Catalonia, about the time when "Don Quixote" was written.

Ros'à-lĭnd. 1. The poetic name of a youthful mistress of Spenser. She is described by him as of great beauty, and as occupying a position of honour and dignity, though her parentage was humble. In the "Shepherd's Calendar," he bewails her ill usage, and, in the sixth book of the "Faëry Queen," — where she is undoubtedly intended by Mirabel, — he retaliates it. Her real name was long unknown; but within a few years it has been proved that she was Rose Daniel, sister of Samuel Daniel, the poet, and that she married John Florio (see DON ADRIANO DE ARMADO, and HOLOFERNES, 3) in preference to Spenser. *Rosalinde* reads, anagrammatically, *Rose Daniel;* for, according to Camden, "a letter may be doubled, rejected, or contrariwise, if the sense fall aptly;" we thus get rid of the redundant *e*, and have a perfect anagram.

2. A daughter of the exiled duke, in Shakespeare's "As You Like It."

☞ "Rosalind ... has vivacity and wit enough to captivate those who like a woman of spirit; and yet with this there is interwoven so much womanly tenderness and delicacy, she is, in her gayest moods, so truly, sometimes so touchingly, feminine, that she wins more admirers than she dazzles."   R. G. *White.*

Ros′a-line, *or* Ros′a-line. 1. A lady attending on the princess of France, in Shakespeare's "Love's Labour's Lost."

2. A scornful lady, for whom Romeo entertained a dreamy and fanciful passion before he fell in love with Juliet, who was in every respect her opposite. See ROMEO.

Rosamond, Fair. See FAIR ROSAMOND.

Ro′sen-crantz (ro′zn-krănts). The name of a courtier, in Shakespeare's tragedy of "Hamlet."

Ros′I-clear. A character in the "Mirror of Knighthood." See DONZEL DEL PHEBO.

Ros′I-phele. Princess of Armenia, a lady of surpassing beauty, but insensible to the power of love, represented by Gower, in his "Confessio Amantis," as reduced to obedience to Cupid by a vision which befell her on a May-day ramble.

Ross, Man of. See MAN OF ROSS.

Roubigné, Julie de (zhü′le′ dụ roo′bĕn′yȧ′, 34). The title of a novel by Henry Mackenzie, and the name of its heroine.

Rough and Ready. A sobriquet given to General Zachary Taylor (1790–1850), twelfth president of the United States, as expressive of prominent traits in his character.

Round Table. 1. A huge circular marble table, at which, according to the old romancers, King Arthur and his knights were accustomed to sit. It was originally the property of Uther Pendragon, for whom it was made by the sorcerer Merlin; it afterward belonged to Leodegrance, king of Camelard, and came to Arthur as the portion of his wife Guinever, the daughter of that monarch. It was said to have been modelled after one established by Joseph of Arimathea in imitation of that which Jesus had used at the Last Supper. Every knight had his seat, with his name inscribed on it in letters of gold. Some say there were only thirteen seats around it, in memory of the thirteen apostles. Twelve only were occupied, and by knights of the highest fame. The thirteenth represented the seat of the traitor Judas. According to others, there were seats for fifty, sixty, a hundred, or a hundred and fifty; and an empty place — called "the perilous siege" or seat — was left for the sangreal.

☞ "King Arthur stablished all his knights, and gave them lands that were not rich of land, and charged them never to do outrage nor murder, and alway to flee treason. Also, by no means to be cruel, but to give mercy unto him that asked mercy, upon pain of forfeiture of their worship, and lordship of King Arthur, for evermore, and alway to do ladies, damosels, and gentlewomen succour upon pain of death. Also, that no man take no battailes in a wrong quarrel for no law, nor for worldly goods. Unto this were all the knights sworn of the Round Table, both old and young."
               Morte d'Arthur.

☞ The more celebrated members of this order were, Meliadus, Ban, Bohort, Caradoc, Ryence, Pharamond, Lancelot du Lac, Gawain, Tristram, Hector de Marys, Bliomberis, Gaheris, Kay, Sagramour le Desirus, Morhault, Agravaine, Mordred, Dodynas le Sauvage, Dynadam, Perceval, Galahad, Driam, Palamedes, Amoral of Wales, Yvain, Ozanna, Persaunt of Inde (called "of Inde," not as being an Indian, but from the colour he wore,

and for the Remarks and Rules to which the numbers after certain words refer, see pp. xiv–xxxii.

namely, dark blue). Torres, Lavaine, Gareth, Pelleas, Braudiles, Bedivere, Colgrevance, Ladynas, Ironside, Lionel, Lucau.

☞ This ancient order of knighthood was revived by Edward III. at Windsor, upon New-Year's day, 1344, in order to draw the best soldiers of Europe into his interest, with a view to the recovery of France, which descended to him in right of his mother. A huge round table is still preserved in Winchester castle as the identical one around which King Arthur and his knights were accustomed to sit. The tradition that it is such dates back to the beginning of the twelfth century.

"For his own part," he said, "and in the land where he was bred, men would as soon take for their mark King Arthur's *Round Table*, which held sixty knights around it."
Sir W. Scott.

2. A similar table said by French and Italian romancers to have been constructed or instituted by Charlemagne in imitation of that of King Arthur.

Roustem (roos'tem). A famous halfmythical Persian hero, another Hercules, who is said to have lived in the sixteenth century, and to have been a descendant of the celebrated Djamshid. Marvellous exploits are ascribed to him, such as the killing of a thousand Tartars at one blow, the vanquishment of dragons and devils, the capture of whole cities, and the like. [Written also Rustam, Roustam, Rostam.]

Rōw-e'nă. A Saxon princess, ward of Cedric of Rotherwood, in Sir Walter Scott's novel of "Ivanhoe," of which she is the nominal heroine. See REBECCA THE JEWESS.

Rōw'lănd. Another orthography of *Roland*, one of the most famous of Charlemagne's Twelve Peers. To give one "a Rowland for an Oliver" is an old and proverbial expression used to signify the matching of one incredible lie with another. Oliver was also one of Charlemagne's paladins; and the exploits of these renowned heroes are rendered ridiculously and equally extravagant by the old romancers. See ROLAND and ORLANDO.

I promise you that he gave my termagant kinsman a "quid pro quo,"—a *Rowland* for his *Oliver*, as the vulgar say, alluding to the two celebrated paladins of Charlemagne.
Sir W. Scott.

Rōw'lănd, Childe. The hero of an old Scottish ballad, of which only a fragment has been preserved; the youngest brother of the fair Burd Helen, and the same as *Roland*, or *Orlando*, the famous paladin. Guided by Merlin, he undertakes the perilous task of bringing back his sister from Elfland, whither she had been carried by the fairies. See BURD HELEN and ROLAND.

Childe *Rowland* to the dark tower came.
(*Quoted by Shak.*)

Rōw'ley, Thomas. The name of a fictitious priest of Bristol, pretended by Chatterton to have lived in the reigns of Henry VI. and Edward IV., and to have written several remarkable poems, of which Chatterton himself was really the author.

Royalist Butcher. [Fr. *Le Boucher Royaliste.*] A sobriquet given to Blaise de Montluc (1502–1527), a French captain distinguished for his cruelties to the Protestants in the time of Charles IX.

Royal Martyr. Charles I. of England, who was beheaded Jan. 30, 1649, in pursuance of the sentence of death pronounced against him by the High Court of Justice, on the 27th of the same month.

We are at a loss to conceive how the same persons, who, on the 5th of November, thank God for wonderfully conducting his servant King William, and for making all opposition fall before him until he became our king and governor, can, on the 30th of January, contrive to be afraid that the blood of the *Royal Martyr* may be visited on themselves and their children!
Macaulay.

Royal 'Prentice in the Art of Poetry. A name given to himself by James I. of England, who wrote a great many miserable roundels, ballads, sonnets, and other pieces of verse. His first publication was a collection of poems, under the title of "The Essays of a Prentice in the Divine Art of Poesy" (4to, 1584).

Royal Psalmist. A designation often applied to King David, the reputed author of most of the compositions known as "The Psalms."

Rŏz'ĭ-nan'te. [Sp. *Rocinante*, from

rocin, a small, jaded horse, a carthorse, and *ante*, before, formerly.] The name given by Don Quixote to his celebrated steed. See DON QUIXOTE.

☞ "He next visited his horse, which, though he had more corners than a real (being as lean as Gonnella's, that *tantum pellis et ossa fuit*), nevertheless, in his eye appeared infinitely preferable to Alexander's Bucephalus, or the Cid's Bavieca. Four days he consumed in inventing a name for this remarkable steed.... After having chosen, rejected, amended, tortured, and revolved a world of names in his imagination, he fixed upon *Rozinante*, — an appellation, in his opinion, lofty, sonorous, and expressive not only of his former, but likewise of his present, situation, which entitled him to the preference over all other horses under the sun. *Cervantes, Trans.*

In short, bid *Rozinante* change with Pegasus, and you do no more than Mr. Vane's letter held out to Triplet. *C. Reade.*

Rübezahl (rü'bä-tsäl, 51, 70). The name of a famous spirit of the Riesengebirge in Germany, corresponding to the *Puck* of England. He is celebrated in innumerable sagas, ballads, and tales, and represented under the various forms of a miner, hunter, monk, dwarf, giant, &c. He is said to aid the poor and oppressed, and shows benighted wanderers their road, but wages incessant war with the proud and wicked. The origin of the name is obscure. See NUMBER NIP.

Road abounding in gloomy valleys, intricate rock-labyrinths, haunts of sprite *Rübezahl*, sources of the Elbe, and I know not what. *Carlyle.*

Ru'bĭ-cŏn. The ancient name of a small stream — thought to be the modern Pisatello — which formed the boundary between Italy and Cisalpine Gaul. It is celebrated from Cæsar's having hesitated about crossing it with his army, and initiating civil war, in the year 49 B. C. Hence, "to pass the Rubicon" has become a proverbial phrase to denote the taking of the first step in an undertaking from which one cannot or will not recede.

Rŭ'chi-el. [Heb. *ruch*, air, and *el*, god, or mighty one.] In the old Jewish angelology, the name of the angel who ruled the air and the winds.

Rudge, Barnaby. The title of a novel by Charles Dickens, and the name of its hero, a half-witted lad whose companion is a knowing but evil-looking raven.

There comes Poe, with his raven, like *Barnaby Rudge*,
Three fifths of him genius and two fifths sheer fudge. *Lowell.*

Rüdiger (rü'de-gĕr, 51, 58, 64). The faithful squire of Chriemhild in the great epic poem of Germany, the "Nibelungen Lied."

Rug'by. A servant to Dr. Caius, in Shakespeare's "Merry Wives of Windsor."

Ruggiero (rood-jā'ro, 102). A young Saracen knight, born of Christian parents, who figures in Bojardo's "Orlando Innamorato," and in Ariosto's "Orlando Furioso." In the latter poem, he falls in love with Bradamante, a Christian Amazon, and sister to Rinaldo. After numerous adventures, crosses, and narrow escapes, the poet, in the last canto of the poem, makes them marry; and from their union he derives the genealogy of the house of Este. Ruggiero is noted for the possession of a hippogriff, or winged horse, and also of a veiled shield, the dazzling splendour of which, when suddenly disclosed, struck with blindness and astonishment all eyes that beheld it. This he threw into a hidden well, in a nameless forest, in an undiscovered land, after having won too cheap a victory by its accidental exposure. [Written also Ruggieri, Rogero, Ruggero, Ruggeri.]

Rump, The. (*Eng. Hist.*) See PRIDE'S PURGE; see also *infra*.

Rumpelstilzchen (room'pel-stilts'-ken, 71). A character in a German nursery tale, which has been translated into English, and is composed, according to Grimm, of several mutually complementary narratives, originating in Hesse.

☞ Rumpelstilzchen is a dwarf who spins straw into gold for a certain miller's daughter, — a task enjoined upon her,

---

and for the Remarks and Rules to which the numbers after certain words refer, see pp. xiv-xxxii.

under penalty of death, by the king, who, in the sequel, marries her. In her distress, the girl had engaged to give the little man her first child as a reward for the service he had rendered her; but when the fulfilment of the promise was claimed, she grieved so bitterly and pleaded so hard, that he gave her three days in which to find out his name, telling her, that, if she succeeded, she should keep the child. On the first and second days, when he presented himself before her, she repeated all the names she knew; but at each one he said, "That is not my name." Early on the third day, a messenger of the queen accidentally saw him in an out-of-the-way place, where he lived, and overheard him exclaim, "How glad I am that nobody knows my name is Rumpelstilzchen!" The queen, being told of this, was ready for him at his next appearance; and he was so chagrined at finding his secret known as to destroy himself on the spot.

Rump Parliament. (*Eng. Hist.*) A derisive epithet applied to a remnant of the famous Long Parliament of England, which re-assembled on the 6th of May, 1659, after the dissolution of the parliament summoned by Richard Cromwell on the 27th of January, and dissolved by him on the 22d of April, of the same year. [Called also, simply, *The Rump.*]

Rû'pẽrt, Knight. Formerly, and still in some of the villages of northern Germany, a personage clad in high buskins, white robe, mask, and enormous flaxen wig, who, at Christmas time, receives from parents the presents designed for their children, goes about from house to house, every where received with great pomp and welcome, and, calling the children, distributes to each a present. Like St. Nicholas, he is supposed to exercise a secret supervision over children; but more especially he keeps watch over naughty children, and thus answers to the English *Robin Goodfellow*, or *Hobgoblin*. The horseman in the May pageant is in some parts of Germany called Ruprecht, or Rupert.

Rush, Friar. See FRIAR RUSH.

Russian Byron. A name given by his countrymen to Alexander Sergeivitch Pushkin (1799–1837), the most distinguished poet of Russia in the present century. He is said to have not a little of the bold and brilliant genius of his prototype, and, like him, to excel in vigour of imagery and impassioned sentiment.

Russian Mu-răt' (*or* mii'rä'). A name given by the French to Michael Miloradowitch (1770–1820), distinguished in the wars against Napoleon, and accounted one of the boldest and most enterprising and active of the Russian generals of his time.

Rye-house Plot. (*Eng. Hist.*) The name given to an alleged conspiracy to assassinate Charles II. and his brother, the Duke of York (afterward James II.), at a place called Rye-house, between London and Newmarket, as they returned from Newmarket races. The execution of the plot is said to have been frustrated by the king's leaving Newmarket somewhat sooner than was expected.

Ry'ence, King. A knight of the Round Table, king of Ireland, North Wales, and many isles. He sent to King Arthur for his beard, to enable him, with those of eleven other kings, whom he had already discomfited, to purfle his mantle. Meeting with an angry refusal, he entered Britain with a large army, to enforce his demand, but was captured, and sent as a prisoner to Arthur, who, according to some accounts, married his daughter Guinever. [Written also Ryon.]

☞ For the "Key to the Scheme of Pronunciation," with the accompanying Explanations,

S.

Sabreur, Le Beau (lu bō så'brör', 43). See HANDSOME SWORDSMAN.

Så-brī'nå. The virgin daughter of Locrine and Estrildas, thrown into the Severn (Lat. *Sabrina*) by Guendolen, a divorced wife of Locrine. In Milton's "Comus" and Fletcher's "Faithful Shepherdess," she is fabled to have been transformed into a river-nymph, that her honour might be preserved inviolate. See LOCRINE.

To fashion's light tempters, her very thought was as closed as,
"Under the glassy, cool, translucent wave,"
was the ear of *Sabrina* to the comrades of Comus. *Sir E. Bulwer Lytton.*

Sach'ā-ris'så. [From Gr. σάκχαρ, σάκχαρον, sugar, like Melissa from μέλι, honey.] A poetical name given by Waller (1605–1687) to the eldest daughter of the Earl of Leicester, Lady Dorothea Sidney, for whose hand he was an unsuccessful suitor.

Fancy *Sacharissa* beckoning and smiling from the upper window. *Thackeray.*

Sacred Island. An old name of Ireland; the same as *Holy Island*. See HOLY ISLAND, 1.

Sacred War. (*Gr. Hist.*) 1. A war undertaken by the Amphictyonic league — a council established at a very early period for the management of all affairs relative to Greece — for the defence of Delphi against the Cirrhæans. It began B. C. 595, and ended B. C. 587.

2. A war instituted by the Athenians for the purpose of restoring Delphi to the Phocians, from whom it had been taken by the Lacedæmonians. B. C. 448–447.

3. A war in which the Phocians, who had seized Delphi, B. C. 357, were attacked and conquered by Philip of Macedon, as chief of the Amphictyonic league. This is the most celebrated of the Sacred Wars.

Sac'rĭ-pănt, King. 1. King of Circassia, and a lover of Angelica, in the poems of Bojardo and Ariosto.

This is no new thing, said Don Quixote, nor is it difficult to be done. With the same stratagem, *Sacripant* had his steed stolen from under him by that notorious thief Brunello at the siege of Albracca. *Cervantes, Trans.*

2. A personage introduced by Alessandro Tassoni (1565–1635), the Italian poet, in his mock-heroic poem entitled "Secchia Rapita," or "The Rape of the Bucket;" represented as false, brave, noisy, and hectoring. The name is quoted as a synonym with vanity and braggart courage.

Let us hunt up this *Sacripant*, let us beat him as we would the Devil. *Granval, Trans.*

Sæhrimnir (szä-rim'nĕr). (*Scand. Myth.*) A boar whose flesh furnishes food for the banquets of Valhalla. Every day it is served up at table, and every day it is entirely renewed again.

Saga (szä'gä). [From the same root as the Eng. *say.*] (*Scand. Myth.*) The goddess of history.

Sage of Mon'tĭ-cel'lo. An appellation often given, in America, to Thomas Jefferson (1743–1826), third president of the United States, from the name of his country-seat, and in allusion to his wise statesmanship and great political sagacity.

As from the grave where Henry sleeps,
From Vernon's weeping-willow,
And from the grassy pall which hides
The *Sage of Monticello,*
So from the leaf-strewn burial-stone
Of Randolph's lowly dwelling,
Virginia, o'er thy land of slaves
A warning voice is swelling. *Whittier.*

Sage of Samos. See SAMIAN SAGE.

Sag'it-tä-rȳ. A famous imaginary monster introduced into the armies of the Trojans by the fabling writer, Guido da Colonna, whose work was translated by Lydgate. He is described as "a terrible archer, half man and half beast, who neighs like a horse, whose eyes sparkle like fire, and strike dead like lightning." He is evidently the same as the archer-centaur, the sign *Sagittarius* in the zodiac.

The dreadful *Sagittary*
Appals our numbers; haste we, Diomed,
To reinforcement, or we perish all. *Shak.*

---

and for the Remarks and Rules to which the numbers after certain words refer, see pp. xlv-xxxii.

☞ The same name is given in "Othello" (a. i., sc. 1 and 3) to the residence of the military officers at the arsenal in Venice, from the figure of an archer over the door.

Sagramour le Desirus (sag'rȧ-moor lu dā/ze-roos'). A knight of the Round Table, who figures in "Lancelot du Lac," "Morte d'Arthur," and other old romances of chivalry.

Sailor King. A title popularly conferred upon William IV. of England, who entered the navy in 1779, at fourteen years of age, and continued in the service till 1827, having passed from the rank of midshipman to that of captain, by regular promotion, and thence by a merely formal ascent to that of admiral of the fleet in 1801, and that of lord high admiral in 1827.

St. Befana. See BEFANA, LA.

St. Brandan, Island of. See ISLAND OF ST. BRANDAN.

St. Christopher. A saint of the Roman Catholic and Greek churches. Legendary writers place him in the third century, but critical historians reject him as imaginary, and regard his history as wholly fabulous. According to the common account, he was a native of Lycia; but the "Legenda Aurea" (cap. 100) says that he was a Canaanite, and adds, that he was very tall and fearful to look at. So proud was he of his bulk and strength, that he would serve only the mightiest princes, and was ever in search of a stronger master. At length he entered the service of the Devil; but, finding that his new master was thrown into great trepidation and alarm by the sight of an image of Christ, he lost all respect for him, and resolved to seek out and follow the Saviour. For a long time his quest was vain; but he finally found him in a little child, whom he undertook to carry across a deep river, which had no bridge, — or, according to a late Latin hymn, the Red Sea, — and whose weight kept growing greater and greater, until Christopher began to sink under the burden, when the child declared himself to be Christ, and wrought a miracle to prove it. Christopher was convinced, embraced Christianity, performed miracles himself, was martyred, canonised, and became an object of the most eager veneration. The sight of his image was thought to be a protection from sickness, earthquakes, fire, or flood, for the rest of the day, and it was therefore carved and painted in huge proportions on the outside of churches and houses, especially in Italy, Spain, and Germany. His body is said to be at Valencia, in Spain; he has an arm at Compostella, a jaw-bone at Astorga, a shoulder at St. Peter's in Rome, a tooth and a rib at Venice, and many other relics, all enormous, at other places. The Greek church celebrates his festival on the 9th of May; the Roman Catholic, on the 25th of July.

Like the great giant *Christopher* it stands
Upon the brink of the tempestuous wave,
Wading far out among the rocks and sands,
The night-o'ertaken mariner to save.
Longfellow, The Light-house.

St. Distaff. An imaginary saint to whom the 7th of January — the day after the Epiphany, or Twelfth-day — is consecrated in some localities. The Christmas holidays being ended, the distaff and other industrious employments are now resumed. The name occurs in an old ballad, entitled "Wit a-sporting in a pleasant Grove of new Fancies," Lond., 1657.

"Partly worke and partly play
You must on *St. Distaff's* day;
Give *St. Distaff* all the right,
Then give Christmas-sport good night."

St. Fil'o-me'nȧ. The name of a pseudo-saint of the Roman Catholic church, whose worship commenced in the present century. Longfellow has applied the name to Florence Nightingale, probably from its resemblance to the Greek and Latin *philomela*, a nightingale, and also because, in a picture by Sabatelli, St. Filomena is represented as hovering over a group of the sick and maimed, who are healed by her intercession.

☞ In the year 1802, a grave was found in the cemetery of St. Priscilla, by which were the remains of a glass vase that had held blood, the indication of the burial-place of a martyr. The grave was closed by three tiles, on which were the following words, painted in red letters: LVMENA PAXTE CVMFI. There were also rudely painted on the tiles two anchors, three darts, a torch, and a palm-branch. The inscription was read by placing the first tile after the two others, thus, — "Pax tecum Filumena," Peace be with thee, Filumena; and Filumena was adopted as a new saint in the long list of those to whom the Roman church has given this title. It was supposed, that, in the haste of closing the grave, the tiles had been thus misplaced. Thereupon a devout artisan, a priest, and a nun, were all severally visited by visions of a virgin martyr, who told them the story of Diocletian's love for her, of her refusal, and subsequent martyrdom; and explained, that, having been once called Lumena, she was baptised Filumena, which she explained as a daughter of light! Some human remains near the stone being dignified as relics of St. Filomena, she was presented to Mugnano, and, on the way, not only worked many miracles on her adorers, but actually repaired her own skeleton, and made her hair grow. So many wonders are said to have been worked by this phantom saint, that a book printed at Paris in the year 1847 calls her "La Thaumaturge du 19me Siècle;" and she is by far the most fashionable patroness in the Romish church. *Norton. Yonge.*

St. George, Chevalier de. A name assumed by James Francis Edward Stuart, the elder Pretender. See PRETENDERS, THE.

St. Graal, or **San'greàl.** [Old Fr., holy grail; *graal, gréal, grasal,* Pr. *grazal,* from Middle Lat. *gradalis, gradale,* as if from a Latin word *cratalis,* from *crater, cratēra,* a cup.] A vessel made of a single precious stone (usually said to be an emerald), from which our Saviour was supposed to have drunk at the last supper, and which was afterward filled with the blood which flowed from the wounds with which he was pierced at the crucifixion; or, according to some accounts, it was the platter on which the paschal lamb was served at the last Passover which Jesus celebrated with his disciples. It is fabled to have been preserved and carried to England by Joseph of Arimathea. It remained there many years, an object of pilgrimage and devotion; but at length it disappeared, one of its keepers having violated the condition of strict virtue in thought, word, and deed, which was imposed upon those who had charge of it. Thenceforth many knights-errant, particularly those of the Round Table, spent their lives in searching for it, and Sir Galahad was at last successful in finding it. Various miraculous properties are attributed to this dish, by the old romancers, such as the power of prolonging life, preserving chastity, and the like. In some legends, it is said to have been brought down from heaven by angels, and given in charge to a body of knights, who guarded it in a temple-like castle on top of the inaccessible mountain Montsalvage, whence it would be borne away and vanish from their sight, if approached by any but a perfectly pure and holy person. [Called also *Holy Grail.*] See GALAHAD, SIR, and KING PECHEUR.

A sinful man, and unconfessed,
He took the *Sangreal's* holy quest,
And, slumbering, saw the vision high,
He might not view with waking eye.
Sir W. Scott.

St. Hilaire, Marco de (mar'ko' dụ sŏnt ê'lêr', 62, 64). A pseudonym of Émile Marc Hilaire, a French writer of the present day (b. 1790).

Saintine (săn'těn', 62). A pseudonym adopted by Joseph Xavier Boniface (b. 1797), a popular French writer, author of "Picciola" and other well-known works.

St. Le'ǫn. The title of a novel by William Godwin (1756–1836), and the name of its hero, a man who becomes possessed of the elixir of life (by which he has the power of renewing his youth), and the secret of the transmutation of metals into gold,— acquisitions which only bring him misfortunes and much protracted misery.

St. Nicholas. The patron saint of boys. He is said to have been bishop of Myra, in Lycia, and to have died in the year 326. Of his personal history little or nothing is known with certainty. The young were universally taught to revere him, and the

---

and for the Remarks and Rules to which the numbers after certain words refer, see pp. xiv-xxxii.

popular fiction which represents him as the bearer of presents to children on Christmas eve is well-known. He is the *Santa Claus* and the *Kriss Kringle* of the Dutch. [Written also Nicolas.] See KRISS KRINGLE.

☞ "St. Nicholas is said to have supplied three destitute maidens with marriage portions by secretly leaving money at their window, and as his day occurred just before Christmas, he thus was made the purveyor of the gifts of the season to all children in Flanders and Holland, who put out their shoe or stocking in the confidence that Santa Klaus, or Knecht Clobes, as they call him, will put in a prize for good conduct before morning. Another legend described the saint as having brought three murdered children to life again; and this rendered him the patron of boys, especially school-boys."
Yonge.

St. Patrick's, Dean of. See DEAN OF ST. PATRICK'S.

St. Patrick's Purgatory. The subject and locality of a legend long famous throughout Europe. The scene is laid in Ireland, upon an islet in Lough Derg. Here St. Patrick was supposed to have made a cave, through which was a descent into Purgatory for the living sinner who was desirous of expiating his evil deeds while yet in the flesh. The punishments undergone were analogous to those described by Dante in his "Divina Commedia." The interest in this legend and locality tended, perhaps, as much as any thing, to fix the popular notion of an intermediate state of existence. The story was made the subject of a romance in the fourteenth century; and, in Spain, in the seventeenth century, it was dramatised by Calderon. See OWAIN, SIR.

☞ "Who has not heard of St. Patrick's Purgatory, of its mysterious wonders, and of the crowds of devotees who have for ages been attracted by its reputed sanctity? There it stands, with its chapels and its toll-houses; and thither repair yearly crowds of pious pilgrims, who would wash away at once, by a visit to these holy shores, the accumulated sins of their lives." *Wright.*

St. Swith'in. Bishop of Winchester, and tutor to King Alfred, canonised by the Roman Catholic church. He is said to have wrought many miracles, the most celebrated being a rain of forty days' continuance, by which he testified his displeasure at an attempt of the monks to bury him in the chancel of the minster, instead of the open church-yard, as he had directed. Hence the popular superstition, that, if it rain on St. Swithin's day (July 15), it will rain for forty days thereafter.

St. Tam′mȧ-nẏ. An Indian chief, who, in the United States, has been *popularly* canonized as a saint, and adopted as the tutelary genius of one branch of the Democratic party. Tammany, or Tammenund (the name is variously written), was of the Delaware nation, and lived probably in the middle of the seventeenth century. He resided in the country which is now Delaware until he was of age, when he moved beyond the Alleghanies, and settled on the banks of the Ohio. He became a chief sachem of his tribe, and, being always a friend of the whites, often restrained his warriors from deeds of violence. His rule was always discreet, and he endeavoured to induce his followers to cultivate agriculture and the arts of peace, rather than those of war. When he became old, he called a council to have a successor appointed; after which the residue of his life was spent in retirement; and tradition relates that "young and old repaired to his wigwam to hear him discourse wisdom." His great motto was, "Unite in peace for happiness, in war for defence." When and by whom he was first styled *Saint*, or by what whim he was chosen to be the patron of the Democracy, does not appear.

☞ "The Americans sometimes call their tutelar saint 'Tamendy,' a corruption of the name [Tammenund] of the renowned chief here introduced. There are many traditions which speak of the character and power of Tamenund." *Cooper.*

This is the first of May; our shepherds and nymphs are celebrating our glorious *St. Tammany's* day. We'll hear the song out, and then join in the frolic, and chorus it o'er and o'er again. This day shall be devoted to joy and festivity. *Old (Amer.) Play.*

Sakhrat (săk'răt). (*Mohammedan Myth.*) A sacred stone of which a single grain gives miraculous powers to the possessor. This stone is of an emerald colour, and its reflected light is the cause of the tints of the sky. Upon it rests Mount Caf. See MOUNT CAF.

Salamanca, Bachelor of. See DON CHERUBIM.

Să-lā'ni-o. A friend to Antonio and Bassanio, in Shakespeare's "Merchant of Venice."

Să'lă-rī'no. A friend to Antonio and Bassanio, in Shakespeare's "Merchant of Venice."

Sal-mo'neûs. [Gr. Σαλμωνεύς.] (*Gr. & Rom. Myth.*) A king of Elis, son of Æolus, and brother of Sisyphus; celebrated for his arrogance and impiety. He ordered sacrifices to be offered to himself, as if he were a god, and even imitated the thunder and lightning of Jupiter, for which he was struck by a thunderbolt, and punished in the infernal regions.

It was to be the literary *Salmoneus* of the political Jupiter. *Sir E. Bulwer Lytton.*

Salt River. An imaginary river, up which defeated political parties are supposed to be sent to oblivion. [*Cant, U. S.*]

☞ "The phrase, ' To row up Salt River,' has its origin in the fact that there is a small stream of that name in Kentucky, the passage of which is made difficult and laborious as well by its tortuous course as by the abundance of shallows and bars. The real application of the phrase is to the unhappy wight who has the task of propelling the boat up the stream; but, in political or slang usage, it is to those who are rowed up." *J. Inman.*

Sam. A popular synonym in the United States for the Know-nothing, or Native-American, party. The name involves an allusion to *Uncle Sam*, the common personification of the government of the United States.

Sam, Dicky. See DICKY SAM.

Sam, Uncle. See UNCLE SAM.

Samaël (să'mă-el). In the old Jewish demonology, the prince of demons, who in the guise of a serpent tempted Eve. Many Rabbins, however, say that he is the angel of death, who is armed with a sword, or with a bow and arrows. By some, he is identified with Asmodeus.

Sam'bo. A cant designation of the negro race.

No race has ever shown such capabilities of adaptation to varying soil and circumstances as the negro. Alike to them the snows of Canada, the hard, rocky land of New England, or the gorgeous profusion of the Southern States. *Sambo* and Cuffey expand under them all. *Harriet Beecher Stowe.*

Samian Sage. An appellation bestowed upon Pythagoras (about 584-506 B. C.), one of the most celebrated philosophers of antiquity, who, according to the received opinion, was a native of Samos.

Sampson. A servant to Capulet, in Shakespeare's tragedy of "Romeo and Juliet."

Sampson, Dominie. See DOMINIE SAMPSON.

Sam'son (-sn). A judge of Israel in the twelfth century before Christ; famous for his wonderful strength,— which was dependent on the length of his hair,—and for his unfortunate marriage with the artful Delilah, a Philistine, who betrayed him to his enemies. Milton's magnificent classical tragedy of "Samson Agonistes" — that is, Samson the Champion, or Combatant — is founded upon and embodies the Scriptural account of Samson.

Sancho. See PANZA, SANCHO.

Sanction, Pragmatic. See PRAGMATIC SANCTION.

Sand, George (jorj sand, *or* zhoȓzh sŏⁿ, 62). A pseudonym of Madame Dudevant, a distinguished French authoress of the present day (b. 1804). The name Sand was assumed in consequence of Mme. Dudevant's friendship for Jules Sandeau, a young student, conjointly with whom she wrote her first novel, "Rose et Blanche," which was published (1832) with "Jules Sand" on the title-page as the author's name.

San-dal'phŏn. In the Rabbinical system of angelology, one of three angels who receive the prayers of the Israelites and weave crowns from them. Longfellow has made this superstition the subject of a beautiful poem.

Sand'fọ̄rd, Harry. One of the leading characters in Thomas Day's popular juvenile work entitled "The History of Sandford and Merton."

> Now the poor cottager has . . . something of the pleasure which *Sandford* and Merton felt when they had built and thatched their house, and then sat within it, gravely proud and happy. *A. K. H. Boyd.*

San'glā-mōre. The sword of Braggadochio, in Spenser's "Faëry Queen."

Sangrado, Doctor (sȧn-grȧ'tho, 56). The name of a physician in Le Sage's novel of "Gil Blas," who practises blood-letting as a remedy for all sorts of ailments. By Le Sage's contemporaries, this character was generally thought to be intended for the celebrated Helvetius.

> If this will not be sufficient, may we have plenty of *Sangrados* to pour in plenty of cold water till this terrible fermentation is over!
> *Sterne.*

> I was obliged to send for a physician, who seemed to have been a disciple of *Sangrado*; for he scarce left a drop of blood in my body.
> *Smollett.*

> The results were "bad nights and much feverish agitation;" and the remedies were of the usual desperate *Sangrado* order, — bleeding two days in succession, leaving him "almost dead." *Percy Fitzgerald.*

Sangreal. See ST. GRAAL.

Santa Cláus, or **Kláus** (*Dutch pron.* sȧn'tȧ klowss). The Dutch name of *St. Nicholas.* See ST. NICHOLAS.

Sappho of Toulouse (săf'fo, too'- looz'). A title given to Clemence Isaure (b. 1664), on account of a beautiful ode to Spring which she composed.

Săr'ȧs-wă'tĭ. (*Hindu Myth.*) The wife of Brahma, and the goddess of poetry, painting, sculpture, eloquence, and music. [Written also **Seriswattee.**]

Sar-mā'ti-ȧ (sar-mā'shĭ-ȧ). The country of the Sarmatæ, a great Slavic people of ancient times, dwelling between the Vistula and the Don. It is often used in modern poetry as synonymous with Poland.

> Oh, bloodiest picture in the book of Time! *Sarmatia* fell unwept, without a crime;

> Found not a generous friend, a pitying foe, Strength in her arms, nor mercy in her woe.
> *Campbell.*

Sar-pe'dọ̆n. [Gr. Σαρπηδών.] (*Gr. & Rom. Myth.*) A son of Jupiter, and king of Lycia, who went into the Trojan war to assist Priam, and was slain by Patroclus.

Sā'tặn. [Heb., an adversary; Lat. *Sat'a-nas.*] One of the names of the Devil, and that by which in the Bible, in poetry, and in popular legends, he is often designated. According to the Talmud, he was originally an archangel, but revolted from God, together with one third of the host of heaven, on being required to bow down and do reverence to Adam. He was thereupon expelled from heaven, vanquished in battle by Michael and the other angels "who kept their first estate," and cast with all his crew into the abyss of hell. Satan is the most conspicuous figure in Milton's sublime epic, the "Paradise Lost," and he figures also in the "Paradise Regained" of the same author. Those mediæval writers who reckoned nine kinds of demons, placed Satan at the head of the fifth rank, which consisted of cozeners, as magicians and witches. Wierus makes him leader of the opposition in the infernal empire, of which Beëlzebub was considered the sovereign. See DEVIL, THE.

☞ "The legendary Satan is a being wholly distinct from the theological Lucifer. He is never ennobled by the sullen dignity of the fallen angel. No traces of celestial origin are to be discovered on his brow. He is not a rebellious æon who was once clothed in radiance; but he is the fiend, the enemy, evil from all time past in his very essence, foul and degraded, cowardly and impure: his rage is oftenest impotent, unless his cunning can assist his power. Equally dramatic and poetical is the part allotted to Satan in those ancient romances of religion, 'The Lives of the Saints.' But in the conception of the legendary Satan, the belief in his might melts into the ideal of his character. Amidst clouds of infernal vapour he develops his form, half in allegory, and half with spiritual reality; and his horns, his tail, his saucer-eyes, his claws, his taunts, his wiles, his mal-

ice, all bear witness to the simultaneous yet contradictory impressions to which the hagiologist is compelled to yield."
Pulgrave.

☞ "Milton has carefully marked in his Satan the intense selfishness, the alcohol of egotism, which would rather reign in hell than serve in heaven. To place this lust of self in opposition to denial of self or duty, and to show what exertions it would make, and what pains endure, to accomplish its end, is Milton's particular object in the character of Satan. But around this character he has thrown a singularity of daring, a grandeur of sufferance, and a ruined splendour, which constitute the very height of poetic sublimity." *Coleridge.*

Satanic School. A name often given to a class of writers whose productions are thought to be characterised by an impatience of all restraint, a disgust at the whole constitution of society, an impassioned and extravagant strain of sentimentality, and a presumptuous scorn of all moral rules, as well as of the holiest truths of religion. Southey, in the preface to his "Vision of Judgment," was the first to use this degrading appellation. Of the writers who have been included under it, Byron, Shelley, Moore, Bulwer, Rousseau, Victor Hugo, Paul de Kock, and George Sand are the most prominent.

☞ "Immoral writers, . . . men of diseased hearts and depraved imaginations, who, forming a system of opinions to suit their own unhappy course of conduct, have rebelled against the holiest ordinances of human society, and, hating that revealed religion which, with all their efforts and bravadoes, they are unable entirely to disbelieve, labour to make others as miserable as themselves by infecting them with a moral virus that eats into the soul. The school which they have set up may properly be called the *Satanic School;* for, though their productions breathe the spirit of Belial in their lascivious parts, and the spirit of Moloch in their loathsome images of atrocities and horrors, which they delight to represent, they are more especially characterised by a Satanic spirit of pride and audacious impiety which still betrays the wretched feeling of hopelessness wherewith it is allied." *Southey.*

This ["Werther"] and "Goetz von Berlichingen" . . . have produced incalculable effects,—which now, indeed, however some departing echo of them may linger in the wrecks of our own Mosstrooper [imitation of Sir Walter Scott's "Lay of the Last Minstrel"] and *Satanic Schools*, do at length all happily lie behind us. *Curlyle.*

Sat'urn. [Lat. *Saturnus*, cognate with *serere*, to sow, *sator*, a planter.] (*Gr. & Rom. Myth.*) The first king of Latium, who came to Italy in the reign of James. He was afterward worshipped as the god of agriculture, and of civilisation and social order. At a very early period he was identified with the *Cronos* of the Greeks, and hence was said to be the son of Cœlus and Terra, and the husband of Ops, or Cybele. He was dethroned and imprisoned by his brother Titan, but was set at liberty and reinstated in his rights by his son Jupiter, who, however, afterward deposed him and divided his kingdom with Neptune and Pluto. Saturn fled to Italy, where his reign was so mild that men called it "the golden age."

Sat'y-râne, Sir. A knight, in Spenser's "Faëry Queen," who helps Una escape from the satyrs who rescued her from the lust of Archimago.

And passion, erst unknown, could gain
The breast of blunt *Sir Satyrane.*
Sir W. Scott.

Sat'yrs, or **Sā'tyrs.** [Gr. Σάτυροι, Lat. *Satyri.*] (*Gr. & Rom. Myth.*) Woodland deities with horns, pointed ears, tails, and goat's feet. They are described as fond of wine and every kind of sensual pleasure.

Säun'dĕrs, Clerk. The hero of a well-known Scottish ballad.

Säun'dĕrs, Richard. A feigned name under which Dr. Franklin, in 1732, commenced the publication of an Almanac, commonly called "Poor Richard's Almanac," of which the distinguishing feature was a series of maxims of prudence and industry in the form of proverbs.

☞ "I endeavoured to make it both entertaining and useful. . . . And, observing that it was generally read, scarce any neighbourhood in the province being without it, I considered it as a proper vehicle for conveying instruction among the common people, who bought scarcely any other books. I therefore filled all the

little spaces that occurred between the remarkable days in the calendar with proverbial sentences, chiefly such as inculcated industry and frugality as the means of procuring wealth, and thereby securing virtue; it being more difficult for a man in want to act always honestly, as, to use here one of those proverbs, 'It is hard for an empty sack to stand upright.' These proverbs, which contained the wisdom of many ages and nations, I assembled and formed into a connected discourse prefixed to the Almanac of 1757, as the harangue of a wise old man to the people attending an auction. The bringing all these scattered counsels thus into a focus, enabled them to make greater impression. The piece, being universally approved, was copied in all the newspapers of the American continent; reprinted in Britain, on a large sheet of paper, to be stuck up in houses; two translations were made of it in France, and great numbers bought by the clergy and gentry, to distribute gratis among their poor parishioners and tenants. In Pennsylvania, as it discouraged useless expense in foreign superfluities, some thought it had its share of influence in producing that growing plenty of money which was observable for several years after its publication."
Franklin's Autobiography.

Saw'ney. A sportive designation applied by the English to the Scotch. It is a corruption of *Sandie*, the Scottish abbreviation of *Alexander*.

I muse how any man can say that the Scotch, as a people, are deficient in humour! Why, *Sawney* has a humour of his own so strong and irrepressible that it broke out all the stronger in spite of worldly thrift, kirk-session, cutty-stool, and lectures.
Hartley Coleridge.

Saxon Switzerland. A name commonly given to the mountainous region of the kingdom of Saxony southeast of Dresden. Although the scenery is highly picturesque, its mountains are of no great elevation, the highest not exceeding 2000 feet.

☞ "To readers of a touring habit, this Saxon country is perhaps well known. For the last half-century, it has been growing more and more famous, under the name of ' Saxon Switzerland' (*Sächsische Schweitz*), instead of ' Misnian Highlands' (*Maissnische Hochland*), which it used to be called. A beautiful enough and extremely rugged country; interesting to the picturesque mind. Begins rising, in soft hills, on both sides of the Elbe, a few miles east of Dresden, as you ascend the river; till it rises into hills of wild character, getting ever wilder, and riven into wondrous chasms and precipices;... torn and tumbled into stone labyrinths, chasms, and winding rock walls, as few regions are. Grows pinewood, to the topmost height; pine-trees far aloft look quietly down upon you, over sheer precipices, on your intricate path." *Carlyle.*

Scæv'o-lă. [Lat., diminutive of *scæva*, the left-handed.] A surname or sobriquet of Caius Mucius, a young Roman patrician, who made his way into the camp of King Porsena to kill him, and, on his intention being discovered, burned off his own right hand, to show that he did not fear torture or death.

Scan'dĭ-nā'vĭ-ă. The classic name of the great peninsula of northern Europe, consisting of Sweden and Norway; often used in modern poetry.

Scapino (skȧ-pe'no), or **Scā'pin** (*Fr. pron.* skȧ'păⁿ', 62). [From It. *scappino*, a sock, or short stocking.]
1. A mask on the Italian stage; represented as a cunning and knavish servant of Gratiano, the loquacious and pedantic Bolognese doctor.
2. A valet in Molière's comedy, " Les Fourberies de Scapin."

Both were angry, and a war began, in which Frederick stooped to the part of Harpagon, and Voltaire to that of *Scapin*. *Macaulay.*

Scăr'ă-môûch'. [Originally the name of a celebrated Italian comedian.] A military personage in the old Italian comedy, derived from Spain, and dressed in the Spanish or Hispano-Neapolitan costume. His character is that of a great boaster and poltroon, and in the end he always receives a beating from Harlequin. The term is used in a general way to stigmatise a buffoon or braggadochio.

Scaramouch is to have the honour of the day, and now marches to the engagement on the shoulder of the philosopher. *Dryden.*

Scarlet, Will. One of the companions of Robin Hood, as appears from an old ballad.
"I have heard talk of Robin Hood,
    Derry, derry, derry down;
And of brave Little John,
Of Friar Tuck, and *Will Scarlet*,
Stokesby, and Maid Marian.
    Hey down."

Scarlet Woman. In the controversial writings of the Protestants, a common designation of the church of Rome, intended to symbolise its vices and corruptions. The allusion is to the description contained in *Revelation*, xvii., where it is said, that "the woman ... is that great city which reigneth over the kings of the earth."

Scathe'looke. The name of one of Robin Hood's followers. See RONIN HOOD.

Scheherezade, Queen (she-he′re-zād′; *Fr. pron.* shā′hā′rā′zâd′). The fictitious relater of the stories in the "Arabian Nights' Entertainments." The sultan of the Indies, exasperated by the infidelity of his wife, resolves to espouse a new sultana every evening, and to strangle her in the morning, to prevent the accidents of the day. At length, Scheherezade, the daughter of the vizier, solicits the hand of this indulgent bridegroom, interrupts the progress of these frequent and sanguinary nuptials, and saves her own life, by the relation of tales in which she awakens and suspends the sultan's curiosity night after night, till he at length repents of his vow, and recalls it.

Pray consider, even the memory of the renowned *Scheherezade*, that empress of tale-tellers, could not preserve every circumstance, *Sir W. Scott.*

If we may borrow another illustration from *Queen Scheherezade*, we would compare the writers of this school to the jewellers who were employed to complete the unfinished window of the palace of Aladdin. *Macaulay.*

Schlemihl, Peter (shlā′meel, 61). The title of a little work by Chamisso (1781-1838), and the name of its hero, a man who sells his shadow to an old man in gray (the Devil) who meets him just after he has been disappointed in an application for assistance to a nobleman. The name has become a by-word for any poor, silly, and unfortunate fellow.

Scholastic Doctor. An honorary title given by his admirers to Anselm of Laon (b. 1117), a celebrated French theologian.

Sco′gan, John. A favourite buffoon of the court of Edward IV. A collection of his jests was published by the notorious Dr. Andrew Borde.

Sco′ti-ă (sko′shĭ-ă). A modern Latin name of Scotland, often used by the poets. It was formerly, and for a long time (some say from the second to the tenth century), applied to Ireland, which was sometimes called *Scotia Magna*, or *Major*, to distinguish it from *Scotia Minor*, or Scotland. Old historians derive the name from that of Scota, wife of a legendary king of Ireland. Venerable Bede says that Scotland bore the name of Caledonia until A. D. 258, when it was invaded by a tribe from Ireland, and called Scotia.

Scottish Ho′garth. A title given to David Allan (1744-1796), whose skill as an artist lay in depicting the familiar and the humourous.

Scottish Homer. A title given by his literary friends to William Wilkie (1721-1772), author of "The Epigoniad."

Scottish Solomon. James VI. of Scotland and I. of England. See SOLOMON OF ENGLAND, 2.

Scottish Ten′i-ērs. A name given to Sir David Wilkie (1785-1841), a Scottish painter who ranks among the most celebrated masters of the Dutch school.

The scales fell from his eyes on viewing the sketches of a contemporary, the *Scottish Teniers*, as Wilkie has been deservedly styled. *Sir W. Scott.*

Scottish The-oc′rĭ-tus. A name often given to Allan Ramsay (1685-1758), a popular and eminently national Scottish poet. His "Gentle Shepherd" is, perhaps, the finest dramatic pastoral in the language.

Scourers. See TITYRE TUS.

Scourge of God. [Gothic *Godegesil*, Lat. *Flagellum Dei.*] A title often given to Attila, king of the Huns, and the most formidable of the invaders of the Roman empire. It is first found in the legend of St. Loup, written in the eighth or ninth century by a priest of Troyes.

☞ "He was the son of Mundzuk, and, with his brother Bleda, ... attained, in A. D. 434, to the sovereignty of all the northern tribes between the frontier of Gaul and the frontier of China, and to the command of an army of 500,000 barbarians. In this position, partly from the real terror it inspired, partly from his own endeavours to invest himself, in the eyes of Christendom, with the dreadful character of the predicted Antichrist, and in the eyes of his own countrymen with the invincible attributes attendant on the possessor of the miraculous sword of the Scythian god of war, he gradually concentrated on himself the awe and fear of the whole ancient world, which ultimately expressed itself by affixing to his name the well-known epithet of 'The Scourge of God.' The word seems to have been used generally at the time to denote the barbarian invaders; but it is not directly applied to Attila in any author prior to the Hungarian Chronicles, which first relate the story of his receiving the name from a hermit in Gaul. The earliest contemporary approaches to it are in a passage in Isidore's Chronicle speaking of the Huns as '*Virga Dei*,' and in an inscription at Aquileia, written a short time before the siege in 451, in which they are described as '*imminentia peccatorum flagella*' [the threatening scourges of sinners]." *A. P. Stanley.* Ihre (" Glossarium Suiogothicum," *sub voce* "Gisl") suggests that *Godegesil* — usually derived from *Goth*, God, and *gesil*, rod, whip, scourge — may probably come from the Gothic words *Goth*, God, and *gesal*, given, corresponding to the Gr. Θεόδοτος, Lat. *Deodatus*, a common title of the kings and emperors who were Attila's contemporaries. The epithet would then convey no injurious meaning.

Scourge of Princes. An appellation given to Pietro Aretino (1492-1556), an Italian author, who distinguished himself as a satirist.

Scrambling Committee. A name given to the "patriots" of Ireland, in the Irish parliament, who were received into favour by the Duke of Devonshire, viceroy in 1755, and who signalised themselves for their rapacity in regard to the division of the surplus revenue.

Scri-ble'rus, Cornelius (9). The name of the father of Martinus Scriblerus; noted for his pedantry and his oddities and absurdities about the education of his son. See SCRIBLERUS, MARTINUS.

Scri-ble'rus, Mar-ti'nus (9). A celebrated personage whose imaginary history is related in the satirical "Memoirs of the Extraordinary Life, Works, and Discoveries of Martinus Scriblerus," usually published in Pope's works, but chiefly, if not wholly, written by Arbuthnot. The design of this work, as stated by Pope, is to ridicule all the false tastes in learning, under the character of a man of capacity that had dipped into every art and science, but injudiciously in each.

Being a world-schoolmaster (and, indeed, a *Martinus Scriblerus*, as we here find, more ways than one), this was not strange in him. *Carlyle.*

Scrog'gen. A poor hack author celebrated by Goldsmith in his "Description of an Author's Bed-chamber."

Otway could still die of hunger, not to speak of innumerable *Scrogginses* (*Scroggens*), whom "the Muse found stretched beneath a rug." *Carlyle.*

Scrub. An amusing valet in Farquhar's comedy, "The Beaux' Stratagem."

Scyl'la. [Gr. Σκύλλα.] (*Gr. & Rom. Myth.*) 1. A daughter of Nisus, who, for love of Minos, cut from her father's head a purple lock, on the preservation of which his life depended, and was changed in consequence into a lark.

2. A daughter of Phorcus, changed by Circe, who was jealous of her, into a frightful sea-monster, and placed on a rock on the Italian coast opposite Charybdis on the coast of Sicily.

Search, Edward. A pseudonym under which Abraham Tucker (1705-1774), an English metaphysician, published his "Light of Nature Pursued."

Searcher, The. A surname or sobriquet given to Dr. Robert Fludd (1574-1637), on account of his investigations in medicine, mathematics, philosophy, &c.

Searle, January. A pseudonym adopted by George Searle Phillips, a popular writer of the present day, author of "The Gypsies of the Danes' Dike."

Se-bast'ian. 1. A character in Shakespeare's "Tempest."

☞ For the "Key to the Scheme of Pronunciation," with the accompanying Explanations,

2. A character in Shakespeare's "Twelfth Night."

Se-ces'si-ă (se-sesh'ĭ-ă). A popular collective name applied to the States which attempted to secede from the American Union, in 1860-61. The inhabitants received the cant name of "The Secesh."

Second Au-gŭs'tĭne. A title given to St. Thomas Aquinas by his admiring scholars. See ANGELIC DOCTOR.

Sed'ley, Amelia. A marked figure in Thackeray's "Vanity Fair;" an impersonation of virtue without intellect. She is contrasted with Becky Sharp, who is an impersonation of intellect without virtue. The one has no head, the other no heart.

Seekers. A name originally given to the Quakers, or Friends, from their seeking the truth.

Self-denying Ordinance. (*Eng. Hist.*) The name given to an act or resolution of the Long Parliament, passed Dec. 9, 1644, whereby the members bound themselves not to accept certain executive offices, particularly commands in the army. The effect of this ordinance was the transference of power, first in the army and then in the State, from the Presbyterian to the Independent party.

Se'lim. 1. The hero of Byron's "Bride of Abydos;" brought up as a son, but treated with great cruelty, by his uncle, the pasha Giaffer, who has secretly destroyed his own brother, Abdallah, Selim's father, by poison. The discovery of the fondness of his beautiful daughter, Zuleika, for her supposed brother, fills Giaffer with rage and jealousy. He informs Zuleika, in the presence of Selim, of his intention to marry her immediately to Osmyn Bey; but she voluntarily gives a promise to Selim, in private, never to marry against his wishes. At his urgent request, she meets him at night in a favourite grotto in the harem gardens. He appears, not as a pasha's son, but as the chief of a band of pirates, informs her that he is not her brother, declares his love, and proposes that she should fly with him, and become the companion of his adventures and toils, the sharer of his joys and triumphs, when distant voices and flashing torches announce betrayal and pursuit. Selim is shot while endeavouring to join his followers on the beach; but he dies not unrevenged, for Zuleika cannot survive her lover, and Giaffer is left in childless desolation.

2. The hero of Moore's "Lalla Rookh." See LALLA ROOKH.

Sem'e-le. [Gr. Σεμέλη.] (*Gr. & Rom. Myth.*) A daughter of Cadmus and Thebe, and mother of Bacchus by Jupiter.

Se'mĭr'ă-mis. [Gr. Σεμίραμις.] A celebrated queen of Assyria, wife and successor of Ninus. She built the walls of Babylon, was slain by her own son, Ninyas, and was turned, according to the popular belief, into a pigeon.

Se-mĭr'ă-mis of the North. 1. A name often given to Margaret (1353-1412), daughter of Waldemar III., king of Denmark, and a most politic and able ruler. By the death of her father and of her son, his successor, she became queen of Denmark; and, by the death of her husband, Haco VIII., king of Norway, she succeeded to the throne of that kingdom also. She then turned her arms against Albert, king of Sweden, who was unpopular with his subjects, defeated him, and made him prisoner, upon which she was acknowledged queen of Sweden. She is said to have possessed considerable beauty of person, and unusual powers of fascination.

From Scotland it [the name Margaret] went to Norway with the daughter of Alexander III., whose bridal cost the life of Sir Patrick Spens; and it . . . remained in Scandinavia to be the dreaded name of the *Semiramis of the North*, and was taken as the equivalent of Astrid and Grjotgard.   *Yonge.*

2. A title given to Catharine II., empress of Russia (1729-1796), a powerful and ambitious sovereign, who administered with great energy the internal affairs of the empire, while carrying on extensive and important wars with other nations. Her sensuality was extreme, and she lived a life of open and unrestrained vice.

Sentry, Captain. One of the members of the fictitious club under whose auspices and superintendence the "Spectator" was professedly issued.

September Massacre. (*Fr. Hist.*) An indiscriminate slaughter of loyalists confined in the Abbaye and other prisons, which took place in Paris, September 2-5, 1792, on receipt of the news of the capture of Verdun. The number of victims was not less than 1200, and by some is placed as high as 4000.

Seraphic Doctor. [Lat. *Doctor Seraphicus.*] An appellation given to St. Bonaventura (1221-1274), an Italian scholastic theologian of the order of Franciscans, and one of the most eminent of Roman Catholic divines. He was so called on account of the religious fervour of his style. Dante places him among the saints in his "Paradiso," and, in 1587, he was ranked by Sixtus V. as the sixth of the great doctors of the Church. His own order is as proud of him as the Dominicans are of Thomas Aquinas.

What do I care for the *Doctor Seraphic*,
With all his wordy chaffer and traffic?
Longfellow.

Seraphic Saint. An appellation bestowed upon St. Francis d'Assisi (1182-1226), founder of the order of the Franciscans. "Of all the saints," says Dean Milman, "St. Francis was the most blameless and gentle."

Sĕr′ă-pis. [Gr. Σαράπις, Σεράπις.] (*Myth.*) An Egyptian deity, afterward worshipped also in Greece and Rome; at first a symbol of the Nile, and so of fertility; later, an infernal god.

Sĕr-ġes′tus. One of the companions of Æneas; the reputed progenitor of the Sergian family at Rome. He took part in the naval games at Drepanum, in Sicily, on the occasion of the anniversary of Anchises's death, and commanded the "Centaur," but ran upon the rocks, and with difficulty preserved the vessel and crew.

Servant of the Servants of God. [Lat. *Servus Servorum Dei.*] A style or appellation assumed by Pope Gregory I. (544-604) in his letters, and retained by his successors. By "the servants of God," the bishops are intended.

Set′e-bos. A deity mentioned in Shakespeare's "Tempest" as worshipped by Sycorax, the mother of Caliban.

His art is of such power,
It would control my dam's god *Setebos*.
Shak.

☞ Shakespeare did not invent this false god; he had found him in the travels of his time, in which he is mentioned as a deity of the Patagonians,— an evidence, in addition to others, that Shakespeare had been reading books of American discovery before he wrote "The Tempest."

The giants, when they found themselves fettered, roared like bulls, and cried upon *Setebos* to help them.
Eden's Hist. of Travayle.

Seven against Thebes. (*Gr. & Rom. Myth.*) The leaders of an expedition designed to place Polynices on the throne of Thebes, from which he had been driven by his brother Eteocles. (See ETEOCLES.) Their names were Adrastus, Amphiaraus, Capaneus, Hippomedon (Argives); Parthenopæus (an Arcadian); Polynices (a Theban); Tydeus (an Æolian). The expedition was a failure, as the chiefs were arrogant and boastful, and despised signs sent by the gods; but a second expedition, conducted by their more pious sons, — the *Epigoni*, — who acted in obedience to the will of heaven, was crowned with success. One of the noblest dramas of Æschylus is entitled "The Seven against Thebes."

Seven Champions of Christendom. St. George, the patron saint of England; St. Denis, of France; St. James, of Spain; St. Anthony, of Italy; St. Andrew, of Scotland; St. Patrick, of Ireland; and St. David, of Wales. They are often alluded to by old writers. "The Famous History of the Seven Champions of Christendom" is the work of Richard Johnson, a ballad-maker of some note at the end of the sixteenth and the beginning of the seventeenth centuries.

☞ For the "Key to the Scheme of Pronunciation," with the accompanying Explanations.

Seven Cities, Island of. See ISLAND OF THE SEVEN CITIES.

Seven-hilled City. One of the names by which Rome has for many ages been designated. It was originally built upon seven hills, several of which have, in course of time, so far disappeared that they are now hardly recognizable.

Seven Sages. 1. See SEVEN WISE MEN OF GREECE.

2. Characters in an ancient English metrical romance having this appellation for its title.

☞ A young Roman prince having rejected improper advances made by his step-mother, the latter falsely accuses him of having attempted to offer her violence, and persuades her husband to order his death; but the prince's instructors, the Seven Sages, preserve his life by each telling the emperor, his father, on successive days, a story which as often induces him to delay the execution, though each night the queen counteracts the effect they have produced by telling a story which changes her husband's mind. At the end of seven days, the prince, who has all the while abstained from speaking, in obedience to information obtained by consulting the stars, tells a story which leads his father to have the queen brought to judgment and put to death. The romance of the Seven Sages is of great antiquity, and probably of Indian origin. Versions exist in Arabic, Hebrew, Greek, Latin, French, German, and other languages. In English there are two metrical versions, and also one in the humble form of a chap-book, under the title of "The Seven Wise Masters."

Seven Sleepers. According to a very widely diffused legend of early Christianity, seven noble youths of Ephesus, in the time of the Decian persecution, who, having fled to a certain cavern for refuge, and having been pursued, discovered, and walled in for a cruel death, were made to fall asleep, and in that state were miraculously kept for almost two centuries. Their names are traditionally said to have been Maximian, Malchus, Martinian, Denis, John, Serapion, and Constantine. Their relics are said to have been conveyed to Marseilles in a large stone coffin, which is still shown there in St. Victor's church. The church has canonised the Seven Sleepers, and has consecrated the 27th of June to their memory. The Koran relates the tale of the Seven Sleepers, — deriving it probably from the same source as the Christian legend, — and declares that out of respect for them the sun altered his course twice a day that he might shine into the cavern.

☞ "By the Seven Sleepers are commonly understood seven Christians of the third century of our era, who were put to death for the faith of Jesus Christ. The event happened at Ephesus, in Asia Minor, in the reign of the emperor Decius. ... More than two centuries after, ... their bodies having been found in a cavern where they had been enclosed, they were taken out, and exposed to the veneration of the faithful. The legend, in speaking of their death, said, following the usual form, that they had fallen asleep in the Lord. The vulgar took occasion thence to say that these holy martyrs were not dead; that they had been hid in the cavern, where they had fallen asleep; and that they at last awoke, to the great astonishment of the spectators. Such is the origin of the legend of the Seven Sleepers. At Ephesus, the spot is still shown where this pretended miracle took place. As a dog had accompanied these seven martyrs into their retreat, he has been made to share the celebrity of his masters, and is fabled to have remained standing all the time they slept, without eating or drinking, being wholly occupied with guarding their persons. The Persians celebrate annually the feast of the Seven Sleepers, and their names are regarded as powerful talismans against the decrees of fate. Their dog has not been forgotten; and, to recompense him for his zeal, he has been intrusted with the care of letters missive and correspondences, and admitted to Paradise with the ram which Abraham sacrificed in place of his son, with the ass of Balaam, with the ass upon which our Lord entered Jerusalem upon the Day of Palms, and with the mare upon which Mohammed mounted miraculously to heaven." *Reinaud.*

Tressilian's fellow hath ever averred, that to wake the earl were death, and Masters would wake the *Seven Sleepers* themselves, if he thought they slept not by regular ordinance of medicine. *Sir W. Scott.*

Here, however, we gladly recall to mind that once we saw him laugh; once only; perhaps it was the first and last time in his life;

but then such a peal of laughter,—enough to have awakened the *Seven Sleepers!* *Carlyle.*

"Whoever it is, has knocked three times, and each one loud enough to wake the"—he had such a repugnance to the idea of waking the dead, that he stopped even then, with the words upon his tongue, and said, instead—"the Seven Sleepers." *Dickens.*

Seven Wise Masters. See SEVEN SAGES, 2.

I think he [Don Quixote] is one of the *Seven Wise Masters.* I thought he knew nothing but his knight-errantry, but now I see the devil a thing can escape him: he has an oar in every man's boat, and a finger in every man's pie. *Cervantes, Trans.*

Seven Wise Men of Greece. Famous Greeks of the sixth century B. C., distinguished for their practical sagacity and their wise maxims or principles of life. Their names are variously given; but those most generally admitted to the honour are Solon, Chilo, Pittacus, Bias, Periander (in place of whom some give Epimenides), Cleobulus, and Thales. They were the authors of the celebrated mottoes inscribed in later days in the Delphian temple: "Know thyself" (*Solon*); "Consider the end" (*Chilo*); "Know thy opportunity" (*Pittacus*); "Most men are bad" (*Bias*); "Nothing is impossible to industry" (*Periander*); "Avoid excess" (*Cleobulus*); "Suretyship is the precursor of ruin" (*Thales*).

Seven Wonders of the World. A name given to seven very remarkable objects of the ancient world, which have been variously enumerated. The following classification is the one most generally received: 1. The Pyramids of Egypt; 2. The Pharos of Alexandria; 3. The walls and hanging gardens of Babylon; 4. The temple of Diana at Ephesus; 5. The statue of Jupiter by Phidias, at Olympia; 6. The Mausoleum erected by Artemisia, at Halicarnassus; 7. The Colossus of Rhodes.

Seven Years' War. (*Ger. Hist.*) A war carried on by two alliances, headed respectively by Austria and Prussia, which commenced in 1756, and was brought to a close—without any material advantages gained by any party—by the peace of Hubertsburg, Nov. 15, 1763. It is remarkable for the extraordinary campaigns of Frederick the Great, the Prussian king.

Seyd. A fierce and revengeful pasha in Byron's poem of "The Corsair." See GULNARE, 1.

But a scene ensued like that in the hall of Seyd. *Sir W. Scott.*

Sey'ton (-tn). An officer attending Macbeth, in Shakespeare's tragedy of this name.

Sganarelle (sgä'nȧ'rel'). 1. The hero of Molière's comedy, "Le Mariage Forcé." He is represented as a humourist of fifty-three or four, who, having a mind to marry a fashionable young woman, but feeling some instinctive doubts and scruples, consults several of his friends upon this momentous question. Receiving no satisfactory counsel, and not much pleased with the proceedings of his bride elect, he at last determines to give up his engagement, but is cudgelled into compliance by the brother of his intended.

☞ The plot of this play is founded on an adventure of the Count de Grammont, who, when leaving England, was followed by the brothers of *la belle* Hamilton, who, with their hands on the pommels of their swords, asked him if he had not left something behind. "True," said the count, "I forgot to marry your sister;" and instantly went back to repair his lapse of memory by making her Countess de Grammont.

2. A simple-minded valet in Molière's "Festin de Pierre," who is ever halting between the fear of being drubbed by his master, Don Juan, and the far deeper horror of abetting or witnessing his crimes. See DON JUAN.

3. The same name occurs in several of Molière's other plays ("Le Cocu Imaginaire," "L'École des Maris," &c.), and is usually assigned to a bluff, wilful, and domineering character.

De Pradt answered by saying that ... the country was in the situation of the wife of *Sganarelle* in the farce, who quarrelled with a stranger for interfering with her husband when he was beating her. *Sir W. Scott.*

Shac'ạ-bac. See BARMECIDE, THE.

Shȧf'ton, Sir Pier'cie (2). A fantastical character in Sir Walter Scott's

"Monastery;" drawn in imitation of the pedantic courtiers of Queen Elizabeth's reign, and made to talk in the unnatural and high-flown style which Lyly rendered fashionable by his "Euphues." He turns out to be grandson of one Overstitch, a tailor.

> His [Johnson's] speech, like *Sir Piercie Shafton's* euphuistic eloquence, bewrayed him under every disguise. *Macaulay.*

Shakespeare of Divines. An epithet sometimes applied to Jeremy Taylor (1613–1667), one of the greatest ornaments of the English pulpit. His devotional writings are characterised by a fervid eloquence and an affluence and aptness of illustration that entitle them to the praise of belonging to the loftiest and most sacred description of poetry, "of which," as Heber remarks, "they only want what they cannot be said to need, the name and the metrical arrangement."

> Old Chrysostom, best Augustine,
> And he who blent both in his line,
> The younger Golden Lips or mines,
> Taylor, the *Shakespeare of Divines*.
> *Emerson.*

Shallow. A country justice, in Shakespeare's "Merry Wives of Windsor," and in the Second Part of "King Henry IV.;" a braggart, a liar, a rogue, and a blockhead. It is supposed that this character was intended as a satirical portrait of Sir Thomas Lucy, of Charlecote, near Stratford-upon-Avon, who is said to have prosecuted Shakespeare for a youthful misdemeanour.

> A nurse of this century is as wise as a justice of the quorum and cust-alorum in *Shallow's* time. *Macaulay.*

Shan'dy, Captain. The uncle of Tristram Shandy, in Sterne's novel of this name; the same as *Uncle Toby.* See UNCLE TOBY.

> When Mr. Southey takes up his pen, he changes his nature as much as *Captain Shandy* when he girt on his sword. *Macaulay.*

Shan'dy, Dinah. See DINAH, AUNT.

Shan'dy, Mrs. Elizabeth. The mother of Tristram Shandy, in Sterne's novel of this name. She is the ideal of nonentity, a character profoundly individual from its very absence of individuality.

Shan'dy, Tris'tram. The nominal hero of Sterne's novel, "The Life and Opinions of Tristram Shandy, Gent."

> The author proceeds, with the most unfeeling prolixity, to give a minute detail of the civil and common law, of the feudal institutions, of the architecture of churches and castles, of sculpture and painting, of minstrels, of players, of parish clerks, &c., &c.; while poor Chaucer, like *Tristram Shandy*, can hardly be said to be fairly born, although his life has attained the size of half a volume.
> *Sir W. Scott.*

Shan'dy, Walter. The name of Tristram Shandy's father, in Sterne's novel entitled "The Life and Opinions of Tristram Shandy, Gent." By reading antiquated books he has got his head filled with absurd or idle fancies and theories; but all his notions are thwarted, and the exact opposite of what he wishes takes place. He believes in the virtue of a substantial nose, and his son's is crushed by the accoucheur who attends upon his wife. A leading article of his creed is that the characters of mankind are greatly influenced by their Christian names. Trismegistus he thinks the most propitious name in the world, and Tristram the very worst; yet his son accidentally gets christened Tristram.

> ☞ "He [Sterne] . . . supposed in Mr. Shandy a man of an active and metaphysical, but at the same time a whimsical, cast of mind, whom too much and too miscellaneous learning had brought within a step or two of madness, and who acted, in the ordinary affairs of life, upon the absurd theories adopted by the pedants of past ages. He is most admirably contrasted with his wife, well described as a good lady of the *poco-curante* school, who neither obstructed the progress of her husband's hobby-horse, — to use a phrase which Sterne has rendered classical, — nor could be prevailed upon to spare him the least admiration for the grace and dexterity with which he managed it." *Sir W. Scott.*

> The project of mending a bad world, by teaching people to give new names to old things, reminds us of *Walter Shandy's* scheme for compensating the loss of his son's nose by christening him Trismegistus. *Macaulay.*

> Foolish enough, too, was the college tutor's surprise at *Walter Shandy*, how, though unread in Aristotle, he could nevertheless argue, and, not knowing the name of any dialectic tool, handled them all to perfection. *Carlyle.*

aud for the Remarks and Rules to which the numbers after certain words refer, see pp. xiv–xxxii.

Sharp, Becky. A female sharper, who is a prominent character in Thackeray's "Vanity Fair;" distinguished by her intriguing disposition, her selfishness, good-humour, energy, perseverance, cleverness, and utter want of heart and moral principle. See SEDLEY, AMELIA.

With *Becky Sharp*, we think we could be good, if we had five thousand a year. *Bayne.*

Shepherd Kings. [Called also *Hykshos*, or *Hyksos*.] A name often given to a tribe of Arabian or Phœnician shepherds who are said to have invaded Lower Egypt about two thousand years B. C., and to have overthrown the reigning dynasty. They maintained their authority, according to some accounts, about two hundred and sixty years, when they were expelled by the Egyptian rulers of Upper Egypt. Some writers, however, wholly deny the existence of any such race of kings; others hold that the captive Jews, the descendants of Jacob, are intended by this designation; and various other theories have been advanced in explanation of this vexed question.

Shepherd Lord. Lord Henry Clifford (d. 1543), of the English house of Lancaster, and the hero of much legendary narration. To save him from the vengeance of the victorious York party, his mother put him in charge of a shepherd, to be brought up as one of his own children. Afterward, on the accession of Henry VII. (being then at the age of thirty-one years), he was restored to his birthright and possessions. In the "White Doe of Rylstone," Wordsworth speaks of

"The gracious fairy
Who loved the *Shepherd Lord* to meet
In his wanderings solitary."

Shepherd of Banbury. The ostensible author of a work entitled "The Shepherd of Banbury's Rules to judge of the Changes of Weather, grounded on Forty Years' Experience, &c. By John Claridge, Shepherd," first published in 1744, and reprinted in 1827. It is a work of great popularity among the English poor, and is attributed to Dr. John Campbell, author of "A Political Survey of Britain." It is mostly a compilation from "A Rational Survey of the Weather," by John Pointer, rector of Slapton in Northamptonshire.

Shepherd of Salisbury Plain (sŏlz'-bŭr-ĭ). The hero of a very popular tract having this name for its title, and written by Mrs. Hannah More; distinguished for his homely wisdom and simple Christian piety. The original of this character was one David Saunders, who, with his father, had kept sheep upon Salisbury Plain for a hundred years.

Shepherd of the Ocean. A name given by Spenser, in his poem, "Colin Clout's come Home again," to his friend Sir Walter Raleigh, celebrated for his maritime expeditions and discoveries.

Shipton, Mother. See MOTHER SHIPTON.

Short-lived Administration. (*Eng. Hist.*) A name popularly given to an administration formed by the Hon. William Pulteney, which expired on the 12th of February, 1746, two days after its partial formation. [Called also, in derision, *Long-lived Administration.*]

Shufflebottom, Abel. A pseudonym of Robert Southey (1774-1843), under which he wrote several amatory sonnets and elegies.

Shylock. A sordid, avaricious, revengeful Jew, in Shakespeare's "Merchant of Venice." See PORTIA.

Of course, not Louis XVI. alone, but all monarchs, might be justly put to death in Carnot's estimation; because they are naturally the objects of fear to their subjects; because we hate those we fear; and because, according to the kindred authority of *Shylock*, no man hates the thing he would not kill.
Sir W. Scott.

Sicilian Vespers. (*Hist.*) A name given to a memorable massacre of the French which began at Palermo, in Sicily, March 30, 1282, at the hour of vespers on Easter Monday, and extended throughout the island. Sicily was at this time subject to Charles of Anjou, whose soldiers had made themselves hateful to the Sicilians. The result of the insurrection was, that the authority of Charles was completely overthrown, and the islanders placed themselves under the protection of the king of Aragon.

Sick Man of the East. A name popularly given to the Turkish empire, which, under Soliman the Magnificent (1495-1566), reached the summit of its prosperity, and has ever since steadily declined. At the present day, Turkey is mainly indebted for its existence to the support of foreign powers.

☞ The expression, "Sick Man," as applied to Turkey, originated with the emperor Nicholas of Russia. He is represented to have said to Sir George Seymour, the British *chargé d'affaires*, in a conversation at St. Petersburg, on the 11th of January, 1844, "We have on our hands a sick man, a very sick man. It would be a great misfortune, I tell you frankly, if, one of these days, he should happen to die before the necessary arrangements were all made. But this is not the time to speak to you of that." The conversation then broke off, but was renewed on the 14th of the same month, when the emperor observed, "Turkey, in the condition which I have described, has by degrees fallen into such a state of decrepitude, that, as I told you the other night, eager as we all are for the prolonged existence of the man (and that I am as desirous as you can be for the continuance of his life, I beg you to believe), he may suddenly die upon our hands." And again, at another interview, on the 21st inst.: "I think your government does not well understand my object. I am not so eager to determine what shall be done when the sick man dies, as I am to determine with England what shall not be done upon that event taking place. . . . I repeat to you that the sick man is dying; and we can never allow such an event to take us by surprise. We must come to some understanding." (*Annual Register* for 1853, p. 248, *et seq.*) The minutes of Sir George Seymour's conversations with the emperor having been laid before parliament by the English ministry in the course of the debates that immediately preceded the declaration of war against Russia, the expressive appellation, "Sick Man of the East," was caught up and circulated by the press, till it has become an established national sobriquet.

Sid'ro-phel. A poetical name given by Butler, in his "Hudibras," to William Lilly, a distinguished astrologer of the seventeenth century. Some, however, have supposed that under this name Butler intended to refer to Sir Paul Neal, a conceited virtuoso, and a member of the Royal Society, who constantly affirmed that Butler was not the author of "Hudibras."

The last inroad of these pretended friends to cleanliness was almost as fatal to my collection as Hudibras' visit to that of *Sidrophel*.
Sir W. Scott.

How I became a prophet, it is not very important to the reader to know. Nevertheless, I feel all the anxiety which, under similar circumstances, troubled the sensitive *Sidrophel*.
Macaulay.

Siegfried (szeck'freet, 58, 65). The hero of various Scandinavian and Teutonic legends, particularly of the old German epic poem, the "Nibelungen Lied;" a young warrior of peerless physical strength and beauty, and in valour superior to all men of his time. He cannot easily be identified with any historical personage. In an old saga, he is represented as having slain a dreadful dragon, and bathed in its blood, whereby his skin became as hard as horn, except in one spot, where a leaf intervened. But he is most celebrated for having vanquished the ancient fabulous royal race of the Nibelungen, and taken away their immense treasures of gold and gems. He woos, and finally wins, the beautiful Chriemhild, but is treacherously killed by the fierce and covetous Hagen, who seeks the treasures of the Nibelungen, and who skilfully draws from Chriemhild the secret of the spot where alone Siegfried is mortal, and fatally plunges a lance between his shoulders in a royal chase. Siegfried is noted for a cape which rendered its wearer invisible, and for a wonderful sword named Balmung. The former he obtained from the dwarf Alberich; the latter he is said to have forged, while yet a boy, at a traitorous smith's in the depths of a primeval forest. See BALMUNG, BRUNEHILD, CHRIEMHILD, and HAGEN.

☞ "In this colossal figure are combined what Greece divided, — heroic strength and the passion for travel, Achilles and Ulysses." *Michelet, Trans.*

Sif. (*Scand. Myth.*) Wife of Thor,

famous for the beauty of her hair, which Loki cut off while she was asleep. Thor compelled him to get her a new head of hair made of gold, that should grow like natural hair. This he obtained from the dwarfs.

Sig'is-mun'dạ. [It. *Ghismonda.*] 1. The heroine of one of the tales in Boccaccio's "Decamerone," which relates her love for a page named Guiscardo, and the secret, accidental discovery of their guilt by her father, Tancred, prince of Salerno, who afterward upbraids her with her conduct, and, finding her insensible to shame and reproof, sends her Guiscardo's heart in a golden cup, whereupon the princess drains a poisonous draught, after having poured it on her lover's heart.

☞ No tale of Boccaccio has been so often translated and imitated as this. In English it is best known through the "Sigismunda and Guiscardo" of Dryden.

The pale widow whom Captain Richard, in his poetic rapture, compared to a Niobe in tears, to a *Sigismunda*, to a weeping Belvidera, was an object the most lovely and pathetic which his eyes had ever beheld. *Thackeray.*

2. The heroine of Thomson's tragedy of "Tancred and Sigismunda," the groundwork of which is the tale — founded on fact — of "The Baleful Marriage" ("*Le Mariage de Vengeance*") in "Gil Blas."

Siguna (sze-goo'nä), *or* **Sigyn** (sze'-gin). (*Scand. Myth.*) The wife of Loki, celebrated for her constancy to him. She sits by him in the subterranean cavern where he is chained, and holds out a vase to catch the venom dropped by the serpents which hang over him. When she goes out to empty the vessel, the poison falls on his limbs, and his writhings cause earthquakes.

Sigurd (sze'goord). The hero of an old Scandinavian saga or legend, the foundation of the celebrated German epic, the "Nibelungen Lied." He discovered Brynhild, a beautiful *valkyria*, encased in complete armour, and lying in a death-like sleep, to which, for some offence, she had been condemned by Odin. Sigurd awoke her by ripping up her corselet, fell in love with her, engaged on oath to marry her, and took his departure. He subsequently met with Gudrun, whom her mother caused him to marry by giving him a charmed potion which made him forget Brynhild. This ill-starred union was the cause of unnumbered woes. *Sigurd* is the Icelandic or Old Norse form of *Siegfried.* See SIEGFRIED.

Sikes. A ruffian in Dickens's "Oliver Twist."

Silence. A country justice, in the Second Part of Shakespeare's "King Henry IV.;" a man of untamable mirth when he is tipsy, and of asinine dulness when he is abstinent.

Like Master *Silence*, he had been merry twice and once in his time. *Sir W. Scott.*

Silent Sister. A name given to Trinity College, Dublin, on account of the little influence it exerts in proportion to its resources.

Trinity College itself held its ground and grew wealthy only to deserve the name of the *Silent Sister*, while its great endowments served effectually to indemnify it against the necessity of conforming to the conditions under which alone its example could be useful to the whole nation. *Goldwin Smith.*

Neither Oxford nor Cambridge, I am certain, would blush to own my labours in this department [classical criticism and exegesis]; and yet I was an alumnus of her whom they used to style the *Silent Sister. Keightley.*

Si-le'nus. [Gr. Σειληνός.] (*Gr. & Rom. Myth.*) The foster-father, instructor, and companion of Bacchus; represented as a jovial old man, with a bald head, pug nose, and rubicund visage, and generally as intoxicated, and therefore riding on an ass or supported by satyrs. His fondness for sleep and music, and his lasciviousness, are prominent traits in his character. He is further described as a prophetic deity.

The tile-beard of Jourdan is shaven off; his fat visage has got coppered, and studded with black carbuncles; the *Silenus*-trunk is swollen with drink and high living. *Carlyle.*

Sil'ū-rist, The. Henry Vaughan (1621-1695), a British poet of some note; — so called because born among the Silures, or people of South Wales.

Sil-vā'nus. (*Rom. Myth.*) A deity presiding over woods, forests, and fields. [Written also S y l v a n u s.]

In shadier bower
More sacred and sequestered, though but feigned,
Pan or *Sylvanus* never slept. *Milton.*

Silver Age. [Lat. *Argentea ætas.*] (*Gr. & Rom. Myth.*) One of the four ages into which the history of mankind was divided by the ancient poets. It was ruled over by Jupiter, and was marked by the change of the seasons, and the division and cultivation of lands. See BRAZEN AGE and GOLDEN AGE.

Silver-fork School. A name which has been given to novelists of the Theodore Hook class; that is, those who attach great and undue importance to the etiquette of the drawing-room, and the mere externals of social intercourse. Among the more distinguished writers of this class are reckoned Mrs. Trollope, Lady Blessington, and Sir Edward Bulwer Lytton.

Silverpen. A *nom de plume* adopted by Eliza Meteyard (b. 1824), an English authoress. It was originally bestowed upon her by Douglas Jerrold.

Silver-tongued, The. 1. An epithet applied to Joshua Sylvester (1563-1618), the translator of Du Bartas's "Divine Weeks and Works."
2. The same epithet has been applied to William Bates (1625-1699), an eminent Puritan divine, reckoned the most polished writer, if not the best scholar, of the whole body of ministers who retired from the church in 1662, on the passage of the Act of Uniformity, and formed what is sometimes called the "Dissenting Interest."

Sil'vi-â. The name of a lady beloved by Valentine, in Shakespeare's "Two Gentlemen of Verona."

Simple. A servant to Slender, in Shakespeare's "Merry Wives of Windsor."

Simple Simon. The subject of a well-known popular tale of early and unknown authorship.

☞ "Simple Simon's misfortunes are such as are incident to all the human race, since they arose 'from his wife Margery's cruelty, which began the very morning after their marriage;' and we therefore do not know whether it is necessary to seek for a Teutonic or Northern original for this once popular book." *Qu. Rev.*

Sind'bad the Sailor. A noted character in the "Arabian Nights' Entertainments," in which is related the story of his seven strange voyages and his wonderful adventures. [Written also, less correctly, S i n b a d.]

☞ On his first voyage, he disembarked on what was supposed to be a small green island, but was in reality only a huge sea-monster, which, when a fire was kindled on his back, in order to dress some food, dived under water, and left Sindbad and his companions struggling for life in the midst of the ocean. Sindbad himself escaped, but most of the others were drowned. On the second voyage, he landed on an island to procure water, strayed from his companions, fell asleep, was given up as lost, and left to perish. Discovering a monstrous bird, called a roc, or rukh, sitting on its egg, he tied himself to one of its legs, and was carried the next day to the main land, and deposited in a valley strewn with diamonds, but unluckily shut in on every side by lofty and precipitous mountains. From this awkward situation he extricated himself by a stratagem similar to that by which he had escaped from the island. On the third voyage, he fell among gigantic hairy savages, with whom he had an adventure precisely like that of Ulysses in the land of the Cyclops. (See POLYPHEMUS.) On his fourth voyage, he suffered shipwreck on the coast of a country of which the king took him into favour, but compelled him, though he had a wife living in Bagdad, to marry a lady of the court. Upon the death of this lady, he was buried alive with her in a deep pit, according to an irrevorsible custom of the country, but was fortunate enough to discover a long passage which led to an opening on the sea-shore, whence he escaped to his own land. On his fifth voyage, he fell into the power of the Old Man of the Sea. (See OLD MAN OF THE SEA.) On the sixth voyage, his ship got into a rapid current, which, aided by a strong wind blowing over directly toward the shore, carried her to the foot of an inaccessible mountain, where she went to pieces. Sindbad, having survived his comrades, made a raft, committed himself to a river of fresh water running out of the sea into a great cavern at the base of the mountain, floated for some days in perfect darkness, and when he at last came out into the light, found himself in the island of Ceylon. Undismayed by so many misfortunes, he made a seventh voyage, was attacked by corsairs, sold into slavery, and employed in shooting elephants from a tree. After a time, he was attacked by a troop of these animals, was caught, and carried to a hill-side completely covered with tusks and bones of elephants, and then suffered to depart unharmed. For communicating this discovery to his master he received his freedom, and was sent home to Bagdad, loaded with riches.

This is the first George,— first triumph of the Constitutional Principle, which has since gone to such sublime heights among us,— heights which we at last begin to suspect might be depths, leading down, all men now ask, Whitherwards? A much admired invention in its time, that of letting go the rudder, or setting a wooden figure expensively dressed to take charge of it, and discerning that the ship would sail of itself so much more easily, which it will, if a peculiarly good seaboat, in certain kinds of sea — for a time, till the *Sindbad* " Magnetic Mountains" begin to be felt pulling, or the circles of Charybdis get you in their sweep, and then what an invention it was! *Carlyle.*

Singing Tree. See PARIZADE.

Single-speech Ham′il-tŏn. A byname given to William Gerard Hamilton (1729-1796), an English statesman.

☞ " It was on this night [November 13, 1775] that Gerard Hamilton delivered that *single speech* from which his nickname was derived. His eloquence threw into the shade every orator except Pitt, who declaimed against the subsidies for an hour and a half with extraordinary energy and effect." *Macaulay.*

☞ " The preceding generation had greatly esteemed the man called ' Single-speech Hamilton; ' not at all for the speech (which, though good, very few people had read), but entirely for the supposed fact that he had exhausted himself in that one speech, and had become physically incapable of making a second: so that afterward, when he really *did* make a second, every body was incredulous; until, the thing being past denial, naturally the world was disgusted, and most people dropped his acquaintance." *De Quincey.*

Singular Doctor. [Lat. *Doctor Singularis.*] A title given to William Occam (or Ockham), an English nominalistic philosopher of the latter part of the thirteenth and beginning of the fourteenth centuries, distinguished for his trenchant logic. He was the greatest of the later schoolmen. His philosophy rested to a considerable degree upon a famous principle called from him " Occam's razor;" namely,

" *Entia non sunt multiplicanda,*" Entities — that is, real existences representing general ideas, or the terms used to denote the genera and species of things — are not to be unnecessarily multiplied.

Si′nŏn. [Gr. Σίνων.] (*Gr. & Rom. Myth.*) A crafty Greek, who induced the Trojans to take into their city the fatal Wooden Horse, which was filled with armed enemies. See WOODEN HORSE.

Sin′trăm. The hero of a German romance written by Baron La Motte Fouqué, entitled " Sintram and his Companions," — a tale of the old life of mediæval Europe, suggested to the author by Albert Dürer's engraving of the Knight, Death, and Satan.

Si′rens (9). [Lat. *Sirenes,* Gr. Σειρῆνες.] (*Gr. & Rom. Myth.*) Three sister sea-nymphs, who usually resided on a small island near Cape Pelorus, in Sicily, and, by their melodious singing, enticed ashore those who were sailing by, and then killed them. Later writers represent them as presiding over the music of the spheres. Their names are usually given as Parthenope, Ligeia, and Leucothea.

Sir Oracle. See ORACLE, SIR.

Sister Anne. A sister of Fatima, the seventh and last of the wives of Blue-beard. This unfortunate lady having been condemned to death by her husband, obtained the favour of a brief delay; and her sister Anne ascended the highest tower of the castle to watch for her brothers, who were expected about that time to make them a visit, and who, happily arriving at the last moment, rescued their sister, and put Blue-beard to death. See BLUE-BEARD.

If Painting be Poetry's sister, she can only be a *Sister Anne*, who will see nothing but a flock of sheep, while the other bodies forth a troop of horsemen with drawn sabres and white-plumed helmets. *Hare.*

Ah! why was there no clairvoyant *Sister Anne* to cry that she saw "somebody coming," — to tell the desolate girl, staring from her window into the unfriendly night, that succour was afoot! *Theo. Winthrop.*

Sĭs′ў-phus. [Gr. Σίσυφος.] (*Gr. & Rom. Myth.*) A son of Æolus, and husband of Merope, famous for his fraud and avarice. He was punished in the lower world for his wickedness by having to roll up-hill a large stone, which, as soon as he had reached the top, always rolled down again.

With many a weary step, and many a groan
Up the high hill he heaves a huge round stone;
The huge round stone, returning with a bound,
Thunders impetuous down, and smokes along the ground. *Pope's Homer.*

Siva (se'vā). [Sansk. *Civa*, happiness, final bliss.] (*Hindu Myth.*) The supreme being, in the character of the avenger or destroyer; the third person in the *Trimurti*, or trinity, of the Vedas.

Siward (se'ward). Earl of Northumberland, and general of the English forces, in Shakespeare's tragedy of "Macbeth."

Sixteen-string Jack. A nickname popularly given to John Rann, a noted English highwayman, who, after having been several times tried and acquitted, was at last hanged at Tyburn on the 30th of November, 1774. He was remarkable for foppery in his dress, and particularly for wearing breeches with eight strings at each knee.

Boswell. "Does not Gray's poetry, sir, tower above the common mark?"
Johnson. "Yes, sir; but we must attend to the difference between what men in general cannot do if they would, and what every man may do if he would. *Sixteen-string Jack* towered above the common mark."
Boswell's Life of Johnson.

Skeggs, Miss Carolina Wilhelmina Amelia. A character in Goldsmith's "Vicar of Wakefield;" a false pretender to gentility, who boasts of her aristocratic connections and acquaintance, and prides herself upon her taste for Shakespeare and love of musical glasses, but who turns out to be no better than she should be.

Skidbladnir (skid'blăd'nêr). [Old Norse *skid*, a thin plank, and *blad*, a leaf.] (*Scand. Myth.*) The name of a ship, made by the dwarfs and given to Frey. It was so capacious that it would hold all the gods, with their weapons and armour, and, when the sails were set, it always had a fair wind. When not required for navigation, it could be folded up like a piece of cloth.

Skim'ming-tŏn. A word of unknown origin, but supposed to be the name of some notorious scold of the olden time. [Written also **Skimmerton** and **Skimitry**.]

☞ The word is used only in the phrase, "To ride Skimmington," or "To ride the Skimmington," employed to describe a species of mock triumphal procession in honour of a man who had been beaten by his wife. It consisted of a cavalcade in which the man (or, according to old authorities cited by Nares, the man's next neighbour) rode behind a woman, with his face to the horse's tail, holding a distaff in his hand, at which he seemed to work, the woman all the while beating him with a ladle, and those who accompanied them making hideous noises with frying-pans, bull's-horns, marrow-bones, cleavers, and the like. "As the procession passed on," says Sir Walter Scott, "those who attended it in an official capacity were wont to sweep the threshold of the houses in which fame affirmed the mistresses to exercise paramount authority, which was given and received as a hint that their inmates might, in their turn, be made the subject of a similar ovation."

Skĭm'pole, Hăr'ŏld. A character in Dickens's "Bleak House;" a plausible, mild-mannered sponger upon his friends; said to have been suggested by some of the more prominent traits in the character of Leigh Hunt, though not intended as a portrait of him.

From Paris, he wrote to his "dear Lydia" one of those warm, affectionate letters which are delightful to read, and which, it is apparent, no one with a particle of the *Harold Skimpole* leaven in his frame could have written. *Percy Fitzgerald.*

Slaw'ken-bĕr'ġi-us, Hä'fen. The name of an imaginary author,— distinguished by the length of his nose, — who is quoted and referred to in Sterne's "Life and Opinions of Tristram Shandy, Gent.," as a great authority on all learning connected with the subject of noses. A quaint and singular tale — professedly extracted from his writings — about a man with an enormously long nose is introduced into the work by way of episode.

No nose can be justly amputated by the

and for the Remarks and Rules to which the numbers after certain words refer, see pp. xiv–xxxii.

public, not even the nose of *Slawkenbergius* himself. *Carlyle.*

Slay-good, Giant. See GIANT SLAY-GOOD.

Sleek, Aminadab. A character in the comedy of "The Serious Family," by Morris Barnett.

Sleeping Beauty in the Wood. [Fr. *La Belle au Bois dormant,* Ger. *Dornröschen.*] The heroine of a celebrated nursery tale, written in French by Charles Perrault, which relates how a princess was shut up by fairy enchantment, to sleep a hundred years in a castle, around which sprang up a dense, impenetrable wood, and how, at the expiration of the appointed time, she was delivered from her imprisonment and her trance by a gallant young prince, before whom the forest opened itself to afford him passage.

☞ Grimm derives this popular and widely diffused tale from the old Northern mythology, and finds its prototype in the sleeping Brynhild, and her awakening and deliverance by Sigurd. Dunlop thinks it was suggested by the story of Epimenides, the Cretan poet, who, when a boy, is said to have been sent out by his father to fetch a sheep, and, seeking shelter from the mid-day sun, went into a cave. He there fell into a sleep in which he remained for fifty-seven years. On waking, he sought for the sheep, not knowing how long he had been sleeping, and was astonished to find everything around him altered. When he returned home, he found to his great amazement, that his younger brother had in the mean time grown an old man. Tennyson has given an exquisite metrical version of the story of the Sleeping Beauty. See EPIMENIDES and SIGURD.

Like the prince in the nursery tale, he [Alfieri] sought and found the *Sleeping Beauty* within the recesses which had so long concealed her from mankind. *Macaulay.*

These precincts of Klein-Schnellendorf . . . are silent, vacant, yet comfortably furnished, like *Sleeping Beauty's* castle. *Carlyle.*

Sleipnir (szlĭp'nĕr). (*Scand. Myth.*) The name of Odin's horse, the noblest of his race, who carries his master over land and sea. He is of a gray colour, has eight legs, and typifies the wind, which blows from eight principal points. [Written also S l e i p n e r.]

Slender. A character in Shakespeare's "Merry Wives of Windsor."

☞ "In this play the English gentleman, in age and youth, is brought upon the stage, slightly caricatured in Shallow, and far more so in Slender. The latter, indeed, is a perfect satire, and, I think, was so intended, on the brilliant youth of the provinces, such as we may believe it to have been before the introduction of newspapers and turnpike roads; awkward and boobyish among civil people, but at home in rude sports, and proud of exploits at which the town would laugh, yet, perhaps, with more courage and good-nature than the laughers." *Hallam.* "Slender and Sir Andrew Aguecheek are fools, troubled with an uneasy consciousness of their folly, which, in the latter, produces a most edifying meekness and docility, and, in the former, awkwardness, obstinacy, and confusion." *Macaulay.*

By my faith, Dick, thou hast fallen into poor *Slender's* blunder; missed Anne Page, and brought us a great lubberly postmaster's boy. *Sir W. Scott.*

Slick, Sam. The title and hero of various humourous narratives, illustrating and exaggerating the peculiarities of the New-England character and dialect, written by Judge Thomas Chandler Haliburton (d. 1865), a native of Nova Scotia. Sam Slick is represented as a Yankee clock-maker and peddler, full of quaint drollery, unsophisticated wit, knowledge of human nature, and aptitude in the use of what he calls "soft sawder."

Slipslop, Mrs. One of the leading female characters in Fielding's novel of "Joseph Andrews;" a woman of frail morals.

Slop, Doctor. See DOCTOR SLOP.

Slough of Despond. In Bunyan's "Pilgrim's Progress," a deep bog into which Christian falls, and from which Help extricates him.

☞ "The name of the slough was Despond. Here, therefore, they wallowed for a time; and Christian, because of the burden that was on his back, began to sink into the mire. This miry slough is such a place as cannot be mended; it is the descent whither the scum and filth that attends conviction for sin doth continually run, and therefore it is called the Slough of Despond; for still, as the sinner is awakened about his lost condition, there arise in his soul many fears, and doubts and discouraging apprehensions, which all of them get together, and

☞ For the "Key to the Scheme of Pronunciation," with the accompanying Explanations,

settle in this place, and this is the reason of the badness of this ground." *Bunyan.*

Every thing retrograded with him towards the verge of the miry *Slough of Despond*, which yawns for insolvent debtors.
Sir W. Scott.

Sly, Christopher. A tinker, in the "Induction" to Shakespeare's "Taming of the Shrew."

It was a good commonty, as *Christopher Sly* says; nor were we sorry when it was done. *Thackeray.*

Enough, his poor Eminence [Cardinal Louis de Rohan] sits in the fittest place, in the fittest mood: a newly awakened *Christopher Sly;* and with his "small ale" too beside them. *Carlyle.*

Small-back. A cant name in Scotland for Death, usually delineated as a skeleton.

Men have queer fancies when old *Smallback* is gripping them; but *Small-back* must lead down the dance with us all in our time. *Sir W. Scott.*

Small-beer Poet. A nickname given by Cobbett to William Thomas Fitzgerald (1759-1829), a poetaster, satirised by Lord Byron in his "English Bards and Scotch Reviewers," and parodied by Horace Smith in the "Rejected Addresses."

Small-endians. See BIG-ENDIANS, THE.

Smec-tym'nu-us. The title of a celebrated pamphlet containing an attack upon episcopacy, published in 1641. This work was written by five Presbyterian divines, and the title was formed from the initial letters of their names,— Stephen *M*arshall, *E*dmund *C*alamy, *T*homas *Y*oung, *M*atthew *N*ewcomen, and *W*illiam *S*purstow. [Written also, but improperly, S m e e t y m n u s.]

Smel-fuñ'gus. A name given by Sterne to Smollett, who, in 1766, published a volume of "Travels through France and Italy," filled with illiberal and splenetic observations upon the institutions and customs of the countries he visited. "The chronicle of his journey," says Fitzgerald, "from the first day to the last, is literally one prolonged snarl." The nickname — the composition of which is obvious — became exceedingly popular in England, much to the annoyance of Smollett. It is sometimes, though rarely, used in a general way to designate an ill-tempered antiquary, or a mousing and inappreciative historian.

The lamented *Smelfungus* travelled from Boulogne to Paris, from Paris to Rome, and so on; but he set out with the spleen and jaundice, and every object he passed by was discoloured or distorted. He wrote an account of them, but 't was nothing but the account of his miserable feelings.
Sterne, Sentimental Journey.

Smelfungus, denouncing the torpid vacuity of Voltaire's biographers, says he never met with one Frenchman, even of the literary classes, who could tell him whence this name Voltaire originated. *Carlyle.*

Smike. A broken-spirited *protégé* of Nicholas Nickleby, in Dickens's novel of that name.

Smith, Wayland. See WAYLAND SMITH.

Smoky City. A name sometimes given to Pittsburg, an important manufacturing city of Pennsylvania. The use of bituminous coal occasions dense volumes of smoke to fill the air in and around the place, soiling the garments of passengers, and giving the buildings a dark and sooty appearance.

Smol'kin, or **Smul'kin.** The name of a fiend or evil spirit mentioned in Shakespeare's "King Lear," a. iii., sc. 4. See FLIBBERTIGIBBET, 1.

Snare. A sheriff's officer, in the Second Part of Shakespeare's "King Henry IV."

Sneak, Jerry. The name of a henpecked pin-maker, a noted character in Foote's farce, "The Mayor of Garratt."

From Lucifer to *Jerry Sneak* there is not an aspect of evil, imperfection, and littleness which can elude the light of humour or the lightning of wit. *E. P. Whipple.*

If, in the logic of character, Iago or *Jerry Sneak* be the premises, it is impossible to find Bacon in the conclusion. *Atlantic Monthly.*

Sneer. A carping character in Sheridan's "Critic," with just wit enough to make him mischievous.

Sneerwell, Lady. A character in Sheridan's "School for Scandal," given to gossip and slander.

Snod'grăss, Augustus (2). One of the Pickwick Club, in Dickens's novel, "The Pickwick Papers;" a sort of poetic nonentity.

---

and for the Remarks and Rules to which the numbers after certain words refer, see pp. xiv-xxxii.

Snout. A tinker, in Shakespeare's "Midsummer-Night's Dream."

Snug. A joiner, in Shakespeare's "Midsummer-Night's Dream," who takes part in the "Interlude."

> The jest is as flat and dull as that of *Snug* the joiner, when he acts the lion barefaced.
> *Sir W. Scott.*

Sofronia (so-fro'ne-ä). A young Christian of Jerusalem, who is the heroine of one of the most touching episodes in Tasso's "Jerusalem Delivered."

☞ "The Mahommedan king of Jerusalem [Aladin], at the instigation of Ismeus, a magician, deprives a Christian church of its image of the Virgin, and sets it up in a mosque, under a spell of enchantment, as a palladium against the Crusaders. The image is stolen in the night; and the king, unable to discover who has taken it, orders a massacre of the Christian portion of his subjects, which is prevented by Sofronia's accusing herself of the offence. Her lover, Olindo, finding her sentenced to the stake in consequence, disputes with her the right of martyrdom. He is condemned to suffer with her. The Amazon Clorinda, who has come to fight on the side of Aladin, obtains their pardon in acknowledgment of her services; and Sofronia, who had not loved Olindo before, now returns his passion, and goes with him from the stake to the marriage-altar." *Leigh Hunt.*

Sol. [Lat., the sun.] (*Rom. Myth.*) A surname of Apollo. See APOLLO.

Solar City. See CITY OF THE SUN.

Soldiers' Friend. A surname popularly given in England to Frederick, Duke of York (1763-1827), the second son of George III., and commander of the British troops in the Low Countries at the period of the French Revolution. It was through his exertions that the system of favouritism was abolished, and political opinions were no longer made a ground of preferment. In 1814, he was publicly thanked by parliament for his excellent administration of the army.

Solemn Doctor. [Lat. *Doctor Solemnis.*] An honorary appellation given by the Sorbonne to Henry Goethals (1227-1293), a eminent schoolman who was a member of that famous theological faculty.

Solemn League and Covenant. (*Eng. & Scot. Hist.*) A bond of union adopted by the Scottish parliament in 1638, and by the English parliament in 1643. Its main object and specific obligation was support of the Church of Scotland, and extirpation of popery and prelacy. Charles II. subscribed to the covenant on his coronation, in 1651; but, at the Restoration, it was declared null by act of parliament, and was burned by the common hangman.

Solid Doctor. A title conferred upon Richard Middleton (d. 1304), an English theologian of the order of the Cordeliers; — so called from his extensive learning. See PROFOUND DOCTOR, 2.

So-li'nus. Duke of Ephesus, in Shakespeare's "Comedy of Errors."

Solomon of England. 1. An appellation bestowed upon Henry VII. (1457-1509), first of the Tudor kings of England, whose reign, conducted upon pacific principles, was, upon the whole, beneficial to his country, and gave an opportunity for the nation to flourish by the development of its internal resources.

2. The same title has been satirically awarded to James I. (1566-1625), on account of his pedantry and puerility. Buchanan, his instructor, said that he "made him a pedant because he could make nothing else of him." Sully aptly termed him "the wisest fool in Christendom." "He was, indeed," says Macaulay, "made up of two men, a witty, well-read scholar, who wrote, disputed, and harangued, and a nervous, drivelling idiot, who acted."

Solomon of France. 1. An appellation conferred upon Charles V. (1336-1380), king of France. He was also called "The Wise."

2. A title bestowed upon Louis IX., or St. Louis (1215-1270), who summoned to his council the most able and virtuous men of his kingdom, put an end to many ecclesiastical abuses, and was always intent upon promoting the happiness of his subjects.

☞ For the "Key to the Scheme of Pronunciation," with the accompanying Explanations,

Som'nus. [Lat.] (*Gr. & Rom. Myth.*) A deified personification of sleep; described as the son of Nox and Erebus.

Son of God. A title in common use among the Jews in the time of our Saviour as a designation of the expected Messiah. It was assumed by Jesus, as expressing the peculiar and intimate relationship between himself and the Father. See *Matt.* iii. 17.

Son of Man. A designation of himself made use of by our Lord, who was, "according to the flesh," the son of the Virgin Mary, and the reputed son of Joseph, her husband, and through them both "of the seed of David." But commentators are far from being agreed as to the precise import of the term.

Son of the Last Man. A name commonly given, in the time of the English Commonwealth, to Charles II., whose father, Charles I., was popularly called the "Last Man." The designation is applied to Charles II. in a parliamentary offer of reward for his apprehension. See LAST MAN.

Sons of Thunder. See BOANERGES.

Sordello (sor-del'lo, 102). A celebrated Provençal poet whom Dante and Virgil meet in Purgatory, sitting alone, with a noble haughtiness of aspect, and eying them like a lion on the watch. On finding that Virgil is his countryman, he springs forward to embrace him with the utmost joy, and accompanies him part-way on his journey. Browning has used the name as the title of a poem containing an account of Sordello's progress in experience and education till he reaches the stature, name, and fame of poet. He chooses him as in some sort an ideal man, who is identified with the cause of liberty and human progress, and exemplifies the highest and best results of human culture. See FARINATA.

So'si-ä (so'shI-ä, 23). A servant of Amphitryon, or Amphitruo, in Plautus's play of this name. Mercury, availing himself of his power to assume disguises at pleasure, figures in the play as the double of Sosia, who is, in consequence, led to doubt his own identity. Hence, by an extension of the term, the name is given to any person who closely resembles another. Molière and Dryden have both adapted the "Amphitruo" of Plautus to the modern stage.

My right honourable father, sending for this other *Sosia* . . . from France, insisted, in the face of propriety, that he should reside in his house, and share, in all respects, in the opportunities of education by which the real *Sosia* . . . hath profited in such uncommon degree. *Sir W. Scott.*

Again the book is brought, and in the line just above that in which he is about to print his second name (his rescript), his first name (scarce dry) looks out upon him like another *Sosia*, or as if a man should suddenly encounter his own duplicate. *Charles Lamb.*

So'si-ï (so'shI-î, 23). The name of two brothers, famous booksellers at Rome in the time of Horace.

Sotenville, M. de (mos'e-ö' dü so'-tŏu'vĕl', 43, 62). [That is, Fool in the city.] A pompous, stolid, provincial French noble of the seventeenth century, who figures in Molière's comedy of "George Dandin," and who aggravates his intrinsic insignificance and vacuity by aping the manners of the court *noblesse*. See DANDIN, GEORGE.

South, Esquire. A name given to the Archduke Charles of Austria, in Arbuthnot's humourous "History of John Bull."

South Britain. A popular designation of England and Wales, or all that part of the island of Great Britain lying south of Scotland, which is often called North Britain.

South Sea. The name originally given, and still sometimes applied, to the Pacific Ocean, which was discovered in 1513 by Vasco Nuñez de Balboa, the Spanish governor of Darien. Crossing the isthmus on an exploring expedition, he arrived, on the 29th of September, at a mountain, from the summit of which, *looking south*, he beheld the boundless expanse of the ocean stretched out before him, while the northern portion was shut out from his view. He named it, therefore, *Mar del Sur*, or the South Sea.

South-Sea Bubble. A name popularly applied to a stupendous stock-jobbing scheme, in England, in 1720, characterised as "the most enormous fabric of national delusion ever raised amongst an industrious and prudent people." The South-Sea Company, a trading corporation, having exclusive privileges, offered to buy up the government annuities, with a view to the reduction of the public debt. The proposal was accepted; great numbers of people hastened to invest in the stock of the company, which rose to an extraordinary premium, when, on the 29th of September, this greatest of bubbles burst. Merchants, lawyers, clergymen, physicians, passed from their dreams of fabulous wealth, and from their wonted comforts, into penury. "Some died of broken hearts; others removed to remote parts of the world, and never returned."

Spanish Brû′tus. An epithet conferred upon Alphonso Perez de Guzman (1258–1320), a distinguished general of Spain. It is related, that, on one occasion, while besieged within the walls of a town, he was threatened by the enemy with the death of his son, who had been taken prisoner, unless he would surrender the place; to which he replied by throwing a dagger over the walls, and refusing to surrender. This incident has been dramatised by Lope de Vega.

Spanish En′ni-us. A title given to Juan de Mena (1412–1456), who owes his great fame to his having been the first who introduced into Castilian verse some of the refinements of Italian taste.

Spanish Fury. (*Hist.*) A name given to the attack upon Antwerp by the Spaniards, Nov. 4, 1576, which resulted in the pillage and burning of the place, and a great massacre of the inhabitants.

Spanish Jack. A noted felon executed at Maidstone (Eng.), April 18, 1756, for stealing. He was born at Alicant in Spain, and his real name was Bli Gonzales. He afterwards went to England, where he had connections, who induced him to change his name to John Symmonds.

Spanish Main. A name popularly given, by the early English voyagers and the English colonists of the West India Islands, to the coast along the north part of South America, from the Mosquito territory to the Leeward Islands. The term is often erroneously thought to apply to the Caribbean Sea, — a double mistake, for the word *main* is not used, in this phrase, as seems to have been supposed, in the sense of *main ocean*, but of *main land*; and besides, the Caribbean Sea, though commonly regarded as a portion of the Atlantic, is not, properly speaking, a part of the *main ocean*, having almost the character of an inland sea.

A parrot, from the *Spanish Main*,
Full young and early caged came o'er,
With bright wings, to the bleak domain
Of Mulla's shore.   *Campbell.*

☞ In the following citations, the name is incorrectly used : —

Then up and spake an old sailor,
Had sailed the *Spanish Main*,
"I pray thee put into yonder port,
For I fear the hurricane." *Longfellow.*

Under which diabolical ensign he was carrying me and little Em'ly to the *Spanish Main* to be drowned.   *Dickens.*

Spanish Molière (mo′lē-êr′). A name given to Leandro Fernandez Moratin (1760–1828), a Spanish dramatic poet, who took Molière for his model.

Spasmodic School. A name which has been given in ridicule to certain popular authors of the present day, whose productions are, in a greater or less degree, distinguished by an overstrained and unnatural style, and abound, more or less, in extravagant and forced conceits. In this school are commonly included Carlyle, Gilfillan, Tennyson, Bailey (the author of "Festus"), and Alexander Smith; and these writers have been cleverly satirised in "Firmilian, a Spasmodic Tragedy," by Professor William Edmonstoune Aytoun.

Spectre of the Brock′en. [Ger. *Brockengespenst.*] A singular colossal apparition seen in the clouds, at certain times of the day, by those who ascend the Brocken, or Blocksberg, the highest mountain of the

Hartz range, in Prussian Saxony. This remarkable optical phenomenon — which was formerly regarded with superstitious admiration and awe — is merely a gigantic projection of the observer's shadow upon misty clouds opposite to the rising or the setting sun.

Speed. A clownish servant of Valentine, and an inveterate punster, in Shakespeare's "Two Gentlemen of Verona."

Spens, Sir Patrick (spenss). The hero of a famous old Scottish ballad, represented as having been sent in the winter time, by the king of Scotland, on a mission to Norway, and as having been lost, with his whole crew, in mid-ocean, on the homeward voyage.

☞ "The name of Sir Patrick Spens is not mentioned in history; but I am able to state that tradition has preserved it. In the little island of Papa Stronsay, one of the Orcadian group, lying over against Norway, there is a large grave, or *tumulus*, which has been known to the inhabitants, from time immemorial, as 'the grave of Sir Patrick Spens.' . . . The people know nothing beyond the traditional appellation of the spot, and they have no legend to tell. Spens is a Scottish, not a Scandinavian, name. Is it, then, a forced conjecture, that the shipwreck took place off the iron-bound coast of the northern islands, which did not then belong to the crown of Scotland?" *Aytoun.*

Sphinx. [Gr. Σφίγξ.] (*Gr. & Rom. Myth.*) A monster described as having a human head and the body of a lion, and sometimes as having wings also. It used to propose the following riddle to travellers, and tear in pieces those who could not solve it: "What is that which has one voice, and at first four feet, then two feet, and at last three feet, and when it has most is weakest?" Œdipus explained the enigma by saying that it was man, who, when an infant, creeps on all fours, when a man, goes on two feet, and, when old, uses a staff, a third foot; and the Sphinx thereupon destroyed herself.

Spid'I-reen'. An imaginary ship sometimes mentioned by sailors.

Spo'rus (9). A name under which Pope satirises John, Lord Hervey, in the "Prologue to the Satires." See LORD FANNY.

Let *Sporus* tremble. — What! that thing of silk?
Sporus, that mere white curd of asses' milk?
Satire or sense, alas! can *Sporus* feel?
Who breaks a butterfly upon a wheel? *Pope.*

Squab, Poet. See POET SQUAB.

Square, Mr. The name of a "philosopher" in Fielding's novel "The History of Tom Jones, a Foundling."

Squeers. An ignorant, brutal, avaricious Yorkshire pedagogue; in Dickens's novel of "Nicholas Nickleby." See DOTHEBOYS HALL.

Squintum, Doctor. See DOCTOR SQUINTUM.

Squire of Dames. A personage introduced by Spenser in the "Faëry Queen" (Bk. III., canto vii., stanza 51, *et seq.*), and whose curious adventures are there recorded. The term is often used to express a person devoted to the fair sex.

My honest *Squire of Dames*, I see
Thou art of her privy council. *Massinger.*
And he, the wandering *Squire of Dames*,
Forgot his Columbella's claims.
Sir W. Scott.

Squire Western. See WESTERN, SQUIRE.

Squob, Poet. See POET SQUAB.

Stag'I-rite. [Gr. Ὁ Σταγειρίτης, Lat. *Stagirites.*] A surname given to Aristotle (B. C. 384–332), from Stagira in Macedonia, the place of his birth. [Often improperly written Stagyrite.]

See physic beg the *Stagirite's* defence;
See metaphysic call for aid on sense. *Pope.*
Plato's lore sublime,
And all the wisdom of the *Stagirite*
Enriched and beautified his studious mind.
Wordsworth.

Staph'y̆-lă. One of the *dramatis personæ* in Plautus's "Aulularia."

Starvation Dun-dăs'. Henry Dundas, the first Lord Melville; — so called from having first introduced the word *starvation* into the English language, in a speech in parliament, in 1775, on an American debate.

Starveling. A tailor in Shakespeare's "Midsummer-Night's Dream."

---

and for the Remarks and Rules to which the numbers after certain words refer, see pp. xlv-xxxii.

Stă-tī'ră (9). The heroine of La Calpreuède's romance of "Cassandra." She was the daughter of Darius, and the most perfect workmanship of the gods. Oroondates became enamoured of her, and, after many adventures, succeeded in obtaining her hand.

S. T. C. The initials of Samuel Taylor Coleridge (1772-1834), the celebrated English poet and philosopher. He is sometimes designated by them instead of his name.

Stee'nie. A nickname for *Stephen*, given by James I. to George Villiers, Duke of Buckingham, in allusion to his fine face. "And it was," says Hearne, "a very singular compliment to the splendour of his beauty, having reference to *Acts* vi. 15, where it is said of St. Stephen, 'All that sat in the council, looking steadfastly on him, saw his face as it had been the face of an angel.'"

Stel'lă. [Lat., the star.] 1. A name given by Sir Philip Sidney, in a series of exquisitely beautiful amatory poems entitled "Astrophel and Stella," to Penelope Devereux, — afterward Lady Rich, — at one time the loadstar of his affections, and generally admitted to have been the finest woman of her age. She was a sister of Lord Essex. See ASTROPHEL.

2. A poetical name given by Swift to Miss Esther Johnson, whose tutor he was, and whom, in 1716, he privately married. The name Esther (related to the Greek ἀστήρ, Lat. *aster*) signifies *a star*.

Sten'tor. [Gr. Στέντωρ.] (*Gr. & Rom. Myth.*) A Grecian herald in the Trojan war, whom Homer describes as "great-hearted, brazen-voiced Stentor, accustomed to shout as loud as fifty other men."

With this design, he raised up his cudgel for the defence of his head, and, betaking himself to his heels, began to roar for help with the lungs of a *Stentor*. *Smollett.*

Steph'ă-no. 1. A drunken butler, in Shakespeare's "Tempest."

2. A servant to Portia, in Shakespeare's "Merchant of Venice."

Stĕrn, Daniel (4). A *nom de plume* of Marie de Flavigny, Countess of Agoult, a popular French authoress of the present century.

Stĕr'o-pēṣ. [Gr. Στερόπης.] (*Gr. & Rom. Myth.*) One of the Cyclops. See CYCLOPS.

Stewart, Walking. See WALKING STEWART.

Sthe'no. [Gr. Σθενώ.] (*Gr. & Rom. Myth.*) One of the three Gorgons. See GORGONS.

Stich, Tom. The subject of an old tract, or "merry history," composed in the seventeenth century. It consists of a collection of anecdotes respecting a young tailor who was a favourite with the ladies.

Stiles, John. See STYLES, TOM.

Stińk'o-mă-lee'. A cant name for London University; originated by Theodore Hook. He gave it this appellation for the double reason that some question about *Trincomalee* (in Ceylon) was agitated at the time, and that the institution was in ill odour with the members of other Universities because it admitted students from all denominations.

Only look at *Stinkomalee* and King's College! Activity, union, craft, indomitable perseverance on the one side; indolence, indecision, internal distrust and jealousies, calf-like simplicity, and cowardice intolerable on the other. *Noctes Ambrosianæ.*

Stock'well Ghost. A name given to a supposed supernatural agent who produced a train of extraordinary disturbances in the village of Stockwell, near London, in the year 1772, by which the inhabitants were thrown into the utmost consternation. The author of the imposture, a servant-girl by the name of Anne Robinson, was at length detected, and the magic she employed found to be only an unusual dexterity aided by the simplicity and credulity of the spectators.

Stonewall Jackson. A sobriquet given, during the great American Rebellion, to Thomas Jonathan Jackson (1824-1863), a general in the service of the insurgents. The appellation had its origin in an expression used by the rebel General Bee, on trying to rally his men at the battle of Bull Run, July 21, 1861,— "There is Jackson, standing like *a stone wall.*" From that day he was known as "Stonewall Jackson," and his command as the "Stonewall Brigade."

Storm-and-Stress Period. [Ger. *Sturm-und-Drang Zeit.*] In the literary history of Germany, the name given to a period of great intellectual convulsion, during the last quarter of the last century, when the nation began to assert its freedom from the fetters of an artificial literary spirit. Goethe's "Goetz von Berlichingen" gave a powerful impulse to this movement, which was increased by the appearance of Schiller's "Robbers." The period derives its name from a drama of Klinger (1753–1831), whose high-wrought tragedies and novels reflect the excitement of the time.

☞ "The wisdom and extravagance of the age united in one stream. The masterly criticisms of Lessing, the enthusiasm for Shakespeare, the mania for Ossian and the Northern mythology, the revival of ballad literature and parodies of Rousseau, all worked in one rebellious current against established authority. There was one universal shout for 'nature.' With the young, nature seemed a compound of volcanoes and moonlight. To be insurgent and sentimental, explosive and lachrymose, were the true signs of genius." *Lewes.*

☞ "Great indeed was the woe and fury of these Power-men [*Kraftmänner*]. Beauty to their mind seemed synonymous with strength. All passion were poetical, so it were but fierce enough. Their head moral virtue was Pride; their *beau idéal* of Manhood was some transcript of Milton's Devil. Often they inverted Bolingbroke's plan, and, instead of 'patronising Providence,' did directly the opposite, raging with extreme animation against Fate in general, because it enthralled free virtue, and, with clenched hands or sounding shields, hurling defiance towards the vault of heaven." *Carlyle.*

Stormy Cape, *or* **Cape of Storms.** [Port. *Cabo Tormentoso.*] The name originally given to the Cape of Good Hope, in 1486, by Bartholomew Diaz, the celebrated Portuguese navigator. Its present name, for better augury, was substituted by King John II.

Jew Hirsch, run into for low smuggling purposes, had been a *Cape of Storms*, difficult to weather; but the continual lee-shore were those French,— with a heavy gale on, and one of the rashest pilots! *Carlyle.*

Strap, Hugh. A simple, generous, and faithful friend and adherent of Roderick Random, in Smollett's account of the adventures of that notorious personage. See RANDOM, RODERICK.

☞ "We believe there are few readers who are not disgusted with the miserable reward assigned to Strap in the closing chapter of the novel. Five hundred pounds (scarce the value of the goods he had presented to his master) and the hand of a reclaimed street-walker, even when added to a Highland farm, seem but a poor recompense for his faithful and disinterested attachment."
Sir W. Scott.

Stre'phŏn. The name of a shepherd in Sir Philip Sidney's "Arcadia," in love with the beautiful shepherdess Urania; used by the poets of a later day as the name of any lover.

Strephon and Chloe languish apart; join in a rapture; and presently you hear that Chloe is crying, and *Strephon* has broken his crook across her back. *Thackeray.*

Struld'brugs. The name of certain wretched inhabitants of Luggnagg, described in Swift's imaginary "Travels" of Lemuel Gulliver as persons who never die.

Now it came to pass, that, about this time, the renowned Wouter Van Twiller, full of years and honours, and council-dinners, had reached that period of life and faculty which, according to the great Gulliver, entitles a man to admission into the ancient order of *Struldbrugs.* *W. Irving.*

Sturm – und – Drang Zeit (stoŏrm-ŏŏnt-drăng tsit). See STORM-AND-STRESS PERIOD.

Styles, Tom, *alias* **John a-Styles.** A fictitious character formerly made use of in actions of ejectment, and commonly connected with *John o' Noakes*. See NOAKES, JOHN O', also DOE, JOHN. [Written also Tom a Styles, Tom o' Styles, John Styles, and John Stiles.]

☞ In the Middle Ages, the phrase John at Style was in common use to denote a plebeian ; and it still survives in a slightly altered form in the saying, 'Jack Noakes and Tom Styles.'

Peter Stuyvesant read over this friendly epistle with some such harmony of aspect as we may suppose a crusty farmer reads the loving letter of *John Stiles*, warning him of an action of ejectment. *W. Irving.*

I have no connection with the company further than giving them, for a certain fee and reward, my poor opinion as a medical man, precisely as I may give it any day to Jack Noakes or *Tom Styles*. *Dickens.*

He [Doctor Burton, the "Doctor Slop" of Sterne's "Tristram Shandy"] . . . was often seen along the Yorkshire bridle-roads, thus strangely mounted, hurrying away to assist the ladies of *Tom o' Styles* or John Noakes, in their illness. *Percy Fitzgerald.*

Stym-phā'li-ạn Birds. See HERCULES.

Styx. [Gr. Στύξ.] (*Gr. & Rom. Myth.*) One of the rivers of hell, around which it flowed nine times. The gods held it in such veneration that they were accustomed to swear by it, and such an oath was inviolable.

Subtle Doctor. [Lat. *Doctor Subtilis.*] A name given to Duns Scotus, a famous schoolman of the thirteenth and fourteenth centuries, celebrated for his "keenness and versatility in detecting invisible distinctions, in multiplying hypotheses which differed from each other only in some verbal incidents, in untwisting every thought and proposition as by an intellectual prism, in speculating upon themes above the reach of human knowledge, and in the multiplication of ingenious theories without proof to sustain them or utility to recommend them."

Sucker State. A cant name given, in America, to the State of Illinois, the inhabitants of which are very generally called *Suckers*, throughout the West. The origin of this term is said to be as follows:—

"The Western prairies are, in many places, full of the holes made by the 'craw-fish' (a fresh-water shell-fish, similar in form to the lobster), which descends to the water beneath. In early times, when travellers wended their way over these immense plains, they very prudently provided themselves with a long, hollow reed, and, when thirsty, thrust it into these natural artesians, and thus easily supplied their longings. The craw-fish well generally contains pure water; and the manner in which the traveller drew forth the refreshing element gave him the name of 'Sucker.'" *Providence Journal.*

Sullen, Squire. A brutal husband in Farquhar's "Country Blockhead."

Parson Barnabas, Parson Trulliber, Sir Wilful Witwould, Sir Francis Wronghead, Squire Western, *Squire Sullen*,—such were the people who composed the main strength of the Tory party for sixty years after the Revolution. *Macaulay.*

Super Grammaticam. A name sometimes given to Sigismund (1367-1437), emperor of Germany.

"At the opening of the Council [of Constance, 1414], he 'officiated as deacon,' actually doing some litanying 'with a surplice over him,' though Kaiser and King of the Romans. But this passage of his opening speech is what I recollect best of him there : ' Right reverend Fathers, *date operam, ut illa nefanda schisma eradicetur,*' exclaims Sigismund, intent on having the Bohemian Schism well dealt with, which he reckons to be of the feminine gender. To which a Cardinal mildly remarking, '*Domine, schisma est generis neutrius* ' (*Schisma* is neuter, your Majesty), Sigismund loftily replies, '*Ego sum Rex Romanus, et super grammaticam !*' (I am King of the Romans, and above grammar !) — for which reason I call him in my Note-books Sigismund *Super Grammaticam*, to distinguish him in the imbroglio of the Kaisers." *Carlyle.*

Surface, Charles. A character in Sheridan's comedy, "The School for Scandal;" represented as an extravagant rake, but generous, warm-hearted, and fascinating.

Surface, Joseph. A mean hypocrite, in Sheridan's comedy, "The School for Scandal," who affects great seriousness, gravity, and sentimentality.

Surtur (soor'toor). (*Scand. Myth.*) A formidable giant, who, with flames collected from Muspelheim, is to set fire to the universe at Ragnarök. See RAGNARÖK.

Surya (soo're-ä). (*Hindu Myth.*) The god of the sun.

Swan, The Mantuan. See MANTUAN SWAN.

Swan of Avon, Sweet. An epithet conferred upon Shakespeare by Ben Jonson, in some well-known commendatory verses originally prefixed to the second folio edition of Shakespeare's works, printed in 1632.

For the "Key to the Scheme of Pronunciation," with the accompanying Explanations,

Swan of Căm-brāī' (*or* kön'brü', 62). An epithet bestowed, on account of the graces of his style, upon Fénelon (1651–1715), Archbishop of Cambrai, and a writer of fervid eloquence.

Swan of Lichfield. A title given to Miss Anna Seward (1747–1809), an English poetess of some distinction.

Swan of Păd'u-ă. A name given to Count Francesco Algarotti (1712–1764), a native of Venice, a man of much information and taste, and, in his day, an esteemed writer.

☞ " His respectable books on the opera and other topics are now all forgotten, and crave not to be mentioned." *Carlyle.*

Swan of the Me-an'dẽr. An epithet applied to Homer, on account of the harmony of his verse, and on the supposition that he was a native of Asia Minor, of which the Meander is one of the chief rivers.

Swedish Nightingale. A name popularly given to Jenny Lind (Madame Goldschmidt, b. 1821), a native of Stockholm, and one of the most celebrated of female vocalists.

Sweet Singer of Israel. A title applied to King David. See ROYAL PSALMIST.

Sweet Singer of the Temple. An epithet often applied to George Herbert (1593–1633), author of "The Temple: Sacred Poems and Private Ejaculations," and one of the most charming and gifted, though quaint, poets of England.

Swẽr'gă. (*Hindu Myth.*) A terrestrial paradise situated on the summit of Mount Meru (*q. v.*); the delightful abode of Indra, and a place of frequent resort for the other gods.

Swing. A fictitious and much-dreaded name signed to incendiary threats in the rural districts of England, about fifty years ago.

Swiv'el-lẽr, Dick. A careless, light-headed fellow in Dickens's novel of the "Old Curiosity Shop," whose flowery orations and absurdities of quotation provoke laughter, but whose real kindness of heart enlists sympathy.

Sword of God. A surname of Khaled, the conqueror of Syria between the years 632 and 638. He was so called by Mohammed.

Swordsman, The Handsome. See HANDSOME SWORDSMAN.

Syc'o-răx. A foul witch mentioned, in Shakespeare's "Tempest," as the dam of Prospero's slave, Caliban.

Joining, however, the various merits of these authors [Wycherley, Vanbrugh, Farquhar, Congreve], as belonging to this period, they form a galaxy of comic talent scarcely to be matched in any other age or country, and which is only obscured by those foul and impure mists which their pens, like the raven wings of *Sycorax*, had brushed from fern and bog. *Sir W. Scott.*

If you had told *Sycorax* that her son Caliban was as handsome as Apollo, she would have been pleased, witch as she was.
Thackeray.

Sylvanus. See SILVANUS.

Symmes's Hole. An enormous opening imagined by Captain John Cleve Symmes (d. 1829), a visionary American theoriser, to exist in the crust of the earth at 82° north latitude. Through this opening, he thought a descent might be made into the interior of the globe, which he supposed to be peopled with plants and animals, and to be lighted by two small subterranean planets, — named Pluto and Proserpine, — which diffused a mild radiance. According to Humboldt, Captain Symmes publicly and repeatedly invited Sir Humphry Davy and himself to explore this underworld.

☞ It is stated by the same authority, that similar fantastic notions were entertained by the celebrated astronomer Halley, in the latter part of the seventeenth century, and by the learned Norwegian satirist and dramatist Holberg, in the eighteenth century.

Sym-pleg'ă-dēs. [Gr. Συμπληγάδες, the justling rocks.] (*Gr. & Rom. Myth.*) Two huge floating rocks in the Euxine Sea, which at times were driven together by the winds, and crushed all that came between them. The "Argo," however, succeeded in passing through in safety, losing only a portion of her stern; and the islands thenceforth became fixed. See ARGO.

---

and for the Remarks and Rules to which the numbers after certain words refer, see pp. xlv–xxxii.

Syntax, Doctor. See DOCTOR SYNTAX.

Sy′phax. One of the *dramatis personæ* in Addison's tragedy of "Cato."

> Waverley ... could not help bursting out a-laughing, as he checked the propensity to exclaim, with *Syphax*,—
> "Cato 's a proper person to intrust
> A love-tale with!" *Sir W. Scott.*

Sy′rinx (9). [Gr. Σῦριγξ.] (*Gr. & Rom. Myth.*) A nymph beloved by Pan, and changed at her own request into a reed, of which Pan then made his flute.

☞ For the "Key to the Scheme of Pronunciation," with the accompanying Explanations,

T.

Taf'fy. A sobriquet for a Welshman, or for the Welsh collectively. The word is a Welsh mispronunciation of *Davy*, a diminutive of *David*, one of the most common of Welsh names.

Tailors of Tooley Street, The Three. See THREE TAILORS OF TOOLEY STREET.

Tál'bọt, Lying Dick. A nickname given to the celebrated Irish Jacobite, Tyrconnel, who filled the highest offices in Ireland during the last period of the rule of James II. and the early period of William III.

Talking Bird, Singing Tree, and Yellow Water. See PARIZADE.

> Friedrich is loyally glad over his Voltaire; eager in all ways to content him, make him happy, and keep him here, as the *Talking Bird*, the *Singing Tree*, and the *Golden Water* of intelligent mankind; the glory of one's own court, and the envy of the world. *Carlyle.*

Tā'lus. [*Gr.* Τάλως.] A brazen man made by Vulcan for Minos, to guard the island of Crete. Spenser, in the "Faëry Queen," represents him as an attendant upon Artegal, and as running continually round the island of Crete, administering warning and correction to offenders by flooring them with an iron flail. His invulnerable frame, resistless strength, and passionless nature, typify the power which executes the decrees of justice and the mandates of magistrates.

> They [the Puritans] went through the world like Sir Artegal's iron man, *Talus*, with his flail, crushing and trampling down oppressors, mingling with human beings, but having neither part nor lot in human infirmities; insensible to fatigue, to pleasure, and to pain; not to be pierced by any weapon, not to be withstood by any barrier. *Macaulay.*

Talvi (tăl'vee). A *nom de plume* assumed by Mrs. Robinson, — wife of Dr. Edward Robinson, — a well-known authoress of the present day, born in Germany; formed from the initials of her maiden name, *T*herese *A*lbertine *L*ouise *von* *J*akob.

Tammany, St. See ST. TAMMANY.

Tam of the Cowgate. A sobriquet given to Sir Thomas Hamilton (d. 1563), one of the ablest and most learned of Scotch lawyers.

Tam'o-rặ. Queen of the Goths, in Shakespeare's "Titus Andronicus."

Tannhäuser, Sir (tản'hoi-zĕr, 38). [*Ger. Ritter Tannhäuser.*] A famous legendary hero of Germany, and the subject of an ancient ballad of the same name. The noble Tannhäuser is a knight devoted to valorous adventures and to beautiful women. In Mantua, he wins the affection of a lovely lady, Lisaura, and of a learned philosopher, Hilario, with whom he converses frequently upon supernatural subjects. Enchanted by the marvellous tales related to him by his preceptor, he wishes for nothing less than to participate in the love of some beauteous elementary spirit, who shall, for his sake, assume the form of mortal woman. Hilario promises him that he shall kiss even Venus herself, the queen of love and of lovers, if he will have courage to venture upon the Venusberg. The infatuated Tannhäuser sets forth and ascends the mountain, upon hearing of which Lisaura plunges a dagger into her heart. Long does Tannhäuser tarry among the delicious enchantments of the Venusberg; but, at last, moved to repentance, he asks and obtains permission to depart. He hastens to Mantua, weeps over the grave of his gentle Lisaura, and thence proceeds to Rome, where he makes public confession of his sins to Pope Urban. The pope refuses him absolution, saying he can no more be pardoned than the dry wand which he holds can bud forth and bear green leaves. Tannhäuser, driven to despair, flees from Rome, and vainly seeks his former preceptor, Hilario. At this juncture, Venus appears before him, and, with seductive smiles, lures him back to the mountain, there to remain until the day of judgment. Meanwhile, at Rome the dry wand has sprouted and borne green leaves.

Urban, alarmed at this miracle, sends messengers in search of the unhappy knight; but he is nowhere to be found.

☞ This Tannhäuser legend is very popular in Germany, and is often alluded to by German writers. Tieck, in his "Phantasus," has made it the subject of a narrative, and Wagner of a very celebrated opera. The name of the trusty Eckhardt is frequently joined with that of Tannhäuser, as a companion, and by some they are considered to be identical. See ECKHARDT, THE FAITHFUL.

Tan'tạ-lus. [Gr. Τάνταλος.] (*Gr. & Rom. Myth.*) A son of Jupiter, and king of Lydia, Phrygia, or Paphlagonia; punished in the infernal regions with insatiable hunger and thirst, and placed up to his chin in water, under an overhanging fruit-tree; but whenever he attempted to drink or eat, the water or fruit retreated from his lips. His crime is differently stated: the common account is, that, to test the omniscience of the gods, he served up the limbs of his son Pelops (see PELOPS) at a banquet to which he had invited them; some, however, say that he divulged secrets which Jove had confidentially communicated to him; others allege that he stole nectar and ambrosia from the table of the gods, and gave them to his friends; while others again attribute to him inordinate pride, and the possession of too great wealth. The punishment of Tantalus has passed into a proverb, and from it we have derived the word *tantalise*, that is, to hold out prospects or hopes which cannot be realised.

Tap'ley, Mark. The body-servant of Martin Chuzzlewit, in Dickens's novel of this name; noted for his irrepressible jollity, which always showed itself most when his affairs were at the worst.

Charles [VII. of France], who was the *Mark Tapley* of kings, bore himself with his usual jollity under this afflicting news.
Rev. John White.

Tap'per-tit, Simon. An ambitious and conceited apprentice in Dickens's novel of "Barnaby Rudge."

Tar'tạ-rus. [Gr. Τάρταρος.] (*Gr. & Rom. Myth.*) The infernal regions, or, according to some, that part of them where the impious and guilty were punished for their crimes.

Tartuffe (tar-tüf'; *Fr. pron.* tar'tüf', 34). A common nickname for a hypocritical impostor, or knave, who uses the garb of religion to cover his deceit. It is derived from a celebrated comedy of the same name by Molière, in which the hero, a hypocritical priest, is so called. Some say that the character of Tartuffe depicts the confessor of Louis XIV., Père La Chaise, whom Molière once saw eating truffles (Fr. *tartuffes*, It. *tartufi*) with great relish. Great opposition was made to the appearance of the play; but at length, in 1667, Molière succeeded in bringing it on the stage; and for three months "Tartuffe" was performed uninterruptedly, and with great applause. A comedy under the title of "Lady Tartuffe" has been brought out in Paris with success by Mme. Delphine de Girardin.

All types of all characters march through all fables; tremblers and boasters; victims and bullies; dupes and knaves; ... *Tartuffes* wearing virtuous clothing; lovers and their trials, their blindness, their folly and constancy.
Thackeray.

Swiss Pache, on the other hand, sits sleek-headed, frugal; the wonder of his own alley, and even of neighbouring ones, for humility of mind, and a thought deeper than most men's; sit there, *Tartuffe*, till wanted!
Carlyle.

Tattle. A character in Congreve's comedy, "Love for Love;" represented as a half-witted beau, vain of his amours, yet valuing himself for his secrecy.

Teacher of Germany. An epithet often applied to Philip Melanchthon (1497–1560), the celebrated reformer, who was so greatly admired as an instructor that students flocked to him from all parts of Germany, and, indeed, from almost every portion of Europe.

Tearless Battle. See BATTLE, THE TEARLESS.

Tear-sheet, Doll. A strumpet, in the Second Part of Shakespeare's "King Henry IV."

☞ For the "Key to the Scheme of Pronunciation," with the accompanying Explanations,

Seigneur and shoe-black, duchess and *Doll Tear-sheet*, flung pell-mell into a heap, ranked themselves according to method. *Carlyle.*

Tea'zle, Lady (te'zl). The heroine of Sheridan's comedy, "The School for Scandal," and the wife of Sir Peter Teazle, an old gentleman who marries late in life. She is represented as being "a lively and innocent, though imprudent, country girl, transplanted into the midst of all that can bewilder and endanger her, but with still enough of the purity of rural life about her heart to keep the blight of the world from settling upon it permanently."

Tea'zle, Sir Peter. A character in Sheridan's play, "The School for Scandal;" husband of Lady Teazle.

Spite and enmity thinly disguised by sentiments as benevolent and noble as those which *Sir Peter Teazle* admired in Mr. Joseph Surface. *Macaulay.*

Tel'a-mŏn. [Gr. Τελαμών.] (*Gr. & Rom. Myth.*) An Argonaut, son of Æacus, brother of Peleus, father of Ajax and Teucer, and king of Salamis. He was the first to scale the walls of Troy when Hercules took that city in the reign of Laomedon. He also took part in the famous Calydonian hunt, for a notice of which see MELEAGER.

Te-lem'a-chus. [Gr. Τηλέμαχος.] (*Gr. & Rom. Myth.*) The only son of Ulysses and Penelope. After the fall of Troy, he went in quest of his father, accompanied by Minerva in the form of Mentor.

Tel'fer, Jamie. The hero of a Scottish ballad which contains a spirited account of one of the forays so common on the border during the reigns of Mary and James VI.

Tel'lus. (*Rom. Myth.*) A personification of the earth, viewed in relation to its productiveness. [Called also *Terra.*]

Tem'pe. [Gr. Τέμπη.] A romantic valley between Mount Olympus and Mount Ossa, in Greece, through which the Peneus escapes into the sea.

They would have thought, who heard the strain,
They saw, in *Tempe's* vale, her native maids,

Amidst the festal-sounding shades,
To some unwearied minstrel dancing.
Collins.

Tempest, The. [Fr. *La Tempête.*] A sobriquet conferred, on account of his bravery and martial impetuosity, upon Andoche Junot (1771-1813), one of Napoleon's generals, who was educated for the law, but in 1792 enlisted in the army as a volunteer.

Temple, Laun'ce-lŏt. A pseudonym of John Armstrong (1709-1779), the English poet.

Templeton, Laurence. A pseudonym under which Sir Walter Scott published his "Ivanhoe," the work being dedicated by Laurence Templeton to the Rev. Dr. Dryasdust.

☞ "There was no desire or wish to pass off the supposed Mr. Templeton as a real person. But a kind of continuation of 'The Tales of my Landlord' had been recently attempted by a stranger; and it was supposed this Dedicatory Epistle might pass for some imitation of the same kind, and thus putting inquirers upon a false scent, induce them to believe they had before them the work of some new candidate for their favour." *Sir W. Scott.*

Te'reūs. [Gr. Τηρεύς.] (*Gr. & Rom. Myth.*) A king of Thrace, husband of Progne, whose sister Philomela he violated, for which he was changed into a hoopee.

Termagant. [It. *Tervagante, Trivigante;* Old Fr. *Tervagant.* Ritson suggests its derivation from the Lat. *ter,* thrice, and *vagare* (p. pr. *vagans*), meaning, in the lower age of Latinity, to go or turn round, — a very ancient ceremony in magical incantations; and he supposes *Termagant* to be a corruption of *Tervagant,* just as *cormorant* is a corruption of *corvorant* (?), and *malmsey* of *malvesie.* Ugo Foscolo says: "*Trivagante,* whom the predecessors of Ariosto always couple with Apollino, is really Diana *Trivia,* the sister of the classical Apollo, whose worship, and the lunar sacrifices which it demanded, had been always preserved amongst the Scythians." According to Panizzi, *Trivagante,* or *Tervagante,* is the Moon, or Diana, or Hecate, "wandering under three names."] An imaginary being, supposed by the crusaders, who confounded Mahometans with pagans, to be a Mahometan deity. This imaginary personage was introduced into early English plays and moralities, and was represented as of a most violent character, so that a ranting actor might always appear to advantage in it. Hence, Hamlet says of one too extravagant, "I would have such a fellow whipped for o'erdoing Termagant."

Tĕr'mĭ-nus (4). (*Rom. Myth.*) A deity who presided over boundaries. His worship is said to have been instituted by Numa.

Tĕrp-sĭçh'o-re. [Gr. Τερψιχόρη.] (*Gr. & Rom. Myth.*) One of the Muses; the one who presided over dancing.

Tĕr'rą. (*Rom. Myth.*) A personification of the earth; the same as *Tellus*.

Terror of the World. [Lat. *Metus Orbis*.] An epithet given to Attila, the famous king of the Huns, by his contemporaries. See SCOURGE OF GOD.

Tĕr'rȳ Ălts. A lawless body in Clare, Ireland, who sprang up after the Union, and committed various outrages. Similar societies were "The Thrashers," in Connaught, "The Carders" (so called from flaying their victims with a wool-card), &c. See CAPTAIN RIGHT and CAPTAIN ROCK.

Te'thys. [Gr. Τηθύς.] (*Gr. & Rom. Myth.*) A daughter of Cœlus and Terra, and the wife of Oceanus, to whom she bore the Oceanids and the river-gods.

Teu'çęr. [Gr. Τεῦκρος.] (*Gr. & Rom. Myth.*) 1. A son of the river-god Scamander, and the first king of Troy.

2. A son of Telamon of Salamis, and brother of Ajax. He was the best archer among the Greeks at the siege of Troy.

But, thought he, I may, like a second *Teucer*, discharge my shafts from behind the shield of my ally.
Sir W. Scott.

Teufelsdröckh, Herr (hĕr toi'fels-drök, 43, 46). [Ger., Devil's dung.] An eccentric German professor and philosopher, whose imaginary "life and opinions" are given in Carlyle's "Sartor Resartus." "The Philosophy of Clothes" is represented as forming the subject of his speculations. "To look through the Shows of things into Things themselves he is led and compelled." The design of the work is the exposure of the illusions and shams which hold sway so extensively over the human intellect and the social life of man.

Thaisa. A daughter of Simonides, in Shakespeare's "Pericles."

Thal'ą-bą. The hero of Southey's poem entitled "Thalaba, the Destroyer."

Thą-les'tris. [Gr. Θάληστρις.] (*Gr. & Rom. Myth.*) A queen of the Amazons.

"A perfect *Thalestris!*" said the emperor: "I shall take care what offence I give her."
Sir W. Scott.

Thą-lī'ą. [Gr. Θάλεια.] *4Gr. & Rom. Myth.*) 1. One of the Muses; the Muse of comedy.

2. One of the Graces. See GRACES.

Thal'i-ard. A lord of Antioch, in Shakespeare's "Pericles."

Tham'muz. (*Myth.*) The name under which the Phœnicians and Syrians worshipped Adonis. He was killed by a wild boar on Mount Libanus, and was said to revive and be slain again every year. His death happened on the banks of a river named after him Adonis, which at a certain season of the year acquired a reddish tinge. By this circumstance his feast was regulated.

Thammuz came next behind,
Whose annual wound in Lebanon allured
The Syrian damsels to lament his fate
In amorous ditties all a summer's day;
While smooth Adonis from his native rock
Ran purple to the sea, supposed with blood
Of *Thammuz* yearly wounded. *Milton.*

Tham'ȳ-ris. [Gr. Θάμυρις.] (*Gr. & Rom. Myth.*) A Thracian poet of such overweening conceit that he boasted he could surpass the Muses themselves in song; in consequence of which he was deprived of his sight and of the power of singing. He was therefore represented with a broken lyre in his hand. See MÆONIDES.

Thaumaste (to'mȧst', 30, 40, 94). The name of a great English scholar in Rabelais' celebrated satirical romance. He went to France to argue by signs with Pantagruel, and was overcome by Panurge.

Tháu′mă-tur′gus. A surname given to Gregory, a native, and afterward bishop, of Neo-Cæsarea, in Cappadocia, in the third century, on account of the numerous miracles ascribed to him by his early and his mediæval biographers.

Tháu′mă-tur′gus of the West. An appellation given to St. Bernard (1091-1153) by his admiring disciples. His ascetic life, solitary studies, and stirring eloquence, made him, during his lifetime, the oracle of Christendom. He became widely known in connection with the disastrous crusade of 1146, which was urged on by his fervid zeal. Innumerable legions, fired by his burning words, hurried to the East, almost depopulating, in many places, castles, towns, and cities.

Thek′lă (*Ger.* pron. tĕk′lä). The daughter of Wallenstein, in Schiller's drama of this name. She is an invention of the poet.

Thélème (tă′lăm′, 31). A name under which Voltaire has personified the will, in his composition entitled "Thélème and Macare."

Thélème, Abbey of. The name of an imaginary establishment in Rabelais' "Gargantua," stored with every thing which could contribute to earthly happiness, and given by Grangousier to Friar John, as a recompense for his services in helping to subject the people of Lerné.

☞ "The Abbey of Thélème is the very reverse of a Catholic religious house, being an edifice consecrated to the highest state of worldly civilisation. As the discipline of Gargantua represents Rabelais' notion of a perfect education, so may we suppose the manners of the abbey show what he considered to be the perfection of polished society. Religious hypocrites, pettifogging attorneys, and usurers are excluded; gallant ladies and gentlemen, and faithful expounders of the Scriptures, are invited by the inscription over the gate. The motto of the establishment is, '*Facey que vouldras*,' [Do what thou wilt]; and the whole regulations of the convent are such as to secure a succession of elegant recreations, according to the pleasure of the inhabitants." *For. Qu. Rev.*

Now in this *Abbey of Thélème*,
Which realised the fairest dream
That ever dozing bull-frog had. *Lowell.*

He appeared less to be supplicating expected mercies, than thankful for those already found, as if . . . saying the "*gratiæ*" in the refectory of the *Abbey of Thélème*. *Putnam's Mag.*

The′mis. [Gr. Θέμις.] (*Gr. & Rom. Myth.*) The goddess of justice, a daughter of Cœlus and Terra. She was also a prophetic divinity.

Against these Bailliages, against this Plenary Court, exasperated *Themis* every where shows face of battle. *Carlyle.*

Theodorus (the′o-do′rus, 9; *Fr.* pron. tă′o′do′rüss,′ 102). The name of a physician, in Rabelais' romance of "Gargantua." At the request of Ponocrates, Gargantua's tutor, he undertook to cure the latter of his vicious manner of living, and accordingly purged him canonically with Anticyrian hellebore, by which medicine he cleared out all the foulness and perverse habit of his brain, so that he became a man of great honour, sense, courage, and piety.

Thĕr-sī′tēs. [Gr. Θερσίτης.] (*Gr. & Rom. Myth.*) The ugliest and most scurrilous of the Greeks before Troy. He spared, in his revilings, neither prince nor chief, but directed his abuse principally against Achilles and Ulysses. He was slain by Achilles for deriding his grief for Penthesilea. The name is often used to denote a calumniator. Shakespeare introduces him in his play of "Troilus and Cressida," exhibiting him as a sarcastic humourist who lays open the foibles of those about him with consummate address.

In the midst of this chuckle of self-gratulation, some figure goes by, which *Thersites* too can love and admire. *Emerson.*

The′seŭs (28). [Gr. Θησεύς.] 1. (*Gr. & Rom. Myth.*) A son of Ægeus, and king of Athens, who, next to Hercules, was the most celebrated of the heroes of antiquity. He vanquished the Centaurs, slew the Minotaur, and escaped from the labyrinth of Crete by means of a clew of thread given him by Ariadne. He was further distinguished for his friendship for Pirithous. See ARIADNE, HIPPOLYTUS, and PIRITHOUS.

2. Duke of Athens; a character in Shakespeare's "Midsummer-Night's Dream."

Thes'tў-lis. [Gr. Θέστυλις.] A female slave mentioned in one of the Idyls of Theocritus ; hence, any rustic maiden.

And then in haste her bower she leaves
With *Thestylis* to bind the sheaves.
Milton.

The'tis. [Gr. Θέτις.] (*Gr. & Rom. Myth.*) A sea-nymph, daughter of Nereus and Doris, wife of Peleus, and mother of Achilles.

Theuerdank (toi'ĕr-dȧnk). [Ger., dear thanks.] A sobriquet of Maximilian I., emperor of Germany (1459–1519); also the title of a German poem first printed at Nürnberg in 1517.

Third Founder of Rome. A title given to the Roman general Caius Marius, on account of his repeated triumphs over the public enemies of his country, particularly for his successful conduct of the Jugurthine war, and for his decisive victories over the combined forces of the Ambrones and Teutones, near Aquæ Sextiæ (Aix), in 102 B. C., and over the Cimbri, on the plain of Vercellæ (Vercelli), in 101.

Thirty Tyrants, The. (*Rom. Hist.*) A fanciful designation given to a number of adventurers, who, after the defeat and captivity of Valerian, and during the reign of his weak successor, Gallienus (A. D. 260–267), aspired to the throne, and by their contests threatened to produce a complete dissolution of the empire. The name was first applied to them by Trebellius Pollio, one of the writers of the Augustan Chronicle, who has given the biographies of the different usurpers. The analogy between these adventurers, who sprang up suddenly, without concert or sympathy, in diverse quarters of the world, each struggling to obtain supreme dominion for himself, and the Thirty Tyrants of Athens, who, on the termination of the Peloponnesian war, received the sway over that city from the Spartan Lysander, is purely imaginary. Even the numbers do not correspond; and the Latin historian is forced to include the names of women and children, and many doubtful names, to complete the parallel.

☞ The following list comprises all who have been mentioned by different authors:—

Cecrops.	Macrianus, father and son; and
Antoninus.	
Cyriades.	Quietus, another son.
Postumus, father and son.	Ballista.
	Odenathus.
Lælianus, or Lollianus.	Herodes, his son.
Marius.	Herennianus, ⎫ other
Victorinus, father and son.	Timolaus, ⎬ sons.
	Vabalathus, ⎭
Victoria, or Victorina.	Mæonius.
	Zenobia.
Tetricus, father and son.	Piso.
	Valens.
Ingenuus.	Æmilianus.
Regalianus.	Saturninus.
Aureolus.	Celsus.
Trebellianus.	Firmus.

Thirty Years' War. (*Ger. Hist.*) A collective name given to a series of wars between the Protestants and the Catholics in the first half of the seventeenth century. It began with an insurrection of the Bohemians, in 1618, and ended with the peace of Westphalia, in 1648, spreading from one end of Germany to the other, and leaving the country one wide scene of desolation and disorder. The house of Austria was at the head of the Catholic party, while the chief support of the Protestants was Gustavus Adolphus.

This'be. [Gr. Θίσβη.] (*Gr. & Rom. Myth.*) A beautiful maiden of Babylon, beloved by Pyramus. They lived in adjoining houses, and, as their parents would not let them marry, they contrived to communicate through an opening in a wall. Once they agreed to meet at the tomb of Ninus. Thisbe was first on the spot, but, seeing a lioness, she became frightened, and ran off, dropping in her haste a garment, which the lioness found and soiled with blood. When Pyramus arrived and saw it, he imagined that Thisbe was killed, and so made away with himself; while she, gaining courage, after a time returned, and, finding his dead body, likewise killed herself. Shakespeare has burlesqued the story of Pyramus and Thisbe in the Interlude in his "Midsummer-Night's Dream."

The wall he sets 'twixt Flame and Air
(Like that which barred young *Thisbe's* bliss),
Through whose small holes this dangerous pair
May see each other, but not kiss.
T. Moore (on *Davy's Safety-Lamp*).

Thomas the Rhymer. The name under which Thomas Learmont, of Ercildoune, a Scotchman,— born during the reign of Alexander III., and living in the days of Wallace, — is generally and best known.

☞ "This personage, the Merlin of Scotland, and to whom some of the adventures which the British bards assigned to Merlin Caledonius, or The Wild, have been transferred by tradition, was, as is well known, a magician, as well as a poet and prophet. He is alleged still to live in the land of Faëry, and is expected to return at some great convulsion of society, in which he is to act a distinguished part, — a tradition common to all nations, as the belief of the Mahommedans respecting their twelfth Imaum demonstrates." *Sir W. Scott.*

Tho'pas, Sir. The hero of the "Rime of Sir Thopas," one of Chaucer's "Canterbury Tales," containing an account of the adventures of a knight-errant, and his wanderings in search of the queen of Faëry. [Written also, erroneously, T o p a z.]

Bad as *Sir Topaz*, or Squire Quarles, —
Matthew did for the nonce reply, —
At emblem or device am I. *Prior.*

Thor. [Old Norse *Thôrr*, contracted from *Thonar*, Old Saxon *Thunar*, A.-S. *Thunor*, Old High Ger. *Donar;* all from the same root as *thunder*.] (*Scand. Myth.*) A son of Odin and Frigga; the god of war, and in that capacity the defender of the gods against the frequent attacks of the Giants. He drives a golden chariot drawn by two white he-goats, and, when it rolls along the heavens, it causes thunder and lightning. His principal weapon, and that on which much of his power depends, is a mace or hammer called Mjölnir. He has also a famous belt, which, when on him, doubles his strength, and a pair of steel gauntlets, which are of great use to him, as Mjölnir is almost always red-hot. The fifth day was sacred to this god, and hence it was called Thor's day, our *Thursday.* See MJÖLNIR.

Thorn'hill, Sir William, or **Squire.** See BURCHELL, MR.

This worthy citizen abused the aristocracy much on the same principle as the fair Olivia deprecated *Squire Thornhill;* — he had a sneaking affection for what he abused.
Sir E. Bulwer Lytton.

Thorough. An expressive name given by the Earl of Strafford (Thomas Wentworth), one of the privy councillors of King Charles I., to a vast and celebrated scheme projected by himself, and designed to make the government of England an absolute or despotic monarchy.

Thorough Doctor. [Lat., *Doctor Fundatus.*] An honorary appellation conferred upon William Varro, an English Minorite and scholastic philosopher of the last half of the thirteenth century.

Thoth. (*Egypt. Myth.*) The god of eloquence, and the supposed inventor of writing and philosophy; represented as having the body of a man, and the head of a lamb or ibis. He corresponds to the *Mercury* of the Greeks and Romans.

Thoughtless, Miss Betsey. The heroine of a novel of the same name by Mrs. Heywood (1696-1758), supposed to have suggested the plan of Miss Burney's "Evelina." She is represented as a virtuous, sensible, and amiable young lady, but heedless of ceremony, ignorant of etiquette, and without experience of the manners of the world. She is consequently led into many awkward situations, most mortifying to her vanity, by which the delicacy of an amiable and devoted lover is at length alarmed, and his affections almost for ever alienated.

Thrā'so. [Lat.; Gr. θράσων, a braggart, from θρασύς, bold, over-bold.] The name of a swaggering captain in Terence's "Eunuch." From this name is derived the adjective *thrasonical*.

Three Calendars. Three sons of kings, disguised as begging dervises, who are the subject of tales in the "Arabian Nights' Entertainments."

> Jeanie went on opening doors, like the second *Calendar* wanting an eye, in the castle of the hundred obliging damsels, until, like the said prince-errant, she came to a stable.
> *Sir W. Scott.*

Three-fingered Jack. The nickname popularly given to a famous negro robber, who was the terror of Jamaica in 1780. He was hunted down and killed in 1781.

Three Kings of Cologne. See COLOGNE, THE THREE KINGS OF.

Three Tailors of Tooley Street. Three characters said by Canning to have held a meeting for redress of popular grievances, and to have addressed a petition to the house of commons, beginning, "We, the people of England." Tooley Street is in London, in the parliamentary borough of Southwark.

> What a queer fish Mr. Taylor must have been! Where is he now? Why, he (your servant) is Taylor — Jeremy Taylor — Tom Taylor — Taylor the Water-Poet — Billy Taylor — the *Three Tailors of Tooley Street* — ... and — he is asleep!
> *Sala.*

Thresher, Captain. The feigned leader of a body of lawless persons meeting as confederates, who attacked the collectors of tithes and their underlings in Ireland about the year 1806, in consequence of the exactions of the latter in the counties of Mayo, Sligo, Leitrim, and part of Roscommon. Their threats and warnings were signed Captain Thresher.

Thrym. (*Scand. Myth.*) A giant who fell in love with Freyja, and stole Thor's hammer, hoping to receive her hand as a reward for returning it. See MJÖLNIR.

Thumb, Tom. [Fr. *Le Petit Poucet*, Ger. *Daumling.*] The name of a diminutive personage celebrated in the legendary literature of England. He is said to have been buried at Lincoln, where a little blue flag-stone was long shown as his monument, which, however, has been displaced and lost.

☞ In the Bodleian Library there is a work bearing the following title: "Tom Thumb his life and death: wherein is declared many marvailous acts of manhood, full of wonder and strange merriments. Which little knight lived in King Arthur's time, and famous in the Court of Great Brittaine. London: printed for John Wright, 1630." It begins thus: —

> "In Arthur's court *Tom Thumbe* did line,
>   A man of mickle might,
> The best of all the Table Round,
>   And eke a doughty knight.
>
> "His stature but an inch in height,
>   Or quarter of a span;
> Then thinke you not this little knight
>   Was prou'd a valiant man?"

☞ "As to Tom Thumb, he owes his Christian name, most probably, to the spirit of reduplication. Some Teuton, or, it may be, some still remoter fancy, had imagined the manikin, called, from his proportions, Daumling, the diminutive of *Daum*, the same word as our *thumb*; while the Scots got him as Tamlane, and, though forgetting his fairy proportions, sent him to Elfland, and rescued him thence just in time to avoid being made the 'Teind to hell.' As Daumling, he rode in the horse's ear, and, reduplicated into Tom Thumb, came to England, and was placed at Arthur's court, as the true land of Romance; then in France, where little Gauls sucked their Latin *pollex* as their *pouce*, he got called 'Le Petit Poucet,' and was sent to the cave of an ogre, or *orco*, — a monster (most likely a cuttlefish), — straight from the Mediterranean, and there performed his treacherous, but justifiable, substitution of his brother's night-caps for the infant ogresses' crowns, and so came to England as Hop-o'-my-Thumb, too often confounded with the true Tom Thumb." *Yonge.*

☞ "On ballad authority we learn that 'Tom a lyn was a Scoottsman born.' Now . . . Tom-a-lin, otherwise Tamlane, is no other than Tom Thumb himself, who was originally a dwarf, or dwergar, of Scandinavian descent, being the Thaumlin, *i. e.* Little Thumb, of the Northmen. Drayton, who introduces both these heroes in his 'Nymphidia,' seems to have suspected their identity. . . . The prose history of Tom Thumb is manufactured from the ballad; and by the introduction of the fairy queen at his birth, and certain poetical touches which it yet exhibits, we are led to suppose that it is a *rifacciamento* of an earlier and better original." *Qu. Rev.*

Thunderbolt of Italy. A sobriquet or epithet given to Gaston de Foix

☞ For the "Key to the Scheme of Pronunciation," with the accompanying Explanations,

(1489-1512), nephew of Louis XII. of France, and commander of the French armies in Italy, where he gained a series of brilliant victories, and distinguished himself by the celerity of his movements.

Thunderer, The. A popular appellation of the London "Times;" — originally given to it on account of the powerful articles contributed to its columns by the editor, Edward Sterling.

Thundering Legion. [Lat. *Legio Fulminatrix.*] A name given to a Roman legion, A. D. 179, from the prayers of some Christians in it having been followed, it is said, by a storm of thunder, lightning, and rain, which not only enabled them to relieve their thirst, which had been excessive, but tended greatly to discomfit the Marcomanni, the invading enemy.

☞ This legend has been the subject of considerable controversy ; and, though there would appear to have been some foundation for the story, it is certain that the name "Thundering Legion" existed long before the date when it is said to have originated.

Thu'ri-o (9). A foolish rival to Valentine, in Shakespeare's "Two Gentlemen of Verona."

Thwackum. A famous character in Fielding's novel, "The History of Tom Jones, a Foundling."

While the world was resounding with the noise of a disputatious philosophy, the Baconian school, like Allworthy, seated between Square and *Thwackum*, preserved a calm neutrality, half scornful, half benevolent, and, content with adding to the sum of practical good, left the war of words to those who liked it. *Macaulay.*

Thy̆-es'tĕṣ. [Gr. Θυέστης.] (*Gr. & Rom. Myth.*) A son of Pelops and Hippodamia, and brother of Atreus, with whose wife he committed adultery. In requital of this act, Atreus invited his brother to a feast, at which he made him ignorantly eat the flesh of his own son. Thyestes consulted an oracle,' to learn how he might avenge himself; and having been told that his offspring by his own daughter should avenge him, he begot by her Ægisthus, who afterward slew Atreus.

A natural repast; in ordinary times, a harmless one ; now, fatal as that of *Thyestes*.
Carlyle.

Thȳr'sis (4). [Gr. Θύρσις.] The name of a herdsman in Theocritus; also, a shepherd mentioned in Virgil's seventh Eclogue, who has a poetical contest with Corydon; hence, in modern poetry, any shepherd or rustic.

Hard by, a cottage chimney smokes
From betwixt two aged oaks,
Where Corydon and *Thyrsis*, met,
Are at their savory dinner set. *Milton.*

Tibbs, Beau. See BEAU TIBBS.

Tib'ĕrt, Sir. A name given to the cat, in the old romance of "Renard the Fox." See RENARD.

Tickler, Timothy. One of the interlocutors in Wilson's "Noctes Ambrosianæ;" an idealised portrait of an Edinburgh lawyer named Robert Sym (1750-1844).

Tiddler, Tom. A personage well known among children from the game of "Tom Tiddler's ground." One of Dickens's minor tales is entitled "Tom Tiddler's Ground."

Tiddy-doll. A nickname given to Richard Grenville, Lord Temple (1711-1770), in the pasquinades of his time.

Til'bu-ri'nṣ. [Latinised from the Eng. *Tilbury.*] A character in Sheridan's play, "The Critic," whose love-lorn ravings constitute the acme of burlesque tragedy. She is the daughter of the governor of Tilbury Fort.

An oyster may be crossed in love, says the gentle *Tilburina*, — and a drover may be touched on a point of honour, says the Chronicler of the Canongate. *Sir W. Scott.*

Like *Tilburina* in the play, they [Mrs. Radcliffe's heroines] are "inconsolable to the minuet in Ariadne." *Dunlop.*

Til'bu-ry Fort, Governor of. A character in Mr. Puff's tragedy of "The Spanish Armada," in Sheridan's dramatic piece entitled "The Critic;" "a plain matter-of-fact man; that 's his character."

Though the parliamentary major stood firm, the father, as in the case of the *Governor of Tilbury*, was softened, and he agreed that his friends should accept a compromise.
Sir W. Scott.

Tim'i-ăṣ. The name of a character in Spenser's "Faëry Queen," intended

and for the Remarks and Rules to which the numbers after certain words refer, see pp. xiv-xxxii.

to represent the spirit of chivalrous honour and generosity.

☞ "The affection of Timias for Belphœbe is allowed, on all hands, to allude to Sir Walter Raleigh's pretended admiration of Queen Elizabeth; and his disgrace, on account of a less platonic intrigue with the daughter of Sir Nicholas Throgmorton, together with his restoration to favour, are plainly pointed out in the subsequent events. But no commentator has noticed the beautiful insinuation by which the poet points out the error of his friend, and of his friend's wife. Timias finds Amoret in the arms of Corflambo, or sensual passion: be combats the monster unsuccessfully, and wounds the lady in his arms." *Sir W. Scott.*

Ti'mon. [Gr. Τίμων.] An Athenian who lived in the time of the Peloponnesian war, noted as an "enemy to mankind." He is mentioned by Plutarch, Lucian, Aristophanes, and other Greek writers, but is best known to English readers as the misanthropical hero of Shakespeare's "Timon of Athens."

☞ "The story [in Shakespeare] is treated in a very simple manner ...:— in the first act, the joyous life of Timon, his noble and hospitable extravagance, and the throng of every description of suitors to him; in the second and third acts, his embarrassment, and the trial which he is thereby reduced to make of his supposed friends, who all desert him in the hour of need; in the fourth and fifth acts, Timon's flight to the woods, his misanthropical melancholy, and his death." *Schlegel, Trans.*

When he [Horace Walpole] talked misanthropy, he out-Timoned *Timon*. *Macaulay.*

Tin-clā'ri-ăn Doctor, The Great (9). A title assumed by William Mitchell, a white-iron smith, or tinplate worker, of Edinburgh, who published many indescribable books and broadsides there and in Glasgow at the beginning of the last century. "The reason why I call myself *Tinclarian Doctor*," quoth he, "is because I am a Tinklar, and cures old Pans and Lantruns." His great work, the "Tinkler's Testament," was dedicated to Queen Anne.

Tin-tag'el. A strong and magnificent castle situated on the coast of Cornwall; said to have been in part the work of giants. It is renowned in romance as the birthplace of King Arthur, and the residence of King Mark and Queen Isolde. Its walls were washed by the sea, and immediately below it were extensive and beautiful meadows, forests abounding with game, and rivers filled with fish. According to Dunlop, some vestiges of this castle still remain. [Written also T i n t a g g e l and T i n t a d i e l.]

Tin'to, Dick. 1. The name of a poor artist in Scott's novels, "The Bride of Lammermoor" and "St. Ronan's Well."

2. A pseudonym adopted by Frank Boott Goodrich (b. 1826), a popular American author.

Tip'pe-cā-nōe'. A sobriquet conferred upon General William Henry Harrison, afterward president of the United States, during the political canvass which preceded his election, on account of the victory gained by him over the Indians in the battle which took place on the 6th of November, 1811, at the junction of the Tippecanoe and Wabash Rivers.

Tī-rănte' the White. The hero of a fine old romance of chivalry, composed and published in the fifteenth century. His name is derived partly from his father, and partly from his mother, the former being "lord of the seigniory of Tirania, on the borders of England," the latter, Blanca, daughter of the Duke of Brittany.

Tī-re'sĭ-ăs (23). [Gr. Τειρησίας.] (*Gr. & Rom. Myth.*) A celebrated blind soothsayer of Thebes who lived to a great age. He plays a prominent part in the mythical history of Greece. His blindness is said to have been sent upon him for some offence which he unintentionally gave to Minerva or to Juno, or because he imprudently revealed to men things which the gods did not wish them to know.

Thee, Sion, and the flowery brooks beneath ...
Nightly I visit; nor sometimes forget
Those other two equalled with me in fate, —
So were I equalled with them in renown, —
Blind Thamyris and blind Mæonides;
And *Tiresias* and Phineus, prophets old.
Milton.

Tirso de Molina (tēr'so dā mo-lē'nä). A pseudonym of Gabriel Tellez

☞ For the "Key to the Scheme of Pronunciation," with the accompanying Explanations,

(1570–1648), a Spanish monk and dramatist. His *chef-d'œuvre*, a comedy founded on the legend of the world-famous Don Juan de Tenorio, is one of the most remarkable plays in the dramatic literature of Spain.

Tisbina (tĕz-be'nȧ). See Prasildo.

Ti-siph'o-ne. [Gr. Τισιφόνη.] (*Gr. & Rom. Myth.*) One of the three Furies; a minister of the vengeance of the gods, who punished the wicked in Tartarus. See Furies.

Ti'tạn. [Gr. Τιτάν.] (*Gr. & Rom. Myth.*) A son of Cœlus and Terra, elder brother of Saturn, and father of the Titans, giant deities who attempted to deprive Saturn of the sovereignty of heaven, and were, by the thunderbolts of Jupiter, the son of Saturn, hurled into Tartarus. By some poets, Titan is identified with Hyperion, Helios, or Sol; but this point is involved in obscurity.

Ti-tā'ni-ȧ. (*Fairy Myth.*) Wife of Oberon, and queen of the fairies.

☞ "The Shakespearian commentators have not thought fit to inform us why the poet designates the fairy queen 'Titania.' It, however, presents no difficulty. It was the belief of those days that the fairies were the same as the classic nymphs, the attendants of Diana. . . . The fairy queen was, therefore, the same as Diana, whom Ovid ('Met.' lii. 173) styles Titania." *Keightley.*

Her figure, hands, and feet, were formed upon a model of exquisite symmetry with the size and lightness of her person, so that *Titania* herself could scarce have found a more fitting representative. *Sir W. Scott.*

Tit'cŏmb, Timothy (tit'kum). A *nom de plume* adopted by Josiah Gilbert Holland (b. 1819), a popular American author and journalist.

Ti-tho'nus. [Gr. Τιθωνός.] (*Gr. & Rom. Myth.*) A son of Laomedon, king of Troy. He was so beautiful that Aurora became enamoured of him, and persuaded the gods to make him immortal; but, as she forgot to ask for eternal youth, he became decrepit and ugly, and was therefore changed by her into a cicada.

Tit'marsh, Mī'chȧ-el Ăn'ġe-lo. A pseudonym under which Thackeray, for a series of years, contributed tales, essays, and sketches to "Fraser's Magazine," all "distinguished by shrewd observation, exquisite style, and the play of keen wit and delicate irony over a hard and philosophic meaning." He afterward published several volumes under the same name. He is said to have been called "Michael Angelo" by a friend who admired his broad shoulders and massive head, and to have added "Titmarsh" by way of contrast and depreciation.

Let whosoever is qualified tell forth the peculiar experiences of those classes [the fashionable classes] in any serious form that may be possible; and let what is ridiculous or despicable among them live under the terror of *Michael Angelo Titmarsh*. *Masson.*

Titmouse, Mr. Tittlebat. The hero of Warren's "Ten Thousand a Year;" a vulgar, ignorant coxcomb of the lowest order, a linen-draper's shopman suddenly exalted, through the instrumentality of certain rascally attorneys, who discover a defect in a pedigree, to the third heaven of English aristocracy.

We who have not had the advantage of personal observation, supposed "gent." to be fitly given up to the use of those execrable animals who are the triumphs of John Leech's pencil, and the butts of his gentlemen,—in short, the *Tittlebat Titmice* of the English part of the British nation. *R. G. White.*

Tit'ȳ-re Tūṣ. Under this name, and under those of Muns, Hectors, Scourers, and afterwards Nickers, Hawkabites, and Mohawks, dissolute young men, often of the better classes, swaggered by night about London, towards the latter end of the seventeenth century, breaking windows, upsetting sedans, beating quiet citizens, and rudely caressing pretty women. Several dynasties of these tyrants, after the Restoration, according to Macaulay, domineered over the streets. The Tityre Tus took their name from the first line of the first Eclogue of Virgil,—

"Tityre tu patulæ recubans sub tegmine fagi."

Tit'ȳ-rus. [Gr. Τίτυρος, a Doric form of σάτυρος, a satyr.] A character in Virgil's first Eclogue, borrowed from the Greeks, among whom this was a common shepherd's name. He is thought to represent Virgil himself.

Chaucer is affectionately commemorated under this name in Spenser's "Shepherd's Calendar."

*Heroes and their feats
Fatigued me, never weary of the pipe
Of Tityrus, assembling, as he sang,
The rustic throng beneath his favourite beech.*
Cowper.

Tit′y-us. [Gr. Τιτυός.] (*Gr. & Rom. Myth.*) A famous giant, son of Jupiter and Terra. His body was so vast, that it covered nine acres of ground. For attempting the chastity of Latona, or, as some say, of Diana, he was punished in the infernal regions by having two vultures or serpents kept feeding upon his liver, which was made to grow again continually.

Tizona (te-tho′nä, 70). The name of a sword of the Cid. See CID, THE, and COLADA.

To′by. The name of a dog in the common English puppet-show of "Punch and Judy." See PUNCH.

☞ "In some versions of the great drama of 'Punch,' there is a small dog,— a modern innovation,— supposed to be the private property of that gentleman, whose name is always Toby. This Toby has been stolen in youth from another gentleman, and fraudulently sold to the confiding hero, who, having no guile himself, has no suspicion that it lurks in others; but Toby, entertaining a grateful recollection of his old master, and scorning to attach himself to any new patrons, not only refuses to smoke a pipe at the bidding of Punch, but, to mark his old fidelity more strongly, seizes him by the nose and wrings the same with violence; at which instance of canine attachment the spectators are deeply affected." *Dickens.*

Toby, Uncle. See UNCLE TOBY.

Todd, Lau′rie. A poor Scottish nail-maker,— the hero of Galt's novel of the same name, founded on the autobiography of Grant Thorburn,— who emigrates to America, and, after some reverses of fortune, begins the world again as a backwoodsman, and once more becomes prosperous.

Tod′gers, Mrs. M. A character in Dickens's novel of "Martin Chuzzlewit;" the proprietor of a "Commercial Boarding-House" in London.

Tom-à-lin. The same as *Tom Thumb.* See THUMB, TOM.

☞ The name is sometimes written, in ignorance of its etymology, *Tom-a-Lincoln*. An old book, formerly very popular, relates "The most pleasant History of Tom-a-Lincoln, that ever renowned soldier, the Red Rose Knight, surnamed the Boast of England, showing his honourable victories in foreign countries, with his strange fortunes in Faëry Land, and how he married the fair Angliterra, daughter to Prester John, that renowned monarch of the world." It was written by Richard Johnson, and was entered on the books of the Stationers' Company, December 24, 1599.

Tom, Dick, and Harry. An appellation very commonly employed to designate a crowd or rabble.

Tomès, M. (mos′e-ô′ to′mä′). A character in Molière's "L'Amour Médecin."

M. Tomès liked correctness in medical practice. *Macaulay.*

Tom Long. See LONG, TOM.

Tom Noddy. A name given to a fool, in various parts of England.

Tom o' Bedlam. A name given to wandering medicants discharged from Bethlem Hospital on account of incurable lunacy, or because their cure was doubtful.

Tooley Street, The Three Tailors of. See THREE TAILORS OF TOOLEY STREET.

Toots, Mr. An innocent, honest, and warm-hearted creature in Dickens's "Dombey and Son," "than whom there were few better fellows in the world." His favourite saying is, "It's of no consequence."

Topaz, Sir. See THOPAS, SIR.

Top′sy. A young slave-girl in Mrs. Stowe's novel, "Uncle Tom's Cabin," who is made to illustrate the ignorance, low moral development, and wild humour of the African character, as well as its capacity for education.

The book was not deliberately made; but, like Topsy, it "growed." *R. G. White.*

Tormes, Lazarillo de (lä-thä-reel′yo dä tor′mĕs, 70, 82). The hero of a Spanish novel of the same name, by Diego Hurtado de Mendoza (d. 1575), a novel of low life, the first of a class well known in Spanish literature under the name of the *gusto picaresco*,

☞ For the "Key to the Scheme of Pronunciation," with the accompanying Explanations,

or the style of the rogues, and made famous all over the world in the brilliant imitation of it, Le Sage's "Gil Blas."

<small>Faithfully executed, [It] would exhibit . . . the type of the low-minded, merry-making, vulgar, and shallow "Yankee," the ideal Yankee in whom European prejudices find, gracefully combined, the attractive traits of a Gines de Passamonte and a Joseph Surface, a *Lazarillo de Tormes* and a Scapin, a Thersites and an Autolycus. *W. H. Hurlbut.*</small>

Tot'ten-hăm in Boots (tŏt'tn-ăm). A popular toast in Ireland in the year 1731, during the administration of the Duke of Dorset. The government, being anxious to free themselves from the control of the Irish parliament, attempted to obtain a grant of the supplies for twenty-one years; but they were out-voted by a majority of one. The casting vote was given by Mr. C. Tottenham, of New Ross, who had come up from the country without having had time to change his dress, which was considered a remarkable breach of etiquette.

Touchstone. A clown, in Shakespeare's "As You Like It."

<small>Arlecchino is, . . . in his original conception, . . . a buffoon or clown, whose mouth, far from being eternally closed, as amongst us, is filled, like that of *Touchstone*, with quips, and cranks, and witty devices, very often delivered extempore. *Sir W. Scott.*</small>

Touchwood, Lady. A character in "The Belle's Stratagem," a comedy by Mrs. Crowley.

<small>The Dorimants and the *Lady Touchwoods*, in their own sphere, do not offend my moral sense; in fact, they do not appeal to it at all. *Charles Lamb.*</small>

Touchwood, Pĕr'e-grīne. A touchy old East Indian, who figures in Scott's novel of "St. Ronan's Well."

<small>That Boswell was a hunter after spiritual notabilities, that he courted such and longed to be near them, that he first (in old *Touchwood* Auchinleck's phraseology) "took on with Paoli," and then took on with a schoolmaster, that he did all this, and could not help doing it, we count a very singular merit. *Carlyle.*</small>

Tox, Miss. A grotesque character in Dickens's "Dombey and Son;" a little, lean old maid, of limited independence, and "the very pink of general propitiation and politeness."

Tram, Tom. The hero of an old work entitled "The Mad Pranks of Tom Tram, Son-in-law to Mother Winter; whereunto is added his Merry Jests, Odd Conceits, and Pleasant Tales; very delightful to read." This work was probably written in the seventeenth century. It was for a long time very popular, and continued to be republished until within thirty or forty years.

<small>All your wits, that fleer and sham,
Down from Don Quixote to *Tom Tram.*
Prior.</small>

Tranchera (trän-kä'rä). [It., from the Fr. *trancher*, to cut.] The name of a sword of Agricane, which afterward came into the possession of Brandimart.

Trā'ni-o. A servant to Lucentio, in Shakespeare's "Taming of the Shrew."

Translator General. A title borne by Philemon Holland (d. 1636), the translator of Livy, Pliny, Plutarch, Suetonius, Xenophon, and other Greek and Latin authors. It was given to him by Dr. Thomas Fuller, in his "History of the Worthies of England."

Trap'bois. A superannuated usurer in Sir Walter Scott's novel of "The Fortunes of Nigel," "who was believed, even at his extreme age, to understand the plucking of a pigeon as well [as], or better than, any man of Alsatia."

<small>It was as dangerous to have any political connection with Newcastle as to buy and sell with old *Trapbois*. *Macaulay.*</small>

Trap'bois, Martha. A cold, decisive, masculine woman in Scott's "Fortunes of Nigel."

Trav'ẽrs. A retainer of the Earl of Northumberland, in the Second Part of Shakespeare's "King Henry IV."

Tre-mont'. The original name of Boston, Massachusetts; — given to it on account of the three hills on which the city was built. [Called also *Trimount*, or *Trimountain*.]

☞ By many persons erroneously pronounced trem'ŏnt, or tre/mŏnt.

Trim, Corporal. Uncle Toby's attendant, in Sterne's novel, "The Life and Opinions of Tristram Shandy, Gent.;" distinguished for his fidelity and affection, his respectfulness, and his volubility.

☞ "Trim, instead of being the opposite, is, in his notions, the duplicate of Uncle Toby. Every fresh accession of the captain's military fever infected the corporal in a like degree; and, indeed, they keep up a mutual excitement, which renders them both more eager in the pursuit than either would have been without the other. Yet, with an identity of disposition, the character of the common soldier is nicely discriminated from that of the officer. His whole carriage bears traces of the drill-yard, which are wanting in the superior. Under the name of a servant, he is in reality a companion; and he is a delightful mixture of familiarity in the essence and the most deferential respect in forms. Of his simplicity and humanity, it is enough to say that he was worthy to walk behind his master." *Elwin.*

Selkirkshire, though it calls the author Sheriff, has not, like the kingdom of Bohemia, in *Corporal Trim's* story, a seaport in its circuit. *Sir W. Scott.*

Trimmers. A memorable set of politicians contemptuously so called by the two great parties in the time of William III. The chief of this junto was Halifax, who assumed the nickname as a title of honour, and warmly vindicated its dignity, because, as he remarked, every thing good 'trims' between extremes.

Trin'cu-lo. A jester, in Shakespeare's "Tempest."

Conscious that a miscarriage in the matter would, like the loss of *Trinculo's* bottle in the horse-pool, be attended not only with dishonour, but with infinite loss, she determined to proceed on her high emprise with as much caution as was consistent with the attempt. *Sir W. Scott.*

Trinity Jones. A sobriquet of William Jones, of Nayland (1726–1800), distinguished for his treatises in defence of the doctrine of the Trinity and also for having originated "The British Critic."

Trin'o-vănt, or **Trin'o-van'tum.** An old name of London, corrupted from *Troja Nova* (New Troy), the name given to it by Brutus, a legendary or mythical king of England, who is said to have been the founder of the city, and the great-grandson of Æneas. [Written also T r i n o b a n t and T r o y n o v a n t.]

For noble Britons sprong from Trojans bold,
And *Troynovant* was built of old Troy's ashes
cold. *Spenser.*

Triple Alliance. (*Hist.*) 1. A treaty entered into in 1688, by Great Britain, Sweden, and the United Provinces, for the purpose of checking the ambition of Louis XIV. of France.
2. A treaty between George I. of England, the United Provinces, and Philip, Duke of Orleans, regent of France, designed to counteract the plans of Alberoni, the Spanish minister. It was signed in 1717.

Trip-tol'e-mus. [Gr. Τριπτόλεμος.] (*Gr. & Rom. Myth.*) A favourite of Ceres, who taught him husbandry. He was a great hero in the Eleusinian mysteries. Plato makes him one of the judges in the lower world.

Trissotin (trĕs'so'tăn', 62). [That is, Thrice fool, or Fool cubed, from *tri*, thrice (used in composition), and *sot*, fool, blockhead.] The name of a poet and coxcomb in Molière's comedy, "Les Femmes Savantes."

☞ Under this character, Molière satirised the Abbé Cotin, a personage who affected to unite in himself the rather inconsistent characters of a writer of poems of gallantry and of a powerful and excellent preacher. His dramatic name was originally *Tricotin*, which, as too plainly pointing out the individual, was softened into *Trissotin*.

We hardly know any instance of the strength and weakness of human nature so striking and so grotesque as the character of this haughty, vigilant, resolute, sagacious bluestocking [Frederick the Great], half Mithridates and half *Trissotin*, bearing up against a world in arms, with an ounce of poison in one pocket, and a quire of bad verses in the other. *Macaulay.*

Tris'trăm, Sir. One of the most celebrated heroes of mediæval romance. His adventures form an episode in the history of Arthur's court, and are related by Thomas the Rhymer, as well as by many romancists. He is noted for having been the seducer of his uncle's wife. Tradition long ascribed to him the laws regulating the practice of venery, or the chase, which were deemed of much consequence during the Middle Ages. See ISOLDE. [Written also T r i s- t a n, T r i s t r e m.]

☞ "The original meaning of the name is said to have been *noise, tumult;* but, from the influence of Latin upon Welsh, it came to mean *sad*. In Europe, it reg-

☞ For the "Key to the Scheme of Pronunciation," with the accompanying Explanations,

ularly entered the ranks of the names of sorrow, and it was, no doubt, in allusion to it, that Don Quixote accepted the sobriquet of 'The Knight of the Rueful Countenance.'" *Yonge.* In "Morte d'Arthur," the name is explained as signifying *sorrowful birth,* and is said to have been given to Tristram by his mother, who died almost as soon as she had brought him into the world.

"Thou canst well of wood-craft," said the king after a pause: "and hast started thy game and brought him to bay as ably as if *Tristram* himself had taught thee."
Sir W. Scott.

Tri'tŏn. [Gr. Τρίτων.] (*Gr. & Rom. Myth.*) A powerful sea-deity, son of Neptune and Amphitrite; a green-haired being, with the upper part of the body human, and the lower part that of a fish. At the bidding of his father, he blows through a shell to rouse or calm the sea. Later writers speak of a plurality of Tritons.

Great God! I'd rather be
A pagan suckled in a creed outworn;
So might I, standing on this pleasant lea,
Have glimpses that would make me less forlorn;
Have sight of Proteus coming from the sea,
Or hear old *Triton* blow his wreathéd horn.
Wordsworth.

Triv'ă-gănt. The same as *Termagant,* a supposed deity of the Mohammedans, whom our early writers seem to have confounded with pagans. See TERMAGANT.

Triv'i-ă. [Lat., from *ter* (in composition *tri*), three, and *via,* way.] (*Rom. Myth.*) A name given to Diana, because her temples were often erected where three roads met.

Troil, Brenda. See BRENDA.

Troil, Magnus. A character in Sir Walter Scott's novel of "The Pirate;" a Zetlander of wealth and rank, but of neglected education, brought up among inferiors and dependents, and having, in consequence, both the vices and the virtues naturally produced by such limited social intercourse.

Troil, Minna. See MINNA.

Trŏ'ĭ-lŭs. [Gr. Τρωϊλος.] (*Gr. & Rom. Myth.*) A son of Priam and Hecuba, slain by Achilles. He is the hero of Chaucer's poem of "Troilus and Cresseide," and Shakespeare's play of "Troilus and Cressida." There is no trace of the story of Cressida among the ancients.

☞ "This [the vehement passion of Cressida] Shakespeare has contrasted with the profound affection represented in Troilus, and alone worthy the name of love; affection, passionate indeed, — swollen with the confluence of youthful instincts and youthful fancy, and growing in the radiance of hope newly risen, in short, enlarged by the collective sympathies of nature, — but still having a depth of calmer element in a will stronger than desire, more entire than choice, and which gives permanence to its own act by converting it into faith and duty. Hence, with excellent judgment, and with an excellence higher than mere judgment can give, at the close of the play, when Cressida has sunk into infamy below retrieval and beneath hope, the same will which had been the substance and the basis of his love, while the restless pleasures and passionate longings, like sea waves, had tossed but on its surface, — this same moral energy is represented as snatching him aloof from all neighbourhood with her dishonour, from all lingering fondness and languishing regrets, while it rushes with him into other and nobler duties, and deepens the channel which his heroic brother's death had left empty for its collected flood." *Coleridge.*

Tro-pho'ni-us. [Gr. Τροφώνιος.] (*Gr. & Rom. Myth.*) A celebrated architect who, with his brother Agamedes, is said to have built the temple of Apollo at Delphi. After death, he was worshipped as a hero, and had a famous oracle in a cave near Lebadia, in Bœotia, which was entered only in the night.

Trotwood, Mrs. Betsy. A kind-hearted but ogreish-mannered aunt, in Dickens's novel of "David Copperfield."

Trŭl'lĭ-bĕr, Parson. A fat clergyman in Fielding's "Adventures of Joseph Andrews;" noted for his ignorance, selfishness, and sloth.

Trun'nion, Commodore Hawser (trun'yun). The name of an eccentric naval veteran in Smollett's novel, "The Adventures of Peregrine Pickle." He is represented as having retired from service in consequence of injuries received in engagements; yet he retains his nautical and military habits, keeps garrison in his house, which is defended by a ditch and entered through a draw-bridge, obliges his servants to sleep in hammocks and to take turns on watch all the year round, and indulges his humour in various other odd ways.

Try'a-môur', Sir. The hero of an old metrical romance, and a model of all knightly virtues and good qualities.

Tu'bal. A Jew, friend to Shylock, in Shakespeare's "Merchant of Venice."

Tuck, Friar. See FRIAR TUCK.

Tulk'ing-horn, Mr. A lawyer in Dickens's novel of "Bleak House," in possession of family secrets which are of no importance to any body, and which he never divulges.

<small>Finally, it is said to the phonotype, In the words of *Tulkinghorn*, "I tell you, I do not like the company you keep." *Thomas Hill.*</small>

Tupman, Tracy. A character in Dickens's "Pickwick Papers;" represented as a member of the Pickwick Club, and as a person of so susceptible a disposition that he fell in love with every pretty girl he met.

Turcaret (tür/kä/rĭ', 34). A character in a comedy of the same name by Le Sage; a coarse and illiterate man who has grown rich by stock operations. The name is proverbially applied to any one who grows suddenly rich by means more or less dishonest, and who, having nothing else to show, makes a display of his wealth.

Turk Gregory. The name given by Falstaff, in Shakespeare's historical play, "1 Henry IV." a. v., sc. 3, to Pope Gregory VII. (the belligerent Hildebrand), who became a by-word with the early reformers for vice and enormity of every description.

Turnip-hoer. A nickname given to George I., because, it is said, when he first went to England, he talked of turning St. James's Park into a turnip ground.

Tur'nus. A king of the Rutuli in Italy, slain in single combat by Æneas, who was his rival for the hand of Lavinia, daughter of King Latinus. See LAVINIA, 1.

Turpentine State. A popular name for the State of North Carolina, which produces and exports immense quantities of turpentine.

Tur'pin, Dick. A noted English felon, executed at York, for horse-stealing, April 10, 1739. His celebrated ride to York, on his steed Black Bess, is graphically described in Ainsworth's "Rookwood," but a great portion of the description is said to have been written by Maginn.

Tur'vey-drop, Mr. A character in Dickens's novel of "Bleak House;" represented as living upon the earnings of his son, who has a most slavish reverence for him as a perfect "master of deportment."

Tu'tĭ-vil'lus. An old name for a celebrated demon, who is said to have collected all the fragments of words which the priests had skipped over or mutilated in the performance of the service, and to have carried them to hell.

Twelve Apostles of Ireland. A name given to twelve Irish prelates of the sixth century, who appear to have formed a sort of corporation, and to have exercised a kind of jurisdiction or superintendence over the other ecclesiastics or "saints" of the time. They were disciples of St. Finnian of Clonard.

☞ Their names were as follows: 1. Ciaran, or Kieran, Bishop and Abbot of Saighir (now Seir-Keiran, King's County); 2. Ciaran, or Keiran, Abbot of Clonmacnois; 3. Colum-cille (or St. Columba) of Ily (now Iona); 4. Brendan, Bishop and Abbot of Clonfert; 5. Brendan, Bishop and Abbot of Birr (now Parsonstown, King's County); 6. Columba, Abbot of Tirdaglas; 7. Molaise, or Laisre, Abbot of Damhlris (now Devenish Island, in Lough Erne); 8. Cainnech, Abbot of Aichadhbo, Queen's County; 9. Ruadan, or Rodan, Abbot of Lorrha, Tipperary County; 10. Mobi Clairenech, or the Flat-faced, Abbot of Glasnooidhan (now Glasnevin, near Dublin); 11. Senell, Abbot of Cluain-Inis, in Lough Erne; 12. Nannath, or Nennith, Abbot and Bishop of Inismuige-Samh (now Inismac-Saint), in Lough Erne.

Twelve Peers. Famous warriors of Charlemagne's court; — so called from the equality which reigned among them. They were also termed "paladins," a term originally signi-

---

☞ For the "Key to the Scheme of Pronunciation," with the accompanying Explanations,

fying *officers of the palace.* Their names are not always given alike by the romancers. The most famous of them were Orlando, Rinaldo, Astolfo, Oliver, Ogier le Danois, Ganelon, Florismart, Namo, Otuel, Ferumbras, Malagigi. See these names.

Twickenham, Bard of. See BARD OF TWICKENHAM.

Twist, Oliver. The hero of Dickens's novel of the same name; a poor boy born and brought up in the workhouse of an English village, starved, beaten, and abused by every body, but always preserving a saint-like purity and lovableness, even under circumstances of the deepest misery, and when surrounded by the very worst of evil influences.

Twitcher, Harry. A sobriquet popularly given to Lord (Henry) Brougham (b. 1778), on account of a partial *chorea*, or tic, in the muscles of his face.

Don't you recollect, North, some years ago, that Murray's name was on our title-page; and that, being alarmed for Subscription Jamie [Sir James Mackintosh] and *Harry Twitcher*, he took up his pen, and scratched his name out, as if he had been emperor of the West signing an order for our execution?
Noctes Ambrosianæ.

Twitcher, Jemmy. 1. The name of a character in Gay's "Beggar's Opera."
2. A nickname given to John, Lord Sandwich (1718–1792), by his contemporaries.

When sly *Jemmy Twitcher* had smugged up his face
With a lick of court whitewash and pious grimace,
A-wooing he went where three sisters of old,
In harmless society, guttle and scold. *Gray.*

Two Eyes of Greece, The. A name given by the ancients to Athens and Sparta, the most celebrated of all the Grecian cities.

Behold,
Where on the Ægean shore a city stands,
Built nobly; pure the air, and light the soil;
Athens, *the eye of Greece*, mother of arts
And eloquence, native to famous wits
Or hospitable. *Milton.*

Two Kings of Brentford, The. See BRENTFORD, THE TWO KINGS OF.

Two-shoes, Goody. See GOODY TWO-SHOES.

Tyb'alt. A nephew to Lady Capulet, in Shakespeare's tragedy of "Romeo and Juliet."

Were we to judge of their strength in other respects from the efforts of their writers, we should esteem them very unworthy of Dryden's satire, and exclaim, as *Tybalt* does to Benvolio,—
"What! art thou drawn among these heartless hinds?" *Sir W. Scott.*

Tỹ-bur'ni-$. [A Latinised form of *Tyburn.*] A cant or popular name given to the Portman and Grosvenor Square districts in London.

Ty'deŭs. [Gr. Τυδεύς.] (*Gr. & Rom. Myth.*) A son of Œneus, king of Calydon, and father of Diomedes. He was one of the seven chiefs who besieged Thebes, where he greatly distinguished himself. See SEVEN AGAINST THEBES.

Tỹ-di'dês. [Gr. Τυδείδης.] (*Gr. & Rom. Myth.*) A patronymic of Diomedes, the son of Tydeus. See DIOMED.

Tyn-dā're-us (9). [Gr. Τυνδάρεος.] (*Gr. & Rom. Myth.*) A king of Sparta, husband of Leda, and the reputed father of Castor and Pollux. See CASTOR.

Tyn-dăr'I-dæ. [Gr. Οἱ Τυνδαρίδαι.] (*Gr. & Rom. Myth.*) A patronymic of Castor and Pollux, the sons of Tyndareus. See CASTOR.

Tyne'mąn. [That is, losing man.] A surname given to Archibald IV., Earl of Douglas, from his many misfortunes in battle.

Ty'phǫn. [Gr. Τυφῶν.] 1. (*Gr. & Rom. Myth.*) A famous fire-breathing giant, struck by Jupiter with a thunderbolt, and buried under Mount Ætna. [Written also T y p h o e u s (tī-fo'ŭs).]
2. See OSIRIS.

Tyr (tĕr, *or* tēr). (*Scand. Myth.*) A son of Odin, and younger brother of Thor. He was a warrior deity, and the protector of champions and brave men; he was also noted for his sagacity. When the gods wished to bind the wolf Fenrir, Tyr put his hand into the demon's mouth as a pledge that the bonds should be removed again. But Fenrir found that the gods had no intention of keeping their word, and revenged himself in some degree by biting the hand off.

---

and for the Remarks and Rules to which the numbers after certain words refer, see pp. xiv–xxxii.

U.

Uggero (ood-jū′ro). See OGIER LE DANOIS.

Ugolino (oo-go-le′no). [It. *Ugolino de' Gherardeschi.*] A Pisan noble of the thirteenth century, and leader of the Guelphs. Having been defeated in an encounter with Archbishop Ruggieri, a leader of the Ghibelline faction, he is said to have been imprisoned, together with his sons, in the tower of the Gualandi (since called the Tower of Hunger), where they were left to starve, the keys having been thrown into the Arno. Dante has immortalised the name and sufferings of Ugolino. He is represented as voraciously devouring the head of Ruggieri, in hell, where they are both frozen up together in a hole in a lake of ice.

Nothing in history or fiction — not even the story which *Ugolino* told in the sea of everlasting ice — approaches the horrors which were recounted by the few survivors of that night [spent in the Black Hole of Calcutta].
Macaulay.

Woe to him who has found
The meal enough: if *Ugolino's* full,
His teeth have crunched some foul, unnatural thing,
For here satiety proves penury
More utterly irremediable.
Mrs. E. B. Browning.

Ulen-Spiegel (oo′len-spe′gel). See OWLE-GLASS, TYLL.

Ulivieri (oo-le-ve-ā′ree). See OLIVER, 1.

Ullur (or ōōl′loor). (*Scand. Myth.*) A warlike deity who presided over single combats, archery, and the chase. He was accustomed to run so rapidly on snow-shoes, that no one was a match for him. [Written also Uller and Ullr.]

Ul-ri′ca. A hideous old sibyl in Sir Walter Scott's "Ivanhoe."

U-lys′sēs. [Gr. 'Οδυσσεύς.] (*Gr. & Rom. Myth.*) A son of Laertes, king of Ithaca; husband of Penelope, and father of Telemachus; distinguished above all the Greeks at the siege of Troy for his craft and eloquence. On his way back to Ithaca, after the fall of Troy, he was exposed to incredible dangers and misfortunes, and at last reached home without a single companion, after an absence of twenty years. His adventures form the subject of Homer's "Odyssey." See CIRCE, PENELOPE, and POLYPHEMUS.

U′na. A lovely lady in Spenser's "Faëry Queen," intended as a personification of Truth. The name Una signifies *one*, and refers either to the singleness of purpose characteristic of truth, or to the singular and unique excellence of the lady's character. See RED-CROSS KNIGHT.

The gentle lady married to the Moor,
And heavenly *Una* with her milk-white lamb.
Wordsworth.

Mindful oft
Of thee, whose genius walketh mild and soft
As *Una's* lion, chainless though subdued,
Beside thy purity of womanhood.
Mrs. E. B. Browning.

Uncle Sam. A jocular or vulgar name of the United States government.

☞ "Immediately after the last declaration of war with England, Elbert Anderson, of New York, then a contractor, visited Troy, on the Hudson, where was concentrated, and where he purchased, a large quantity of provisions, — beef, pork, &c. The inspectors of these articles, at that place, were Messrs. Ebenezer and Samuel Wilson. The latter gentleman (invariably known as 'Uncle Sam') generally superintended in person a large number of workmen, who, on this occasion, were employed in overhauling the provisions purchased by the contractor for the army. The casks were marked 'E. A. — U. S.' This work fell to the lot of a facetious fellow in the employ of the Messrs. Wilson, who, on being asked by some of his fellow-workmen the meaning of the mark (for the letters U. S., for United States, were then almost entirely new to them), said 'he did not know, unless it meant Elbert Anderson and Uncle Sam,' — alluding exclusively, then, to the said 'Uncle Sam' Wilson. The joke took among the workmen, and passed currently; and 'Uncle Sam' himself, being present, was occasionally rallied by them on the increasing extent of his possessions. . . . Many of these workmen, be-

☞ For the "Key to the Scheme of Pronunciation," with the accompanying Explanations,

ing of a character denominated 'food for powder,' were found, shortly after, following the recruiting drum, and pushing toward the frontier lines, for the double purpose of meeting the enemy and of eating the provisions they had lately laboured to put in good order. Their old jokes accompanied them, and before the first campaign ended, this identical one first appeared in print; it gained favour rapidly, till it penetrated, and was recognised, in every part of the country, and will, no doubt, continue so while the United States remain a nation." *Frost.*

Uncle To'by. The hero of Sterne's novel, "The Life and Opinions of Tristram Shandy, Gent.;" represented as a captain who had been wounded at the siege of Namur, and forced to retire from the service. He is celebrated for his kindess and benevolence, his courage, gallantry, and simplicity, no less than for his extreme modesty, his love-passages with the Widow Wadman, and his military tastes, habits, and discussions. It is thought that he was intended as a portrait of Sterne's father, who was a lieutenant in the army, and whose character, as sketched by his son, is the counterpart of Uncle Toby's.

☞ "But what shall I say to thee, thou quintessence of the milk of human kindness, thou reconciler of war (as far as it was once necessary to reconcile it), thou returner to childhood during peace, thou lover of widows, thou master of the best of corporals, thou whistler at excommunications, thou high and only final Christian gentleman, thou pitier of the Devil himself, divine Uncle Toby! Why, this I will say, made bold by thy example, and caring nothing for what any body may think of it who does not, in some measure, partake of thy nature, that he who created thee was the wisest man since the days of Shakespeare; and that Shakespeare himself, mighty reflector of things as they were, but no anticipator, never arrived at a character like thine." *Leigh Hunt.*

☞ "My Uncle Toby is one of the finest compliments ever paid to human nature. He is the most unoffending of God's creatures; or, as the French express it, *un tel petit bonhomme!* Of his bowling-green, his sieges, and his amours, who would say or think any thing amiss?" *Hazlitt.*

Uncle Tom. The hero of Mrs. Harriet Beecher Stowe's novel entitled "Uncle Tom's Cabin;" a negro slave, distinguished for unaffected piety and the faithful discharge of all his duties. His master, a humane man, becomes embarrassed in his affairs, and sells him to a slave-dealer. After passing through various hands, and suffering great cruelties, he finds relief in death.

Underground Railroad. A popular embodiment of the various ways in which fugitive slaves from the Southern States of the American Union were assisted in escaping to the North, or to Canada, before the abolition of slavery took place; often humourously abbreviated U. G. R. R.

Undertaker, The General. See GENERAL UNDERTAKER, THE.

Undertakers. Parties in the Irish parliament, in the last century, who bargained with the government to carry its measures, and who received in return places, pensions, and profitable jobs.

Un-dine' or **Un'dine** (*Ger. pron.* oonde'nă). The name of a water-nymph who is the heroine of La Motte Fouqué's romance of the same name, one of the most delightful creations of German fiction. Like the other water-nymphs, she was created without a soul, which she could gain only by marriage with a mortal. By such marriage, however, she became subject to all the pains and miseries of mortal men.

Unfortunate Peace. (*Hist.*) The peace of Cateau-Cambresis (April 2, 1559), negotiated by England, France, and Spain. By this treaty, Henry II. of France renounced all claim to Genoa, Corsica, and Naples, agreed to restore Calais to the English within eight years, and to give security for five hundred thousand crowns in case of failure.

U'ni-gen'I-tus. (*Ecclesiastical Hist.*) The name given to a famous bull issued by Pope Clement XI., in 1713, against the French translation of the New Testament, with notes by Pasquier Quesnel, priest of the Oratory, and a celebrated Jansenist. The bull began with the words, "*Unigeni-*

and for the Remarks and Rules to which the numbers after certain words refer, see pp. xiv-xxxii.

tus Dei Filius," and hence the name given to it.

Unique, The. See ONLY, THE.

Universal Doctor. [Lat. *Doctor Universalis.*] 1. An honorary title given by his admirers to Alain de Lille (1114–1203), one of the greatest divines of his age.
2. A designation applied, in allusion to his extensive and profound learning, to Thomas Aquinas (1227–1274). See ANGELIC DOCTOR and DUMB OX.

Unlearned Parliament. See PARLIAMENT OF DUNCES.

U-rā′ni-ă. [Gr. Οὐρανία.] (*Gr. & Rom. Myth.*) One of the Muses; the one who presided over astronomy.

U′ră-nids (9). [Gr. Οὐρανίδαι.] (*Gr. & Rom. Myth.*) The descendants of Uranus; by some identified with the Titans. See TITAN.

U′ră-nus (9). [Gr. Οὐρανός.] (*Gr. Myth.*) One of the most ancient of the gods, husband of Tellus or Terra, and father of Saturn; the same as the *Cœlus* of the Romans.

Urban, Sylvanus, Gent. The fictitious name under which the "Gentleman's Magazine" is edited, and by which is expressed its universality of town and country intelligence.

True histories of last year's ghost,
Lines to a ringlet or a turban,
And trifles for the "Morning Post,"
And nothing for *Sylvanus Urban*.
Praed.

Here, through *Sylvanus Urban* himself, are two direct glimpses, a twelvemonth nearer hand, which show us how the matter has been proceeding since. *Carlyle.*

Urganda (oor-gän′dä). The name of a potent fairy in the romance of "Amadis de Gaul," and in the romances of the Carlovingian cycle and the poems founded upon them. In the Spanish romances relating to the descendants of Amadis, she is invested with all the more serious terrors of a Medea.

This *Urganda* seemed to be aware of her own importance, and perfectly acquainted with the human appetite. *Smollett.*

This ancient *Urganda* perceived my disorder, and, approaching with a languishing air, seized my hand, asking in a squeaking tone if I was indisposed. *Smollett.*

We will beat about together, in search of this *Urganda*, ... who can read this, the riddle of thy fate, better than ... Cassandra herself. *Sir W. Scott.*

Urian, Sir (yoo′ri-an, 9; *Ger. pron.* oo′re-än). [Ger. *Herr Urian.*] Among the Germans, a sportive designation of a man who is very little thought of, or who is sure to turn up unexpectedly and inopportunely. In Low German, the name is applied to the Devil.

U′ri-el (9). [Heb., fire of God.] An angel mentioned in the second book of *Esdras*. Milton makes him "regent of the sun," and calls him "the sharpest-sighted spirit of all in heaven."

Ur′să Mā′jŏr. A nickname given by Boswell, the father (Lord Auchinleck), to Dr. Johnson.

☞ "My father's opinion of Dr. Johnson," says his biographer, "may be conjectured from the name he afterwards gave him, which was 'Ursa Major.' But it is not true, as has been reported, that it was in consequence of my saying that he was a *constellation* of genius and literature." Goldsmith remarks: "Johnson, to be sure, has a roughness in his manner; but no man alive has a more tender heart. He has nothing of the bear but his skin."

Ur′su-lă. A gentlewoman attending on Hero, in Shakespeare's "Much Ado about Nothing."

Useless Parliament. [Lat. *Parliamentum Vanum.*] (*Eng. Hist.*) A name given to the first parliament held in the reign of Charles I. It met June, 18, 1625, adjourned to Oxford, August 1, on account of the plague, and, having offended the king, was dissolved on the 12th of the same month.

Utgard (ŏŏt′gard). [Old Norse, outer ward or enclosure.] (*Scand. Myth.*) A circle of rocks surrounding the vast ocean supposed to encompass the earth, which was regarded as a flat circular plane or disk; the abode of the Giants; the same as *Jötunheim*.

Utgard - Loki (ŏŏt′gard-lo′kee). (*Scand. Myth.*) The king of Utgard, and chief of the Giants. See LOKI.

U′thẽr. Son of Constans, one of the

fabulous or legendary kings of Britain, and the father of Arthur. See IGERNA.

And what resounds
In fable or romance of *Uther's* son,
Begirt with British and Armoric knights.
Milton.

Mythic *Uther's* deeply wounded son,
In some fair space of sloping greens,
Lay, dozing in the vale of Avalon,
And watched by weeping queens.
Tennyson.

U-to'pi-å. [From Gr. οὐ, not, and τόπος, a place.] A term invented by Sir Thomas More (1480–1535), and applied by him to an imaginary island which he represents to have been discovered by a companion of Amerigo Vespucci, and as enjoying the utmost perfection in laws, politics, &c., in contradistinction to the defects of those which then existed elsewhere. The name has now passed into all the languages of Europe to signify a state of ideal perfection.

☞ "The second book ... gives a geographical description of the island; the relations of the inhabitants in social life, their magistrates, their arts, their systems of war and religion. On the latter subject, — which could hardly be expected from the practice of the author, — the most unbounded toleration is granted. The greater part of the inhabitants believed in one Spirit, all-powerful and all-pervading; but others practised the worship of heroes and the adoration of stars. A community of wealth is a fundamental principle of this republic, and the structure [is] what might be expected from such a basis." *Dunlop.*

☞ "That he [Sir T. More] meant this imaginary republic seriously to embody his notions of a sound system of government, can scarcely be believed by any one who reads it and remembers that the entirely fanciful and abstract existence there depicted was the dream of one who thoroughly knew man in all his complicated relations, and was deeply conversant in practical government." *J. H. Burton.*

---

and for the Remarks and Rules to which the numbers after certain words refer, see pp. xiv-xxxii.

V.

Vadius (vā'de-ŭs', 102). The name of a grave and heavy pedant in Molière's comedy, "Les Femmes Savantes."

☞ The character of Vadius is supposed to be a satire on Ménage, an ecclesiastic celebrated for his learning and wit. It is said, however, that Ménage bore the attack upon his pedantry with such perfect good humour and good sense that Molière always refused to acknowledge that he had taken him for his model in constructing the character of Vadius.

Val'en-tine. 1. One of the heroes in the old romance of "Valentine and Orson," which is of uncertain age and authorship, though it probably belongs to the fifteenth century. See ORSON.

Do not think you will meet a gallant *Valentine* in every English rider, or an Orson in every Highland drover. *Sir W. Scott.*

2. One of the "Two Gentlemen of Verona," in Shakespeare's play of that name.

3. A gentleman attending on the Duke in Shakespeare's "Twelfth Night."

4. One of the characters in Goethe's "Faust." He is a brother of Margaret, whom Faust has seduced. Maddened by his sister's shame, he interrupts a serenade of Faust's, attacks him, is stabbed by Mephistopheles, falls, and expires uttering vehement reproaches against Margaret.

Val-häl'lă. [Icel. *valhöll*, hall of the slain, from *valr*, slaughter, and *höll*, a royal hall, Old Saxon and Old High Ger. *halla*.] (*Scand. Myth.*) The palace of immortality, inhabited by the souls of heroes slain in battle. [Written also V a l h a l l and W a l- h a l l a.]

Val-kȳr'i-ŏr, or **Val'kȳrṣ.** [Old Norse *valkyrja*, from *vale*, crowds of slain, and *kiöra*, *kera*, to select; A.-S. *välcyrie*, Ger. *Warlküren*, *Walkyren*, or *Walkyrien*.] (*Scand. Myth.*) Beautiful and awful maidens, messengers of Odin, who visit fields of battle to carry off to Valhalla the souls of heroes who fall. At the banquets of Valhalla, they hand round to the guests mead and ale. [Written also V a l k y r i a s.]

Valley of Humiliation. In Bunyan's "Pilgrim's Progress," a valley in which Christian was attacked by Apollyon, who nearly overpowered him, but was at length wounded and put to flight.

Valley of the Shadow of Death. In the "Pilgrim's Progress" of John Bunyan, the valley through which Christian, after his encounter with Apollyon, was obliged to pass on his way to the Celestial City. "Now this valley is a very solitary place; the prophet Jeremiah thus describes it: 'A wilderness, a land of deserts and pits, a land of drought, and of the Shadow of Death, a land that no man' (but a christian) 'passeth through, and where no man dwelt.'" See *Psalm* xxiii. 4.

One would have thought Inverary had been the *Valley of the Shadow of Death*, the inferior chiefs showed such reluctance to approach it. *Sir W. Scott.*

Van-dyck' of Sculpture. A designation conferred upon Antoine Coysevox (1640-1720), a French sculptor, on account of the beauty and animation of his figures.

Vă-nes'să. [Compounded of *Van*, the first syllable of *Vanhomrigh*, and *Essa*, diminutive of *Esther*.] A poetical name given by Swift to Miss Esther Vanhomrigh, a young lady who had fallen in love with him and proposed marriage. How her declaration of affection was received is related in Swift's poem of "Cadenus and Vanessa." See CADENUS.

Vanity. 1. An established character in the old moralities and puppet-shows.

2. A town in Bunyan's "Pilgrim's Progress," on the road to the Celestial City.

☞ For the "Key to the Scheme of Pronunciation," with the accompanying Explanations,

Vanity Fair. In Bunyan's spiritual allegory, "The Pilgrim's Progress," the name of a fair which was held all the year round in the town of Vanity. "It beareth the name because the town where it is kept is lighter than vanity (*Ps.* lxii. 9), and also because all that is there sold, or that cometh thither, is vanity." Thackeray has made use of this name as the title of a satirical novel.

☞ The origin and history of this fair are thus described: "Almost five thousand years ago there were pilgrims walking to the Celestial City, and Beëlzebub, Apollyon, and Legion, with their companions, perceiving by the path that the pilgrims made that their way to the city lay through this town of Vanity, they contrived here to set up a fair, — a fair wherein should be sold all sorts of vanity, and that it should last all the year long. Therefore, at this fair are all such merchandise sold as houses, lands, trades, places, honours, preferments, titles, countries, kingdoms, lusts, pleasures; and delights of all sorts, as harlots, wives, husbands, children, lives, blood, bodies, souls, silver, gold, pearls, precious stones, and what not. And, moreover, at this fair there is, at all times, to be seen jugglings, cheats, games, fools, knaves, rogues, and that of every kind. And, as in other fairs of less moment, there are several rows and streets, under their proper names, where such and such wares are vended, so here, likewise, you have the proper places, rows, streets, (namely, countries and kingdoms,) where the wares of this fair are soonest to be found. . . . Now, as I said, the way to the Celestial City lies just through this town where this lusty fair is kept; and he that would go to the city and yet not go through this town, must needs go out of the world."

I charge you to withdraw your feet from the delusion of that *Vanity Fair* in whilk ye are a sojourner, and not to go to their worship, whilk is an ill-mumbled mass, as was weel termed by James the Sext. *Sir W. Scott.*

Vā'pǐ-ăns. A name — probably a feigned one — occurring in Shakespeare's "Twelfth Night," a. ii., sc. 3. See PIGROGROMITUS.

Vă-rī'nă. A poetical name given by Swift to Miss Jane Waryng, for whom, in early life, he professed an attachment. It is a Latinised form of Waryng.

Vă-rû'nă. (*Hindu Myth.*) The ruler of the ocean; represented as a white man riding on a sea-monster, with a club in one hand and a rope in the other.

Vath'ek. The hero of William Beckford's celebrated novel of the same name; a haughty and effeminate monarch, led on by the temptations of a malignant genie, and the sophistries of a cruel and ambitious mother, to commit all sorts of crimes, to abjure his faith, and to offer allegiance to Eblis, the Mohammedan Satan, in the hope of seating himself on the throne of the pre-Adamite sultans.

We saw men, who, not yet in the vigour of life, were *blasé* with its pleasures; men with the poisoned youth, *Vathek*-like, to find themselves some day with fires, unquenchable and agonising, in the place of those hearts they had silenced, perverted, and destroyed.
Putnam's Mag.

Ve (vee, *or* vā). (*Scand. Myth.*) One of the three deities who took part in the creation of the world; a brother of Odin and Vili.

Veal, Mrs. An imaginary person whom De Foe feigned to have appeared, "the next day after her death, to one Mrs. Bargrave, at Canterbury, on the 8th of Sept., 1705," — one of the boldest and most adroit experiments upon human credulity that ever was made.

Vegliantino (vāl-yăn-te'no, 77). The name of Orlando's horse.

Venerable Bede. See BEDE, THE VENERABLE.

Venerable Doctor. [Lat. *Doctor Venerabilis.*] A title given to William de Champeaux, a celebrated philosopher and theologian of the twelfth century, regarded as the first public professor of scholastic divinity, and the founder of scientific realism.

Venerable Initiator. [Lat. *Venerabilis Inceptor.*] An honorary appellation conferred upon William of Occam (d. 1347), a famous English scholastic philosopher.

Venice of the West. A name sometimes given, rather inappropriately, to Glasgow, the chief city of Scotland.

A bird proper, on the shield argent of the city of Glasgow, has been identified with the resuscitated pet of the patron saint. The

---

and for the Remarks and Rules to which the numbers after certain words refer, see pp. xiv-xxxii.

tree on which it is there perched is a commemoration of another of the saint's miracles. . . . Another element in the blazon of the *Venice of the West* is a fish, laid across the stem of the tree, "in base," as the heralds say.
J. H. Burton.

Ve'nus. (*Gr. & Rom. Myth.*) The goddess of love and beauty, said to have sprung from the foam of the sea. She was the wife of the deformed blacksmith Vulcan, but was not remarkable for her fidelity to him. Her amour with Adonis is particularly celebrated. By the Trojan Anchises, she became the mother of Æneas, and hence was regarded by the Romans as the progenitor of their nation. See ÆNEAS.

Ve'nus-berg. See ECKHARDT, THE FAITHFUL.

Věr'gěș (4). A watchman and night-constable, in Shakespeare's "Much Ado about Nothing," noted for his blundering simplicity.

Vermilion Sea. A name formerly given to the Gulf of California, on account of the red colour of the infusoria it contains.

Věr'non, Die (*or* Di-an'ą). The heroine of Sir Walter Scott's novel of "Rob Roy;" a young girl of great beauty, talents, and excellence of disposition, to which are superadded pride of high birth, and the enthusiasm of an adherent to a persecuted religion and an exiled king. She is excluded from the ordinary wishes and schemes of other young ladies by being predestined to a hateful husband or a cloister, and by receiving a masculine education, under the superintendence of two men of talent and learning.

Věr-tum'nus. [Lat., from *vertere*, to turn, to change, to transform.] (*Rom. Myth.*) The god of the seasons, and of their manifold productions in the vegetable world. He fell in love with Pomona, and, after vainly endeavouring to get access to her under a thousand different forms, at last succeeded by assuming the appearance of an old woman. In this guise, he recounted to her lamentable stories of women who had despised the power of love; and, when he found that her heart was touched, he suddenly metamorphosed himself into a beautiful youth, and persuaded her to marry him.

Very Christian Doctor. See MOST CHRISTIAN DOCTOR.

Very Methodical Doctor. See MOST METHODICAL DOCTOR.

Very Resolute Doctor. See MOST RESOLUTE DOCTOR.

Ves'tą. [Gr. Ἑστία.] (*Gr. & Rom. Myth.*) A daughter of Rhea and Saturn, and sister of Ceres and Juno. She was the goddess of fire, and she also presided over flocks and herds. Her mysteries were celebrated by maidens, called vestal virgins, who kept a fire constantly burning on her hearth or altar, and who were required to lead lives of perfect purity.

Véto, M. et Mme. (mos'e-ö' å mȧ'-dȧm' vȧ'to'). Injurious names often given by the anarchists of the French Revolution to Louis XVI. and his queen, Marie Antoinette. The expression originated in the indignation of the people at the *veto* allowed the king on the resolves of the National Assembly. The name occurs in the celebrated song, "La Carmagnole," which, with the accompanying dance, was performed at popular festivals, executions, and outbreaks of popular discontent during the Reign of Terror.

That is the pass ye have brought us to. And now ye will break the prisons and set Capet *Veto* on horseback to ride over us. *Carlyle.*

Ve'tus. A *nom de plume* of Edward Sterling (1773 - 1847), an English writer.

☞ "He [Sterling] now furthermore opened a correspondence with the 'Times' Newspaper; wrote to it, in 1812, a series of Letters under the signature of Vetus: voluntary Letters I suppose, without payment or pre-engagement, one successful Letter calling out another; till Vetus and his doctrines came to be a distinguishable entity, and the business amounted to something. Out of my own earliest Newspaper reading, I can remember the name Vetus as a kind of editorial hacklog on which able editors were wont to chop straw now and then. Nay, the Letters were collected and reprinted; both this first series, of 1812, and then a second of next year." *Carlyle.*

☞ For the "Key to the Scheme of Pronunciation," with the accompanying Explanations,

Vi′æ Dol′o-ro′sæ. [Lat., way of pain.] A name popularly given, since the Christian era, to the road at Jerusalem leading from the Mount of Olives to Golgotha, which Jesus passed over on his way to the place of crucifixion. Upon this road are situated the house where the Virgin Mary was born; the church erected upon the spot where she fell when she beheld Jesus sink under the weight of the cross; the house of St. Veronica, upon whose veil, employed to wipe away his blood and sweat, the image of his face was miraculously impressed; and many other objects consecrated by Christian traditions. The road, which is about a mile in length, terminates at the Gate of Judgment.

Vicar of Bray. A name originally given to an English clergyman who was twice a Papist and twice a Protestant in four successive reigns. It is now commonly applied to one who deserts his party when it is no longer for his safety or his interest to remain in it.

☞ Bray is a village in Berkshire. "The vivacious vicar hereof," says Fuller, "living under Henry VIII., Edward VI., Queen Mary, and Queen Elizabeth, was first a Papist, then a Protestant, then a Papist, then a Protestant again. He had seen some martyrs burned (two miles off) at Windsor, and found this fire too hot for his tender temper. This vicar, being taxed by one for being a turncoat and inconstant changeling, 'Not so neither,' said he; 'for, if I changed my religion, I am sure I kept true to my principle, which is to live and die the Vicar of Bray.'" According to Haydn, the name of this consistent personage was Symon Symonds; according to a Mr. Brome ("Letters from the Bodleian," vol. ii., part i, p. 100), it was Simon Alleyn, or Allen. The former is said to have held the vicarage from 1533 to 1558; the latter from 1540 to 1588. Another statement gives the name as Pendleton; and it is related that, in the reign of Edward VI., Lawrence Sanders, the martyr, an honest but mild and timorous man, having expressed a fear that his own strength of mind was not sufficient to endure the persecution of the times, Pendleton answered, that, for himself, he would see every drop of his fat and the last morsel of his flesh consumed to ashes ere he would swerve from the faith then established. He, however, changed with the times, saved his fat and his flesh, and became rector of St. Stephen's, whilst the mild and diffident Sanders was burnt at Smithfield. Townsend ("Manual of Dates") says that the story in regard to the Vicar of Bray is not borne out by the church records, the living not having been held by the same person for so long a period as that required to prove the truth of the anecdote. The celebrated song of the "Vicar of Bray," though founded on the historical fact, makes the vicar a subject successively of Charles II., James II., William III., Anne, and George I., and a political as well as religious renegade. It is said (Nichols' "Select Poems," 1782, vol. viii., p. 234) to have been written by an officer in Colonel Fuller's regiment, in the reign of George I.

He [Sbult] obeyed, he says, not as in any respect an enemy of the king (Louis XVIII.), but as a citizen and a soldier, whose duty it was to obey whomsoever was at the head of the government, as that of the *Vicar of Bray* subjected him in ghostly submission to each head of the church *pro tempore*.
Sir W. Scott.

Vicar of Christ. A title assumed by the pope of Rome, who claims to exercise a delegated authority as the representative or vicegerent of Christ.

Vicar of Wakefield. The hero of Goldsmith's novel of the same name. See PRIMROSE, THE REV. DOCTOR.

Thus an era took place in my life, almost equal to the important one mentioned by the *Vicar of Wakefield*, when he removed from the Blue room to the Brown. *Sir W. Scott.*

Vice, The. A grotesque allegorical character who invariably figures in the old English mysteries and moralities which preceded the rise of the regular modern drama. He was fantastically accoutred in a long jerkin, a cap with ass's ears, and a dagger of lath. His chief employment was to make sport for the multitude by leaping on the back of the Devil, — another personage always introduced into these plays, — and belabouring him with his dagger till he roared. The Devil, however, always carried him off in the end. He bore the name sometimes of one particular vice, and sometimes of another; but was generally called "The Vice," simply. He was succeeded in his office by the fool and the clown, and is now best remembered by the allusions which occur in the plays of

Shakespeare to his character and office.

Vidar (ve′dár). (*Scand. Myth.*) The god of wisdom and of silence. His look is so penetrating that he reads the most secret thoughts of men. He wears very thick shoes, and hence is sometimes called "the god with the thick shoes."

Vil. (*Scand. Myth.*) The brother of Odin and Ve, who, with him, were the progenitors of the Asir race.

Vin-cen′ti-o (vin-sen′shĭ-o). 1. The Duke of Vienna in Shakespeare's "Measure for Measure." He commits his sceptre to Angelo (with whom Escalus is associated in a subordinate capacity), under the pretext of being called to take an urgent and distant journey; and, by exchanging the royal purple for a monk's hood, observes *incognito* the condition of his people, and especially the manner and effect of his vicegerent's administration.

2. An old gentleman of Pisa, in Shakespeare's "Taming of the Shrew."

Vinegar Bible. A name given to an edition of the Bible published in 1717 at the Clarendon Press, Oxford. By a ludicrous misprint, the title of the twentieth chapter of *Luke* was made to read, "Parable of the *Vinegar*" instead of, "Parable of the *Vineyard;*" hence the name.

Vin′länd. A name given, according to Snorro Sturleson, by Scandinavian voyagers, to a portion of the coast of North America discovered by them toward the close of the tenth century, well wooded, and producing agreeable fruits, particularly grapes. It is thought to have been some part of the coast of Massachusetts or Rhode Island.

Vī′o-lá. A lady in love with Duke Orsino, in Shakespeare's "Twelfth Night."

☞ "As for her situation in the drama (of which she is properly the heroine), it is, shortly, this: She is shipwrecked on the coast of Illyria; she is alone, and without protection, in a strange country. She wishes to enter into the service of the Countess Olivia; but she is assured that this is impossible, 'for the lady, having recently lost an only and beloved brother, has abjured the sight of men, has shut herself up in her palace, and will admit no kind of suit.' In this perplexity, Viola remembers to have heard her father speak with praise and admiration of Orsino, the duke of the country; and, having ascertained that he is not married, and that, therefore, his court is not a proper asylum for her in her feminine character, she attires herself in the disguise of a page, as the best protection against uncivil comments, till she can gain some tidings of her brother. . . . To pursue the thread of Viola's destiny: she is engaged in the service of the duke, whom she finds 'fancy-sick' for the love of Olivia. We are left to infer (for so it is hinted in the first scene) that this duke . . . had already made some impression on Viola's imagination; and when she comes to play the confidante, and to be loaded with favours and kindness in her assumed character, that she should be touched by a passion made up of pity, admiration, gratitude, and tenderness, does not, I think, in any way detract from the genuine sweetness and delicacy of her character; for '*she never told her love.*' . . . Viola, then, is the chosen favourite of the enamoured duke, and becomes his messenger to Olivia, and the interpreter of his sufferings to that inaccessible beauty. In her character of a youthful page, she attracts the favour of Olivia, and excites the jealousy of her lord. The situation is critical and delicate; but how exquisitely is the character of Viola fitted to her part, carrying her through the ordeal with all the inward and spiritual grace of modesty."

Mrs. Jameson.

Vī′o-len′tá. A character in Shakespeare's "All 's Well that Ends Well."

Violet, Corporal, *or* **Daddy.** [Fr. *Caporal la Violette,* or *Papa la Violette.*] A name given to the emperor Napoleon Bonaparte, by his partisans in France, after his banishment to Elba, and designed to be expressive of their hope that he would return in the spring (of 1815). The flower and the colour were publicly worn by them as a party distinction.

Virginie (vêr′zhe′ne′, 64). The heroine of Bernardin de St. Pierre's romance entitled "Paul et Virginie," — "a tropical Arcadian romance which [for a time] reigned supreme over French, English, and German imaginations of a certain calibre, and rendered the name *Virginie* triumphant in France."

Virgin Modesty. A surname given by Charles II. to the Earl of Rochester (John Wilmot), because he blushed so easily.

Virgin Queen. An appellation popularly given to Queen Elizabeth (1533–1603). She may, in fact, be said to have assumed it; for, on the 10th of February, 1559, less than three months after her accession to the throne, in a speech which she made to the privy council and a deputation from the house of commons, who had requested her, in the name of the nation, to be pleased to take to herself a husband, she said that for herself it would be enough "that a marble stone should declare that a queen, having reigned such a time, lived and died a virgin." Historians, however, agree that her right to the title is at least questionable, even if it be not demonstrably ill-founded. See MAIDEN QUEEN.

Virgins, The Eleven Thousand. See ELEVEN THOUSAND VIRGINS, THE.

Vish'nŭ (6). [Sansk., from *vish*, to pervade, to extend through nature.] (*Hindu Myth.*) One of the chief deities of the later religion, and the second person of the holy *Trimurti*, or triad; regarded as the preserver, while Brahma is the creator, and Siva the destroyer. He accomplishes the objects of his providence by successive avatars or incarnations, in which he appears and acts on earth. Nine of these have already taken place; in the tenth, which is yet to occur, he will appear on a white horse, with a flaming sword, for the everlasting punishment of the wicked. Buddha and Juggernaut are both regarded as avatars of Vishnu.

Vitalis (ve-tä′lis). A name assumed by Erik Sjöberg (1794–1828), a distinguished Swedish lyric poet. By this pseudonym he intended to convey the notion of "*Vita lis*," Life is a struggle.

Viv′i-ăn. Mistress of the enchanter Merlin. She forms the subject of one of the poems in Tennyson's "Idylls of the King." See LADY OF THE LAKE, 1, MERLIN, and LANCELOT DU LAC. [Written also Vivien, Viviana, and Viviane.]

Voland, Squire (fo′länt, 56, 67). [Ger. *Junker Voland*.] Among the Germans, a familiar name for the Devil.

Vol-po′ne. [It., an old fox.] The title of a play by Ben Jonson, and the name of its chief character.

Volscius, Prince. See PRINCE VOLSCIUS.

Voltaire, The German. See GERMAN VOLTAIRE.

Voltaire, The Polish. See POLISH VOLTAIRE.

Vol′tĭ-mănd. The name of a courtier, in Shakespeare's tragedy of "Hamlet."

Völund (vö′loont). (*Scand. Myth.*) A renowned smith, corresponding to the Vulcan or Dædalus of classical mythology. Like Vulcan, he was lame, was always busy at the forge, and executed all kinds of smith-work, from the finest ornaments in gold to the heaviest armour. See WAYLAND SMITH.

Vor′tĭ-ġēr. Seneschal of Constans (a fabulous king of Britain), and usurper of the throne after Constans had been killed by his subjects.

Vul′căn. [Lat. *Vulcanus*.] (*Gr. & Rom. Myth.*) A son of Jupiter and Juno, — according to some accounts, of Juno alone, — and the husband of Venus. He was the god of fire, and the patron of blacksmiths and all workers in metal. His workshop was supposed to be under Mount Ætna; and there, assisted by the Cyclops, he forged the thunderbolts of Jupiter, and arms for the gods and for celebrated heroes. See MULCIBER.

W.

Wăd'măn, Widow. The name of a lady, in Sterne's novel of "Tristram Shandy," who tries to secure Uncle Toby for a husband.

Waggoner Boy. A popular sobriquet of Thomas Corwin (b. 1794), an American statesman. While yet a lad, General Harrison and his army were on the northern frontier, almost destitute of provisions, and a demand was made on the patriotism of the people to furnish the necessary subsistence. The elder Corwin loaded a waggon with supplies, which were delivered by his son, who remained with the army during the rest of the campaign, and who is said to have proved himself "a good whip and an excellent reins-man."

Wagner (väk'nẽr, 58, 68). The name of a character in Goethe's "Faust." This name is not original with Goethe, but was borrowed by him from old legends, in which it occurs under the form of Cristoph Wagner, who is represented to have been the attendant, or *famulus*, of Faust.

☞ "Wagner is a type of the *philister* and pedant; he sacrifices himself to books, as Faust does to knowledge. He adores the letter. The dust of folios is his element, parchment the source of his inspiration. ... He is one of those who, in the presence of Niagara, would vex you with questions about arrow-headed inscriptions; who, in the presence of a village festival, would discuss the origin of the Pelasgi." *Lewes.*

Wakefield, Pindar of. See GEORGE A-GREEN.

Walking Stewart. The sobriquet of John Stewart, an English traveller, born in the first half of the eighteenth century, died in 1822. This celebrated peripatetic travelled on foot through Hindostan, Persia, Nubia, Abyssinia, the Arabian Desert, Europe, and the United States.

☞ "A most interesting man, whom personally I knew; eloquent in conversation; contemplative, if *that* is possible, in excess; crazy beyond all reach of hellebore (three Anticyræ would not have cured him), yet sublime and divinely benignant in his visionariness; the man who, as a pedestrian traveller, had seen more of the earth's surface, and communicated more extensively with the children of the earth, than any man before or since; the writer, also, who published more books (all intelligible by fits and starts) than any Englishman, except, perhaps, Richard Baxter, who is said to have published three hundred and sixty-five, *plus* one, the extra one being, probably, meant for leap-year." *De Quincey.*

Walpurgis (väl-poor'gis, 58, 68). The name of the female saint who converted the Saxons to Christianity. May-day night is dedicated to her, and is popularly thought to be the occasion of a great witch festival on the summit of the Brocken, in the Hartz mountains, — a superstition supposed to have originated in the secret celebration of heathen rites, in remote places, by those who adhered to the ancient faith when their nation was forcibly converted to Christianity.

Wăm'bȧ. The "son of Witless," and the clown or jester of Cedric of Rotherwood, in Sir Walter Scott's "Ivanhoe."

Wandering Jew. See JEW, THE WANDERING.

Wantley, Dragon of. See DRAGON OF WANTLEY.

Ward, Artemus. A pseudonym adopted by Mr. Charles F. Browne, an American humourist of the present day, author of a series of popular comic productions purporting to be written by an itinerant showman, and remarkable for their perverse orthography.

War of 1812. (*Amer. Hist.*) A name commonly given to the war between the United States and Great Britain, which began on the 18th of June, 1812, and ended, Feb. 17, 1815, on the ratification by congress of the treaty of peace concluded at Ghent

☞ For the "Key to the Scheme of Pronunciation," with the accompanying Explanations,

on the 24th of the preceding December.

War of Liberation. (*Ger. Hist.*) The name commonly given to the war undertaken by the Germans, in 1813, to throw off the French yoke, in consequence of the destruction of Bonaparte's grand army in the Russian campaign of 1812.

War of the Barons. (*Eng. Hist.*) An insurrection against the authority of Henry III., which broke out in 1262, and was excited by his faithlessness and the oppressions of his favourites. The barons were headed by Simon de Montfort, whose death, in 1265, at the battle of Evesham, occasioned their submission.

War of the Seven Captains. See SEVEN AGAINST THEBES.

War of the Succession. (*Hist.*) A celebrated struggle between England, France, Austria, and the United Provinces, to determine whether Philip, Duke of Anjou (grandson of Louis XIV. of France), or the Archduke Charles (son of the Emperor Leopold I.), should succeed to the throne of Spain, left vacant by the death of Charles II. It commenced May 4, 1702, and ended with the peace of Utrecht, March 13, 1713, by which Philip was acknowledged and confirmed as king. The contest was signalised by the splendid achievements of the Duke of Marlborough.

War of the Three Henries. (*Fr. Hist.*) A war between Henry III. king of France, Henry de Bourbon, king of Navarre, and Henry, duke of Guise, growing out of a project of the last to exclude the king of Navarre from his right of succession to the French throne.

Wars of the Roses. (*Eng. Hist.*) A name given to the intestine wars which raged in England from the reign of Henry VI. to that of Henry VII. (1452–1486). It refers to the badges or emblems of the parties to the strife, — that of the house of York being a white rose, and that of the house of Lancaster a red rose.

Washington of Colombia. A name given to Simon Bolivar (1785–1831), who established the independence of the Spanish provinces of Venezuela and New Granada, which were thereupon united into a republic, called Colombia, of which he was chosen the first president.

Wăs′tle, William (wŏs′l). A pseudonym of John Gibson Lockhart (1794–1854), under which he contributed to "Blackwood's Magazine."

Water-poet. A title assumed by John Taylor, an English poet (1580–1654), who for a long time followed the occupation of a waterman on the Thames.

Wăt′ling Street. A name very generally given in England, during the Middle Ages, to the *Via Lactea*, or "Milky Way." It occurs in Chaucer's "House of Fame," Book II.:—

"Se yondir, lo, the galaxie,
The wiche men clepe the milky way,
For it is white; and some, parfay,
Y-callin it han *Watlinge-strete*."

In "The Compleynt of Scotland," the comet, it is said, "aperis oft in the quhyt circle, the quhilk the marinalis callis *Vatlanstreit*." The name occurs again, in the translation of the "Æneid" by Gawain Douglas:—

"Of every sterne the twinkling notis he,
That in the still hevin move cours we se,
Arthuris house, and Hyades, betaikning rane,
Watlingestrete, the Horne, and the Charlewane,
The feirs Orion with his golden glave."

This, however, was only an application of the word, not its proper and original meaning. The real Watling Street was a road extending across South Britain in a general direction from east to west. Beginning at Richborough or Dover, it ran through Canterbury to London, and thence across the island to Chester. It is yet, in some parts, an important highway, and the portion which ran through London still preserves the old name. Under the Britons, Watling Street existed as a simple forest-lane or track-way; the Romans made a great military road of it; and the Anglo-Saxons adopted it, as they did all the Roman roads and bridges in every part of the island.

☞ The origin of the name is uncertain. By some the street is supposed to have been called, in honour of *Vitellius*, the *Via* (or *Strata*) *Vitellina*, of which the modern name is an Anglo-Saxon corruption. According to Camden, it was named after *Vitellianus*, who directed the work, and whom the Britons, in their language, called *Guetalin*. Florence of Worcester (Chron. *sub. an.* 1013) derives the name from the *Wætlings*, or sons of King Wætla, who, Wright says, "was, no doubt, a personage of the Anglo-Saxon mythology." Grimm offers no explanation, but merely remarks, "Who the Wætlings were, and how they came to give their name both to an earthly and a heavenly street, we do not know." This glittering pathway in the sky has, in other countries, been called after roads on earth. By the Italians, it was denominated the "*Santa Strada di Loretto*." Aventin, a German writer in the sixteenth century, calls it "*Euringstrasse*," and makes it belong to a mythical King Euring on the Danube.

Wāy′lặnd Smith, *or* **Wāy′lặnd the Smith.** A mythical and invisible farrier — the *Völund* or *Wieland* of Northern fable — whose name has been handed down to the present time by English traditions. He haunted the Vale of White-Horse, in Berkshire, where three squarish flat stones supporting a fourth are still pointed out as his stithy. His fee was sixpence, and, unlike other workmen, he was offended if more was offered him. Sir Walter Scott, by a strange anachronism, introduces him into the romance of "Kenilworth" as a living person of the reign of Elizabeth. See VÖLUND *and* WIELAND.

Weeping Philosopher. An epithet given to Heraclitus, a native of Ephesus, who flourished about 500 years B. C. He was of a gloomy and melancholy disposition, and is said to have been perpetually shedding tears on account of the vices of mankind.

☞ The name of Democ′ritus, the laughing philosopher, being often coupled with that of Heracli′tus, the weeping philosopher, many speakers are apt to accent the latter, incorrectly, on the second syllable.

Weird Sisters. Three witches, in Shakespeare's tragedy of "Macbeth."

☞ "The Weird Si creation of Shakespear Caliban, — fates, furies witches being the cl wholly different from of witches in the con and yet present a su semblance to the creat udice to act immediate Their character consis tive, disconnected fro are the shadowy obs anomalous of physica less of human nature, ers without sex or kin

Weissnichtwo (vĭs′ [Ger., I-know-not-Scot. *Kennaquhair*. in Carlyle's "Sarto place (probably me spoken of as contai in which Herr Teuf fessor. See TEUFEL:

Wel′lẽr, Samuel. man, in Dickens's c wick Papers;" des ome of London low agreeable and entert is an inimitable com plicity, quaint humo

☞ "The far-famed sponds to no reality. and bred is apt to be t uninteresting of being for him the gloss of no fifteen years old. He scum of a *nil admirar* specimen, shrivelled a timate result of his pri ons collected more jok men in London woul and bestowed the wh Sam."

Wel′lẽr, Tony. Th Weller, in Dickens' pers;" a represent: broad-brimmed, gre waistcoated, red-fac lish stage-coachmen

Well-founded Doc *tor Fundatissimus.*] appellation conferre his profound learnin Romanus (d. 1316), Colonna, Archbishop general of the Aug

Well-languaged Da IEL, THE WELL-LA

Werther (wĕr'tĕr, 4; *Ger. pron.* vĕr'-tĕr, 64, 68). The hero of Goethe's sentimental romance, "The Sorrows of Werther," in which he portrays the character of a young and highly endowed spirit who has become disgusted with life.

☞ "'Werther,' infusing itself into the core and whole spirit of literature, gave birth to a race of sentimentalists who have raged and wailed in every part of the world till better light dawned on them, or, at least, exhausted nature laid itself to sleep, and it was discovered that lamenting was an unproductive labour." *Carlyle.*

The practical, not the sentimental, is Friedrich's interest, not to say that *Werther* and the sentimental were not yet born into our afflicted earth. *Carlyle.*

Western, Miss Sophia. The sweetheart of Tom Jones, in Fielding's "History of Tom Jones, a Foundling."

Western, Squire. A jolly country gentleman in Fielding's "History of Tom Jones, a Foundling."

☞ "Amongst these [the characters of the story], Squire Western stands alone; imitated from no prototype, and in himself an inimitable picture of ignorance, prejudice, irascibility, and rusticity, united with natural shrewdness, constitutional good-humour, and an instinctive affection for his daughter,—all which qualities, good and bad, are grounded upon that basis of thorough selfishness natural to one bred up from infancy where no one dared to contradict his arguments, or to control his conduct." *Sir W. Scott.*

There now are no *Squire Westerns*, as of old, And our Sophias are not so emphatic, But fair as them or fairer to behold. *Byron.*

Rants which in every thing but diction resembled those of *Squire Western*. *Macaulay.*

Conceive a rugged, thick-sided *Squire Western*, of supreme degree,—for this *Squire Western* [Frederick William I., of Prussia] is a hot Hohenzollern, and wears a crown royal,— conceive such a burly *ne plus ultra* of a Squire, with his broad-based rectitudes and surly irrefragabilities. *Carlyle.*

Western Reserve. A name popularly given to a tract of country reserved by the State of Connecticut, at the time of the cession of the North-west Territory to the United States. Disputes arose, after the war of the Revolution, between several of the States, respecting the right of soil in this territory, which were only allayed by the cession of the whole to the United States, Connecticut reserving a tract of 3,666,921 acres near Lake Erie. In 1800, jurisdiction over this tract was relinquished to the federal government, the State reserving the right to the soil, and disposing of it in small lots to settlers (from which sales she obtained her magnificent school-fund), while the Indian titles to the rest of the soil were bought up by the general government.

Westminster, Long Meg of. See LONG MEG OF WESTMINSTER.

Westminster's Glory. See ENGLAND'S PRIDE AND WESTMINSTER'S GLORY.

Weth'ẽr-ell, Elizabeth. A pseudonym adopted by Miss Susan Warner, an American writer of the present day, author of "The Wide, Wide World" and other works.

Whar'ton, Eliza (-tn). The heroine of a novel of the same name, founded on fact, by Mrs. Hannah Foster, an American authoress.

Whar'ton, Grace (-tn). A pseudonym adopted by Mrs. Anthony Todd Thomson (*née* Katharine Byerley), a popular and voluminous author of the present day.

Whar'ton, Philip (-tn). A pseudonym adopted by J. P. Thomson, a popular English author.

Whirling Rocks. See SYMPLEGADES.

Whis'ker-ăn'dos, Don Fe-rō'lo. The lover of Tilburina, in Sheridan's farce of "The Critic."

I dare say I blushed; for I . . . had christened him *Don Ferolo Whiskerandos*. *Thackeray.*

Whiskey Insurrection. (*Amer. Hist.*) A name given to an outbreak in Western Pennsylvania, in 1794, resulting from an attempt to enforce an excise law passed in 1791, which imposed duties on domestic distilled liquors. The insurrection spread into the border counties of Virginia, and called forth two proclamations from President Washington, which had no effect. It was finally suppressed by

General Henry Lee, governor of Virginia, with an armed force.

Whistlecraft, William and Robert. A *nom de plume* of John Hookham Frere (1769-1846), an English author and statesman.

White Devil of Wallachia. A sobriquet given by the Turks, to whom he was a great terror, to George Castriota (1404-1467), a celebrated Albanian chief, commonly called Scanderbeg, that is, Bey, or Prince, Alexander.

White House. In the United States, a name popularly given to the executive, or presidential, mansion, at Washington, which is a large building of freestone, painted white.

White Lady of Av′e-nel. A kind of tutelary spirit protecting the fortunes of a noble family in Sir Walter Scott's novel, "The Monastery."

> Noon gleams on the lake,
> Noon glows on the fell;
> Wake thee, oh, wake,
> White Maid of *Avenel.*
> *Sir W. Scott.*

White Rose. A common designation of the house of York, from its emblem, which was a white rose. See WARS OF THE ROSES.

White Rose of Ra′by̆. Cecily, wife of Richard, Duke of York, and mother of Edward IV. and Richard III.; — so called in allusion to her private character, as well as to the distinguishing colour of the Yorkists in the Wars of the Roses. She was the youngest of twenty-one children. A novel of some popularity entitled "The White Rose of Raby," was published in 1794.

Whit′ting-tŏn, Dick. The hero of a famous old legend, in which he is represented as a poor orphan boy from the country, who went to London, where, after undergoing many hardships, he attracted the notice and compassion of a rich merchant, who gave him a situation in his family as an assistant to the cook. Here he led a miserable life, abused by the cook, and sleeping in the garret, which was overrun with rats and mice. At length, having obtained a penny, he purchased a cat. His master, shortly after, being about to send a ship to sea, gave all the servants permission to send a venture in her. Dick had nothing to risk but his cat, and sent her. The ship was driven to the coast of Barbary, where the master and chief mate were invited to court. At an entertainment given to them by the king, rats and mice swarmed over the tables, and disputed with the guests possession of the banquet. The captain thereupon sent for Dick's cat, which, being produced, made a terrible havock among the vermin, and was gladly purchased by the king at a very high price. With the money thus acquired, Dick commenced business, and succeeded so well that he finally married his former master's daughter, was knighted, and became lord mayor of London. This tradition has probably no foundation in fact, though there was a real Sir Richard Whittington, who was thrice mayor of London in the reign of Henry V.

☞ According to Mr. H. T. Riley ("Rerum Britannicarum Medii Ævi Scriptores, Munimenta Gildhallæ Londinensis," vol. i., "*Liber Albus*," Preface, p. xviii.), in the fourteenth century and the beginning of the fifteenth, trading, or buying and selling at a profit, was known to the more educated classes in England under the French name *achat*, which they wrote, and probably pronounced, *acat*. To *acat* of this nature, Whittington was indebted for his wealth ; and as, in time, the French became displaced by the modern English, the meaning of the word probably was lost, and thereby opportunity was given to some inventive genius, at a much later period, of building a new story upon the double meaning of an obsolete word. By Sir William Ouseley, the story is said to be founded on an Oriental narrative ; and it is related in a Persian MS., according to Halliwell, that, in the tenth century, one Keis, the son of a poor widow of Siraf, embarked for India with his sole property, a cat; there he fortunately arrived at a time when the palace was so infested by mice or rats that they invaded the king's food, and persons were employed to drive them from the royal banquet. This cat was useful in the same manner as Whittington's, and its owner was similarly rewarded. In a "Description of Guinea,"

1665, it is recorded "how Alphonso, a Portuguese, being wrecked on the coast of Guinney, and being presented by the king thereof with his weight in gold for a cat to kill their mice and an oyntment to kill their flies, which he improved, within five years, to £6000 on the place, and returning to Portugal, after fifteen years traffick, became the third man in the kingdom." See further in Keightley's "Tales and Popular Fictions," pp. 241-266.

Wicked Bible. A name given to an edition of the Bible published in 1632 by Barker and Lucas, because the word *not* was omitted in the seventh commandment. The printers were called before the High Commission, fined heavily, and the whole impression destroyed.

Wick'field, Agnes. The heroine of Dickens's "David Copperfield," one of the most charming female characters in the whole range of fiction.

Wieland (ŷee'lănt, 56, 68). A famous Northern smith; the same as *Völund.* See VÖLUND and WAYLAND SMITH.

☞ In a contest with a smith named Amilias, as to who would manufacture the best sword, he clove Amilias down to the waist with a blade of such sharpness that it cut through steel helmet and armour and body, and yet Amilias did not feel it; but, on attempting to rise from his seat, he discovered its effects by falling asunder. This sword was called Balmung.

Wife of Bâth (2). One of the pilgrims who are represented by Chaucer in his "Canterbury Tales" as travelling from Southwark to Canterbury, and each relating a story on the road for the common amusement. The "Wife of Bath's Tale" seems to have been taken from that of Florent, or Florentius (*q. v.*), in Gower's "Confessio Amantis;" or perhaps from an older narrative in the "Gesta Romanorum," or some such collection, from which the story of Florent was borrowed.

Oh, she is well attended, madam, replied the dame, who, from her jolly and laughter-loving demeanour, might have been the very emblem of the *Wife of Bath.*   *Sir W. Scott.*

Wife of Keith, Wise. See WISE WIFE OF KEITH.

Wild, Jonathan. A notorious English robber, who was executed in 1725. He is chiefly known to readers of the present day as the hero of Fielding's novel, "The History of Jonathan Wild."

☞ "In that strange apologue, the author takes for a hero the greatest rascal, coward, traitor, tyrant, hypocrite, that his wit and experience, both large in this matter, could enable him to devise or depict; he accompanies this villain through all the actions of his life, with a grinning deference and a wonderful mock respect, and does not leave him till he is dangling at the gallows, when the satirist makes him a low bow, and wishes the scoundrel good-day." *Thackeray.* "It is not easy to see what Fielding proposed to himself by a picture of complete vice, unrelieved by any thing of human feeling, and never, by any accident even, deviating into virtue; and the ascribing a train of fictitious adventures to a real character has in it something clumsy and inartificial on the one hand, and, on the other, subjects the author to a suspicion that he only used the title of 'Jonathan Wild' in order to connect his book with the popular renown of that infamous depredator." *Sir W. Scott.* "It has been justly remarked by Mr. Murphy, that Fielding wrote 'The History of Jonathan Wild' for a noble purpose, and one of the highest importance to society. A satire like this strips off the spurious ornaments of hypocrisy, shows the beauty of the moral character, and will always be worthy the attention of the reader who desires to rise wiser or better from the book he peruses."   *Roscoe.*

Wildair, Sir Harry. The hero of Farquhar's comedy of the same name, and also of his "Constant Couple." He is represented as an airy gentleman, affecting humourous gayety and great freedom in his behaviour, but not altogether profligate or unfeeling.

Wild Boar of Ardennes (ar'den', or ar'den). [Fr. *Le Sanglier des Ardennes.*] A sobriquet given to William, Count of La Marck (d. 1485), on account of his ferocity and the delight he took in haunting the forest of Ardennes. According to Sir Walter Scott, who introduces him into "Quentin Durward," he was remarkable for an unusual thickness and projection of the mouth and upper jaw, and for huge protruding side-teeth, which gave him a hideous and brutal expression of countenance.

Wild Boy, Tho. A savage creature found, in November, 1725, in the forest of Hertswold, Hanover, and supposed to be at that time about thirteen years old. He was accustomed to walk on all fours, and would climb trees like a squirrel. His food consisted of wild plants, leaves, grass, moss, and the bark of trees. Many efforts were made to reform his savage habits, but with little success, nor could he be taught to utter one distinct syllable. He commonly went by the name of Peter. His death took place in February, 1785.

Wildfire, Madge. The sobriquet of a prominent character in Sir Walter Scott's novel, "The Heart of Mid-Lothian," whose real name is given as Margaret Murdockson. She is described as having been a beautiful, but very vain and giddy girl, crazed by seduction and the murder of her infant, and exhibiting in an exaggerated degree those weaknesses of character to which she owed her misery.

Wild Huntsman. [Fr. *Le Grand Veneur*, Ger. *Der Wilde Jäger*.] The subject of a popular and widely diffused tradition concerning a strange and spectral hunter who appears by night, surrounded by dogs, and sometimes with a train of attendants, driving on the chase. The well-known cheer of the hunter, the cry of his hounds, and the tramp of his horse's feet, are distinctly audible. The superstition probably has its origin in the many and various strange sounds which are heard in the depths of a forest during the silence of the night. In Germany, this tradition has been made the subject of a ballad by Bürger, entitled "Der Wilde Jäger," which has been translated into English by Sir Walter Scott, under the name of "The Wild Huntsman." In this poem, the hunter is represented not as driving, but as himself driven by the Devil, from whom he seeks to escape. The French have a similar tradition concerning an aërial hunter who infests the forest of Fontainebleau. Some account of him may be found in Sully's "Memoirs," in which he is styled *Le Grand Veneur*. Father Matthieu relates, that the shepherds of the neighbourhood hold it to be the hunt of St. Hubert, which is also heard in other places. The superstition would seem to be quite general. In a Scottish poem entitled "Albania," there is a poetical description of this phantom chase. In England, the tradition seems to have established itself under the figure of *Herne the Hunter*, as in Shakespeare's "Merry Wives of Windsor."

Wil'kins, Peter. The hero of a work entitled "The Voyage of Peter Wilkins," written by Robert Pultock, about the year 1750. He is a mariner, who, like Robinson Crusoe, is thrown on a distant uninhabited shore, after undergoing various calamities at sea, and who is furnished with stores, utensils, and provisions, from the wreck of the ship in which he sailed. His solitary abode is in a beautiful twilight country frequented by a race of flying people, or beings provided with a sort of elastic natural investment which will open and shut at pleasure, thus furnishing the possessor with wings or a dress, according to the requirement of the moment.

☞ "The hero's name was most likely suggested by that of a celebrated advocate of the possibility of flying, — Wilkins, Bishop of Chester." *Leigh Hunt.*

I cannot image to myself whereabout you are. When I try to fix it, *Peter Wilkins's* Island comes across me. *Charles Lamb.*

Wil'let, John. A burly and obstinate English country innkeeper of the last century, who figures in Dickens's novel of "Barnaby Rudge."

William of Clöûdeslïe. A famous North-country archer celebrated in an old "popular history," and in a poem which has been reprinted by Ritson and by Percy.

Williams, Caleb. The title of a novel by William Godwin (1756-1836), and the name of its hero.

Will-with-the-Wisp. Another name for *Jack-with-the-Lantern*, *q. v.*

Wil'mọt. 1. A character in Lillo's "Fatal Curiosity."

2. (**Arabella.**) A lady beloved

☞ For the "Key to the Scheme of Pronunciation," with the accompanying Explanations,

by George Primrose, in Goldsmith's "Vicar of Wakefield."

Wil'mọt Proviso. (*Amer. Hist.*) A name popularly given in America to an amendment to a bill placing $2,000,000 at the disposition of President Polk to negotiate a peace with Mexico. It was introduced in the national house of representatives, on the 8th of August, 1846, by the Hon. David Wilmot, a Democratic representative from Pennsylvania, and was in these words: "Provided, that, as an express and fundamental condition to the acquisition of any territory from the republic of Mexico by the United States, by virtue of any treaty which may be negotiated between them, and to the use by the executive of the moneys herein appropriated, neither slavery nor involuntary servitude shall ever exist in any part of said territory, except for crime, whereof the party shall first be duly convicted." The bill with this amendment attached was passed in the house by a vote of 87 yeas to 64 nays, but failed in the senate in consequence of the arrival of the hour for the final adjournment of the session before a vote could be reached. At the next session of congress (1846–47), a bill appropriating $3,000,000 for the same purpose as before had a similar provision affixed to it by the senate, but was rejected in the house by a vote of 102 to 97. On the termination of the war, the practical question involved in the Wilmot Proviso, whether the introduction of slavery should be allowed or prohibited in the territories newly acquired from Mexico, became the source of great agitation throughout the country.

Wimble, Will. The name of a celebrated character in the "Spectator," distinguished for his delightful simplicity and good-humoured officiousness. He is said to have been intended for a Mr. Thomas Morecroft, who died at Dublin, July 2, 1741.

Wimbledon, Philosopher of. See PHILOSOPHER OF WIMBLEDON.

Wih'kle, Mr. Nathaniel (wingk′l). One of the club, in Dickens's "Pickwick Papers;" represented as a cockney pretender to sporting skill.

Wih'kle, Rip Van (wingk′l). The name of one of the Dutch colonists of New York, whose adventures are related in Washington Irving's "Sketch-book." He is represented as having met a strange man with a keg of liquor in a ravine of the Kaatskill Mountains, and as having obligingly assisted him to carry the load to a wild retreat among the rocks, where he found a company of odd-looking personages playing at ninepins, with the gravest of faces and in the most mysterious silence. His awe and apprehension having by degrees subsided, he ventured, when no eye was fixed on him, to steal a taste of the beverage which he had helped the strange man bring along. He repeated the draught so often that at length his senses were overpowered, and he fell into a deep sleep, which, strange to say, lasted for twenty years, though they seemed to him but as one night. Meanwhile, remarkable events had taken place: his wife had died, his daughter was married, his former cronies were dead, or scattered, or much the worse for the wear and tear of time; and, more than all, there had been a war of revolution, the colonies had thrown off the yoke of the mother country, and were now known as the United States of America. See EPIMENIDES; KLAUS, PETER; and SLEEPING BEAUTY IN THE WOOD.

Winter King. A title derisively given to Frederick V., elector palatine (1596–1632), who was elected king of Bohemia by the Protestants, in 1619, and was defeated, and his reign brought to an end, in 1620.

☞ "What kind of a 'King of Bohemia' this Friedrich made, . . . and what sea of troubles he and his entered into, we know: the '*Winter-König*' (Winter King, fallen in times of *frost*, or built of mere frost, a *snow*-king altogether soluble again) is the name he gets in German Histories." *Carlyle.*

Winter Queen. A mocking appellation given to Elizabeth, daughter of James I. of England, and wife of

Frederick, elector palatine. See *supra.*

Wise Men of Gotham. See GOTHAM.

Wise Men of Greece, The Seven. See SEVEN WISE MEN OF GREECE.

Wise Men of the East. See MAGI, THE THREE; also, COLOGNE, THE THREE KINGS OF.

Wise Wife of Kĕith. A popular designation given to one Agnes Simpson, or Sampson, a Scottish woman executed about the latter part of the sixteenth century for witchcraft, and especially for taking part in an alleged conspiracy against the life of the king, James VI. See Scott's "Letters on Demonology and Witchcraft," Letter IX.

Wishfort, Lady. A character in Congreve's comedy, "The Way of the World;" distinguished for her mixture of wit and ridiculous vanity.

Witchfinder General. A title assumed by one Matthew Hopkins, an impudent and cruel wretch, who, for three or four years previous to 1647, travelled through the counties of Essex, Sussex, Norfolk, and Huntingdon (in England), pretending to discover witches, superintending their examination by the most unheard-of tortures, and compelling them to admit and confess matters equally absurd and impossible, the issue of which was the forfeiture of their lives.

☞ At first the current of popular feeling was strongly with Hopkins; but at length it set against him with such violence, that he was seized and subjected to his own favourite test of swimming, and, happening to float, was convicted of witchcraft, and put to death. He has been pilloried by Butler in "Hudibras" (Part II., canto 3).

Witch of Atlas. The heroine of Shelley's poem of the same title.

Witch of Balwery, The Great. See GREAT WITCH OF BALWERY.

Witch of Ed'mŏn-tŏn. The heroine of a tragi-comedy of the same name by William Rowley, assisted by Ford and Dekker. It was published in 1658.

Witch of Endor. A divining woman consulted by King Saul, when, having become disheartened and discouraged by the general defection of his subjects, and being conscious of his own unworthy and ungrateful disobedience, he despaired of obtaining counsel and assistance from the offended Deity, who had previously communicated with him through his prophets. At the direction of Saul, she called up the spirit of Samuel, who foretold the defeat and death of the king.

With'ring-tŏn, Roger. A gallant squire celebrated in the ballad of "Chevy Chase." His legs having been smitten off, he continued to fight "upon his stumps." [Written also W i d d r i n g t o n.]

Some stone saints were brought on their marrow-bones, like old *Widdrington* at Chevy Chase. *Sir W. Scott.*

Witling of Terror. A nickname given to Bertrand Barère (or Barrère), in the time of the first French Revolution. See ANACREON OF THE GUILLOTINE.

But though Barère succeeded in earning the honourable nicknames of the *Witling of Terror* and the Anacreon of the Guillotine, there was one place where it was long remembered to his disadvantage that he had, for a time, talked the language of humanity and moderation. *Macaulay.*

Wit'would, Sir Wilful (wĭt'wŏŏd). A character in Congreve's comedy, "The Way of the World."

Parson Barnabas, Parson Trulliber, *Sir Wilful Witwould,* Sir Francis Wronghead, Squire Western, Squire Sullen,— such were the people who composed the main strength of the Tory party for sixty years after the Revolution. *Macaulay.*

Wizard of the North. A name often given to Sir Walter Scott (1771–1832), in allusion to the extraordinary charm and descriptive power of his writings, which excited unbounded enthusiasm on their first appearance, and which still retain a large measure of their original popularity.

☞ "Sir Walter Scott earned the title of 'Wizard of the North' by the magic power which reproduced old Scotland, refought its battles, remounted its steel-harnessed warriors, re-enacted its Border feuds, repeopled its Highlands, restored the dark days of its Covenanters, revived

its by-gone superstitions, raised Claverhouse and his troopers from the dead."
Christ. Examiner.

Wo'den. (*Myth.*) The German and Anglo-Saxon form of *Odin*. See ODIN.

Wolfland. A nickname sometimes given to Ireland, in the time of William III., in consequence of a prevalent belief that wolves abounded there to an extraordinary extent.

Wolverine State. The State of Michigan;—popularly so called from its abounding with wolverines.

Wonderful Doctor. [Lat. *Doctor Mirabilis.*] Roger Bacon, a celebrated philosopher and mathematician of the thirteenth century;—so named on account of his extensive knowledge. [Called also *Admirable Doctor.*] See ADMIRABLE DOCTOR.

Wonderful Parliament. (*Eng. Hist.*) The name given to a parliament which met on the 3d of February, 1388, and which, by playing into the hands of the Duke of Gloucester, thwarted an attempt made by the king (Richard II.) to assume the reins of government in fact as well as in seeming.

Wood, Babes, *or* **Children, in the.** See CHILDREN IN THE WOOD.

Wood, Babes of the. See BABES OF THE WOOD.

Wooden Horse. (*Gr. & Rom. Myth.*) A monstrous image of a horse, made of wood and filled with Greeks, which the Trojans were induced to take into their city by the artful representations of Sinon, a pretended deserter from the Grecian army, who asserted that it had been constructed as an atonement for the stealing of the Palladium by Ulysses and Diomed, and that, if the Trojans should venture to destroy it, Troy would fall, but if, on the contrary, they were to draw it with their own hands into the city, they would gain the supremacy over the Greeks. Though warned, by Laocoon, Calchas, and Cassandra, that he was an impostor, the Trojans took the advice of Sinon, and drew the horse within the walls. In the night, Sinon stole forth and unlocked a concealed door in the horse, and the Greeks, rushing out, opened the city-gates to their friends waiting without, who poured in, and thus gained possession of Troy.

Worldly-Wiseman, Mr. One of the characters in Bunyan's "Pilgrim's Progress," who converses with Christian by the way, and endeavours to deter him from proceeding on his journey. See CHRISTIAN.

Worthies, The Nine. Famous personages often alluded to, and classed together, rather in an arbitrary manner, like the Seven Wonders of the World, the Seven Wise Men of Greece, &c. They have been counted up in the following manner:—

THREE GENTILES.	1. Hector, son of Priam.
	2. Alexander the Great.
	3. Julius Cæsar.
THREE JEWS.	4. Joshua, conqueror of Canaan.
	5. David, king of Israel.
	6. Judas Maccabæus.
THREE CHRISTIANS.	7. Arthur, king of Britain.
	8. Charlemagne.
	9. Godfrey of Bouillon.

In Shakespeare's "Love's Labour's Lost," a. v., sc. 2, Hercules and Pompey appear as two of the Nine Worthies.

Ay, there were some present that were the *Nine Worthies* to him, I' faith. *Ben Jonson.*

Wray, Enoch (rā). The "Village Patriarch," in Crabbe's poem of that name. He is represented as having numbered a hundred years, and as being poor and blind; but he has become the chronicle of his neighbourhood, and is reverenced by all for his meek resignation, his wisdom, and his elevated piety.

Wronghead, Sir Francis. A character in Colley Cibber's comedy of "The Provoked Husband."

Wū-o'tăn. (*Myth.*) The same as *Odin*, or *Woden*. See ODIN.

X.

Xan'a-dû (zăn'ă-doo). The name of a city mentioned in Coleridge's poem of "Kubla Khan." It is an altered form of *Xaindu*, the residence of the Khan Kublai, as given in Purchas's "Pilgrimage," from which book the idea of the poem was derived.

Xan-tip'pe. [Gr. Ξανθίππη.] The wife of Socrates, the famous Grecian philosopher; so notorious a termagant that her name has passed into a proverb. [Written also, less usually, but more correctly, X a n t h i p p e.]

Xavier (zav'i-ẽr; *Fr. pron.* zä've-ā'). A *nom de plume* of Joseph Xavier Boniface (b. 1797), a popular French writer. See SAINTINE.

Xu'ry (zu'rў, 9). A Moresco boy, in De Foe's romance of "Robinson Crusoe;" servant to Crusoe.

Xury and Friday . . . can never be to him the realities they once were.   *Macaulay.*

Y.

Yā'hoo. A name given by Swift, in his satirical romance entitled "Travels into several Remote Nations of the World, by Lemuel Gulliver," to one of a race of brutes having the form and all the vices of man. The Yahoos are represented as being subject to the Houyhnhnms, or horses endowed with reason. See HOUYHNHNMS.

Art thou the first who did the coast explore?
Did never *Yahoo* tread that ground before?
   Pope.

The filthiest and most spiteful *Yahoo* of the fiction was a noble creature when compared with the Barrère of history.   *Macaulay.*

Yama (yä'mȧ). [*Sansk.*, a twin.] (*Hindu Myth.*) A fierce and terrible deity, the lord of hell and the tormentor of the wicked; originally conceived of as one of the first pair from whom the human race is descended, and the beneficent sovereign of his descendants in the abodes of the blest. He is represented as of a green colour, with inflamed eyes, sitting on a buffalo, clothed in red garments, a crown on his head, and a club in his hand.

Yăr'I-co. See INKLE, MR. THOMAS.

Yellow Dwarf. [Fr. *Le Nain Jaune.*] A hideous pygmy who figures in a fairy tale originally written in French by the Countess d'Aunoy (1650–1705). He was so called on account of his complexion, and his living in an orange-tree. He abducts a beautiful princess, and stabs her lover, whom chance has thrown into his power, before her eyes, whereupon she expires from excess of grief.

Yellow Jack. Among sailors, a common personification of the yellow fever. Although used as a proper name, it is probable that the original meaning of the appellation was nothing more than *yellow flag*, a flag being termed a *jack* by seamen, and *yellow* being the colour of that customarily displayed from lazarettos, or naval hospitals, and from vessels in quarantine.

Yel'lōw-ley, Trip-tol'e-mus. An agricultural enthusiast, of mixed Scottish and Yorkshire blood, who figures in Sir Walter Scott's novel, "The Pirate."

Yellow Water. See PARIZADE.

Yen'dys, Syd'ney. A literary name adopted by Sydney Dobell (b. 1824), an English poet of the present day. Yendys is merely *Sydney* reversed.

Ygg'drȧ-sil. (*Scand. Myth.*) An ash-tree, called "the tree of the universe," under which the gods assem-

☞ For the "Key to the Scheme of Pronunciation," with the accompanying Explanations,

ble every day in council. Its branches spread over the whole world, and tower up above the heavens. It has three roots, one of which reaches to the Asir, another to the frost-giants where was formerly Ginnunga-gap, and the third stands over Niflheim. See NIDHÖGG and NORNS.

Y-guërne' (4). Another spelling of *Igerna*. See IGERNA.

Ymir (ee'mĕr). (*Scand. Myth.*) The first of all beings, a giant and the progenitor of the giant race. He was slain by Odin, Vili, and Ve, and from his body the world was constructed. He is a type of chaos. [Written also Y m e r.]

Yŏr'ick. 1. The king of Denmark's jester, mentioned in Shakespeare's "Hamlet," a. v., sc. 1. Hamlet, picking up his skull in a church-yard, apostrophises it, moralising upon death and the base uses to which we may return.

2. A humourous and careless parson, in Sterne's famous novel of "Tristram Shandy;" represented as of Danish origin, and a descendant of the Yorick celebrated by Shakespeare.

☞ "Yorick, the lively, witty, sensitive, and heedless parson, is the well-known personification of Sterne himself, and, undoubtedly, — like every portrait of himself drawn by a master of the art, — bore a strong resemblance to the original. Still, however, there are shades of simplicity thrown into the character of Yorick which did not exist in that of Sterne. We cannot believe that the jests of the latter were so void of malice prepense, or that his satire flowed entirely out of honesty of mind and mere jocundity of humour." *Sir W. Scott.*

Yorke, Oliver. The name assumed by the editor of "Fraser's Magazine," when it was first started.

Thou too, miraculous Entity, that namest thyself *Yorke* and *Oliver*, and, with thy vivacities and genialities, with thy all-too Irish mirth and madness, and odour of palled punch makest such strange work, farewell; long as thou canst, fare-*well*! *Carlyle.*

Young America. A popular collective name for American youth, or a personification of their supposed characteristics.

☞ "What we call ' Young America ' is made up of about equal parts of irreverence, conceit, and that popular moral quality familiarly known as ' brass.' "
J. G. Holland.

Young Chevalier. A title popularly given to Charles Edward Stuart, grandson of James II., and a claimant for the crown of England. He is otherwise known as the Younger Pretender. See PRETENDERS, THE.

Young England. A collective designation given some thirty years ago to a number of persons of rank and character in England, who attempted to give a new form and application to Tory principles. One of their chief aims was the revival of the manners of mediæval times, which they held to have been destroyed or greatly changed and injured by the growth of a commercial spirit among the higher classes. Their cry was, —

"Let wealth and commerce, laws and learning, die,
But give us back our old nobility."
Ld. John Manners.

☞ "Young England was gentlemanly and cleanly, its leaders being of the patrician order; and it looked to the Middle Ages for patterns of conduct. Its chiefs wore white waistcoats, gave red cloaks and broken meat to old women, and would have lopped off three hundred years from Old England's life, by pushing her back to the early days of Henry VIII. . . . Some of the cleverest of the younger members of the aristocracy belonged to the new organisation, and a great genius [B. Disraeli] wrote some delightful novels to show their purpose, and to illustrate their manner of how-not-to-do-it in grappling with the grand social questions of the age. . . . Young England went out as soberly and steadily as it had lived. The select few who had composed it died like gentlemen, and were as polite as Lord Chesterfield in the act of death. Some of them turned Whigs, and have held office under Lord Palmerston ; and others are Tories, and expect to hold office under Lord Derby, when he shall form his third ministry." *C. C. Hazewell.*

Young Europe. An association organised April 15, 1834, by delegates from the various national leagues, "Young Italy," "Young Switzerland," &c., on the basis of the political, social, and religious views advanced by Mazzini, and with the avowed design of exciting the nations of Europe to rise against their despotic rulers.

Young France, Spain, Switzerland, Poland, &c. Social and literary parties which sprang into being, in nearly all the countries of continental Europe, in consequence of the political agitations resulting from the French Revolution of 1830, and whose aim was to reconstitute society, literature, the arts, in short, every thing, upon a new basis. See YOUNG ITALY, also, YOUNG EUROPE.

Young Germany. A name assumed by a revolutionary and literary school in Germany which claimed to represent the tendencies of modern thought, and to embody the political sympathies and aspirations consequent upon the late revolutionary struggles in Europe. Heinrich Heine (1800–1856) may be regarded as the best exponent of this school. The other principal representatives of Young Germany were Karl Gutzkow, Heinrich Laube, Gustav Kühne, and Theodor Mundt. The organisation was broken up after the failure of the revolutionists of 1848–49.

Young Ireland. A name adopted by a party of Irish malcontents, about the year 1840, who were in sympathy with the progressive movements instigated by O'Connell, — himself a member of the organisation, — but who ridiculed his renunciation of physical force in seeking political reforms, and who were impatient to initiate insurrection and war.

Young Italy. [It. *La Giovine Italia.*] The name assumed by an association of Italian refugees in France, who seceded from the "Charbonnerie Démocratique," — a secret political union founded shortly after the Revolution of July, and which endeavoured to make Paris the centre of all political movements. The league was organised mainly at the instigation of Mazzini, who was dissatisfied with the centralising tendency of the Charbonnerie. It was instituted at Marseilles, — at that time the head-quarters of the Italian refugees, — in 1830, and its main object was to republicanise the Italian peninsula. The motto of Young Italy was " Now and Ever," and its emblem a branch of cypress.

Young Roscius, The (rosh'I-us). An epithet conferred upon William Henry West Betty, an English actor, who made his *début* at the Belfast Theatre, August 1, 1803, when not twelve years old. In fifty - six nights he drew £34,000. After winning immense popularity, and accumulating an ample fortune, he retired from the stage in 1807.

Ysaie le Triste (e'zā' lụ trēst). A valiant knight of the Round Table, son of Tristan, or Tristram, of Leonnoys, and Yseult, or Isolde, the wife of King Mark of Cornwall. His adventures are the subject of an old French romance published at Paris in 1522.

<small>I did not think it necessary to contemplate the exploits of chivalry with the gravity of *Ysaie le Triste*, or the productions in which they are detailed with the sad and sorrowful solemnity of the Knight of the Woful Countenance. *Dunlop.*</small>

Yseult (iz'oolt), **Ysolt** (iz'ọlt), **Ysolde** (iz'ọ̄ld), or **Ysoude** (iz'ood). See ISOLDE.

Yvetot, King of. See KING OF YVETOT.

☞ For the "Key to the Scheme of Pronunciation," with the accompanying Explanations,

Z.

Zadig (ză'dĕg'). The title of a famous novel of Voltaire, and the name of its hero, a wealthy young Babylonian. The work is intended to show that the events of life are placed beyond our control.

Zad'ki-el. 1. According to the Jewish Rabbins, the name of one of the angels of the seven planets; the angel of the planet Jupiter.
2. A pseudonym of Lieutenant Morrison, of the British navy, a writer of the present day.

Zang'bar. The name of a fabled island in India. The Persian *zangi* signifies an Egyptian, Ethiopian, or savage. The root is probably the same as that of the country Zanguebar, on the east coast of Africa.

Ză-no'ni. The hero of Sir Edward Bulwer Lytton's novel of the same name; one of a secret brotherhood who possess a knowledge of the means of communicating with spiritual beings, of prolonging life to an indefinite term, and of copying many of the processes of nature, such as the production of gold and precious stones.

Ze-lu'co. The hero of a novel of the same name by Dr. John Moore (1730–1802), the object of which is to prove, that, in spite of the gayest and most prosperous appearances, inward misery always accompanies vice. Zeluco is the only son of a noble family in Sicily, accomplished and fascinating, but spoiled by maternal indulgence, and at length rioting in every prodigality and vice.

Ze'phŏn. [Heb., the searcher of secrets.] The name of a cherub in Milton's "Paradise Lost," a "strong and subtle spirit," "severe in youthful beauty," whom Gabriel despatched, together with Ithuriel, to find Satan, after his escape from "the bars of hell." See ITHURIEL.

Zeph'y-rus. [Gr. Ζέφυρος.] (*Gr. &* *Rom. Myth.*) A personification of the west wind, described as a son of Æolus and Aurora, and the lover of Flora; the same as *Favonius*. See FAVONIUS. [Written also, in an Anglicised form, Z e p h y r.]

Zerbino (dzĕr-be'no, 64, 70). A famous warrior in Ariosto's poem of "Orlando Furioso." He is represented as the son of a king of Scotland, and as the fast friend of Orlando.

Ze'tĕṣ. [Gr. Ζήτης.] (*Gr. & Rom. Myth.*) A son of Boreas and Orithyia; generally described as a winged being. With his brother Calais, he accompanied the Argonautic expedition, and drove the Harpies from Thrace. Hercules is said to have killed them with his arrows near the island of Tenos.

Ze'thus. [Gr. Ζῆθος.] (*Gr. & Rom. Myth.*) A son of Jupiter and Antiope, and twin brother of Amphion.

Zeūs (6). [Gr. Ζεύς.] (*Gr. Myth.*) The Greek name of *Jupiter*, the king of gods and men. See JUPITER.

Zeyn Alasnam, Prince. See ALASNAM.

Zim'rī. A nickname under which Dryden satirised the Duke of Buckingham, in his "Absalom and Achitophel," in return for Buckingham's attack on him in "The Rehearsal." See BAYES.

Zī-pan'gī, *or* **Zī-pan'grī.** See CIPANGO.

Zobeide (zo-bād'). A lady of Bagdad whose history is related in the story of the "Three Calendars" in the "Arabian Nights' Entertainments." The caliph Haroun-Al-Raschid became enamoured of her, and married her.

Zo'i-lus. [Gr. Ζώιλος.] A grammarian of antiquity whose place of birth and the age in which he lived are not known with any degree of certainty. He is celebrated for the extraordinary asperity with which he commented on the poems of Homer. He appears also to have assailed Plato and Isocrates. His name has become proverbial for a captious and malignant critic, and has given rise to the words *Zoilean* and *Zoilism.*

Zo'phi-el. [Heb., spy of God.] In Milton's "Paradise Lost," an angelic scout, "of cherubim the swiftest wing."

Zorphéo (zor-fā'). A fairy, in the romance of "Amadis de Gaul."

Zu-lēi'kā. 1. A pattern lover whose courtship and fortunes are a staple subject of description or allusion with the Persian bards.

2. The name of the heroine of Byron's poem, "The Bride of Abydos." See SELIM.

☞ "Never was a faultless character more delicately or justly delineated."
Geo. Ellis.

☞ For the "Key to the Scheme of Pronunciation," with the accompanying Explanations, and for the Remarks and Rules to which the numbers after certain words refer, see pp. xiv-xxxii.

INDEX

OF THE REAL NAMES OF PERSONS, PLACES, ETC., WHOSE NICKNAMES, PSEUDONYMS, OR POPULAR APPELLATIONS, ARE GIVEN IN THE PRECEDING DICTIONARY.

"Qui sera en cherche de science, si la pesche où elle se loge." — MONTAIGNE.

Aartsen, Peter. Long Peter.
Abernethy, John. Doctor My-book.
Abraham. Father of the Faithful.
Ahyla and Calpe. See GIBRALTAR, ROCK OF, AND JEBEL ZATOUT.
Accolti, Bernardo. The Only Aretino.
Adair, Serjeant. Junius (?).
Adams, John Quincy. Old Man Eloquent.
Adams, William T. Oliver Optic.
Addison, Joseph. Atticus, Clio.
Ægidius Romanus. See ROMANUS, ÆGIDIUS.
Æschylus. Father of Tragedy.
Aëtius. Last of the Romans.
Africa. Afric.
Agamemnon. King of Men.
Agoult, Countess of. (*Marie de Flavigny*.) Daniel Stern.
Aiken, Margaret. Great Witch of Balwery.
Ailly, Pierre d'. Eagle of French Doctors, Hammer of Heretics.
Albani, Francesco. Anacreon of Painters.
Albert (*Margrave of Brandenburg and Culmbach*). Achilles of Germany, or German Achilles.
Alboquerque, Affonso de. Portuguese Mars.
Alcaforada, Mariana. Portuguese Nun.
Alexander the Great. Madman of Macedonia.
Alfonso I. (*of Spain*). Catholic Majesty.
Algarotti, Count Francesco. Swan of Padua.
Algiers. Argier.
Ali (*uncle of Mohammed*). Lion of God.
Allahabad. Holy City.
Allan, David. Scottish Hogarth.
Allen, Ralph. Allworthy, Man of Bath.
Allen, *or* Alleyn, Simon. Vicar of Bray (?).
Amazon. King of Waters.
America. Columbia, New World.

American Indian (*The*). Red Man.
Amory, Thomas. English Rabelais.
Anastasius. New Moses.
Andouins, Diane d'. (*Countess of Guiche and Grammont.*) Beautiful Corisande.
Andreas, Antony. Dulcifluous Doctor.
Angus, Archibald, Earl of. Good Earl.
Anjou, Duke of. (*Philip Bourbon.*) Philip Baboon.
Anjou, René d'. See RENÉ D'ANJOU.
Anne (*queen of James I.*). Oriana.
Anne, Queen. Brandy Nan, Mrs. Morley.
Anscharius. Apostle of the North.
Anselm of Laon. Scholastic Divine.
Antioch. Queen of the East.
Antoninus, Marcus Aurelius. The Philosopher.
Apollonius of Alexandria. Prince of Grammarians.
Apperley, Charles J. Nimrod.
Appiani, Andrea. Painter of the Graces.
Aquinas, St. Thomas. Angelic Doctor, Angel of the Schools, Dumb Ox, Eagle of Divines, Father of Moral Philosophy, Fifth Doctor of the Church, Second Augustine, Universal Doctor.
Arabia. Araby.
Arcadia. Arcady.
Aretino, Pietro. Scourge of Princes.
Argyleshire. Morven (?).
Aristarchus of Samothrace. Coryphæus of Grammarians.
Aristophanes. Father of Comedy.
Aristotle. Pope of Philosophy, Stagirite.
Arkansas (*State*). Bear State.
Armstrong, John. Launcelot Temple.
Armstrong, William. Kinmont Willie.
Arrom, Cecilia. Fernan Caballero.
Artaxerxes. King of Kings.
Arteveld, Jacob. Brewer of Ghent.

Arthur (*King*). Flower of Kings.
Ascham, Roger. Father of English Prose.
Assisi, St. Francis d'. Seraphic Saint.
Athanasius, St. Father of Orthodoxy.
Athens. City of the Violet Crown.
Athens and Sparta. The Two Eyes of Greece.
Atlanta. Gate City.
Attila. Scourge of God, Terror of the World.
Auersperg, Anton Alexander von Anastasius Grün.
Augustine, St. Bishop of Hippo.
Augustine, *or* Austin, St. Apostle of the English.
Aureolus, Peter. Eloquent Doctor.
Austria, Charles, Archduke of. Esquire South.
Avicenna. Prince of Physicians.
Awbeg. Mulla.
Aytoun, William E. Augustus Dunshunner.
Aytoun (William E.) and Martin (Theodore). Bon Gaultier.

Baalbec. City of the Sun, *or* Solar City.
Babelmandeb. Gate of Tears.
Bacon, Roger. Admirable, *or* Wonderful, Doctor.
Baconthorp, *or* Bacondorp, *or* Bacon, John. Resolute Doctor.
Bagouly. Pactolus.
Bagshaw, William. Apostle of the Peak.
Balkh. Mother of Cities.
Ballantyne, James. Aldiborontephoscophornio.
Ballantyne, John. Rigdum Funnidos.
Balsamo, Joseph. Count de Cagliostro.
Baltimore. Monumental City.
Bandarra, Gonçalo Annes. Portuguese Nostradamus.
Bank of England. Old Lady of Threadneedle Street.
Bank-of-England Note. Abraham Newland.
Barbadoes. Little England.
Barère, Bertrand. Anacreon of the Guillotine, Witling of Terror.
Barham, Richard. Thomas Ingoldsby.
Baron, Michael. French Roscius.
Barre, Isaac. Junius (?).
Barros, João de. Portuguese Livy.
Barth, *or* Bart, Jean. French Devil.
Barton, Bernard. Quaker Poet.
Barton, Elizabeth. Holy Maid of Kent.
Basselin, Oliver. Father of the Vaudeville.
Bassol, John. Most Methodical Doctor.
Batavia. Queen of the East.
Bates, William. The Silver-tongued.
Bath (*Eng.*). Mount Badon (?).
Bayard, Chevalier. (*Pierre de Terrail.*) Good Knight without Fear and without Reproach.
Becket, Gilbert. Lord Belchan, *or* Bateman (?).
Bede. The Venerable.
Beham, Hans Sebald. Little Master.
Behn, Aphra, *or* Aphara. Astræa.

Bell, Adam. Abraham-Cupid (?).
Bellay, Joachim du. Prince of the Sonnet.
Benares. Holy City.
Benton, Thomas H. Old Bullion.
Berkshire (*Eng.*). Mount Badon (?).
Berlichingen, Goetz von. Iron Hand.
Bermuda Islands. Bermoothes.
Bernard, St. Honeyed Teacher, Last of the Fathers, Mellifluous Doctor, Thaumaturgus of the West.
Betty, William H. W. Young Roscius.
Bible. (*Genevan*) Breeches Bible; (*London*, 1578) Dotted Bible; (*Oxford*, 1717) Vinegar Bible; (*Barker and Lucas's*, 1632) Wicked Bible.
Billaut, Adam. Master Adam.
Bitzius, Albert. Jeremias Gotthelf.
Blackwood, William. Ebony.
Blackwood's Magazine. Ebony, Maga.
Blake, Joseph. Blueskin.
Blücher, Lebrecht von. Marshal Forwards.
Boleslas I. (*of Poland*). Cœur de Lion.
Bolivar, Simon. The Liberator, Washington of Colombia.
Bonaparte, Napoleon. Armed Soldier of Democracy, Boney, Corporal Violet, Father Violet, General Undertaker, Heir of the Republic, Jean d'Épée, Jupiter Scapin, Little Corporal, Man of Destiny, Nightmare of Europe, The Other One.
Bonaparte, Napoleon Francis Charles Joseph. King of Rome.
Bonaparte. See NAPOLEON, PRINCE.
Bonnventura, St. Seraphic Doctor.
Boniface, Joseph Xavier. Saintine, Xavier.
Boniface, St. Apostle of Germany.
Bonnivard, François de. Prisoner of Chillon.
Borde, Andrew. Merry-Andrew.
Bordeaux, Duke of. (*Henri Charles Ferdinand Marie Dieudonné d'Artois.*) Miraculous Child.
Bossuet, Jacques Bénigne. Eagle of Meaux.
Boston (*U. S.*). Athens of America, City of Notions, Hub of the Universe, Modern Athens, Puritan City, Tremont *or* Trimountain.
Boston State-House. Hub of the Universe.
Boswell, James. Bozzy.
Bourbonnais, Charles, Duke of. Constable de Bourbon.
Bourdaloue, Louis. King of Preachers.
Bourette, Charlotte. La Muse Limonadière.
Bourgogne, Antoine de. Great Bastard.
Bourgogne, Louis, Duke of. Great Dauphin.
Bourgogne, Louis, Duke of (*son of the preceding*). Little Dauphin.
Boyd, A. K. H. Country Parson.
Boyd, Hugh. Junius (?).
Boyle, Richard. Great Earl of Cork.
Bozzaris, Marco. Leonidas of Modern Greece.
Bradley, Edward. Cuthbert Bede.
Bradwardine, Thomas. Profound Doctor.
Brentano, Elizabeth. Bettina.
Bridgewater, Duke of. (*Francis Egerton.*) Father of British Inland Navigation.

Britain. Albion, Mistress of the Seas.
British Isles. Old Country.
British Review. My Grandmother's Review.
British Soldiers. Red-coats.
Brontë, Anne. Acton Bell.
Brontë, Charlotte. (*Mrs. Nicholls.*) Currer Bell.
Brontë, Emily. Ellis Bell.
Brooklyn. City of Churches.
Brooks, Maria. Maria dell' Occidente.
Brougham, Henry, Lord. Harry Twitcher.
Brown, Launcelot. Capability Brown.
Browne, Charles F. Artemus Ward.
Browne, Halbot K. Phiz.
Brydges, Grey. (*Lord Chandos.*) King of Cotswould.
Buchanan, James. Old Public Functionary.
Buckingham, Duke of. (*George Villiers.*) Steenie.
Buckingham, 2d Duke of. (*George Villiers.*) Zimri.
Buda. Key of Christendom.
Buffalo. Queen City of the Lakes.
Bultadœus, John. Wandering Jew.
Bulwer Lytton, Edward Robert. Owen Meredith.
Bunbury, Mrs. See HORNECK, CATHARINE.
Bunyan, John. Bishop Bunyan.
Burdett, Sir Francis. England's Pride and Westminster's Glory.
Burgoyne, John. Chrononhotonthologos, Sir Jack Brag.
Burke, Edmund. Junius (?).
Burleigh, Walter. Plain and Perspicuous Doctor.
Burns, Robert. Bard of Ayrshire, Peasant Bard.
Burritt, Elihu. Learned Blacksmith.
Burton, Robert. Democritus Junior.
Byron, Commodore John. Foul-weather Jack.

Cairo. City of Victory.
Calcutta. City of Palaces.
California (*Gulf*). Vermilion Sea.
California (*State*). Golden State.
Calpe and Abyla. See GIBRALTAR, ROCK OF, AND JEBEL ZATOUT.
Cambrai, Peace of. Ladies' Peace.
Camden, William. British Pausanias.
Cameron, Donald. Gentle Lochiel.
Cameron, Sir Evan. Lochiel.
Camoens, Luis. Portuguese Apollo.
Campbell, John. Shepherd of Banbury (?).
Campbell, Mary. Highland Mary.
Campbell, Robert. See MACGREGOR, ROBERT.
Campbell, Thomas. Bard of Hope.
Canaan. Promised Land.
Canada. New France.
Canadians. Cannucks.
Canadians (*The French*). Jean Baptiste.
Cannæ (*Battle-field of*). Field of Blood.
Canning, George. Cicero of the Senate.
Cape of Good Hope. Head of Africa, Lion of the Sea, Stormy Cape.
Carew, Bampfylde Moore. King of Beggars.

Carlisle. Carduel.
Carlyle, Alexander. Jupiter Carlyle.
Carvalho, Sebastião Jose de. (*Marquis de Pombal.*) Great Marquis.
Cassius, Caius. Last of the Romans.
Castlereagh, Lord. (*Robert Stewart.*) Derrydown Triangle.
Castriota, George. White Devil of Wallachia.
Cateau-Cambresis, Peace of. Unfortunate Peace.
Catharine II. (*of Russia*). Modern Messalina, Semiramis of the North.
Catinat, Nicholas. Father Thoughtful.
Cenci, Beatrice. Beautiful Parricide.
Cervantes Saavedra, Miguel de. Cid Hamet Benengeli.
Chambord, Comte de. Miraculous Child.
Champeaux, William de. Pillar of Doctors, Venerable Doctor.
Chandos, Lord. See BRYDGES, GREY.
Charles, Archduke of Austria. See AUSTRIA, CHARLES, ARCHDUKE OF.
Charles I. (*of England*). Last Man, Man of Blood, Royal Martyr.
Charles II. (*of England*). Merry Monarch, Old Rowley, Son of the Last Man.
Charles II. (*of France*). Most Christian King, or Majesty.
Charles II. (*of Spain*). Lord Strutt.
Charles IV. (*of Moravia*). Parsons' Emperor.
Charles V. (*of France*). French Solomon, or Solomon of France.
Charles V. (*of Spain*). Picrochole (?).
Charles XII. (*of Sweden*). Alexander of the North, Madman of the North, Quixote of the North.
Chatham, Earl of. See PITT, WILLIAM.
Chatterton, Thomas. Marvellous Boy, Thomas Rowley.
Chaucer, Geoffrey. Father of English Poetry, Flower of Poets, Tityrus.
Chiabrera, Gabriello. Italian Pindar.
Chicago. Garden City.
China. Cathay, Celestial Empire, Flowery Kingdom, Middle Kingdom.
Chinese (*The*). John Chinaman.
CHRIST. Good Physician, Good Shepherd, King of Kings, Kriss Kringle, Prince of Peace, Son of God, Son of Man.
Christian II. (*of Denmark and Sweden*). Nero of the North.
Christian III. (*of Denmark*). Father of his People.
Christopher III. (*of Denmark, Sweden, and Norway*). King of Bark.
Christ's Hospital (*London*). Blue-coat School.
Chrysostom, St. John. Glorious Preacher.
Chubbuck, Emily. See JUDSON, MRS. EMILY.
Chulkhurst, Mary and Elizabeth. Biddenden Maids.
Churchill, John. See MARLBOROUGH, DUKE OF.

Cicero, Marcus Tullius. Father of his Country.
Cincinnati. Losantiville, Porkopolis, Queen City, Queen of the West.
Clare, John. Peasant Poet of Northamptonshire.
Clark, McDonald. Mad Poet.
Clay, Henry. Mill-boy of the Slashes.
Clement XIV. (*Gian Vincenzo Ganganelli*.) Protestant Pope.
Cleopatra. Queen of Queens.
Cleveland. Forest City.
Clifford, Henry, Lord. Shepherd Lord.
Clifford, Rosamond. Fair Rosamond.
Clodia. Lesbia.
Clootz, Baron Jean Baptiste. Anacharsis Clootz.
Cobbett, William. Peter Porcupine.
Coello, Alouzo Sanches. Portuguese Titian.
Coffin, Robert Barry. Barry Gray.
Coffin, Robert S. Boston Bard.
Cold-Bath Fields, Jail of. English Bastille.
Coleridge, Samuel Taylor. S. T. C.
Collins, John. English Mersenne.
Columba, St. Apostle of the Highlanders.
Confederate Soldiers. Johnny Rebs.
Confederate States. Secessia.
Connecticut (*State*). Freestone State, Land of Steady Habits, Nutmeg State.
Constitution (*The Frigate*). Old Ironsides.
Cordova, Gonsalvo de. See GONSALVO DE CORDOVA.
Corinensis, Ricardus. See RICHARD OF CIRENCESTER.
Corinna. Lyric Muse.
Cork. Athens of Ireland, Drisheen City.
Corwin, Thomas. Waggoner Boy.
Cosmo de' Medici. See MEDICI, COSMO DE'.
Cotin, Abbé. Trissotin.
Courtray (*Battle of*). Battle of Spurs.
Cowper, William. Bard of Olney.
Coysevox, Antoine. Vandyck of Sculpture.
Crichton, James. Admirable Crichton.
Croly, Mrs. J. C. Jennie June.
Cromwell, Oliver. Old Noll, Man of Sin.
Cromwell, Thomas. Maul of Monks.
Cromwell's Soldiers. Ironsides.
Cruden, Alexander. Alexander the Corrector.
Cuba. Key of the Gulf, Queen of the Antilles.
Cumberland, Duke of. Bloody Butcher.
Cumberland, Richard. English Terence, Sir Fretful Plagiary.
Cunningham, Allan. Mark Macrabin (?).
Cusa, Nicolas de. Most Christian Doctor.
Cuzco. Holy City.
Cyril, St. (*of Alexandria*). Champion of the Virgin, Doctor of the Incarnation.
Cyril, St. Apostle of the Slaves.
Czacki, Thaddeus. Polish Franklin.

Damiens, Robert François. Robert the Devil.
Daniel, Rose. Rosalind.
Daniel, Samuel. Well-languaged Daniel.
Davaux, Jean Baptiste. Father of the Rondo.

David. Man of Blood, Royal Psalmist, Sweet Singer of Israel.
Davidoff, Dennis. Black Captain.
Death. Davy Jones, King of Terrors, Smallback.
Delaware (*State*). Blue Hen, Diamond State.
Democritus of Abdera. Laughing Philosopher.
Denis, St. Apostle of the French.
De Quincey, Thomas. English Opium-eater.
Derby, Earl of. (*Edward Geoffrey Smith-Stanley*.) Hotspur of Debate.
Derby, George H. John Phœnix, Gentleman.
Desbillons, François Joseph Terasse. Last of the Romans.
Desforges, Evariste Désiré. French Tibullus.
Desmoulins, Camille. Attorney-General to the Lantern.
D'Espréménil. Crispin-Catiline.
Detroit. City of the Straits.
Devereux, Penelope. Stella.
Devil (*The*). Auld Ane, Auld Clootic, Auld Hangie, Auld Hornie, Black Man, Eblis, Evil One, Father of Lies, Lord Harry, Lucifer, Nickie-Ben, Old Bendy, Old Gentleman, Old Harry, Old Nick, Old One, Old Scratch, Satan, Sir Urian, Squire Voland. See SATAN.
Dickens, Charles. Boz.
Dickinson, John. Pennsylvania Farmer.
Disraeli, Benjamin. Dizzy.
Dobell, Sydney. Sydney Yendys.
Dobson, William. English Tintoret, English Vandyck.
Dodge, Mary A. Gail Hamilton.
Dogs. (Of Fingal) Bran; (of Llewellyn) Gelert; (of the Seven Sleepers) Al Rakim.
Donald of Islay. Lord of the Isles.
Dorat, Jean. French Pindar.
Doria, Andrea. Father of Peace.
Douglas, Archibald. Bell-the-Cat, Great Earl.
Douglas, Archibald IV., Earl of. Tyneman.
Douglas, Ellen. Lady of the Lake.
Douglas, Margaret, Countess of. Fair Maid of Galloway.
Douglas, Stephen A. Little Giant.
Douglas, William of. Flower of Chivalry.
Dowling, Vincent. Long Scribe.
Draper, Elizabeth. The Bramine.
Dryden, John. Bayes, Poet Squab.
Dublin University Magazine (*Editor of*). Anthony Poplar.
Duchesne, André. Father of French History.
Dudevant, Mme. George Sand.
Du Guesclin, Bertrand. Eagle of Brittany.
Dundas, Henry. (*Lord Melville*.) Starvation Dundas.
Dundee, Viscount. See GRAHAM, JOHN.
Dunning, John. (*Lord Ashburton*.) Junius (?).
Dunois, Jean. Bastard of Orleans.
Duns Scotus. Subtle Doctor.

Durand de St. Pourçain. Most Resolute Doctor, or Resolute Doctor.
Dürer, Albert. Prince of Artists.
Dutch (The). Nic Frog.
Dyer, Samuel. Junius (?).

Eastern Hemisphere. Old World.
East India Company. John Company, or Mother Company.
Eden. Aidenn.
Edinburgh. Auld Reekie, City of Palaces, Dun Edin, Edin or Edina, Embro, Maiden Town, Modern Athens, Northern Athens, Queen of the North.
Edinburgh, Jail of. Heart of Mid-Lothian.
Edmund II. Ironside.
Edward I. (of England). English Justinian.
Edward, Prince of Wales (son of Edward III.). Black Prince.
Edwards, George. Father of Ornithologists.
Egerton, Francis. See BRIDGEWATER, DUKE OF.
Egypt. Land of Bondage.
Eleanora of Brittany. Damsel of Brittany.
Eldon, Lord. (John Scott.) Old Bags.
Eliot, John. Apostle of the Indians.
Elis. Holy Land.
Elizabeth (of England). Belphœbe, Gloriana, Good Queen Bess, Maiden Queen, Oriana, Virgin Queen.
Elizabeth (of Bohemia). Goody Palsgrave, Queen of Hearts, Winter Queen.
Elizabeth Petrowna (of Russia). Infamous Northern Harlot.
Elliott, Ebenezer. Corn-law Rhymer.
Emma (of Normandy). Gem of Normandy.
England. Loegria or Logres, Merry England, Ringing Island, South Britain.
England, Bank of. See BANK OF ENGLAND.
England, King of. Defender of the Faith.
English (The). Bono Johnny, Godon or Godam, John Bull, Nation of Shopkeepers.
Este, Prince of. Azo.
Ethelwold of Winchester. Father of Monks.
Eusebius of Cæsarea. Father of Ecclesiastical History.
Evans, Mary A. See LEWES, MARY A.

Faber, John. Hammer of Heretics.
Fabius Maximus Verrucosus, Quintus. Cunctator.
Faneuil Hall. Cradle of Liberty.
Faulkner, George. Atticus.
Fénelon. (François de Salignac de la Mothe.) Swan of Cambrai.
Fenner, W. Martin Mar-Prelate (?).
Ferdinand II. (of the Two Sicilies). Bomba.
Ferdinand V. (of Spain). Catholic Majesty.
Ferguson, Richard. Galloping Dick.
Fermor, Arabella. Belinda.
Fessenden, Thomas G. Christopher Caustic.
Field, John. Martin Mar-Prelate (?).
Finch, Heneage. (Lord Nottingham.) Father of Equity.
Fitzgerald, Elizabeth. Fair Geraldine.
Fitzgerald, William T. Small-beer Poet.

Flavigny, Marie de. See AGOULT, COUNTESS OF.
Fleet Prison (London). Fleta.
Florida. Peninsular State.
Florio, John. Don Adriano de Armado, Holofernes, The Resolute.
Fludd, Robert. The Searcher.
Foix, Gaston de. See GASTON DE FOIX.
Foote, Samuel. English Aristophanes, Modern Aristophanes.
Forrester, Alfred II. A. Crowquill.
Fouquet, Nicolas. Man with the Iron Mask (?).
Fox, Charles James. Carlo Khan, Man of the People.
France. Gallia, La Belle France.
France, King of. Most Christian King, or Majesty.
Francis I. (of France). Father of Letters.
Francis, Sir Philip. Junius (?).
Francis d'Assisi, St. See ASSISI, ST. FRANCIS D'.
Franklin, Benjamin. Richard Saunders.
Fraser's Magazine (Editor of). Oliver Yorke.
Frederick V. (Elector Palatine). Goodman Palsgrave, Winter King.
Frederick the Great. Alaric Cottin, Der Alte Fritz, Philosopher of Sans-Souci.
Frederick William (of Brandenburg). Great, or Grand, Elector.
Fremont, John C. The Path-finder.
French (The). Jean, or Johnny, Crapaud, Robert Macaire.
French Canadians. See CANADIANS (THE FRENCH).
French Peasantry. Jacques Bonhomme.
Frere, John Hookham. William and Robert Whistlecraft.
Frith, Mary. Moll, or Mall, Cutpurse.
Fry, Elizabeth. Female Howard.

Galway. City of the Tribes.
Ganganelli, Gian Vincenzo. See CLEMENT XIV.
Garcilaso de Vega. Prince of Spanish Poetry.
Garrick, David. English Roscius.
Gaston de Foix. Thunderbolt of Italy.
Gautama. Buddha.
Gay, John. Orpheus of Highwaymen.
Geneva Bible. See BIBLE.
Gentleman's Magazine (Editor of). Sylvanus Urban, Gent.
George I. (of England). Turnip-hoer.
George III. Farmer George.
George IV. First Gentleman of Europe.
George, Lake. Horicon.
George, Prince (of Denmark). Est-il-possible.
Germain, Lord. See SACKVILLE, LORD GEORGE.
Germans (The). Cousin Michael.
Germany. Almain.
Germany, Heir of the Emperor of. King of the Romans.
Gerson, Jean de. Most Christian Doctor.
Ghika, Helena. (Princess Koltzoff-Massalsky.) Dora D'Istria.

Gibraltar, Rock of. Key of the Mediterranean.
Gibraltar, Rock of, and Jebel Zatout. Pillars of Hercules.
Gildas. British Jeremiah.
Giles de Laval. Blue-beard.
Gillies, Robert Pearce. Kempferhausen.
Gilmore, James R. Edmund Kirke.
Gilpin, Bernard. Apostle of the North, Father of the Poor.
Girardin, Delphine do. Le Vicomte Delaunay.
Glasgow. City of the West, Venice of the West.
Glasgow (*Inhabitants of*). Mordecai Mullion.
Glastonbury. Avalon.
Glover, Catherine. Fair Maid of Perth.
Goderich, Viscount. (*Frederick Robinson.*) Goosey Goderich, Prosperity Robinson.
Godoy, Manuel de. Prince of the Peace.
Goethals, Henry. Solemn Doctor.
Goethe, Johann Wolfgang von. German Voltaire, The Master.
Goetz von Berlichingen. See BERLICHINGEN, GOETZ VON.
Goldoni, Carlo. Italian Molière.
Goldschmidt, Mme. See LIND, JENNY.
Goldsmith, Oliver. Goldy, Inspired Idiot.
Gomorrah and Sodom. Cities of the Plain.
Gonsalvo de Cordova. Great Captain.
Gonzales, Bli. See SYMMONDS, JOHN.
Good Hope, Cape of. See CAPE OF GOOD HOPE.
Goodrich, Frank B. Dick Tinto.
Goodrich, Samuel G. Peter Parley.
Gordon, Duke of. Cock of the North.
Gougon, Jean. French Phidias.
Gower, John. The Moral Gower.
Graham, James. (*Marquis of Montrose.*) Great Marquis.
Graham, John. (*Viscount Dundee.*) Claverhouse.
Great Britain. See BRITAIN.
Gregory I. (*Pope*). Servant of the Servants of God.
Gregory VII. (*Pope*). Turk Gregory.
Gregory, St. (*of Armenia*). The Illuminator.
Gregory of Neo-Cæsarea. Thaumaturgus.
Gregory of Rimini. Authentic Doctor.
Grenville, George. Gentle Shepherd.
Grenville, Richard. See TEMPLE, LORD.
Grey, Lord. Artegal.
Guernsey. Holy Island.
Guesclin, Bertrand du. Eagle of Brittany.
Guilford. Astolat.
Guinarda, Pedro Rocha. Roque Guinart.
Guinegate (*Battle of*). Battle of Spurs.
Gustavus Adolphus. Lion of the North.
Guzman, Alphonso Perez de. Spanish Brutus.
Guzman, Fernan Nuñez de. Greek Commentator.
Gwyn, Mary. See HORNECK, MARY.

Hafiz. Anacreon of Persia, *or* Persian Anacreon:

Hales, Alexander. Fountain of Life, Irrefragable Doctor.
Hales, John. The Ever-memorable.
Haliburton, Thomas C. Sam Slick.
Hall, Joseph. Christian Seneca, English Seneca.
Halpine, Charles G. Private Miles O'Reilly.
Hamann, Johann Georg. Magician of the North.
Hamilton, Alexander. Publius.
Hamilton, Patrick. First Scotch Reformer.
Hamilton, Sir Thomas. Tam of the Cowgate.
Hamilton, William Gerard. Junius (?), Single-speech Hamilton.
Hannibal. Bluff City.
Hardenberg, Friedrich von. Novalis.
Harley, Robert. (*Earl of Oxford and Mortimer.*) Harlequin.
Harrison, William H. Tippecanoe.
Harrow, William. Flying Highwayman.
Harvey, Gabriel. Hobinol.
Hassan Ben-Sabbah-el-Homairi. Old Man of the Mountain.
Haynau, Julius Jakob von. Austrian Hyena.
Heaven. Celestial City, New Jerusalem.
Heber, Richard. Atticus.
Hébert, Jacques René. Le Père Duchesne.
Heenan, John C. Benicia Boy.
Henley, John. Orator Henley.
Henry I. (*of England*). Beauclerc.
Henry II. (*of Germany*). King of the Romans.
Henry IV. (*of France*). King of Brave Men, Le Béarnais.
Henry VII. (*of England*). Defender of the Faith, Solomon of England.
Henry VIII. (*of England*). Blue-beard, Bluff Hal, *or* Burly King Harry, Defender of the Faith.
Henry de Londres. Burnbill.
Henry the Minstrel. Blind Harry.
Heraclitus. Weeping Philosopher.
Herbert, George. Sweet Singer of the Temple.
Herbert, Henry W. Frank Forester.
Herodotus. Father of History, Father of Lies.
Hervey, Lord. Lord Fanny, Sporus.
Hesiod. Ascræan Sage.
Hilaire, Émile Marc. Marco de St. Hilaire.
Hildebrand. See GREGORY VII.
Hill, Sir John. Mrs. Glasse (?).
Hippocrates. Father of Medicine.
Hobbes, Thomas. Philosopher of Malmesbury.
Hogg, James. Ettrick Shepherd.
Holland. Batavia.
Holland, Josiah G. Timothy Titcomb.
Holland, Philemon. Translator General.
Holman, James. Blind Traveller.
Homer. Father of Epic Poetry, Father of Poetry, Father of Song, Mæonides, Melesigenes, Swan of the Meander.
Hood, Robin. Locksley.
Hooker, Richard. The Judicious.

Hopkins, Matthew. Witchfluder General.
Horneck, Catharine. Little Comedy.
Horneck, Mary. Jessamy Bride.
Horne Tooke. See TOOKE, JOHN HORNE.
Horns. (Of Heindall) Gjallar; (of Orlando) Olivant.
Horses. See STEEDS.
Hortensius, Quintus. King of the Courts.
Howard, Lord William. Belted Will.
Howard, Sir John. Jockey of Norfolk.
Howe, John. Platonic Puritan.
Howe, Richard, Earl. Black Dick.
Hubert, St. Apostle of Ardennes.
Hudson, George. Railway King.
Hughes, John. Buller of Brazenose.
Hume, Joseph. Adversity Hume.

Illinois. Garden of the West, Prairie State, Sucker State.
Illinois (*Southern*). Egypt.
India. Ind.
Indiana. Hoosier State.
Indianapolis. Railroad City.
Indre-et-Loire. Garden of France.
Iowa. Hawkeye State.
Ireland. Emerald Isle, Erin, Green Isle, Hibernia, Holy Island, Innisfail, Isle of Saints, Old Country, Sacred Island, Scotia, Woltland.
Irenæus, St. Apostle of the Gauls.
Irving, Edward. Doctor Squintum.
Irving, Washington. Diedrich Knickerbocker, Fray Antonio Agapida, Geoffrey Crayon, Esq., Jonathan Oldstyle.
Irving (Washington), Irving (William), and Paulding (James K.). Launcelot Langstaff.
Isabella (*of Valois*). Little Queen.
Isaure, Clemence. Sappho of Toulouse.
Ishmonie. Petrified City.
Isocrates. Old Man Eloquent.
Italy. Garden of Europe.
Iturbide, Augusto. Napoleon of Mexico.

Jackson, Andrew. Old Hickory.
Jackson, Thomas J. Stonewall Jackson.
Jacobi, Friedrich Heinrich. German Plato.
James I. (*of England*). English Solomon, or Solomon of England, Royal 'Prentice in the Art of Poetry, Scottish Solomon.
James V. (*of Scotland*). Goodman of Ballengeigh.
James VI. (*of Scotland*). See JAMES I. (OF ENGLAND).
James and John (*the sons of Zebedee*). Boanerges, or Sons of Thunder.
Janin, Jules Gabriel. King of Feuilletons.
Japan. Cipango, Zipangi, or Zipangri (?).
Jasmin, Jacques. Barber Poet, Last of the Troubadours.
Java. Queen of the Eastern Archipelago.
Jebel Zatout and Rock of Gibraltar. Pillars of Hercules.
Jefferson, Thomas. Sage of Monticello.
Jenings, Mrs. E. Wycliffe Lane.
Jerusalem. City of David, City of Peace, City of the Great King, Holy City.

Jews (*Portuguese, of the fifteenth century*). New Christians.
Joachim II. (*of Brandenburg*). Hector of Germany.
Joan (*Countess of Salisbury, and afterward wife of Edward the Black Prince*). Fair Maid of Kent.
Joan of Arc. La Pucelle, Maid of Orleans.
John III. (*of Brandenburg*). Cicero of Germany, or German Cicero.
John V. (*of Portugal*). Most Faithful Majesty.
John, St. Beloved Disciple.
Johnson, Anna C. Minnie Myrtle.
Johnson, Esther. Stella.
Johnson, Samuel. Great Cham of Literature, Great Moralist, Leviathan of Literature, Ursa Major.
Johnstone, Mrs. Meg Dods.
Jones, Inigo. English Palladio, English Vitruvius.
Jones, O. Devonshire Poet.
Jones, William. Trinity Jones.
Jonson, Ben. Rare Ben Jonson.
Judson, Mrs. Emily. Fanny Forester.
Junot, Andoche. The Tempest.

Kansas. Garden of the West.
Keats, John. Adonais.
Kendal, Duchess of. The Maypole.
Kentucky. Dark and Bloody Ground, Corn-cracker.
Keokuk. Gate City.
Khaled. Sword of God.
King, Edward. Lycidas.
Klopstock, Friedrich Gottlieb. German Milton.
Know-nothings. See NATIVE AMERICANS.
Knox, John. Apostle of the Scottish Reformation.
Koltzoff-Massalsky, Princess. See GHIKA, HELENA.
Krasicki, Ignatius. Polish Voltaire.
Kyle. Coila.
Kyrle, John. Man of Ross.

Labé, Louise. Beautiful Ropemaker, Captain Loys.
Labrador. Estotiland.
Lacépède, Count. (*Bernard Germain Étienne de la Ville.*) King of Reptiles.
La Chaise, Père. Tartuffe (?).
Lactantius, Lucius Cœlius. Christian Cicero.
Lafayette, Marquis de. Grandison Cromwell.
La Marck, William, Count of. Wild Boar of Ardennes.
Lamb, Charles. Elia.
Lancaster, House of. Red Rose.
Lances. See SPEARS.
Landon, Letitia Elizabeth. L. E. L.
Lanoue, François de. Iron Arm.
Laval, Giles de. See GILES DE LAVAL.
Law, John. Paper King.
Laynez, Rodrigo. The Cid.
Learmont, Thomas. Thomas the Rhymer.

Lee, Ann. Mother Ann.
Lee, Charles. Junius (?).
Lee, Henry. Light-horse Harry.
Lee, Nathaniel. Mad Poet.
Legendre, Louis. Peasant of the Danube.
Leipsic (*Battle of*). Battle of the Nations.
Leo VI. The Philosopher.
Leopold (*of Anhalt-Dessau*). Old Dessauer.
Le Sieur, Eustace. French Raphael.
Lessing, Gotthold Ephraim. Father of German Literature.
Leucate. Lover's Leap.
Lever, Charles J. Cornelius O'Dowd, Harry Lorrequer.
Lewes, Mary A. George Eliot.
Lewis, Matthew G. Monk Lewis.
Ligne, Prince de. Prince of Coxcombs.
Lilburne, John. Free-born John.
Lille, Alain de. Universal Doctor.
Lilly, William. Erra Pater, Sidrophel.
Limerick. City of the Violated Treaty.
Lincoln, Abraham. Rail-Splitter.
Lind, Jenny. (*Mme. Goldschmidt*.) Swedish Nightingale.
Lindisfarne. Holy Island.
Linley, Miss. (*Mrs. R. B. Sheridan*.) Maid of Bath.
Lippincott, Sara J. Grace Greenwood.
Liverpool (*Inhabitants of*). Dicky Sam.
Lloyd, Charles. Junius (?).
Lockhart, John G. Peter Morris, William Wastle.
Lockhart, John Hugh. Hugh Little-John.
Lombard, Peter. Master of Sentences.
London. City of Masts, Cockagne, Lubberland, Modern Babylon, Trinovant or Trinovantum, Weissnichtwo (?).
London University Stinkomalee.
Londres, Henry de. See HENRY DE LONDRES.
Longinus, Caius Cassius. See CASSIUS, CAIUS.
Lorenzo de' Medici. See MEDICI, LORENZO DE'.
Louis V. (*of France*). Le Fainéant.
Louis VIII. Cœur de Lion.
Louis IX. (*St. Louis*). Solomon of France, or French Solomon.
Louis XI. Most Christian King, *or* Majesty.
Louis XII. Father of his People.
Louis XIV. Le Grand Monarque, Lewis Baboon.
Louis XVI. M. Véto.
Louis XVIII. King of England's Viceroy.
Louisiana. Creole State.
Louis Napoleon. See NAPOLEON III.
Louis Philippe. Citizen King, Napoleon of Peace.
Louisville. Fall City.
Lowell. City of Spindles.
Lowell, James R. Hosea Biglow.
Luke, St. Beloved Physician.
Lulle, *or* Lully, Raymond. Illuminated Doctor.
Lytton, Edward Robert. See BULWER LYTTON, EDWARD ROBERT.

Macdonald, *or* Mac Ian. Glencoe.

Macdonald (*of Glengarry*). Glengarry.
Macgregor, Robert. Rob Roy.
Mackenzie, Henry. Addison of the North, Man of Feeling.
Maerlant, Jakob. Father of Dutch Poetry.
Maginn, William. Modern Rabelais, Sir Morgan Odoherty.
Mahomet. Macon, Mahoun, *or* Mahound.
Mahony, Francis. Father Prout.
Maine. Lumber State, Pine-tree State.
Mairone, François de. Illuminated Doctor.
Manuel I. (*of Trebizond*). Great Captain.
Margaret (*daughter of Eric II. of Norway*). Maid, *or* Fair Maid, of Norway.
Margaret (*of Denmark*). Semiramis of the North.
Maria (*daughter of Robert, king of Naples*). Fiammetta (?).
Marie Antoinette. Mme. Véto.
Marignano (*Battle of*). Battle of the Giants.
Marius, Caius. Third Founder of Rome.
Marlborough, Duchess of. (*Sarah Churchill*.) Atossa, Mrs. Freeman.
Marlborough, Duke of. (*John Churchill*.) Handsome Englishman, Humphrey Hocus.
Martin (Theodore) and Aytoun (William E.) Bon Gaultier.
Marvell, Andrew. British Aristides.
Mary I. (*of England*). Bloody Mary.
Mary (*of Modena*). Queen of Tears.
Massachusetts. Bay State.
Mathew, Theobald. Apostle of Temperance.
Matilda (*Plantagenet*). Lady of England.
Matthioli, Count. Man with the Iron Mask (?).
Maura, Sta. See STA. MAURA.
Maximilian I. (*of Germany*). Last of the Knights, Pochi Danari, Theuerdank.
Mecca. Holy City.
Medici, Cosmo de'. Father of his Country.
Medici, Lorenzo de'. Father of Letters.
Medina. City of the Prophet, Holy City.
Melanchthon, Philip. Teacher of Germany.
Melendez Valdes, Juan. Restorer of Parnassus.
Mena, Juan de. Spanish Ennius.
Menedemus. Eretrian Bull.
Meteyard, Eliza. Silverpen.
Michigan (*State*). Lake State, Wolverine State.
Mickiewicz, Adam. Polish Byron.
Middleton, John. Child of Hale.
Middleton, Richard. Profound, *or* Solid, Doctor.
Midway Oak (*Battle of*). Battle of the Thirty.
Milan. Little Paris.
Milburn, William H. Blind Preacher.
Milky Way. Watling Street.
Miller, Joseph. Father of Jests.
Miloradowitch, Michael. Russian Murat.
Mind, Godefroi. Raphael of Cats.
Mirabeau, Marquis de. (*Victor Riquetti*.) Friend of Man.
Mirabeau, Viscount de. (*Boniface Riquetti*.) Barrel-Mirabeau.

Mississippi (*River*). Father of Waters.
Mississippi (*State*). Bayou State.
Mississippi (*Valley*). Garden of the World.
Mitchel, Ormsby M. Old Stars.
Mitchell, Donald G. Ik Marvel.
Mitchell, William. Great Tinclarian Doctor.
Mogridge, George. Old Humphrey.
Moir, David M. Delta.
Monmouth, James, Duke of. Absalom, Protestant Duke.
Montbars. The Exterminator.
Montluc, Blaise de. Royalist Butcher.
Montmorency, Anne, Duke of. French Fabius.
Montreal. Island City.
Montrose, Marquis of. See GRAHAM, JAMES.
Moore, Thomas. Anacreon Moore, Thomas Brown the Younger, Thomas Little.
Moratin, Leandro Fernandez. Spanish Molière.
Mornay, Philippe de. Huguenot Pope.
Morning Post (*London*). Jeames.
Morris, James M. K. N. Pepper.
Morrison, Lieut. Zadkiel.
Mucius, Caius. Scævola.
Murat, Joachim. Handsome Swordsman, King Franconi.
Murray, or Morny, Earl of. (*James Stewart.*) Good Regent.
Murray, John. Emperor of the West.

Naples. Regno.
Napoleon III. (*Louis Napoleon.*) Badinguet, Boustrapa.
Napoleon, Prince. (*Napoleon Joseph Charles Bonaparte.*) Prince Plon-plon.
Napoleon Bonaparte. See BONAPARTE, NAPOLEON.
Nash, Richard. King of Bath.
Nashville. City of Rocks.
Nasmyth, Patrick, or Peter. English Hobbema.
Native Americans. Hindoos, Know-nothings, Sam.
Neal, John. Jehu O'Cataract.
Neal, Sir Paul. Sidrophel (?).
Negroes. Cuffee, Quashee, Sambo.
Nelson, Horatio. Hero of the Nile.
Neo-Cæsarea, Gregory of. See GREGORY OF NEO-CÆSAREA.
Nevil, Richard. See WARWICK, EARL OF.
Newell, Robert H. Orpheus C. Kerr.
New Brunswick (*Inhabitants of*). Blue-Noses.
New England and Nova Scotia. Drogio.
New Hampshire. Granite State.
New Haven. City of Elms, or Elm City.
New Orleans. Crescent City.
New York (*City*). Empire City, Gotham, New Amsterdam.
New York (*State*). Empire State, Excelsior State, New Netherlands.
Ney, Marshal. Bravest of the Brave.
Nicholas, St. Boy-bishop, Kriss Kringle.
Nicholls, Mrs. See BRONTÉ, CHARLOTTE.
Nightingale, Florence. St. Filomena.
Ninian, St. Apostle of the Picts.

Norbury, Earl of. Hanging Judge.
Normandy. Land of Wisdom.
Normandy, Robert, Duke of. Robert, or Robin, the Devil.
Northallerton (*Battle of*). Battle of the Standard.
North Carolina. Old North State, Turpentine State.
Norway and Sweden. Scandinavia.
Norwich, Bishop of. See SPENSER, HENRY.
Nottingham, Lord. See FINCH, HENEAGE.
Nova Scotia. Acadia.
Nova Scotia and New England. Drogio.
Nova Scotians (*The*). Blue-Noses.

Occam, William of. Invincible Doctor, Singular Doctor, Venerable Initiator.
O'Connell, Daniel. Irish Agitator, The Liberator.
Ohio (*State*). Buckeye State.
Oldham, John. English Juvenal.
Omar I. Emperor of Believers.
Orleans (*Battle of*). Battle of the Herrings.
Orleans, Louis Philippe Joseph, Duke of. Égalité.
Orpheus. Father of Poetry.
Otterburn (*Battle of*). Chevy Chase (?).
Oxford, Earl of. See HARLEY, ROBERT.

Pacific Ocean. South Sea.
Paige, Eldridge F. Dow, Jr.
Palæologus, Andronicus. Father of his Country.
Palestine. Holy Land.
Palestine (*Western*). Land of Promise, or Promised Land.
Palestrina, Giambattista Pietro Aloisio da. Father of Music.
Palmerston, Lord. (*Henry John Temple.*) Pam.
Paoli, Pasquale de. Corsica Paoli.
Paris. Lutetia.
Parrhasius. King of Painters.
Parton, Sarah P. Fanny Fern.
Patrick, St. Apostle of Ireland.
Patterson, Robert. Old Mortality.
Paul, St. Apostle of the Gentiles, Prince of the Apostles.
Paulding, James K. See IRVING.
Peel, Sir Robert. Orange-Peel.
Pekin. Cambalu.
Pendleton, Rev. Mr. Vicar of Bray (?).
Pennsylvania. Key-stone State.
Penrose, Elizabeth. Mrs. Markham.
Penry, or Ap Henry, John. Martin Mar-Prelate (?).
Pepin the Short (*of France*). Most Christian King, or Majesty.
Percy, Harry. Hotspur.
Perrers, or Pierce, Alice. Lady of the Sun.
Perth. Fair City.
Peter, St. Prince of the Apostles.
Petersburg. Cockade City.
Pezza, Michele. Fra Diavolo.
Philadelphia. City of Brotherly Love, Quaker City.
Philip of Anjou. See ANJOU, DUKE OF.

Phillips, George S. January Searle.
Phillips, Katharine. The Matchless, or Incomparable, Orinda.
Philo Judæus. Jewish Plato.
Philopœmen. Last of the Greeks.
Pierce, Alice. See PERRERS, ALICE.
Pigalle, Jean Baptiste. French Phidias.
Pinkerton, John. Robert Heron.
Pinto, Ferdinand Mendez. Prince of Liars.
Pitt, William. (*Lord Chatham.*) Great Commoner, Junius (?).
Pittsburg. Iron City, Smoky City.
Plantagenet, Edith. Fair Maid of Anjou.
Plantagenet, Humphrey. Good Duke Humphrey.
Plantagenet, Matilda. Lady of England.
Plato. Athenian Bee.
Plymouth Colony. Old Colony.
Poland. Sarmatia.
Pole, Michael de la. Beloved Merchant.
Poniatowski, Joseph. Polish Bayard.
Pope (*The*). Lord Peter, Man of Sin, Servant of the Servants of God, Vicar of Christ.
Pope, Alexander. Bard of Twickenham.
Porphyry. The Philosopher.
Portland (*Maine*). Forest City.
Portman and Grosvenor Square Districts (*London*). Tyburnia.
Portugal. Lusitania.
Pot, Philippe. Cicero's Mouth.
Powis, Lucia. Castara.
Pratt, Samuel J. Courtney Melmoth.
Presbyterians (*The*). Blue-Skins.
Procter, Bryan W. Barry Cornwall.
Puget, Pierre. Michael Angelo of France.
Pushkin, Alexander Sergeivitch. Russian Byron.
Putnam, Israel. Old Put.
Pym, John. King Pym.
Pythagoras. Samian Sage, or Sage of Samos.

Quakers, or Friends. Seekers.
Quebec. Gibraltar of America.
Queen's Camel. Camelot.

Rabelais, François. Alcofribas Nasier, Curate of Meudon, Father of Ridicule.
Raleigh, Sir Walter. Shepherd of the Ocean.
Ramsay, Allan. Scottish Theocritus.
Rann, John. Sixteen-string Jack.
Rathbone, Mrs. Richard. Mary Powell.
Redden, Laura C. Howard Glyndon.
René d'Anjou. Good King René.
Rhode Island. Little Rhody.
Ricardus Corinensis. See RICHARD OF CIRENCESTER.
Rich, John. Lun.
Rich, Lady. See DEVEREUX, PENELOPE.
Richard I. (*of England*). Cœur de Leon, Le Noir Fainéant.
Richard II. (*of England*). Defender of the Faith.
Richard of Cirencester. Monk of Westminster.
Richter, Jean Paul Friedrich. Jean Paul, The Only.
Rimini, Gregory of. See GREGORY OF RIMINI.

Roberts, John. Junius (?).
Robin Hood. See HOOD, ROBIN.
Robinson, Frederick. See GODERICH, VISCOUNT.
Robinson, Mary. Beauty of Buttermere.
Robinson, Mary Darby. English Sappho, Perdita.
Robinson, Mrs. Edward. Talvi.
Rochester (*New York*). Flour City.
Rochester, Earl of. (*John Wilmot.*) Virgin Modesty.
Roderick. Last of the Goths.
Rogers, Samuel. Bard of Memory.
Roman Catholic Church. Mystical Babylon, Scarlet Woman.
Romanus, Ægidius. Well-founded Doctor.
Rome. Eternal City, Imperial City, Mistress of the World, Nameless City, Queen of Cities, Seven-hilled City.
Ronsard, Pierre de. Prince of the Ode.
Rosenhagen, Rev. J. Junius (?).
Rousseau, Jean Jacques. Jean Jacques, J. J.
Royal Marines. Mistress Roper.
Rügen. Holy Island.
Rupert, Prince. Mad Cavalier.
Russell, Lord John. (*Earl Russell.*) Finality John.
Russia. Northern Bear, Northern Giant.
Russians (*The*). Ivan Ivanovitch.
Ruysbroek, Jean. Divine Doctor, Ecstatic Doctor.

Sacheverell, Lucy. Lucasta (?).
Sackville, Lord George. Junius (?).
St. Hilaire, Comte de. (*Louis Vincent Joseph Le Blond.*) Roland of the Army.
St. Louis (*Missouri*). Mound City.
St. Martin, Louis Claude de. Philosopher of the Unknown.
St. Pourçain, Durand de. See DURAND DE ST. POURÇAIN.
Sampson, Agnes. See SIMPSON, AGNES.
Sandwich, John, Lord. Jemmy Twitcher.
Sta. Maura. Lover's Leap.
Sarpi, Peter. Father Paul.
Satan. Belial, Prince of Darkness, Prince of the Power of the Air. See DEVIL.
Saunders, David. Shepherd of Salisbury Plain.
Savannah. Forest City.
Saxony (*South-eastern*). Saxon Switzerland.
Scanderbeg. White Devil of Wallachia.
Schwerin, Count von. Little Marlborough.
Scotch (*The*). Nation of Gentlemen, Sawney.
Scotland. Albania or Albany, Albyn, Caledon or Caledonia, Coila, Land of Cakes, North Britain, Scotia.
Scott, Adam. King of the Border.
Scott, John. See ELDON, LORD.
Scott, Sir Walter. Border Minstrel, or Minstrel of the Border, Captain Cuthbert Clutterbuck, Chrystal Croftangry, Great Magician, Great Unknown, Jedediah Cleishbotham, Laurence Templeton, Malachi Malagrowther, Peter Pattieson, Wizard of the North.

Scotus, Duns. See DUNS SCOTUS.
Scoville, Joseph A. Walter Barrett, Clerk.
Settle, Elkanah. Doeg.
Seward, Anna. Swan of Lichfield.
Seymour, Charles. (*Duke of Somerset.*) Proud Duke.
Shadwell, Thomas. Mac Flecknoe.
Shaftesbury, Earl of. Achitophel.
Shakespeare, William. Bard of Avon, Sweet Swan of Avon.
Sharp, Samuel. Mundungus.
Sharpe, Richard. Conversation Sharpe.
Shelburne, Lord. Malagrida.
Shelley, Percy B. Poet of Poets.
Sheppard, Elizabeth S. Mme. Kinkel.
Shield of Arthur. Pridwin.
Sicily. Garden of Italy, Granary of Europe.
Sicinius Dentatus. Roman Achilles.
Sidmouth, Viscount. (*Henry Addington.*) The Doctor.
Sidney, Lady Dorothea. Sacharissa.
Sidney, Sir Philip. Astrophel, English Petrarch, Philisides.
Sigismund (*emperor of Germany*). Super Grammaticam.
Simmons, Thomas. Man of Blood.
Simpson, Agnes. Wise Wife of Keith.
Sjöberg, Erik. Vitalis.
Smith, Seba. Jack Downing.
Smith, Sydney. Peter Plymley.
Smith, William. Father of English Geology.
Smolensk. Key of Russia.
Smollett, Tobias. Smelfungus.
Society of Medical Observation (*in Paris*). Mutual Admiration Society.
Sodom and Gomorrah. Cities of the Plain.
Solomon. The Preacher.
Somerset, Duke of. See SEYMOUR, CHARLES.
Sophie Charlotte (*of Prussia*). Republican Queen.
Sophocles. Attic Bee, Attic Homer.
Soult, Marshal. Old Fox.
South Carolina. Palmetto State.
Southern States (*U. S.*). Dixie.
Southey, Robert. Abel Shufflebottom, Espriella.
Spain. Hispania, Iberia.
Sparta and Athens. The Two Eyes of Greece.
Spears. (Of Arthur) Ron; (of Odin) Gungnir.
Spenser, Edmund. Colin Clout, Prince of Poets.
Spenser, Henry. (*Bishop of Norwich.*) Fighting Prelate.
Springfield (*Illinois*). Flower City.
Spurzheim, John Gaspar. Dousterswivel.
Steeds. (Of Alexander the Great) Bucephalus; (of Apollo and the Muses) Pegasus; (of Argalia) Rabicano; (of the four sons of Aymon) Bayard; (of Bevis of Southampton) Arundel; (of the Cid) Bavieca; (of Don Quixote) Aligero Clavileño *and* Rozinante; (of Sir Launcelot Greaves) Bronzomarte; (of Mohammed) Al Borak; (of Odin) Sleipnir; (of Orlando) Brigliadoro *and* Vegliantino;
(of Rinaldo) Bayard; (of Ruggiero, *or* Rogero) Frontino; (of Siegfried) Grane; (of Tristram) Passetreul.
Steele, Sir Richard. Nestor Ironside.
Sterling, Edward. Vetus.
Sterne, Lawrence. The Bramin, English Rabelais.
Stevenson, John H. Lord of Crazy Castle.
Stewart, James. See MURRAY, *or* MORAY, EARL OF.
Stewart, John. Walking Stewart.
Stoddart, John. Doctor Slop.
Stowe, Harriet B. Christopher Crowfield.
Strother, David H. Porte-Crayon.
Stuart, Charles Edward. Young Chevalier, Younger Pretender.
Stuart, James Francis Edward. Chevalier de St. George, Elder Pretender.
Sturleson, Snorro. Northern Herodotus.
Sunderland, Anne, Countess of. Little Whig.
Swain, Charles. Manchester Poet.
Sweden and Norway. Scandinavia.
Swift, Jonathan. Cadenus, Dean of St. Patrick's, English Rabelais, Presto; M. B., Drapier.
Swiss (*The*). Colin Tampon.
Switzerland. Helvetia.
Swords. (Of Agricane) Tranchera; (of Arthur) Caliburn, *or* Excalibar; (of Bevis of Southampton) Morglay; (of Braggadochio) Sanglamore; (of Charlemagne) La Joyeuse; (of the Cid) Colada *and* Tizona; (of Doolin of Mayence) Merveilleuse; (of Edward the Confessor) Curtana; (of Frithiof) Angurvardel; (of Hako I.) Quern-biter; (of Lancelot of the Lake) Aroundight; (of Ogier le Danois) Curtana; (of Orlando, *or* Roland) Durandal, *or* Durlindana; (of Sir Otuel) Corrouge; (of Rinaldo) Fusberta; (of Ruggiero, *or* Rogero) Balisardo; (of Siegfried) Balmung, Gram, Mimung; (of Thoralf Skolinson) Foot-breadth; (of Wittich) Mimung.
Sylvester, Joshua. The Silver-tongued.
Sym, Robert. Timothy Tickler.
Symmonds, John. Spanish Jack.
Symonds, Symon. Vicar of Bray (?).
Syrus, Ephraem. Prophet of the Syrians.

Tamerlane. Prince of Destruction.
Tammenund. St. Tammany.
Tatler (*Editor of the*). Isaac Bickerstaff.
Tauler, John. Illuminated Doctor.
Taylor, Jeremy. Shakespeare of Divines.
Taylor, John. Water-poet.
Taylor, Zachary. Rough and Ready.
Tellez, Gabriel. Tirso de Molina.
Temple, Lord. (*Richard Grenville.*) Lord Gawky, Tiddy-doll.
Terpander. Father of Greek Music.
Texas. Lone-Star State.
Thackeray, William M. George Fitz-Boodle, Michael Angelo Titmarsh.
Thompson, Mortimer. Q. K. Philander Doesticks.

Thomson, J. P. Philip Wharton.
Thomson, Mrs. Anthony T. Grace Wharton.
Throckmorton, or Throgmorton, Job. Martin Mar-Prelate (?).
Times, (*The London*). The Thunderer.
Timour. See TAMERLANE.
Titus (*emperor of Rome*). Delight of Mankind.
Tooke, John Horne. Philosopher of Wimbledon.
Triulty College (*Dublin*). Silent Sister. .
Trowbridge, J. T. Paul Creyton.
Troy. Ilium, or Ilion.
Tucker, Abraham. Edward Search.
Turkey. Sick Man of the East.
Tyrconnel. Lying Dick Talbot.

Udall, John. Martin-Prelate (?).
Uncas. Last of the Mohicans.
United States. Columbia, Uncle Sam.
United States (*Frigate*). Old Waggon.
United States (*People of*). Brother Jonathan.
United States Flag. Old Glory.
Uther. Pendragon.

Van Buren, Martin. Little Magician.
Vanhomrigh, Esther. Vanessa.
Varro, Marcus Terentius. Most Learned of the Romans.
Varro, William. Thorough Doctor.
Vaughan, Henry. The Silurist.
Vaughan, Thomas. Dangle.
Vendôme Beaufort, François de. King of the Markets.
Venice. Bride of the Sea.
Vermont. Green-Mountain State.
Vernon, Admiral Edward. Old Grog.
Victoria, or Victorina. Mother of the Camps.
Vida, Marco Girolamo. Christian Virgil.
Villiers, George. See BUCKINGHAM, DUKE OF.
Virgil. Mantuan Swan.
Virginia. Mother of Presidents, Mother of States, Old Dominion.
Vivian. Lady of the Lake.
Voltaire, François. Apostle of Infidelity, Philosopher of Ferney.

Wales. Cambria.
Wales, Edward, Prince of. See EDWARD, PRINCE OF WALES.
Walker, John. Elocution Walker.
Walker, John. Hookey Walker.
Walpole, Sir Robert. Robin Bluestring, Grand Corrupter.
Walton, Izaak. Father of Angling.
Warner, Susan. Elizabeth Wetherell.
Warwick, Earl of. (*Richard Nevil*.) Kingmaker.
Warwick and Eccleston Square Districts (*London*). Cubitopolis, Mesopotamia.
Waryng, Jane. Varina.

Washington. City of tances.
Washington, George. Father of his Count:
Wayne, Anthony. Mad
Webster, Daniel. Exp(stitution.
Wedell, C. H. Leonida:
Wellington, Duke of. Great Duke, Iron D
Welsh (*The*). Taffy.
Western Hemisphere.
Western Reserve. New
Westminster Review. I
West Virginia (*Northern*
White, John. Century
White, Rev. John. Pa ter.
Whitefriars. Alsatia.
White Mountains. Cry
Whitfield, George. Doc
Whittier, John Greenlea
Wieland, Christoph Mar taire.
Wilbrord, or Willibrod, Frisians.
Wild, Henry. Arabia: Tailor.
Wilkes, John. Junius (
Wilkie, Sir David. Scot
Wilkie, William. Scott:
William I. (*of England*)
William IV. Sailor Kin
Williams, John. Tony
Williams, Rev. John. I
Williams, Renwick. Th
Wilmot, John. See Roc
Wilson, John. Christo] Mordecai Mullion.
Winchcomb, John. Jac
Winchester. Camelot (?
Wisconsin. Badger Stat
Wise, Henry A. Harry
Wolcott, John. Peter P
Worcestershire. Garder
Wordsworth, William. Mount.
Wycliffe, John de. Eva Doctor, Morning St tion.

Xavier, St. Francis: Ap
Xenophon. Attic Muse

Yellow Fever. Yellow J
York, Cecily, Duchess (Raby.
York, Frederick, Duke of
York, House of. White

Zaragoza, Agustina. M:
Zenobia. Queen of the 1
Zoroaster. Bactrian Sa;

www.ingramcontent.com/pod-product-compliance
Lightning Source LLC
Chambersburg PA
CBHW022146300426
44115CB00006B/366